Making Theatre: A Life of Sharon Pollock

Enjoy your wonderful journey
Mom 06/08

Congratulations - your
dedication & determination
will take you far!
Dad 06/08

Sharon Pollock, ca 1986.

Courtesy of Sharon Pollock.

Making Theatre

A Life of Sharon Pollock

SHERRILL GRACE

TALONBOOKS

Talonbooks
P.O. Box 2076, Vancouver, British Columbia, Canada V6B 3S3
www.talonbooks.com

Typeset in Scala and printed and bound in Canada.

First Printing: 2008

The publisher gratefully acknowledges the financial support of the Canada Council for the Arts; the Government of Canada through the Book Publishing Industry Development Program; and the Province of British Columbia through the British Columbia Arts Council and the Book Publishing Tax Credit for our publishing activities.

LIBRARY AND ARCHIVES CANADA CATALOGUING IN PUBLICATION

Grace, Sherrill E., 1944-
    Making theatre : a life of Sharon Pollock / Sherrill Grace.

Includes bibliographical references and index.
ISBN 978-0-88922-586-2

    1. Pollock, Sharon. 2. Dramatists, Canadian (English)—20th century—Biography.
3. Theatrical producers and directors—Canada—Biography. 4. Actors—Canada—Biography.
I. Title.

PS8581.O34Z64 2008   C812'.54   C2008-901053-1

In Memory of Rick McNair
(1942–2007)

&

for all those who make Canadian theatre—
past, present, and future

CONTENTS

LIST OF ILLUSTRATIONS

Poster by Scott McKowen for the Grand Theatre production of *Blood Relations*, 1989
Cover

Sharon Pollock, ca 1986   *Frontispiece*

LIST OF ABBREVIATIONS

Unless otherwise indicated, quotations from the plays are from the three-volume *Collected Works (CW)* and are cited by play title abbreviation followed by *CW*, volume number, and page. See the Bibliography for other editions.

AT: *Angel's Trumpet*
BR: *Blood Relations*
C: *Constance*
DF: *Death in the Family*
D: *Doc*
ED: *End Dream*
FLC: *Fair Liberty's Call*
G: *Generations*
GIS: *Getting It Straight*
KMI: *Komagata Maru Incident*
KT: *Kabloona Talk*
MJ: *Man Out of Joint*
MP: *Moving Pictures*
MW: *The Making of Warriors*
OTH: *One Tiger to a Hill*
PD: *Prairie Dragons*
SJ: *Saucy Jack*
SLL: *Sweet Land of Liberty*
W: *Walsh*
WSC: *Whiskey Six Cadenza*

All references to the Sharon Pollock Papers in Special Collections at the University of Calgary are provided in parentheses by box, folder, and page number.

PREFACE AND ACKNOWLEDGEMENTS

As Robert Fulford noted in 1997, the "boom" in biography of Canadian artists and intellectuals did not begin until the 1990s. A decade later, we still have very little biography for our performing, and not much more for our visual, artists. Performers' memoirs and autobiographies, while not numerous, have been published more frequently, but biographies remain rare. While I cannot explain this relative lack, I suspect the reasons are various: Canadians are wary of exposing their own or others' lives; we are also suspicious of heroics and hagiography, and biography skirts around the edges of both. The unfortunate consequence of this reticence or modesty is our continued underestimation of our accomplishments, especially in the arts.

Unlike the biographers of Glenn Gould or Virginia Woolf, who have influenced my approach, my subject is a *living* female Canadian artist working in contemporary theatre, so my practical challenges and joys are closer to those of Margaret Atwood's biographers. Pollock's story is far from over so some things are just not known yet because they haven't happened. Other things cannot be said because there are people whose privacy and sensibilities must be respected, and I decided at the outset to place my focus on the work and to allow private details to remain private, unless they in some way illuminate a play or a public decision made by Pollock herself. This is both an ethical and an aesthetic decision on my part. But writing a *living* life has major rewards, as I have discovered, because I have been able to talk with, observe, and listen to Sharon Pollock, interview many people who know her well or worked with her at some point and have stories to tell—of pot-bellied pigs, white rats, red wine, detective movies, political arguments, and the sharing of hard work to make theatre. I have been blessed with access, assistance, and advice.

In a 1991 interview, Pollock insisted that "to be authentic … one needs to tell the story in such a way that it acknowledges the position of the originator" (Zimmerman, 1991, 35). She was, of course, speaking about plays, but as her literary biographer I have taken this proviso to heart. This biography is *a* life, not *the* life; I must stress that it is my version of the life of a roughly contemporary Canadian woman working in the theatre, which is still a largely male-dominated domain, especially in the area of playwriting. Because of what I have in common with her (in class, race, education, historical moment, and nationality), I think I am able to understand my subject. Because we are both women, I see some of the hurdles that she had to face and overcome to build a successful career. What I have never known from the inside, from behind the scenes as she has, is the process of making theatre, so perhaps my biggest adventure and most of my discoveries lie there in what was for me a largely unexplored country.

In this biography I begin in the theatre and will keep returning to it. You will find genealogy here and a narrative that advances decade by decade through the lives of this woman as she works in Canadian theatre, but you will *not* find a tidy year-by-year chronology because the narrative is woven to capture her lived experience of remembering, creating, and moving back and forth in time and space. I have also tried to let Sharon change, to accept that I will never know all her selves, to enjoy the ones I have discovered, and to leave her on the brink of new adventures as she goes on making theatre. If this biography of Sharon Pollock prompts others to write biographies of our performing artists, I will feel that one of my goals has been accomplished.

The research for *Making Theatre* has taken several years and has been supported by many organizations and individuals. A list of individuals interviewed and works consulted is provided in Sources, and full references can be found in the Bibliography. However, there are some acknowledgements that I wish to stress here. I owe enormous thanks to the Social Sciences and Humanities Research Council of Canada for research funding and to the Canada Council Killam Foundation for the Killam Research Fellowship that gave me time to travel, conduct interviews, and write, and assisted with the publication of this book. It is also a great pleasure to acknowledge the archives that hold Pollock materials—manuscripts, letters, production materials and photographs—and to thank their curators or managers who so generously granted me access to documents and files, but I would like to make special note of the Sharon Pollock Archive at the University of Calgary, an indispensable resource; the Stratford Festival Archives; the National Arts Centre Archives; the Archives of both CBC radio and television, as well as the archives of Concordia University's Centre for Broadcast Studies; the Glenbow Museum Archives; the Paul Fleck Library Archives at the Banff Centre; and the New Brunswick Provincial Archives. I am eternally grateful to the librarians in the Inter-Library Loan division of the UBC Library for their patience and diligence in tracking down a host of minute bibliographical details.

To Sharon's family—her brother, Peter Chalmers, who went out of his way to assist me on several occasions, and his wife Donna, Sharon's children, Jennifer, Melinda, Michele, and Kirk, and her sister Susan Chalmers-Gauvin—I am deeply grateful. They helped when they could, shared some wonderful stories of growing up with Sharon, and provided me with vital information about the history and life of the Garry Theatre. Never did they question my access to information. To Sharon herself, of course, I owe unique thanks. It cannot be easy to have someone pestering you with questions about the past when you are deeply engaged with present work or future plans, and in Sharon's case this focus on the present and near future is of paramount importance. She is always busy, full of new ideas, and over-booked with commitments, but on many occasions she agreed to sit down with me to answer questions, or to smooth my way with potential interviewees, or check details, dates, and facts. I suspect that my sleuthing has puzzled and amused her, but I hope she will not be disappointed with the final result should she ever find the time to read it.

Inevitably, there are individuals it was impossible to interview: in some cases, like those of Catherine Adams, Fred Diehl of the CBC, Alexander Gray, Larry Lillo, Graham McPherson, Susan Wright, or John Juliani, they had died before I was able to contact them or to realize that I should do so; in a very few cases, I was unable to establish contact or set up an interview because my inquiries were not answered or because the person had moved or was seriously ill. The person whose silence I especially regret is Ross Pollock, but my efforts to reach him were of no avail.

It is a personal pleasure to thank my colleagues and students, many of whom have been supportive and helpful in numerous ways. I have been fortunate in that I knew I could rely on their knowledge and good judgment on all matters theatrical, and I thank them for listening to me and, in some cases, for reading drafts and offering wise advise: George Belliveau, Gail Bellward, Diane Bessai (who provided much more than interview information), Donna Coates, Jane Cowan (my wise and patient editor), Jim DeFelice (for tapes, xeroxes, and good conversations), Mark Diotte, Joyce Doolittle (and what good dinners with wine we shared), Ron Fedoruk, Albert-Reiner Glaap, Gabriele Helms (a dear friend and the first to work with me on Pollock's plays, who did not live to see the completion of this research), Yashmin Kassam (for once again, cheerfully, preparing one of my manuscripts in electronic form), Ric Knowles, Ira Nadel, Glen Nichols, Anne Nothof, Harjot Oberoi, Malcolm Page, Damiano Pietropaulo, Angela Rebeiro, Denis Salter, Karl and Christy Siegler for their support of this book and their long commitment to Canadian theatre, Jerry Wasserman (who corrected me on many occasions and advised on many others), Dominique Yupangco (for expert help with scans, power point, and image preparation), Cynthia Zimmerman (good friend and editor of Pollock's collected plays), the late Yoshinari Minami, and colleagues in many countries who listened to me present my ideas in the early form of conference papers and who shared their reactions and insights with me. It is perhaps risky to single out one person for special praise and thanks, but in the case of this biography and in light of the years spent working on it, I do want to acknowledge my former graduate student Michelle La Flamme. While preparing her own dissertation, Michelle helped as my research assistant, and she was always patient, good-humoured, enthusiastic, and persistent in tracking down an elusive fact or date; we met weekly and I could not have managed without her.

It has become common for an author to thank his or her family, but in this case my thank-you is more than a gesture. My daughter, Elizabeth Grace, drove me to research locales near Toronto and to interviews in the city; she took photographs, attended performances of Pollock plays, and together with her partner Susan Vella provided food, drink, accommodation, and excellent company on my many research trips east. My husband, John Grace, provided encouragement and took far better photographs of Fredericton sites than I could; he is also an experienced playgoer with a keen critical eye, so discussing productions with him is always illuminating. Theatre is a communal activity, meant to be shared, and I am fortunate to have such articulate companions.

Sherrill Grace
Vancouver 2008

PART I

CHAPTER I

Writing Lives and Making Theatre

I began to think in a mad way that a biography was a kind of snuff movie.
—A.S. BYATT, *The Biographer's Tale*, 190

The could-have, might-have mode so dear to (some) contemporary biographers [is] a mode we might call the prurient wishful subjunctive.   —MARJORIE GARBER, *The Seductions of Biography*, 15

Maybe everything I've said in interviews, speeches, bars, lecture halls, kitchens, hotel and living rooms, on stage and off, in answer to some variation on why me and theatre, is a lie. Maybe I make theatre because I make theatre. Maybe I'll stop when I die. Maybe all this is a lie.
—SHARON POLLOCK, "A Memoir," 17

I: Writing a Life

Biography is very popular these days. Although the genre has been around for a very long time, today there seem to be more and more ways of writing biographies and more and more people whose life stories are worth writing. No longer must biographies be about great men in public life; no longer must the subject of a biography be safely dead; and it is no longer absolutely necessary to write a life as if it had some unified purpose or some kind of ultimate goal. Biographers have also changed their methods: these days, they (or I guess I should say *we*) are more likely to pry behind hitherto decorously covered areas. We are not only interested in what people did or how they rose to power, but in why they chose their paths in life, on how a multitude of social, familial, and political forces influenced the life, and on the many different selves there actually are within one individual. I trace much of this shifting perspective on the writing of biography back to Virginia Woolf because more than any other modern writer Woolf argued that, like novelists, biographers had to tell good stories, that great men were no longer the only worthy subjects, and that the biographee might have many lives and multiple selves.

Virginia Woolf's views have been important to me as I have wrestled with how to tell my story of Sharon Pollock's life because Pollock is a woman and very much alive. She is also a great writer, or, as she might prefer to be called, a serious maker of theatre. She has produced a major body of fine works for the stage including *Walsh, Blood Relations, Doc, Fair Liberty's Call*, and *Moving Pictures*, plus numerous plays for children and for radio and television. Much of this work is beautifully written and crafted, and all of it is serious drama that places high demands on the actor, director, designer, and audience. She is herself a fine actor and an accomplished director; she has been an artistic director and in the 1990s she founded her own theatre. Her administrative service to Canadian theatre, like her mentoring of young playwrights, is generous and indefatigable. In short, she has done what not even Alan Ayckbourn has done. In his recent biography of Ayckbourn, Paul Allen claims that Ayckbourn "is probably unique in being capable of doing every job in the theatre (except perhaps front-of-house)" (60), but Pollock has done every job including front-of-house. She has, as Woolf would say, many selves, and she has reinvented herself several times and led many different lives.

Fascinating as these multiple selves and frequent reinventions might be, the *sine qua non*, for writing—and reading—a biography of Sharon Pollock is her writing. If she were not an excellent playwright with a large number of produced and *published* plays, we would not bother, as is clear if we think of Tom Thomson. Canadians have invented stories about him shamelessly, obsessively, pruriently, reverently, but we would never have bothered if he were not a splendid artist. It is the work that makes the difference, that and the times through which the artist lives. And in the case of Sharon Pollock, or simply *Sharon* (as I have come to think of her), those times were momentous. Between 1965, when she first took seriously to the boards, and today, the arts of Canadian theatre (as well as the art of theatre in Canada) have blossomed until it is possible for us to look back with pride on the variety and quality of our theatre. And she was there. To tell her story is to tell something of that larger story in which she has been such a significant character; it is, in short, to tell a part of our collective story as a people or a nation.

Like Margaret Atwood's, Sharon's is a success story about challenges met and hurdles overcome and constant striving to do more and be better and reach people and make a difference through art. At the beginning of her biography of Atwood, *The Red Shoes*, Rosemary Sullivan explained that she wanted "to write about a woman who had managed to take control of her artistry and her life" (3), to tell the story of a healthy, successful female artist instead of a depressed, suicidal or murdered one, and I can understand this sentiment. I can understand it because it seems that so many biographies of women are littered with disasters and self-destructive impulses and because Sharon's story might well have been much less successful or healthy than it has turned out to be. So while I do not offer this biography of one person, however remarkable, as a model or a morality tale, I do think we can pay attention to it with pride and learn much about our own history and identity in the process. Like Atwood's story, Pollock's is the story of an entire generation, albeit one that was making theatre, rather than poetry or fiction, in Canada.

A biographer's challenges, pitfalls, and choices are many, and on these choices depends the very nature of the narrative *art* of biography. Once I had decided to assume the biographer's role and chosen my subject, my immediate challenge was *how* to tell this story in a way that would preserve the *life* in the term life-story. At one extreme biography may produce a chronological account of facts, places, dates, and external events; in this kind of narrative the biographer assumes an objectivity and forensic disinterest in the private person whose life is being charted. At the other extreme is the kind of highly speculative biography that relies heavily on the biographer's imaginative invention of what might have been said or felt or done. These extremes are the ones that Byatt and Garber warn against. Biography can also begin at *the* beginning—or *a* beginning arbitrarily decided upon by the biographer—and move forward from genealogy to childhood to maturity. To tell the life-story this way imposes linearity on it and implies a cause and effect process through which we try to explain and make sense of, to tidy up and organize, as it were, the messiness of lived experience. Biography can lean on external concepts and theories, such as Freud's, to locate the *essence* of the subject that will explain why the writer writes or the painter paints or the man of action becomes a general, an explorer, or a prime minister, or it can place greater emphasis on time and place than on psychology, and thereby define the character at the centre of the biography as a product of social forces. But somewhere between these poles of psychology and sociology sits what biographer Marion Shaw calls "that web of connectedness which radiates out from the subject and without which the subject is life-less" (245). Inhabiting that web are the "invisible presences" that, as Shaw suggests, the biographer must somehow "capture." Although I am a tad uneasy with this web and presences metaphor because it implies that the biographer is rather spider-like (which swings perilously close to Byatt's warning about snuff movies), Shaw's point reminds me that Sharon's story is also the story of those invisible presences—some of whom she herself has called "the many brave spirits."

In approaching this biography, I knew from the start that I wanted to situate Sharon's life and work in the context of her time and place, and that this would take me from the Maritimes to Vancouver and most places in between and make me consider much of the history of Canadian theatre from the mid-1960s to the present. Whether at Banff, Stratford, the National Arts Centre, the Vancouver Playhouse, Theatre New Brunswick, the Manitoba Theatre Centre, and Tarragon Theatre, not to mention theatres in Calgary and Edmonton, or on CBC radio and local television, through her plays, her acting, her directing, and her administration, she has played roles in all these dramatic worlds. A biography could not do justice to all this activity in so many parts of the country, not to mention in other countries, but with careful attention to the places and histories of which this one story is a part, I felt I might capture aspects of Sharon living her life. In *Wondrous Strange: The Life and Art of Glenn Gould*, Kevin Bazzana captured masterfully the society that influenced Gould, that in some ways made him what he was. The streets of Toronto, the neighbourhoods, the sights, sounds, and smells, all come to life around Bazzana's Gould who, in turn, steps onto that richly furnished stage as a lively, complex, three-dimensional person. And in her monumental *Virginia Woolf*, Hermione Lee beautifully negotiates many potential traps to present a woman writer about whom so much has already been written, a famous artist whom we think we know, and who is often described as mad and a suicide, no matter how brilliant, with such respect and sensitivity that Virginia seems to step off the page and elude any neat summing up. While I have learned much from other biographies and biographers, I have always kept these two exemplary works in mind because they avoid the extremes of contemporary biography that Byatt and Garber describe (in my epigraphs to this chapter) and succeed in creating vibrant stories of artists, one a performing artist, the other a woman writer, who, like Sharon Pollock, travelled widely and yet chose to remain at home in the places that defined them.

Perhaps it may seem odd, in these early years of the twenty-first century, for a biographer to think back to Virginia Woolf, but that is what I do because she had trenchant things to say about biography. For me, however, it was less Woolf's comments on biography that came to mind than one of her most famous essays called, rather blandly, "Professions for Women." This essay was first delivered as a lecture in 1931 to a women's group, and looking back at it today I would rename it "Killing the Angel in the House." In it, Woolf describes the obstacles facing a professional woman in the early twentieth century, especially a woman whose profession is literature, and she explains that the literary profession offers "fewer experiences for women than ... any other, with the exception of the stage" (149). As we know, these limitations on women seeking professional lives as writers did not stop Woolf, and they would not stop Pollock. However, as Woolf goes on to explain, the most dangerous, undermining presence for a woman writer is not the literary or even the stage professions themselves, but the Angel in the house—this "intensely sympathetic," "immensely charming," "utterly unselfish" creature who "never had a mind or a wish of her own" (150). This creature haunted Virginia Woolf. The minute she took pen in hand, the Angel would flutter around warning: "Never let anyone guess you have a mind of your own." This state of affairs proved impossible, so after a protracted struggle, Woolf just seized the creature by the throat and did her in. Only then was she able to speak her mind on all subjects and become a professional writer.

But what has this to do with Sharon Pollock, a Canadian born in 1936 who, by the age of thirty knew she wanted to be a writer—of plays no less—and by the age of forty was a produced and published playwright? Surely she was not pestered by some Victorian phantom, especially when a pre-eminent female writer like Virginia Woolf had already dispatched the creature! Surely no one and no thing as ephemeral as a ghostly Angel would presume to tell Sharon Pollock not to reveal that she had a mind of her own! But the Angel in the house has more than a cat's nine lives, and she reappeared frequently in Sharon's life, sometimes in demonic form to threaten, sometimes in cherubic form to cajole, and sometimes cunningly disguised as Ariel so she could drop down from the flies, not to inspire but to undermine and insist that the realities and exigencies of a woman's life in the home (and in the theatre) must take precedence over artistic interests and creative ambitions— in short, that a proper woman must know how to behave. For Sharon, these exigencies began in childhood and continued through marriage and the arrival of six children—a test that Virginia never had to face. When the plays started coming, the babies stopped, but Sharon continued to hear the internalized voice of the Angel criticizing her when she turned her attention away from her family to her work. Moreover, this phantom haunted Canadian theatre houses, so that when a woman like Sharon stepped forward to direct or to manage a theatre as artistic director, the Angel would whisper criticisms—loudly—from the boardroom, the wings, and the other side of the footlights. She might even descend from the gods, dressed as Wotan, to admonish this woman, who not only had a most definite mind of her own but also possessed a strong, assertive voice and was determined to use them in both her domestic and professional houses.

Sharon's life-story, then, is not only the story of contemporary Canadian theatre and of one person's contributions over a period of forty-plus years, it is also the story of a woman daring to aspire to the profession Woolf described as virtually barred to women: writing for the theatre. This aspect of her biography cannot be casually dismissed any more than it can become the cause for a feminist argument on my part. The facts speak for themselves and the facts include these realities. In addition to the intimidating Angel in theatre houses, there were no *major* female playwrights in Canada to whom Sharon could turn for support or inspiration in the sixties or seventies, and there were very few women who played roles of any significance in professional Canadian theatre until later still. Talented actresses were emerging, but none of the major Canadian professional theatres and theatre companies to arrive on the scene in the 1970s and 1980s was led by a woman (the exception here was the new Vancouver Playhouse where Joy Coghill began a term as artistic director in 1967) or produced many plays by women. Sharon's generation of writers is also that of Margaret Laurence, P.K. Page, Mavis Gallant, Margaret Atwood, Alice Munro, and Carol Shields, and it is these women who established the national and international careers for professional women writers in Canada that we now take for granted. However, while this generation of women writers had minds of their own and powerful voices, they did not ask to be seen and heard on the stages of this country as Sharon did. Thus, her story is also one of trail-blazing that cleared the way for some of the remarkable Canadian women who now write for the stage. Again, I recall Rosemary Sullivan writing about Margaret Atwood and reminding me that Atwood believed in her self and in her art. The same is true of Sharon who tells a story— apocryphal only in its details—of herself at about twenty-six, standing at the sink washing dishes, and thinking: "I am too this ... I am not enough that ... I shouldn't argue this [or] that. I know exactly who I'm *supposed* to be and all I have to do is turn myself into it. Then ... all of a sudden I said 'I am a valid person as I am ... My life is as valid as his is and if I don't do something else I'll kill myself, literally or metaphorically ... So there's a choice: kill myself or allow myself to be born and live" (see Dunn, 2, and Appendix 3, 411).

Robert Kroetsch once asked how one grows a poet, but I have often asked: how does one grow a playwright? Plays, unlike poems or novels, must be performed; others must sanction your work, at least to the extent that it gets produced, with live actors, putting your text to the ultimate test. If you were Samuel Beckett, Arthur Miller, or David Mamet, you received an excellent university education and then travelled and explored without any strings attached. Amongst the women playwrights of Sharon's generation, only Caryl Churchill comes close to experiencing this kind of privilege. If you were Harold Pinter, Alan Ayckbourn, Sam Shepard, or Timothy Findley, you took another route, one less academic but, nonetheless, enabling; you attended RADA or Stratford or worked with established directors and theatre companies in London and New York. Above all, there was no Angel breathing down your neck in either house and you did not live a life resembling the one that drove Anne Bancroft mad in the British film classic *The Pumpkin Eater*. Just as the young Peggy Atwood may have been traumatized by that other film about female duty, *The Red Shoes*, so I imagine Sharon standing at the kitchen sink in her late twenties and confronted with images from *The Pumpkin Eater* of Bancroft's isolated housewife, who is betrayed by her self-important, writer husband and is surrounded by demanding children. Either you submit and die (going mad is a version of this), or you escape from the pumpkin into the night wearing the red shoes of art ... and live.

As Woolf said in *Orlando*, "a biography is considered complete if it merely accounts for six or seven selves, whereas a person may well have a thousand" (218), and I shall try to account for as many of Sharon's as possible. She has invented and reinvented herself at least as often as Mavor Moore did; in addition to being an actor, a director, an artistic director, and an award-winning playwright, she is a daughter, a mother, a grandmother, a wife and lover, a friend, a mentor, a lecturer, an adjudicator, and the rescuer of wounded animals. She has done all this and remained in Canada, an inspiration to younger theatre artists, a champion of many causes, and the creator of plays that delight, challenge, and inform. Uniting these selves is her passionate commitment to her work in the theatre, to the spirit and honesty of her art. Others have described her as angry, generous, loving, demanding, funny (in her own special way), imaginative, and formidably intelligent and hard-working, but all have summed her up with the word *passion*. If it is true that certain life-stories help to shape the ways in which a nation and its history are defined or intersect powerfully with the larger cultural meanings of their time and place, then Sharon Pollock's life may be one of those significant stories. Against a backdrop of considerable political turmoil, injustice, and trauma, within Canada and abroad, Sharon has carried out her self-appointed task—to make us see (as Conrad would have said), through the art of theatre, what life can mean—with passionate commitment. I have tried to keep this background in mind as I read or think about her plays and about the decisions she has made because she is so profoundly connected to the world around her and so precise in her responses to historical and current events. But at the same time, I have tried to keep the theatre at centre stage in the chapters that follow. The play is the thing, after all, in which to catch Sharon Pollock, if catch her I can, for she does not stay still for long and she is never satisfied with repeating herself.

II: Making Theatre

At 8:00 P.M. on Monday, 6 December 2004, in the theatre of the Timms Centre for the Arts at the University of Alberta in Edmonton, the house lights went down, and then a spot light picked out an elderly woman sitting in a chair at a desk on a dark stage (see Illus. 1), with two younger women, barely visible, standing behind her. The woman was wearing drab clothes, an old sweater, and glasses, and she was reading a letter. She was *not* "Sharon Pollock." The woman on stage was Nell Shipman in old age, and the play that was about to begin was *Moving Pictures*:

1. Sharon in the role of Shipman in the 2004 production of *Moving Pictures* at the Timms Theatre of the University of Alberta. This image is from the opening moments of the play as the elderly Shipman reflects on the news about her health and begins to think back over her life.
    Photograph by Ed Ellis.

NELL: Play.
SHIPMAN: Can't.
NELL: Come on plaaay.
SHIPMAN: Can't.
NELL: Can so. Play! (*MP,CW* III, 83)

Moving Pictures is about the silent film actor and independent filmmaker Nell Shipman (1892–1970). During its premiere with Theatre Junction in Calgary in 1999, I had watched the play with Sharon from the audience. On that night she was keenly observant, assessing, looking *at* the play, judging it with an experienced eye to see how theatre is made to work well. On this night, however, she was on stage helping to make theatre in the play she wrote about a woman who had devoted her life to creating art but who must now, in the present moment of the play, observe, assess, and judge that life—*her life*—because it might soon be going to end. *Moving Pictures* is a biographical play, but it is also autobiographical, and with a sixty-eight-year-old Pollock playing Shipman (who died at seventy-eight) the complexities and layers of experience that were being realized and brought to life on the magical space of the stage were, quite simply, stunning. As I sat in the audience on this December night in 2004, I realized that I was witnessing the uncanny essence of theatre as life. Pollock was playing Shipman and this Shipman embodies Pollock's words—yes—but so much more. If, as R.H. Thomson once said, "biography on stage is biography with breath," then there it was unfolding, building, breathing in front of me.

But there was no time for me to reflect on all these matters at that moment because the play was rushing forward to its motivating challenge: Shipman has just read a letter from her doctor with an alarming report on her health, and this bad news will first immobilize, then galvanize her. Her younger self, Nell, prompts her—"Play."—but she cannot. Instead, Shipman turns angrily on Nell to demand that *she* "make something" of this bad news: "Do you think you could write a script about dying!" (*MP*, 85) The anger and bitterness, not to mention the stakes, in this argument continue to build as Shipman confronts her younger self with being a "lousy mother," with failing in her career, with never listening, with lying, and now with the prospect of death. At this point on that December evening, there was a tense pause. I leaned forward to listen: "Now as The End looms up there on the screen— what can *you* make of it?" Shipman hisses at Nell, fully expecting to defeat her. But Nell snaps back: "What can you make of it?" And the play has begun!

Making theatre, like living one's life, is a process of making a story full of others' stories or, as Shipman pointedly reminds Nell—full of *subtext*. Nell will try to make her life-story up from the beginning with the help of Helen, Shipman's teenaged, ingénue self, but Shipman will trip Nell up repeatedly, forcing other, hidden versions of the autobiography to the surface, making Nell *"acknowledge true family history"* (95). At times, this play feels like a battle as Shipman and Nell turn on each other, disagree, and jab accusations at each other as if they were knives. Intermittently, the ebullient optimism of young Helen displaces the recriminations and disappointments of her older, quarrelling selves, but as the minutes race by and the tension builds, as the layers of self-deception are stripped away, it becomes clear that this play is not about fighting, but about the conflicting inner voices or selves that haunt this old woman who was once young, beautiful, carefree, and full of dreams, who then became a mature star, bruised by life but confident, charging ahead with her career, her writing, her creative vision, and then ... somehow ... ended up utterly alone, old, destitute, holding a letter with bad news that obliges her to relive and retell and reassess what it all means. *Moving Pictures* is not, at least not on the surface, about the playwright at all. No indeed, that was not Sharon Pollock on the stage because Sharon is not alone, old, or destitute. This play is her version of someone else's life or her version of Macbeth's lament that life is but a poor player that struts and frets his hour upon the stage or, perhaps more indirectly, it is Sharon's response to *Krapp's Last Tape* or *Endgame*, and her appeal to us to reflect on our lives while we still have time to do so.

All these thoughts came to me later because, as I watched Sharon play the part of Shipman in *Moving Pictures* that night, I was swept up in the inexorable forward movement of the story and in the ruthless, uncompromising determination of this older woman who faces her younger selves, her betrayals of others, her pain, her failures, and—yes—her victories, in short as she works through the conflicting yet complementary versions of her own life. As an actor, Sharon propelled the dramatic action, playing to the other two much younger women who perform Nell and Helen and to the young men whose presence she conjures up from her past to perform on the stage of her mind. She egged them on, challenging them and eliciting an intense concentration that kept them interacting with each other. Because this play exists in Shipman's mind and memory, she is the dramatic linchpin, the fulcrum through which all the emotions of the play must pass. It is an exhausting role because even when Shipman is silently watching the others playing, when Nell or Helen take over the story, even when Shipman's back is turned to the audience, she *is* the action that she has created and is reliving. She must register every moment and communicate what she feels to the other actors and to us.

Much as I enjoyed this performance, I found myself analyzing it and marvelling at how entirely Sharon could be *in* this role and be oblivious of herself as the author. Up on the stage, Shipman was turning the tables on Nell and forcing her to acknowledge something about her father. But it was the words "Daddy" and "Mummy" that snagged my attention because this is how Sharon speaks of her parents, and these words reminded me that there was a deep undercurrent of connection between the character of Shipman and the playwright who was performing the part that night. What I witnessed that evening, however, was not confession but *art* and the discipline of theatre training that enabled the actor, Sharon Pollock, to leave the playwright behind and to submerge herself in the created part. No, that was not "Sharon Pollock" on the stage, and yet it was. To arrive at that paradoxical position required a journey through rehearsals, writing, research, and, above all, life.

Being a fly on the curtain during rehearsals for the 2004 production gave me glimpses into who Sharon is as a person because this biographical play is also intriguingly autobiographical and, on this occasion, she was interpreting Shipman *as she imagined her to have been*: as stronger and older than the more delicate woman Lory Wainberg presented in this role for the 1999 premiere, and as a tough, practical woman who could, and did, sink her arms into frigid lake water to make mush for her animals. This business of animals is just one of the many points at which the lives of Nell Shipman and Sharon Pollock intersect because Shipman built her reputation on her talent for working with animals (bears and dogs among others) without electric prods; she cared personally for the animals, and Sharon, like Emily Carr, is famous for keeping a menagerie of animals, abled and disabled, conventional and highly unconventional. One of the other parallels between these women that only impressed me as I watched the rehearsals was that this play is about a woman who says she is dying, a woman—an artist—at the end of her life who asks herself if all the sacrifices were worth while and what, if any, meaning her life and life's work holds. When Sharon was writing this play, she knew she had serious heart problems, but through its premiere in 1999 and the premieres of the two plays that followed, she pushed ahead. If time was running out, she would bloody well see these plays through production. And she did. That she recovered from heart surgery to write, direct, and to act again (never mind in such a demanding, personally resonant role) is a blessing. Like *her* Shipman, she kept going; she met the challenge put to her by Nell: "The beginning, the middle, the bits in between, then the end, make something of it! Go on!" (*MP*, *CW* III, 86). Moreover, like Helen, Sharon began in the theatre as an actor touring imported, often second-rate plays, until she decided to write her own. Like Nell, Sharon confronted and challenged the established order, burned many bridges behind her, and stubbornly followed her own creative vision. Like Nell, albeit in theatre not cinema, she went independent during the Garry years. Like Helen and Nell, for better or worse, she divided her life between her work and her partners and children. And, like Shipman, at least like *her* Shipman, the past haunted her in the shapes of "Mummy" and "Daddy."

Although *Moving Pictures* in many ways recapitulates Sharon's own career up to 1999, explores many of her most important themes, and pushes her artistic practices in new directions, for a biographer it invites two fascinating questions: how did she arrive at this point, this pinnacle in her life's work and, insofar as her life resembles Helen-Nell-Shipman's, how did she find the courage to choose this life and how did she find the energy to always "go on"? After so many major stage plays and other pieces for children's theatre, radio, and television, her themes are familiar. They include the relationship of the individual to authority, the injustices we inflict on each other through prejudice, ignorance, and fanaticism, the sacrifices incurred by people (artist or anyone else) who pursue their vision regardless of the cost, the ubiquitous interpenetration of the public and the private, the personal and the political, and the constant need to find, or better still, *make* meaning through stories and storytelling. It may be dangerously close to a cliché to phrase it this way, but it is nevertheless true to say that in all her work Sharon Pollock struggles to articulate aspects of the human condition, and she always conducts her search for meaning with humour. Although *Moving Pictures* is an intimate play, a personal life-story, best presented in a small theatre space, it also demonstrates Sharon's capacity to establish both a layering of personal time with almost a century of socio-cultural history and to choreograph space so that a physical stage is transformed from the inside of a woman's mind into the ground on which a range of different events occurs, to a film studio, a farm in Idaho, and more. Space, like time, in Sharon's plays can be as narrow as one mind or as expansive as the world. Where did she learn this craft?

If we are to believe her (despite her warnings in the passage I quoted at the beginning), she decided to write plays in Acme, Alberta, in the summer of 1967, and the story is familiar because Sharon has told it many times. The story of Acme—more fondly, if irreverently, dubbed "Acne" by Sharon—has been recounted in essays, interviews, lectures, speeches and in private conversations, and it is a story about touring plays to small towns during the mid-1960s. Acme (and to be fair, that is its name), is tiny. You can find it on a good map about 40 kilometres due west of Drumheller or about 60 kilometres, as the crow flies, northeast of Calgary. If you are setting out for Acme from Calgary, as Sharon did once upon a time, you should go east from Calgary on the Trans Canada (Highway 1) and turn north on to Highway 9 at Interlake. Your route will take you straight north past Dalroy and Irricana to Beiseker, where the 9 meets the 72. But you do not want either of these roads because it is only a minor road, the 806, that will take you the remaining few kilometers to Acme.

In the 1960s, as today, Acme, Alberta was a very small place, but it did have a school, and actors touring plays would come into town to perform (at least that is how the story goes). However, the only place to put on plays was the school gym, and the only place to change or put on make-up was the locker-room, and the only plays that would put bums on seats were ... well, in the 1960s, they were not Canadian. The plays were all from elsewhere (England or the United States, London or New York) and the actors were expected to sound like Brits or Americans or like some odd mid-Atlantic alien. "The only voice and accent one never used," as Sharon has put it, "was the Canadian voice and accent, the Canadian voice as it was heard when it fell from the lips of white Canadians ... People found nothing odd about its absence in our theatres for virtually no plays were set in Canada" ("Evolution of an Authentic Voice," 116). By a series of steps I will describe later, Sharon found herself in Acme, Alberta sometime during the summer of 1967, with the MAC 14 Touring Company's production of *Mary, Mary* under the direction of Victor Mitchell who had arrived in Calgary to start up a drama department at the University of Calgary. The professional actors of this touring group were also part of Mitchell's short-lived, loosely organized troupe, the Prairie Players, that included Sharon, Michael Ball, Bob Haley, and Jaimie Eberle and they did what their name suggests: they played the Prairies, going to small-towns in southern Alberta and British Columbia with MAC 14 productions like *The Knack* (which they toured in the summer of 1966), *Mary, Mary*, and *Wicked John and the Devil*. The players travelled in a yellow school bus, loaned to them (with driver) by the school board, and this vehicle carried them, their sets, costumes, and everything. They would arrive at the theatre before the show, quickly unload and put up the set, change into their costumes, and go forth to perform. The performance over, they would strike the set themselves, change, pack up the bus, and retire to some little flea-bag hotel (as Bob Haley recalls) for the night. Next day they set forth once more to repeat this process. If lucky, they earned $35.00 per week for these gigs.

But before one begins to feel that the poor Prairie Players, or the MAC 14 group, were an especially hapless and exploited lot, it is well to remember that summer stock and touring theatre companies, even famous ones led by star actor-managers, experienced much of this same rough and ready work in North America well into the twentieth century. This is not a glamorous life. The touring experiences that Helen remembers in *Moving Pictures*—"Provide my own ward-robe ... pay my own way ... Cheapest hotels. [...] Mattress this thin! [...] And the smell?" (*CW* III, 94)—are part of the deal. As a rising star at the turn of the twentieth century, Pauline Johnson "appeared in theatres, hotel dining lounges, church basements, schoolrooms, drill sheds, and drawing rooms," and she often slept in bedrooms "with cockroaches, bed bugs, and rats" (Grey, 217). Hers was an exhausting round of one-night stands, of dressing in barbershops, and of poor food, cold trains, and constant change. Margaret Anglin, who made and lost a fortune, had similar experiences even when touring with the great James O'Neill, and during the 1940s Amelia Hall worked like a Trojan all winter for her beloved Canadian Repertory Theatre in Ottawa only to become an itinerant actor, grateful for work with groups like the Straw Hat Players in the summers. Vernon Chapman tells similar tales of woe in *Who's in the Goose Tonight?*, but Fred Euringer sums it up best: As a stock and non-equity actor in the 1950s, he was glad to earn $20.00 to $25.00 for a week that required rehearsals for an upcoming play, followed by learning lines for next day's play, topped off with an evening performance of yet another play. The day's work did not end there because it was the actors who took the show down before leaving the theatre to learn more lines until 2:00 A.M., after which they snatched some sleep and began the routine all over again the next day. What astonishes me is that anyone did this and that some of them loved it. Many gave up this gruelling pace and token pay, but those who stuck it out had remarkable dedication as well as talent. None of these actors (with the exception of Pauline Johnson, who included her own work in her shows) appears to have worried about the origins of the material they were performing in or what playwright's lines they were studying into the small hours. Few, if any, of the plays were about Canada or written by Canadians, and the actors were expected to mimic others' voices and accents. And this brings me back to Sharon, MAC 14, the Prairie Players, Acme, Alberta, and *Mary, Mary*, a slick fifties New York domestic comedy.

One night after some show in some small-town, Sharon Pollock decided to become a writer. She decided she had had enough of reproducing somebody else's stories and that she could tell her own, and *our*, stories, while speaking in her own voice. She decided to become a playwright, a Canadian playwright no less. Now, there are many nuances and modifiers to qualify these nouns—stories, plays, voices, Canadian—but they will emerge later, when I consider the plays she did go on to write. For now, it is enough to say that Sharon decided. Or so the story goes. But I will let her tell it in her own words:

> I was touring Western Canada with *Come Blow Your Horn* or *Mary, Mary* or something similar, and I'd played almost every grain elevator town in the West. On this occasion I was in Acne, Alberta—that's actually the name of the place—population 250, and we had about 265 out to the show, which was nice. I was changing after the performance in a basement locker room. The air was rich with the scent of runners and stale jock straps. That was an aroma I'd grown to know if not love on tour. I was an actress, and I naively thought I was going to change the world and that the theatre was the place to do it.... Anyhow, as I was removing my make-up, it began to dawn on me that changing the world with Neil Simon was a long-range project to which I was not prepared to commit my life. As I was taking in this stunning thought, there was a knock at the door. There was a girl of 14 or 15 standing there. She wanted my autograph and as I moved the old runners out of the way and we leaned on the locker to sign my name on her program she said to me, "Miss Pollock, how did you get where you are today?" I answered. "By bus." But then I thought. "You deserve better than this, and God damn it I sure do."

This version of the story appeared in a 1982 essay called "Canada's Playwrights: Finding Their Place" (34–35), and in it Sharon dates her decision at about 1971, but the transformation from actor to writer (who would remain an actor) actually began earlier, in 1967 when she was touring Western Canada, and the passion that led her into making theatre began earlier still. But that night in that town, the accidental encounter, and the girl's eager question—whether real or apocryphal—have gathered, with time and repetition, the patina of legend. Who was that girl? Did she leave "Acne"—no, Acme—Alberta? Does she know today where Sharon Pollock has got to? *Did she keep that signed program?* Has she attended a Pollock play, in Calgary, say, or in Edmonton? How can one thank her for being the unintentional thorn in the side that provoked the actor to become the playwright? Would Sharon have turned to writing her own plays anyway, without this push? I am certain the answer to this question is: yes. But I am equally certain that the girl from Acme (or Bragg Creek or

Balzac—why not Balzac!—or Bon Accord) existed and asked her question and received that abrupt answer: "By bus." I am certain because this sounds like Sharon's voice and because it is also characteristic of her to wish she had not been so abrupt and offered so little hope to a young person, who after all had dreams, and because she really did believe that young Canadians deserved better.

Sharon, at this stage in her life, was no longer in her teens and she had five youngsters of her own (with a sixth on the way, or soon to be, depending on the exact date of this Acme performance), so she had a considerable stake in the future. She also knew that she had to make up for lost time—lost that is to the writing of plays. She must have known this as well in the early sixties, when she found herself back in Fredericton, New Brunswick, living under her father's roof once more, a single parent with a fifth child just a baby in arms, because that is when and where the story of Sharon Pollock and the making of theatre really begins. She had taken another momentous decision, thrown off the spectre of Virginia Woolf's Angel, and left her unhappy marriage. She had decided to live rather than die, literally or metaphorically, and her new life took her into the box office of the Beaverbrook Playhouse on the main street of Fredericton, only a few blocks from Mary Sharon Chalmers' family home.

From the box office to the stage would not take long, and once on stage as Dandini in the 1964 Christmas pantomime, *Cinderella*, or as Lady Brute in *The Provok'd Wife*, or in a supporting role in *Mary, Mary* with a handsome young actor called Michael Ball, it took very little time for this new life to emerge. The Beaverbrook Playhouse would soon become Theatre New Brunswick. The beautiful young woman would catch the handsome young actor's eye. And the actress playing "a well-adjusted, healthy rich girl" in *Mary, Mary* would get her first Equity card, with a group called "The Company of Ten," and be singled out in the local newspaper as a "rising star." The process of becoming Sharon Pollock, actor, director, playwright, had begun.

CHAPTER 2

Family Matters

When I tell people I was born in Fredericton, I am always met with the observation that it is impossible to be accepted into Fredericton society—that it is snobbish and cliquish. I sympathize because I felt all of that when I lived there. Many people do. —MARY PRATT, 53

My past in New Brunswick is a ghost story. —SHARON POLLOCK, IN HOFSESS, 1980, 60

If Sharon had deliberately sought out a place in which to be born, as distinct from a place to call home, she could scarcely have chosen a place within Canada more different from Calgary, where she has lived since the mid-1960s, than Fredericton, New Brunswick. When she moved to Calgary in 1966, she moved to, or found, the place where she would feel most at home, and she has often said in interviews that "you don't always come from the place you're born in" (see Nothof, 2000, 181). But *home*, as the place in which she was born, was in the Maritimes beside the legendary Saint John River, with its generations of Canadian settler history, thousands of acres of forest, and rivers rich in Atlantic salmon. These New Brunswick rivers have melodious, magical names—Miramichi, Restigouche, Oromocto, Nashwaake, Tantramar—in comparison with which Alberta's Bow, Red Deer, Oldman, and Saskatchewan seem literal and prosaic. If the distance between New Brunswick and Alberta was a stretch, then the shift from tiny, elegant, mature, ethnically homogeneous Fredericton to sprawling, raw, brash, ethnically complex, upstart Calgary must have been a shock. Sharon's departure from the place of her birth and her ancestors was deliberate and apparently liberating, although she would stage her departure twice, first in 1956 and again in 1966.

How then explain why she has returned there often, like her contemporary, fellow artist Mary Pratt, when both women escaped its constraints first through marriage and then through art and fame? Why is Fredericton's appeal so powerful? The city, and by extension the province, whether as provocation or inspiration, haunts three of her finest plays—*Blood Relations*, *Doc*, and *Fair Liberty's Call*—and Sharon has said, quite simply and directly, that her past in New Brunswick is "a ghost story." So it is worthwhile exploring that distant home ground to explain its hold on her, and it is certainly important to understand the time and the place that shaped her first twenty years and surrounded and influenced her parents. Everyone with whom I have spoken who has spent any time in New Brunswick or, like Mary

Pratt and Sharon Pollock, grew up in Fredericton has stressed the importance of family, but my title for this chapter was given to me by Glen Nichols, a friend and colleague at the Université de Moncton, who told me never to forget that in that part of Canada, in the twenty-first century as much as in the late eighteenth, family matters. Which means that heritage, history, genealogy, class, and names matter, and that the ghosts of New Brunswick and Fredericton must be given their due.

To *visit* Fredericton today is to discover a small, manicured, pastoral city of considerable beauty. It sits on the edge of the Saint John River and rises gradually up the gently sloping hills to the southwest. From the university and the hospital near the crest of these hills the summer panorama looking east to the river resembles nothing so much as certain late-nineteenth century paintings by John Fraser, Homer Watson, and Lucius O'Brien. In winter it is easy to imagine a Cornelius Krieghoff scene played out on the streets and frozen curve of the river below. On the northeast side of the Saint John sit Devon and Marysville, now incorporated into the city of Fredericton, but for generations considered the wrong side of the river. The two sides of the water have long been connected by picturesque bridges strong enough to withstand the heavy ice of winter and spring breakup, and one of these bridges, the former CN railway bridge, now maintained as a trail and pedestrian bridge, involves one of Sharon's more troubling ghosts. Fredericton's main street, Queen, runs parallel to the river and has no high rise towers or postmodern architecture. There is nothing to obstruct the view up- and down-river. Like the other major streets of Fredericton, it is steeped in history. In fact, everywhere you walk in the compact downtown area you find evidence of the past, from the eighteenth century military presence of the beautifully preserved Officers' Square and Garrison District to Saint Anne's Point, nestled against the river just beyond the Garrison, where the earliest French settlement in this area began. The Old Public Burial Ground lies two short blocks southwest of Queen bordering Regent Street; elegant Waterloo Row and the Loyalist Cemetery are no more than a leisurely ten-minute stroll beside the river as it swings north and east past the nineteenth century Legislature and the delicate spires of Christ Church Cathedral or, coming closer to the present and into the twentieth century, past the Lord Beaverbrook Hotel, the Beaverbrook Art Gallery, and the Playhouse (also created by Beaverbrook and home to Theatre New Brunswick).

The streets to the east and south of Queen bear other important names that commemorate the city's and the province's historic loyalties to the Crown and those English-speaking colonists (the United Empire Loyalists) who fled north after the American Revolution: King, Brunswick, George, and Charlotte, with cross streets called Westmoreland, York, Carleton, and Regent. Brunswick is for the royal House of Brunswick (and the German duchy of Brunswick-Lunenburg), which gave the province its name; George and Charlotte, are for the King and Queen, and Carleton for the British officer, Colonel Thomas Carleton, whose brother Sir Guy Carleton led the United Empire Loyalists (UEL) out of the rebel colonies into a new home in 1783 and, in 1785, became a founding father and the first lieutenant-governor of the newly created province. Beaverbrook Street lies further up the hill, but downtown Fredericton has been indelibly marked by the money and vision of this feisty, entrepreneurial, successful little man from Newcastle, New Brunswick—first known simply as Max Aitken—who would become a newspaper tycoon and a British Lord but, like so many New Brunswickers, never forget his roots.[1] Fredericton itself was named for Prince Frederick, the second son of King George III.

When Fredericton, chosen as the capital of the new province in 1788, became an ecclesiastic centre in 1845, it was called "the celestial city," and the nickname still makes sense. At least it does in summer and fall when the city's wide, quiet, residential streets, perfumed with lilac and lined with stately elms seem redolent of peace, harmony, and safety. Mary West Pratt (1935–), that other eminent Canadian artist of Sharon's generation to be born in Fredericton, grew up in a house on Waterloo Row and she has given the city another, more earthy, but equally positive epithet: "the city in which to be a child" (Pratt, 49). Sharon Chalmers (1936–) grew up on Grey Street, about two blocks away from Mary West, and while Grey Street is less historic or prestigious than Waterloo Row, it is nonetheless impressive for its large houses, groomed gardens, and genteel beauty. Many of the families in this area are from the professional class and include lawyers, doctors, or professors at the University of New Brunswick just a short distance up the hill. As a child and teenager, Sharon walked, bicycled, and drove her father's green Packard on these streets, but if Fredericton was a good place for Sharon, like Mary West, to be a child, the same cannot be said for the Chalmers' family house on Grey Street. Calm, decorous, orderly surfaces can hide disorder and distress, at least to the visitor or mere passerby.

To this day, and certainly to an outsider, New Brunswick appears to be a province of divided loyalties. An invisible and yet palpable line seems to separate English-speakers and French-speakers, Protestants and Catholics, Tories and Liberals, the UEL counties of York, Sunbury, Charlotte, Kings, Queens, and Saint John lying to the south and west of the province from the northern and coastal counties of Madawaska, Restigouche, Gloucester (with the Pénisule Acadienne), Kent, and Albert. The centre of New Brunswick is sparsely populated, criss-crossed with scenic roads and picturesque rivers, and it contains the province's highest mountain (Mount Carleton at 820 metres) and Carleton Provincial Park (see Illus. 2). Almost 90 percent of New Brunswick is still forested with spruce, fir, white pine and northern hardwood; it is a wilderness paradise, and New Brunswickers are enthusiastic hunters and fishers. But it is the names of the towns and cities circling this natural preserve that are so telling: to the west and south of Fredericton are Woodstock, Canterbury, McAdam, St. Stephen, St. Andrews, and, along the Bay of Fundy at the river's mouth, Saint John; then, further east and north, past Sackville, with historic Fort Beauséjour strategically nestled in Cumberland Basin where Nova Scotia meets New Brunswick, you find Dieppe across from Moncton, then Cap Pelé, Sainte Antoine, Richibucto, Sainte Louis-de-Kent and Baie Sainte-Anne. If you wish you can follow the coastal road into the heart of modern New Brunswick's Acadie or you can cut across country from the city of Miramichi directly to Bathurst and further on to tiny, coastal Belledune, two towns that entered Sharon's history in the mid-nineteenth century.

These divided loyalties, like the patterns of settlement, pre-date the arrival of Europeans in the early seventeenth century because the Maliseet and Mi'kmaq First Nations, to whom these lands and resources belonged, shared their territory. The Maliseet controlled the inland

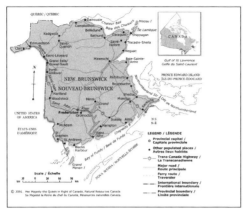

2. Map of New Brunswick showing places
    connected with Sharon's story: Fredericton and
    the Saint John River, Minto, Saint John,
    Miramichi, and to the north Bathurst and
    Belledune.
    © 2001. *Her Majesty the Queen, Natural
    Resources Canada. Reproduced with permission of
    Natural Resources Canada, courtesy of the Atlas
    of Canada.*

and river areas, notably along what the white settlers would call the Saint John River, and the
Mi'kmaq lived along the coast. When Sharon revisited this early New Brunswick history in
Fair Liberty's Call, it was the Maliseet (called by the settlers, the red-painted people) who
inhabited the forest edges of her white refugees' new world and were sensed by Joan Roberts,
the only member of the Loyalist group in the play to acknowledge her predecessors in the
land around Saint Anne's Point and Fredericton. But the United Empire Loyalists were not
the first Europeans to settle in what would become New Brunswick. When about 14,000 of
them arrived between 1783 and 1784 as refugees from the victorious American rebels, the
Indians, the French, and a few hundred English settlers were already there. As early as 1611,
tiny Acadian French communities had sprung up along the north shore of the Bay of Fundy
and near the mouth of the Saint John, and by 1700 the area's small European presence was
largely French and concentrated along the Bay. The Maliseet were still secure in their upriver
centre at Meductic, and they lived peaceably with the French who had spread as far up river
as Saint Anne's Point by 1730.

The first serious disruption of this pastoral cooperation came in the mid-1750s in what
remains to this day one of the darkest periods in pre-Confederation Canadian history. For
many reasons having mostly to do with eighteenth century wars in Europe between England
and France and with the constant jockeying for power and wealth in the colonies, at least
8,000 French settlers were driven out of Acadia (which included areas in modern Nova
Scotia, Maine and Quebec, as well as New Brunswick) in 1755, the villages in which those
two thousand or so who escaped expulsion took refuge were ordered burned by Colonel
Monckton (the British officer in charge of the expulsion), and both the small French
population and their Maliseet neighbours were driven north. Some French fled to the
Madawaska area adjacent to the future Quebec; the Maliseet withdrew from Saint Anne's
Point up river to Kingsclear, where an Indian reservation exists today. By 1763, when the
defeat of New France was assured on the Plains of Abraham and the Treaty of Paris signed,
the lines were drawn. The British had gained control of the interior along its major riverway;
English settlers (mostly pioneers from Massachusetts) began to arrive and establish small
communities as far upriver as Maugerville as early as 1762–63. The First Nations were soon

3. Members of the George W. Chalmers family with, from left to right, Sharon's Uncle Robert Chalmers, his wife Ruth, seated on the beach, Sharon's Aunt Lillian, and her husband Jeff behind her, Sharon's father Everett, and beside him her grandfather George Chalmers. Missing from this photograph are grandmother Mary Chalmers and Lillian's twin sister Marian. *Photograph (ca 1936), courtesy of Sharon Pollock.*

unable to resist the invaders, and the antipathy between French and English was sealed by tears, blood and fire. Ethnic, demographic, and geographic separations that mark the province today were firmly planted in the soil and psyche of New Brunswick. For many generations it would not be easy to be French there; indeed, as *may* have happened with Sharon's maternal ancestors, some changed their names and religious affiliation to join the English Protestant majority. And it would never again be easy to be Maliseet or Mi'kmaq in New Brunswick.

When New Brunswick became a province, separate and independent from Nova Scotia in 1784, the Loyalists moved quickly to consolidate their position. The divisions already present in the territory were enshrined in legal documents of treaty, escheat, and borders, and entrenched in institutions of government, church, the law, and the schools. Fredericton, the military centre, won out over Saint John as the provincial capital, and a group of fifty-five elite UEL (known as the petition or committee of "55"), pretty much took control of the future by maintaining their own interests. They were a Maritime equivalent of Upper Canada's Family Compact. By fiat of the new Lieutenant Governor Carleton, only the Church of England could perform marriages, and the "55" ensured that only English would be taught in the schools, that only members of this Family Compact would receive large land grants, and that slavery for Black Loyalists would be reinstituted under the label *indentured service. Spem Reduxit*—Hope was Restored—the motto of the new province applied chiefly to the few who held power. The great majority of Loyalists, like the English pioneers who had arrived before them, were farmers and labourers. Only a few were Harvard-trained lawyers, military leaders, or educated professionals, but these men, with names like Chipman, Willard, and Winslow, and their families became a local aristocracy which ruled the province until responsible government arrived almost fifty years later.

Mary Sharon Chalmers' roots go back into the pioneer years of New Brunswick's history, and possibly pre-date the arrival of the Loyalists, but were not part of the UEL élite stock. When her parents, Eloise Elizabeth Roberts (1913–54) and George Everett Norris Chalmers (1905–93), married, two pioneer New Brunswick families, each with New Brunswick family

4. The George Chalmers home in its original location beside the Gibson Train Station (ca 1925). The house was moved to Union Street, a few blocks away, and the verandahs were no longer in place by the time Sharon visited her grandparents there.
Postcard photograph reproduced with permission from Taylor and Rodger, Fredericton: A Postcard Trip to the Past *(126).*

connections, consolidated their heritage of Protestant faith, Tory politics, English and Scots ethnicity, and British loyalty, as well as a shared appreciation for education and service. On the Chalmers side it seems fairly certain that the original patriarch, John Chalmers (?–1882) from Ayrshire, Scotland, emigrated to New Brunswick in 1831 with four brothers, and they settled in Belledune (Beresford Parish, Gloucester County), a tiny coastal community on the Baie de Chaleur about 25 kilometres due north of Bathurst (see Illus. 2). From this time forward, the line is comparatively clear: John and his wife Mary had two sons and five daughters, and their second son, Hugh, born in Belledune in 1835, would be Sharon's great-grandfather; Hugh Chalmers and his first wife Phoebe Wilson (who brings the Wilson name into the genealogy on the Chalmers side) were the parents of George Wilson Chalmers (1875–1951), and George was Sharon's paternal grandfather. George Chalmers and Mary Sinclair Branch (1880–1940), were married in July 1904 and their first child, George Everett Norris Chalmers, was born on 5 June 1905 in Belledune. In 1905, George W. Chalmers was working as a telegraph operator, possibly for the Intercolonial Railway, and Mary's occupation would have been wife and mother. After George Everett, twin daughters, Marion and Lillian, were born in 1907 and a second son, Robert Hugh, arrived in 1912, by which time the family had moved to Devon on the east side of the river facing Fredericton (see Illus. 3).

The late nineteenth and early twentieth centuries were important for the expansion of the railways everywhere in Canada, but especially in New Brunswick because of its distance from economic centres like Halifax and Montreal, and the Fredericton area quickly became a significant railway hub. By the time WWI broke out, George Chalmers was thirty-nine, with a wife and four children. He needed steady work, which he had with the railway, and he advanced to become the Stationmaster at the CNR Gibson Train Station in Devon. This position, at an important railway junction, provided security, responsibility, and a comfortable home for his family, but not élite status. The house (see Illus. 4), originally located a short distance from the track and the railway bridge crossing the river to the Fredericton side, was substantial and attractive, and before it was moved to Union Street, where young Sharon and her brother would visit, it had a spacious verandah.

Judging from official records, the New Brunswick Chalmers line started during a period of considerable British immigration, and the Chalmers men brought with them their Presbyterian faith and British loyalties. They were successful, respected farmers with enough education to become local magistrates and elders with the church (as John Chalmers was), property owners, and managers, which is how one would characterize George W. Chalmers' position. The other family trait of note, at least one that appears on the record for the male line, is the "disease or condition directly leading to death"—"heart failure" for Hugh and "myocardial degeneration" for George W. Now these terms can, and did, cover a variety of problems leading to death, but this recurrence suggests a congenital heart problem passed down through Sharon's father to Sharon herself.

The Roberts line has been harder to confirm, but much more intriguing to explore. One of the first questions I asked Sharon and her brother Peter was whether Eloise, their mother, was a Roberts, by which I meant a *Fredericton* Roberts of the Charles G.D. Roberts clan. Their answer, like that of other family members and those Fredericton residents whom I queried on the subject, was either that they did not know or that they did not think so. When I learned from Sharon that her mother wrote poetry, it seemed possible, even likely, that Eloise and Sir Charles might be kin. However, despite frustrating blanks in the Eloise Roberts family tree, the genealogical facts are these: Roberts is a fairly common British name and there are many Roberts families in New Brunswick. More importantly, George Roberts, grandfather of the Canadian Confederation poet, was educated at Oxford and had moved to New Brunswick from England, with his English wife, Emily Goodridge, by 1832, when their son, the poet's father, George Goodridge Roberts, was born; George was well educated and a deacon, then a rector of the Anglican church, and his poet-son, Charles (1860–1943), who was born in Douglas (a short distance upriver from Fredericton), grew up in the Tantramar area and in Fredericton, graduated from the University of New Brunswick, and celebrated New Brunswick's beauty in poems like "Tantramar Revisited." He *was related*, on his mother's side, to fellow poet Bliss Carman but *not* to Eloise.

My next avenue of investigation took me back to the arrival of the United Empire Loyalists in 1783 because Roberts is a typical Loyalist name. In her book, *The Loyalists of New Brunswick*, Esther Clark Wright lists Roberts as a family that had lived in the American colonies for some generations by the time of the Revolution, when some of them fled to British North America and New Brunswick. If Eloise's poetry did not confirm a connection to Sir Charles, then surely her daughter's choice of the name Roberts for the Loyalist family in *Fair Liberty's Call* implied a UEL lineage. Moreover, Eloise was born in Chipman, the town northwest of Fredericton on the Salmon River that was named for Ward Chipman, a founding father of the province, a leader of the UEL and of the "55," and a wealthy Harvard-educated lawyer. All this information prompted me to believe that, on the male side, at least, Eloise was descended from those hardy, courageous refugees who gave up so much for their principles and chose to build new homes in the wilderness, where they could retain their allegiance to the King.

I wish I could confirm *absolutely* that this is the Roberts lineage because it suggests a romantic story full of pride, endurance and hope: *Spem Reduxit!* It is also a success story because those UEL Roberts did build new lives and a new country. But most of all I wish this because Eloise Roberts Chalmers is a powerful and very troubling presence in the story I am telling. It would be satisfying to portray her life as, in some respects, heroic, and as a success story. It would be satisfying, but I cannot make this claim for her. Whatever successes she enjoyed she appears to have forged for herself, and she inspired an intense desire for success in her daughter Sharon.

So where and how do I find the lines that run to Eloise Chalmers, neé Roberts? County census records suggest that the correct Roberts line may have included francophone roots because genealogical data lead back to the name Robear, likely a phonetic spelling of the French name Robert, in Kent County. At some point after 1861, one Peter Robear (French, Church of England, and probably born in Quebec) and his wife Abigail (of Scots descent, born in New Brunswick) anglicized their name to Roberts. They had three sons (John, Peter, and Benjamin) and a daughter. This daughter, Elizabeth (Robert) Roberts (born in 1845), appears in an 1881 Kent County census as having four children: Fredric, Allas (or Alice), John (born ca 1877–78), and Robert. She is not listed with a husband, so she may have been a widow or unmarried. A John Roberts, specifically John William Roberts, born in Richibucto, Kent County on 30 April 1878, was Eloise's father and almost certainly Elizabeth Roberts' second son.[2] Questions remain, but it is possible, given the history of New Brunswick and the deep-rooted antipathies between French and English settlers (whether pre-Loyalist or Loyalist), that Sharon's maternal Roberts ancestry included some French blood, and it is also possible that families with French names like Robert (also found in Quebec) anglicized their names to blend in with the dominant group. When intermarriage between French and English *Protestants* occurred (as happened with Peter and Abigail), then there was even more reason for the Robert family to adapt.

Whatever the case may be, this genealogical detour has no special significance in Sharon's story, except for the ironic light it throws on her father's impatience with French-Canadians. When John William Roberts (1878–1919) of Richibucto married Agnes Jane Dann (1882–1983) of Springfield, the family they established was Church of England and staunchly royalist. This couple had five children: Rena Donna (1904–87), Edward Clare (1907–85), Beatrice Irene (1909–?), William (whose dates I have not been able to confirm), and Eloise Elizabeth, the youngest, most talented, and, by all accounts, most beautiful of the Roberts daughters. At the time of their marriage in 1903, John Roberts and Agnes Dann Roberts were living in Hampton and Springfield respectively (towns in Kings County), and John was a millman, presumably employed with one of the southern New Brunswick timber companies that were struggling to survive the early twentieth-century decline in the lumber industry before the pulp and paper boom of the 1920s, and certainly not a member of the establishment. By the time John enlisted with the 20th Battalion of the Canadian Infantry, New Brunswick Regiment, on the 28th of November 1914, he was thirty-six years old, Eloise was eighteen months old, and the family was living in Chipman. His attestation paper indicates that he had served for one year, probably as a reservist, with the Third Battalion Royal Canadian Regiment, and that he was declared "fit" to serve. He was tall (six feet), well built, and with brown hair and eyes. Very little else is known, except that he survived,

5. Sharon, seated in front of
   her father, Everett, with her
   mother, Eloise, and brother
   Peter.
   *Photograph (ca 1940–41)
   courtesy of Peter Chalmers.*

returned home a sick man, and died of tuberculosis on 29 May 1919, leaving Agnes to raise her five children alone. As Desmond Morton explains in *Fight or Pay: Soldiers' Families in the Great War*, medical examinations at the time were often cursory, or even fraudulent, and TB, which was poorly diagnosed anyway, may well have begun before he enlisted. Certainly soldiers who were returned with TB received scant attention, hospital facilities were very poor, and families received little or no support.

Eloise would barely know this man who, upon his return from the war and according to family lore, slept in a tent outside, perhaps to shield his children from his illness. In a deed dated 14 November 1918, he left the family farm—"that Piece or parcel of land lying and being in the Parish of Chipman ... together with all Houses, Outhouses, Barns, Buildings,

Edifices, Fences, Improvements, Profits, Privileges and Appurtenances ... unto the said Agnes Jane Roberts her heirs and Assigns." In six months he was dead and this farm, passed from Agnes to her son Edward Clare, would become a place loathed by Sharon, loved by her brother, financially supported by their father, Everett Chalmers, and reincarnated, almost beyond recognition, in *Blood Relations*. Grandmother Roberts, who lived past one hundred, held her family together, saw her son William off to WWII, and buried her youngest child, Eloise, the one whose education, talent, and beauty promised so much. According to the family, her grief was inconsolable.

At the time of their wedding on 17 July 1935, Eloise and Everett Chalmers were an impressive couple. They were both well educated, good looking, charismatic, and optimistic about their future. Eloise, twenty-two at the time of her marriage, had completed her early education with high grades and gone on to train as a Registered Nurse at the Saint John General Hospital; she was the only one of her siblings to achieve so much. Everett was thirty, a graduate of the University of New Brunswick in Science with his medical degree from McGill, and he was taking further specialist training when he and Eloise married. In one version of their meeting, they saw each other in Montreal's Royal Victoria Hospital sometime between 1933 and 1935 and fifty years later this version would find its way into *Doc*; in another version, apparently reported by Everett late in life and repeated by others in the family, they met in Saint John, where he first saw her sitting on a park bench looking alone and forlorn. Exactly how or when scarcely matters now, of course, but the existence of versions reminds me of the complexity and conflicting details of stories and memories. What is certain is that these two people, born and bred in New Brunswick and trained in medicine, had a lot in common. After they moved to Fredericton, where Everett began his practice in general medicine and surgery in 1936 and where their first child, Mary Sharon, was born on 19 April 1936, Eloise would have to begin a new life as wife, daughter-in-law, and mother (see Illus. 5). Their second child, christened John Everett Brian, was born on 19 October 1937, and Eloise Roberts Chalmers would never work as a nurse again.

***

In hindsight it is easy to see that 1936, the year in which Sharon was born, was an ambivalent, if not downright ominous, and pivotal one in Western history. The decade that lay ahead would produce the fury of WWII, the horror of the Holocaust, and destructive air raids on England. Canadians were still struggling with the impact of the 1929 crash, the Depression, and the devastating droughts on the Prairies. There was no medicare, no social security system, and unemployment was high, especially in economically-depressed New Brunswick. The 1935 "On-to-Ottawa Trek" that began in Vancouver had floundered in Ottawa when R.B. Bennett (originally from New Brunswick) offered little support and then decided to arrest the leaders. The riots that erupted on 1 July 1935 in Regina, where the protesters were awaiting news from Ottawa, revealed the capacity for political and police repression in Canada and fuelled grassroots anger and despair across the country. This almost mythic confrontation between the people and the state eventually provided Sharon with material for two plays and inspired the creation of one of her more memorable satiric characters—the trekker called "Goose." William Lyon Mackenzie King was returned as Prime Minister in October 1935, partly as the nation's rejection of Bennett's failures of compassion and policy, and he held onto power until 1948, steering the country through the terrible years of the war on the strength of shrewd political manoeuvring, procrastination, and séances with his dogs and his dead mother. In England and Europe, various other instabilities and pressures were mounting. On the death of George V, Edward VII was crowned King of England, but in less than a year he abdicated to marry the American commoner Wallis Simpson, and his younger brother George VI became King on December 11th. For Canadians like the Roberts and Chalmers families, these royal affairs were immensely interesting and significant.

Far more important, however, was the outbreak of the Spanish Civil War on 17 July 1936, three months after Sharon's birth. As the world now knows and as novelists like Malcolm Lowry and Hugh MacLennan have shown us, this war was the harbinger of worse to come. In Lowry's *Under the Volcano*, set in Mexico, where Trotsky had fled into exile (and was soon assassinated), Western civilization was perched on the edge of an abyss; in MacLennan's *The Watch That Ends the Night*, the hero goes to Spain to support the republican forces. That hero, called Jerome Martell, born in a New Brunswick logging camp, a veteran of WWI, and a gifted surgeon, was based, in part, on Dr. Norman Bethune (1890–1939), who had practiced thoracic surgery at Montreal's Royal Victoria Hospital in the 1930s before departing for Spain in 1936. It is hard to imagine that Everett Chalmers did not know Bethune during these years and perhaps even admire him. Their politics could scarcely have been more different—Bethune became a Communist in 1935 and Chalmers was always a staunch Conservative—but as doctors they both believed in the need for improved services and medical reform. Unlike MacLennan's hero, Bethune died young serving this vision in China; like Sharon's character "Doc," Chalmers would live to realize many of his dreams for medicine in his home town. Both men chose public service over private duty or happiness, and with considerable cost. Meanwhile, Germany was mobilizing under Hitler, as Leni Riefenstahl's films, especially *Triumph des Willens* (1935) about the 1934 Nuremburg rallies, should have made clear, if the Nazi displays of power in Berlin during the 1936 Olympic Games did not. Regardless of how peaceful Fredericton may have been at the time, anxiety, turbulence, and war provided the context and backdrop for the Chalmers marriage and for the generation of children born during the 1930s.

By comparison with the dark forces massing in Europe, life in North America, while certainly hard for many, was comparatively benign. South of the border, the popular Franklin Delano Roosevelt was re-elected president and a great American playwright, Eugene O'Neill, won the Nobel Prize for literature. A novel that would go on to enjoy another life as a film had won the Pulitzer Prize, and Eloise Chalmers who was an avid reader would not have missed *Gone with the Wind*. Closer to home, where we had been told that Canada came of age on Vimy Ridge and the twentieth century belonged to Canada, the cultural scene was more productive than terms like the "Dirty Thirties" and "Ten Lost Years" (as Barry Broadfoot called the 1930s) would imply. In 1936 the Canadian Broadcasting Corporation, the CBC, was established from its 1932 roots as the Canadian Radio Broadcasting Commission. In 1936 the first Governor General's Award for fiction was won by Bertram Brooker for *Think of the Earth*. In 1936 Mazo de la Roche was a hit in England with her *Whiteoaks of Jalna* saga, *Canadian Poetry Magazine* began publication, and *The University of Toronto Quarterly* (founded in 1931) started its annual "Letters in Canada" reports. Also in 1936, Toronto's competing newspapers, the *Globe* and the *Mail*, buried their political differences and merged, as *The Globe and Mail*, in a bid to become Canada's national newspaper.

The 1930s, in fact, were anything but stagnant. The Group of Seven had disbanded in 1932, but was replaced by the Canadian Group of Painters; the first of the Massey Lectures was given that same year; and the third national Canadian political party of stature was founded when the Co-operative Commonwealth Federation (the CCF, today the NDP), formed under the leadership of Methodist Minister and social reformer J.S. Woodsworth. Frederick Phillip Grove published his best novel in 1933, that classic portrayal of prairie life, *Fruits of the Earth*, and in 1933 Emily Carr, whose career finally blossomed in the thirties, painted *Lillooet Indian Village* and broke through the prejudice that discouraged women from professional lives as artists in Canada. For Carr, "real success [was] to feel down in your soul that the thing you have striven for has been accomplished" (qtd in Shadbolt, 196), but it would take another fifty or more years for the two women artists born in Fredericton in that decade to feel this success.

If the arts were on the move in the thirties, on the stages of the country very little of *Canadian* substance was happening as yet. But there were promising signs of life: Herman Voaden, a nationalist and avant-garde director and playwright, published *Six Canadian Plays* in 1930; the first finals of the Dominion Drama Festival (DDF) were held with considerable pomp and ceremony in Ottawa in 1933, the same year that a small extension program from the University of Alberta put on its first amateur plays in the mountain resort community of Banff. Both the DDF and the Banff School of Fine Arts would play important roles not only in the future of Canadian theatre but also in Mary Sharon Chalmers' life. The one sour theatrical note struck in that otherwise artistically propitious year of 1933 was the Toronto reception given to a Progressive Arts Club play called *Eight Men Speak*. Because it was an openly left-wing play about the loss of civil rights by leaders of the Canadian Communist Party, word of its impending production caused hysteria and the Toronto police closed it down on the night of December 4th after its only performance. Clearly, Canadians, or at least their government, did not feel secure or at ease. As the decade wore on the government in Ottawa closed its eyes and ears to the worsening plight of the Jews in Germany, while those who did see what was coming grew more and more anxious. *The War of the Worlds*, Orson Welles's famous Mercury Theatre radio program of October 1938, caused an international panic, which if nothing else indicated the jittery state of peoples' imaginations. Canada's National Film Board, begun in 1939 and today one of the country's finest institutions, was created with propaganda in mind as Canada geared up for war.

In the years leading up to and then through the war, Fredericton seems to have been a safe and tranquil place. Yet, common sense says that it must have harboured the same kinds of tensions that John Murrell portrays so tellingly in *Waiting for the Parade* and Anne Wheeler captures in *Bye, Bye Blues*. There were curfews, blackout curtains, drills, sirens, and shortages, and there were alarming rumours, like the one about Moncton becoming a target for German bombs. Nevertheless I see it as a civilized oasis in a terrifying world. Little girls like Mary West and Sharon Chalmers were quite safe playing in cemeteries, walking to their first schools, or enjoying a spectacle like the great circus parade of 1938 that marched and danced through Fredericton with its elephants, painted ladies, clowns, and acrobats, and its fabulous cages with real lions and tigers. They could explore the parks, attend classes in the playgrounds, or even be taken to inspect the Coleman Frog crouched in its glass case and presiding over the lobby of the Barker House Hotel on Queen Street. True, as Mary Pratt remembers, the children's Hilroy scribblers had the standard war pictures on their covers and they were encouraged to collect pink war stamps and stick them in special books, but real hardship or serious threat was remote for the girls of Waterloo Row and Grey Street. As they grew up, they could easily visit the library, go to the movies, attend Sunday school, sing in the church choir, or ride a bike without fear of serious mishap, and in winter they could skate or ski or hike.

With her brother's arrival on the scene, only eighteen months after her own birth, Sharon got a playmate, or at least a younger protégé to advise, boss about, and read to. Peter was born on 19 October 1937, and here I must pause to explain. Eloise's only son was christened John Everett Brian Chalmers—John presumably for his grandfather Roberts, Eloise's father, Everett for his own father, and Brian for reasons that are now unclear—but at the age of ten he and his mother had his name legally changed to Peter Dann Chalmers. This name change was significant in several ways: Eloise must have persuaded Everett to agree to such a step, even though it represented a son's tacit rejection of a father with whom he would never be close; it signalled the acknowledgement of a beloved grandparent, Eloise's mother, Agnes Dann Roberts; and, most important, it illustrated the exceptionally strong bond between this mother and her young son, a bond that the grown man still cherishes. Today no one recalls why the boy's first name John was replaced by Peter or why Brian was also dropped.

The couple's first home was a rented place on George Street across from Fredericton's historic Old Burial Ground, where Sharon later recalled playing boisterously—to the dismay of the neighbours. When her brother was born, she was sent over to her Chalmers grandparents on the Devon side of the river, and when she was still pre-school aged, the family moved into their own home at 63 Grey Street, the house in which Sharon would live until she left for Toronto in 1956. This house on Grey Street (see Illus. 6) looks today very much as it did in the early 1940s, except that the property around it was more extensive and Eloise grew splendid roses in her garden. Buying such a place was concrete evidence that Everett was able to live in a neighbourhood and a style appropriate to his professional success, and he could afford to hire people to help in the house and the yard. There were numerous pets—a monkey, as well as more conventional ones like cats and dogs—beautiful silver, fine furnishings, and all the accoutrements needed for the social life of a doctor and his wife in small but formal and status-conscious Fredericton.

While storms were erupting in Europe and throughout the Western world during these years, they were also gathering behind the curtains at 63 Grey Street, and signs of this domestic discord soon became clear. Fredericton residents who knew the family and family

6. The Fredericton home in which Sharon grew up at 63 Grey Street. Although the property around the house was sold and developed in the 1980s, the house itself looks much as it did in Sharon's youth.   *Photograph by J. Grace, 2006.*

members—not to mention Everett himself and Sharon's brother—insist that what Sharon portrayed in *Doc* was true, literal fact, and a faithful recreation of life in that house prior to Eloise's death. But I will put questions of truth aside until it is time to consider the play and simply warn here against a too literal reliance on fiction to produce or reproduce facts. What *Doc* recreates is the atmosphere inside that house, the quality of bewildered pain endured by a young girl who may have, like Mary West, found Fredericton a fine place to be a child but nevertheless knew something entirely different and threatening about childhood. The discrepancy between the private world inside the house and the public world outside—the safe streets, well-groomed gardens, friends, school, carefree visits to the library in the Legislative Building or to the movies, escapades of skating on the river or skiing down the hill below the Arts Building at the University—was striking and real. Inside the house, Eloise Chalmers was becoming seriously depressed, suicidal, and an alcoholic. Her husband was rarely home; he could not be there because he had a medical practice to build in an era when doctors made house calls night and day and diseases like polio could not be prevented. Moreover, he lived in a small city surrounded by isolated farms, where accidents with machinery occurred often and women still died in childbirth; he *had* to spend time on the road.

To begin to understand the tragedy unfolding inside the home, one must try to remember what life was like in that time and place. New Brunswick was poor, behind the times in economic growth and development, largely rural and resource-based, and socially conservative. The 1929 crash and Depression hit the province hard and the industrial boom of the war effort that would galvanize other parts of Canada, bringing prosperity and new freedom to women, in particular, was much less evident in New Brunswick. Unemployment hovered near 20 percent during the 1930s, the province was deeply in debt, and poverty levels rose sharply. Put simply, times in New Brunswick were hard. But New Brunswick was also intensely loyal to Britain and proud of its military past that stretched from the eighteenth century to WWI, a legacy visibly celebrated in its streets, monuments, and historic sites. Patriotism was high, along with unemployment, so that when Canada declared war on Germany on 10 September 1939, enlistment was more brisk than it had been for the Great War. Records suggest that close to half the eligible men of New Brunswick signed up, among them Eloise's brother William Roberts, who became a sniper, and Everett's younger brother, Dr. Robert Chalmers, who served with the Royal Canadian Army Forces Medical Corps. Everett tried to enlist but was rejected because his medical examination indicated signs of diabetes. As the war dragged on reports of the exploits of New Brunswick's Carleton and York Regiment dominated the news at home, especially when the Regiment participated in the famous Italian campaign of 1943–44 and the costly push up the Liri Valley to Ortona and the Hitler Line. From today's perspective, it may be hard to reconstruct what daily life was like at that time, but we know that Allied propaganda was fierce, that Canadian men walking the streets in civilian dress were challenged and, as the casualties mounted, resented for not doing their part. Doc Chalmers must have felt he should double his efforts on the home front, where there was also a staggering amount to do.

New Brunswick's socially conservative and rural outlook was not encouraging for women. Like other Canadian women they got the federal vote in 1918; the right to vote provincially came a year later. However, in New Brunswick women were not *permitted* to run for political office until 1934, and no woman was elected to office in the province until 1948, when Edna Steele of Saint John became the first female city councillor. The Bench was no better: New Brunswick's first woman judge, Muriel Fergusson of Fredericton, was appointed in 1935, but no other female judge was appointed until 1980.[3] Prior to WWII, illiteracy was higher in New Brunswick than anywhere else in Canada (Soucoup, 226), and highest of all among Acadian New Brunswickers. It was not until the 1960s, in fact, when Louis Robichaud, a Liberal and the first Acadian Roman Catholic to be *elected* premier, took office that some of these old inequities were addressed: his government passed an Official Languages Act, making New Brunswick bilingual, created the Université de Moncton in 1963 and introduced many social reforms. Robichaud was defeated by the Conservatives under Richard Hatfield in 1970, and Doc Chalmers, a staunch Conservative, who had begun his active interest in local politics immediately after the war, was finally able to make an impact on provincial politics.

As a woman, Eloise had few options: she came from a working class background and lived in a profoundly sexist era; as the wife of an important doctor in a small city that placed great value on appearances, she was expected to entertain, to play bridge, and to join the IODE (the Independent Order of Daughters of the Empire). Because she was married with children and a husband who was fully employed she was not wanted in the labour force (a state of affairs common across Canada after 1945); and Everett Chalmers opposed her wish to return to her profession, even though he knew that she was an excellent nurse. The prejudices and social constraints of the day dictated against her retaining an independent identity or a sense of self-worth outside the home. Her socially sanctioned role during the war years was to keep the home fires burning, buy war bonds, and support the war effort. After 1945, war propaganda quickly gave way to a new rhetoric of domesticity defining and limiting women's proper role, with magazines, radio programs, advertisements, and the images of popular culture, notably in films, all loudly proclaiming that a happy, healthy woman belonged in the home and that a woman who rejected or disliked this life was unfit, even dangerous. She would come to a bad end or die, like Norma Shearer in the popular 1948 film *The Red Shoes*, and be justly punished for daring to want a career *and* a family.

Other events than the war in Europe, New Brunswick's inadequate health care, and women's rights were pressing in on the family as early as 1940 when tragedy struck on a pleasant summer day in quiet Fredericton. Eloise, Everett, and their two youngsters had moved into the house on Grey Street at about this time, so financially they were prospering, and the news from overseas, albeit grim, was not personally devastating—both Uncle Bill Roberts and Uncle Bob Chalmers were alive. However, at about 5:00 in the afternoon on Monday, August 5th, only a few blocks from the family's home, Mary Branch Chalmers, Everett's mother and the grandmother for whom Sharon was named, drowned in the Saint John River in what may have been a bizarre accident. Grandmother Chalmers was sixty when she stepped onto the south end of the CN railway bridge that spans the river joining Fredericton, at the bottom of University Street (see Illus. 7), with Station Street, in Devon on the north side of the river, about a block from Barker Street where she lived. It was broad daylight on a fine summer's day. The train from Minto was waiting on the Devon side because the swing-span in the bridge had been raised to allow the motorship *D.J. Purdy* from Saint John to proceed upriver. A YMCA instructor was teaching a lifesaving class by the river bank, young men were canoeing in the afternoon sun, and on the south shore Mrs. J. Bacon Dickson of 44 Waterloo Row was sitting on her verandah enjoying the view across the river and the activities on the bridge. Presumably Mary Chalmers was on her way home. She may have been visiting her daughter-in-law and grandchildren on Grey Street just a short walk from the south end of the bridge; if we can trust the story in *Doc*, she may have wanted to see her son and not been able to find him.

But this is speculation. What is certain is reported in the *Fredericton Daily Gleaner* for Tuesday, August 6th, and the account is disturbing. Mrs. Dickson told the police that as she sat on her verandah her "attention was attracted by a figure on the bridge about four spans from the Devon end," and she became alarmed. Then she "saw the figure leap feet first and strike the water some twenty feet below." The caretaker of the bridge, who operated the swing-span and knew Mary Chalmers, had watched her come on to the bridge and spoken to her, but then he "was horrified to see [her] moving toward the side of the bridge and down to the cap of a pier" from which she "jumped." As the waiting train slowly pulled onto the bridge, the crew saw a woman in the water on the lower, south side of the bridge and rushed

7. The old CN railway bridge across the Saint John River, seen from downriver on the Devon side with Fredericton in the distance. In August 1940, Mary Chalmers, Sharon's paternal grandmother, fell from the bridge when she was crossing from the Fredericton side and drowned. Today it is called the Trail Bridge and is a recreation pathway for pedestrians and cyclists that is part of the Trans Canada Trail.   *Photograph by J. Grace, 2006.*

to do what they could to help; they threw a mattress down to the water as a flotation device but "the woman in the water made no apparent effort to save herself." According to the paper:

> The death was witnessed by several persons none of whom was close enough to do anything or to render any aid during the brief time the victim floated on the surface. Death must have ensued shortly as craft which hurried to the scene, reaching it in a few minutes, were unable to find trace of the body. Dragging operations were begun by the R.C.M.P., last evening two boats engaging, and other craft were also at the scene. The body was not located. Hundreds gathered on the river banks and watched as soon as word of the fatality spread.

Everett Chalmers was among those in the "other craft" and he continued to search into the night and the next day. Mary Chalmers's body was eventually recovered downstream and the coroner, Charles MacKay, recorded the death as an "accident" caused by "drowning," although suicide (and homicide) are options provided on the legal registration form, and he listed "myocarditis" and "general ill health" as the "morbid conditions" contributing to the death.

At the bottom of the newspaper column describing this local tragedy, the surviving relatives are listed as her retired husband and four children, and Mary is described as a member of the Gibson Memorial United Church "in which she was very active." Beside this column one large headline announces AIRCRAFT OUTPUT IN BRITAIN GROWS and the article reports that the R.A.F. have dropped more than 3,000 bombs on Germany, and another reads—HITLER APPOINTS NEW AMBASSADOR—who, as the item explains, will go to occupied Paris which fell to the Nazis in June. At other points on the page there are advertisements for "Slipp & Flewelling's Sausage," internationally famous Omega watches, and Nova Scotia Pack Apple Juice. These juxtapositions, abrupt, arbitrary, and incongruous, are stark reminders that the private grief and shock of this individual death, which would haunt the family and play a small but strategic role in *Doc*, made little impact on the daily business of Fredericton life and was of no consequence at all on a national or international stage preoccupied by war.

What really happened on the bridge that day and what Mary Chalmers *intended* to do when she climbed down onto a pier cap are impossible to know. The Minto train was not on the bridge so she was not in danger; the newspaper spoke of "conjecture as to what caused Mrs. Chalmers to go to the side of the bridge and apparently leap into the water"; and Everett is quoted as saying that "his mother suffered from heart-trouble [and] this could have caused dizziness." Privately, he spoke of depression due to menopause. But to this day, people in Fredericton, including Sharon's brother and family acquaintances, believe that Mary Chalmers committed suicide. Whatever the cause, it seems unlikely that such a spectacular, shocking death, and the attention and gossip it attracted, would not have caused grief, consternation, and possibly recriminations within the Chalmers family. For Mary's husband George, the shock must have been terrible, and at four years of age Sharon was old enough to register some of this distress and to remember this grandmother clearly.

By 1940, when grandmother Chalmers died, the family comprised Eloise, Everett, Sharon, and little Peter. Shortly after this time, three additional people joined the household as regular if not permanent members: Mary and Hazen Arbeau who worked for the Chalmers, and a girl called Elaine, who was a few years older than Sharon and especially close to Eloise. The precise relationship between Eloise and this young woman is a matter of conjecture. She was understood to be a favourite niece, the daughter of Eloise's older sister Beatrice, and she apparently came to live with her relatives in Fredericton to attend a good high school, a move by no means uncommon for country girls of the day. However, the strong physical resemblance between Eloise and Elaine and their obvious affection for each other have led to the suspicion that Elaine was, in fact, Eloise's daughter from before her marriage.[4] As far as Sharon's story is concerned, Elaine's arrival meant that Sharon had to share her mother's attention, not only with Peter, but with an older sister/daughter figure (see Illus. 8). It is tempting to imagine Sharon recreating Elaine in the character of Lizzie Borden's older sister, Emma, in *Blood Relations*, who sides with the stepmother but who also acted as a mothering figure for the younger Lizzie when their own mother died. It is tempting, except for the facts: Lizzie Borden had a sister called Emma, so one did not have to be invented. As for the dramatic tensions between the two characters, the layers of affection and resentment in their relationship, and the striking contrast in their natures ... well, in *Blood Relations* these elements are fictional, there to serve the play, but they could have been inspired, as much of the deeply rooted power of this play is, by Chalmers' family matters.

8. A family evening out ca 1946–47. Left to right: Sharon, Elaine, Eloise, Everett, and Peter.
Photograph courtesy of Peter Chalmers.

Mary and Hazen Arbeau worked for the Chalmers family for about twenty years, from circa 1940–41 to 1961. Mary was the housekeeper and maid, and she was devoted to Eloise. Judging from her vivid memories of these years, Eloise returned this affection, relied on Mary, and confided in her. Hazen was the gardener and did assorted maintenance chores. The couple had their own home and a son, but they arrived early in the morning, and Mary was sometimes in the house during the evenings and at night. Like anyone who works in close daily contact with a family over many years, Mary Arbeau saw what was happening in the home, and while the details may have faded (she was ninety-one when we met), I was impressed, as I listened to her talk, by the depth of her emotion when remembering Eloise. In terms corroborated by many others who knew Eloise, even at her worst, Mary wanted me to understand that she was a *beautiful*, loving, kind, and very intelligent woman. She loved her garden, was an excellent cook, read widely and played the piano a little, and she loved Everett. Yes, Mary told me, Eloise hid bottles of liquor around the house and she, Mary, would find and confiscate them. Yes, Eloise was sent away for treatment many times, to Montreal, Connecticut, and to the provincial psychiatric hospital in Saint John, which was an appalling place with bars on all the windows; she was even hospitalized in Fredericton's Victoria Hospital. And yes, Mary hesitated, then insisted: Everett was unfaithful and one night Eloise took Mary with her in the car over to Devon, where they both saw his car parked outside another woman's house, the same woman who called Eloise at home to taunt her. Recalling this evening and Eloise's despair, she explained that she had urged Eloise to take her children and leave Fredericton or, at least, to move out and find a job, but that Eloise could not be persuaded to do either. Such a step was, after all, rare in the 1940s, especially for a woman with Eloise's position who lived in a city like Fredericton, where maintaining appearances and family ties mattered.

Hazen Arbeau, despite his long years with the family, seems to have played a more minor role in the drama unfolding inside the house. Mary recalled him arriving at about 7:00 one morning to find that Eloise had fallen when drunk and become stuck somehow and unable to move; it was Hazen who rescued her and, in Mary's view, saved her life. Hazen Arbeau died in 1960 or 1961, shortly before Mary left her position with the Chalmers, and it was at about this time that Sharon wrote a brief sketch of this man who clearly made an impact on her imagination. The sketch is short, just over two typed pages, and it is titled "The Order of Things." The narrator, now grown and recalling this figure from her past, begins emphatically: "I met him when I was quite young, about four I believe, and I hated him even then." Her reasons for hating Murray, as the man in the story is called, were that he was ugly and stupid, or seemed so to her:

> He was tall but his humped shoulders and bent posture made him appear much shorter as well as giving him a threatening air. His arms were unnaturally long, and his hands hung and danced about when he walked as if they were attached to coiled springs. My eyes were continually drawn to his face when he was near, and I catalogued each feature, and debated which was ugliest and why. He had a low, sloping forehead, and heavy eyebrows, no two hairs of which grew in the same direction.... His teeth were numerous and of varying colours.

To make matters worse, this man came "from the North Shore and could not read or write.... For this I hated him."

But the narrator is telling this story in retrospect and the story has a moral. She goes on to describe how she and her girlfriends mocked Murray before pausing to describe her self:

> I was a pretty child and an only child, the centre of my mother's life and the apple of my father's eye. My parents had a preconceived idea of a sort of perfect type of adult and I was raised to fit this mould. We were extremely happy, relaxed and content with each other. Often we were pointed out and referred to as an example of a harmonious family.

Years later this pretty, only child would return home from university and accompany her parents and Murray when they close the country cottage for the winter. As she sits reading while he works in the yard, she still finds him repulsive, that is, she does until something he says causes her to look again: "Suddenly he uttered a hoarse whisper, 'Look, look at the sky!'" A spectacular fall sunset was unfolding across the sky, but she had been oblivious to this beauty until he spoke. "Ain't it beautiful,' he breathed." As she stared at him, seeing him transformed by the setting sun and with tears in his eyes, she was silently rebuked for her cruelty and ignorance: "I stared at him and my throat felt tight and prickly. I somehow was an intruder in a strange world. He belonged."

Sharon did not publish this story, but she may have sent it to her father who sent it back to her with the following handwritten note, dated 1987, at the end: "Sharon—I found this recently when cleaning out a desk. I don't know whether your mother wrote it or not. It seems familiar?—Dad." Everett Chalmers' uncertainty about who wrote this sketch is understandable when one checks the name and address typed at the top of the first page: E. Roberts, Site K, Keswick, Ontario. For some reason, Sharon Pollock, as she was called by the time she lived in Keswick, Ontario in the early sixties, had called herself "E. Roberts," but there is no doubt that *she* wrote "The Order of Things" and there is no doubt that this is a portrait of Hazen Arbeau. There is also no question but that the girl and the "harmonious family" described here bear, at best, a qualified resemblance to Sharon Chalmers and the family of 63 Grey Street, Fredericton. What, if anything, can be made of this slight foray into narrative with its caricature of the hired help, its saccharine picture of the girl and her parents, and the clear moral judgement made about class pretensions and insensitivity at the end? Can it tell us anything about Sharon Pollock the playwright? And why, more importantly perhaps, would the adult woman use her dead mother's name as a pseudonym? Sharon has said that she often put "E. Roberts, which was my mother's name," on her earliest prose sketches and stories because she was "trying to work through my feelings about my mother in some unconscious or subconscious way" (see Hohtanz, 1987, 6), but how using her mother's name would help is another matter. Possibly this naming enacted her wish to do something *for* this lost mother, to give her a surrogate voice and existence, to compensate for what her mother had lacked; or perhaps it allowed her to distance and control a range of powerful, largely negative feelings about Eloise. The naming, in short, seems to be an act of recuperation (in love) and appropriation (in hatred and fear) in one gesture. And this gesture would recur, as we shall see, well into the 1990s, when "E.E. Roberts" would reappear in connection with Sharon's work. While it is unwise to overemphasize the importance of slight early pieces in a writer's oeuvre and it would be irresponsible to scour this story for psychological explanations of the person who wrote it, questions raised here are not going to evaporate, and some of them are easier to answer (if only partially) than others. I believe that this use of her mother's name indicates the psychological and symbolic importance of Eloise for her daughter and that the implied criticism of pretension, that the need, even in such a brief piece, to focus on social and ethical issues, are integral to Sharon's view of life and inevitably part of her work.

Her school years were, in many ways, the usual mix of discovery, mischief, adventure, boredom, and routine. Regardless of her mother's private state, many of Sharon's childhood experiences were perfectly standard for a girl of her time, place, and class. Her teachers recognized her intelligence and strong personality. She was not bookish, but she read voraciously and indiscriminately, developing a lasting passion for history, on the one hand, and for murder mysteries on the other. She was shy when called on to speak publicly. She fretted about her hair, her clothes, and even about the plaid shoelaces her mother brought her from New York: "I had put them into my saddle shoes," she recalls, "but no one in the

9. Dinner at Montreal's famous restaurant Au Lutin Qui Bouffe, 18 October 1946. This recalls the photograph Catherine describes in *Doc*, but it does not exactly replicate Catherine's description. *Photograph courtesy of Peter Chalmers.*

rest of the school was wearing plaid shoelaces, and that didn't mean that I thought I was ahead of the game; I thought I was terribly outside the game" (see Appendix 3, 411). She wore the "Madawaska" skirts and twin sweater sets popular at the time; she was the envy of other girls (like Mary West) because she had expensive toys; she suffered the indignity of having braces on her teeth; she attended Christ Church Cathedral with her family and sang in the choir; she played the piano at the Charlotte Street school while her classmates trouped into assembly.

Although she did not belong to groups, she had a few close friends and, as a teenager, she had boyfriends, attended street dances in Phoenix Square, sometimes went to parties, and found as many opportunities as possible to drive her father's car. She argued with her brother over the usual things, especially the car, cadged money from her father, who seldom refused her, and she could be catty—about other girls at school, about a particular French teacher who was a bore, and about poor Hazen Arbeau—but she disapproved of this behaviour, even when young. Out of her messy bedroom an increasingly beautiful, well-dressed teenager would emerge. She was, in short, healthy, active, privileged, and as happy as teenaged girls ever are. It would be a mistake to forget all the ways in which Mary Sharon Chalmers led a perfectly normal life. What's more, her family experiences were often happy ones. Although Eloise and Everett did not take their children to serious plays, they did go to popular musicals in New York—*Annie Get Your Gun, South Pacific, Oklahoma!*—and they sometimes took both Sharon and Peter to see stand-up comics in Montreal dinner clubs like Au Lutin Qui Bouffe, where Everett ordered her "pink lady" cocktails and Eloise was photographed (an image described in *Doc*) feeding the piglet from a baby's bottle (see Illus. 9). There were family trips in the green Packard; one that Peter recalls in 1952 took them to Banff for a medical convention, then on to Vancouver, and home through the United States. There were hunting trips and fishing holidays at the family's camp on the Miramichi, where Eloise liked to hunt and fish, pleasant weeks at the summer cottage near Fredericton on the

10. The 1951 staff of Fredericton High School's yearbook, *The Graduate*. Sharon is standing second from left in the back row; Mary (West) Pratt is seated first on the left in the front row. *Courtesy of Fredericton High School Library.*

Saint John River, and trips to New Brunswick's beaches and parks. Peter recalls a trip to Fundy National Park shortly after it opened in 1948, when the family was featured in tourist advertisements for the park looking like that happy family in "The Order of Things."

Sharon's first school was the Charlotte Street primary school, an attractive two-story building of red brick dating from 1884, only a few minutes walk from her home. Her high school years were divided between Fredericton High School (FHS), then at the corner of George and Regent streets, and an Anglican private girls' school in Quebec's Eastern Townships called King's Hall. The girls in her year, or a year ahead or behind her, at FHS were mostly from established, professional Fredericton families—Beth Cattley, Jane Hickman, Pam McCready, Jennifer Prosser, and Mary West—and those with whom I have talked recall Sharon clearly (see Illus. 10). She was, above all, exceptionally intelligent, strong-willed, sometimes critical of her teachers, at least by the time she reached high school, and always outspoken. She was also very generous, ready for any adventure or escapade and, by her early teens, she smoked Players Export (no filters) and swore vividly, if not quite as constantly as her father. Male and female friends and acquaintances alike, remember her as beautifully dressed and very good-looking, although who she resembled depends on who you talk to. Some say she looked like Eloise, who had dark auburn hair, large wide-set brown eyes, a lovely figure and, when dressed (often in green) to go out, looked like a movie star. Others insist that she was very much like Everett in both looks and manner. And those I have spoken with who knew her well in those years agree that she adored and emulated her father and was not close to her mother.

Of course I have asked Sharon and her childhood friends when she started writing or if she had an early interest in plays or theatre. Her writing, apparently, began early, but a special interest in dramatic literature or theatre came somewhat later. There was a Drama Club at FHS, as was common in high schools of the day, and in grade 10 she was its president, but she cannot recall any of the plays the club put on and the school yearbooks I have seen are no help. In any case, recitations, public speaking, and various school performances were standard features of primary and secondary school education (elocution, after all, was still taught and valued), and children were simply expected to participate whether or not they had an ounce of ability. Sharon does recall becoming shy and red-faced when called on to perform in this way during high school. There were also annual plays and revues at King's Hall for which she would "emcee," but acting or studying drama (beyond the requisite Shakespeare) or writing plays was still many years down the road. She began other kinds of writing, however, at least as early as age ten. Nancy Drew books, featuring that clever, courageous girl detective with the handsome successful father and conveniently dead mother, were popular reading for Sharon's generation, so she wrote what she described to me as "Nancy Drew type stories" in lined scribblers. These stories provided a fantasy outlet into a world where there were no family problems, a housekeeper to do the chores, and an indulgent father who paid the bills: Nancy, the daddy's girl and super-sleuth, had it all. Like Eloise, Sharon also wrote poems in small booklets, one of which was returned to her years later by a former teacher and neighbour. (It now appears to have vanished along with the scribblers.) This booklet contained, in Sharon's words, "twelve pages of bad, childish poetry," but the child had decorated the booklet with a copyright sign, ©, and a set of numbers resembling those used by publishers on the copyright page. According to Jane Hickman, her closest friend, the idea of becoming a writer was serious for Sharon from this early age, when the girls formed what they called "The Secret Two Club" because they both wanted to be writers instead of housewives or teachers like the adult women around them. When they weren't plotting careers and escapes from Fredericton domesticity, they amused themselves with stories that Sharon wrote.

By the time she reached high school, Sharon had decided to go public by publishing little prose pieces in *The Graduate*, the Fredericton High School Yearbook. One appeared in the "Literary Section" of the 1950–51 yearbook, the same year she represented her class on the Student Council and was a member of the "Year Book Staff," and it is an admonishing little number called "Shaking Hands":

> There are many ways of shaking hands. Some are pleasant; some decidedly unpleasant. Perhaps you may have the honour of receiving guests at a large social affair. One becomes quickly acquainted with the various types after an hour or more of hand shaking. A small frail frightened man enters the room. Seeing your outstretched hand, he glances furtively around and extends his, which seems like a slightly damp, pliable dishcloth. This type of hand shaking is often accompanied by chills and shivers running over your backbone. Next enters a large, husky woman, who flits from group to group in the room rather like a waterbug skimming over the surface of a pond. With cries of ecstasy she descends upon you, thrusts her hand into yours with a vicelike grip and pumps your arm up and down for several minutes while uttering shrieks of joy because she has located you. A slightly normal looking man, whose name is probably Smith, Jones or Brown, offers a natural hand shake, which is firm enough to get a good grip, and lasting only a few seconds. Hand shakes of this sort quickly erase any horrors previously endured through

a sense of duty to your hostess. Perhaps it would be a good idea to classify one's own method
of the age old custom of offering hands as a greeting, before condemning your neighbour.

Sharon Chalmers, D1

The similes of dishcloths and waterbugs are clumsy, but the point of the story is clear: those
who live in glass houses shouldn't throw stones and anyone with limp wrists and sweaty
palms had best think twice before shaking hands with Miss Chalmers.

Before Sharon left Fredericton for King's Hall, she and Jane had found other ways than
clandestine writing and dreaming in their Secret Two Club to flout genteel behaviour and
escape the expectations of female conformity. The most astonishing of their adventures, at
least by today's urban standards, occurred when Jane and Sharon were sent off to Montreal
by train un-chaperoned. They were just eleven and twelve at the time and Sharon, who made
regular visits to the orthodontist, knew the route to his office. But this time the girls stayed
overnight in a downtown hotel, with Everett paying the bill and providing the pocket money.
Nothing daunted by the big city, they made a time of it, hired a calèche for a drive around
Old Montreal (see Illus. 11), lingered at a fairground, spent every cent they had except the
return bus fare to the hotel, and then missed their bus stop on the trip back. What seemed
like hours of walking and miles later, they arrived at their room safely, exhausted, but
jubilant.

Other adventures had somewhat less happy endings. One day, after skiing on the hill in
front of the Arts Building at the University of New Brunswick, Jane and Sharon ended up
in a vigorous fight. Sharon pelted Jane with snowballs; Eloise insisted that Sharon go over
to Jane's house and apologize; when Sharon arrived at the door to do her duty, Jane clobbered
her over the head with a ski. Whereupon Sharon announced that she would never again
apologize—a decision she has, by and large, kept to. But they did make up, and they certainly
found other ways of acting up. On one occasion (at least as Jane recalls it), Sharon led a
group of ten- or eleven-year-old girls (all daughters of leading families) into the local Zellers
store on a balloon-stealing mission. Balloons had been unavailable during the war, so these
bright items were highly desirable. Unfortunately, however, the manager caught them
balloon-handed and called Jane's father, a lawyer, who proceeded to lecture them on the fate
of thieves and to threaten them with something called Juvenile Court, which Sharon heard
as "Jewish Court." The girls, who understood what had happened to the Jews in Europe,
were terrified. A few years later, now in grade 10, the two sallied forth on a more major
adventure, this time with serious consequences. For three weeks, they skipped school and
slipped into the local cinema by a back door to watch the movies for free. When they were
finally caught a huge fuss ensued. They were temporarily suspended from FHS and
grounded at home; then Sharon was removed from the school and sent to King's Hall, while
Jane, who was sent back to FHS, was forced to memorize *Macbeth* for punishment.

Sharon never studied again at FHS, but she did attend the graduation dance there in June
1954 on the arm of a tall, handsome young chap called Murray Allen. He had once been
Jane's beau, but Mr. Hickman regarded him as unsuitable and during Sharon's absence
from Fredericton, her boyfriend, Tom Bennett, left the city to train for the RCMP. But now

11. An adventure in Montreal, ca 1948. Jane and Sharon look very mature and proper for two teenagers from "F'ton" on the loose in the big city.
Photograph courtesy of Jane (Hickman) Green.

Murph was available. As he recalls it, when Sharon came home from King's Hall, she needed a partner for the dance at her former high school so she asked him, and she did so in a dramatic and memorable way. He had checked into a hotel in Black's Harbour, a two-hour drive from Fredericton, and he was preparing to play baseball with the Black's Harbour Brunswicks when his team mates called him down to the lobby because "a good-looking broad" driving a green Packard convertible was asking for him. It was Sharon, driving Everett's car, and after he got his coach's permission, the baseball player and the doctor's daughter sped back to Fredericton for the dance. The guys on the team were impressed, and so was Murph Allen.

In Jane Hickman's recollection of the early fifties and of Sharon's departure for King's Hall, it was playing hooky from FHS that prompted Everett to pack his daughter off to the private school on the assumption that the school could not be challenging enough if she could skip so much and still get good grades. Murph Allen remembers this differently. He recalls an occasion on which Sharon wanted Tom Bennett to run away with her so they could put Fredericton well behind them—in the mind set of the day, a male companion was needed for a girl to make her escape; however, Tom was not up to this challenge (shades of Dr. Patrick in *Blood Relations*) and reneged, but Murph Allen suspects that Everett realized his daughter's restlessness (or recklessness) and wanted to remove her from temptation. However, there is at least one other plausible reason for Sharon's abrupt departure: Eloise. At some point during the late forties family matters had so deteriorated that home life was a nightmare. As Sharon would later recall, the family was "so unable to communicate [or] be assured of each other's love that we filled the house with animals to fulfil those functions for all of us" (see Zwarum, 33). Others have described the home, the mother, and the mother/daughter relationship more directly. Apparently there were times, during the day, when Eloise would appear before Sharon and her friends from somewhere in the house clad in a silk dressing gown, drunk and ranting, and waving a knife. There were also times,

12 Mary Sharon Chalmers, aged ca nine
   months, with her mother, Eloise.
   Photograph courtesy of Peter Chalmers.

during the night, when she tramped through the rooms brandishing her rifle and terrifying everyone in the house (her husband was out) or rushed into the street in her nightdress, as if berserk. And there were times when she slashed her wrists. Her son would come home from school and listen intently because if the water was running in an upstairs bathroom, it meant that a disaster was in process; more than once he had to intervene. For Peter, who adored his mother, these scenes were heartbreaking, as well as frightening. Sharon's reaction was anger, but she would not talk about the situation; no one in the family would. She and her mother fought a lot, sometimes to the point of screaming and physical blows. Sharon would find and confiscate liquor bottles; Eloise would protest and rage. Eloise appears to have preferred her son; Sharon gravitated to her dashing, successful, generous, but largely absent father.

It is dangerous to read a photograph too closely for any fact or truth (and family photographs are among the most staged and fictional representations of life), but an early photograph of Eloise with Sharon, at about nine months, shows a less than radiant, happy young mother holding on to a baby that almost seems to be pushing her away (see Illus. 12). Mother and child do not look at each other (something or someone else has the baby's attention) or even seem to share the same space. Perhaps it is only in hindsight that such a photograph can seem so prophetic, but in later life the adult daughter would openly acknowledge her negative feelings about this alcoholic mother. Through the writing of *Doc*, she would also come to understand her mother's suffering and, to a degree, forgive her for the pain Eloise caused others during those years. In the forties and fifties, very little was known about alcoholism, and female alcoholics were an especially taboo subject. Today, however, it is well recognized that adult children of alcoholic parents are traumatized by the situation and that daughters of alcoholic mothers suffer more than sons. But Sharon did have another role model in her life and I want to bring Everett back on stage before trying to understand Eloise's death and its impact on her daughter.

When Sharon's first national theatre success took place, Dr. George Everett Chalmers was there in a front-row seat. The place was Stratford; the play was *Walsh*; the date was 24 July 1974, opening night in the Third Stage Theatre. Interviewed later, Doc Chalmers said—

> I wouldn't know whether it's any good or not; I don't know anything about that sort of thing.... Sharon always had her nose in a book; she was always writing poetry. If she has any talent she inherited it from her mother, not from me. Her mother was artistic. That's where she gets it. (Webster, 1974, 50)

There is no reason to doubt his disclaimer. Eloise *was* artistic: she wrote poetry, she painted (painting was considered good therapy), and she was a lively storyteller. However, if Sharon inherited literary talent from Eloise, she inherited her determination to succeed, her tenacious hold on survival, and her boundless energy from her father. She wanted, from an early age, to be like him. The role model her mother presented was hardly positive. But if Eloise is now impossible to know, except through her haunting presence in others' lives, Everett Chalmers is something of a conundrum. He was highly respected by many, reviled by some, loved by his patients and some of his family members, especially his two daughters, and resented by others. He described himself to a few people close to him as a man unable to love (a comment that could mean many things, from an inability to demonstrate affection or tenderness to an intransigent refusal to give himself intimately to anyone), and yet he loved his children in his own way. He was there for them if they needed his help, and he could talk intimately, at least in his latter years, with his daughter Susan from his second marriage. He also came to see that he had failed Eloise, if not as a husband, then certainly as a doctor, and he would devote a considerable part of his life to the study of addiction and to the modernization of its treatment.

An old friend with whom I spoke described him as "an angel and a devil," which is one way of summing up this contradictory, colourful, complex, ruthlessly honest, hard-working, and deeply flawed man. By all accounts (from friends and enemies), he was a brilliant doctor and a pioneer in the betterment of medical practice and health services in New Brunswick. He fought for a provincial polio clinic after two outbreaks (the worst in 1941 and another a decade later) devastated an unprotected population by formally joining the provincial Tories and running for office. As chief surgeon in Fredericton's old Victoria Hospital, he fought to improve sanitary conditions. He championed medical specialization at a time when the idea was revolutionary, and he attracted young specialists to join him. In other words, Dr. Everett Chalmers rocked the medical establishment boat in New Brunswick, but he got results. He did not bill poor patients. He made house calls at all hours of the night. His concern for his patients became legendary. Also legendary in small-town Fredericton were other aspects of the man. For starters, he swore, constantly, loudly, and vividly in all circumstances. And he drank, even by the standards of an era when heavy social drinking was the norm, and for a time after Eloise's death this drinking became a problem. He was arrogant, domineering, a man's man who played hard—in sports, work, and life—and wanted to win. And he had affairs. On this business people who knew him and Eloise divide. Those who sympathized with Eloise and recognized her abilities and thwarted potential, blamed Everett for causing her collapse, first through emotional neglect and then through physical betrayal. Those who admired Everett (and his young daughter was one of them) tended to excuse the private failures of the husband, whose wife, after all, was too ill or too drunk to be a wife or was away undergoing treatment, and to praise the public achievements. *She* has been described to me as a "lady"; *he* as a "ruffian." But I find it impossible to square these labels with images of Eloise wandering the house, drunk, brandishing her rifle or with images of Everett who could operate so quickly and deftly that his patients suffered a minimum of trauma. Real people are just too complex to categorize, and blame is a mug's game. Sharon has said, quoting her father, that if he had died or fallen ill, Eloise would have taken charge with great competence and strength. And in another set of circumstances that may well have been true.

The facts and the circumstances, however, were different. In 1949, while she struggled to hold on to her life, he plunged into provincial politics for the Conservative Party (he had been in municipal politics from 1945 to 1949), and by 1959 he was president of the New Brunswick Progressive Conservative Association. In 1956 he married again, this time to Winnifred (née Winchester) Hickey, and Pegi, as she was called, was also beautiful and also an alcoholic. Like Everett, Pegi brought two children to this marriage, which then produced two more—George Everett Jr. (1957–) and Susan (1960–). In 1960 he was elected to the provincial legislature in the first of five consecutive victories, and in 1976 he officially opened Fredericton's DECH—the Doctor Everett Chalmers Hospital (see Illus. 13). When he died there on 26 April 1993, the flags flew at half mast. During his long career and life he received many awards and honours, including an LLD from the University of New Brunswick, the Distinguished Citizen of Fredericton Award and, in 1983, he was named an Officer of the Order of Canada. In his obituary, he was praised as "a legendary figure in the health care arena," "a truly great man," "a thinker and a leader," and "a people's person" who made New Brunswick "a better place." The funeral service was held in the Gibson Memorial United Church in Devon, not far from where he grew up and where he had worshipped as a boy and had continued to attend services as a man. It was the same church in which the service for his mother had been held fifty-three years earlier. Everett Chalmers is buried beside Eloise in the Fredericton Rural Cemetery, with one large headstone to mark the grave. On the front it reads: "Dr. Everett Chalmers, MD, MC, 1905–1993, and his wife Eloise E., 1913–1954." There are no messages of loving memory, no quotations from scripture, and no Latin inscriptions. The only decoration is on the back of the stone where a rifle crossed with a fishing rod has been carved in simple relief.

13. a) Everett relaxing on the steps of the family fishing camp on the Miramichi River, ca 1945.
Courtesy of Sharon Pollock;

b) This portrait of Dr. Everett Chalmers hangs in the foyer of the DECH (the Doctor Everett Chalmers Hospital) in Fredericton. It was painted by R. Benn in 1976.

Of course, the public facts of a career do not tell the entire life-story, and there are two other accounts of Doc Chalmers that deserve attention. Sharon's, in *Doc*, will be considered later. Right now I want to turn to *Gentlemen, players, and politicians* (1970) by Dalton Camp, the New Brunswick-born political backroom boy and Tory strategiser. Among other things, this memoir is an analysis of Canadian politics after WWII and the rise of the Progressive Conservatives to federal power under John Diefenbaker after years of Liberal rule. The book is also something of an exposé of behind-the-scenes PC manoeuvrings in New Brunswick's provincial affairs from 1949 on, and possibly the most colourful, outrageous Tory of them all was Doc Chalmers. Early in his narrative, Camp describes his arrival in Fredericton in the winter of 1949. As he looked out of his window in the Lord Beaverbrook Hotel to the streets below, he saw

wasted men, the withering years upon them, bundled against the cold ... consumed by idleness, their women worn by harsh routine, bearing the pallor of self-neglect, the children with bad teeth, the early beginning of a life cycle of decay; store windows displaying the hideous litter of cheap merchandise, malevolently designed for lives of quiet despair, for an existence amid an abandoned culture, in a ghetto of memory. (Camp, 27)

Several years later, on the eve of an election, Camp returned to Fredericton and once more stood at a window in the Beaverbrook, but this time he was looking downriver, away from the city streets, towards "the familiar span of the old CN railbridge that hovered over the river" (199), and he remembered a physics professor from UNB who drowned near the bridge while trying to rescue two boys who had fallen into the water.

These passages from Camp's book testify to the social situation that Everett Chalmers found in Fredericton and New Brunswick after the war, but I read them with a shock of recognition because I too have stayed in the Beaverbrook and stood at my window looking down from rooms facing upriver to the city and downriver to that railway bridge. I have only been there in late spring, summer, and early fall, so I saw natural beauty instead of pitiable squalor, but my sense of Fredericton as a sleepy conservative backwater that modern times had passed by was very strong, and the death associated, in my mind, with that bridge was one of the reasons for my coming to Fredericton at all.

What Dalton Camp does that I cannot is to conjure up into his smoke-filled room the figure of Dr. Everett Chalmers. "He was impressive on sight," Camp says, "exuding confidence, his tanned face radiating cheer." This time it is summer and Chalmers, "clothed in an impeccable white suit, looks like Clark Gable about to meet Carole Lombard at the Ritz" (71). But the good doctor has come to this political meeting with his own agenda and his own way of expressing himself … with "electrifying versatility" in four-letter words:

> I'll tell you about the goddam Liberal health program. A woman comes to see me, see, she's half out of her fucking mind, with this Christless lump in her breast. So I take a section, see, because she probably has cancer but no way in God's world I can operate on her until I damn well know what's wrong with her.
>
> Well, Jesus, I have to ship the goddam tissue to Saint John, on the fucking bus, see, and wait, Christ, three days to a goddam week while this poor woman is half out of her mind—maybe she's a mother, see, or has to work for a goddam living—but I can't tell her whether she has cancer or whether I have to remove the goddam breast or what the hell I'm going to do to her because the fucking Grits refuse to give us a clinic in this Christless city. And I've told those bastards a hundred times: for Christ's sake stop building fucking liquor stores and give your goddam doctors a decent chance to practice medicine and save a few fucking lives. (71–72)

His point made about Doc Chalmers' rhetoric, Camp goes on to extol the doctor's documented proof of Liberal neglect of the polio situation and medical services in general, and to describe how this profane surgeon performs on radio in a political speech crafted (and sanitized) by Camp and aimed at drumming up Tory support and ousting the local Liberals in the election.

Chalmers, it would seem, was a hit with listeners, and Camp was relieved to hear him "speak for fifteen minutes without lapsing into profanity" (75). Neither man could have predicted what lay ahead in public or private life, but Camp realized he had bagged a winning Tory "with an unexpected element of the theatrical in him" (75). As for Chalmers, his only recorded response to his radio debut was: "I never knew so goddam many people listened to the fucking radio. Christ, I can't even eat my meals for answering the phone." And if all this doesn't sound vaguely familiar to anyone who knew or knows Sharon Pollock or has read, or seen, *Doc* or *Whiskey Six Cadenza*, then it soon will. More than one member of the Chalmers family had an undiscovered theatrical bent and an "electrifying versatility" with language.

***

When Sharon began her last two years of high school at King's Hall in 1952, she left behind in Fredericton an increasingly traumatic and difficult situation. Eloise was not well and would be dead in less than two years. Mary Arbeau was there to take what care of things she could; Peter was in high school at FHS and absorbed much of the daily emotional brunt of the unfolding domestic tragedy; Everett was busy with his medical practice and provincial politics. By sending Sharon away to school, her father had removed her, at least when school was in session, from a destructive home life and a deteriorating mother/daughter relationship. King's Hall, called "Compton" by the Old Girls, was established in 1874 in a quiet rural setting near Lennoxville in Quebec's Eastern Townships.[5] The area was then, and still is to some degree, an English Protestant enclave in French Catholic Quebec with gently rolling hills, farms, tiny picturesque villages like Hatley and Compton, and lakes with large summer homes owned by wealthy Westmount families. The Headmistress, or Lady Principal, was Miss Adelaide Gillard, who ruled the school for thirty-eight years (1930–1968). She was a university-educated Canadian from Ontario, a devout Anglican, and a staunch royalist. Judging from her letters and from reports of her by Old Girls, she was very traditional in her principles and values, but also seriously dedicated to providing women with a well-rounded education that would prepare them, not only to be good Christian wives and mothers, but also productive, patriotic citizens. The teachers were a mix of Canadian and British women, the French teacher came from France, and the curriculum in the years after WWII was extensive. In addition to the academic subjects needed for matriculation—English, History, French, German, Latin, Spanish, Mathematics, and Science—the regular regime included Gymnastics, Dancing, Games (which meant swimming, tennis, riding, skiing, skating, soccer and other team sports), Music (girls could prepare for the McGill Conservatory examinations in piano, violin, and voice), Elocution, Drawing, Painting, and Crafts.

During the 1950s the school experienced considerable growth (enrollments reached 130 and 148) and expansion, acquiring excellent facilities such as a renovated science laboratory, a swimming pool, and a modernized physical plant. But it retained its traditional priorities as well: the girls attended regular services at the Anglican parish church of St. James the Less, and the school maintained its own farm, which produced milk, garden vegetables, meat, and maple syrup from its two hundred maple trees. When punishments were called for, physical labour on the farm was ready to hand. In a word, Compton was a *special* school and the students were privileged. They were also strictly supervised in all matters: they could not write letters unless the addressees had parental approval; they could not bring food into the school (fruit and the occasional birthday cake excepted); they could under no circumstances read books not available in the school library; and they could not leave the school unsupervised. However, they were taken on trips to see plays or attend concerts at Bishop's College or in Sherbrooke, and cultural events and visiting speakers came to them. They had regular concerts, guest lectures, theatre performances, and Saturday night movies.

Sharon's first year, 1952–53, was exceedingly full, and she participated in several ways. She was on the soccer team, she contributed a report on the Hallowe'en party, which reads more

14. Snapshot of Sharon in her "Matric" year, 1954, from the King's Hall, Compton, yearbook *Per Annos*. Her favourite saying (often attributed to Mark Twain) is: "Whenever I feel like working I lie down until the feeling passes away." Her "probable destination" is "Leader of the Opposition." Although the saying would never apply to Sharon, the probable destination is not far off the mark.
Photograph courtesy of the Archives, Bishop's College School.

like a story than a factual account (like the reports by other girls), and she wrote one literary sketch, called "Lament of a Clock-Watcher," for the "Literary" section of the school magazine *Per Annos*. The plays produced at Compton that year were *To Each Generation* by Dora Smith Conover and J.M. Barrie's chestnut, *Shall We Join the Ladies*, and the movies shown were *The Lavender Hill Mob* (with Alec Guiness), *The Man in the White Suit*, *The Promoter*, *The Ivory Hunter*, *Outpost in Malaya* (with Colette Colbert), and *Blanche Fury*—this last item, a 1948 gothic melodrama from Britain about a governess who marries into a wealthy family, was apparently the great favourite. In *Per Annos* for 1953–54, Sharon has less of a presence. She is shown as a member of the "Matrics" class, and she roomed in Montcalm House, was an editor of the magazine that year, and played baseball and volleyball. The descriptive entry on her (according to the genre of the yearbook) gives her identifying expression as—"Whenever I feel like working, I lie down until the feeling passes"—while her ambition is to become "First Lady Prime Minister" and her "probable destination" is "Leader of the Opposition" (see Illus. 14). Whoever tagged her probable destination (if not Sharon herself) came close to getting it right. Her only literary contribution to the magazine is a short, short story called "Things I Like To Do" (see Appendix 1).

As I read through these years of *Per Annos*, the predictable question keeps surfacing: what, if anything, might these pictures and stories tell me about the future playwright? While I think they do shed some light on Sharon's future, I cannot see anything to suggest that she would become a major writer. It is only with hindsight that I can detect something characteristic in a piece like "Lament of a Clock-Watcher," a lively, ironic, autobiographical sketch about her exam-writing fears:

> When I am writing an exam, it seems that clocks have a peculiar fascination for me. I had entered the room calm, cool, and confident. Now, thanks to the endless tick-tock, tick-tock, tick-tock of that leering face on the wall, I am reduced to a doddering, panic-stricken fool whose chances of passing are slim.

And the sketch ends perfectly with—"I am convinced that time will pass, but will I?" There are no tell-tale traces of genius here, but what catches my eye is the economy of this writing, its ironic tone, and the author's capacity to capture a state of mind without lapsing into sentimentality or cliché. "Things I Like To Do," although longer and more complex, has many of the same traits: it is energetic, economical, unsentimental, and personal, with an honesty of feeling and simplicity of detail that do indeed make it stand out from the surrounding pieces of poetry and prose of her fellow students. The two "likes" Sharon describes in this piece are ones she has carried with her through the rest of her life—"walking in the rain at night" and driving a car. The latter activity, in contrast to the solitary walking, "requires four friends, one convertible, and a hot dry day." This extroverted pleasure is common amongst teenagers, and the girls' trip to the beach, driving fast, their hair disheveled, faces sun burned, and the author's laconic answer to her mother's question—"Where did you go?—"O-o-o-o-oh, I don't know—some lake or other, I guess."—are not surprising. What is less expected is how well this "adventure in being young" is described and how tightly balanced the two experiences are: a solitary night walk in the rain with a raucous, convivial, joy ride in the sun. But if the joy ride is typical, I am not sure that the night walk alone, at least for a teenaged girl, is. "Things I Like To Do" is not the first writing Sharon produced, but it is representative enough that I have included it in Appendix 1. Although she would become known as a playwright, she has always written prose sketches or short, short stories, and she threatens (promises?) to produce a novel one of these years.

Sharon's recollections of Compton are somewhat mixed. English was taught by Hugh MacLennan's sister, Frances, and the teachers tried their best to get the New Brunswick accent out of her speech, an effort Sharon successfully resisted because I still hear New Brunswick, or at least Fredericton, in her accent and cadences—flat vowels, a rising interrogative note to sentences, and a blunt directness of address. (In fact, I hear her voice in that drawled answer from "Things I Like To Do": "O-o-o-o-oh, I don't know.") Someone commented on a report card that Miss Chalmers was "cryptically critical of the staff," which is consistent with the views of earlier teachers who had noted her outspoken nature and intelligence. Recalling this report card, Sharon chuckled, appreciating the unintended alliteration as much as the prim, futile admonishment. Her French classes two days per week required hefty doses of dictation, at which she felt utterly hopeless. And yet, she did well, even in this dreaded French exercise. History was another matter. Because she read so widely, even as a youngster, she was not only happy (as Everett later put it) with her nose in a book, but she had developed, very early, a taste for narrative that included serious history, historical biography, and popular fiction—mystery stories and crime fiction and detective novels. Today we need to remember that Sharon's generation did not grow up with television, so children had to read and amuse themselves. Radio was the dominant technology of the period and would, in time, become important in her career, but at Compton her great joy was history and her favourite place in the school was the library (see Illus. 15). Her history teacher, Miss Mary Morris, must have been an astute and sympathetic woman because she encouraged Sharon's interest in history by allowing her to read historical biography in the library instead of doing homework in her room. It is not surprising then that history became a passion, the library a refuge, and Miss Morris the focus of her happiest memories of Compton. History has remained, after theatre and *with* theatre, one of the central interests in Sharon's life.

15. The Library at Compton was Sharon's refuge and favourite place to read between 1952 and 1954. This photograph is reproduced, courtesy of the Archives, Bishop's College School, from a brochure providing information to parents and prospective students of King's Hall Boarding School for Girls.

In Quebec during the 1950s high school students who were bright and intended to continue on to university completed their secondary schooling with matriculation examinations at the end of their final year. But Sharon's last two months at Compton were disrupted when she was summoned home on the 10th or 11th of May to be at Eloise's death bed. She was away from school for nearly three weeks, after which she returned to Compton to prepare for and write her final examinations. Sharon has commented on her mother's death and her reaction to it in interviews, but when I asked her about this death in the context of her school year, she recalled the trauma in terms of a completely different event. There was an American girl, called Diana, at Compton that year and she was picked on by all the other girls. Her classmates "bullied and teased her" and spoke of her as "demented"—which recalls scenes from Margaret Atwood's novel *Cat's Eye* or Joan MacLeod's play *The Shape of a Girl*. No one wanted to room with Diana or befriend her. When Sharon was called back to Fredericton for Eloise's funeral, her classmates taunted her with the prospect of having to room with Diana when she returned to the school. This is not, in fact, what happened, but the cruelty of the threat and the victimization of the unfortunate Diana has stayed with Sharon into adulthood. It is a small episode, perhaps, no more than one of those minor scars from childhood and youth, but it is also significant because it highlights the kind of injustice that would preoccupy the creative writer in the years ahead. But at Compton she was not, as far as she can recall or I can discover, writing plays or acting or directing for any of the school's dramatic presentations. She emceed for school revues and she wrote letters home to her father, to Murph Allen, and to Jane; however, few of these letters have survived and her two years at Compton, with occasional trips into Montreal to see the orthodontist or trips back to Fredericton on holidays, were solitary, even lonely, ones.

Although the family and some friends knew that Eloise Chalmers was ill, her death, when it came, was a devastating shock. She had tried to play the role of the Fredericton doctor's wife, joined the IODE, and hosted formal teas (with the sterling silver service, fine china cups, and dainty sandwiches, crumpets, or cakes). She had two fine, healthy children and was a gracious, intelligent, and beautiful woman (see Illus. 5, 9, 12, and 16). So what went

16. Eloise Roberts Chalmers, ca 1936.
This studio portrait of Eloise shows her to have been a remarkably attractive woman.
Photograph courtesy of Peter Chalmers.

wrong? The facts I have been able to gather are few, and the versions of what caused or contributed to her decline are many and contradictory. Even the *precise* cause of her death is unclear. And perhaps precise details do not matter after all. What does matter is the long-lasting and largely negative impact of her life, and especially of the way she died, on her children. While she was alive, she was increasingly frustrated by her inability to work at her chosen profession and increasingly hurt and depressed by the deterioration of her marriage. She was frequently sent away to "dry out" and for psychiatric assessment. Years after her death, Everett would tell his children that IQ tests carried out during those assessments showed Eloise to be "brilliant," and that he realized far too late how frustrated such a woman would be when forced to do mindless socializing instead of productive work. She painted, apparently, and she wrote poetry. Sharon found some of her poems after her death, and Everett told Susan that Eloise and Sharon had exchanged poem-letters during the early years when Eloise was sent away. In life and in death, Eloise Chalmers was a powerful, charismatic, and disturbing figure. According to Susan, Everett's second family believed that the house on Grey Street was haunted by her presence.

When Sharon got the call to return to Fredericton, her mother was already in hospital. Eloise died in the Victoria Public hospital on Wednesday, the 12th of May, 1954, three days after swallowing poison at home and after three days of excruciating pain. Her official

"Registration of Death" certificate gives the direct cause of death as "Acute Nephritis" (kidney failure) and the antecedent cause as "Toxemia." There is nothing recorded in the box used to indicate what caused an "external" (meaning violent) death, such as accident, suicide, or homicide, and yet her dying was violent. The only other information provided is her address, date of birth, exact age at time of death—"41 years and 12 days"—her sex, her nationality, and ethnic origin, and her husband's and parents' names. Opposite "trade, profession" the document reads: "Housewife." The obituary in Thursday's *Gleaner* (for May 13th) is brief. Eloise is described as the "widely known" wife of Dr. G. Everett Chalmers, the daughter of the late John W. Roberts and Mrs. Roberts of Chipman, and the mother of Sharon and Peter. The other surviving relatives listed are her two brothers, Claire and William, and her two sisters, Rena and Beatrice. Her education is mentioned—"she was trained and graduated by the school of nursing of the Saint John General Hospital"—but the only personal passage is the following:

> Mrs. Chalmers was a great enthusiast of the outdoors and took an active part in golfing, salmon and trout fishing and hunting. Keenly interested in hockey, Mrs. Chalmers missed few games at the local arena and gave freely of her means and interest to encourage the junior hockey teams for school boys of all ages.

Her body was "resting at home until Friday morning at 11 o'clock," and the service was held in St. Anne's parish church. There was no photograph with the obituary.

At this point I must turn, briefly, to personal recollections of this woman's passing because "Acute Nephritis" and "Toxemia" tell the layman nothing about the dying. Peter Chalmers, who was sixteen, remembers coming home from school, probably on Monday the 10th to discover that his mother had eaten a sandwich filled with, what he thinks may have been silver polish, washed this down with a cup of tea, and retired to an upstairs room.[6] Mary Arbeau recalls making Eloise a cup of tea and finishing her ironing before leaving the house for a period of time. It was not until the next morning, when Everett asked Mary to search the house for any toxic substance that might be missing that she discovered the silver polish cream was used up. Others have told me that Eloise swallowed carbolic acid or rose fertilizer, but these seem less likely than silver polish (or possibly an arsenic powder), either because they are not readily accessible (carbolic acid) or not fatally toxic (fertilizer), whereas silver polish (perhaps containing a mercury compound) or an arsenic-based insecticide or weed killer could easily be in the home. When her kidneys failed, her entire system closed down, and her painful death was appalling to watch. As a trained nurse, she must have known what the clinical consequences of her actions would be and how devastating such a death would be for Everett, who was unable to save her, and for her family.

Peter blamed his father for not being more vigilant about dangerous household products— and for much else besides. For Sharon, the grieving process and grief itself seem to have been blocked. In interviews she has described her horror at the funeral, where people wept and said things she found hypocritical, sentimental, or simply untrue. So profoundly did this funeral upset her that she would not attend her father's in 1993; one such *event* was enough.

17. Sharon Chalmers, 1954. For her graduation photograph Sharon has a new hair cut and looks older and more sophisticated than the girl in *Per Annos* (Illus. 14).
Photograph courtesy of Peter Chalmers.

In a 1983 interview with John Hofsess, she explained her feelings about Eloise then, during her mother's life, and later, when she herself had become a mother with a successful career:

> For years I disliked my mother intensely. Her drinking embarrassed me. When she died we found bottles secreted all through the house. She drank anything—even perfume. I remember once, when I was about 11, I poured a bottle of rum down the sink. My mother couldn't believe it. She cried. [...] From about the time I was seven or eight, she was frequently sent away to 'rest homes' to dry out. I've never been particularly sympathetic to illness or weakness and here was this woman in full-blown, self-indulgent disintegration.
>
> [...] As I grow older, however, I think I understand my mother better. I see now what a difficult position she was in. She came from a very large and poor family in New Brunswick. She was the only one to get an education. No sooner did she graduate as a nurse than she married my father ... and her career was terminated. Her whole personality was geared to striving ... yet suddenly she was expected to retire and play the role of a doctor's wife—gracious, idle, nothing much to do. (3)

However one classifies Sharon's feelings about her mother, they were strong, deep, and long-lasting. This failed mother-daughter relationship and the spectacle of Eloise's death and funeral provided Sharon with hard, formative lessons and deep emotional scars. From Eloise she learned what, above all, she did not want to become—a pitiable victim and a mother who was not there for her children. She also learned anger. Eloise left her little else. She died intestate; in the legal language of the probate court, she was "neither seized nor possessed of any real estate," and her personal property was estimated as worth about "Fifteen Thousand, Two Hundred and Twenty-eight Dollars and twenty-six cents."

CHAPTER 3

The Angel in the House

It was she who bothered me and wasted my time and so tormented me that at last I killed her.
—VIRGINIA WOOLF, "PROFESSIONS FOR WOMEN," 150

Anger fuels a lot of work, not just my own. It's anger about how things are and the sense you have
about how they ought to be ... anger leads to action. —SHARON POLLOCK, APPENDIX 3, 409

I: Leaving Home

In the summer of 1956 Sharon left Fredericton as Sharon Pollock, and the decade ahead would be full of false starts and new beginnings. Two years after her mother's death she had secured a husband, had a baby daughter, and completed about a year and a half of university education. She took with her, as a wedding present, her mother's silver service but also a great deal of hurt and anger. The husband was acquired at the University of New Brunswick; the hurt and anger were accumulated from her years as the daughter of an alcoholic mother; and in some ways this precipitous, early marriage and her mother's emotional legacy are connected.

In the 1950s young women were expected to marry, settle down, and have children, regardless of their abilities, interests, or temperaments. Certainly it is what Everett anticipated, and Sharon has said that the big questions at the time for her and her girlfriends were who they would marry and what their names would be; they hoped, as she jokingly put it, that their names would not be dreadful ones like Hickman or Pollock. By 1963, in a letter to her father, she was not joking when she wrote that a woman "chooses a dog with more care than a husband"—a dismaying but honest and blunt remark. In 1956 she wanted, above all, to get away. Away from gossipy, staid Fredericton; away from her father's changing household; and away from the family "ghost story." According to middle-class rules for women in the 1950s, a husband was the ticket out, especially if his education and career required him to move. This fate was a far cry from the hopes and dreams of the Secret Two Club, but most of the Fredericton girls of Sharon's generation, including Jane, married young, had children, and moved away. It is important to allow for this social expectation in weighing the influence of Eloise's example on Sharon's choices and decisions between the fall of 1954 and the winter of 1955, when she married a UNB Forestry student and football player called Ross Douglas Pollock.

In September 1954, when Sharon entered the first year of the general Arts program at UNB, Ross Pollock was in his fourth year of the five-year Forestry program in the Faculty of Applied Science. Presumably he had come to UNB because its Forestry program was very good, and he appears in several photographs in the yearbook, called *Up the Hill*, with his Forestry class and with the football team, the "Red Bombers." Sharon is not in the yearbook, but records for 1954–55 and 1955–56 confirm that she enrolled in the fall of 1954 as Mary Sharon Chalmers and in the fall of 1955 as Mary Sharon Pollock. Ross and Sharon were then listed as living at 63 Grey Street, and Mary Arbeau, who was among the first to know that the young couple had eloped, recalls Ross "living in" with Sharon for almost two years; they shared her bedroom and ate most of their meals on Everett's tab at a local restaurant. The university they attended was still small enough to be friendly, intimate, and unthreatening. A new president, Dr. Colin Mackay (New Brunswick born and bred, a WWII veteran, and one of the first graduates of UBC's Law School) arrived in 1953 intending to put UNB on the map of modern Canadian universities. The student body was growing (across the country, returning soldiers led to a large influx of students), excellent faculty were being hired, and spirits were high. How much, if any, of this growth and excitement touched the freshman population is hard to say, but in the Faculty of Arts there were opportunities to study with some distinguished scholars. Professor Robert Cattley, the father of one of Sharon's FHS classmates, taught Classics and Ancient History; Dr. Desmond Pacey, who pioneered the academic study of Canadian Literature, was Head of English and a neighbour of the Chalmers. The younger faculty members included men like Alec Lucas and Fred Cogswell (both in English and both to become important players in the emerging fields of Canadian literary history and poetry), James Chapman and Lovell Clarke (both in History), and Alvin Shaw, whose discipline was Romance Languages but whose passion was the theatre. In a university where the Applied Sciences, especially Forestry, were predominant, the Arts Faculty attracted notable public attention. Items in the student newspaper *The Brunswickian* featured Desmond Pacey's 1955 election to the Royal Society of Canada, the unveiling of "Poet's Corner," with a plaque and poems celebrating two famous alumni, Roberts and Carman, and lively reports on the annual "Red 'n Black Revue" and on the serious plays produced by the UNB Dramatic Society under the direction of Professor Shaw—Robertson Davies' *Fortune My Foe* in 1953 and a spectacular *Antigone* in 1954.

Sharon's name does not appear in the newspapers I saw in connection with either the revues or any of the plays directed by Shaw, but she is referred to *very obliquely* in a comment about Ross. Facing his graduation picture in the 1956 *Up the Hill*, we are told that in his fourth year (1954–55), "Ross presented us all with a surprise and since then he has been a member of the ranks of the few 'old married men' of the class." Sharon Pollock registered for the fall term of 1955 in the category "Arts (Special)," but by the summer of 1956 Jennifer had been born, Ross had graduated, and they had moved to Toronto. That same fall (1955), Peter entered UNB, where his father hoped he would take Science and Medicine, but Peter rebelled. After two years, he left to pursue his own path and became a pilot with the former

Canadian Pacific Airlines.[1] Everett was remarried, in February of 1956, to Pegi (Winnifred) Hickey, and for Peter the situation was intolerable. Moreover, the house on Grey Street was crowded, with Everett, Sharon and Ross, Peter, the new Mrs. Chalmers with her two youngsters (a daughter Jerilyn, and a son, Bryant), and numerous family pets. Sharon's recollections of the months between the fall of 1954 and her departure as a wife and mother less than two years later are sketchy. She remembers enjoying her university classes in History with Dr. Chapman and in Classics with Professor Cattley; she could debate politics with Chapman, and she wrote a paper for Cattley in which she "argued that 'off-ing' Socrates was a good thing." Her English classes made little lasting impression, and she heard nothing about Canadian literature or *The Fiddlehead*, the UNB literary magazine, begun in 1945, in which she would later publish a short story. Despite the brevity of her university education and her regret at not having more exposure to advanced studies, it was already clear that she was capable of learning on her own regardless of the obstacles that were soon to appear.

When Sharon met Ross he was both a senior student and a "jock," which gave him status and cachet and placed him at the centre of UNB campus life. Forestry was the star discipline then, and a man who played quarterback for the Red Bombers was bound to attract female attention. Judging from his photographs in *Up the Hill*, especially his graduation photograph, he was dark, of average height and slight build, with a charming smile (see Illus. 18). Recalling her feelings at that time, Sharon told me that she was "enamoured" of him, but she has also explained that she thought she could help him or make him happy because his childhood had been desperately unhappy. Ross quickly became, in her eyes and through the early years of their marriage, something of a mission, someone for whom she felt responsible. If Sharon had been listening, Virginia Woolf would have warned her not to believe the Angel in the house, but Sharon was *not* listening, and she told him very little about her own childhood. Once their daughter was born, she must have felt she had not only performed the role expected of her—by her father, by society, and by herself—but also that this new responsibility was her chance to do a perfect job, as Eloise had not, of being a wife and mother. Before she left Ross in 1964, she had five children, Jennifer (1956–), Kirk (1957–), Melinda (1959–), Lisa (1961–), and Michele (1963–); however, the marriage was in trouble by about 1959–60. Why things went wrong is a complex question, one for which I only have Sharon's answers because I have not been able to talk with Ross.[2] What I know of his life between 1954 and 1964 I have had to piece together from records at UNB, Sharon's memories, a few letters (only one by Ross), and scattered recollections of him by Sharon's family, friends, and acquaintances.

Ross Douglas Pollock was born in Toronto in 1932 or 1933, the second of two children. Apparently his mother was emotionally unstable and either unable or unwilling to care for her new baby or his older sister. Ross was raised by an aunt; his sister was raised by the Pollock grandparents, with whom his father may also have lived. According to Sharon's memories, Ross and his sister were told never to speak to their mother who was occasionally seen in the neighbourhood watching them at play or school. At the time of her breakdown, right after Ross's birth, she may have been persuaded to relinquish her rights to her children. Ross's father, Douglas Pollock, worked for Ontario Hydro and was absent much of the time,

18. Ross Douglas Pollock. Ross Pollock graduated in Forestry from the University of New Brunswick in May 1956.
This photograph is from the university yearbook, Up the Hill, *and is reproduced courtesy of Archives and Special Collections, Harriet Irving Library, UNB (UA RG 85).*

but later when Ross and Sharon had their children, he would turn up, unannounced, with fancy presents for them. He also owned a summer cottage in the town of Keswick, north of Toronto on Lake Simcoe, and Ross, Sharon, and their rapidly growing family holidayed there during the summers in the late fifties. As for the Pollock genealogy, I have not been able to confirm any details, but they may have been a pioneer Ontario family of Irish or Scots background, and the Pollock grandparents told Sharon that a relative had fought with William Lyon Mackenzie in the 1837 rebellion.

When Ross arrived at UNB in the fall of 1951, he joined the football team and the Campus Police Force right away. He also belonged to the track team and in his third year (the year before he met Sharon), he briefly managed the girls' basketball team. Sports were his chief extracurricular interest and, so far as I can tell, he had no interest in literary, dramatic, or political activities on campus. He graduated in May 1956 with a second class BSc. in Forestry. Personal recollections of him, though few, do provide some small sense of the man. One woman who was at UNB with Ross and Sharon and lived in the same neighbourhood, described him to me as good-looking and sensuous, but with a weak character. Another described him as not especially attractive and engrossed in football. Peter Chalmers remembers not liking Ross even at this early stage and finding him a bully. At one point when the two came to blows Peter (who was several years his junior) knocked Ross down.

Of course, every story has at least two sides, but whatever troubled Ross Pollock, assuming that something did, he later became openly abusive to Sharon and seemed less stable as the ten-year marriage progressed. When the couple first moved to Toronto, he found work with Ontario Hydro and was away a fair bit. Their first home was a modest rented apartment on

Queen St East, in an area that was not then gentrified, and it was a far cry from what Sharon Chalmers had grown up with. Kirk, their second child and only son, was born on May 12th in 1957, the third anniversary of Eloise's death. At some point, probably in late 1957, they moved closer to the University of Toronto because Ross had decided to do an MBA, and they rented an upstairs apartment in a house on Robert Street in the "the Village," which was a bit of an improvement over Queen but nonetheless fairly poor student digs. Sharon recalls that the people below them were Trotskyites and that she enjoyed political debates with them and began to read a wide range of political material. Ross, however, had right-wing views and disapproved of these people and of Sharon's reading. These were the years when they were able to spend their summers at the Keswick cottage, and when they moved into their own home in the summer of 1958, they found a place in Keswick, which Everett paid for.

Both the house and Keswick were a great improvement over what they had had in Toronto, but they could not have purchased a house anywhere without Sharon's father's help. The home was registered in Sharon's name, a point to keep in mind when we wonder why she stayed as long as she did in an increasingly difficult marriage. But things started well enough. In a letter to his father-in-law, dated 23 July 1958, with the return address of Wynhurst Gardens, RR#2, Keswick, Ontario, Ross writes that he and Sharon "are so happy to be in our own place thanks to you" and goes on to describe their fun on the beach, how darkly Sharon and Kirk tan, and the antics of their six cats. The letter is cheerful, with particular news of Kirk—"a strong, strong-minded, happy, determined & aggressive boy" who will soon end "Jennifer's days of [being] the 'leader'"—and with numerous business details regarding mortgage rates, taxes, and insurance. He reports that they purchased the house below the market value (at $17,500.00), that he is taking the bus into Toronto to his new job with New York Life Insurance at Bay and Adelaide, and then goes on to discuss the stock market and the price of mining shares, with one interesting exception. According to Ross, the employment situation for young men with university degrees is grim: he gives four examples of classmates or acquaintances, who have not found appropriate work or have spent many weeks looking for a job. It seems likely that in just a few years, after a move from New York Life to Sun Life, Ross was unemployed. Sharon remembers her surprise and alarm when she called his Sun Life office one day in 1964, shortly before she fled Keswick, only to be told that he no longer worked there. For some time, Ross had been travelling into Toronto as if he were going to work and staying there during the week, when in fact he had lost his job.

Between the summer of 1958 and the summer of 1964, Sharon's next three children were born. The Wynhurst Gardens house was full and busy, and they lived on a shoestring, but Keswick offered the family a great deal—pleasant natural surroundings, decent schools, recreation and, as Sharon soon discovered, a small, local amateur theatre group and a nearby professional summer theatre. During her years in Toronto, Sharon had few distractions; she saw a few Fredericton friends, like Jane Hickman and Pam McCready, who visited or lived nearby, and family members visited at least twice, but she was otherwise pretty much on her own with two children under three and very little money. Toronto in the mid-fifties could scarcely have been described as lively or progressive, so perhaps she did not miss much. And yet, an intellectual and artistic life was percolating under the city's dull surface. The Crest Theatre and the Canadian Players had both started in 1954 and were in full swing by 1956–57. Not far to the west, Stratford had opened its tent doors in 1953 and, by the summer of 1957, had its stunning Festival Theatre.

In fact, artists and arts groups were organizing as never before in Canada at this time: the National Ballet of Canada was founded by Celia Franca in 1951 and the Royal Winnipeg Ballet began in 1953; in 1952 the CBC began its television operations in Toronto and founded the CBC Symphony Orchestra; Jean-Louis Roux and Jean Gascon started the Théâtre du Nouveau Monde in Montreal in 1951, and the Frederic Wood Theatre opened at the University of British Columbia in 1953. Also in 1953, Joy Coghill and Myra Benson founded Holiday Theatre in Vancouver, the first professional theatre for children in Canada and the theatre that produced some of Sharon's earliest plays; Tom Hendry and John Hirsch founded the Manitoba Theatre Centre in 1958, the same year that the Canadian Opera Company began its career in Toronto. A Canadian branch of Actors' Equity (an American organization) was formed in 1955, and the Canadian Theatre Centre was founded in Toronto the next year with Mavor Moore as its first chairman; Ernest Macmillan (also in Toronto) published *Music in Canada* in 1956, and some important Canadian arts magazines were founded at about the same time (the *Tamarack Review* and the *Canadian Music Journal* in 1956 and *Canadian Literature* in 1959). In 1957 Jack McClelland announced plans for his important New Canadian Library paperback series, and Glenn Gould, defying Cold War protocols and Soviet repression, gave his now legendary Moscow concert—on May 12th (that resonant Chalmers' date)—of proscribed contemporary music by Webern, Berg, and Krenek. The first four titles in the New Canadian Library entered this world in 1958 without fanfare, but Gould's Russian success was in all the newspapers and the *Toronto Daily Star* praised him as an artist turned cultural ambassador.

Strait-laced Toronto was especially lively in the "Village" area near the University of Toronto, and it is ironic that Ross attended the university in 1958 instead of Sharon, who would have thrived in such an atmosphere. Marshall McLuhan and Northrop Frye were both lecturing then; poets like Jay Macpherson, Margaret Avison, and Douglas LePan were active and E.J. Pratt was still on hand. Young writers like Margaret Atwood and Dennis Lee, who entered the university in 1957, had begun to write, to wear bohemian black, and to read their poems in cafés and bars with poets like Gwendolyn MacEwen. The folk-music scene had arrived in the Village, along with Ian Tyson, and so had many young painters, like Harold Towne, who were keen to *épater la bourgeoisie*. Sheila Watson, who was writing her doctoral dissertation on Wyndham Lewis with McLuhan, lived not far away and published *The Double Hook* in 1959, the same year that Hugh MacLennan won a Governor General's Award for *The Watch That Ends the Night*. James Reaney was also in town, on leave from his university position in Winnipeg, to write his dissertation with Frye and teach seminars on poetry, myth, and drama. Perhaps most significantly, at least as far as the future of the Arts was concerned, the 1950s saw the submission to the federal government of *The Report of the Royal Commission on National Development in the Arts, Letters, Humanities, and Social Sciences* in 1951, and the Massey/Levesque Report (as it is more familiarly known after its co-chairmen) championed Canadian cultural nationalism with special attention to the theatre, in which Massey had a personal interest. The Report led directly to the creation of the Canada Council in 1957 and to a debate about government support of the Arts that involved Sharon in the years ahead and that has continued to the present. It might be pleasing to imagine Sharon enjoying the intellectual and artistic life of Toronto in the late fifties—studying with McLuhan and Frye, enjoying Ian Tyson at a local hang-out, discussing ideas and smoking cigarettes over scotch with Sheila Watson, sharing her affinity for animals with Glenn Gould and following his career on radio, or taking in a play at the Crest—but none of these things happened.

By 1959, when George Luscombe founded Toronto Workshop Productions, she was living miles from the city with her third child, Melinda, just a baby, Kirk in his terrible twos, Jennifer not yet in school, and a menagerie of pets to care for. If she had begun to contemplate a different life for herself, the popular culture of the late fifties would not have encouraged her, even if Ross had, or if the Angel had not been firmly in control. The Pollock household had a television, so Sharon was able to watch murder mysteries and American male adventure series like *Route 66*, which hardly endorsed positive images of women, and most popular movies of the period—*Rebel Without a Cause* (1955), *The Blackboard Jungle* (1955), *Night of the Hunter* (1955), or *The Wild One* (1954) in which Marlon Brando and his motorcycle gang terrorize small towns—celebrated male violence and rebellion, and presented such threatening images of home, school, and neighbourhood streets (with an evil Robert Mitchum stalking kids in *Night of the Hunter*) that any sane mother would stay home and lock the doors. In Margaret Atwood's description of these years, jazz and rock 'n' roll were male preserves, the Beat poets wanted their women "cookin' and smilin' and payin' the rent," the term "'artist' meant male painter," and a woman who wanted to be an artist had Freudian hang-ups, not talent (*Moving Targets*, 148).

However, even under these circumstances Virginia Woolf's ingratiating Angel, who held such sway over Sharon's life, was not the only voice whispering advice in her ear. Thanks to her left-wing neighbours on Robert Street and her own curiosity, she was reading widely and keeping abreast of politics through the newspapers and the radio. The Korean War, to which Canada had sent troops, ended in 1953 and the Cold War was fully underway with the American-built DEW (Distance Early Warning) line stretching across the Canadian North by 1954. Another nine years of Liberal rule under Louis St. Laurent, who had replaced King in 1948, came to an abrupt end in 1957 when John Diefenbaker's Conservatives swept into power. Also in '57, the Soviet Union launched its first space ship Sputnik I, Lester Pearson won the Nobel Peace Prize, and Frank Scott, poet and lawyer, challenged Duplessis' infamous Quebec Padlock Law—and won. By 1961 the Berlin Wall had gone up, a powerful reminder of worsening international affairs, the arms race, and the hovering threat of a nuclear war. Closer to home, that is, to home in New Brunswick, politics had a more personal appeal because of Everett Chalmers' involvement. Judging from the four letters I have seen from her years in Ontario, Sharon corresponded regularly with her father and called home often, although more often than not home meant calling or writing "care of" the hospital or clinic rather than the house on Grey Street. One of the predictable topics in these letters was political affairs, and her views, at least in these letters, appear to have been pro-Conservative and anti-French, whether from loyalty to Everett or as her own considered opinion. Between 1957 and 1963 there were four federal elections, which kept party rivalries in the headlines, and in New Brunswick during these years, as Dalton Camp has explained, the struggle to renew the PCs and eventually to topple the Liberals under Robichaud was fierce. Doc Chalmers campaigned and won in a series of provincial elections beginning in 1956, and Sharon maintained a keen interest in his successes. "How goes both elections [federal and provincial]?" she asked him in an April 1963 letter before describing her own situation: "I figure our P.C. candidate this time has a better chance than last time. The damn Toronto papers are so biased a person can't tell how the rest of the country's going. I hope that Robichaud goes out on his ear. I'm sick to death of hearing about French-Canadians. There should only be one kind of Canadian." And while Sharon came in later life to hold more sympathetic views regarding "French-Canadians," or any other ethnically or linguistically categorized group, her belief in "one kind of Canadian" remained constant. Although she came to see geographical regions as necessarily distinct, she developed sincere doubts about the ethics of stressing other forms of difference.

These few letters home, together with her recollections of those years, provide limited but important insights into her life and into the pressures that finally drove her to leave the husband, the marriage, and Ontario in 1964, and these pressures were crucial because without them I doubt that there would be the Sharon Pollock we know today. Each letter is addressed "Dear Daddy" and signed "Love Sharon," and each contains descriptions of the children, her household chores and health, bits of news about friends or about Ross or his sister, and *always* inquiries and comments about Peter, Everett himself, and, as the years passed, about his new family, especially young George Everett, Jr., and Susan. These letters read like an ongoing conversation of which I have not seen the other side; they are frank, warm, and generally matter-of-fact. Only occasionally does she write more personally of her love and concern for him as, for example, in January 1958, when she tells him: "if anything should ever come up don't forget me because I can always come if you want me to—I want everything to be right for you and I expect it will be, but I just want you to know that I'm always here." She also encloses things for him such as newspaper editorials about the 1963 election and a note from Jennifer to her "Grandad," and there are amusing asides about the children, as well as reports on their health. It is these brief comments that illustrate her life clearly: "Kirk is screaming his head off"; Jennifer has developed a stutter and "Dr. Spock—the mother's bible—says it's common"; "the kids all have horrid coughs"; she despairs of being able to help them with their math, and after Michele arrives she writes that this infant is "awake all day [and] Lisa [just two years older] wants to put her in the garbage." She will interrupt a letter to get Ross's lunch, to attend to a child's needs, to do the laundry, and even to wax the floors—by hand.

Admittedly, such a sparse and one-sided correspondence makes it impossible to reconstruct the years between 1958 and the end of 1963 fully, but the general picture that emerges is one of constant domestic work and exhaustion, mitigated by a devotion (albeit tinged with irony and humour) to her children, and a thinly veiled longing for "F'ton," as she calls her home town, expressed in a desire to return there in the summer for visits or, in 1963, for a school reunion, or even, she hints, permanently. Underneath lies a hard kernel of anxiety centred on Ross, who is changing jobs or is in need of money, which she gives him, explaining to Everett that she has done so just in case Ross should mention it to him. Everett was sending her cheques, as well as clothes for the children, and he was also providing emotional and medical support. A letter she wrote him, dated 10 December 1963, explains why she needed such help. Ross, it seems, had developed some bizarre suspicions and alarming reactions that suggest a degree of paranoia. As she tells her father, Ross interrogates her about who comes to the house during his absences; when she goes "across the street or next door to a neighbour's, he hides and watches me come home," and "he keeps asking me what I'm smiling about or what I'm scowling about when I've got no expression on my face at all." After giving Everett these examples of her husband's erratic behaviour, she asks her father for sleeping pills, explaining that she cannot sleep when Ross "stands in the dark looking out the window" and tells her that "he feels like something is going to happen." Then she apologizes for burdening Everett with her problems, which she fears sound too much like those of his more neurotic patients, and she reflects, with surprising detachment (given the frightening episodes she has just described), on how much luckier she is than Ross "with all his crack pot ideas" and "mental anguish." It would be easier to feel sorry for him, she confesses, if she did not have to live with him. How Everett reacted to this letter, I do not know, but any parent would be concerned. When she went on to tell her father that she hated Ross—"not any deep, burning hate, but just a quiet, every-day hate, if you know what I mean"—he may have urged her to return to Fredericton. What she does not tell him, at least not in this letter, is what she has told me (and others) in conversations and interviews. Ross's behaviour was not confined to standing at windows or questioning her every move and expression. He became violent and on more than one occasion either tried to kill her or seemed about to do so. And she retaliated by fighting back verbally, physically, and on one occasion by trying to do him in. Her plan involved hoarding birth control pills that Everett had been sending in an effort to stop the arrival of more babies, then to grind them up in her husband's dinner. Perhaps she thought this dose of hormones might precipitate a heart attack (the contraceptive dosage was much higher in the early sixties than now), but it is only after the fact that this Lucretia-Borgia-strategy seems funny. At the time it was all too real and part of a violent marital breakdown. The older children witnessed some of this violence and remember seeing their father threaten their mother with a knife, possibly when Sharon was pregnant with Michele. It would not be long before the danger to her self and the children reached a point where she gathered them up and, with her family's help and on the pretext of attending a wedding in Fredericton, she left.

About seven years later, when she was living in British Columbia and her career as a writer had been launched, Sharon would write a short story, called "If at first," in which the wife, Leslie Mitchell, tries repeatedly to dispatch her loathsome husband, George. Written as if it were a confiding monologue or a series of first-person diary entries, it is a clever, amusing murder spoof in which all Leslie's homicidal plots backfire: George shifts in his chair just as she pulls the trigger of the pistol she has aimed at his head (the bullet shatters a picture of her dear mother); he gives the chicken paprika she has laced with poison to her beloved dog (it dies); he adroitly sidesteps her manoeuvres with the car (she gets whiplash); and when she tries to electrocute him in the bath, she trips, falls, and breaks her wrist on the toilet bowl. To add injury to insult, George finally plans, executes, and gets away with her murder when he contrives to have her fall off a cliff during a holiday in the Rockies. We learn of Leslie's demise from an obituary. But the source of humour in this story lies less in the zany plot than in the matter-of-fact tone of voice, the unselfconscious understatement, the descriptive details, and in the snatches of dialogue that capture the frustration of this marriage, reflect ironically on Leslie's state of mind, and provide a portrait of George that is both ludicrous and menacing. This passage near the beginning illustrates some of these qualities, which she refined for her plays:

> It's terrible to live with someone so irritating that one would run the risk of hanging just to be rid of him. He's driven me to it, so whatever follows is his fault. Any logician would tell you that. Once I tried to discuss it with him. I said, very reasonably, I said, "George, if you had a business partner, and you suddenly discovered that you could not bear that partner, what would you do? You would dissolve that partnership, wouldn't you, George?"
> And what did he say.
> "I never knew you didn't like Fred."
> That is what he said.
> "I never knew you didn't like Fred." [...]
> It's at a time like this that I wonder how I control myself. The urge to pick up a rather heavyish lamp is almost overpowering.

Perhaps more interesting than these qualities of her prose and even more promising for her future work, this story, written less than a decade after her separation from Ross, indicates her capacity to distance herself from personal experiences, laugh at herself, and *fictionalize* aspects of her own life.

Before she achieved that distance, however, and during those times when Ross was either away in Toronto working or pretending to work, she had a busy life and a new activity had caught her attention. The first indication I have found that Sharon was actively interested in live theatre is in an April 1963 letter to her father when she notes, almost as an afterthought, that "a drama group that I belong to is putting on a revue in May. I'm directing a bunch of high school kids in a couple of skits. The blind leading the blind." This "drama group" was a local amateur theatre company run by Keswick residents and headed by Joe Dales, who became the mayor of Keswick and twenty years later wrote to congratulate Sharon on winning the Governor General's Award for *Blood Relations*. At some point in 1962–63 Sharon had joined this group, and she had also discovered another theatre attraction in the Red Barn Theatre just a few miles north of Keswick in Sutton (see Illus. 19). The Red Barn, Canada's oldest professional summer theatre, started in 1949 and is still in operation. As the name suggests the theatre is a charming old barn, now a heritage building, and it caters to summer tourists by offering good productions of classic British comedies, musicals, and

19. The Red Barn
    Theatre, Sutton,
    Ontario, is a short
    drive from where
    Sharon was living in
    Keswick in the early
    sixties. The theatre
    still looks much as it
    did at that time.
    *Photograph by E.
    Grace, 2003.*

murder mysteries. But in the early 1960s when Sharon discovered it, the seasons were more challenging: *The Glass Menagerie*, for example, was staged there in 1962 with a young Timothy Findley as Tom, and in 1964 the irascible Nathan Cohen came up from Toronto expressly to see the Harlequin Players' production of *Kiss Mama Goodbye*. Somehow she found the time and the energy not only to attend plays at the Red Barn but also to act and direct with the Keswick group, and these outlets and activities may have caused further friction between her and Ross. He had no interest in such things, and he may have become, like the husband in Sam Shepard's *Lie of the Mind*, resentful of her involvement in a world that excluded him or jealous of her friendships with members of the group. With his own life increasingly uncertain, his need to maintain control over something—his wife and children—may have become an obsession. The questions raised by this domestic situation, however, are many and familiar. Why did she stay as long as she did? Why did she have so many children? What finally precipitated her decision to flee? How did she manage to escape and how did Ross react?

Some of these questions can be partially answered. She left in June 1964 after a particularly terrifying episode when she had to seek safety with a next-door neighbour. Everett and Pegi helped her get back to Fredericton by plane. And Ross did eventually follow them to Fredericton, where he created another violent scene and had to be taken away from the Chalmers home by the police and sent back to Toronto at Everett's expense. In the months immediately following her departure, lawyers became involved when he tried to gain access to some of the children and fought to have Sharon returned to him. He appears to have held on to the house and furnishings, even though the house was in Sharon's name and most of those furnishings were hers, and he continued to make demands despite claims made by the Fredericton lawyer representing Sharon that he was not working, had cashed the Family Allowance cheques meant for the children, and had refused to allow movers to enter the Keswick home for Sharon's belongings. When his legal threats failed, Ross seems to have abandoned his children. For many years after, Sharon recalls, she was afraid he would show up or that she might suddenly encounter him on the street, and she never forgave his refusal to help the children or show any interest in their futures. To her this was the ultimate wrong. Moreover, her disbelief and anger at his apparent lack of concern for his children may help to explain why she stayed in the marriage as long as she did. Having grown up in a family with a mother who could not be counted on to be there, she knew first hand how much pain that kind of home life caused a child, and she had set as her goal the creation of a safe, loving, consistent and reliable home. Moreover, she owned the home they lived in and she was establishing a viable, even happy life in Keswick when Ross was not around. Walking away from all that could not have been easy, but the decision to save herself and the children, to value her life above his, to *live* instead of die, when it came, was swift and final. Sharon Pollock did not kill herself, as Sylvia Plath did in February of 1963; she did not kill her husband with her concoction of birth control pills and chili con carne; and she was not killed by her husband, as poet Pat Lowther would be. Instead, she killed the Angel in the house who kept telling her to behave, to remain silent, and above all not to have a mind or a life of her own.

II: Leaving Home Again

Back in Fredericton, Sharon had time to reflect on all that had changed for her since 1954. The mom and pop domestic bliss promised by Doris Day and Betty Crocker had turned out to be a fraud. Prince Charming was worse than a failure. Now she was a single mother with five youngsters, no university degree, no job, no prospects, and no money—never mind a room—of her own. Things did not go better with Coca Cola, as the sixties jingle insisted, and worse still, she was back in the house on Grey Street where Eloise had eaten her fatal sandwich and lain in the coffin prior to her funeral. But at least the children were safe, and she could, with effort and guts and luck, make a new start. During these first months back on home ground she clarified in her own mind the principles and priorities that would guide her for the rest of her life. Giving up, as Eloise had done, first to domestic anonymity and then to alcohol and suicide, were simply not options. *Looking after* the children, as distinct from merely *providing for* them, was essential. Being able to turn to her father illustrated the value of parental strength and reliability. And some parts of her nature—a stubborn resilience, an exuberant interest in life, a basic tough practicality—precluded the grand gesture of putting her head in an oven like Plath or walking into a river like Woolf. Sharon was not then, and is not now, one to feel sorry for her self. She decided to take control of her life and full responsibility for her children, and never again surrender that control to anyone else. Pushing her towards this new sense of identity was the experience of escaping an abusive marriage, but I believe that Eloise's life and death—her influence and her example— were even more decisive, if less obvious, incentives.

Beginning in the 1970s, clinical and theoretical studies of addiction, especially of alcoholism, have increased until what was once a taboo subject is openly discussed and treated. Associations exist today to help recovering alcoholics, with parallel organizations for families and for the adult children of alcoholics. In an effort to understand Eloise and the impact of her disease on her daughter, I have explored the literature on these subjects, but I remain skeptical about psychoanalytic generalizations because they seem arbitrary, and often ignore fundamental social factors such as class, historical and cultural influences, and gender. Nevertheless, when handled with care, these studies can shed light on Sharon's reactions to her mother and her fierce determination to survive and succeed after the break-up of her marriage.[3] Amongst the many frequently reported characteristics of adult children of alcoholics, a few are worth noting. Daughters of alcoholic mothers seem more severely affected than sons because they are deprived of a mature role model and lack a *positive* image of female identity. They are often expected, by a father or brothers, to take over a mother's duties in the home, to be silent, and to put up with things. The evidence suggests that daughters of alcoholic mothers will more often escape into early marriages than the general population, and if they have children at all, they will have several in an effort to create the kind of family life that they were denied. Because they grew up conditioned (even more than the daughters of non-alcoholic parents) to repress their own needs and to look after others, they expect to assume this kind of role as adults. More specifically, and here the clinical evidence does not distinguish between daughters and sons, children of alcoholic parents grow up with much more than the average degree of unresolved anger: girls appear to internalize their anger, while boys more often rebel openly, and girls tend to blame themselves for their parents' problems. Both sexes develop feelings of insecurity accompanied by an inability to trust other people, a deep-rooted suspicion of and resistance to authority and, finally, the need, often amounting to an obsession, for control. Experts argue that a childhood once complicated by secrecy, lack of trust, and anger and guilt, and disturbed by feelings of rejection by a parent that results in low self-esteem and insecurity, will produce an adult who insists on self-control (against their own anger and fear) and the control of things and people around them because control props up a fragile sense of identity.

Does this describe Sharon Pollock in the summer of 1964 or at any time thereafter? Does it describe her in ways that are unique or clearly linked to her childhood? Well, yes ... and no. Complex human beings cannot be neatly explained, labeled, or summarized. That said, I have found from interviews with many people who have known her well over considerable periods of time, and in comments she has made about her self, that anger and control come up frequently: "I have always attempted to control the world," she once said, "or to control myself by analyzing things" (see Zimmerman, 1991, 38). As for the anger, well Sharon has frequently commented on this aspect of her personality in interviews and through her plays: "If I didn't write plays," she once said, "I would be in jail" (Hofsess 52), but because she had the skill and knowledge to express her rage at the way things are, she could channel her anger into creative rather than destructive acts. Virginia Woolf once said that "a woman writing thinks back through her mothers" (A Room of One's Own, 96), and insofar as Sharon thought back through Eloise, or through Mary Chalmers, she began the process of controlling the spectres of self-defeat and loss when she returned to Fredericton in 1964. It must have been a shock to find herself back where she started and had hoped never again to be, this time with responsibility not only for five other people but for herself and for proving that Eloise's fate would not be hers. The miracle is that she found the wherewithal to transform her rage into the productive, aesthetically separate (from self) beauty of art. And she found her way, her *métier*, in Fredericton's new Beaverbrook Playhouse.

By 1959 Max Aitken, Lord Beaverbrook, had created the Beaverbrook Art Gallery, a gracious one-storey building on the banks of the Saint John River, and he had begun its permanent collection with pieces from his own and his friend Sir James Dunn's private collections of historical Canadian and modern European art. On the other side of Queen Street, directly across from the Lord Beaverbrook Hotel, he and Dunn saw another opportunity to leave a mark on Fredericton by funding something else of lasting value—a theatre. And so the Beaverbrook Playhouse was built and opened with a grand gala on 26–27 September 1964. The building is elegant with a classical façade and a large mural depicting fifty-six life-sized figures in costumes and masks, commissioned by Beaverbrook from Irish painter Sidney Smith, dominating the foyer. The original building had a good-sized house with seating for 750 on the main floor and a balcony for another 250, a proscenium stage and space for a small orchestra pit. The lack of a fly gallery limited the kinds of plays that could be produced, but the theatre, nonetheless, was a splendid addition to the artistic life and cultural potential of the city and the province. Alexander Gray, an experienced Canadian director and artistic director fresh from work in England was hired as the first general manager, and he brought with him his wife, the actor Elizabeth Orion, plus an exciting vision for future developments that soon included the creation of a resident acting company. Sharon had arrived back in her home town at a propitious moment.

Within weeks of her return, she landed her first job—running the Playhouse box office—and she soon had other theatre tasks to attend to. As the daughter of Doc Chalmers, she was well placed to know some of Fredericton's VIPs, among them Robert Tweedie, who was on the new board, and the rather alarming owner of the Fredericton *Daily Gleaner*, Brigadier Michael Wardell, and both men helped her. Tweedie suggested she apply for the position of Lady Dunn's "secretary" at the Playhouse, where she would take charge of guest lists and the like, but the Brigadier was the man she had to deal with on a regular basis because he represented Lady Dunn in all Playhouse business. Wardell was a large, terrifying man who screamed at people and would remove his black eye patch and clean his eye socket in public. But Sharon liked him because he reminded her of her father, and he appears to have liked or, at least, tolerated her. She has recalled for me occasions on which a cat that had been adopted by the theatre scrambled up the burlap walls in the long gallery, where the theatre hung paintings, and that she, like everyone else, worried about the Brigadier finding out. But the man liked cats and never made a fuss over these feline workouts. By October that year, Sharon had added acting to her work at the theatre with a role in Gray's first production, *Little Lambs Eat Ivy*.

Beaverbrook had stipulated that the Playhouse was to be a rental facility that would make money, but Gray and Orion wanted to establish a semi-professional acting company, so they found a way around the restrictions on funding and programming to found "The Company of Ten" with themselves, Alvin Shaw from UNB, Doreen Grinstead, Sharon Pollock, and a few local actors and people from the UNB Drama Society. The Company followed *Little Lambs Eat Ivy* with a Broadway hit by William Gibson, *Two for the Seesaw*, the Christmas pantomime *Cinderella* and, in 1965, *The Provok'd Wife*, *Separate Tables*, *Mary, Mary*, and *A Man for all Seasons*. By the end of the year, and with Gray's contract renewal in doubt, he and Orion left Fredericton and the Company of Ten dissolved. For the moment, Beaverbrook's rental concept had trumped an artistic director's vision, but this disruption of the Playhouse was short-lived. In 1968 Walter Learning was hired as general manager and he moved quickly to establish a professional Equity company and to form Theatre New Brunswick (TNB) in 1969. From this point on, TNB grew and developed rapidly: the company began touring the province, expanding its repertoire, and by 1972 the theatre added the fly gallery with Tom Forrestall's impressive mural of bright bands of colour. This is the theatre building, the vision, and the company that Sharon would inherit when she returned to Fredericton and to TNB as artistic director in 1988. But much would transpire before then, so I want to return to the first year in the life of the Playhouse, its box office, stage, and the Company of Ten because all these places and people contribute to the larger story of Sharon Pollock making theatre.

Sharon recalls that, once she had started to act for Alexander Gray, she juggled rehearsals and performances with the tasks of taking minutes, carrying out other secretarial duties, and setting up and running the box office—a tiny cubicle in the middle of the lobby—which handled the tickets for a constant round of films, recitals, and other visiting engagements quite separate from play productions. The opening festival program lists Sharon Pollock as "Box Office Manager," and Doreen Grinstead (a founding member of the Company of Ten and Gray's "Personal Assistant") described for me the excitement and hectic routine of those months. Everyone worked hard, including Sharon, who would show up at the theatre, Doreen recalls, in a small Volkswagen with all her kids and various pets. By this point, shortly after her return to Fredericton, she had moved across the river to a house in Devon that Pegi Chalmers owned, where she could re-establish a home base for herself and her children. I have located few details about the theatre's first play, *Little Lambs Eat Ivy*, except that it was directed by Gray with Elizabeth Orion, Alvin Shaw, and Sharon Pollock in the cast. However, the Company of Ten's next play received newspaper coverage with photographs of Sharon in the lead female role of Gittel Mosca in *Two for the Seesaw* and enough narrative to provide some sense of her ability on stage. The play itself is described as a drama that will appeal to serious theatre lovers because it tells a realistic story about two people who find love and meaning in life, and Gray is quoted as saying he believes that his actors (Sharon Pollock and Don Lord) will rise to the occasion: "This is a big challenge for them [because] these two parts would tax the abilities of the most seasoned professionals, but I am confident that Sharon and Don will do well. They are both, to my mind, good potential professional actors." Gray was taking a risk, forced on him by the last-minute cancellation of Clifford Odet's *The Country Girl*, and Sharon was learning some basic lessons in the vicissitudes of theatre. Two reviewers praised Sharon's portrayal of the lonely, uninhibited young woman as "outstanding" and "exceptionally fine," and the production itself as "thought-provoking" and "exciting," but a more critical reviewer recognized that neither actor was experienced enough

20. Sharon Pollock in her first publicity photograph when she began acting with the Fredericton Playhouse in 1965.
Photograph courtesy of Sharon Pollock.

to do the play justice and that more rehearsal time was needed. The Company's work was no match for the Broadway production that had starred Anne Bancroft as Gittel, but Sharon Pollock had made a respectable stage debut in a play with some substance (see Illus. 20).

Judging from the newspapers, Sharon made a bit of a splash in the next Playhouse production—the Christmas pantomime *Cinderella*. Pantomime has a long tradition in Europe, and British panto, with its spectacle, broad humour, dancing, familiar songs, and local references, is especially popular at Christmas. Because men cross-dress as women and vice versa, it provides an opportunity to put young women with good figures and shapely legs in very short skirts and flesh-coloured tights, and Sharon, despite her five children had, in Doreen Grinstead's words, "a gorgeous figure." The principals in the panto that year in Fredericton were Elaine Fowler (an English major at UNB) as "Prince Charming," Catherine McKinnon (a soprano with the Don Messer Show) as "Cinderella," and Sharon Pollock as "Dandini" and, predictably, the production photographs showed lots of leg. One newspaper piece, noting that pantomime was a novelty for New Brunswick, explained its conventions, stressed the contemporary version as "a musical extravaganza for children" that "can appeal to all ages" and called the production an "outstanding success." Other reviews had headlines like "Cinderella Surprises, Delights Audience" and "Christmas Extravaganza"; there was coverage of rehearsals, features on members of the cast (the men playing Cinderella's ugly step-sisters were a real hit), and calls for another pantomime the following year. And there was another one—the perennial favourite *Aladdin*—but the plays for 1965 came first, and Sharon gained valuable experience in three of these, one of which (*Mary, Mary*) eventually prompted her to write plays herself and also brought a new partner into her life. The two plays she performed in before *Mary, Mary* were *The Provok'd Wife*, a Restoration comedy by John Vanbrugh, and Terence Rattigan's *Separate Tables*—from seventeenth-century to twentieth-century British comedy in the space of two months—both witty, fast-paced, satiric portrayals of marital relations and social manners, and plays (especially Vanbrugh's) that have more than a few resonances with her short story "If at first." Sharon played Lady Brute, the provoked wife of the title, with Michael Harling as the ill-tempered, wife-loathing Sir John, Elizabeth Orion as the ageing, frivolous Lady Fanciful, and Carol Friolet as the wise and worthy Belinda. Fredericton's audiences seem to have been enchanted by the make-up, elegant costumes, and the sets designed by Orion, and the reviews praised the Company of Ten and Gray's production, calling the period piece "something new and different" and a "solid success." After opening night, on February 26th, the Fredericton *Daily Gleaner* featured Sharon looking beautiful and perplexed as she considers taking revenge on her surly husband by finding a lover. *Separate Tables* (comprising two one-act plays, "Table By the Window" and "Table Number Seven," with its hapless Major Pollock) was also enthusiasti-cally received, and Sharon attracted special attention for learning the tricks of her role as a waitress by consulting a local Zeller's waitress and received praise for her performance, which D.F. Rowan described as "crisp, controlled and a pleasure to watch."

The Playhouse ran each play for three nights, and neither went on tour, in part because of the winter weather but also because touring to the rest of the province was not as important as it would become for TNB. However, by May 1965, when Gray's Company of Ten staged Jean Kerr's comedy *Mary, Mary*, this practice seems to have changed. In fact, a number of things were changing for Sharon, as well as for the Playhouse. *Mary, Mary* did go on tour that May; the Company was hailed as New Brunswick's "first professional touring company"; and Gray hired a handsome young actor, recently graduated from the National Theatre School in Montreal to perform in it. The actor was Michael Ball, born in Ottawa in 1943 and raised in Victoria, B.C., where he discovered theatre in the Oak Bay high school, was encouraged by Victor Mitchell, and decided to become an actor. Several years later, Michael told Ray Conlogue that he knew early what he wanted to do, so he dropped out of high school to study at the National Theatre School from 1961 to 1964. Shortly after he arrived in Fredericton on his first acting gig, or so the story goes, he spied a beautiful girl in the box office and, in an effort to get her attention, he leaned over the counter accidentally hitting an alarm button. He got the girl's attention all right and, as he told me in our interview, they "really hit it off." At some point, either during rehearsals for *Mary, Mary* or after its short run and tour, Michael, Sharon, the children, and assorted cats and dogs, began their life together in a house owned by Everett in Marysville, a town adjacent to Devon and today part of greater Fredericton.

Meanwhile, *Mary, Mary* also hit it off with local audiences. This popular Broadway play is about a New York publisher called Bob, his new girlfriend, Tiffany, and his forthright, but unhappy, ex-wife, Mary. In Gray's production, Elizabeth Orion played Mary opposite Ron Braden as Bob, her indecisive, former husband. Promotion materials for the Playhouse premiere described Braden and Michael Ball (in the role of Dirk, a friend of Bob's and an actor who falls in love with Mary) as "two of Canada's leading young actors," and both men, along with Orion, were professionals. The two amateurs in the play were UNB student, Graham Whitehead (who played Oscar, a lawyer and family friend), and "Sharon Pollock, rising Playhouse star," in the role of the perky, rich girlfriend. They made a handsome cast but the play itself is light fare, "a sparkling comedy" about well-to-do New Yorkers sorting out their marriage problems, with little depth or serious purpose. After trying out the British accents required for *The Provok'd Wife* and *Separate Tables*, the actors now mimicked a Manhattan drawl as best they could, and their audiences apparently loved them. When *Mary, Mary* went to Woodstock, a small city upriver from Fredericton, the performance was halted several times by applause. The local newspaper praised Orion but also reminded its readers that "Sharon Pollock, remembered for her role in *Cinderella*, was well cast in her role as a well adjusted, healthy rich girl." For Sharon this must have been heady stuff. She was being billed in popular plays, directed by an experienced professional, and acting alongside some fine professional colleagues. Although the season's three plays were all domestic comedies, the differences in style, accent, historical period, and staging gave her a crash course in the importance of sharp dialogue, spatial dynamics on stage, and pacing, as well as insight into the kind of subject matter she would *not* want to use in her own work. By November 1965 she had signed her first Equity card for her role in *Aladdin*, but it would take another three years or so and several more performances of plays like *Mary, Mary* before she had had her fill of sparkling comedies from England and the United States.

There was one more play for Gray and his Company that summer—*A Man for All Seasons*—and there was another Christmas panto—*Aladdin and His Wonderful Lamp* in which Michael played the Emperor of China, Ed Stephenson from Toronto played the Widow Twankey, Elizabeth Orion played the "Genie of the Ring," and Sharon played the naughty Prince Pekoe. In describing this lively production, Doreen Grinstead recalled one of those priceless moments in children's theatre when the rules of theatre decorum and the observance of illusion proved too much for a young audience member to bear. At the point when Aladdin is lost in the cave and wails—"Oh what am I going to do"—this totally engrossed youngster sang out, "rub the lamp," and the whole house and cast erupted in such laughter that the child wept with embarrassment. Behind the scenes, however, more serious things were beginning to unravel. By Christmas, Gray and Orion had left Fredericton under circumstances that are far from clear. Vernon Chapman believes that the problems that arose between Gray and the board of directors were to blame, and if that is the case, it would prove prophetic for more than one artistic director at the Playhouse. But Gray and Orion had made a remarkable contribution to theatre in New Brunswick and, while they could not have foreseen it, they provided invaluable practical training in the art of making theatre that helped produce Sharon Pollock. She still speaks with pleasure and gratitude of that training. Vernon Chapman's summary of the first year and a half in the life of the Fredericton Playhouse provides a better picture than anything I can conjure up of just what the Company of Ten achieved:

> From the Playhouse opening in September 1964 to Christmas 1965, by using The Company of
> Ten and the Patrons of the Playhouse, Gray had produced three plays [my count is six] and two

large-cast Christmas pantomimes. With the invaluable assistance of Doreen Grinstead and Sharon Pollock, he had also managed the day-to-day running of the Playhouse. By 1965 the Stratford Festival, the Canadian Opera Company, and the National Ballet had become aware of the Beaverbrook Playhouse and begun to bring their touring productions on a regular basis. The Playhouse had given the culture of New Brunswick a hefty shot-in-the-arm, and Alex Gray had begun the process of making it into a home for a professional theatre company. (533)

***

When the 1965 Christmas festivities were over and the final curtain had come down on *Aladdin*, Sharon prepared to leave Fredericton again. Michael Ball had received the call from Victor Mitchell, who was starting a new drama program at the University of Calgary, offering him a job starting in early January, and Sharon was going with him. She was going as Sharon *Pollock*, of course, and taking the three eldest children (Jennifer, Kirk, and Melinda) with her; the two youngest, Lisa and Michele stayed behind with Everett and Pegi for a while because Lisa needed an operation. Sharon was going as her own person, and as an actor, and she kept the name Pollock for several reasons. Pollock was her children's name, even though they came to see Michael as the father figure in their lives; she was an Equity member and would soon be writing professionally under this name; and, most decisively of all, she was not divorced from Ross Pollock. When a marriage failed in Canada in the 1960s, the only grounds for divorce was adultery and establishing (or staging) those grounds was an ugly business. If children were involved it could also be risky. Neither she nor Ross chose to pursue this route, at least not at this time.[4] Moreover, when she met Michael in the spring of 1965, she knew she did not want to commit herself to another formal marriage. Nevertheless their partnership was a happy one for many years, produced one more child (Michael's daughter and Sharon's youngest—Amanda), and proved to be a mutually stimulating professional relationship with him acting in most of the stage plays she wrote. But if Sharon was beginning again she was doing so under circumstances that appeared, on the surface at least, to be unusual if not downright foolhardy. She would be thirty in April of 1966 and she was throwing in her lot with a man seven years her junior; she had five children but no career as yet. However well-intentioned, optimistic, and in love they must have been, neither Michael nor Sharon was going to become rich making theatre in Calgary in the 1960s. What she did have working for her—as did Michael—was a hell of a lot of courage, determination, and hope. She may also have felt a sense of urgency: ten years had passed in which, despite the joys of her children and the excitement of discovering theatre, she had suffered further trauma, acquired even more reasons for mistrusting others, but accomplished little professionally.

Leaving Fredericton again put physical and psychological distance between herself and her memories. It also entailed another separation from the father she loved and who had provided so much support. Everett, however, had forged ahead with his own life, remarrying and having two more children as well as advancing his medical career and succeeding at politics. As usual, his life was extremely busy. Sharon's rather wistful assurances in her January 1958 letter that she wanted him to be happy and would always be there for him seemed beside the point. In any case, the Chalmers home was full enough. Pegi was already showing signs of being an alcoholic and possibly bipolar; she had done what she could to assist Sharon and Ev's grandchildren and was struggling to cope with two more children of her own. There was no place for Sharon in this household, which Peter had left years ago and refused to re-enter. But leaving Fredericton again did not mean leaving Eloise and the family ghost story, which now included Ross, behind. Nor did it mean wiping the emotional slate clean of anger, guilt, and fear. In the decade ahead, Sharon continued to be haunted by the double trauma of her mother's abandonment and her husband's abuse, subjects that could not be talked about or acknowledged for the damage they caused. If Eloise's example—or failure to provide a positive example—contributed to Sharon's choice of a domineering husband who was insecure and violent, then the mother had multiplied her daughter's reasons for disliking and rejecting her, although what the daughter needed most was to love, understand, and forgive her mother, to make amends and find a place for her lost mother in her own life.

Earlier I mused on what Sheila Watson and Sharon Pollock might have talked about *if* they had met on the streets around the University of Toronto in the late fifties. And Sheila Watson comes to mind again as I try to imagine Sharon's position at the end of 1965. In January 1956, during her sojourn in Paris, at an especially dark time in her own marriage and three years before her breakthrough with *The Double Hook*, Watson wrote the following wise warning in her journal:

> It is absolutely necessary to liquidate all anger, chagrin, or contempt before writing. In short, a writer must have mastered the emotions before he can use the insight which the emotion has given him. (see Flahiff, 165)

These words ring true, simply and unequivocally true. An artist must move beyond, must transcend, anger, grief, and contempt, before he or she is able to use the insights of experience in the creation of art. As she packed for Calgary, Sharon was still packing an enormous amount of anger, grief, and contempt. Before she could write well she had to look these emotions in the face and discover sources of compassion and forgiveness within herself. Only then would she be able to make reparation.

Why *reparation*? Because, as psychoanalyst Melanie Klein explains, "making reparation is ... a fundamental element in love and in all human relationships" (68). It goes hand in hand, according to Klein, with the aggression and hate a person can feel towards a parent who has let them down or a spouse who has failed them. I turn to psychoanalysis with caution to help me situate Sharon as she embarks on the next stage of her journey, but Klein, unlike many Freudians, does not presume to find in psychoanalysis an etiology for creative genius. Instead she stresses the mother/child connection and recognizes and accepts the multiplicity of normal adult identity and the relationships that shape that identity. We become who we are, says Klein, not only through our childhood experiences but also through our ongoing interactions with others and our capacity to rewrite earlier scripts of anger and blame—that is to make reparation and through reparation forgive ourselves. Perhaps most important, since Sharon was on the brink of becoming an artist, is Klein's notion that an adult's desire to make reparation for the loss of a loved one and for their anger with that loved one will "be expressed in creative and constructive ways" (107). In this way, Klein does not so much account for creativity, let alone for artistic talent, as map the route taken by an individual who may have artistic potential. Many other factors contribute to artistic success, and some of these may be accidental, but the desire for reparation must be there, together with the need to manage strong emotion by controlling it in art, if that potential is going to be realized. Which brings me back to Sheila Watson's warning and to Sharon Pollock's position.

In December of 1965, as she prepared to leave the place of her birth once more, she was taking with her not only her children, a new partner, a new career, and an Equity card but also a symbolic trunk full of unopened letters (to invoke an image from *Doc*) and a mass of unresolved anger, unexamined guilt, and barely suppressed insecurity and fear. Somehow, somewhere over the next twenty years, she found a way, the tools if you will, to exploit, explore, and redirect the trauma of her abandonment, betrayal, and loss into creation instead of destruction. She found a way to "liquidate anger," as Sheila Watson put it, or, in Sharon's words, to let off her rage at "the way things are" by making theatre. By 1965 she was about to recreate herself as a woman who could accept, even like, herself in her various roles of mother, lover, actor, and playwright. To do this she would need some luck, a lot of talent, and the ability to work exceedingly hard, but she would also need to make reparation, which she began to do by finding a voice of her own.

CHAPTER 4

Finding a Voice of Her Own

The playwright, the crucial member of the drama, is the most neglected in this country. As long as he is blocked, stifled, and not allowed to be productive, the Canadian theatre will be insignificant.
—NATHAN COHEN QUOTED IN EDMONSTONE, 198

To me, the writer was the essence of what I thought could be a Canadian theatre. ... But radio is not enough—there must also be a living stage. —ANDREW ALLAN, QUOTED IN GOODWIN, 6, 13

I began to write because I felt I had no voice, even though I was working as an actor.
—SHARON POLLOCK, QUOTED IN ZIMMERMAN, 1991, 37

I: Playing the Prairies

When Sharon landed in Calgary in early January 1966, she was ready to start again, if not entirely on her own terms, then at least on terms she helped to make. Years later she told John Hofsess that she wanted her children to grow up "in a new land without the heavy psychological baggage of the family in New Brunswick" (Hofsess, 1980, 3), a comment that speaks volumes about her state of mind and hope for the future. Going west gave her the physical and emotional distance she needed from New Brunswick and its ghost stories to establish a firm sense of herself and her abilities. It freed her to find a voice of her own that would, in time, marshall and transform into art all the voices she had ignored or rejected or tried, unsuccessfully, to silence. Going west quickly proved to be one of the most fortunate and formative moves of her life.

Calgary, like many other Canadian cities in the mid-1960s, was poised to develop an arts scene, and professional theatre was central to this development. Many factors contributed to the sense of excitement and purpose that galvanized the arts in Canada, and theatre people in particular at this time: the organizational and financial impact of the Canada Council; the keen sense of national pride inspired by the 1967 centenary; a series of major arts commissions or premieres, which marked that birthday, such as Glenn Gould's CBC sound documentary *The Idea of North*, Mavor Moore's and Harry Somers' opera *Louis Riel*, and the premieres of George Ryga's *The Ecstasy of Rita Joe* in Vancouver and, in 1968, Michel

Tremblay's *Les Belles Soeurs* in Montreal; the hoopla surrounding Expo 67 which put Canada and Canadian culture on a world stage; and the proactive presence of the CBC, which provided the closest thing Canada has ever had to a *national* theatre or even to a national stage for the arts. The 1960s also saw a number of significant *foundings* and publications that paved the way for an even greater blossoming in the seventies: the Shaw Festival in 1962; Neptune Theatre in Halifax in 1963, the same year that the Vancouver Playhouse opened its doors; Vancouver's Arts Club Theatre in 1964; Edmonton's Citadel in 1965; Regina's Globe Theatre in 1966; and the National Arts Centre, Theatre Passe Muraille, Theatre Calgary, and Theatre New Brunswick, all in 1969. Also during this decade, the National Theatre School opened in Montreal (1960); an important meeting of the Canadian Conference of the Arts was held in Kingston (1961); the first Charlottetown Festival (with an all-Canadian program) took place (1964); CEAD (Centre d'essai des auteurs dramatiques) began operations and Carl Klinck published the first *Literary History of Canada* (both in 1965). Ironically, given the mounting nationalist sentiment amongst anglophone Canadian artists, arts groups, and intellectuals, George Grant published *Lament for a Nation* in 1965, and only time will tell if his Cassandra-like message was prophetic. In the late sixties, however, this book served as a rallying cry for an entire generation—Sharon's generation.

Simply noting a series of events or meetings or premieres or publications and naming a few representative organizations and people cannot do justice to an entire decade, but it does demonstrate that the momentum was building that would turn the 1970s into a watershed that transformed Canadian theatre—by which I mean plays written, produced, directed, and performed by Canadians—into the richly successful activity we enjoy today. This kind of accounting also reminds us that the artistic life of the country was not the exclusive preserve of Toronto or Montreal, so that when we turn to the 1970s we are prepared to see and appreciate the sheer geographical spread of creativity to which Sharon contributed and from which she drew support. This point is important because it is clear that she was not disadvantaged by living in Western Canada. On the contrary, places like Calgary, Vancouver, and Edmonton, where she lived and worked between 1966 and 1976 before settling permanently in Calgary in 1977, provided ideal environments for her growth as a playwright. In interviews through the seventies, eighties, and nineties, she was repeatedly asked why she stayed in Calgary—the implication being that Toronto was the best place to be—and the question was perfectly understandable, if also quickly answered. People asked because the alternative theatre scene in Toronto exploded into life in the seventies, so, of course, it seemed the place to be. Unless, that is, you were happier living elsewhere and were able to work there with talented colleagues, challenging opportunities, and a network of professional support. Calgary, Vancouver, and Edmonton offered her all these opportunities. Moreover, a quick glance through the chronology of events and theatre seasons prepared by Denis Johnston in *Up the Mainstream: The Rise of Toronto's Alternative Theatres* (1991) suggests to me that from the late 1960s and through the 1970s, the Toronto theatre scene was dominated by a group of men—talented, dedicated, and in some instances visionary—who championed the work of other men, especially in playwriting. By contrast, in Calgary, Vancouver, and Edmonton during these years, there was more room for an ambitious, talented woman to make her mark, in part because the field was less crowded and in part because there was somewhat less of an entrenched old boys' system operating in these western cities, the kind of system that seems to have erased, as Paula Sperdakos argues, Dora Mavor Moore from Toronto's theatre history. In the most basic sense, there was more freedom and more space out west, and Sharon found these qualities stimulating and enabling. By great good fortune, she arrived on the scene when Victor Mitchell, Fred Diehl, and Joyce Doolittle were lighting artistic fires in Calgary, when Christopher Newton, Larry Lillo, Dorothy Jones, and Don Shipley could provide vital encouragement and practical stage experience in Vancouver, and when her path would cross, at the most propitious moments, with those of Harold Baldridge, Lucille Wagner, and Douglas Riske in Calgary, Jim DeFelice and Diane Bessai in Edmonton, Don Williams in Vancouver, and Tom Hendry at Banff. Sharon's story between 1966 and 1976 (and after) is also their story, and it is the story of the growth of a distinctly non-centrist anglophone Canadian theatre, using Western Canadian voices and stories.

But the 1960s was not a decade to be primarily remembered, in Canada or anywhere else, for its creativity or prosperity. Too much was happening of grave political and military concern for celebration or complacency to characterize the period. The Cuban Missile Crisis of 1962 signalled the escalation of Cold War hostilities and reminded North Americans about the ever-present threat of sudden, mass annihilation. The assassination of John F. Kennedy in 1963 transformed a single public tragedy into one of those moments by which individuals date their private lives. The Vietnam War was underway and dominated North American news until the fall of Saigon in 1975. Student protests and violent state repression, especially in the United States and France, illustrated, among other things, how fragile our democracies were, how disposable our civil rights could be, and how wide the gulf had become between the generations born before and after WWII. Uncensored, horrifying photographs, graphic print journalism, and film coverage from Vietnam revealed the appalling consequences of war, for Vietnamese civilians and American GIs, as never before (or since) in the history of war reporting. In the summer of 1968, the Warsaw Pact forces invaded Czechoslovakia, and the Soviet army marched through Prague to suppress the famous "Prague Spring" reforms; Martin Luther King, Jr., and Robert Kennedy were assassinated in 1968; and, in Canada, that peaceable kingdom to the north, the FLQ crisis was worsening in Quebec with bombs in mail boxes, terrorist manifestoes, and eventually the kidnappings and murder that pushed Prime Minister Pierre Elliott Trudeau to invoke the War Measure's Act on 16 October 1970. This crisis reminded Canadians that even at home civil liberties could be abrogated in one swift government move. None of this international and national violence, state and military oppression, or social turmoil escaped Sharon's notice. During and immediately after WWII she was too young to register or comprehend the realities of war, genocide, atomic bombs, or, at home, the violations of personal rights and liberties, but this time she was paying full attention and stockpiling examples of violence and injustice that would inform both her approach to playwriting and her choice of specific themes and images.

It is no overstatement to describe Sharon as a "news junkie." She constantly listens to and watches the CBC, CNN, and local news, and she can usually be found awake before everyone else and reading the morning paper. History and politics have always been central interests in her life and art, and during the sixties and seventies she was living through, and raising young children in, the worst times of the post-WWII generation. From the very beginning then, which for her serious playwriting starts in 1968–69, she created theatre out of her socio-political orientation to the world and her passionate belief that theatre could make a difference—possibly even make the world a safer, better place. This orientation and passion are fundamental to her work, whether she is writing for children or adults, for radio or the stage, or, by the mid-seventies, for television. To understand why she makes the kind of theatre she does, it is necessary to pay close attention to her integration of the private experience of New Brunswick ghost stories (or, indeed, the haunted personal stories of historical figures) with the public observance of contemporary history, a type of bearing witness to her time and place. With Sharon Pollock, the public power politics of history cannot be separated from the private realm of the family or from the individual's conscience or consciousness. Between 1968–69 and 1976, she wrote and had produced four major stage plays (two of which required extensive historical research), eight children's plays, six original radio plays, and three scripts for television, and almost all of these works address social, political, and cultural issues. By any measure her output was astonishing, but when I add that she was also acting, teaching, rapidly involving herself in theatre administration, moving from rented house to rented house in three cities, scrambling to help pay the bills, and raising six children, then this productivity confirms her tremendous energy and sense of mission. Equally important is the fact that she was immersing herself in theatre work, learning on the fly—*by doing*—experimenting with form and subject matter, discovering her strengths as a writer, and honing her skills. By the late seventies she was ready to create the play that would consolidate her status as a major Canadian and a leading contemporary playwright: *Blood Relations*.

***

When Alberta joined Confederation as a separate province in 1905 (the same year as Saskatchewan), Edmonton became the provincial capital and the rivalry that still characterizes relations between Edmonton and Calgary was underway. Edmonton, famous as the "Gateway to the North," the site of the University of Alberta (founded in 1907), and the home of the best Fringe Theatre Festival in Canada, of Wayne Gretsky, and the West Edmonton Mall, has usually seemed relatively sophisticated and cultured compared to its brash rival. To think of Calgary is to think of the "Greatest Outdoor Show on Earth"—the Calgary Stampede— its reputation for rednecks, and the 1988 Winter Olympics (something of a turning point in the city's sense of itself and the occasion of a small Pollock contretemps). However, there is one incident in particular that I feel represents the essence of Calgary's (former) reputation, and it occurred on an evening in April 1975. As Brian Brennan tells the story, a "deeply troubled" local pilot and "would-be country singer" called

Cal Cavendish decided to protest the injustice of his life (his pilot's licence had been revoked and his music career was stalled) by flying very low over Calgary and "manurewritingbombing" the city (*Boondoggles*, 133). For three hours he swooped around the city and buzzed the Calgary Tower before dumping his load of manurewritingcoated records on city streets. Why manure? "'It was a cow town and I figured it could take a joke,' said Cavendish" (133).

In 1966 Calgary was still young and small; its population was well under half a million, and the overwhelming majority of its people were white and English-speaking. It was dominated, as it had been since its incorporation in 1893, by the CPR, which made Calgary the major transportation hub of the West, and then, from 1924 (with a major oil discovery in nearby Turner Valley) by the oil and gas industries. But if it was small and homogeneous, it was also becoming wealthy, and over the next forty years that wealth would transform Calgary from a "cow town" into a vibrant metropolis of a million people, the financial centre of Western Canada, and home to an impressive array of cultural institutions. I first saw Calgary in the summer of 1977, well before I had heard of Sharon Pollock, and I was not impressed. After many years in Montreal, it seemed to me a raw, loud, physically unappealing place, and I was glad to be passing through. Since then, however, my opinion has changed, as has the city, which Richard Rhodes describes as "a hub connected to the rest of the world ... and running on global time" (38). Certainly, I will never forget my impression of Calgary in the late summer of 2005 as I drove through it on my way to Banff, following the highway as it climbs slowly out of the Bow Valley and into the gently rising foothills. It was early in the morning when I reached the ranches beyond the suburban sprawl and paused to look back at the city. I had been preoccupied with the thought that this was the road that Sharon had taken many, many times until I turned to see the morning sun shining directly on the distant cluster of distinctive, individual silver and glass towers rising out of the valley. How to describe that sight? At that hour of the morning and from my distance and angle, downtown Calgary, balanced on the curve of the earth, had a startling, surreal beauty, and as I watched the light dancing on those towers, I remembered a phrase, coined by my friend and colleague Laurie Ricou, to capture the abrupt incongruity of modern civilization on the Canadian Prairies: "vertical man, horizontal world." Calgary is a triumph of verticality, flaunting its growth and wealth, challenging the heavens and the earth to deny its energy and power. Calgary is as far as it gets from Fredericton. Calgary is, as it already was in 1966, the right place for Sharon Pollock.

Victor Mitchell, fresh from his postgraduate studies at Stanford was hired by the new University of Calgary (until 1966 it was a branch of the University of Alberta) in 1965 to develop a drama program. Because he had so little to start with—a broom closet (approximately) for an office, no campus theatre, no faculty members, no support staff, and only a few students from the Faculty of Education—he was literally starting from scratch. He began by taking three important steps: he hired Joyce Doolittle to teach; he invited Michael Ball, whom he had known in Victoria, to teach and act; and he started a small theatre troupe called the Prairie Players. He also built bridges with local amateur and semi-professional theatre groups such as the conservative Allied Arts Centre Theatre and the much more lively MAC 14. Between January 1966 and the fall of 1968, MAC 14, the Prairie Players, and

Mitchell's university-based productions provided Sharon with something approaching a crash course in the best of modern English and American drama with plays by Beckett, Pinter, Osborne, Miller, Albee, and Williams. Sharon became active with all these theatre groups, touring southern Alberta and parts of British Columbia with the Prairie Players, and acting in some of the plays done by Mitchell at the university, but she made her first local headlines with MAC 14, Joyce Doolittle, and Anne Jellicoe's *The Knack*.

The MAC 14 Theatre Society formed in February 1966 from the merger of the Musicians and Actors Club of Calgary, or MAC (a company that began in 1963), with a theatre group called Workshop 14. Its purpose was to establish a permanent theatre and a company that could present a regular, professional season of plays for Calgarians, and by 1965 they were successful with plays like *The Miracle Worker* and *A Streetcar Named Desire*. Victor Mitchell was on the board of directors, Dr. Betty Mitchell (no relation, but the grand dame of local theatre), was the Honorary President, Joyce Doolittle was directing and writing plays, and both Sharon and Michael were acting. In fact, many of the young people involved in MAC 14 went on to pursue careers as actors, directors, professors, or writers. While they certainly staged lighter fare in each of the seasons for which I have seen records—with *Barefoot in the Park*, *Dial 'M' for Murder*, *Breath of Spring*, *Present Laughter*, *Mary, Mary* and plays for children like *Wicked John and the Devil* (starring Sharon Pollock and Michael Ball) and *The Sorcerer's Apprentice*, written by Doolittle with Dukas's music, they by no means flinched from serious modern classics—*Ghosts, Major Barbara*—and challenging contemporary pieces—*Death of a Salesman, A View from the Bridge, Luther*, and *A Taste of Honey*. MAC 14 began touring in the summer of 1966 with *Mary, Mary* and declared that one of its objectives was "to encourage Canadian writing"; it produced a musical by W.O. Mitchell called *Wild Rose* and some original scripts by Doolittle. But the event that put MAC 14 and Calgary theatre people on the national map was the 1966 Dominion Drama Festival.

When Joyce Doolittle decided to direct an extra production in the 1965–66 season, she chose Jellicoe's *The Knack* and cast Robert Haley, Michael Ball, Sharon Pollock, and James Eberle for the four parts. Michael and Sharon won best actor and actress in the national finals in Victoria in May, Haley won best actor in the regional festival, and Eberle won the prize for best actor under twenty-five. Although Doolittle did not bring home the trophy for best director—that went to André Brassard—*The Knack* won the award for best production, and the team created a sensation at home. All this made Calgary begin to look, as Doolittle later said, like "a cow town with culture" (1985, 7). Then *The Knack*, with some changes in the cast but with Sharon and Michael still on board, was produced again in Calgary before playing at the Manitoba Theatre Centre in the fall of 1966 (see Illus. 21). Recalling the play in 2003, Victor Mitchell described the cast as "the most talented foursome" he had ever met because they could speak and act with precision.

On first reading this play (I have not seen a production), I found it difficult to understand what all the fuss was about. Nevertheless, it definitely influenced the first stage play Sharon wrote—"A Compulsory Option"—and both Joyce Doolittle and Jim Eberle have since convinced me that in terms of dialogue and pacing it is almost like music. *The Knack* is a three-act British comedy, first produced in 1961, with four characters—three callow young

21. After winning at the 1966 Dominion Drama Festival finals in Victoria, B.C., *The Knack* toured to the Manitoba Theatre Centre. Left to right: the Director, Joyce Doolittle, Douglas Riske (who replaced James Eberle from the DDF production), Robert Haley, Sharon, and Michael Ball.
Photograph courtesy of Joyce Doolittle.

men, Tom, Tolan, and Colin, who share a small London flat and are having problems deciding where to put the furniture. Tom is sarcastic and manipulative; Tolan (played by Michael) is aggressive and mildly predatory; and Colin is nice and well-meaning. Enter Nancy (played by Sharon), a seventeen-year-old girl who has arrived in the big city and is somewhat hysterical and dense. The guys argue; Tolan watches for girls passing the window and exits and enters by the window to track his quarry because the bed blocks the door; and Nancy ends up in the flat, on a ladder, in the midst of the confusion, screaming "rape." In a successful production, everything depends on rapid fire dialogue, deadpan delivery, and strategic pauses. Jim Eberle recalled the production as "quite magical," and in live performance the stage business with the bed provided a counterpoint to the dialogue. But the play, which was popular in a more sexist, politically incorrect era, when the Beatles were the rage and improv theatre was the fashion, now seems superficial and glib. The theme, if I can call it that, is one of youthful male confusion, but there is no point to the play, and the "knack" of the thing lies entirely in stagecraft: the play taught Sharon a few things about pacing, dialogue, and performance.

Meanwhile, living conditions for the Ball/Pollock family were far from comfortable. They began by renting a townhouse on Trelle Drive near the airport before moving downtown to a larger, but nearly derelict, and sparsely furnished rental house on 8th Street SW, a short distance from the Armouries. This house (long since demolished) is the one most fondly (if that's the right word) remembered by Sharon, Michael, and close friends like Jim Eberle, who describes himself as "like a fixture" there in 1967 and 1968. In winter there were more icicles inside than outside, and because there was so little yard space around the house, its windows looked directly onto an apartment complex, with the pretentious name of "Place Concorde" that Sharon dubbed "Place Discord." And yet the house, like every house she

22. Sharon with James Eberle in *The Recruiting Officer*, directed by Victor Mitchell at the University of Calgary, February 1968. *Photograph courtesy of James Eberle*

lived in, was in other ways a home and a haven because it was full of children, activity, noise, and animals, including a little rag dog called "Fang" and an assortment of cats (injured, sick, or stray) that Sharon could not turn away. Although everyone with whom I have spoken who has been in one of her homes agrees that the atmosphere, albeit noisy and confusing at times, was characterized by tolerance, good humour, respect for the children and, above all, love, it is once again Victor Mitchell who described that rented place most clearly when he told me that "an aura of peace and love permeated their slum home." To help pay the bills, Sharon ran the Ticket Wicket in the downtown Hudson's Bay department store and did other odd jobs, but the poverty of those years, coming on the heels of her separation from Ross Pollock, helped to politicize her in more immediate, personal ways than any general reading, current news, or her father's political campaigns could ever do. She was seeing how the other half lives, experiencing first hand the hardships of no pay, or low pay, no social safety net, and lousy housing, and she was developing a keen sympathy for the underdog, the social outcast, and those who were treated as second class citizens by the powers that be. She has said of these years that "we existed on a terribly marginal level" and that she "began to believe that the theatre was a way people were able to gain some compassion and insight into a reality other than their own" (see Hohtanz, 1987, 8).

By November 1967 she had produced her own centennial project, her sixth child, Amanda (better known as Bear, for Amanda-Pooh-Bear), finished touring with that crazy, shoestring operation called the Prairie Players, and performed in the MAC 14 touring production of *Mary, Mary* in Acme, Alberta. The Prairie Players did not survive the fall of 1967, but their demise did not mean the end of Sharon's acting. Between 1967 and 1969, both she and

23. Sharon as Maddy (left of centre top) and James Eberle (right of centre bottom) as Dan in the innovative stage production of Samuel Beckett's radio play *All That Fall* for the new Theatre Department at the University of Calgary. Chris Hampton directed and the set was designed by W.S. Eddelman. The production was billed as a world premiere and it received three performances during the 1967-68 Season. *Photograph courtesy of the Theatre Department, University of Calgary.*

Michael performed in radio plays for Fred Diehl in his CBC Calgary studio and in plays for Victor Mitchell at the university. It was for Fred Diehl that she would write her first produced scripts, "Split Seconds in the Death of," "Thirty-one for Two," and "We to the gods," and it was through the university that she discovered Samuel Beckett who, with Pinter, has had the greatest impact on her work. Mitchell had already hired Michael for roles in some of the classics he directed, like *Volpone*, and begun to use Sharon as well for roles in George Farquhar's restoration comedy *The Recruiting Officer* (see Illus. 22), N.F. Simpson's popular absurdist play *A Resounding Tinkle*, and John Osborne's *Look Back in Anger*, but the two productions that everyone remembers from those years are Beckett's *Endgame* and *All That Fall* (see Illus. 23), both done in the 1967–68 season and directed by Chris Hampton, another Mitchell hire and a Beckett expert. By 1967 the Drama department finally had a good theatre on campus (Calgary Hall with a combined proscenium/thrust stage), which made it physically possible to stage everything from period classics to minimalist Beckett, and it was Beckett who made the lasting impression.

In *Endgame* that year, Jim Eberle played Hamm opposite Bob Haley's Clov, with Sharon and Michael as Nell and Nagg. The idea of these two stuck in their respective trash cans is rather incongruously hilarious now when they are at the top of their respective fields, but at the time everyone in the cast was getting, as Eberle put it, a thorough education in theatre by performing in such a rich, demanding play. *All That Fall* was another matter. This time there was no languishing in a trash can with almost nothing to say. For Sharon, the role of old Maddy Rooney was a gift. Jim Eberle played Dan Rooney, her blind, querulous husband, and most of the play consists of Maddy and Dan talking as they walk home from the train station. But the points to remember about *All That Fall* are that it is a radio play, first broadcast by the BBC in January 1957, and that Beckett was notoriously difficult about productions of his plays. Somehow Chris Hampton talked Beckett into allowing this live stage production, and so Sharon got the chance to work *inside* a small masterpiece of contemporary theatre under the eye of a talented, innovative director who knew Beckett's work well and was keen to try for a technically sophisticated design and production (Illus. 23). Since she was already writing small sketches at home and would soon be creating radio plays for Diehl, *All That Fall* could not have entered her life at a more propitious moment.

The lessons she learned from this play are not the kind that invite identifications of this Beckett character with that Pollock character, or that suggest precise verbal or thematic links. Nevertheless, there are influences in matters of technique and in something I would call *tone* or perspective rather than theme as such. But let me explain. When Beckett's play opens, Mrs. Rooney is trudging along a country road on her way to meet Mr. Rooney's train because, being blind, he needs her help to get home. She is talking to herself and, indeed, much of what is said in the play, by Maddy or Dan, is almost like talking to one's self. She even wonders whether her manner of speaking—her actual choice of words—is not "bizarre" (13). And it is. Her response to a friend, who asks if she and her husband would like to buy a load of dung, is to wonder out loud, in an apparent *non sequitur*—"Dung? What would we want with dung at our time of life?" (13). In her own inimitable way, Maddy Rooney is a philosopher; she is also a woman with many griefs, from one of which her husband will try to shield her and himself. His train has been delayed, but in response to her questions about the cause, he is evasive, and their conversation, if it can be called that, wanders. When the cause of the delay is finally revealed, right at the end, by a boy from the train station who has run after them to return a ball to Mr. Rooney, we learn that a child was killed by a fall from the train. Hearing this, the old couple drags off again in silence, and we are left to find some meaning in their oblique references or seemingly tangential fragments of talk about dung, fertility, childlessness, death, and derangement. *All That Fall* has an extraordinary richness of language and allusion, but its meaning is carried less by its slim story line, or dialogue, which as often as not shows the characters talking past one another or to themselves, than by the Rooneys' parallel ruminations on life and religion or such apparently trivial things as dung or the weather. Maddy is a study in the compressed art of character creation; she is in a sense crazy, or crazed, but she is also attuned to the underlying tragedy of existence and the injustice of life. She exists, vividly and powerfully, not in anything she does, but in the bizarre way she speaks, and it is this existence of complex character in words alone (instead of actions) that I also find in several of Sharon's most complex and fascinating female characters—from Goose, in her earliest work, to Eme in *Getting It Straight*, Joan Roberts in *Fair Liberty's Call*, Shipman in *Moving Pictures*, and Constance in the radio play *Constance Kent*.

Beckett has remained important to Sharon. Friends remember her quoting him at length and making punning allusions to his plays: thus, her scrap book became her "krap book." She has directed *Krapp's Last Tape* and certainly knows *Happy Days* and *Waiting for Godot*. Her preference for serious, even philosophical themes (so-called big subjects) over lighter or comic ones of social manners, has an echo in Beckett's work, as does her poetic language and ability to create ambiguity through allusion and symbol. And yet, her views on human nature and on making theatre are radically different from his. Although *Getting It Straight* invites comparison with *Happy Days*, and *Moving Pictures* could be described as her response to *Krapp's Last Tape*, the similarities only serve to illuminate the profound and strategic differences. But I will leave further elaborations of my Beckett/Pollock comparison until later; for the moment, it is equally important to note that she was also discovering Pinter and Miller and that aspects of Pinter's dramaturgy, notably his manipulation of time, have parallels in her work, as do Miller's use of historical subjects and his interest in the moral tension between the individual and society. But before I leave *All That Fall*, there is one more Beckettian lesson Sharon may have learned from her work on this play—how to get maximum effect out of radio as a medium for drama. *All That Fall* is a play that one hears more than sees, even on the page; it is difficult to read, let alone perform the piece, without being aware of its rich, intimate soundscape.

Both Michael and Jim Eberle remember that Sharon began writing plays in about 1967–68. Michael recalls the meticulous, daily, hard work that went into drafting and rewriting, a reiterative process that she has always followed. Jim describes her early writing, possibly of "A Compulsory Option," from a more personal perspective. Because he was so often in the house on 8th Street, he was available as a reader, and Sharon would give him, his girlfriend, and Michael, scenes she was working on and ask them to read and comment. Then she would hover, alert and defensive. If they reacted visibly, she would demand: What? What? Whereupon they would struggle to be favourable, or at least diplomatic. But if the criticisms seemed sharp or relevant, she would storm out of the room, only to return later with a peace offering of food. She would argue, protest, fly off the handle, and she never apologized, but she would come back and pick up cheerfully where the group had left off. The first plays to be completed and produced were the radio plays for Fred Diehl, and Michael credits Diehl as one of the earliest supporters of her work. He and Sharon met Diehl shortly after they arrived in Calgary because he needed actors, so when Sharon expressed scorn for the quality of the scripts, he invited her to do better. She took up the challenge and wrote "Split Seconds in the Death of," directed and produced by Diehl and broadcast nationally by the CBC on 22 November 1970.

By 1970 the golden years of radio drama were coming to a close; some would say they had already gone. Andrew Allan, the godfather of Canadian radio plays and playwrights, had left the scene; television had become the media darling in the late fifties and sixties with programs like *Gunsmoke*, *I Love Lucy*, and the *Ed Sullivan Show* to attract audiences. The many actors and writers who had started with Andrew Allan (or with Rupert Caplan and Esse Ljungh)—among them Fletcher Markle, Lister Sinclair, John Drainie, Lorne Greene, Christopher Plummer, and Jane Mallett—had shifted to television or the stage, moved to the United States, or left the broadcast business altogether. The time when a radio play could attract more listeners than *Hockey Night in Canada* (as happened in the late forties) was over. According to Howard Fink, the CBC created 8,000 drama broadcasts, 3,500 of which were original Canadian plays, between 1939 and 1959, and by the early 1970s, "CBC radio drama became a less public, more intimate and subjective, perhaps even more experimental medium" (1982, 19). Nevertheless, Canadians of Sharon's generation grew up on radio drama—*Just Mary*, *Jake and the Kid*, *Wayne and Shuster*, and *The Shadow* (a popular American detective series that produced the characters of Lamont Cranston and his alter ego "The Shadow," whose menacing laugh I can still hear), a variety of American soaps, and Andrew Allan's *Stage*. Mary Jane Miller argues that this wealth of radio material was a major influence on our writing and production of stage plays because it showed what could be achieved through the creation of complex soundscapes—using the human voice, sound effects, music, and strategic pauses and silences.

This influence was especially significant for non-naturalistic writers who wanted to explore subjective realities and poetic language, or documentary writers keen to incorporate current events or historical facts in innovative stories set in the present, and Sharon Pollock was rapidly becoming both non-naturalistic and documentary in her approach to drama. Radio drama provided—and still does—a greater freedom from realism and the physical, visual constraints of the stage; at the same time, it offered greater artistic control, or what Fink calls "aesthetic unity," the kind of control that made Glenn Gould so happy in the recording studio. At the documentary end of the spectrum, an excellent play like Reuben Ship's *The Investigator* (1954) about the McCarthy era demonstrated radio's capacity to dramatize contemporary crises, while Allan's justly famous production of *Mr. Arcularis* (first aired in 1949 and frequently rebroadcast), adapted by Gerald Noxon from a Conrad Aiken story, illustrates the ability of radio to transform a soundscape into a dreamscape. This play unfolds in the mind of a man dying on an operating table; as he dies he hears snatches of conversation from the doctors who are working on him overlaid with voices from his past and with his own voice as a remembered sound and as a present remembering vehicle. We, intimate eavesdroppers as it were, are captured by this consciousness and pulled by his voice into this purely subjective, imagined world. Allan's *Mr. Arcularis* was a *tour de force* and probably an influence, along with *All That Fall*, on Sharon's first scripts. Moreover, what Allan achieved with this play showed men like Diehl what radio drama at its best could do.

"Split Seconds in the Life of" reveals its debt to *Mr. Arcularis*, but it also gives ample evidence of the kind of artist Sharon would become. The play is about George, an Indian who has left his reservation and come to the city in search of answers to personal questions about native spirituality and identity. He is the victim of a hit and run accident and the action takes place in his mind in a series of flashbacks as he lies dying. The scenes he recalls include a meeting with Joe, a former friend from the "Rez," who warns him against trying to assert his native identity instead of assimilating with the white majority; a visit to a bar, where George and Joe are taunted and insulted by white racists; attempts to negotiate his way through the red tape of employment offices, where he meets a man called Everett Roberts (an interesting combination of Sharon's family names); and an attempt to get a job on a construction site, where he is rejected by the white foreman. Judging from her comments in a preliminary description of the script, it is clear that Sharon was aware of and able to use the aural resources of radio (54.10.10): she calls for an opening "interval of silence sufficient to [create] anxiety" for the audience, who will be forced to wait expectantly for the first sounds. She calls for the traffic noises to be introduced softly so the listener "leans towards the set" and then to build gradually until the traffic noise increases "a feeling of tenseness." After several seconds of noise, she calls for screeching brakes that drown out all the traffic sounds, followed by a woman's scream. This scream rises over the sounds of the brakes and traffic and "segues to reverb," which then shifts into an Indian song before stopping abruptly. Between this dramatic opening and the screeching brakes at the end of the play lie the split seconds in the life of George.

This "exercise in imagination," as the announcer describes the play, is a fascinating example of a novice playwright creating a complex script that demonstrates a clear grasp of medium, dramatic structure, and audience participation, and that explores several themes or issues of lasting importance for her work. Despite certain weaknesses, it is not an amateurish effort. Here, in her first script, Sharon pushes the boundaries of realist narrative, searching for a form that will allow her to position an individual crisis within a wider context of prejudice, abuse, and disenfranchisement, and experimenting with sound effects such as reverb, music, and overlapping or layered voices, which are among the most powerful and characteristic qualities of her stage plays. Also of continuing interest to her are the interrelated problems of racism, oppression, and the treatment of First Nations peoples in Canadian history and contemporary society. Whether she was responding, in part, to a play like *The Ecstasy of Rita Joe* or commenting on the plight of native men on the streets around her in Calgary, "Split Seconds in the Death of" is her first attempt to represent a First Nations character in a First Nations story and her only attempt to represent experience from within that character's own psyche by creating a voice and point of view for him. In 1970, unlike today, white writers could and did create such characters, voices, and stories, and, for its time, Sharon's play is both politically aware and socially sensitive. But this focus, what some might now call appropriation, is also the weak point of the script because her attempts to articulate George's spiritual quest or to incorporate trickster figures like Coyote and Raven (who appears as the foreman to lure George into the traffic) into the story seem contrived. In *Walsh* and *The Making of Warriors* she recreated First Nations peoples and stories from history, but she confined the dramatic focus and the perceiving, experiencing centre of these plays to the white characters who need to learn about their own ignorance. In *Generations* and *Fair Liberty's Call* she also included a First Nations presence but refrained from using it to condemn oppression.

On the one hand, "Thirty-one for Two" has all the strengths of "Split Seconds" and none of the weaknesses; on the other, it is not tackling such tragic material or treating its subject with such solemnity. Again Fred Diehl directed and produced it in his CBC Calgary studio for "Studio 71 Soundstage," and it was broadcast nationally on 7 February 1971. A production script for this play survives in the CBC Concordia Archives and there is a brief scenario, as well as a tape of the production, with the Pollock papers (54.4.1), so I have been able to listen to the play several times.[1] And what a delight it is! The plot is complex but clever and tight and shot through with irony; the characters are small-town film noir *stereotypes*, but they are created with economy and energy, and the dialogue is fast paced. The story, which comments on recent political events (the October 1970 FLQ Manifesto, the kidnapping of

British Trade minister James Cross, and the kidnapping and murder of Pierre Laporte), twists and turns, holding a listener's attention until its final, surprise ending.

The title, "Thirty-one for Two," comes from the counting of points in a cribbage game. The player who makes thirty-one first, ending the hand and cutting off her opponent, experiences the kind of satisfaction she might also feel with a checkmate in chess or a trump in bridge. The carefully chosen title serves several functions, not the least of which are its realistic signal that the activity underway as the play opens is something as innocuous as a cribbage game and its symbolic reference to the more serious political games being played all around us. The context of the play is precise: the year is about 1970, and terrorist activities are rife in our safe, cozy Canada. As the play opens, four people are chatting as they play cribbage—Peter Roberts (again Sharon uses family names), his wife, Liz, and their friends, Don and Betty—with a radio playing in the background. The game is interrupted by a news bulletin reporting that government buildings have been bombed and a diplomat killed by some radical protest group. Then, both the game and the radio are drowned out by a racing heart beat and a blast. When the focus returns to the cribbage game, Peter and Don discuss this news and recall their own more radical views in 1952 when they lost their jobs. Peter grows agitated and angry and expresses his sympathy for the so-called terrorists who are struggling (as he once did) against injustice. He exclaims that he is once more ready to challenge the powers that be. But Don disagrees, telling him that violence is not the way to right wrongs; Peter's wife, Liz, joins the argument, disapproving of his extreme views. The voices fade, then a telephone rings loudly, insistently. Time has passed and it is the dead of night. Peter and Liz are wakened from a deep sleep. When Peter answers the phone, he (and we) hear a suave, menacing, Shadow-like voice (played by none other than Andrew Allan) thanking Mr. Roberts for his support of the "Organization" and instructing him on how to take delivery of a special package that will arrive at his house tomorrow—a trunk with "perishable" contents.

From this point on, the play spirals into a web of coercion, threats, and terrorizing activities by men who are little more than goons. The sound effects are at times spectacular, and the complex layering of past and present, waking and dreaming, inner and outer realities leaves the listener both amused by the gothic twists and turns and thoroughly involved in the rapidly deteriorating situation in the Roberts home. "Thirty-one for Two" combines elements of murder mystery and detective spoof in a story with serious consequences and an underlying moral theme. The serious consequences erupt at the very end when the "Geezer" (the boss of the "Organization" with the Shadow-like voice) calls to tell Peter that his men (the goons who delivered the ominous trunk) have been arrested and that Peter is now viewed as an informer. The menacing voice makes it clear that Peter will pay, and he does. The play ends back at the cribbage table with a game in progress and the radio playing music, but suddenly the broadcast is interrupted and the radio broadcaster announces that there has been a fatal hit and run accident involving a teenaged boy in the Roberts' neighbourhood. The boy is Peter's son, his murder a message from the Organization. But what a message! A play that seemed to combine elements of film noir, mystery story, intrigue and suspense, using wonderful sound effects for an entertaining story has turned very dark indeed, and the moral of the story overtakes its entertainment value. Insofar as the events we have overheard really happened and are not just a figment of Peter's disturbed imagination or fantasies about political activism, then "Thirty-one for Two" clearly warns against do-gooder bourgeois liberals involving themselves in violent protests or revolutionary style efforts to topple those in power. We never do find out for certain what was in the mysterious trunk, but we are told enough to guess that the body of the diplomat was inside, and this clear connection with the FLQ crisis strips away any vestige of mere murder mystery fun. "Thirty-one for Two" has forced its listeners to rethink their political views and agree with Liz when she tells her husband that "there are situations in which we can't be neutral," and that in *this* situation one must uphold the established social order and the rule of law.

"We to the gods," the third of her radio plays, produced by Diehl on 9 May 1971, is the least substantial of these early scripts, but it does illustrate the range of her interests and her exploration of genre. This piece combines fantasy, in which the gods roll the dice of fate to determine the deaths of famous historical figures, such as Abraham Lincoln and Archduke Franz Ferdinand of Austria, with her abiding interest in history and the often violent intersection of the private lives of individuals with the juggernaut of public events. Invariably, the individual loses to the impersonal forces of history, here represented as the "gods." Sharon's allusion to Gloucester's observation in *King Lear*—"As flies to wanton boys, are we to th' gods; They kill us for their sport" (IV, 1, lines 35–36)—would resonate with listeners, but her choice of an historical figure like the Archduke, whose assassination in Sarajevo triggered the Great War, underscores her desire to connect an isolated violent act with a web of deadly repercussions for humanity at large. Her treatment of historical figures in "We to the gods" points forward to the central dilemma in *Walsh*, just as "Thirty-one for Two" foreshadows both the subject and the mixed style (political satire with historical documentary) of *The Komagata Maru Incident*, and "Split Seconds in the Death of" prefigures several later plays. Together these little-known pieces show her exploring issues and styles she would revisit and refine in the stage plays. In them we can see her interest in history, her concern for the treatment of the First Nations and other oppressed or colonized groups or individuals, and her fascination with the dilemma of individual conscience facing the forces of institutional power. As far as narrative structure, dramatic effects (especially aural ones), dialogue, and character creation are concerned, these scripts show her experimenting to see how form serves content. The radio plays, when placed beside her first two stage plays—"A Compulsory Option" and "And Out Goes You?"—represent a significant, flexible start to her career. Through them she was beginning to exercise a voice of her own. Like so many playwrights of her generation in England, the United States, and Canada, she developed her craft this way, and the structural flexibility and aesthetic freedom from realism basic to radio drama by the 1970s carried over into her writing for the stage. Radio was by no means the only influential factor on the kind of playwright she would become, but it was one all the same, and she continued to write for radio, and to adapt her stage plays for radio (and *vice versa*) well into the 1990s.

During the summer months of 1968, 1969, and 1970, Sharon and Michael left their rented house on Manora Drive in north east Calgary (the home they bought in 1978 where

Sharon still lives), for holidays on Vancouver island. They packed their belongings, including Sharon's typewriter and the pets, into the secondhand seven-passenger Volkswagen bus
Michael bought in 1968, and headed off to visit with Michael's parents in Victoria, camp in
nearby McDonald Park, and treat the children to a vacation. Getting there, however, was
something of an adventure, and Michael has provided a dramatic account of their arrival:

> When the door of the van opened it was like an explosion. Two adults, six children, two dogs
> (Fang and Arthur Pole), seven or eight cats ... two guinea pigs, two mice (I inherited them from
> a production of *Dracula*; one was named Harker, because he lives in Harker's cell in the play,
> the other was his understudy), and for a while we had a turtle as well, but one day one of the dogs
> drank the turtle water and finished off the turtle like an olive at the end of a martini.... We used
> to go to my parents when we needed baths. (see Hofsess, 1980, 58)

These holidays cost little—no fees were charged in campgrounds then—and introduced
Sharon and the kids to the milder climate of the southwest corner of the province. However,
they were not exactly idylls of rest and carefree fun. On the first of these jaunts, Sharon
found herself lying in a tent on hard ground just a few days after having had her tubes tied
and an ovary removed. Her description of the situation in a letter to Jane Hickman was witty
but not calculated to encourage a camping life. "We are making do in a couple of tents," she
wrote, "in a torrential downpour that's been going on for a week and a half." Her stitches
hurt; she had developed a cold, so coughing and blowing her nose hurt; and the spacer on
the typewriter was "on the blink again." And yet cheerfulness kept breaking through—or if
not exactly cheerfulness, then a sardonic wit and a dose of practicality: she tells Jane that she
is writing radio scripts because she can earn up to $2,000 for a five-part series, which will
pay the rent for a year.

Unbelievable as it sounds, in the midst of all this chaos, Sharon was writing more than
letters and radio scripts. She was writing short prose pieces that combined autobiographical
short stories with reflective essay-like narratives, and it was during this period that she wrote
"If at first," the satiric sketch about the wife who tries to bump off her husband described
earlier, and a rather fine short story that she published in *The Fiddlehead* in 1973 called "How
Things Are" (see Appendix 1). This story is about a woman who is camping and meets a
little girl in the campground, a pale, undernourished, strange child whose family has camped
across the country all the way from Minto, New Brunswick, the small town where Sharon's
Roberts relatives lived. It is a magic word for the narrator, who is unquestionably Sharon.
For her, the word Minto conjures up "a great warm wash of Maritime kinship" (83), but for
the child, there is no such fond nostalgic association. What the woman sees on the child's
face when she speaks about Minto is "mute anguish at how things are, and a sick yearning
for how they ought to be" (Appendix I, 385). The story ends without any explanation as to
how things are for this child beyond the flash of insight the woman gains into her
vulnerability and hopelessness. Several other first person sketches survive from this time,
all of them undated and all portraying personal events from these years (54:10–15, 22, 23).
Three pieces describe the perils of camping with such dark humour that they are classics of

their kind and sharp reminders that Sharon can be extremely funny. In one, all eight members of the family wake up to find they have spent "a fair portion of the night rolling, with unerring precision, in the remains of long-dead camp fires" and must now make a dash for the ferry to Vancouver Island without benefit of shower or washbasin. In another, some tough decisions must be made about what can be packed into the bus and what must be jettisoned, and when "Chairman Michael" opts to throw out the mattresses instead of Melinda—daughter number two—no one will speak to him "for the first 200 miles."

A much more somber note is struck by a first-person narrative about her decision to terminate a seventh pregnancy—the operation she alluded to in her letter to Jane. Such an experience is profoundly private and painful, but in writing about it, Sharon reports on the humiliation (despite legislation passed in 1969, she is required to have Michael's consent), the medical bullying, and her unwavering determination not to have more children they cannot afford, in terms that extend beyond the personal. She has thought through her decision in ethical terms and she concludes with an affirmation of social commitment: "What I bring from this is a realization of my responsibility towards, and solidarity with, other women and their children." It would take another ten years or so before she was prepared to champion a woman in one of her plays, but "How Things Are" and this auto-biographical sketch illustrate her increasing attention to gender inequity and the basic powerlessness of women and children in contemporary society.

II: Early Stage Plays

When Michael had the chance to act in *The Lion in Winter* at Vancouver's Arts Club Theatre in the fall of 1971, they moved to British Columbia. Among the scripts Sharon brought with her was "A Compulsory Option," which won the Alberta Department of Culture playwriting competition earlier that year and was the first of her plays to be staged. The other early plays followed rapidly—"And Out Goes You?" *Walsh, The Komagata Maru Incident*, and several plays for children. The places they rented in British Columbia between 1971 and 1976 were a real step down from the Manora Drive house in Calgary, and their first place, in the suburb of Delta, so shocked her brother Peter when he visited her there that he tried to give her enough money to get out. Sharon, however, seemed, if not oblivious to these conditions, at least accepting of them because she was focused on other things. They did move again, this time to a place at 116 Granville Street in New Westminster near the federal maximum security penitentiary (now closed), where the hostage-taking occurred that would inspire *One Tiger to a Hill*, but life was very much hand to mouth. Michael was acting; Sharon was writing furiously and taking on a host of other jobs to earn money; and the children pitched in as best they could, the older ones caring for the younger ones and all of them coping with busy parents and a peripatetic lifestyle. Although descriptions are sparse, I have been given glimpses into their home life by the older children and by some of their Vancouver friends. Moreover, Sharon's and Michael's descriptions of the trips in the van and the camping experiences, together with her comments on other personal events in interviews, letters, and published and unpublished stories, all help me to reconstruct some sense of her life during these apprentice years. The public reception of her theatre work and the Vancouver theatre scene more generally must be cobbled together from reviews of her play productions, where these exist, from a few published studies, and from the reminiscences of those who participated.

But there are some aspects of her Vancouver years, apart from the poverty, that spurred her to write, although they did not determine what she would write about, and these emerge with such clarity that I consider them defining qualities of her personality. The first and last of these is her commitment to her children. No matter how poor the surroundings or frantic the pace, friends and colleagues who visited the Ball/Pollock home tell the same story: Michael was calm, quiet, even reserved; Sharon was loud, full of opinions and arguments, and often angry about current events or theatre issues; but the couple seemed happy together, there was always something to eat—indeed, talking non-stop Sharon would sweep a swarm of cats from the kitchen counter to put together a fine meal—and the children were surrounded by an atmosphere of love, patience, and respect, which meant that their inter-ruptions and questions were not dismissed. Sharon has said of these years, and of her domestic life generally, that she always felt responsible for everything in the house and guilty if she could not make others happy or comfortable. On the one hand, she has described herself as "a hard person to be supportive of," while on the other she would protest in periodic rants: "if Shakespeare lived in this house he never would have written a line" or "if I opened a vein I'd be lying there and no one would ever notice until they ran out of clean clothes" (see Dunn, 1976, 5–6). Clearly, the Angel in the house was still a nuisance, but she was slowly losing her grip on this woman writer.

Sharon's working routine was calculated to defeat, or at least circumvent, the Angel. She would rise early in the morning to have a few quiet hours to write, and the kids would return from school in the afternoon to find her asleep on the kitchen floor, where she had tried to continue working because the sheer discomfort might keep her from falling asleep. There was no way she was going to have a room of her own, so she learned to work in the midst of chaos, without demanding silence or special consideration. She would sit down at the dining room table, push the laundry to one side, shoo away the pets, and write. It helped that she could also fix a look of apparent attention on her face and mutter automatic phrases of semi-acknowledgement and be somewhere else, inside her head, writing. As the years passed she gave up the kitchen floor, but the domestic and working patterns established at this time remained in place, so that when Shipman, in *Moving Pictures*, accuses her younger self, Nell, of not listening, the behaviour is familiar. To a degree, Sharon is speaking about herself:

> SHIPMAN [*to Nell*]: Do you know what everyone hates? ... They hate it when you do that ... I said they hate it when you do that! [...] I said everyone hates it! When your eyes glaze over. When they know you're not paying one bit of attention to anything they're saying. [...] They hate it! I hate it! And you've always done it! As long as I can remember! (18)

Another defining characteristic of these years was her determined promotion of her plays and her assertive networking within the theatre community in Vancouver, Edmonton, Calgary, and Banff, and this networking established what have become basic features of her career—her promotion of others' work, her arts advocacy, and her deep understanding of the collaborative nature of theatre. And I want to stress this last point because I have often been told that Sharon was prickly or demanding and that she seemed very angry much of the time (about professional incompetence, the theatre hierarchies and protocols, and social issues), and that this manner did not help her career. While there may be some truth in this claim, when those who worked with her at the time, like Christopher Newton, Dorothy Jones, Richard Ouzounian, Harold Baldridge, or Tom Hendry, reflect back on these years, they are quick to add that her anger and assertiveness served much more than merely personal interests. Her acute sense of responsibility for others, which caused her to lament her domestic fate, carried over into her professional life. She threw herself into the theatre worlds in these western centres determined to build a career, yes, but also to make a difference for others and for Canadian theatre. To be sure, she did not suffer fools gladly (she still doesn't), but her passion for making excellent theatre and for helping others was clear and, there-fore, respected, even by those who found her abrasive manner hard to take.

The Vancouver theatre scene in the late sixties and early seventies was surprisingly lively, and I say *surprisingly* because, judging from complaints in the newspapers, there appears to have been little provincial government or general public support for any of the arts. No one has yet done for Vancouver what Denis Johnston did for Toronto in *Up the Mainstream*, but according to Renate Usmiani, there was a vibrant alternative theatre in Western Canada dur-ing this period, with about forty small companies active in Vancouver alone between 1965 and 1971. Tamahnous, founded in 1971, is perhaps the best known of these, but John Juliani had started Savage God at Simon Fraser University as early as 1966. The Vancouver Playhouse was doing very well—Ryga's *The Ecstasy of Rita Joe* in 1967 was, in fact, contro-versial, powerful, and very important—and under Christopher Newton, who arrived from Calgary to be the artistic director in 1973, other provocative *Canadian* plays received full productions. Holiday Theatre for children had amalgamated with the Playhouse in 1968 to become Playhouse Holiday, and although it did not survive beyond 1976, in its last years it continued to commission and produce Canadian plays for children and to tour British Columbia schools with the help of federal Local Initiatives Program and Opportunity For Youth grants. The Arts Club Theatre was well established; Pamela Hawthorn's New Play Centre opened its doors in 1972; Carousel Theatre and Green Thumb both began in 1975; UBC's Theatre Department was training young men and women who would make their careers in the theatre, and it was producing lively seasons. Beyond Vancouver, Tom Kerr's Western Canada Theatre opened in Kamloops in 1974, and Victoria's Bastion Theatre was founded in 1976 by Don Shipley and Pat Armstrong. Behind this activity lay decades of amateur theatre, created and managed largely by women whose names, like Dora Mavor Moore's, are too easily forgotten, but whose stories deserve to be told when Vancouver's theatre history is finally written—Jesse Richardson, Dorothy Somerset, Margaret Rushton, Yvonne Firkins, and Joy Coghill (in the years before she became artistic director of the Playhouse and an acclaimed actor). Talonbooks, one of Canada's two pre-eminent publishers of drama, began in 1967, and Talon enters Sharon's story with its publication of *Walsh* in 1973.

Among the people who were active in Vancouver theatre in the early seventies, a few played a crucial role in Sharon's career. She has included several of them in her own tally of "many brave spirits," among them Pamela Hawthorn, Christopher Newton, Don Shipley, Dorothy Jones, Richard Ouzounian, and the late Larry Lillo. Also important were some of those who passed through to act or direct or do administration before moving on. There was fairly extensive newspaper coverage, with good illustrations, of theatre events in the city by men like Bob Allen and Christopher Dafoe, and some arts reporters chastised the local powers-that-be for their neglect of the arts. In one case, Robert Sunter ran a full-page spread in *The Vancouver Sun* under the title "Starvation of the Arts, B.C. Style," in which he speculated that W.A.C. Bennett, the Social Credit premier of the day, was a "Yahoo." From interviews, I have concluded that while theatre was active there was little interest in Canadian plays in Vancouver during the early seventies or, at least, nothing to compare with the alternative theatre scene in Toronto. But Playhouse Holiday's mandate called for such work, and during his time in Vancouver Winnipeg-born director Ray Michal did children's plays by Eric Nicol, James Reaney, Betty Lambert, and George Ryga. In short, Vancouver had no paucity of talented theatre practitioners and a variety of good theatre spaces. It could, and did, attract some of the most innovative and important of Canadian directors and writers, as Jim Hoffman and Ginny Ratsoy illustrate so well in their anthology *Playing the Pacific Province.* There were dynamic people in key positions, and they were ready to support new plays about Canada by Canadian playwrights. Sharon Pollock entered this scene at precisely the right moment.

Volume one of Sharon's collected plays begins with *Walsh*, which means that several of her earliest stage plays remain unpublished. But these plays were produced and, in many cases, reviewed; scripts have survived, and a brief consideration of them is useful because it provides an idea of where and how she began to write for the stage. "A Compulsory Option," the play that had won the Alberta playwriting award in 1971, premiered at Vancouver's New Play Centre in August of 1972 as one of three plays to mark the opening of the Centre. Pamela Hawthorn had returned to Vancouver in the late sixties eager to direct new plays, and she soon reconnected with two theatre people at UBC, Sheila Neribe and Doug Bankson, and together they founded the New Play Centre. By January of 1971, with a $500.00 grant from the Koerner foundation and an office that, Hawthorn told me, she ran out of the bottom drawer of her bedroom dresser, they were poised to begin. All they needed were new plays. Bankson was especially keen to support Canadian playwrights, so when Hawthorn began looking for new *Canadian* scripts to direct and develop, she was pleased to find that "A Compulsory Option," which carried the endorsement of an award, was available. During its first few seasons the Centre mounted its plays in the old Vancouver Art Gallery on West Georgia Street in a very basic space hardly conducive to anything other than the most minimal theatre; thus, by necessity and good luck, Sharon's first stage play—directed by Hawthorn and starring Michael Ball—had a simple design using folding chairs, platforms, and one back wall with a window and a door. This may not have been conventional "poor theatre," but it was close, and the production received qualified praise from Christopher Dafoe ("First production almost a play") and Ray Chatelin. Hawthorn remembers that the script was relatively accomplished and funny, and that it worked well in production, but she does not recall Sharon either attending rehearsals or doing any rewriting. As fate would have it, however, this little play had legs and it received four more productions—in Edmonton, Toronto, Lennoxville, and Kamloops—before being relegated to the status of an historical footnote.

"A Compulsory Option" is a two-act satire about three male teachers who arrive in an unnamed town to take up their positions in the local school. They are expected to share a two-bedroom, furnished apartment, and the action takes place in the living room as, one by one, the men arrive with their belongings. Pete Chalmers (again, a family name) teaches History and plays the ordinary, sane guy; Bob Enns, a former student activist, teaches English and suffers from a severe, if ludicrous, case of paranoia; Leslie Lawrence teaches Physical Education and appears to be outrageously gay. The plot turns on Bob's conviction that some-one in authority is spying on him and is out to get him, so his new roommates are potential suspects. Pete quickly allays Bob's suspicions, but the mincing Leslie, who spends a lot of time in the bathroom and seems to find Bob attractive, becomes the immediate target of Bob's bullying and accusations. Bob enters and exits the apartment through the window because he thinks an assassin could be lurking behind the door; he hides behind the curtains to survey the street outside; he refuses to eat for fear of being poisoned, and he keeps a stash of weapons for use in a possible ambush. When Pete is drawn into the realm of Bob's paranoid fantasies, he *accidentally* shoots and injures Leslie, who returns to the apartment in the second act after a time in hospital, only to become the focus of Bob's aggressive suspicion again. However, in a sudden reversal at the end of the play, Leslie shoots Bob, while a terrified Pete looks on, and Leslie gets the last word: "(*with no trace of affected speech*) It was an accident." Like Pete, the audience is left wondering if Leslie was, indeed, out to get Bob, who was right to think that he was in danger, or if Bob's persecution drove the seem-ingly gentle, forgiving Leslie to this act of retribution. The play offers no answers, but it does suggest that all experience is contradictory, that nothing is what it appears to be, and that we cannot trust our perceptions: Leslie may not be gay after all, or he may be but his sexual orientation cannot be stereotyped by his voice, dress, or mannerisms, and accidents may or may not be accidental. Even the oxymoron of the title reminds us that language itself is unreliable.

In many ways "A Compulsory Option" resembles *The Knack*. The snappy dialogue, the slapstick routines with the window and the guns, and the zany, improbable plot all suggest that in this, her first stage play, Sharon was trying out a style and a structure that she knew would work in production. The play is rather dated now, especially in its representation of homosexuality and of a McCarthy-like atmosphere of persecution. But there is more here than an awkward first attempt at a full-length stage play because the portrayal of an individual's suspicion of a vague, all-powerful authority is a constant theme in her work, and the hints of botched political activism, espionage, and even terrorism connect this play with "Thirty-one for Two," *The Komagata Maru Incident* and her most recent play, *Man Out of Joint.* Indeed, reading "A Compulsory Option" now I find the play uncomfortably relevant. Bob's threatening behaviour and guns are all too familiar; his demand that Leslie answer his incomprehensible questions because, as he says, "we're running a security check," has renewed significance in our post-World Trade Centre world of international terrorism, torture, detention camps, and secret service activity. A play like *The Knack* is hilarious from start to finish, but "A Compulsory Option" is, in the final analysis, disturbing rather than funny. The light it throws on contagious anxiety, violent coercion, and an obsession with weapons illuminates contemporary society as well as providing a darkly comic assessment of sixties obsessions. In her 1976 interview with Margo Dunn, Sharon reflected on "A Compulsory Option" and concluded that it was the only one of her plays (to date) that she would change, and in light of her future development the nature of the change she described to Dunn is worth noting. With this first play she had treated theatre as if it were not illusion, but by 1976 she had come to see it in more Brechtian terms and to prefer plays that were clearly artistic illusions and that emphasized their non-realist or even anti-realist nature. Now, she told Dunn, she would rewrite "'A Compulsory Option' from inside Bob's head" (see Dunn, 4).

Perhaps "A Compulsory Option" should be dusted off, rewritten as Bob's paranoid fantasy, and tested in a new production. Judging from the reviews of the productions it received in the 1970s, it could be well done and enjoyable, and one production demonstrated what should *not* be changed in the script. The October 1975 production in Edmonton, directed by Keith Digby, was praised by Keith Ashwell, who described it as a "very clever, very virile and very, very funny play" and noted that it was more than mere farce because underlying the comic turns, which he says Digby and the actors executed beautifully, "is a black commentary" on society, and there is an "unsettling logic" to the characters' conversation. Two years later, in February 1977, Hrant Alianak directed the play for Theatre Passe Muraille, but this time the play was panned. Gina Mallett was especially savage, calling the piece "inane," the writing miserable, the acting weak, and the direction "vacuously cute." John Fraser was more forgiving; although he found the plot pointless, he praised the acting and aspects of the design. In hindsight Alianak regrets the changes he made—with Sharon's permission it must be said—and when we discussed the play he wondered if these changes might have contributed to what he now thinks of as a disaster. For starters he retitled the play "No! No! No!" thereby handing Mallet her negative review headline: "No! No! No! a thousand times No!" And for reasons he can no longer recall, he cast the character of Leslie as an aggressive, unprepossessing woman. If the gender shift was an attempt to remove any hint of homophobia, it may have missed the mark because, then as now, gay-bashing is an ugly reality. The title change was equally misguided because it removed a clear indication of the contradictions underlying the play's plot, thereby reducing it to the mere "Silly Comedy" of the sub-title: "No! No! No! A Silly Comedy." Fortunately, when it opened at the Lennoxville Festival in July 1977, everything went much better. The play was cast with Leslie as a man, the title was restored, and the reviews were generally positive. Myron Galloway called it a "riotous fantasy" and was delighted with William Davis's direction and the "brilliant" acting. However, David Sherman, writing in the *Sherbrooke Record*, called the play "objectionable,"

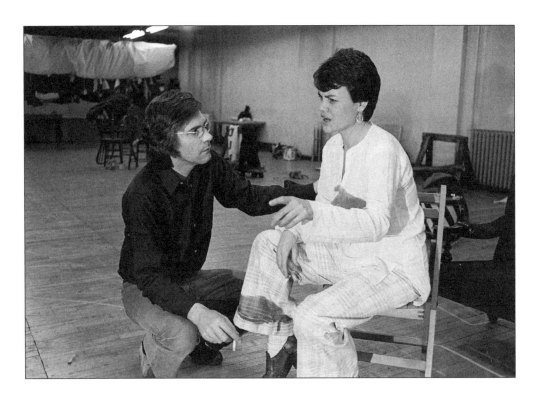

24. Christopher Newton and Sharon discuss "And Out Goes You?" during rehearsals for the March
1975 Vancouver Playhouse production directed by Newton.   *Photograph by Glen Erikson.*

and he left the theatre during the second act. Precisely what he found so objectionable is unclear, but he leaves no doubt that it is the play, not the acting or directing, that he disliked.

"And Out goes You?" Sharon's second play to receive a full production but *not* publication, has a much more complex plot and a more interesting subterranean connection with Sharon's later work. It is a baggy monster of a play, bulging with colourful characters, frenetic stage business, and political satire. Nevertheless, it deserves attention for what it tells us about the playwright, about a figure called "Goose," who will metamorphose into one of Sharon's most important characters—Eme in *Getting It Straight*—and about the state of theatre, notably plays about Canadian subjects, in Vancouver in the early seventies. "And Out Goes You?" premiered on 24 March 1975 at the Vancouver Playhouse, with an excellent eight-person cast (including Irene Hogan as Goose, John Gardiner, Owen Foran, Michael Ball, Lally Cadeau, Alex Diakun, Kenneth Farrell, and Norman Browning) and a great deal of advance publicity. It was directed by Christopher Newton, who worked closely with Sharon on the script (see Illus. 24), and designed by Jack Simon, with lighting by Graham Cook. For Sharon, this collaborative situation was ideal: she and Newton already knew each other from the late sixties in Calgary when Newton arrived there to work with MAC 14 and then shifted over to Theatre Calgary; he was aware that she was writing plays and was keen to support new Canadian work with political bite; she had confidence in his ability and was ready to work with and learn from him. Newton was among those who encouraged her at this critical juncture to create plays based on Canadian history or on contemporary politics, as he had himself in two plays he wrote during this period—"You two stay here, the rest come with me" and "Where are you when we need you, Simon Fraser?"—so she could be confident that her own longstanding interest in both history and politics would receive his attention and support. *Walsh*, which Newton saw in its earliest drafts, was the major play to emerge from this convergence of professional interests and theatre connections, but Newton was also directly involved in *The Komagata Maru Incident*, which he commissioned and Larry Lillo directed. Newton wanted plays on difficult, *local* Canadian issues, and, as he explained to me, other Vancouver writers refused to tackle such subjects. But not Sharon. Even with "And Out Goes You?"—despite its weaknesses—he recalls that "she came through for me."

The plot of "And Out Goes You?" (it must have the question mark) is anything but simple. It revolves around the machinations of a group of British Columbia politicians and developers from the early seventies immediately recognizable to contemporary audiences as Dave Barrett, the NDP premier, Bill Bennett, the Social Credit leader of the Opposition, and former cabinet minister Philip Gagliardi.[2] The government, represented by "the Premier" and his bureaucrat-stooge (called Bob Handle because he is expected to handle the situation) and big business, represented by "The Chairman" (played by Michael Ball, who apparently did a good imitation of Bill Bennett), are the bad guys who want to execute a humane form of expropriation of homes in an east end, working-class area of the city. But when they arrive at the O'Riley house they are in for a surprise. The O'Rileys are quite a bunch. They include Mildred O'Riley, known as Goose, who has been in a coma-like state since 1935, her son George, who fought in the Second World War, her grandson Richard, an ex-postman with piles of undelivered mail stashed in the house, Frankie, who marches about banging a drum, and Elizabeth, the only one with a job and a practical understanding of the real world beyond their doors. When the play opens, the O'Rileys are getting ready to hold a commemorative celebration of the 1 July 1935 Regina Riot that brought a violent end to the "On-to-Ottawa Trek" and left Goose, who was hit in the head by an RCMP bullet, in her present state.[3] Since that day, the family has kept Goose strapped to a stretcher, which they rotate so she will not get bedsores, and every year they hold their own Remembrance Day ritual with marching, songs, and political rants. George, who seems to think he is back in the war, leads his manic troops in a "Keystone Cop rendition" of a march while they all sing "Men of Harlech"; then Goose is brought in and the family re-enacts the Regina Riot while reciting a litany of social wrongs inflicted on the poor, the unemployed, immigrants, and the generally downtrodden of Canada, by governments, the police, and big business.

Into this melée comes the bureaucrat Bob Handle. His job is to induce these people to sign away their property rights so that the government and their cronies in business can develop the area. Needless to say, Bob is overwhelmed by this family and mesmerized by the spectacle of Goose. His protests that he is "here on government business, a plain expropriation, a better than fair price, a lot of money" (54:4.2, 21f) are ignored until he threatens to expose their treatment of Goose unless someone in the family agrees to forge her signature

25. A scene from "And Out Goes You?" The powers-that-be concoct a scheme to swindle the
residents of a poor Vancouver neighbourhood; first step is to insist that everyone "Know Your
Place!" Left to right: Norman Browning as Bob Handle, the late Owen Foran as The Premier, and
Michael Ball as The Chairman.   *Photograph by Glen Erikson.*

on the expropriation agreement. Then the premier and the chairman of "BeeBee Construction" arrive to make personal house calls on the neighbourhood's residents—the premier to
solicit votes in the upcoming election and the chairman to assess the demolition requirements. When Elizabeth remarks to the chairman that he looks "like the leader of the
opposition," his snappy reply is: "I am the leader of the opposition." And when she then
asks if he isn't in "a conflict of interest," he fires back that "there's no conflict with my
interests" (28). The two hot shots begin to extol the benefits of their plans; they set up a
scale model of the development project, pass out lapel buttons saying "Know Your Place" (see
Illus. 25), and insist on meeting the owner of the house. Through all this Goose, still
strapped to her stretcher, has been propped up in a corner and disguised as a coat rack, so
it is her grandson who comes in crossdressed as the lady of the house and talking in a
throaty, American drawl, a ploy that provides the play with a few cracks at American
influence on Canadian society. The premier and the chairman leave to swindle the next
homeowner, and in the free-for-all that ensues in the O'Riley house, Frankie and Richard try
to escape with Goose only to trip and drop the stretcher. To everyone's amazement, this

accident jolts Goose back to full consciousness; she lets out a loud oath—"Jasus H. Christ!"—gets up, goes over to the liquor, and pours her self a stiff drink. "After 40 years," she declares, "me throat's a bit dry" (44).

From this point on, Goose, who has heard all that has been said but been unable to protest, takes over. She chastises her family for letting themselves be "royally screwed" (45), upbraids the "boys" for forgetting the battle and the cause of 1935, and accuses Elizabeth of selling out to the powers-that-be. She then explains what the real working- class situation is in one of her long, rousing, thirties-style songs, while the "boys" rally round and join in:

> Now we're findin' out there's just one kind of war,
> It's one goin' on 'tween the rich and the poor.
> I don't know a lot about what you'd call class,
> But the upper and the middle can all kiss my ass! (53)

When the premier and the chairman turn up again, fleeing from the excited citizens in the street, Goose forces them to sit down for the "premiere and farewell performance" of a little play about humane expropriation by the "East End People's Theatre dedicated to the Moral Uplift of the Masses and Sundry Others" (64f).

What follows is a guerrilla-theatre style satire of local politicians like flying Phil Gagliardi, the minister of highways (played by George who announces, in an all-too-familiar exclamation, "I'm not drivin' fast, I'm flyin' low"), a mocking portrayal of a meeting of the provincial legislature, and a slapstick routine on election politicking, fraud, and patronage. The action degenerates into a series of comic pratfalls and jokes, until Goose calls for order and the premier and the chairman are taken prisoner, tied up, and charged with "arrogance, hypocrisy, and possession of an India-rubber conscience" (87f). But if Goose trusted in this little play within the play to catch the conscience of either man, she is mistaken. The minute his gag is removed, the chairman threatens to have Goose incarcerated in "an institute for the criminally insane" (87f). As police cars, sirens blaring, surround the O'Riley house, Richard retrieves a package from his piles of undelivered mail that contains a gun—but the item is no more than a toy "crack-a-joke" gun—while Goose goes to the kitchen with her "anarchist Cookbook" to make a cake-bomb. Predictably, at the critical moment, Bob Handle, the bureaucrat, frees his bosses, and they seize the cake, but it fails to explode, and the play races to an anti-climactic end: the premier and the chairman escape completely unscathed and unchanged; Goose is shot as she opens the front door to lead her family in a protest and ends up prone and silenced once more; Bob Handle has earned himself a ministerial position for reverting to type and aiding his bosses; and the rights of the poor are exactly where they were when the play opened.

It is not easy to judge this play from the surviving script. However, other documents do help to establish a context for how the play was presented and meant to be received. In an effort to inform reviewers and theatre-goers about the kind of play they were going to see, the Playhouse prepared a "study kit" that contained a collage of recent newspaper headlines alluding to scandals and government corruption, statements from members of the cast, and notes from the playwright on the connection between politics and theatre. Newton provided a comment on the style of the play, followed by a variety of attempts to define or describe political satire. This material was intended to educate an uninformed or inexperienced audience about a type of play with which they were assumed to be unfamiliar—political satire. However, these materials may have raised expectations that the play did not meet. "And Out Goes You?" is not "Guerrilla Theatre," as defined by Ronnie Davis in the study kit, nor is it political satire, if that term means a work with a clear moral argument and a social alternative to the system or ideology being satirized in the text. The kit may well have confused rather than enlightened audiences.

Nevertheless it contains two comments that were helpful, and neither of them presses the connection between political satire and Sharon's play. In his brief comment from "The Actor's Page," Michael Ball says that he does not "think the play is political theatre in the conventional definition" and he goes on to note that "it may be wrong to call it a 'political play'" (54:4.6). In her own remarks, Sharon goes to some lengths to warn against a simplistic categorization of what she was trying to do or, more importantly, what theatre can ever do. In an opening gambit that she often repeated in the years ahead, she explains that, in her view, "all theatre is political insofar as any play is an attempt to communicate the playwright's viewpoint to an audience" (n.p.). From there, she goes on to outline her views on playwriting and on how the playwright must move an audience rather than tell them what to think. Since this short essay is one of the earliest public statements she has made about her art, it is worth quoting at some length:

> I don't believe we learn through our heads; we learn through our guts, our emotional and physical experiences. No one goes to the theatre to be told what to think. We go to be moved, touched, amused, excited (or angered) and through this experience to gain awareness and insight into ourselves, into others, into motivations, and into familiar and alien environments. An audience may be moved by George's re-enactment of the Regina Riot, or his day at Dunkirk, and experience, in some small way, his experience as a casualty of the Depression and the economic system that spawned it. An audience may laugh at the Premier's and the Chairman's pomposity, and recognize more readily the politician's condescension when next they are recipients of it in reality. AND OUT GOES YOU? may appear more political than a French farce because it deals with people in a political situation [...] but the play will succeed or fail not on the validity of the politics, but on the audience response to the specifics of the play: the characters, the situation, the plot. ("Notes from the Playwright")

The actual program for the play put a slightly different spin on the politics by highlighting the historical events underlying the plot. On the one hand, the program was illustrated by a documentary photograph of the Regina Riot with a caption that read: "It's Dominion Day, 1935, in Regina, but the flags have all been torn down by the men who want action, not slogans. Two thousand relief workers are in open warfare with the Mounties. One hundred stores have been damaged. Ten persons have been wounded and forty more arrested. But the Depression still goes on." On the other, Newton told theatre-goers that the play they were about to see was neither "naturalistic comedy" nor "theatre of the absurd," but a "very funny play" about those "who find life empty" and an "old revolutionary" (Goose) who cares about life and living conditions. He concludes by noting that while the play takes place in Vancouver and is "about people who bear a slight resemblance" to local politicians, it is primarily about issues that Canadians should recognize as important.

So where does all this earnest setting-of-the-stage leave us? Well, despite perfunctory nods to Brecht, Shaw and Joan Littlewood, I remain unsure what to call this play. Perhaps it should have been compared with the more gently comic vision of Stephen Leacock or with the kind of routines Canadians saw on television by that inimitable duo Johnny Wayne and Frank Shuster. There is a tradition of Canadian comic-political-satire that sends up individuals and situations without attacking anyone too harshly or offering radical solutions to problems. It is a tradition in which Canadians laugh at themselves for their foibles and failings, a tradition in which nothing is sacred but no babies are thrown out with the bath water. In the final analysis, however, the play is flawed, and, for all its boisterous energy and lively production, it met with mixed reviews. The acting was highly praised, with Irene Hogan's Goose, Owen Foran's premier, and Michael's caricature of a company chairman, receiving special kudos, and Newton's directing was applauded, but reviewers thought the play missed its target. In their thoughtful comments, Bob Allen, Christopher Dafoe, and Ian Caddell, all faulted the play *as political theatre*. Allen complained that the piece did not "hang together" and did not hit its targets sharply. Caddell, calling his review "Pollock play funny, but … ," regretted that it was not tough enough, and Dafoe was even more precise in his description of what misfired in "And Out Goes You?" He explains that although we get "a fleeting impression that some aspect of the truth has been identified and fixed … nothing happens" and he goes on to describe what he understands as genuine political theatre, such as Agitprop that "dealt in absolutes of good and evil." What's more, Dafoe recognizes that such absolutes are not what Sharon Pollock is establishing, and he suggests that because she sees so clearly through simple opposites she is actually pronouncing a plague on both houses in her attempt to "give shape to our dismay and confusion." I would agree.

What Sharon was doing in this play proved to be entirely consistent with the kind of playwright she has become—someone interested in ideas, history, and contemporary social and political questions but who, nonetheless, refuses to divide the world into neat categories or absolutes. The power of authority, no matter who exercises it or what institutions or ideologies claim it, is always her prime concern; the impact of such power on the lives of individuals always worries her. In this she has been entirely consistent throughout her career: theatre, like life, is always political, and she is acutely aware of different, at times contradictory, sides to every argument. Which is not to suggest that she sees no place for right and wrong, for moral or ethical choices, but that these choices and discriminations must be made, as much as possible, by individuals. She has also continued to believe that theatre exists to move people emotionally, to engage them by entertaining and by trying to make them more aware and more involved in their society: by making them feel, think, or, as Joseph Conrad said, by making them *see*.

"And Out Goes You?" received considerable preliminary work thanks to a Canada Council grant and Newton's influence. Once she had a working script in hand, the play got a professional workshop with Tamahnous under the auspices of the New Play Centre. This process, which she continues to favour, was followed by considerable rewriting during the rehearsal period, at which point she worked closely with Newton. But Sharon was far from finished with the play after its Playhouse run. She pared down the script to create a play called "Mail vs. Female," which received a good production at Calgary's Lunchbox Theatre in 1979. This time Sharon set the play in 1979 Calgary, changed the powers-that-be to the federal Postmaster General and his local bureaucrat, who becomes a woman with the name of Roberta Handal, and reduced the O'Reillys (as the name is now spelled) to a family of three: Goose, the sixty-one year-old Rebel Girl who was shot in the Regina Riot and has been immobilized ever since, and her two brothers—Georgie, the war veteran, and Sonny, a none-too-bright postie who has been hoarding Her Majesty's mail. As with "And Out Goes You?" the Handal character switches allegiances but is finally bribed to side with the authorities, Goose wakens from her sleep when her stretcher is dropped and resumes her revolution-ary protest, the Postmaster General is held hostage, and the play ends when Roberta and her boss escape and Goose is once more felled by a police bullet. What emerges more clearly in this tighter, shorter script is the potential for an older, politicized, feisty female to lead her family against an oppressive, patriarchal system that co-opts young women and silences older, threatening ones. The figure of Goose—this older woman who is both Mother Goose and a would-be activist goosing those in power—is both crazy and yet clear-sighted enough to see through the hypocrisy, lies, and greed of the authorities, both full of loud, angry, energetic left-wing speeches and rousing songs and yet ultimately silent and silenced. Goose stayed with Sharon, survived being silenced in both scripts, merged with a whole set of ideas about the gender wars, nuclear war, and social protest movements, and finally found her voice as Eme in *Getting It Straight*. Insofar as Goose is a precursor of Eme and Eme is, as Sharon has clearly said, her most personal, autobiographical character, then Goose is a Sharon-mask, an avatar for that powerful inner voice of her own rage at the way things are and her frustration at not being able to change them.

III: Enter Miss Borden

To map the subterranean links between Goose and Eme requires a short detour from the Vancouver Playhouse to a completely different forum for Sharon's activities in Vancouver in the early seventies. This detour takes me to Douglas College, where Dorothy Jones (see Illus. 26), who played an important role in Sharon's career during these years, was working and where Sharon would act, direct, and teach, while writing the early version of a major new play. By the summer of 1973, the Ball/Pollock household was already installed in the rented house in New Westminster. Between 1973 and 1976, she was writing children's plays for Playhouse Holiday, preparing radio and television scripts, revising *Walsh*, and becoming actively involved in local theatre administration—all this, in addition to her work at Douglas

26. Dorothy Jones (ca 1988), director
    and theatre instructor at Douglas
    College. Jones directed Sharon in
    plays at the college and was the first
    supporter and director of the script
    that would become *Blood Relations*.
    Photograph courtesy of Dorothy Jones.

College. The evening courses on playwriting and marketing that she was hired to teach, as well as the directing (for example, Neil Simon's *The Gingerbread Lady* in 1975), brought in some badly needed money, but more importantly Jones gave her the chance to act in a College production of *Lysistrata* and in a 1975 musical revue celebration of International Women's Year, called "I Am Woman," and then commissioned a new play about Lizzie Borden that Sharon called "My Name is Lisbeth."

Lizzie Borden and *Blood Relations* are important subjects for another chapter, but there is a line that runs from Sharon's discovery of Maddy in *All That Fall* to that early, untitled autobiographical essay on the subject of abortion and to the 1973 short story, "How Things Are" (about the little girl from Minto), through her work with Dorothy Jones and her creation of Goose in "And Out Goes You?", on to *Blood Relations* and, eventually, to *Getting It Straight*. It has become commonplace to describe Sharon as something of a latter-day feminist who had little interest in women's issues and female characters until she wrote *Blood Relations*. Sharon herself has endorsed this idea in interviews by explaining that at the beginning of her career, she associated *action*—the doing of things in contemporary life and in history— with men, not women, and that she found men's lives more interesting, perhaps more amenable, to the creation of dramatic action on stage: she felt that men did things one could dramatize. Reflecting on these early years, she has also admitted that she did not understand or even sympathize enough with actual women (including herself) to know *how* to create female characters until she tackled the Lizzie Borden story. But, in fact, this sympathy or interest or understanding did not spring up unheralded with the creation of Lizzie. The ground was being prepared by her New Brunswick home life, her marriage to Ross Pollock, and her personal experiences in the late sixties and early seventies, and concrete examples of ways to imagine an active, creative, female identity were provided through the example of professional women like Joyce Doolittle and Dorothy Jones, a play like *Lysistrata*, a revue like "I Am Woman," and her own growing success and self-confidence.

Dorothy Jones started her career at Douglas College in 1973, but she already knew Sharon and Michael. They had first met in the late sixties when Sharon and Michael were touring, possibly with the Prairie Players, and performed a play in Medicine Hat, where Jones was teaching high school drama. In addition to her own professional interest in theatre, Jones was a prairie girl born and bred and she knew her Western Canadian history. She paid close attention to any Canadian play about local history, and she was poised, like Pamela Hawthorn and Christopher Newton, to use Canadian work and to support Western Canadian playwrights. Soon after she arrived at Douglas College, she contacted Sharon about the rights to *Walsh*, and she directed a well-received student production of the play at the College in 1974. In our conversations about these years, Jones vividly recalls Sharon's capacity to be demanding about theatre work as well as her occasional angry eruptions. At the time, Sharon seemed to be uncomfortable with herself, acutely anxious to be right and to be competent, and, at the same time, a person who was always thoughtful, who was devoted to her children and very much in love with Michael; she enjoyed social events and created dinners notable for good food and fun. Prickly she certainly was—Dorothy Jones's term for the Sharon she knew then is "firebrand"—and she was completely possessed by the need to create. Although Sharon never discussed her mother or her family past in Fredericton, she did speak of her father with pride, so what friends like Jones saw was a sometimes aggressive, often anxious woman and artist who needed to succeed, to be capable and responsible, and to be right. Without knowing why, Jones also sensed that Sharon, at least in the early seventies, had greater difficulty respecting and liking women than men. But even at that time, this difficulty was diminishing in part, perhaps, through her work with Jones.

When Jones chose Aristophanes's classic anti-war play, *Lysistrata*, for a spring 1975 production, it was a timely choice. Not only were the horrors of Vietnam fresh in peoples' minds, but it was also International Women's Year—a year in which to remember women's history and to celebrate women who took action against the dominant forces of patriarchal and military authority. Judging from newspaper reviews and production photographs, both the play and its title character were a great success. Nerine Berting began her 3 April 1975 review with the headline "Sharon Pollock stars in saucy production" and described the "hilarious Greek farce" as perfectly "in keeping with International Women's Year and a reminder that Women's Lib is not new." The *Vancouver Sun* reviewed the production on the same day, but in their case it is the production photographs by Ralph Bower that capture attention, even today. In one especially delightful example, Sharon's all-powerful Lysistrata dominates the soldiers who cower under their shields while she plants her foot on them and orders an intimidated Commissionaire to cease his military manoeuvres if he and his men ever want to sleep with their wives again. I find it hard to look at these pictures without thinking that, for all the high spirits and rowdy fun of this production, Sharon was well cast. As a mother she feared for the safety of her own children; as a news junkie she had followed contemporary national and international events with mounting alarm; and, as a playwright, she already believed in the theatre as a way of reaching people and encouraging

27. Sharon as Lysistrata in the April 1975 production of *Lysistrata* at Douglas College directed by Dorothy Jones. Here Sharon reads the riot act to the Commissionaire, played by Derek Bissett. *Photograph by Ralph Bower, courtesy of Dorothy Jones.*

them to reconsider, possibly even change, their ways. And, of course, as a "firebrand" female who was both beautiful to look at and not afraid to raise her voice, she was an ideal Lysistrata (see Illus. 27). Aristophanes's call for an end to war resonated with Sharon's protests against social injustice, violence, the abuse of power, and the oppression of the weak. Over the next decade she struggled with her own Lysistrata-play (variously called "God's not finished with us yet" and "Egg") and experimented with the key figure of a strong, articulate, active woman in several plays before she could finally rest her case with Eme in *Getting It Straight*.

Before the end of International Women's Year, Dorothy Jones directed one more play to mark the occasion. This piece, called "I Am Woman," was a collaborative creation by Dorothy Jones, Sharon Pollock, and Gwyneth Harvey, consisting of songs interspersed with sexist quotations from the past (such as Aristotle's infamous statement that "Woman [is] an inferior Man.") held together by witty banter. College audiences enjoyed the work, and Jones recalls that Sharon had a good singing voice and contributed happily to the piece. But there are two brief speeches, both delivered by Sharon *as Sharon*, that deserve to be cited, so aptly do they capture the woman as she was then ... and is now:

> Men continually study women and know nothing about them. Women never study men and know all about them.

And perhaps more pointedly—

You know something: it makes me wild with rage to be described as a female playwright. You never hear people referring to male novelists or a gentleman playwright. I'm a playwright and a woman—I write about what I know.[4]

Dorothy Jones directed "A Lesson in Swizzelry," one of several children's plays that Sharon wrote in the early to mid-seventies, at the College in April 1975, but this *commedia dell'arte*-style play is a minor, atypical example of Sharon's writing for children. Its reliance on boisterous physical action and familiar figures like Harlequin made it a good vehicle for touring lower mainland schools, which it did in the summers of 1974 and 1975, but it was not the more thought-provoking kind of play she usually created for young audiences. For the moment, however, I want to stay with her adult plays at Douglas College, where an especially significant chapter in Sharon's story was beginning to unfold. Sharon has always been fascinated by murder stories, whether they are popular murder mysteries (in novels, plays or films) or accounts of actual murders. If for no other reason (although there *are* other reasons), the subject of Lizzie Borden was bound to capture her imagination.

The first public statement about her interest in Lizzie I have seen is in a January 1976 bulletin at Douglas College, which announced that Sharon was writing about the infamous Lizzie Borden axe murders of 1892. At this stage, the play-in-progress was still untitled, but Sharon's explanation of her approach to the familiar scandal says a good deal about her personal connection with the basic material. In addition to her "morbid interest in murders" (as she put it in the bulletin), she explained that she had been doing research on the case for several years by reading "everything written about Lizzie Borden, and many related books and articles on murders, women, and the age she lived in." What's more, she saw in the historical Lizzie Borden a frustrated daughter who could not behave as her much-loved father expected her to: "What happened to her is an exaggerated example of what still happens today. Often one realizes what those close to them expect them to be, but have difficulty in becoming that." In the years ahead, as this play changed, grew, and developed into the masterpiece we know as *Blood Relations*, Sharon was frequently asked to comment on the play, but this very early observation says as much about Sharon and what Lizzie meant to her as any of her later explanations. Sharon's reading of Lizzie as a frustrated daughter who feels she cannot measure up to others' expectations and resents their assumption that she should force herself to do so echoes across the first thirty years of Sharon's life: she had been that daughter; she had tried to be a compliant wife; she knew, first hand, the anger and frustration generated by a refusal, or failure, to conform to familial and marital demands; and she had chosen to become her own person and a success on her own terms.

When Sharon's Lizzie Borden play premiered at Douglas College in March of 1976 as "My Name Is Lisbeth," Sharon played Lizzie (see Illus. 28). Before agreeing to Sharon's request to play the role, Dorothy Jones made it clear that she, and she alone, was the director, but, as it turned out, directing Sharon in one of her own plays was not difficult. Over the years ahead, Sharon would often act in her own plays or direct them, and most of those who have either directed Sharon in her own work or acted when she was directing, agree that she has an uncanny ability to separate herself from her position as author and to immerse herself

28. A scene from "My Name is Lisbeth," the first version of *Blood Relations*, directed by Dorothy Jones in March 1976 for Douglas College. Left is Wendy Much as Bridgett; right, Sharon as Lizzie. *Photograph by Ralph Bower, courtesy of Dorothy Jones.*

in the task of being an actor or a director. But this time, playing Lizzie under Jones's direction, was her first attempt to relinquish an author's control and enter the performer's realm. Although no problems arose from this shift in roles, rehearsals were not without a few eruptions. On one particular, unusual (for Vancouver), cold, snowy night, Sharon stormed out of a rehearsal in Surrey's Bear Creek Theatre because she disliked some aspect of Bill Baley's set design. She stomped off into the night, determined to walk home, a distance of about six miles (roughly nine kilometres) that required crossing the Patullo Bridge. Realizing the foolishness, and perhaps danger, of this tantrum, Dorothy got in her car and followed Sharon until she relented and allowed herself to be driven back to the theatre. Baley agreed to think about her suggestions and did, in fact, follow them. In retrospect this image of Sharon in a fit of pique, disappearing into the night, nursing her anger, only to be rescued by a firm, wise (and worried) director, seems right in character. Very likely her suggestions for the set were good ones because she has a strong sense of design, but what really matters in this anecdote is that she returned and picked up the rehearsal where she left off. I doubt that she apologized for the disruption, but I am certain that she did not stay angry for long or hold a grudge. At the end of the year, Sharon and Dorothy parted as good friends and respectful colleagues. Dorothy threw a party for Sharon and Michael before they left for Edmonton, and she still has the gift and card Sharon gave her in thanks for her professional and personal support: the gift was a framed print of a painting by a nineteenth-century artist, Richard Doyle, called "Messenger by Moonlight" that depicts a young woman riding on a hummingbird against a ground of blue-green leaves and a large white moon. Sharon's message on the card reads: "with a great deal of love and appreciation.... Thanks, Sharon." And on the envelope, Sharon provides her interpretation of the painting: "This is Lizzie making her final escape at the end."

As we know, Lizzie's escape was temporary. Sharon's performance of "Lisbeth" told her a lot about the story (especially about *how* to tell the story), and this play continued to grow in Sharon's imagination. However, in 1973 and 1974, Sharon was still in the early stages of learning her craft, and some of the practice she needed came through her commissions for children's plays with Playhouse Holiday. Holiday Theatre had a successful history dating back to 1953, when Joy Coghill and Myra Benson, together with a group of like-minded artists, decided to create a theatre for young people in Vancouver. By 1967, when Joy was still the artistic director of Holiday (she was AD of Vancouver Playhouse from 1967 to 1969), the company created Holiday Playhouse as its educational theatre wing and as a form of bridge with the Vancouver Playhouse; a formal merger with Holiday Theatre took place in 1969. This addition of a theatre-in-education program to Holiday's mandate signalled a growing public awareness of the importance of theatre as a way of reaching children in the schools. It also provided opportunities for commissioning new plays by local writers and for training young, non-equity actors. In its early years, Holiday had drawn extensively upon the classic repertoire of children's material (with dramatizations of *Robin Hood* and *Snow White*, and favourites like *Androcles and the Lion*) or on work by contemporary leaders in the field of children's theatre like Charlotte Chorpenning and Brian Way. However, its mandate also called for the production of plays by Canadian writers, and a glance at their programs and script collection from these years illustrates the remarkable stable of up-and-coming writers and directors whose work was performed by Holiday Theatre: Eric Nicol (whose *Beware the Quickly Who* became a perennial favourite), John Lazarus, Henry Beissel, Betty Lambert, John Hirsch, Paddy Campbell, Rex Deverell, Paul St. Pierre, Lister Sinclair, Tom Hendry, and many others, including Sharon Pollock. Although Holiday Theatre did not survive for long after the merger with the much larger, more prestigious, professional Playhouse, it is important to acknowledge the vital support it gave to Canadian and children's theatre in western Canada. By the time Playhouse Holiday died in 1976, it had made a significant contribution to our theatre history.[5]

Under its first two directors (Ray Michal, 1969–71, and Don Shipley, 1971–74), the emphasis on producing Canadian plays appears to have increased. Sharon's connection with Holiday was limited to 1973 and 1974, when she wrote three original plays, all commissioned for the theatre-in-education program, and three adaptations for the theatre school for drama program: "The New Canadians," "Wudjesay?" and "Superstition Through' the Ages," and adaptations of Oscar Wilde's stories "The Happy Prince," "The Rose and the Nightingale," and "Star Child." "The New Canadians" was produced as part of the first pilot season in the company's theatre-in-education program, and it was based on the grade four curriculum. Sharon worked with director Don Shipley, a group of three actor/teachers, a stage manager, and a musician to create a script that dramatized the lives of three immigrant groups (Icelanders, Mennonites, and Doukhobors) and encouraged the "controlled participation" of the students—a key aspect of the Brian Way philosophy and a demanding task for the actors. Over a three-week period, the play toured to thirty grade four classes in Vancouver schools with the goals of introducing students to the rich minority history of Canadian settler society and of involving the children in active theatre work. The report cards received by the troupe on their first venture into the schools were stunning: one teacher wrote that this was "the best experience" his students had "ever had at school"; another exclaimed that the performances turned "literature into a living vital part of a child's experience." "Wudjesay?", which toured in the spring of 1974, was prepared for students in grades three through seven and focused on the evolution of language and communication. Beginning with simple instruments like drums and moving on to scenes that illustrated the invention of the printing press, the telegraph and telephone, and then of radio and television, the play used narration, mime, and music to explore the meanings of words and how different groups of people learn to communicate with each other. The actors made up one group; the children another. In addition to Sharon and Don Shipley, "Wudjesay?" involved four actor/teachers, a designer, and a musician. Although this play also received an enthusiastic reception from the schools and Bob Allen praised both the production and the theatre-in-education program in the *Vancouver Province* newspaper, signs of financial strain were beginning to surface and Playhouse Holiday was unable to mount its full touring program that year. The steadily increasing problem of resources was a major factor in the theatre's demise.

Sharon accepted a commission to write one other children's play in 1973, the anti-smoking piece called "The Great Drag Race or Smoked, Choked and Croaked," for the British Columbia Tuberculosis-Christmas Seal Society (now the B.C. Lung Association). This play is of particular interest for two reasons: enough correspondence survives to provide some insight into Sharon's position in 1973–74, and the play itself contains a delightful narrator-character that prefigures "T.S." in *The Komagata Maru Incident*. Early in 1973, the Society invited Sharon to submit a script for adjudication on the subject of smoking and explained that the winning script would be performed in local high schools. Sharon replied expressing an interest but stressed that, as a professional playwright, she would only prepare a complete script on commission: "my living is earned through writing," she explained, and "to put it bluntly, my time is money." (54:1.21). She asked them for a contract and set her fee at $500.00. The Society accepted, and by the fall of that year, Sharon delivered "The Great Drag Race" with music by Marjorie Morris. The play is a light-hearted treatment of a serious subject, with a colourful cast of melodrama-style characters. The villains are a businessman called "T.B." who is the boss of "Slayer's Cigarettes"; a "Tweedle-dum and Tweedle-dee" duo of company executives; a salesman with the appropriate name of "Peter Puffalot," and his "sex-pot," Mae West-type assistant called Billie Badbreath. The good guys (or prospective victims) include an older man with emphysema and two young innocents, Adam Adamant and Tessie Trueheart. After much (futile) persuasion from Mr. Puffalot and his brazen side-kick, some witty repartee, several snappy songs, and a good deal of coughing and choking, everyone is saved from a miserable fate, T.B. decides to leave cigarettes and go into the cough drop business, and the Narrator pronounces the moral of the tale: Don't smoke!

I have found no indication that the play toured the schools, and the only performance I know of took place at Gladstone Secondary School in Vancouver's east side, but it is a very clever, fast-paced, funny piece, and its Narrator accounts for a good deal of the energy and forward movement of the plot. The play opens with this Narrator, who should perform "as if he were a circus barker," announcing: "Students and Parents! Ladies and Gents! AN ENTERTAINMENT!!!" He describes himself as the one who "ties it all together," and he introduces each of the other characters, who enter to music and freeze when he is finished with them. Sharon had used a similar kind of character in "Wudjesay?"—a chap called "Mr. Dusty," who begins that play by calling out "Tickets! Tickets! Pass your tickets in at the door!" carries on as a kind of master of ceremonies, and continually steps forward to introduce, clarify, and generally keep things moving. The Narrator in "The Great Drag Race" is many times more adroit and manipulative than Mr. Dusty, but both these characters illustrate the concept of T.S., whose role in *The Komagata Maru Incident* is structurally and thematically crucial.

As her correspondence with the Tuberculosis-Christmas Seal Society demonstrates, by 1973 Sharon considered herself a professional whose time and work should be paid for and respected. She had signed her letter to them not just as Sharon Pollock but also as "Secretary of the Executive of the B.C. League of Playwrights." Her reputation was growing and with it her self-confidence. Several people who knew and worked with her in the Vancouver years have characterized her as supremely self-confident, often strident, and always sure she was right. However, a few individuals who were more perceptive realized that beneath this bravado was a vulnerable, insecure person whose need to succeed had complex roots and motivation. And things were by no means easy. Five hundred dollars for many hours of work (no royalties, no box office returns) was not a big sum; her successes, when they came, did so at the cost of very hard work and poor remuneration, even if we consider these years as her apprenticeship because she was learning on the job. The business letters that survive from this period attest to her efforts to get her plays produced. She was actively sending scripts to the United States and across Canada and asking for professional feedback from members of the theatre community. For example, in a letter to Christopher Newton from the fall of 1973, she raised the subject of *Walsh*, which had already premiered in Calgary and been published, acknowledging that it needed further work and outlining what she would do if he agreed to give it a Playhouse production. She ended the letter assuring him that if he chose not to do the play, her pillow would "require constant wringing" but her respect and feelings of friendship for him would not be affected. As it turned out, he did not pick up the play. In a 1973 letter that she received from Mel Bloom of Mel Bloom & Associates in Beverly Hills, she was advised, in a rather condescending and avuncular tone, to give up writing for the stage and devote herself to movies and television. She "*was* a writer" and a good one, he noted, but he could do "nothing with 'Walsh'." Such letters must have cost a good deal to write and read, but somehow the woman and artist who could seem so confident girded up her emotional loins, stuck to her artistic principles, and carried on.

In a 1974 letter to John Neville, the newly appointed artistic director of Edmonton's Citadel Theatre, she offered her services as a PR writer who could develop an effective advertising policy for the theatre. If hired, she would produce something effective for the Citadel, and he would be subsidizing her playwriting—it was a win-win deal. But it is what she goes on to say in this short message, rather than the deal itself, that I find moving and revelatory:

> I feel as if I have been shut in a closet with a typewriter and a calendar. Every day I change the date and slide five pages under the door. My puritanical work ethic unequivocally states that Canada Council grants are bad for the soul. The rest of me agrees. I find it demeaning to write TV plays with artistic changes dictated by story editors to justify their jobs and plot alterations suggested by executive producers' grandsons. While I enjoy conducting workshops, adjudicating festivals, and directing amateurs, the money is miniscule. If I wish to write for the stage, and I do, I must either become a hack churning out TV, radio, and stage scripts when the bell rings, or find other employment related to the theatre. (54:1. 47)

And she ends this letter, not with a plea, but with a bald statement: "I know the Canadian theatre scene, I care passionately about it.... Let me know if you're interested." If Neville replied, his letter is not with incoming correspondence in the Pollock archive, and Sharon Pollock did not get a PR job with the Citadel Theatre.

However, her claim to know and care about the theatre scene was spot on. In addition to writing, acting, and workshop experience, she had tried her hand at directing, and soon after arriving in Vancouver, she threw herself into administrative work for both the amateur and professional theatre. There is a letter with her papers, dated March 1973 and addressed to the executive of the Vancouver Little Theatre Association (VLTA), which sheds light on her knowledge, her artistic principles, and her ability to address issues directly. At a page and a half of single-spaced type, it must have taken some time and thought to write, and it could not have been easy because she begins by informing the VLTA that, "with regret mixed with relief," she and Michael are resigning as co-artistic directors (54:3. 60). She goes on to explain why and to describe the problems the association should address if it wants to survive. For example, it cannot rely on volunteer help and have these volunteers on their executive because, too often, these people cannot (or will not) do the work; the building is a "firetrap" and so cold that the actors can see their breath during rehearsals; she has personally cleaned out the scene shop (the kind of grunt work she would find herself doing in the 1990s for the Garry Theatre) only to discover piles of junk tossed back in. More importantly, the VLTA had cancelled Saturday evening performances so it could make some rental money on those nights, when, she argues, Saturday night should be the high point for their own productions. Worst of all, in her view, is the "indifference on the part of those who should be most committed," and she gives some hair-raising examples of what she means—a lighting man who suddenly backed out of one production, a make-up person (and member of the executive) who failed to show up for another, and the complete collapse of publicity for yet another. Sharon adds several details of practical and financial information that the theatre will need as it prepares for the rest of the season, which included productions of major plays such as Brendan Behan's *The Hostage*, and she concludes by urging them to consider her points and face the future realistically. This 1973 letter to the VLTA also reveals something of Sharon's views about the role of an artistic director and the relationship between a theatre's AD and its board. Twice in the future she would take on these challenges with professional theatres, and the end result would be the same: disagreements with the board culminating in her resignation.

In other letters from 1973 she speaks out more publicly—or, at least, attempts to—by writing to the editors of both the *Province* and the *Vancouver Sun*. The *Sun* letter was, in fact, addressed "via Mr. Dafoe," and she begins by allowing that it may be the "height of folly for a playwright" to write to the local drama critic ... but then she ploughs ahead. Her complaint is that he has totally misrepresented the efforts of local playwrights in his review for 7 September 1973 called "A dramatic theme, yes; a drama? No," because he describes a minor New Play Centre initiative as the presentation of works-in-progress. His point was that the material he saw, even though he was hardly expecting to see a great Canadian play, was weak. Hers is that these scenes and sketches were never intended as works-in-progress that would showcase the potential (or not) of local playwrights. Moreover, she tells him bluntly that she withdrew her own piece from the "Collage" series (as this project was called) and implies that that the New Play Centre is the source of the problem. This letter shows Sharon Pollock at her caustic but loyal best: something must be said, she tells Dafoe, "in defence of that much maligned animal, the local playwright" (54: 3.61). Her letter to the *Province* is equally direct and much more acerbic. This time her target is the paper's championing of the appointment of foreign-born and -trained artistic directors at Stratford. Apparently, fellow writer, David Watmough, who was serving with Sharon on the executive of the short-lived B.C. League of Playwrights, had protested Stratford's failure to consider a Canadian for their top job or even to consult with the Canadian theatre community before inviting Robin Phillips to take the position. Leaping to Watmough's defence, she accuses the *Province*'s editor of being "snide" in his dismissal of his "legitimate concerns" and she warns them that if they were to apply the standard of Sir Tyrone Guthrie and Shakespeare to their own discipline, they would have to close shop because their journalists "are vastly inferior" to those who write for *The New York Times*. As far as I can tell, the paper chose not to publish her riposte, but it clearly demonstrates that Sharon Pollock had a voice of her own.

The B.C. League of Playwrights was an early attempt to create an organization that would support and represent the interests of local playwrights. It formed in 1972 around a small nucleus of professional theatre people in Vancouver that included Christopher Newton, Peter Hay (who had started the publishing program for Talonbooks in 1969 with Beverley Simon's *Crabdance* and George Ryga's *The Ecstasy of Rita Joe*), David Watmough, Majorie Morris, and Sharon, who was nominated as the secretary/treasurer at their November 1972 meeting. The goals of this executive were to recruit members, to sponsor theatre discussion groups that would be open to the public, to organize workshops, and, above all, to inform the media, the National Film Board, the Canadian Theatre Centre, the Canadian Council for the Arts, and the Playwrights' Co-op of their existence. The discussion of the Playwrights'

Co-op, as recorded in their minutes, makes it clear that they believed the publication of plays to be very important for the promotion of Canadian work, and they also felt confident that their endorsement of scripts would enhance the chance of a script's getting published. Although the League did not last for long (perhaps not beyond 1974), they certainly started with a bang. By the end of their first year they had pulled together statistics on the number of productions of original Canadian plays mounted in British Columbia between 1965 and 1973, and the results were dismal. Several theatres, including the Arts Club, failed to provide any information, and among those that did only the Playhouse could claim six main stage productions—the most significant being their 1967 premiere of George Ryga's *The Ecstasy of Rita Joe*. Simon Fraser University reported forty-three main stage productions; the University of British Columbia had none. In her minutes for the September 1973 meeting, Sharon recorded Watmough's report on a successful meeting of playwrights with representatives of the Canadian Film Development Corporation, and another joint meeting was planned with a dozen or so theatre producers, presumably to enlighten them about the need to mount Canadian plays. From 1972 to 1974, Sharon also served on the Advisory Board of the New Play Centre, so that between meetings of the League and the Centre, her work for the Little Theatre, and her own writing, it is small wonder that the children would come home from school to find her dosing on the kitchen floor.

By 1976 Sharon was ready to move on. She had accepted a one-year teaching position at the University of Alberta and she would spend the first of many summer playwriting sessions at Banff in July that year. As it turned out, Edmonton was just a short stop on her way back to a permanent home in Calgary, and she was glad to leave Vancouver behind. In a 1984 interview with Martin Knelman, she was very clear that it was not her kind of town: "I tend to be a high-energy, pushy person," she told Knelman, "and I thought the laid-back atmosphere of lotusland would be good for me. But in Vancouver I wanted to push people down the escalators. I felt they should be walking faster" (1984, 74). Perhaps "lotusland" in the mid-seventies was a bit "laid-back," although there was nothing slow about her own years there. Three moves, several plays, a host of other activities, and thirteen different schools for one of the children, suggests something closer to a maelstrom of activity. And to be fair, Vancouver had been good to her, offering her experiences, professional training, and public exposure on a scale she had not enjoyed in sixties Calgary. When she left for Edmonton, she took with her invaluable lessons in the art of making theatre (lessons in dramatic structure, temporal and narrative framing through narrator-characters, and pacing), in the role of music within a play, on the scope and power of set design, in the process of research, revision, and collaboration that could transform an idea into a script and a script into a play, and in the politics of theatre in Canada. In one of her suitcases she carried at least three plays-in-the-making—*One Tiger to a Hill*, *Blood Relations*, and *Getting It Straight*, and on her resumé she could list several premieres, the publication of *Walsh*, and several radio and television productions. She had earned a living—scarcely a luxurious one—but she had paid her way.

Most important of all, Sharon Pollock had found her voice. From a woman who said of the 1960s that the voice of "the Colonizer ... carried legitimacy and significance" because "an authentic voice" was "silent" in Canadian theatre ("The Evolution of an Authentic Voice," 116) and as an actor who had personally experienced this silencing and had chaffed against the expectation that she would always assume someone else's voice and tell "somebody else's story," she had become a playwright who chose to write out of her own history, background, and place. Years later she would look back on the sixties and early seventies and remember how she had "moved into writing out of anger and frustration, and out of a need to confirm that the work [she] was doing was important" (see Zimmerman, 1991, 36). And she would recall the first time she ever felt "the wonderful recognition of authenticity": "It was John Murrell's *Great Noise, Bright Light*. I just sat there and said I know this" (Zimmerman, 1991, 69).[6] Murrell recalls that moment too and credits Sharon's support with a critical turning point in his career as a writer. The timing of this mutual recognition of voice, authenticity, reality, and support was the summer of 1976, and Sharon could *hear* this voice because she had already found it herself—in "Thirty-one for Two," "Wudjesay?" "And Out Goes You?" and, above all, in *Walsh*.

PART II

CHAPTER 5

Taking to the Stage:
From Breakthrough to Banff and Beyond

What I write is quite Canadian oriented. I couldn't live in the States. I couldn't work for the States either. I really believe that the artist has a job, a responsibility not just to her/himself but to the society s/he comes from. I represent the kinds of questions some Canadians are asking and my responsibility is here.   —SHARON POLLOCK, INTERVIEW, DUNN, 1976, 6

I write the same play over and over and over again. The stories are different, but it seems to me that what consumes me ... is authority, and individual responsibility, and the inability or the lack of will in terms of conforming to either a morality or behaviour that's imposed from the outside.
                                                         —SHARON POLLOCK, INTERVIEW, WASSERMAN, 1993, n.p.

I: *Walsh* and *The Komagata Maru Incident*

When John Parker reviewed Talonbook's first edition of *Walsh* (1973), he praised both its stage premiere and the published text, and he predicted that there would be many future productions of this "remarkable play" (29–30). He was right. Along with *Blood Relations*, *Walsh* has remained a perennial favourite on amateur and professional stages in Canada and the United States and in university drama courses. It premiered at Theatre Calgary in November 1973 and was most recently produced in the summer of 2005 at the Margaret Greenham Theatre in Banff. During the intervening years, there were major productions of *Walsh* at Stratford (1974) and at the National Arts Centre in Ottawa (1983). In 1986 it was adapted for television, with significant cuts, and it received a controversial revival at Theatre Calgary in 1988. The early 1970s seemed the right moment for a play dealing on an epic scale with a little-known event in Canadian history. The other Canadian history play produced in 1973, Rick Salutin's *1837: The Farmers' Revolt*, was attracting attention and awards in Toronto. But Sharon's play created a stir because of its frank portrayal of relations between Major James Walsh of the North West Mounted Police and Sitting Bull, a chief of the Sioux nation, who led his people into exile in the Canadian west in 1877, and because its sensitive exploration of White/Indian relations was timely. During the early 1970s the

American Indian Movement was gaining profile and momentum and the 1970 film *Little Big Man*, starring Chief Dan George and Dustin Hoffman, was a box office hit. Most importantly, Dee Brown's stunning book *Bury My Heart at Wounded Knee*, first published in 1970, had an instant, widespread, and profound impact.

Walsh marked Sharon's real breakthrough as a playwright of stature. It also provided her with some extremely important lessons in the making of theatre—lessons about casting, about rehearsal time for a big play, about how to present historical information within the dramatic action, about what would, or would not, work in performance, and above all, about the importance of rewriting a play after the benefit of a full, professional production. For Stratford she made major revisions that transformed the history lesson of the first version into a much more theatrical realization of one man's moral dilemma. For the National Arts Centre production, she made some further, more minor alterations. *Walsh*, as we know it now, is the result of these three important productions. It remains a vital, powerful piece of writing with a relevant message and a dramatic structure that recurs, to varying degrees, in most of her later work. Because I see *Walsh* as a breakthrough and a benchmark play in the Pollock oeuvre, I want to linger over its production history and explore its development from Calgary to Stratford to the NAC. But before I examine this stage history, it is worth reviewing the stories of its historical figures, James Walsh and Sitting Bull, and the seventies context for the play, if for no other reason than because the turbulent events of the seventies would stay with Sharon long after she wrote *Walsh* and they would resurface in two later plays—*Sweet Land of Liberty* and *The Making of Warriors*.

The brief historical facts are these: James Morrow Walsh was born on 22 May 1840 in Prescott, Ontario, and he joined the newly formed North West Mounted Police Force in 1873. As Superintendent, he led a NWMP force division West in 1874 and founded Fort Walsh in the Cypress Hills on the border of contemporary Saskatchewan and Alberta. However, by 1877 he had moved his base of operations east to the Wood Mountain area in Saskatchewan, where he took official charge of the Lakota Sioux, led by Chief Sitting Bull, who had escaped north in search of sanctuary after the battle of the Little Big Horn. The Sioux stayed in Canada until the summer of 1881, and Walsh grew to like and respect the chief, but the Canadian government wanted to be rid of these troublesome guests and refused Walsh's requests on their behalf. By 1881 Sitting Bull and his people were starved into surrendering to the Americans, and in 1883, Major Walsh resigned from the NWMP. He went into business in Winnipeg for several years, but he returned to the force for one year during the height of the Klondike Gold Rush, from 1897 to 1898, as Commissioner of the Yukon Provisional District. He died on 25 July 1905 in Brockville, Ontario. Walsh's style and personality as well as his courage, honesty, and sense of fair play no doubt contributed to his friendship with Sitting Bull, who named him White Forehead. Nevertheless, he was unable, in his official capacity and despite his personal sympathies, to save the Sioux.

Tatanka Iyotaka (1831–90), called in English Sitting Bull, a chief of the Hunkpapa Sioux, is famous in American history for his total defeat of General George Armstrong Custer and the Seventh Cavalry division on 25 June 1876. Custer's Last Stand hardly needs recounting here. Suffice it to say that the Sioux, with other tribes, were fighting to protect the sacred

Black Hills against white incursions, when Custer foolishly attacked 7,000 of them with two hundred soldiers; the whites were all killed, and Sitting Bull and his people became wanted criminals in American eyes. Within months, Sitting Bull with about 5,000 of his people had crossed into the Canadian West, where they expected refuge, hunting supplies, and eventually a reservation. Not long after they arrived, the Nez Percé nation attempted to flee north as well, but they were attacked by the American army just forty miles south of the border, and only a small, starving, and wounded group of them succeeded in reaching Sitting Bull's camp at Wood Mountain. By all accounts, Sitting Bull was wise and eloquent, as well as a spectacular warrior and courageous leader. His compassion for the plight of the Nez Percé, hereditary enemies of the Sioux, was deep, and he knew that a return to the United States would end in death for himself and the further degradation of his people. Other factors besides genocide contributed to the deterioration of the plains First Nations in the latter half of the nineteenth century; the dwindling herds of buffalo, a staple of the Sioux diet and the linchpin of their culture, was a major contributing factor. Because the buffalo were scarce (and the Americans set fires to stop the migration north of those that remained), the Canadian government was able to starve Sitting Bull's people into submission, after the American General Alfred Terry, who came north to make a deal, could not cajole them into returning with offers of amnesty and a reservation. By July 1881, many of his starving people had returned to the States and Sitting Bull surrendered his rifle at Fort Buford in Montana. However, instead of being granted his request for a reservation near his beloved Black Hills, he and his family were marched south and held prisoner at Fort Randall for two years before being allowed to rejoin the Sioux.

In 1885, Sitting Bull spent four ignominious months with Buffalo Bill's Wild West show, and in 1890, just two weeks before the massacre at Wounded Knee, he was murdered by a group of Lakota police who had been ordered by white agents to stop him from joining the Ghost Dance ceremony being planned on the Rosebud and Pine Ridge reservations in South Dakota. The Indians hoped that the ritual of the Ghost Dance would help rid their land of the white occupiers, and Sitting Bull's participation at such a ceremony would have imbued it with great spiritual power; therefore, his betrayal and murder was a profoundly political and symbolic act. As we know, these efforts to resist the intruder failed, and eighty years later the American Indian Movement and the Pine Ridge reservation once more received wide public attention and American government repression. What's more, the events of the 1970s again involved Canadians because Anna Mae Pictou Aquash was brutally murdered near Pine Ridge, and Sharon would give us her version of Anna Mae in *The Making of Warriors* (1991).

Sharon had begun to write about Walsh and Sitting Bull as early as 1971–72. Christopher Newton, who had read early drafts of her script, arranged for a workshop session with the New Play Centre and encouraged her to continue with it because he was keen to see plays on Canadian subjects. Materials in the Pollock and Theatre Calgary archives help to date her research and drafts and to track the changes she would make between 1973 and 1974 as the play developed. Harold Baldridge, Alberta born and educated, began his artistic director-ship of Theatre Calgary in 1972, and after reading *Bury My Heart at Wounded Knee*, he very much wanted to find a play on the Canadian years of Sitting Bull's life because such a play would fulfil two immediate needs. As a play by a Canadian writer it would meet Canada Council requirements for a grant and it would also be a play he wanted with both local and contemporary resonance. When he heard, in October of 1972, that a writer living in Vancouver, who was unknown to him, was writing such a play, he contacted her immediately. "Dear Miss Pollock," he wrote: "Bob Haley and several other people, including George Ryga, have mentioned the existence of a new play of yours dealing with ... Sitting Bull ... in Canada. This project fascinates me.... If you have any kind of a draft that you could send me, I would be most appreciative." (54:3.36–37). Sharon replied quickly, sending him "a rather tatty draft of my first two acts," and she went on to tell Baldridge a bit about Major Walsh's "personal history" and his brief time in the Yukon. Then she explained how she saw *her* Walsh: "I believe [he] was destroyed by the unjust policies he carried out on behalf of the Canadian government [and] it is this symbolic destruction of Walsh I would like to show in my third act" (54:3.36–37).

By the spring of 1973, the two were corresponding about her work on the play and the New Play Centre workshop. He wrote in February encouraging her to focus on the character of Walsh, and in June he sent her a contract (54.3.56). *Walsh*, as the play was now called, would have its world premiere in November. Baldridge visited Vancouver at least once to discuss the script with Sharon and he brought her to Calgary during rehearsals. In her version of the story, Sharon stays close to the basic facts while confining herself to the four years that the Sioux spent in the Canadian West and maintaining her primary focus on James Walsh. But she also takes significant and important liberties with the facts in order to concentrate the time-span of her plot and to explore the psychology of Walsh, whom she imagines as a basically decent man trapped by a military code and a political situation over which he has no control. *Walsh* becomes Sharon's first study in the fate of an individual crushed by the superior forces, not of history as such, nor anything as abstract as the gods (as in "We to the gods"), but of the self-serving, callous power of bureaucratic authority and a national policy of appeasement of the Americans. *Her* James Walsh is a man who betrays another man and his own best self when he capitulates to the rules of the organization he serves. He is not quite a Judas figure, but he is nevertheless a moral failure, and as she developed her play and her protagonist's character, she came to see him as a man driven to violence and near madness by his guilt. The question she asks in *Walsh* is not whether the fate of Sitting Bull was right or wrong nor whether Walsh could have saved the day but whether a blind adherence to the rules (or laws) is morally defensible and whether the corruption of a good man, not to mention the expedient sacrifice of hundreds of other people, is worth the price of obedience. In 1973 the play addressed such questions to Canada regarding its contemporary relations with the United States, and the questions remain troublingly pertinent today. To her credit, however, her answers do not come easily or without ambiguity because the play offers a sincere exploration of as many sides of the dilemma as possible.

When *Walsh* opened on Wednesday, 7 November 1973, in Calgary's Arts Centre Theatre, it had a near ideal cast, with August Schellenberg as Sitting Bull and Michael Fletcher as

Walsh, an effective, simple raked set by Richard Roberts, and sensitive directing by Baldridge.[1] But there were problems with the script's use of voiceover readings of official documents and in the slow-moving exposition of historical context. According to Jamie Portman, who attended the opening night performance and had very high praise for the play ("an undeniable red-letter event") and the playwright, some audience members left the theatre after Act One and missed the power and dramatic success of Acts Two and Three. But in criticizing the slow, expository beginning and the contrived voiceover device, Portman put his finger on the key structural problem with this first *Walsh* script. Sharon had not yet learned how to manipulate the storytelling aspect of her dramaturgy, and she had not learned to trust that her audience would understand her methods. With time to reflect on the lessons of this premiere and under the imaginative direction of John Wood, she revised this opening strategy and her changes to Act One emphasized the true moral—and dramatic—centre of her play. At this stage *Walsh* was a conventional three-act play with two intermissions and voiceovers before each of its twelve scenes. As a consequence, it *played* like an episodic history play, if not an actual documentary. The characters of General Terry, Mary Walsh, and Pretty Plume were not yet part of the play, but the crucial character of young Clarence, the new NWMP recruit who serves as the embodiment of Walsh's conscience and the vehicle for the playwright's anguish and moral perspective, was there from the beginning. So was Harry, the philosophical wagon master, who became the narrator-character when the play was revised, and Louis, the Métis scout whose skills and critical comments constantly remind the audience (or the reader) about the racial and political games being played with human lives.

In a short article he wrote about finding and directing *Walsh*, Harold Baldridge explained that he quickly realized that it would be a perfect production for the year of the RCMP's centenary. The Mounties, of course, were no strangers to the stage and screen. Images of unarmed, red-coated officers always getting their man, mushing through the snow (in dress uniform), riding fine black horses called King, and singing charming love songs, were already familiar from dozens of Hollywood films, from radio programs like *Sergeant Preston of the Yukon* (which was also a television series in the fifties), and from popular films like *Rose-Marie* (starring the handsome Nelson Eddie and Jeanette Macdonald in the 1936 sound version). But Sharon Pollock's Mountie did not conform to any of these stereotypes; her James Walsh was a man for the 1970s, a man who was trapped by the system he served and who suffered and failed. What the Force thought about this very human portrayal of Walsh I do not know, but the president of the Calgary RCMP Veterans' Association wrote Baldridge to say that he found the play "top notch" and a "pleasure" to watch. Someone in the Alberta government, with the approval of the RCMP, was also willing to countenance this flesh and blood Walsh because Theatre Calgary received a five thousand dollar grant for the production from the Alberta-RCMP Century Celebrations Committee, which is thanked in the program as a sponsor. Of course, the Mounties were not the only stereotypes that Sharon tackled in this play. Indians were even more stereotyped, and negatively so, in popular literature, Hollywood films, and on radio and television programs from the pre-1970 period. As Daniel Francis reminds us in his discussion of the "imaginary" "Red Coats and Red Skins," when an Indian met a Mountie (in novel, play, or film), he was depicted as a violent savage who was easily cowed by the superior moral force of the unarmed, wise Mountie. The message conveyed by these caricatures created a fictive and expedient story of a rational, civilizing presence in the Canadian West that was initially resisted by the Indians and then welcomed by them. The resulting "image of the grateful Indian," as Francis puts it, "was an essential ingredient" in the evolving myth of national identity because it enabled Canadians to feel righteous about their treatment of these peoples at the same time as they could sharply distinguish a just and gentle Canada from a violent, unjust United States (69). But Sharon Pollock would have none of this. If her James Walsh was an all-too-human man, her Sitting Bull was wise, morally consistent, and anything but meek and grateful.

Baldridge's main concern about preparing this "incredibly complex new play" with its twelve characters and multiple scenes, was time not money: all he had was the standard three weeks for rehearsal:

> Sharon and I had agreed not to do much rewriting before we got into rehearsal with the actors [but] we only had three weeks to mount this incredibly complex new play.... [My] commitment was to get the play on the boards, and there would be time for little more. We did do some rewrites. For example, the difficult scenes between Walsh and Sitting Bull, and likewise between Walsh and MacLeod, were in some cases improvised to seek a more human, accessible level for the actors. Sharon spent the first week with us, talking about the play and then [she] disappeared during the weeks of staging. She was always within reach, however, and indeed one short scene was rewritten over the telephone.... By the third week, we were on set [and] Sharon and I and the actors began to discover all sorts of new possibilities for the play. (119)

Clearly, everyone involved realized that this important new play still needed work, and when I discussed *Walsh* with Baldridge in 2004, he stressed the fact that a three-week rehearsal was far too short for such a script and that he was impressed with the changes made for the Stratford production.

Before I move on to the revised *Walsh*, however, I want to recount two stories about this production. The first comes from Carol Hogg, a staff writer for the *Calgary Herald*, who attended rehearsals and wrote a full-page article, with four photographs, for the Saturday, November 3rd edition—Theatre Calgary could not have asked for better advance publicity. In it, she describes the engagement of the actors with their roles and with the tragic story in moving detail. She notes that Jean Archambault, a young Quebec actor working in English for the first time, did not need to fake an accent for Louis, the Métis scout, and that Denis LaCroix, who played Chief Gall and was himself Cree Métis, wore beaded moccasins during rehearsals to remind him of his own roots and personal link with the events in the play. Like the other actors, his voice often trembled with emotion as he worked on his lines. Sharon had wanted First Nations or Métis actors for the play (and always insisted on the importance of this casting), so this aspect of the production was satisfying. Unfortunately, however, she was not present at the rehearsal that produced the second story, one that Baldridge still recalls vividly as the "most exciting" moment in the entire production. He had invited Walter LeCaine, a Sioux elder in his seventies, to assist them because he was famous as a singer of

Sioux war chants, and Baldridge thought that hearing these chants would help the cast and provide him with a song he could use in the production. Mr. LeCaine sang, accompanying himself on a drum, until he was asked for a death chant. This he would not perform; instead, he played a recording he had taped and while it played he sat weeping in a corner. When the chant ended, he said simply: "So many of them have died." "The actors and I were rooted to the spot," Baldridge recalled, "feeling the weight of guilt that we as Canadians have inherited from the gross mismanagement of Indian affairs. It was an unforgettable moment; it still haunts me" (120).

By the time *Walsh* opened on Stratford's Third Stage (now the site of the Tom Patterson Theatre), it was much less likely to be mistaken for a documentary or well-made history play. It had become an innovative, intensely dramatic piece of theatre that I would describe as expressionist in style, structure, and theme. This *Walsh* recreates the tragic events of the 1870s *in retrospect* and largely from James Walsh's tormented and haunted perspective. Working closely with John Wood, Sharon wrote the important Prologue to the play, altered the structure from the previous, conventional three to a taut two acts, and made a host of minor, but significant, changes. Gone were the intrusive voiceover readings and the history lessons. Instead of an episodic narrative punctuated with facts, the play moved directly, and dramatically, from the Prologue into the first act, which ended on a precarious moral high point of decision that is undercut by portents of disaster. The second act plunges immediately into a precipitous sequence of ironic reversals, tragic betrayals, and ultimate despair. At Stratford, and in Talon's quickly published new edition of the play, Act Two became an emotional roller-coaster that demonstrated how the James Walsh in the Prologue had deteriorated into a pathetic, haunted, shell of a man later in life. Emotionally, thematically, and above all, dramatically, the play now circled back on itself to *enact* the legacy of history for the present. The playwright had learned Henry James's lesson, surely even more important for a play than a novel, that showing is artistically superior to telling. And this is a key lesson she would not forget.

John Wood is one of this country's most gifted and intelligent directors, and he has played an important role in Sharon's story, as well as in the larger story of Canadian theatre history (see Illus. 29). He has directed in theatres across the country and done much to promote plays by Canadians. He has lived in Stratford for many years and it was there, in his home, "The Old Wood House," that I met him and he shared with me his memories of working with Sharon on *Walsh* for Stratford and for the National Arts Centre and on *One Tiger to a Hill* and *Blood Relations*. John Wood has a soft-spoken but formidable presence, so I can well imagine how he and Sharon Pollock would either have hit it off or been at daggers drawn; both are opinionated and talented and neither suffers fools gladly. Fortunately, for Canadian theatre, they got along well. At one point, as we sat at his kitchen table to review his files while he reminisced, a sleek, handsome cat paced through the room—dignified, remote— and I realized that Sharon Pollock and John Wood had at least two essential passions in common: theatre and cats. He loves them, and he also loves large, challenging, serious plays with something of value to say about issues that matter, as does Sharon, and, like her, he is disgusted by the "pudding" served up today in many of our regional theatres.

29. John Wood (ca 1982) directed *Walsh* and *One Tiger to a Hill* at Stratford and during his years as Artistic Director, English Theatre, at the National Arts Centre, he directed new productions of both *Walsh* and *Blood Relations.*
Photographer unknown. Courtesy of the Stratford Shakespeare Festival Archives.

So much in art, as in life, seems to happen by chance. In preparing this biography I have often asked myself "what if?" What if Eloise had not been who she was? What if Sharon Chalmers had not met and married Ross Pollock? What if Christopher Newton had not arrived in Vancouver precisely when he did? And what if John Wood had not been directing for Theatre Calgary between 1972 and 1974 and, thus, been able to catch the premiere of *Walsh?* But he was, and he did, and he was impressed, even though he thought the play did not receive the full-scale treatment it deserved. When the opportunity arose to direct a new Canadian play at Stratford, he saw *Walsh* as an obvious choice, but it needed work and Sharon needed pushing to find the theatricality of her story. He suggested a prologue to replace the voiceovers and exposition, and through the collaboration that followed, she created the fine Prologue we now have, as well as overhauling other aspects of the play. In the end, Wood was pleased with the Stratford production, preferring it in many respects to the one he directed at the Centre, and he is convinced that the play is still relevant today and should be made into a film, for which he would like to do the screenplay.

The Stratford *Walsh* opened on 24 July 1974 in the comparatively small, intimate Third Stage Theatre, with its arena-style, 250-seat house, and ran until August 10th. Although the cast earned considerable praise from most reviewers, McKenzie Porter in the *Toronto Sun* criticized the casting of whites in the Indian roles. For this production Michael Ball played Walsh opposite Derek Ralston's Sitting Bull on an impressive set designed by John Ferguson (see Illus. 30), and the most common comments by reviewers are that Michael was a splendid Walsh and that the set and overall design were truly memorable. The set was

30. Michael Ball as Walsh
with the late Derek
Ralston as Sitting Bull in
a scene from the 1974
Stratford production of
Walsh directed by John
Wood.
*Photograph by Robert C.
Ragsdale. Courtesy of the
Stratford Shakespeare
Festival Archives.*

simple, geometric and abstract, with an expressionist use of platforms, steps, and side ramps; props were minimal, and specific objects (the crate of useless government-issue shovels or Walsh's travelling trunk) were placed near the centre and enhanced with lighting to stress their symbolic significance (general bureaucratic indifference and ignorance in the first case and Walsh's attempted abandonment of the situation, or even his psychological baggage in the second). Such a set complemented what Wood considered a totally new play, one that now existed primarily in Walsh's mind because it gave concrete expression to mental anguish and invited the spectator to imagine the emotions and ghostly presences that haunt *collective* memory and persist in time and place, while only hinting at the actual flat expanse of the prairie landscape. Such a design worked against documentary fact, historical records, and realistic detail, and it facilitated a seamless flow from the Prologue into the rest of the play.

At some stage in the rehearsal process, the director and playwright agreed to run the entire play straight through with no break. Further cuts were called for. The action became even more concentrated and the emotional impact more intense. When push came to shove in production, the play as *living theatre* took precedence over the written text and what worked on stage won the day. This experience amounted to another lesson for Sharon, one that has become basic to her theatre-making process: once into rehearsal a play belongs to the theatre—to the physical stage, the actors, the director—*not* to the playwright. In an interview with Stratford theatre critic Doug Bale, Sharon announced that she would never again write a three-act play because "I've already said the things I feel about the play by the first break," and by the second "I'm beginning to wonder" if there's enough time to get to the bar. Reflecting more seriously on the decision to run the play without an intermission, she explained that the piece had "too much momentum to be suddenly braked in mid-career" and that she "trusted John [Wood] implicitly," so that when he suggested jettisoning the break she agreed. Later in this interview, Sharon provides some further insights into her relationship to her own work. Because Michael was performing the title role, questions about their personal relationship seemed inevitable, and instead of dismissing them as impertinent or irrelevant, she answered thoughtfully. On the one hand, she explained, Michael is more familiar with the play than a stranger would be because "everything I write I pass by him" for his reaction. On the other hand, once he takes on the actor's job, his work is with the director and his professional colleagues. What he must care about is that "what he's doing is good. If that conflicts with my ideas, that's too bad."

The Stratford *Walsh* is, finally, Sharon Pollock's and Major James Walsh's story. When she began to imagine the Prologue that John Wood wanted, she reached back to her earliest research on Walsh's life, research that pre-dated Dee Brown's *Bury My Heart at Wounded Knee*. As she recalled for Jerry Wasserman in 1993, she first read about the man in a book for elementary school children, but the account left her puzzled. She began to dig around for more information: Why had he apparently disappeared from the NWMP force after 1883? And what had he done with his life after those few years with Sitting Bull? When she discovered more of the facts—that he had gone into business but been reinstated by the Force during the Gold Rush—she also learned that as Commissioner he was incompetent and possibly corrupt. And yet, the man as represented by his years in the West and his friendship with Sitting Bull seemed to be "a principled individual," so what happened? "Which is the real man here? Or is this [the man of principle] the real man and something had happened to him that changed him" (see Wasserman, 1993, n.p.). Her task became to unearth, understand, and dramatize what had happened to the human being and, as she told Wasserman, she "identified with" his dilemma. Here was a person who was basically honourable, who tried to follow his conscience and to obey the laws set down by the authorities he served, but who was finally "destroyed by his actions." He sacrificed his own code of honour to do as others expected. In the context of Sharon's work and imagination, Walsh was becoming a tragic version of the satiric Bob or Roberta Handal figures in "And Out Goes You?" and "Mail vs. Female." Moreover, in the moral debate over whether to conform or rebel, a debate that Sharon had observed in her mother's life and had experienced herself, Walsh had chosen obedience to authority and conformity with external expectations. By contrast, Sharon had chosen to refuse to conform; as she put it in her conversations with Margo Dunn and Kathleen Flaherty, she decided *to live*. Because she understood the dilemma and the outcome, *her* James Walsh would follow the path she had not taken; he would become her creation, her fiction, a fiction that portrayed some profound truths about the human condition, which the bald facts of the man's life never could.

As the opening stage instructions in the published text remind us, "the scene [in the Prologue] is from WALSH'S point of view," and "the impression given is similar to that experienced when one is drunk or under great mental stress" (*W, CW* I, 33). We are in a saloon in Dawson city in 1898, and the characters must take their places "quickly and silently, like ghosts" (33). When Commissioner Walsh enters, they relax from a "freeze," but they are all focused on Walsh. Only then does the action begin, which suggests that this figure of authority carries with him the motivation for their present uneasy singing and dialogue and for the story that will unfold when the right button is pressed. That button is the Commissioner's violent outburst against a prospector who is asking for charity that Walsh will not give; in a rage he strikes the man, knocking him to the floor, and "plants a foot" on the man's back. At this moment, which will be matched later in the play, in the confrontation scene between Major Walsh and Chief Sitting Bull, the young Clarence screams from the shadows: "Noooooooo!" (36). Clarence is there throughout the saloon scene, but he exists only in Walsh's memory because in 1881 he had witnessed the Major's violent treatment of the Chief and screamed in protest. This cry, then, is a terrible memory of a scream that only a return to the past will explain. Before the Prologue ends, Harry the wagon-master-cum-philosopher-cum-narrator provides the historical context that the play now offers. Briefly, he recounts Custer's Last Stand and, in no more than a phrase, the flight of the Sioux, and he reminds us that the tune we have heard from the boy playing "the music box" (as Robert Service calls him in "The Shooting of Dan McGrew") is "Garryowen"—General Custer's favourite. This tune will be repeated, along with Walsh's action and Clarence's cry, as the rest of the story is conjured up and replayed in James Walsh's tormented mind. This *Walsh* is a ghost story. Through staging, lighting, and a texture of repeated motifs—of gesture, speech, music—the ensuing drama shows us how a once honourable man fell from a position of respect and distinction into failure, violence, and dishonour, especially in his own eyes.

Sharon never intended to reach inside the mind of Sitting Bull, something she realized that as a twentieth-century, white, middle-class woman she could not do, so the Sioux chief became for her a symbolic, "saint-like figure" (see Wasserman, 1993), who should not be romanticized as a noble savage, but whose existence and eloquent speech illustrate the nature of a particular historical loss and the scope of an historical crime. From *reading* the play, comparing reports on productions (including recent observations by First Nations playwright Kevin Loring), and listening closely to Sharon's comments, I see the figure of Sitting Bull as heightened by Walsh's memory of him. Just as young Clarence represents Walsh's conscience, so Sitting Bull represents the ideals of courage, decisiveness, wisdom, and self-respect that Walsh betrays and that haunt him for the rest of his days.

In preparing its audiences for this journey into the past, Stratford publicity provided some carefully selected information in both its souvenir and house programs. The souvenir program had to cover the entire 1974 festival season, with pride of place understandably given to the main stage productions of *King John*, *Love's Labours Lost*, and *Pericles*, but it did include a short summary of the received history on Sitting Bull's years in Canada, his friendship with James Walsh, and the Canadian government's perfidious treatment of the Sioux. Mindful of American tourists, it did not describe the American treatment of Indians in general or comment upon Sitting Bull's treatment after he returned to the United States. The Little Big Horn became simply the battle in which General Custer and his "dedicated troops were destroyed to a man." Ironically, the house program was even more calculated not to offend, and I say *ironically* because one of the most urgent messages of this play is the warning to Canadians not to sell their own souls to appease American bullies. In addition to the usual information about cast and production and several excellent production photographs, it included a map showing the area south to Little Big Horn and north to Fort Walsh and Wood Mountain to help audience members locate the places referred to in the play, and it described Custer's last battle by stressing the story of the horse, Comanche, which survived the carnage to be paraded, riderless and draped in mourning, by the men of the Seventh Cavalry regiment. There was no information on Major Walsh, but there was one short quotation from Sitting Bull in which he stated why he had entered Canada in the first place ("my people had been persecuted by the Americans") and why he refused ever again to speak to the Americans, and then concluded with his insistence that the country he had left behind was his.

Reviewers, however, were much less circumspect. Bob Allen, writing in the *Vancouver Province* was pleased that Stratford, this "creaking flagship of established Canadian professional theatre," had finally discovered the West and "staged the work of a West Coast writer." Allen had seen the New Play Centre's reading in 1972 and he had praised the Theatre Calgary premiere; he was convinced that the play was important, and he recognized that it was much less about the Sioux than about a decent man who "can't act in a manner consistent with his lofty principles" and about problems facing Canada in 1974. Dave Billington of the *Windsor Star* dismissed Custer as "a villain" and he praised Pollock for telling the world about James Walsh ("a symbol of all that we in Canada like to believe about ourselves") and Sitting Bull (the "Indian mystic and warrior shaman"). But he did not like what he called the "potted history" of the play. Audrey Ashley (in the *Ottawa Citizen*) was more enthusiastic; despite flaws (she found the flashback technique confusing), she praised the actors, called the evening magical in the tradition of Greek tragedy, and concluded that "the real hero of the evening is the director, John Wood." In two pieces for the *Globe and Mail*, the shrewd Herbert Whittaker applauded the acting, the staging, the changes made to the play after the Calgary premiere, and the "dreadful inevitability [of] this wide sweeping tragedy." And so it continued, with the exception of the late Urjo Kareda, at that time a freelance drama critic for the *Toronto Star*. Although he described the play as serious and worthy (in a sense damning it with faint praise), he did not like the Prologue or the clichéd characterization of Sitting Bull. *Walsh*, he said, was a "historydrama thick with atmosphere," but thin on imagination.

Nevertheless, Sharon Pollock had made her debut at one of Canada's two most prestigious national theatres. Up to the mid-seventies Stratford had not welcomed or supported Canadian playwrights. James Reaney had received a few productions in the sixties, with *The Donnellys* given one rehearsal hall performance in 1970, and John Herbert's *Fortune and Men's Eyes* received a grudging single workshop production in 1965, but very little else had been attempted until an adaptation of Roch Carrier's *La Guerre, Yes Sir!* got a respectable run in the Avon Theatre in 1972 and Michael Ondaatje's *The Collected Works of Billy the Kid* was done on the Third Stage in 1973, as was Henry Beissel's innovative puppet-play *Inuk and the Sun*. Stratford did a host of foreign works in translation (by Canadians) and a number of single workshop attempts, but they gave no particular attention to new plays by Canadians until the early 1990s, when Sharon and her work returned to Stratford. That said, she was well enough treated in 1974. They put her, Amanda, and Michael up in the Sanders Hotel (today the elegant Stone Maiden Inn) at 123 Church Street, in a residential area about a fifteen-minute walk from the Third Stage, and put her play in the hands of a talented director and an excellent cast. By the time she reached the National Arts Centre in the early 1980s, John Wood was its (English-language) artistic director and he brought to the Centre his serious commitment to Canadian plays. As for Sharon Pollock, she had become the playwright of the hour.

John Wood gave *Walsh* what is, to date, its largest, most ambitious production on the Centre's main theatre stage in 1983. When the play began its two-week run on May 10th, it was in repertoire with *Who's Afraid of Virginia Woolf* and part of a rich season that included Shakespeare, Chekov, and Coward, as well as other contemporary works like Brian Friel's *Translations*. What's more, it did reasonably well at the box office with an average attendance of about seventy percent of the house. According to NAC records, audiences were responsive and appreciative and on one evening gave the play a standing ovation. The same cannot be said, however, for the critics. I have found many fewer reviews for this *Walsh* than for either of its previous productions, and the reasons may lie in the time of year, the geographical location, or in the tastes and interests of a bilingual national capital. The most thoughtful of the reviewers was Edgard Demers writing in *Le Droit*, who found the play too literal in its treatment of history and wished Pollock had taken more liberties with the facts. Like other reviewers, he was not thrilled with the casting (again, no Métis or First Nations actors), but he praised the set design. Audrey Ashley, who had liked the Stratford production, was less impressed this time. She found the play lacking in energy until the second act, and she resented being lectured at by four actors in the opening scene (a point I will return to). But by far the most savage commentary (indeed, perhaps the worst review, among hundreds of good ones that Sharon's plays have received) came from Adele Freedman in the *Globe and Mail*. Freedman loathed the play and her attack, near the start of the run, may well have discouraged theatergoers and reviewers alike. She described the play as "given to pedagogy and platitudes" and saw "few signs of life in this long-winded production." She bristled at the play's "Big Lessons"; she deplored the set; and she accused the Centre of "mounting the play to capitalize on the issue of native rights raised by the Constitution." (Canada's new, repatriated, constitution, including the Charter of Rights and Freedoms, came into force in the spring of 1982 and a new Indian Act was proclaimed in 1985, making the early 1980s a highly charged political period in the country's history.)

This is a nasty review, but it does raise some important questions: Why did this production not achieve more critical success? What was done differently that may have adversely affected its reception? And was there really so little to approve of? In answer to the first question, I can only suggest that the times had changed enough from the early seventies to make the play's subject seem no longer new or challenging and that other aspects of civil liberties and nationalism (such as Quebec separatism) were uppermost in people's minds. Quite possibly, if *Walsh* was not dated (and I do not believe it was, or is), then its first historical moment had passed, and, in a climate like this, Freedman's review provided the *coup de grâce*. My next two questions are more interesting to ponder—and more revealing. Sharon had continued to work on the script and to make small but important changes. For some reason, she and Wood had decided to move more historical information to the beginning of the play and distribute the details among four characters—McCutcheon, MacLeod, Harry, and Louis.[2] The result was a slow start on the large, stark set, and this beginning would, understandably I think, bore or exasperate critics. Sharon also made minor changes to the cast: Pretty Plume, Sitting Bull's wife, was replaced by Tahca Ska, his daughter, and another NWMP officer was added, but she retained the figure of Mary Walsh and the dream-like scene when Walsh reads a letter from home and responds to his wife's sadness—a scene that adds humanity and complexity to the man's character. Casting was beyond her control because, like Stratford, the NAC drew on its acting company to cast Benedict Campbell as Walsh and Ray Jewers (who spoke with a slight but noticeable British accent) as Sitting Bull. Unfortunately, neither actor found much favour with the critics. The one generally agreed upon bright spot was a young Paul Gross in the role of Clarence. And that leaves the set designed by Sue LePage. Production photographs, and the maquette, suggest that Edgard Demers was right to praise it. LePage created a large raked disc, with a forward thrust, for the main playing area, and behind this she placed ramps and a cyclorama which, when back-lit, gave the sense of a world falling off into space or of a far distant horizon against which the tragic action of the play would unfold. Clearly, this powerful set was a symbolic presence that could have evoked the wide expanses of a prairie landscape, the curve of a so-called new world, the sacred circle of Sioux cosmology, or the vicious circle of Walsh's life and of the play's structure. It may also have given concrete form to Walsh's disturbed state of mind—becoming the stage on which his memories haunt his present. Whatever associations it conjured up, it could in no way have been mistaken for a realistic, let alone a factual or literal, representation of anything. Perhaps, however, it simply dwarfed the characters, over-whelming them and their tragic story instead of complementing or enhancing the play's epic quality.

Whatever went wrong with *Walsh* in 1983, the NAC production was not as successful as the Stratford one, and Wood himself thought the Stratford production was better. If there are lessons in this, however, they have as much to do with the vicissitudes of casting and physical space, the intangible and unpredictable mood of the times, and the vagaries of whatever we mean by *taste*, as they do with the subject or the style of the play. As for the dramatic qualities of the script, the need, real or perceived, to explain a little-known event in Canadian history, cannot be allowed to impede the movement of the plot, even though Canadians' ignorance of their own history is the larger problem.

But if *Walsh* faltered in the NAC production, it fared even less well when it was adapted for the intimate medium of television. In 1986 ACCESS TV, Alberta's public television network, produced a telefilm version of the play cut down to just over fifty-eight minutes. The film was very low-budget (and obviously so) and not even good actors like Douglas Riske, as Walsh, and Rick McNair, as Harry, could make lively theatre out of the simplified, linear narrative. The action looked mechanical, an effect stressed by the opening sequence in which a hand appears from off camera to set up cardboard, cut-out figures of the characters before we shift to an artificial indoors set of painted landscapes. This rather silly business with the toy-like figures is repeated in an otherwise important scene near the end of the play in which Walsh uses a toy train set to rehearse his planned NWMP surprise for visiting dignitaries. In the stage play this scene underlines the depths of cynicism and hypocrisy to which James Walsh has been reduced—he has come to see his life's work as nothing more than a cheap spectacle—but on television this device looks obvious and literal. As a television drama the play was reduced to a history lesson with a clear linear narrative but with little psychological depth, emotional complexity, or moral ambiguity.

When Theatre Calgary decided to mount a new production of *Walsh* in 1988, expectations were high, but behind the scenes and in the wings storms were brewing. A jubilant Calgary hosted the winter Olympic Games that year, and as is customary at these grand events, there was an Olympic Arts Festival to showcase talents beyond the merely athletic. The arts high-light of the Festival was to be a multimillion dollar exhibition, called *The Spirit Sings: Artistic Traditions of Canada's First Peoples*, of First Nations arts and artefacts in the city's beautiful Glenbow Museum. However, members of the nearby Lubicon Lake First Nation were angry with what they saw as white appropriation and commodification of native culture, and they set up pickets around the museum asking the public to boycott the exhibition. Prominent among the protesters were several members of the cast for *Walsh* and Sharon Pollock herself. She agreed with the Lubicon that it was arrogant and hypocritical of governments and the oil business (Shell was a co-sponsor) to mount such an exhibition while refusing to settle land claims or, as Sharon put it, to address "the very real rights of the indigenous people of this continent" (see Woloshen). According to Joyce Doolittle, *The Spirit Sings* was "splen-didly displayed" and attracted record attendance despite the picket lines; however, Sharon had shown where her sympathies lay.

Although *Walsh* was the Pollock play finally chosen as Theatre Calgary's contribution to the Olympics' arts program, it had not been the company's first choice. Sharon had been working on a Lysistrata-inspired script, with a Goose-like figure (recalling the Rebel Girl from "And Out Goes You?") at its centre, since the early- to mid-seventies, and this play, at first called "God's not finished with us yet," came to be known as "Egg." In 1986 Walter Learning had commissioned her to write a Lysistrata type of play to be premiered at the Vancouver Playhouse during Expo '86, the international transportation and communica-tion exposition in conjunction with the British Columbia centennial. But she could not complete the script; this complex piece proved intransigent, and her creative process stalled. With more time, the play to emerge from these years of struggle would be *Getting It Straight*, but in 1985 she could not see her way through the material. Meanwhile, Learning and the Playhouse had announced this new play internationally and the playwright had been paid. At the last minute, and amidst considerable embarrassment, the theatre was obliged to cancel the Pollock work and mount George Ryga's new play *Paracelsus*. But Sharon was not finished with "Egg," so when Martin Kinch, the artistic director at Theatre Calgary, wanted a new work by a major playwright for the Olympics, he commissioned Sharon to complete her script of the hapless "Egg." In the event, he only saw one act and after discussions, they both realized that it was far from ready. Once more the play was cancelled, although this time no promotional work had begun, and *Walsh* was chosen instead because, as Kinch told me, it seemed an appropriate play on an important western subject for a Calgary Olympics. I will revisit the sorry saga of "Egg" when the time comes to consider *Getting It Straight*, but it must be said that it is not unheard of for an artist to miss a deadline or be unable to complete a commission on time. The disappointment and frustration I have heard about on the subject of "Egg" must be viewed with these realities in mind: a work of art cannot be created on demand, and a writer can simply become blocked. There was, however, something about this particular work that refused to take shape, and I believe that this something was personal. Aspects of the script drew on deeply private, painful sources, and until Sharon could face her own emotional investment in the story she could not find the play she needed to write.

Kinch accepted this unfortunate end to his Olympic project with good grace and moved ahead with plan B. But his and Sharon's problems were far from over. He had asked her to do some revisions, which she did, in part, by reshaping the Prologue for presentation in 1980s dress, and this update heightened the relevance of the story and the questions it raises for late-twentieth-century audiences (whether local, Canadian, or international). But irreconcilable differences over directing and casting plagued the entire process. One thing Sharon had learned from hard experience with this play in particular was that casting would be a challenge, so her contract included a casting approval clause, but as the weeks passed and the rehearsal period approached, Sharon and Theatre Calgary could not secure her first or second choice of director, after which disagreements arose over the casting for both Walsh and Sitting Bull. Time was running out and the show had to go on, whether or not she approved decisions. Because she did not approve, she felt that her only recourse was to withdraw her name from all publicity for the play except the house program. It is impossible and unnecessary now to lay blame or settle scores. Suffice it to say that Sharon publicly expressed her support for the theatre artists, who, she said, "are working their asses off to give the best possible show they can" (see Woloshen). Her quarrel, she insisted, was with the management who had violated clauses in her contract that guaranteed her artistic control. This was not the first time, nor would it be the last, that she would find herself in such a position, and her reputation for being difficult or demanding stems, in large part, from her insistence on respect for the artistic integrity of her work (or any other artist's work for that matter). If an artist cannot count on respect for the artistic integrity of a work, then I have to wonder what she or he can cling to. Was Sharon, a senior playwright, as temperamental as Eugene O'Neill, as demanding as Beckett, or as shielded from coercion and interference by a bevy of middle-men as Arthur Miller or Tom Stoppard? I think not. If there is a bright side to this story of *Walsh*, it is that the show did go ahead despite all the noises off.[3]

Reviews of the production were mixed. Stephen Godfrey, in the *Globe and Mail*, liked the play which, he said, "still crackles with theatrical energy [and] soars with important ideas, passionately." He was more reserved about the production, faulting "Keith Turnbull's prosaic staging and monotonous pacing" and sharply criticizing Michael Kirby's Walsh and Ron Cook's Sitting Bull. However, Joyce Doolittle zeroed in on "the amount of historical exposition fed to the audience in a turgid, static first act" (by now a familiar complaint) as the key weakness of the play. She liked the set, the cast, and the acting, and she noted that all the First Nations roles were played by "native actors [who] lent authenticity to a piece about their own history." But when I look for a review that captures the full flavour of a Sharon Pollock play in production, I invariably turn to Brian Brennan, who was not only a perceptive, balanced, and knowledgeable drama critic but who also knew Sharon well, understood her approach to theatre, and had watched her development over the years. While allowing that *Walsh* "is a contemporary play [that] deals with historical material, the issues of Canada-U.S. relations, treatment of refugees and dealings between government and native peoples," which are "as fresh today as they were 100 years ago," he comes down emphatically on the shortcomings of this particular production. Because of its complex historical background and the "ill-defined dilemma" facing Walsh, the play, he insists, *must* have a strong production but, as he makes very clear, this production failed the play: "The cast ... simply isn't strong enough to pull the material out of the quicksands of historical documentation. Keith Turnbull's staging—which makes the show look like a nineteenth century Mountie pageant set on a carpeted ski-jump ... contributes to the overall sense of period-embalmed deadliness" ("Play bogs down").

But I should not leave the play on that sour note. *Walsh* had received a fine and successful production at Stratford, so clearly it could make a powerful theatrical statement about issues of importance. And the issues had not gone away over the fifteen years between its premiere and 1988, a repatriated constitution, Bill of Rights and Freedoms, and a revamped Indian Act notwithstanding. Possibly Brennan is right when he says that the play works best when it is read, but only the test of an inspired production will answer the question and then only for that production. According to Kevin Loring, a young Lillooet playwright, who saw the Banff 2005 production of *Walsh*, the play was still powerful, the figure of Sitting Bull was convincing, and the production itself was galvanizing, especially when the Sioux approached the stage from behind and through the audience—a moment Loring described as hair-raising.

In this early play, and through its many revisions, Sharon articulated one of her abiding concerns about the plight of the basically honourable man who is trapped by his own desire to follow his conscience, who is used and discarded by the system he serves and is finally destroyed by a relentless sequence of events that he is unable to control. This is a timeless subject in Western theatre and film—from the Greeks through Shakespeare (in the history plays, in *Julius Caesar*, and above all in *Coriolanus*) to Verdi (in *Don Carlos*), Ibsen (in *An Enemy of the People*), right up to Michael Frayn (in *Democracy*) and Stephen Spielberg (in *Munich*). Such a man can capitulate and lose his soul or his mind, or he can rebel, in which case he will be ostracized or killed: either way, he is damned. Sharon has said that she has written the same play over and over again, and in this fundamental way she has. Settings and characters change, of course; her male protagonists often become female ones; her choice of actual historical subjects shifts to domestic, artistic, or even overtly autobiographical ones—and then shifts back again to history in *Saucy Jack, Fair Liberty's Call, End Dream*, and *Kabloona Talk*. But the central problem remains, and the question, one of the few really decisive ones in a life, continues to be: How can one person do the right (or the best, or the ethical) thing in a world full of contradictions, ambiguities, and illusions? In writing and rewriting *Walsh*, she also learned a great deal about making theatre, and the most significant aesthetic lessons were that her dramatic stories belonged within a temporal/spatial frame that focused attention on a central, witnessing and remembering character who would have to choose amongst a welter of contradictions, ambiguities, and illusions, as she, or he, tries to find meaning, to control events, and to locate some sense of identity and integrity in life. After *Walsh* she began immediately to apply these lessons to the writing of *The Komagata Maru Incident*, *Sweet Land of Liberty*, and *One Tiger to a Hill*.

***

While *Walsh* marked Sharon's public breakthrough on Canadian stages in the seventies, her next play, *The Komagata Maru Incident*, represented a different, more private and artistic breakthrough. On several occasions she has described this play as *the landmark* play for her because in writing it she began to explore dramatic structure seriously and to realize that she did not want to write naturalistic, well-made plays. As she told Margo Dunn in 1976, she was starting to see that the "'theatrical envelope' must be appropriate for the content of the play" (see Dunn, 4), and she was learning how to design that envelope so that it served the play's subject, so that content and form worked together to convey the kinds of stories she wanted to tell—stories about actual events, stories about Canadian history and place, but also stories about how and why we need to tell stories in the first place. Although she was by no means losing her interest in documented reality, politics, or history *per se*, she was becoming more and more fascinated with philosophical questions about how history is recorded, what is suppressed or misrepresented and *why*, how individuals and groups remember—indeed, how memory works as a living process—and how people come to perceive themselves and others or find meaning in human experience. As a dramatist, her challenge was shifting from finding the facts out of which to make a story to creating the appropriate way (the structure or "theatrical envelope") to present these facts in the process of being perceived, interpreted, remembered, and recombined into a story. I am not suggesting that her characters, as representations of developing, complex human beings, were unimportant to her at this time because they were—Hopkinson, the central character in *The Komagata Maru Incident*, is as complex as and possibly a more sympathetic figure than Walsh—but that she was grappling with dramatically effective ways to show, on stage, how human character develops, how it is perceived, how it is shaped by external events and internal, psychological pressures, and how it remembers, heals, or reinvents itself over time. Perhaps her process of artistic growth is best described as a juggling act: with each new play she wrote she tossed another new ball in the air and tried to keep them all moving until she achieved the balanced performance she would reach, for the first time, with *Blood Relations*.

But structure and philosophy aside, this new play began, as had *Walsh* and "Out Goes You?," with real events and history, a history so shocking, powerful, and little-known that she felt compelled to explain her choice of subject *in print* when the play was published in 1992:

> *The Komagata Maru Incident* is a theatrical impression of an historical event seen through the optique of the stage and the mind of the playwright.... As a Canadian, I feel that much of our history has been misrepresented and even hidden from us. Until we recognize our past, we cannot change our future.[4]

Two points are important here: one is her emphasis on the "optique of the stage and the mind of the playwright"; the other is "our history," and it is to this history that I want to turn.

The *Komagata Maru* was a Japanese-owned freighter that arrived in Vancouver's harbour at Burrard Inlet on 23 May 1914, shortly before the outbreak of the Great War. It had left Hong Kong in April carrying 376 East Indians, most of whom were Sikhs and all of whom were British subjects with the right to enter Canada as immigrants. However, by 1913 close to two thousand Sikhs had already settled in British Columbia, where racial prejudice had been mounting steadily. Ottawa also endorsed anti-Asian sentiments through a variety of measures aimed at restricting the immigration of non-white peoples, from the so-called "head tax," which Chinese immigrants were required to pay, to various Orders-in-Council such as the one stipulating that East Indians could only enter Canada if they travelled directly, by continuous passage, from India (a journey no steamship company provided). The official word in Ottawa, pronounced in 1908 by then Deputy Minister of Labour Mackenzie King (who became Prime Minister in 1921) was that Canada should remain a white man's country. In the music halls, these sentiments were more crudely expressed in a popular song of the day called "White Canada Forever" (see Grace, "Constructing Canada," 9):

> Then let us stand united all
> And show our father's might,
> That won the home we call our own,
> For white man's land we fight.
> To Oriental grasp and greed
> We'll surrender, no never.
> Our watchword be God Save the King
> White Canada Forever.

When the *Komagata Maru* arrived in Vancouver's harbour, the authorities were prepared to act and the newspapers joined the fray by publishing dramatic photographs with inflammatory headlines. The East Indians were described as terrorists and savages who would steal jobs from Canadians and destroy the Canadian way of life. "We are our own masters and have the right to say who shall become citizens of our country," pronounced one editorial in the *Vancouver Sun* on 24 May 1914 (54:7–12). The result of this furor was that all but a few of the passengers were detained on the ship for two months while the courts manoeuvred to make a refusal of these people legal and final. As the weeks passed, there were protest riots that resulted in many casualties, local residents gathered on the shore to watch the spectacle unfolding in the harbour, and conditions on board the ship deteriorated as the summer heat intensified. Allegations and accusations multiplied and at one point those on board hurled lumps of coal on the heads of men in an official boat when it attempted to come alongside for an inspection. Finally, the armed Royal Canadian Navy cruiser *Rainbow* made a show of force and the *Komagata Maru* left the harbour on July 23rd to begin its return journey to Calcutta.

Back on land, the story of William C. Hopkinson, a police officer and immigration inspector working for the immigration department and the NWMP, continued to unfold until he was assassinated by Mewa Singh on 21 October 1914. It was well known that he ran a spy ring of informers within the Sikh community. Less well known, or at least not openly acknowledged at the time, was the fact that he was of mixed race; he had been born in the Punjab to an East Indian mother and an English father. These personal details were especially interesting to Sharon, who came to see her character as a complex young man trapped by his mixed race heritage and corrupted by the racial prejudices of his time, prejudices that he had internalized (in her interpretation of his life and death) as denial and self-loathing. She grew to care about Billie Hopkinson and to sympathize with his dilemma at the same time as she deplored the racist attitudes that created and exploited the man and determined his fate—attitudes that she saw around her in 1970s Canada.

There is little doubt that the Lower Mainland Vancouver area to which Sharon, Michael, and the children had moved in 1971 was still experiencing the kind of racial tensions that had led to riots, labour protests, and the extreme immigration policies of the pre-World War I period. Ted Ferguson, a journalist with the *Sun*, was personally aware of white attitudes and racist attacks on local East Indians, and on their homes and temples, because during the early seventies he was living in the East Indian sector of South Vancouver, not far from the Ball/Pollock household in New Westminster. Despite newspaper reports about attacks on East Indians and the obscenities sprayed on temple walls, the dominant majority and local governments did little to address the situation. White Vancouver either knew nothing of the past or had chosen to forget. Within the Sikh community, however, memories were still fresh and Hopkinson's assassin, Mewa Singh, was considered a martyr. In December 1975, Ferguson published the first serious book on the history of the *Komagata Maru* called *A White Man's Country: An Exercise in Canadian Prejudice*, and while his book and research came too late to influence Sharon's play, she would not have missed Leslie Peterson's full-page article about the book in the 14 December *Sun* called "Our Shame Forgotten" in which Ferguson was quoted at length about the things he had witnessed that led him to delve into the past and write the book. In Ferguson's view, "the atmosphere now, the housing situation, the job-shortage situation are all similar" to the situation in 1914, and the parallels between the two periods were "ominous." It seems that the time was right to revisit this ugly episode, and Sharon's play premiered amidst mounting public attention to a worsening contemporary situation. In January 1976, while the play was still running, two public meetings, sponsored by the Forum for Young Asians, were held at the Vancouver Public Library in an effort to focus attention on current affairs and begin a frank discussion of racism in the city. Sharon participated in those meetings, along with Kathleen Ruff, director of the Human Rights Commission in British Columbia, Raminder Singh, the editor of *Ekta*, Dr. Pauline

Jewett, the president of Simon Fraser University, and a local municipal politician, Art Lee. In newspaper coverage of the meetings, both Ferguson's book and Sharon's play were high-lighted as prompting these discussions. The Playhouse could not have received better publicity for *The Komagata Maru Incident*, and Sharon herself could not have imagined a more propitious sequence of events for a play she dearly hoped would make an impact on the real world beyond the doors of the theatre. When Bob Allen reviewed the production for the *Province*, he picked up the key word from the December article on Ferguson's book and called his review "Play reveals shame of *Komagata Maru*," and he went on to provide a summary of the historical background to the play and to quote Sharon on her intentions with the play and her hopes for the role of theatre.

In her introduction to the play—that brief set of comments from which I quoted earlier and that have been preserved with the published text—Sharon explains that the actual events of the summer of 1914 were "seen through the optique of the stage and the mind of the playwright." In other words, she stresses the theatricality, or "theatre envelope," of the piece and her own personal interpretation of the facts. More important still, she describes the live performance of this play as an "optique" and her position as one of seeing: she uses the stage and her imagination to create perspectives or lenses through which an audience will look at and engage with the play. Because she chooses her words carefully, I see "optique" as an important indicator of the kind of play *The Komagata Maru Incident* is and of my constructed relationship to it. The play is meant to be seen, watched, observed, and I am positioned by the playwright as a spectator. Moreover, my spectatorship mirrors characters on the stage who are spectators *within* the play observing the spectacle unfolding before them and (in history or in imagination) beyond the frame of the theatre. Sharon told Bob Allen she thought of the play "as a kind of racist sideshow with Hopkinson as a sort of MC," and she continued to press her point by saying that she found him to be "a fascinating character [whose] mixed blood raises an interesting perspective." There are many technical ways in which Sharon establishes this situation of sideshow spectacle and the various roles of spectator, as I will show. But at the outset it is important to recognize that with this play, she discovered the framework for presenting the apparent social and psychological truths of dramatic action as relative (contingent on who is watching), multiple (each perceiver, including the playwright, will have her or his view), and dynamic (as the action unfolds, our apprehension of what we see shifts, changes, and hopefully evolves). Some reviewers have described this play as too didactic or sentimental (notably in its final treatment of Hopkinson), but I disagree. The play does use documentary and historical sources, it creates an individual character, in Hopkinson, who illustrates the impact of complex and destructive forces, and it throws a strong light on the subject of prejudice, but as *theatre* it exploits the capacity of the stage to intensify spectacle and to engage spectators in a revaluation of their own positions as much as an evaluation of a performance. And this—the theatrical envelope of spectacle—is where the power of the play lies.

The Komagata Maru Incident opens swiftly when the master of Ceremonies, known only as T.S., takes the stage and addresses the audience directly: "Hurry! Hurry! Hurry! Right this way, ladies and gentlemen! First chance to view the *Komagata Maru!*" (*KMI, CW* I, 101).

Right away the stage is set for the double spectacle about to unfold, and we, the audience, are commandeered as witnesses to what transpires on stage and to what the characters on stage witness in the Vancouver harbour at the foot of Burrard Street during that summer of 1914. The challenge hovering over the play is established immediately: Will we identify with the witnesses on stage (and, if we do, with which ones?), or will we see things differently and draw other conclusions? T.S. ends his opening welcome, so reminiscent of a circus barker's spiel, by introducing the characters, producing their props from his hat or from the inside pocket of his coat, and then activating them with a touch of his cane and, as Sharon indicates in her production note, "the scenes flow together without blackouts and without regard to time and setting" and the "characters never leave the stage" (*KMI* 100). Only T.S. is able to move about freely, to speak directly to us, and to withdraw to the side as he watches his creatures enact the story he has scripted and tightly controls. By the time we have taken our seats, we too are playing the part that T.S. requires; we are co-opted by the structure of the play, which offers no intermission or opportunity to leave or break the spell of what we are about to witness. Throughout the action T.S. reminds us of his manipulative presence. He intrudes frequently as a type of puppet master, and he plays many roles loosely identified as officials within the provincial and federal governments, or within the department of immigration, and even within Hopkinson's mind. Indeed, as the play progresses, he almost functions as the inner voice of Hopkinson's conscience, which has come to remind him that his fate, in the shape of Mewa Singh, "waits at the end of the yard" (131). And I say *almost* functions because, to my eyes, it seems that those in power, represented by the wily T.S., have framed Hopkinson by deliberately leaking his betrayal of those on the boat to the local Sikh community and setting in motion its revenge. To the degree, then, that this repeated announcement of Mewa Singh's unseen presence is part of T.S.'s manipulation of Hopkinson, T.S. is less an aspect of the man's moral conscience and more an internalized and undermining voice of his fear, and we can interpret this connection between the two in either way or, perhaps, as a bit of both. At some moments T.S. is the inner voice of conscience (like Faust's good angel), while at others he represents an inner voice of fear, helplessness, and coercion (like Faust's evil angel).

The main action of the play takes place in a brothel run by Evy, Hopkinson's lover, who sees the larger significance of what is transpiring beyond her windows and walls and tries desperately to warn him about the danger and corruption of the game he is playing. Although she loves him and penetrates his racial drag to remind him of the truth about his East Indian mother (about whom he refuses to speak), in an effort to save him from his internalized racism and self-loathing, she will not endorse his racist views or his espionage. In the central moral confrontation of the play, Hopkinson mocks Evy's ethics and dismisses her as a whore, but she does not back down: "I'm a whore and what you do is offensive to me! What you do would gag me! I'm a whore and when I look at your job, I could vomit!" (115). Ultimately, Evy is unable to help her Billie. Like him, she is trapped by the system that T.S. represents. As a woman in the era before Canadian women were legally recognized persons or had the right to vote, she is voiceless and powerless. As a prostitute she is a social outcast, used by the men who run things and just as disposable as Hopkinson.

The other characters in this sideshow are Sophie, the second prostitute, and Georg Braun, her customer and a German national who has shown up on Canada's west coast just as events in Europe begin to explode. Although they are not fully developed characters, they provide essential perspectives on the crisis unfolding in the harbour and within the brothel. Sophie is shallow and self-serving; for her the spectacle of the *Komagata Maru* is pure entertainment, and she is perfectly content to run spy errands for Hopkinson if she is paid. *Selling* services is her job. Georg is a shadowy presence, possibly an undercover spy for Kaiser Wilhelm or a double agent prepared to betray his own country. He too is looking for personal advantage and cares little about ethics or fair play or prejudice. But there is one more character in *The Komagata Maru Incident*—"A woman, a Sikh immigrant [and] British subject." This woman appears from behind "an open grill-work frame" that should give "both the impression of a cage and of the superstructure of a ship" (100) above and to the rear of the main playing area of the brothel. She too will be *introduced* by T.S. when, with a flourish, he pulls down a sheet covering her platform. Once revealed, the woman looks at and comments on the city of Vancouver, the people lined up on shore, who have come to jeer the passengers and applaud the tactics of the immigration officials. Through this symbolic figure, Sharon achieves several things. She provides information about deteriorating conditions on board the ship and a sympathetic voice (a *mother's* voice because this woman, a widow, has a young son with her) for a group of people who have remained voiceless in Canadian history; she also serves as a touchstone of compassion for Hopkinson who sees, even though he cannot admit it, something of his own past in this woman and her child; and, most importantly, she provides a further crucial perspective on the "incident" of the *Komagata Maru* because she watches those who watch her; she returns their gaze and challenges their vision.

The Komagata Maru Incident ends as it must because regardless of interpretation, Sharon was constrained by the historical record. In that record, the ship did return to India and William Hopkinson did give evidence in the investigation and trial that followed upon the murders of men from the Vancouver Sikh community. On 21 October 1914, he was poised to testify that his former spy, Bella Singh, had killed others in self-defence, but when he entered the Vancouver court house Mewa Singh was waiting for him with loaded pistols. Finally, Hopkinson would meet the fate that historical fact and the dramatic fiction of the play had prepared for him. With T.S. orchestrating the scene, we are told that Mewa Singh fires three times. A "bullet pierces Hopkinson's heart" (137). We do not see Mewa Singh, but we do see Hopkinson collapse at the touch of T.S.'s cane. Predictably, T.S. closes the play with a *"soft-shoe shuffle"* and *"a large but simple bow"* (137), taking full credit for the show before the lights go to black. However, Sharon has not left *her* Hopkinson as a simple stooge, erased by the powers that be, or as a hapless victim of Sikh revenge. She steps in where T.S. cannot to create a tormented, complex man who accepts his death as justly delivered by a fellow man, a Sikh, by having her character tell us that instead of resisting Mewa Singh, he opens his arms to him, says "Now!" and draws on ancient Sikh scripture for his final speech in which he invokes the Hindu god of death (and new life), "the four-armed one" with mace, club, conch, and ankle bells (136). By doing so he embraces his fate and his Sikh heritage, as did Mewa Singh who, in words quoted in the play, declared on the gallows that he was a gentle person, who would only be judged by God, before saying that he offered his neck to the rope "as a child opens his arms to his mother" (137). Like Mewa Singh, Sharon's William Hopkinson "opens his arms" to acknowledge his heritage and to embrace his death.

When *The Komagata Maru Incident* opened at the Vancouver East Cultural Centre on 20 January 1976, it had an excellent director, a fine cast, and extensive publicity. The play, commissioned by Newton for the Playhouse, was presented in the New Company series because it suited their mandate "to produce new plays of a contemporary, if perhaps controversial nature, suitable for an intimate space and a concerned audience" (Playhouse News Release, 2 January 1976). Larry Lillo (1947–93), who had co-founded Tamahnous Theatre in 1971 and was rapidly becoming an important figure in Canadian theatre, directed the play, and Sharon trusted and admired him. The set was designed by Jack Simon and the cast included young actors who have gone on to become popular and successful professionals. The Playhouse produced a detailed study kit with historical facts, a note from Sharon reminding audiences of a recent racist attack on an Indo-Canadian by white youths in Toronto, a discussion of prejudice, and two pages of comments "from the director" in which Lillo described the process necessary to bring a new play to life. "I am often exhausted from working on a scripted play," he explained. "But, with a new play, I leave a ten hour rehearsal period invigorated." Sharon worked closely with Lillo at every step in the kind of creative, collaborative process that she would thereafter always seek and often replicate. However, not all things behind the scenes were rosy. Always uncomfortable with the kind of apologetics that explained the documentary aspects of her work and classified it as historical or political or, worse still, moral, she became incensed by the Playhouse publicity that seemed to reduce her play to a recounting of events and, to add insult to injury, misspelled the words Sikh and Singh.

Shortly after the opening she wrote to Christopher Newton to protest a series of problems with the PR materials and with the house program: she detected a racist undertone to the historical summary, which she also felt misrepresented her play, and she pointed out the inexcusable spelling mistakes. She told him she was unimpressed when a member of the staff called her a bully because she had objected to these problems with the materials. And she went further. When she was only earning $5.00 per performance on tour, the money was not worth sacrificing her principles; she did not want the play to tour and was "even willing to lose money by engaging a lawyer to achieve that end."

In a handwritten postscript, she softened this threat with a personal assurance that her comments were meant only for him and by stating that it was more "honest" to speak up than to hide "in the bathroom biting a towel." Nevertheless, she was angry, and this was not the last time (as we have seen with the Olympics *Walsh*) that she would withdraw her support or threaten legal action. Newton replied on January 28th to say he was sorry the play had not been "a happy experience" for her but he disagreed that the materials were racist. He apologized for the proofreading mistakes, but he did not address her concerns about the misrepresentation, which I feel were well-founded. The play was introduced as being about a documented historical case of racism, and such a framing of the play does reduce the complexity and nuance of Hopkinson's dilemma. As for bullying, Newton reminded her that whatever had happened in the office she could "bully [him] successfully in five seconds let alone ten!" He urged her to agree to the tour and he ended by praising the play itself (he knew where to locate her main interest): "I think it's wonderful and I hope you believe me when I say that everyone shares my feelings."

Reviews of the premiere were mixed. Bob Allen called *The Komagata Maru Incident* "a well-crafted piece of work that says things of particular importance to Vancouverites," and he praised the ensemble acting and excellent set. Max Wyman called the production "a richly theatrical piece of dazzle [by] an angry lady," but he recognized the advances she was making artistically, her compatibility with Lillo's approach, and he encouraged people to see the play: "it tells a graphic story, it will touch your emotions, and, if it doesn't challenge you in the head, well, remember Sharon Pollock still has a long way to go—and she shows every sign of being worth travelling with." Richard Green criticized the play for what he saw as its "irreconcilable mixture of styles." Although the play began by reminding him of a "great piece of documentary theatre," such as Joan Littlewood's *Oh What a Lovely War*, it shifted into Hopkinson's psychological dilemma. Green's reference to Littlewood raises an interesting question about the extent to which Sharon may have been drawing on Littlewood's methods, or, equally possible, on Brecht's in a work like *Threepenny Opera*. However, I would be cautious about simplistic comparisons, especially when they are marshalled (as they are by Green) to diminish the play because, unlike Brecht, Pollock is interested in the complexities of individual conscience and personality and in a theatricality that illuminates the tragic manipulation of experience and the social constraints on individual perception, freedom, and choice. She is not creating documentary or social satire in this play.

This production of *The Komagata Maru Incident* was remounted for Festival Habitat, an arts program created in conjunction with the United Nations Conference on Human Settlements that opened in Vancouver on 31 May 1976. It ran for a week at the David Y.H. Lui Theatre in downtown Vancouver and this time there was no offending publicity or heavy-handed history lesson in the program. Moreover, this time Wyman was unqualifiedly enthusiastic, calling the play brilliant, important, and theatrically moving and successful. In 1977 the play received three new productions—in Kamloops by Western Canada Theatre Company; at the Edmonton Citadel's Rice Theatre; and at Toronto's Factory Lab Theatre. Judging from the reviews, which were generally favourable, the best production was the one in Edmonton. Sharon and Michael were living there that year while she taught at the University of Alberta, and she had come to know professor and director Jim DeFelice well because they were both teaching drama and at times combined their classes. Michael, of course, was available to take on the complex lead role. Moreover, DeFelice valued a serious play on a Canadian subject and he believed this one resonated with contemporary Canadian life. In our interview he recalled the parallels that he had perceived between this story of the East Indians off Canada's west coast in 1914 and the plight of Vietnamese boat people desperately seeking asylum in the late 1970s. In short, *The Komagata Maru Incident* had found its second ideal director, someone who respected the playwright, understood what she was trying to do, and cared about the play and its subject. During its run, the production attracted 99 percent houses, received positive reviews, and relied on nothing more than a standard house program with notes on the cast, a brief statement from the playwright, and one page of "Director's Notes." Obviously the play did not require elaborate explanation to be understood and well received.

Because Sharon's program comments are not the same as those preserved with the published play, I should note in passing that she began by stressing that the stage is an "exciting, dynamic place" for performing passionate plays about things that matter such as the "social inanities of our time, and/or the human condition." Once more she reminds me of Lowry who protested, with equal passion, that in his masterpiece about the human condition, *Under the Volcano*, he was "writing about things that will always mean something and not just silly ass style and semicolon technique" (*Collected Letters* I, 520). Then Sharon stated that the play is not a "re-enactment" of history but "the playwright's impression" of historical events "seen through the matrix of the stage and using expressionistic techniques," and the term "expressionistic" tells us something important about this play and about her kind of theatre. An expressionist play, as the great pre-World War I German dramatists knew, retains the central figure of a suffering individual trapped by the machinery of political and social forces beyond his control but rejects a realist representation of or psychological etiology for his fate. The suffering man (it is almost always a man) is both an individual to be pitied and a symbol of the human condition. Sharon Pollock's Hopkinson has a lot in common with Alban Berg's Wozzeck and Georg Kaiser's Cashier.

There are two more productions of *The Komagata Maru Incident* that I want to mention— its 1979 Alberta Theatre Projects (ATP) production and its 1984 television production by Alberta ACCESS. The ATP production was interesting for several reasons, not the least of which being the dramatically opposed reviews it received. Brian Brennan was thoroughly irritated by what he called the "propaganda" of the play itself, and he chastised Sharon for failing to consider both sides of the story, for ignoring the fact that the Sikh who chartered the ship in the first place was, as he put it, "a militant Indian nationalist with German connections," and for writing a play that was "a didactic history lesson, filled with righteous attitudinizing and presented in pseudo-Brechtian epic style" with "hortatory statements." He liked the set and praised some of the acting, but he described the role of the Woman as "impossible," and he dismissed Evy as a "whore with a heart of gold." Rising to the defence of her play, Sharon fired back with a letter to the editor of the *Calgary Herald*, where Brennan's review appeared, correcting his facts and accusing him of overlooking the "basic injustice" of what had happened in the summer of 1914. She closed by calling his review one-dimensional, insensitive, and "not even redeemed by the presence of a 'whore with a heart of gold'" (54:8.7). Touché! Fortunately, John Hofsess was much more pleased with the play, which he found moving and stimulating. He described the structure of episodes, ironic juxtapositions, and emotional shifts as "original and flexible," even as he recognized that the play was "risky" and demanded a strong production. And, after seeing several performances, he was full of praise for Michael's "commanding" Hopkinson and for the characters (with the exception of the Woman) who he found to be "believable and memorable." He was delighted with John Hamelin's T.S. and claimed that designer Richard Roberts had "done wonders" with the small stage of the old Canmore Opera House where ATP mounted its productions at that time.

As originally cast, this ATP production had Diana Belshaw in the role of Evy but because of the disappearance and death of her mother she had to leave the play and Sharon stepped into the breach for the final week of the run. Understandably, local reporters wondered what differences Sharon found between being the playwright and being an actor in her own play. Sharon's reply was that the writer was more accountable than the actor, who only had to deliver the lines well, whereas the playwright had to take responsibility for writing them in the first place. Unfortunately, little was said about her performance as Evy except that it re-united her with her former co-star (harkening back to *The Knack*) and partner Michael Ball. Sharon continued to take her responsibility as playwright seriously by further refining her "author's notes" in the program to remind audiences about this forgotten event from Canada's past, an event overshadowed by the Great War and excised from history, and to insist on the importance of history. And she repeated her view that "Canadian history has been misrepresented and even hidden from us" and that we must know the past if we hope to change the future.

Perhaps to get this message across to as wide an audience as possible, it is necessary these days to resort to film, but few plays or novels can be successfully adapted. Certainly the success of *Walsh* was limited, and when it came to making a film of *Blood Relations* the result would be worse. But *The Komagata Maru Incident* works as a telefilm. Gene Packwood directed the film version, which was shown on 22 October 1984 as part of the Alberta ACCESS television's Canadian Drama Series, with Blair Haynes as T.S. and Graham McPher-son as Hopkinson. The play had to be cut from its full playing time to fifty-nine minutes (Hopkinson's long speech at the end was just one of the passages dropped), but as a piece of television drama it works extremely well, and its adaptation highlights aspects of its style and structure that can only be captured in a skilled stage production (if at all in live theatre). The kind of spatial fluidity demanded by the play as it shifts in time and space and from perspective to perspective are more easily achieved with a camera that can zoom in on a face, capture an apparent act of magic sleight of hand, or seamlessly bridge the separations between ship and brothel. Haynes was remarkably effective as T.S. because he was able to capture the exact mix of oily seductiveness of a circus barker with the insensitive authority of a bureaucrat and the aggressive bullying tone of a government boss. Being able to watch his expressive face in close-up added power to the performance and to the manipulative system he embodied. But most importantly, the medium of television emphasizes a crucial theme of the play, one that unites the structure and the story—that of a spectacle watched by spectators who are made complicit with what they watch. Without a successful staging of the play's visual theatricality, its necessary reminders that we are watching a performance that is itself being watched from a position within the play, a live performance will miss the point. But in this television film the visual dynamic of looking and being looked at is crystal clear. That said, a problem remains, and not even the fluidity of a moving camera can solve it. As almost all the theatre reviewers had noted, the role of the East Indian Woman on the *Komagata Maru* is problematic. She is, of course, both a symbol of the passengers on the ship and of all who suffer from racial discrimination. She is also a theatrical device since through her comments we get a sense of conditions on board and the mounting anger of the passengers. We need her, moreover, to add humanity and a private, personal resonance to the public persona of Hopkinson: she, with her son, is the rejected East Indian mother to whom, in his dying moments, he opens his arms. However, the Woman does not work as a convincing character. Either she needs to be more realistic—where is that child she talks to?—or she needs to be more abstract, a mere shadowy presence, a ghost even, a memory that exists only in Hopkinson's mind and mind's eye.

Since the mid-1980s, *The Komagata Maru Incident* has received very few professional productions. It was done in London, England in 1985, revived in Edmonton the same year, and performed in the spring of 1987 by the amateur London Actors' Showcase theatre in conjunction with a conference being held at Toronto's Macauliffe Institute of Sikh Studies. Since then, it has not received any serious attention. And yet its relevance has not dissipated. Racism is still with us; terrorism, racial profiling, and exclusionary policies are increasing; and Canadians still do not know their history. This play continues to have a lot to say. What's more, its style and structure, which were innovative, even odd, in 1970s Canada, would be more accessible to today's theatre audiences because we have learned how to play our parts in what are now called meta-theatrical plays that foreground their own theatricality. Whether or not we will see a live production of this play any time soon, Sharon Pollock learned a lot about her art through writing it and working with directors like Lillo and DeFelice. The lessons she learned about structure and about her own interest in a type of theatre that stresses the performance of a role as inseparable from an understanding of life, enabled her to write every stage play after this one, up to and including her most recent play—also about race and individual conscience—*Man Out of Joint*.

II: Making Waves—Television, Radio, and *One Tiger to a Hill*

For Sharon the mid- to late-1970s was a busy time. In addition to the writing, rewriting, and staging of *Walsh* and *The Komagata Maru Incident*, she continued to produce children's plays and to do a number of plays for CBC radio and television. Some of this CBC work was slight: radio scripts like "Waiting" (1973) and "In Memory Of" (1975), or episodes for television series like *The Magic Lie* (1978) and *Country Joy* (1979) brought in badly needed cash but offered little creative scope. *Walsh* and *The Komagata Maru Incident* (under the title "The Story of the *Komagata Maru*") were adapted for radio (and broadcast in 1974 and 1978 respectively), while *Generations*, which did not have its stage premiere until 1980, was first performed as a radio play, aired by CBC Calgary AM on 10 December 1978. But some of these pieces merit closer attention, either because Sharon had enough freedom to do interesting work or because the play went on to win a national award. And she was moving: in 1976 from Vancouver to Edmonton to teach; then, in the spring of 1977, back to Calgary to establish a permanent home; and, in the summer of 1977, to the Banff Centre's School of

Fine Arts for her first season as the Head of the Playwrights' Colony and the beginning of a long and rewarding relationship with the Centre.

Her first two television plays were directed by Don Williams, an Alberta-born actor, director, and writer who cut his theatre teeth with John Hirsch in Winnipeg. He first met Sharon and Michael in a Victoria bar in 1966 when the cast of *The Knack* was celebrating its success in the DDF finals. In my conversation with him he warmly recalled their friendship and the visits he and his wife made to the Ball/Pollock digs in Delta and New Westminster. In particular, he recalled her fascination with a film he was making circa 1969–70 about the Scots-Blood Indian scout, special constable with the NWMP, and hero to the Blackfoot, Jerry Potts, who has been immortalized by Guy Vanderhaeghe in his novel *The Last Crossing* (1996). Williams had hired Michael for this film and Sharon accompanied the two men as they drove the van to various locations for the shoot and discussed the western Canadian history of Potts, Sitting Bull, Walsh, and the NWMP. Thinking back over that time, Williams wondered if that film shoot was not the inspiration for *Walsh*, but whether or not it was, Williams and Sharon clearly shared a passion for history and an appreciation for physical place. When he approached her later for a film script about a policeman, she was immediately interested. He promised her a fairly free hand and a film that would be shot on location, not in a studio; within a few months and after three drafts, she delivered "Portrait of a Pig." And the fun began.

The "Pig" in the title is actually a fine young man called Michael who becomes a good police officer, decent, kindly, and just. By no stretch of the imagination does he deserve the label "Pig," which is hurled at him as he works his beat. The "portrait" of the title refers to the framing device Sharon used to establish Michael's motivation and commitment to his work. In the opening sequence a young Michael and his grandmother witness a terrible car accident, and the child will remember both the violence of the hit and run and the calm kindness of the attending policeman. In the final sequence of "Portrait of a Pig," Michael is shot by his own grandfather when he tries to disarm the old man, who is mentally disturbed and prepared to kill any "Pig" who comes after him. As Michael lies dying, a small boy watches terrified until a kindly policeman gently moves him away. The play touches on many of Sharon's perennial interests—childhood trauma, social responsibility, duty, family tragedy—and the title is clearly ironic. But that is not how the Winnipeg Chief of Police saw things. When Williams visited him to check on certain details, the chief insisted on seeing the script. Furious and unable to read beyond the word "Pig," he refused to co-operate and contacted a journalist friend who panned the play in the newspaper even before it was produced. This must be some kind of record for a playwright. Even *Eight Men Speak* got a premiere before the fur began to fly. I have not been able to locate a video of the production (only the audio portion and a script appear to have survived), which is a shame because despite its advance negative billing, Williams recalls that the play received good ratings from Winnipeg viewers and went on to be pirated in the United States. As Sharon's only cop/murder story to date, "Portrait of a Pig" had quite a life.

Nothing daunted by the film's notoriety and dubious afterlife south of the border, Williams and Pollock teamed up to make one more television film for CBC Winnipeg, and this one does survive complete. What's more, it is delightful, witty, full of humour, irony, and social commentary, and it was beautifully acted and produced. "The Larsons" (shown on 27 November 1976) began its theatrical life on radio as "The B Triple P Plan," directed by Irene Prothroe and broadcast by CBC Calgary on 21 September 1974, but the script really comes into its own as a television drama because it needs to be seen to be funny, never mind to be believed. The plot has many of the hallmarks of a serious Pollock stage play—social critique, an individual who resists an unjust system, and ironic family dilemmas—except that this time the hero is the feisty, larcenous wife of an old age pensioner. The play opens with Teddy and Katie Larsen sitting down to a meagre dinner; the calendar on the wall shows us it is October 27th and all the old folks have to eat is one sardine each and an egg. There is no milk, no coffee, and certainly no cookies. Teddy is disgusted. Determined to improve the situation, Katie puts on her winter gear, bundles Teddy up in several layers of clothing, and the pair sets off for Mitchell's Department store to do a little shoplifting. While Katie pretends to look for an expensive watch or clock radio and persuades the bored clerk to lay these items on the counter, Teddy stages a collapse down the nearby escalator. When everyone rushes to help the old man, Katie bags the goods. We catch up with them as they trudge along the wintry streets and arrive at a pawnbroker's. Cut back to the house: the Larsens have just finished a decent meal and are enjoying real milk in their coffee when an intriguing new government program is announced on their television. It is called HERP for Home Environment Rehabilitation Program, and old age pensioners are encouraged to take parolees into their homes on the government tab. Finally, here is a seemingly honest way for the elderly to supplement their pension cheques and be able to eat properly. The Larsens sign up. Enter Johnny Streeter, a young ex-con who becomes a member of the family and initiates a real estate scam to improve the family finances until, that is, his former gang spots him, whereupon Johnny disappears taking the old couple's savings with him. The show ends with Katie and Teddy welcoming their next HERP-boarder who, to Katie's delight, is an ex-counterfeiter. Dismayed, Teddy tries to turn the young man away, but the curious Katie prevails and in he comes. As the door closes she is quizzing him on his skills, and we can guess what will happen next.

With Jane Mallett as Katie Larsen, George Wright as Teddy, and John Boylan as Johnny, the acting is still a joy to watch and because it was shot on Winnipeg streets, in Eaton's, and in a real house, the film retains a freshness and authenticity impossible to achieve in a studio. As Williams told me, there were items in the newspapers about the sorry plight of pensioners reduced to eating dog food because they were so poor, so the subject was topical and, despite its light touch, the play addressed a real social problem. Sharon went to Winnipeg for some of the filming and Williams found her easy to have around, eager to learn about film-scripts and film-making, and ready to collaborate on the practical adjustments demanded by the medium. Making "The Larsens" must have been fun, and the final product is several cuts above the standard television soaps of the day. In *Turn Up the Contrast*, Mary Jane Miller devotes several pages to Don Williams's films, and she singles out "The Larsens" for its portrayal, "in moving detail," of what life on an old age pension is like (347).

But perhaps the chief pleasure of the piece lies in Sharon's creation of the indomitable Katie Larsen who can take on the system with a smile and beat it at its own game.

Sharon has never written a war play, if one defines such a play as set in the trenches of the Great War like R.C. Sherriff's *Journey's End* (1929). She has, however, written about the impact of past wars on civilians and refugees in *Walsh* and *Fair Liberty's Call*, and in *Getting It Straight* she explored the impact of the horror of war on a woman and mother, who watches the spectacle unfold through the news and is driven mad by the immorality of military aggression. She has also written one play about the consequences of Vietnam: *Sweet Land of Liberty*. The best Canadian drama and fiction (to date) about war has, in fact, been written since 1977 in the shadow of Vietnam and at a remove from the front in both time and experience. Timothy Findley's novel *The Wars* (1977), Jack Hodgins' *Broken Ground* (1998), Jane Urquhart's *The Stone Carvers* (2001), and Joseph Boyden's *Three Day Road* (2005), all recreate scenes from the Great War as traumatic memories framed by an individual or communal need to relocate perspective and find meaning in a contemporary home-front world. They are memory novels by writers who never fought in a war but for whom the present, post-World War One world is haunted and irrevocably altered by the past. The same thing can be said about many of our best war plays from John Gray's and Eric Peterson's *Billy Bishop Goes to War* (1981), R.H. Thomson's *The Lost Boys* (2002), and David French's *Soldier's Heart* (2002) to Vern Thiessen's *Vimy*: either they are memory plays, written by men who have never been soldiers, in which one central character re-enacts or remembers battle scenes or, as in French's play, because a son needs to understand what happened in war to damage his father, that father is finally made to tell his story and, by telling it, frees himself from crippling memories. The same points could be made about novels and plays that represent World War Two such as *The English Patient* (1992) and *Obasan* (1983), or *Burning Vision* (2003). These writers choose the subject of a past war to expose the consequences of violence, to explore the lies and propaganda promulgated during war, or the inhumanity of war, and to reflect upon its apparent inevitability. *Sweet Land of Liberty* very much belongs with these creative reconstructions of war.

Commissioned for CBC radio's "Soundstage" by Calgary's Bill Gray, *Sweet Land of Liberty* first aired nationally on 2 December 1979 and was rebroadcast on 22 April 1990. In 2005 it was published in volume one of Sharon's *Collected Works* and in the early twenty-first century context of terrorism and the American invasion of Iraq it would be a timely play to stage. Set primarily in the haunted memory and mind's eye of an American Marine who has deserted from Vietnam and found his way to Canada, it provided Sharon with a vehicle for exploring a number of post-Vietnam, war-related issues and Bill Gray with an opportunity to push the boundaries of his medium beyond the previous generation's concept of theatre on radio to a new form of *radio drama* that was genuinely *aural* because it made an innovative technological soundscape integral to a play. Gray now lives in Vancouver and runs Raging Ruby Pictures, but in the late seventies and early eighties he was working in Calgary as a director/producer for CBC. During his Calgary years he directed several of Sharon's radio plays, but *Sweet Land of Liberty* was the most exciting and successful; it is the one he remains most proud of, not only because it won an ACTRA (Association of Canadian

Television and Radio Artists) Nellie Drama Award in 1980 for the best radio drama but also because it was very well done *for radio* and still holds up nicely.

The inspiration for the play came from two incongruously disparate sources: Tchaikovsky's music for his ballet *Swan Lake* (1876) and a book about Vietnam by Michael Herr. On the day Gray invited Sharon to lunch to discuss the possibility of her writing a new radio play for him, he brought with him a hand-wound music box that could play this music at different speeds; the device intrigued him so much that he hoped she could integrate the music into a story. The subject on her mind that day, however, was not classical ballet. She told Gray that she had been reading Herr's *Dispatches*, his eyewitness account of working as a journalist embedded with the American army in Vietnam. The familiar music, apart from its beauty, evokes a world of innocence, grace, and romance in which evil and betrayal lead to the death of the swan, but the scenes Herr describes are so violent and horrifying that they produced what he calls "a common failure of feeling and imagination" among the troops and "an alienation beyond tolerance" (44). Nevertheless, Sharon took the music box home with her after lunch that day, and from these extremely dissonant ideas she created her play. Listening to *Sweet Land of Liberty* again (as he was in December 2004 when we met) reminded Gray about the excitement he felt creating this play, his regret that the music box, which Sharon returned to him, ended up broken and discarded, and the profound emotion that this production still evokes.

The play has a double, interconnected plot. Its primary story concerns the fate of Tom, the ex-Marine, Vietnam vet and deserter, who is clearly suffering from post-traumatic stress and shoots himself in the frame scene of the play. The secondary story, which complements Tom's, involves Rena Harris and her young son Stevie. Rena is separated from an abusive husband and is trying to rebuild her life. The lives of these three people connect by sheer accident on a bus from Calgary to Lethbridge, Alberta, where Rena and Stevie live and where Tom will be within easy reach of Writing-On-Stone Provincial Park. While Rena sleeps on the bus, Tom befriends Stevie in whom he sees aspects of his former childhood self. Two weeks later, Rena takes Tom in as a boarder, but she soon begins to understand that he is severely disturbed because of his war experiences and completely estranged from his family, who live in Montana just across the Canada-United States border from Writing-On-Stone Park.

All this information about Tom, Rena, Stevie and their developing affection for each other emerges through a series of memories and explanations prompted by the "cool, uninvolved voice" of an Interrogator character who is investigating Tom's suicide and his desertion from the Marines by questioning mother and son. We also hear testimony from one of Tom's Marine buddies who matter-of-factly describes the massacre at My Lai, the little girl running naked in the road with her skin on fire (an image that became symbolic of war atrocity), and various other horrors before stating simply that "anyone who didn't go crazy in 'Nam was nuts" (*SLL*, *CW* I, 207). Interspersed with the present situation of interrogation are Tom's memories of Vietnam, which are triggered by a phrase or a sound, such as Stevie's innocent shout that he will "Run! Run!" Voices from Tom's war experience frequently erupt into his present to shatter his grip on reality and plunge him into renewed terror and despair. Against this violent, reverberating soundscape, we continually hear snatches of the music box playing *Swan Lake* at different speeds and volumes, fading in and out of earshot. The aural effect of this layered, contrasting world of sharply juxtaposed or eerily blending, overlapping voices and sounds causes the distant and immediate past to flood the interrogation scene with complex emotion and meaning. The play, especially as *heard* through the temporal fluidity of acoustic space, shows us that trauma cannot be easily consigned to the past, that we are haunted by our memories of violence, fear, and death as well as by our sense of guilt and injustice, and that the horrors of Vietnam for those who fought there or whose job it was to report on events will not stay in that distant place but will stalk the survivors (and deserters) however far they flee. *Sweet Land of Liberty* ends with the explosive sound of a gun followed by silence and a dying reverberation. We have returned to the opening sequence of the play in which Tom arrives in Writing-On-Stone Park, climbs to an isolated ledge looking south into the Sweet Grass Hills of Montana and the town where he was born, and prepares to commit suicide by communing with an Indian who represents the ancestors of this land and appears from the shadows of Tom's imagination to tell him, in a phrase that echoes Berger's *Little Big Man,* "Well ... it's a good day to die."

Although this play won the Nellie for best radio drama, it did not meet with unqualified praise from Calgary's reviewers. Dave Greber appreciated the restrained sound effects and the strong story, but Bill Musselwhite found nothing positive to say. He was particularly annoyed by what he saw as "Ms Pollock" presuming to moralize about a "disturbed Vietnam war vet" when the subject "has already been done to death" and the playwright was neither in Vietnam nor knowledgeable enough about such vets "to write with moral authority on the subject." Not even the acting pleased him. However, in my view the cast was uniformly good: Miles Potter played Tom with sensitivity; Heather MacCallum made Rena's story a resonant counterpart to Tom's; Alan Maitland did a fine job as young Stevie, and Michael Ball created a three-dimensional character out of Tom's patriotic father who rejects his son for deserting comrades and country because he cannot grasp the complexity of Tom's position or forgive his son for being human. As the representative of blind obedience to authority, this domineering, unforgiving father embodies the real threat to liberty in both the family and the nation, but Michael brings him off with just enough compassion to make him credible. Whether or not Sharon had the perceived credentials to write about the impact of war is irrelevant. *Sweet Land of Liberty* is less about battle scenes over *there* than it is about the trauma we bring home with us or the wars we foment at home through hypocrisy, ignorance, and arrogant imperialism in the name of liberty. Moreover, through Ross Pollock's behaviour, Sharon could imagine how a father's rejection might injure a son, and the sub-plot of domestic abuse is part of this play for a reason: it illustrates on the private, domestic level the violent resentments and need for power over others that fuel wars. Not until *Angel's Trumpet* in 2001 would Sharon again tackle so openly the theme of domestic marital violence, but this too was a battlefield she knew well, and the central drama of *Sweet Land of Liberty* is not Vietnam *per se* but the far more pervasive war going on all around us and the costs we incur when we demonize others, seek power and control at any price, and choose oppression over liberty. The "sweet land" of this play is not Canada, where Tom lives in exile, or the United States, which betrayed liberty in Vietnam, but the sacred native ground of Writing-On-Stone Park and the Sweet Grass Hills where in death Tom's spirit will be free.

In the late seventies Sharon wrote two interesting children's plays, both of which were commissioned by ATP. Douglas Riske and Lucille Wagner founded the company in 1972 with initial funding from a LIP grant (the federal government's Local Initiatives Program) and further support from Calgary's school boards and the province. Wagner served as the managing director, Riske as artistic director, and ATP's mandate was to develop and produce new Canadian, especially regional, plays. Until it moved into downtown Calgary's Perform-ing Arts Centre in the mid-eighties, ATP made its home in the historic Canmore Opera House, a renovated log structure that had been relocated from Canmore to Calgary's Heritage Park in 1966. Today ATP is a thriving, successful company and its early years are remembered for promoting the work of playwrights like Sharon, John Murrell, Carol Bolt, and Tom Hendry, as well as children's plays by Paddy Campbell.

Sharon was ATP's playwright-in-residence for the 1977–78 season, and she has continued to have a productive relationship with the company, but her first work for them has been largely forgotten. "The Wreck of the National Line Car" (as it was then called), premiered in February 1978, and "Chautauqua Spelt E-N-E-R-G-Y" played from 9 April to 1 June 1979. Both were original plays for children supported by the Calgary Board of Education as part of ATP's Theatre-in-Education Program, and for each ATP prepared detailed history and activity booklets. These booklets illustrate the extensive background research and colourful, interactive follow-up materials prepared by ATP to assist teachers and students with the plays—quizzes, dances, science or social studies spin-off projects or games, puzzles, guest lectures, special outings, and suggestions for dramatic or musical performances. Both plays toured extensively and the kids appear to have enjoyed them, judging from the letters and other items received by ATP. Most of the teachers also reported positively, although a few saw no value in the plays and no place for theatre in education.

Wreck of the National Line (the modified title Sharon gave the play for its publication in the *Collected Works*) is a light-hearted fable about the state of Canadian identity and unity a decade after the centenary. The action takes place on a train in the country of Adanac, which mirrors Canada in more ways than one. The five characters are Spill, the conductor of the National Railway that links all parts of the country, Quill, a prosperous businessman who represents Central Adanac, Tanner, a nouveau-riche type from Flat Adanac who sounds very Albertan, Trout who is poor and comes from Western Adanac, and Boris who "comes from Northern Adanac where people sing and never speak—if they can help it." The set by Richard Roberts must have been delightful, almost the star of the show: it consisted of a three-dimensional map of Canada made of large building blocks that could be easily knocked down in the scene where the country falls apart, a toy train at a railway crossing, and a wheeled cart with benches, a prop box, and a fringed top, that was pulled by a tricycle equipped with horns, whistles, and noise-makers. The characters shout, quarrel, and moan about their troubles, accuse Central Adanac of hoarding all the resources, pull out the constitution and argue about its clauses, and disagree about the merits of the country to the south called BigWhere, which might take over Adanac. When the fracas reaches fever pitch

Boris sabotages the whole mess and brings the map tumbling down. He is buried under the debris, the National Line Car is derailed, and Adanac has broken into its various pieces. Horrified, the others pull Boris from the wreckage, assess the damage, and decide to rebuild Adanac by re-assembling the map. But almost immediately they begin to argue again and to imagine merging with BigWhere—until, that is, they remember that there is no medicare in that country and they would be sent off to wars. Finally, they agree to co-operate in creating a new map for the future; they sing together (Robert Clinton composed the music for Sharon's lyrics), and Adanac is back on track.

Wrapped up in this colourful slap-stick is a pointed message: Canadians must stop quarrelling amongst themselves or they will destroy what they have and lose it all to the United States, and they must redistribute the wealth, share their resources, and build a new future. This is a surprisingly nationalist message, favouring unity and resistance to the United States, coming from a writer who has often said that Canada is basically an administrative convenience. Theatre reviewers complained about the obvious political message, calling the play dull, monotonous, and difficult, and they criticized the acting and the music. Joy-Ann Cohen, writing in the *Herald*, may have put her finger on what really rankled with adults: she claimed that only the scenes of argument and collapse were exciting or dramatic, which suggested to her that destruction was more fun than creation. But I am not so sure: the children's responses (now in ATP's files) show that they were stimulated to think as much as to laugh and to imagine a continuing life for Spill and the passengers on the National Line Car.

"Chautauqua Spelt E-N-E-R-G-Y," as its name indicates, hearkens back to the years between the wars when the famous Chautauqua summer shows would arrive in small towns, set up their tents, and put on a variety of wholesome entertainments—short plays, lectures on science, art, politics, and exploration, musical performances, and sermons. Chautauqua, an American travelling education and entertainment movement that began in 1870, was popular in small, isolated communities across the Canadian Prairies between 1917 and 1935, and Sharon's concept was to celebrate the life of Growden, Alberta, in 1929 by showing how the townsfolk rally around when a Chautauqua performers' disagreement leaves the town with nothing but a collapsed tent and a couple of stage hands. The show must go on, so the locals use their own energy to raise the tent and showcase community talent. The "E-N-E-R-G-Y" of the title is what links the play to the curriculum as the townsfolk demonstrate their mechanical energy (the muscle power needed to raise the tent), their electrical energy (when the lights are up and turned on), and their creative, social energy (as they sing, dance, and perform together). But the play loses its theatrical energy when it lapses into a history lesson about Alberta's energy resources—fossil fuels, oil rigs, and the tar sands. Calgary and Chautauqua had a shared history because between 1917 and 1935 Calgary was the administrative headquarters for the shows, and some of the adults in the audience may have understood and appreciated the historical context for the play. But the story and characters are thin. The piece lacks the motivating energy and political edginess of *Wreck of the National Line*. Perhaps the most appealing aspect of the production was the set designed by Ron Fedoruk. Although the Canmore Opera House was small (after renovations the

31. Ron Fedoruk's set design for "Chautauqua Spelt E-N-E-R-G-Y" was especially effective because it
    replicated the tent-like atmosphere of the original Chautauqua entertainments. This play for
    children was produced by Alberta Theatre Projects in Calgary in April 1979 and directed by
    Douglas Riske.   *The design image is reproduced courtesy of Ron Fedoruk.*

theatre had 198 seats), this space allowed Fedoruk to stage the raising of the Chautauqua tent
directly over the audience (see Illus. 31). Once everyone was seated, the actors unrolled the
drop in the audience's lap and raised it in what Fedoruk described as "a good theatre
moment" that positioned the Canmore audience as Chautauqua spectators.

By the end of the 1970s Sharon had also had two adult plays produced by ATP: *The
Komagata Maru Incident* opened in January 1979 and enjoyed a good run, and *Generations*
received its stage premiere in the Canmore Opera House on 28 October 1980. During the
eighties, however, Sharon's reputation as one of the country's top playwrights would soar
with *Blood Relations*, and her time and energy were increasingly taken up with travel,
administrative work, and the premieres of major new plays with Theatre Calgary—*Whiskey
Six Cadenza* in 1983 and *Doc* in 1984—and with acting (Miss Lizzie in their 1981 production
of *Blood Relations*) and directing for them (the 1983 production of Orton's *What the Butler
Saw*). Some resented her apparent shift in allegiance from ATP to Theatre Calgary at this
time, and it was always a struggle for her to complete scripts on time. But she gave a lot as
well. Riske, who had studied Brian Way's theories on children's theatre, wanted serious,

intelligent plays for children, not fairy tale fluff, and Sharon pushed her stories into the realm of politics, local history, and current affairs, regardless of the age of her audience. For a few years, then, Sharon and ATP were a good fit. Her early support for the company was clear and unqualified. Her plays with them were challenging and innovative. And Riske recalls that the ATP production of *Komagata Maru* provided him with one of the highlights of his directing career.

Once Sharon and Michael had returned to live in Calgary, they not only worked hard but they also threw parties that are still warmly remembered as much for the chaos of the house with its children and pets, as for Sharon's good cooking. These were *occasions*, scenes from "the Michael and Sharon show," as one friend put it. Even local business meetings of the Guild of Canadian Playwrights were intense happenings, and Sharon was the loudest in argument and the first to ask tough questions. At one meeting in her living room, Paddy Campbell watched as Sharon and W.O. Mitchell, who were arguing about contracts *and* drinking, faced off so vociferously that they cleared the room. That is the sort of scene in the making of Canadian theatre history that I wish I could have witnessed because if anyone could match W.O. on booze and argument it was Sharon. John Murrell's sharpest memory of those days, however, is not about meetings, arguments, drinking, or parties. His is a much quieter, sustaining memory. He vividly recalls his conversation with Sharon after ATP's premiere of his first play, "A Great Noise, A Great Light." Reviewers had panned it and he felt demoralized until Sharon reassured him: "This was one of the most important ten-minute periods of my life because *Sharon Pollock* said how fine she thought the play was and how important it was to deal with our own history. Coming from Sharon, whom I respected, it was what I needed to hear to be able to go on."

***

Before they moved to Edmonton in 1976, Sharon and the family had spent three years living in New Westminster near the British Columbia Penitentiary. When a hostage-taking and shoot-out occurred inside "the Pen" in June 1975, the streets surrounding the prison immediately became a site for media and police attention, and Sharon had a front row seat. The affair ended badly with the death of a hostage, Mary Steinhauser, a young classification officer, and the serious wounding of an inmate, but it galvanized Sharon to conduct her own research and to write about life and death in a maximum security prison. The result was *One Tiger to a Hill*. The hostage-taking and its tragic outcome captured front-page headlines and extensive ongoing coverage as reporters tried to clarify how the hostage died and what, precisely, provoked the three inmates to hold fifteen hostages for forty-one hours before a Canadian Penitentiary Service tactical squad stormed the vault. At first, rumours circulated that Steinhauser had been stabbed by an inmate, but an autopsy proved that she had been shot more than once; in other words, she was killed by someone on the tactical squad.[5] As for the inmates, they had been struggling for years to have conditions improved and their basic rights respected, and of particular concern was the extensive use of solitary confinement to the "hole." The three inmates responsible for this hostage-taking were demanding improvements as well as safe passage out of the country. A commission of inquiry headed by B.C. Supreme Court Justice John Farris was appointed to investigate the affair, but his report was not made public and accusations of a government cover-up mushroomed after allegations surfaced that Mary Steinhauser was hated by the guards because she sympathized with the prisoners and may have had a liaison with Andrew Bruce, one of the hostage-takers.

But the drama unfolding in her own neighbourhood was not the only prison disaster that Sharon was reading about in 1975. On 13 September 1971 a protracted hostage-taking and a riot in upstate New York's infamous Attica Correctional Institute had ended in a spectacularly violent shoot-out in which police and prison guards stormed the yard where inmates were holding their hostages and killed twenty-nine inmates and ten hostages. Tom Wicker, a journalist with the *Washington Post*, who had a reputation for understanding and sympathizing with prisoners' views, was called in, at the inmates' request, to assist with mediation. Along with other journalists and mediators, he was sequestered to a yard inside the prison from where he could see the hostage area, hear the men's demands, and watch the unfolding tragedy and the final massacre. In 1975 he published his account as *A Time to Die: The Attica Prison Revolt*. Years later, in her interview with Pat Quigley, Sharon singled out Wicker's account as especially important to her, and when I read the book I could see why. *A Time to Die* provides a tight chronological narrative of the days leading up to and immediately following the six-minute shoot-out. It includes several grainy, but powerful, black and white photographs of the siege, the dead, the debris from the riot, and the treatment received by inmates after the shoot-out (roughly two-thirds of them were non-white, chiefly Afro-Americans), when they were paraded naked in front of the armed guards. Interspersed with this narrative are Wicker's criticisms of the penal system, its laws and overcrowded, ageing facilities, and, more telling still, his personal perspective on the surly, antagonistic guards who brought the observers their food and his account of the prisoners' claims. At one point he describes listening to their requests and hearing them say that because they were being treated worse than dogs, they had decided to at least die like men.

There is one more aspect of Wicker's narrative that is relevant to Sharon's play: he wrote his story in the third person, but he called his witnessing journalist-character "Tom Wicker." Reading this narrative today, when so much has changed in journalistic conventions and eye-witness reporting, and autobiography is so popular, this voice sounds odd, but in his Preface to the 1994 reprint of *A Time to Die*, Wicker explains that he believed the device of setting up his third person narrator-character as "Tom Wicker" would guard against sentimentality while freeing him to be more truthful; his model was Norman Mailer's *The Armies of the Night*. Whether this narrative device works or not in *A Time to Die*, the book inspired Sharon to create an analogous perspective for her play in the narrator-character of Everett Chalmers, the lawyer who is called in to mediate but who ends up helplessly witnessing the violence. Because the Chalmers character is so important in *One Tiger to a Hill* and has received some sharp criticism from theatre reviewers, it is worth paying close attention to what Sharon told Pat Quigley in the 1990 interview conducted on the eve of the play's Stratford debut. In response to Quigley's reflection that Chalmers is the only hope left at the end of the play because he has been changed by the events he witnessed, Sharon admits that she has "often wondered where Chalmers is and who he's telling this story to," and she goes on to explore some possible answers. Perhaps, she muses, there is an inquiry and "Chalmers is basically talking to somebody in a formal situation," or perhaps "he's gone to a psychiatrist about what's happened to him" (see Quigley, 37). Typically, however, Sharon does not stop with two possible explanations of the character, the play's structure, or its meaning.

In a move so natural and characteristic that I can hear her talking, thinking out loud, weighing multiple choices and their consequences for her play's meaning *in the theatre*, she continues:

> However, there is a third possibility, which is perhaps the one I like best: I think of Chalmers as being some ordinary person who got caught up in this, and who this actually happened to, and he's standing up and telling the people who are there in the theatre: "This is what happened to me." I think of Tom Wicker who wrote a very interesting book about the Attica prison. He was very much like Chalmers insofar as he was a left of centre journalist whom the prisoners at Attica asked to become part of the negotiating team. He went through the whole negotiating process and began to suspect what was going to happen, and eventually it did happen: a number of the guards were being held hostage, and they were all killed by the bullets of the force that came in to free them. Nobody was knifed to death. At any rate, his reaction to that was to write a book about the whole situation. And so I think of Chalmers as someone whose reaction to it has been to create a play. I think of him as an ordinary person who has been up at the front of a group like Alcoholics Anonymous and said, "This is something that has happened to me." And as he's telling us, because it's the theatre we're in, we then begin to re-enact it, as opposed to simply standing there talking about it. (qtd. in Quigley, 37–38)

I like this explanation of Chalmers because it positions the character as a Dante or Ancient Mariner figure (or indeed, like Marlowe in *Heart of Darkness* or the Consul in *Under the Volcano*) who comes back from hell or the brink of death to tell us about the horror he has seen and to exhort us to pay attention and learn by participating in the re-enactment as witnesses. Whether or not this witnessing works on stage is another matter and has every-thing to do with the collaborative art of making theatre.

Sharon began her research on the subject in 1975–76 by talking with ex-cons and prison workers in bars and on the streets of Main and Hastings in east end downtown Vancouver, an area of the city that is still dangerous to walk in. This infamous part of Vancouver is home to addicts, prostitutes, and alcoholics, the casualties of an otherwise wealthy, and largely uncaring, city; it is the area that Marie Clements would recreate in her play, *The Unnatural and Accidental Women* (2000) about the native women murdered there between 1965 and 1987. For a while, Sharon walked these streets with a drug dealer so she could see, up close, what this life was like and speak with the street people. As a result of this personal contact, she realized that it was, as she told Quigley, her own "naiveté that allowed [her] to sort of 'hang out' with them," and she felt a range of sharply conflicting emotions, by turns overwhelmed with sympathy for human beings whose lives had been so miserable since childhood and then shaken with revulsion and the need to get such people off the streets because they were dangerous. And through it all she believed that the people she spoke with were honest with her because they knew she was writing about the hostage-taking. But surely this *research* was foolhardy. After all, this middle-class white woman was taking a real risk in her effort to see and understand the underworld that shaped the inmates of the B.C. Pen and the characters in the play she would write. What's more, her very background mitigated against her understanding of their situation or her ability to change their lives. But Sharon Pollock, in one and the same breath, could take the risk *and* reflect on her own naiveté and confusion in doing so.

One Tiger to a Hill was not ready for its premiere until February 1980, when Richard Ouzounian directed it for Edmonton's Citadel Theatre. Ouzounian knew Sharon and Michael from their Vancouver days. He had studied theatre at the University of British Columbia in the early seventies and in 1974 directed Michael in a Frederic Wood Theatre production of Arthur Miller's autobiographical *After the Fall*, a play he suggests as a possible influence on the narrator-character in *One Tiger to a Hill*. He and Sharon often went drinking with Larry Lillo after Playhouse productions to critique the shows and assess the acting. But when his turn came to direct a Pollock work, these nights of shop talk, friendship, and shared experiences could not help much with the mounting of this challenging, new play. Remembering the experience for me, Ouzounian called the production "a fiasco!" The casting was wrong-headed; the rehearsal period too short (an all too familiar problem in Canadian theatres); one night a blood pack that was supposed to explode in the shoot-out scene burst ahead of cue, and, worst of all, panic erupted when the actor hired to play the Métis inmate Tommy Paul had to be replaced one week before opening night. Michael Ball stepped into this breach, died his blonde hair black, and brought it off. But he could not save the show and the company's British-born and -trained actors playing the psychotic inmate Gillie and the lawyer Ev Chalmers could not capture the colloquial Canadian speech required for a credible performance of this very Canadian story. In his review Mark Schoenberg, who would direct the premiere of *Generations* later in the year, was emphatic: "Whatever the flaws in the play, it is far better than the production that the Citadel Theatre" show suggested. On his list of mistakes, he noted that Ouzounian "failed to locate" the dramatic tension; that exploding blood packs (even on cue) and special sound effects did not enhance "dramatic substance"; and that the casting was either "riddled with error" or a downright "horror story." But where Schoenberg faulted the production, Nancy Schelstraete targeted the play itself. She especially disliked what she described as characters used as soap-boxes to harangue the audience. Apparently, in this production, the activist character, Lena Benz, the trigger-happy guard, Hanzuk, and the narrator-character Chalmers, all came downstage to address the audience at some length. Indeed, Chalmers with his "lengthy soliloquies" struck Schelstraete as "a mistake."

So just what does happen in *One Tiger to a Hill*? How is the play as written (and published) structured? And what did it take to transform the play into the highly successful production it was at Lennoxville that summer and at Stratford in 1990? Certainly, in its original published form (in the 1981 volume *Blood Relations and Other Plays*), *One Tiger to a Hill* carried some of the most detailed stage instructions that Sharon has ever provided. The entire action of the piece occurs within the cramped quarters of obviously "*makeshift offices*" in a crowded prison, and all the walls and doors must be "*skeletal*" (*OTH, CW* I, 216). Moreover, "the flow from scene to scene is most important," and she calls for transitions to be created through the lighting. No cross-fades or spots are to be used because the characters, once on stage, remain there in a "soft freeze" when they are not active in a scene, and the shifts from scene to scene and from one playing area to another are anticipated by increasing and diminishing the light, which never fades out completely. The only blackouts occur at the beginning and end of the play and between its two acts. Sound is extremely important for the composite design and mood and thus for the meaning of the play: at the beginning and while the characters take their places, we should hear "*a faint electronic hum* [that builds in volume] *which contains within it the clanking of closing doors, footsteps, and rattling keys,*" and this disturbing "*hum*" will recur, as will other "*theme music ... excerpts chosen from* The B.C. Pen Symphony *composed by J. Douglas Dodd*" (*OTH* 216). Sharon recalls Dodd's music as working wonderfully because it avoided any literal, technological duplication of prison sounds but captured an ambient soundscape that suggested entrapment within a prison environment.

The story itself is fairly straightforward. The title, borrowed from a chapter heading in Robert Ardrey's *African Genesis* and inspired by Sharon's reading of Konrad Lorenz's *On Aggression*, which had a snarling tiger on its cover, invokes the familiar notion that an anti-social person is like the non-social tiger and warns that the most powerful animal in an aggressive species will seek to control its domain at all costs.[6] Most of the action takes place in the present of the hostage-taking. While the prison guard, Hanzuk, watches, the prisoner, Tommy Paul, washes the corridors outside the rehabilitation offices. At the same time, but on another level, the Warden, Richard Wallace, the prison's Head of Security, George McGowan, and a rehabilitation officer, Dede Walker, argue about the death, the night before, of a man being held in solitary confinement. Walker wants an inquiry because she suspects that the man was murdered, but Wallace is noncommittal and McGowan is belligerent; as far as he is concerned, Walker's ideas on reform are "crap." "Look," he snaps, "we're not runnin' Open House with Multiple Listing, we're runnin' a maximum security pen" (*OTH* 221). Back in the rehab office area, a second rehab officer, Frank Soholuk, tries to make Walker accept the reality that there is little either of them can do about the man's death and that her befriending of Tommy Paul (he thinks their relationship is sexual) is stupid and dangerous. As the prison brass faces off and the two rehab officers argue, Hanzuk watches and taunts the prisoner. These three sets of paired characters occupy three increasingly charged spaces until Tommy Paul and a second inmate, the nervous, psychotic Gillie, suddenly make their move. The two convicts have managed to fill bottles with gasoline and they have armed themselves with knives. When Hanzuk is momentarily distracted, they turn on the rehab officers and a teacher, who has come to consult with Soholuk, and take them hostage. The rest of the action unfolds rapidly from there.

By the end of Act One, nothing has changed except the pressure: the lawyer, Ev Chalmers, has arrived to mediate, and Wallace and McGowan are confronted by Lena Benz, the loudmouthed, hard-drinking reformer who has come to bargain with them on behalf of the prisoners. In the office where Tommy and Gillie hold the three hostages we see how volatile the situation has become as the prisoners grow more desperate about their demands, especially their safe exit, and the hostages become more terrified. By the end of the act things have reached an impasse: Wallace is delaying for time but making no promises; McGowan is quietly organizing his plan of attack; Hanzuk waits on the sidelines, no longer in control of his small territory; Gillie erupts in moments of near hysteria; Tommy tries to control the situation and to understand Dede, who has reservations about what he is doing; and Soholuk's fear and anger mount steadily. He blames Dede for leading Tommy on, for refusing to help them break free, and for failing to grasp the gravity of their plight. Like the Warden, she hopes that something will happen to ameliorate the situation. "Sure wait," he sneers at her, "there's always time to die, isn't there!" (*OTH*, 224). And his bitterly ironic remark, really an accusation, not only evokes Wicker's title but points to the narrowing of their options—life or death with little time left to choose and no room to manoeuvre.

Act Two brings no respite. The prisoners and their hostages are only more tired, angry, and desperate. Soholuk calls Walker "an asshole" for sympathizing with convicted murderers. Neither Benz nor Chalmers can wring any guarantees about safe conduct or reforms from Wallace or McGowan, and Chalmers is squeezed into facilitating the ambush of the inmates. Although he suspects the prison officials of laying a trap, he has no choice but to lead Tommy Paul, Gillie, and the hostages out of the rehab office towards the door and the helicopter they hope is waiting to fly them out of the country. In the final moments of the play, as Tommy Paul and Gillie come out holding their hostages at knife point, Hanzuk shoots, Tommy falls to the ground, Dede screams "Nooooo!", and the guard shoots her point blank as she kneels by Tommy's body.

But *One Tiger to a Hill* does not end there. The last words of the play go to Chalmers who comes forward and speaks to the audience, returning us to the retrospective frame of the play: "I remember I stood there," he begins, before asking—"What were the lies? ... Is every-thing lies?" He knows he will leave the prison, return to a *normal* life, pick up where he left off, and with this knowledge "*He weeps.*" (*OTH*, 276). After which ... "*Blackout.*" We have come full circle, back to the opening moments of the play, which began with a "*Blackout*" and the sounds of "*a faint electronic hum.*" The play we have just watched is Chalmers' memory play in which he is a bit player, no more than an ineffectual witness *within* the drama. This frame structure, however, gives Chalmers more purpose because *outside* the play, the prison, and his memories, and after the fact, he can put what happened into some form of ethical perspective and shape the casual curiosity of the passerby into "a resolve to find out what happens to them—to us—when we condemn men to that wastebasket we call the pen" (218). By creating this *replay*, as it were, he forces us to see what he saw and to share in the responsibility for the way things are. Without providing neat answers or telling anyone what to do, let alone think, about such enormous social questions as prison justice and human rights, Sharon Pollock/Ev Chalmers shows us that we too are involved, and she/he asks us to learn about these difficult issues and to care.

It is, of course, no accident that the narrator-character bears her father's name. However, "Ev Chalmers" is less a representation of Dr. Chalmers than a mask for the playwright herself. Unable to identify to any degree with the Mary Steinhauser figure, whose do-good lack of realism makes a bad situation worse, she needed a dramatic double, a voice inside the play, and an ethical position from which to speak in order to dramatize this material. That she created a male character for her remembering narrator is not surprising. As she had said in the 1974 *Beacon Herald* interview about *Walsh* ("Spicing up 'bland pap'"), she liked to write about where the action was, and women were rarely initiators of the action. *One Tiger to a Hill*, like *Walsh* and *The Komagata Maru Incident*, centres on the men; they are the ones who strive, fail, suffer, and must live—if they survive—with their haunted memories. The structure of this play grows clearly out of the revised *Walsh*, so much so that even Dede Walker's anguished cry of protest at the end—"Nooooo!"—recalls Clarence's cry in the earlier play. Gradually, Sharon was discovering that on one important level her plays would be about the processes of memory and imagination, and that the action of her plays, wherever else they were overtly set, would take place on the interior stage of the mind. That "same play" she was writing "over and over again" was a product of her social conscience and was taking place inside her own head.

When Richard Ouzounian insisted on directing *One Tiger to a Hill* at the 1980 Lennoxville summer festival, he did so at some personal risk. Word about the Citadel flop had reached the festival board, and they threatened to fire Ouzounian if he persisted. But persist he did. For starters, he felt he owed Sharon and her play a better production, but he must also have felt the need to redeem his own reputation. This time he had a new cast, a new set, and brilliant lighting by Douglas Buchanan. This time *Tiger* was a stunning success. At its July opening it received a standing ovation, and Keith Garebian not only gave it a rave review in his Festival Lennoxville report for *Scene Changes* but also explained at length what worked so well and why he liked the play. He had seen another play about the same hostage-taking, Christian Bruyère's *Walls* (1978), and he judged *One Tiger to a Hill* to be the better play because where Bruyère moralizes and assigns blame Pollock "questions what happens to all of us [and] incriminates us all." Garebian praised the "sinewy" dialogue, the theatrical strategy of a narrator-character who casts the audience members as witnesses to the events, and the dramatic tension created through a careful control of space on Laurence Schafer's two-tiered set of metal bars, stairs, and dividers. For Garebian, the "whole experience [was] impressively etched by Richard Ouzounian's crisply disciplined direction" that effectively captured and deployed the pervasive tension of the play. For Ouzounian the production was a vindication. For Sharon, who was there on opening night, it was—in her own words to me—"my most wonderful night in the theatre."

The six weeks at Lennoxville that summer were among Sharon's happiest thus far and, in retrospect, they seem rather like the calm before the personal and professional storms that lay just ahead. She was back in the Eastern Townships, not far from her old school, and surrounded by some of the country's loveliest pastoral countryside. She and Michael had rented a house for the season with another couple, fellow actors and friends Fran Gebhard and Guy Bannerman. Fran, Guy, and Michael were all in the company, and while they rehearsed and performed Sharon wrote surrounded by a domestic whirl; her older children, now in their twenties, were either in university or working, but she kept the younger ones with her. According to Gebhard, Sharon never asked for quiet or for a room of her own, and she never complained about the mess. She could get up from breakfast, go to a dining room table piled high with laundry, and lose herself in her work—writing and rewriting, among other things, the play that was soon to become *Blood Relations*. As Fran put it, Sharon could focus in the midst of chaos and nothing discouraged her. Both Fran and Guy remember her as a good cook and always fun to be with because she could drink, argue, and analyse late into the night and never appear tired or hung-over. Her energy seemed inexhaustible. Beside Sharon, Michael was calm, undemonstrative, reserved, and gentle, yet able to tolerate her dominant style. To close friends, the two seemed happy together. When the real Everett Chalmers came to Lennoxville for a visit (and suffered a mild heart attack while there), Sharon was anxious to please him. Father and daughter got along well.

With the end of Lennoxville, Sharon and Michael, Fran and Guy, and Richard Ouzounian dispersed to various gigs across the country, but for a while they continued to stay in close touch, to meet and work together at Banff, in Winnipeg at the Manitoba Theatre Centre (MTC), or in Halifax, where Ouzounian produced both *Doc* and *Blood Relations* at the Neptune in the late 1980s. When *One Tiger to a Hill* received its American premiere at the New York Manhattan Theatre Club in the fall, Fran Gebhard went down to see it on opening night, hoping she would also catch Sharon. However, Sharon was busy at MTC by then; she had decided that things at home were more important than a premiere in New York, and on this occasion she was right. According to Fran Gebhard, the production was wonderful, but Frank Rich, the well-known and crusty theatre critic for the *Times* panned it. He found the play sanctimonious, the direction uninspiring, and the cast barely tolerable. New York notwithstanding, *Tiger* still had legs and it received two more professional productions before disappearing into the wings: in March of 1981 Sharon directed it in a National Arts Centre Atelier workshop production, and in the summer of 1990 John Wood gave it its most convincing and impressive production to date. Wood had wanted to do this prison play in the early eighties, but after seeing it at the Atelier he felt it still needed work, and Sharon agreed. As its director she saw more clearly some of the changes it required. When Wood picked it up for Stratford, he pushed the play still further until it became one of those theatre nights that people in the audience remember years later.

In 1990 David William was the artistic director at Stratford (Sharon was an associate director that year), and he was keen to see Canadian plays and playwrights showcased in Stratford productions. When William asked him to direct *One Tiger to a Hill*, Wood already knew that the script was "flawed but interesting" from its Atelier production, and he had some definite ideas about how the play should be done; the result was not only a theatrical success but a significant turning point in his life because it sparked his personal interest in prison life and in the work of the John Howard Society. When I discussed *Tiger* with him in 2003, he reflected that were he to do the play again, in the light of what he has since learned about prisons, he would make it much "uglier" because the play was "too tame." Indeed, the reality of the Abu Ghraib and Guantanamo prisons is far uglier than this play, or perhaps any play, can represent on stage.

For his *Tiger*, Wood made a number of changes to the script with Sharon's consent, but the most important of them was his addition of a violent, dramatic opening. Instead of beginning with Chalmers and the frame introduction, this production began with a brief scene in which a man in solitary confinement commits suicide. The lights came up sharply on a cage-like cell at centre stage; Desjardins (as this man is called) screamed and slit his wrists, and the shocking moment ended abruptly with a blackout. As a result, there was no doubt about what happened to this inmate because Wood sacrificed the ambiguity that Sharon wanted to create to an attention-grabbing start to the play. Although Sharon was never entirely happy with this directorial decision, in production it worked, not simply because it was sensational but because it established *theatrically* the right emotional tenor and moral perspective for the play. This bold, unambiguous beginning showed the audience exactly what life behind bars could lead to and provided concrete motivation for the other prisoners' and Dede Walker's suspicions. Wood made a number of smaller, less spectacular changes to the script. He cut some lines, especially for Dede and Soholuk, with the result that the tension between them increased, and he moved other lines around, which made Hanzuk seem more present in the plot and more human. He also ran the play with no break between acts, which intensified the oppressive mood of narrowing options and impending disaster. A host of small changes to the soundscape of the play contributed to the cumulative impact, but if I were to single out just one feature of this production as especially noteworthy, it would be the set design and lighting. John Ferguson created a catwalk above a cage or cell-like structure that occupied the centre of the thrust stage. This area served not only for the opening suicide but also for the rehab offices, the captivity space of hostage-taking, and the area in which the dead Tommy Paul and Dede Walker would lie at the end.

Visually, Ferguson made the spaces of imprisonment indistinguishable, one from another, thereby establishing through a visual metaphor the horror of prison life and the moral and psychological link connecting the sequence of events. The design focused the attention of a witnessing audience on the space of incarceration in their midst. Together with the catwalk, where a guard was always on patrol, the production exploited the interaction of observers and observed to reinforce the observers' complicity in and responsibility (as witnesses) for the chain of events unfolding before them. *One Tiger to a Hill* owes nothing to Michel Foucault's discussion of the panopticon in *Discipline and Punish: The Birth of the Prison* and Sharon did not need to read French cultural theory to imagine her play, but this production staged contemporary society's complex, ambivalent relationship with such spaces of incarceration by conflating the stage, the space of theatre itself, with a prison in which its characters (actors/inmates) are always completely under surveillance by guards and by us. Insofar as John Wood wanted to make this play tougher, more hard-hitting, than it was on the page, he succeeded, while at the same time he remained faithful to the spirit of the page and, despite Sharon's opposition to the unscripted opening, to the meaning of the play.

Reviews of the Stratford *Tiger* were mixed and I find them both interesting and puzzling now. Ray Conlogue praised the production but thought the play's subject was somewhat dated because while penitentiary life was as brutal in 1990 as it had been in the seventies, we are no longer certain that the state is always wrong and the criminal always right. This strikes me as an odd premise upon which to base his criticism because it not only assumes that the public once thought violent criminals were "always right" but also suggests that *One Tiger to a Hill* provides a simplistic black and white platform for the writer to "score political points." Jamie Portman found little positive to say. As far as he was concerned, the play was "relentlessly single-minded" and the production was "a rescue operation" with only a few striking moments. In sharp contrast with Conlogue and Portman, Larke Turnbull found the play and the production highly successful—"tense, gripping," "superb" and "compelling" are just some of his adjectives; he insisted that the play enabled him to examine prison life from many viewpoints and that Pollock had presented "no heroes or villains in her story." Did these men see the same play? How could one find the play in production to be simplistic and another find the same piece many-sided in its portrayal of the prison story? While I would agree with Portman and Conlogue that *One Tiger to a Hill* is not Sharon's best play (especially not after *Blood Relations* and *Doc*), I do not agree that the play, as read or performed, presents a simplistic, overly politicized treatment of prisons or criminals. But, clearly, the magic of theatre performance art worked splendidly for some and not at all for others with this play and, as Sharon acknowledges, theatre is a "performance art [that ...] exists only in the time it exists in, and every performance is different" (see Quigley, 40). When I saw it the awkward laughter of young people in the audience was jarring and disruptive, but it underscored the unsettling impact of the play.

As usual for Stratford, the house program was excellent. All the standard items were present, but it also included a thought-provoking set of quotations about prisons and crime. At one extreme was a comment made by a nineteenth-century prison warden who claimed that to "reform a criminal you must first break his spirit"; at the other were quotations from George Bernard Shaw, who called the "modern model prison" a "diabolical den," and from an unidentified Métis inmate, who simply said, "I am human too." However, I want to give Sharon the last word on this production of her play because in the house program space reserved for her commentary she positioned herself in relation to the wider human dilemma it embraced by refusing to take sides or provide answers:

> I talked to a lot of correctional workers, ex-prisoners, inmates, and citizens. I hung out in places I'd never been to where things were done I'd never thought of. I became friends with people who made my heart alternate between bleeding with compassion and pounding with fear. I didn't want to write a play. I wanted to understand. Being what I am, a play is what I ended up writing. It's not docu-drama in any sense, although a real event led me to it. It's an attempt to understand, to see past the walls, to get a picture of the people serving time inside, both those who leave at the end of the shift, and those who don't.

***

"Hello out there." This was Sharon speaking (writing, actually) in the late fall of 1976 to sixteen fellow Alberta playwrights on University of Alberta letterhead from her temporary home in Edmonton. However, she was not writing merely to say hello. Her letter— two single-spaced typed pages—was a call to arms urging her colleagues to attend an emergency meeting to be held in Edmonton on 16 January 1977 to discuss their lack of representation on the management committee of Playwrights' Co-op (54:3–10,2). After summarizing the dire situation they all faced if they lived outside Toronto and stressing the need to rethink the structure of this so-called national organization, she warned them that decisions were being made that would affect their professional careers and she urged them to meet, elect representatives, and send them to the February conference being organized by the Co-op in Toronto. "I don't like the meetings, the paper work, the administrative work ... any more than you do," she confessed, but "I also don't like being a second-class citizen in the theatrical community, and, by way of my non-Toronto residency, in a national organization formed to serve my interests." In the early seventies Sharon had put her toes in the Vancouver waters of theatre politics by chastising the board of the Vancouver Little Theatre and attempting to organize British Columbian playwrights, but this was different. This time she was diving into deeper and far more troubled seas. She was also raising her voice loudly, emphatically, *as an Alberta playwright.*

As it turns out, the Playwrights' Co-op was experiencing severe stresses of its own in 1976. According to Paul Morel's Director's Report, external and internal pressures were such that he felt it was time to recommend dissolution of the Co-op and to replace it with three distinct organizations. In short, professional playwrights who belonged to the Co-op had a crisis on their hands with a serious backlog of unpublished scripts, an overworked, skeleton staff, a steadily increasing membership, inadequate resources to fulfil its mandate, little or no clout with Canadian theatres, and a widespread indifference to Canadian play-writing within the cultural community. Playwrights, Morel warned, must "start ganging up for survival." It was this *cri de coeur*, coupled with Morel's recommendations and proposal for a February 1977 conference of playwrights *for playwrights* that spurred Sharon into action. The Co-op had formed in 1971, thanks to a LIP grant, so it was still in its infancy in 1976, the same year that PACT (the Professional Association of Canadian Theatres) was founded and the Canadian Actors' Equity Association formed its own union. Other branches of theatre artists were coming together in common cause, but the playwrights lagged behind. Talonbooks had been publishing plays since 1969, and three years later the Co-op published its first scripts, but the Co-op was trying to meet too many demands, such as promotion and distribution of scripts, organization of reading tours and workshops, and provision of dramaturgical services, as well as production, copyright, and royalty information. In five years, the Co-op membership had grown from a few dozen to 120 writers, with only seven staff members to assist them. It was too much. Canadian playwrights were now the victims of their own success, small though that success may have seemed at the time. The first practical response to this crisis was the founding of the Guild of Canadian Playwrights in Calgary in 1977.

The forces behind this development were Tom Hendry and Mavor Moore who agreed that the Guild would focus on matters of contracts, copyright, institutional visibility for Canadian playwrights on the national level and the international promotion of Canadian plays. The Co-op would continue to publish scripts, organize reading tours and workshops, and provide dramaturgical services and information. By 1983 the Co-op and the Guild had merged to form the Playwrights Union of Canada, which continued to publish plays under its imprint until 2001, when the union and the press separated. But despite all this dedicated work and organizational manoeuvring, practical problems of inadequate contracts, complicated fee structures, poor royalties, and a paucity of main stage productions continued to plague the theatre community and its writers, who were getting the short end of whatever stick was available to them.

But the final years of the seventies should not be dismissed or characterized as mere doom and gloom. On the contrary, it is now clear that the decade as a whole was possibly the most exciting time yet experienced in Canadian theatre, and Sharon was right in the middle of the action even though she had thrown in her lot with the forgotten West and settled in Calgary. Moreover, she was having a hell of a good time. When John Herbert crashed one of Jim DeFelice's drama classes at the University of Alberta, Jim collected Sharon and off they all went to a bar to drink, debate, and share stories—the most memorable being Herbert's description of one night during a Paris production of *Fortune and Men's Eyes* when, just before the play started, two front row seats that were clearly being held in reserve were suddenly occupied by Jean Genet and Jean-Paul Sartre. (According to Herbert they stayed to applaud the show.) Or, to shift from the sublime to the ridiculous, when Sharon arrived in Banff in the summer of 1976 for her first few weeks as a "fellow" at the Centre's new Playwrights' Colony, she was booted off the campus. She had arrived, you see, with Bear (Amanda) in tow, and Hendry and the other serious writers found children *de trop*. So she and David Fennario, who had had the bad taste to bring his wife, were relocated to tiny one-room cabins in a field on Tunnel Mountain. The one assigned to Sharon and Bear had a hole in the floor boards out of which a gopher would periodically pop and scurry about the room. For Bear this was delightful, and I doubt that Sharon was offended by this visitor. She and Fennario called their digs the "off shoot colony"; they ate their meals (with daughter and wife) at the Centre but returned to their gopher field at night. Memories are made of such ad hoc experiences.

The Playwrights' Colony, which Hendry founded in 1974, was a veritable furnace of creative energy in those years. There was nothing like it anywhere else in the country, and to look back now at the lists of attendees, plays, and productions from those early years is to realize how much talent there was. The other "fellows" in the summer of '76 included Hrant Alianak (who, as Tom Hendry recalls, went around wearing earphones so he could listen to loud urban noises instead of the bucolic peace of the mountain retreat), Tom Cone, and Rick Salutin; Bill Lane and John Neville came in to direct, and Diane d'Aquila, Stephen Markle, and Bill Webster formed part of the acting company. On occasion there was enough noise to satisfy Alianak for, in one story Hendry tells, at the 4th of July dinner in 1976, one of the speakers (who shall remain nameless but who was fairly inebriated) raved about the marvels of American culture until Hendry rose to his feet to toast, in still louder tones, Vietnam and the Vietnamese, causing a hush to fall over the dining hall. Here was another moment to remember. The following year, when it came time for Hendry to move on, he wanted Sharon to take over as Head of the Playwrights' Colony because he knew she could be tough and "not put up with any shit." She returned for a two-year stint as Head, and in 1977 she gathered another stellar team for the colony: Larry Lillo, John Wood, and Mavor Moore all put in directorial appearances; Michael Cook, John Murrell, and Allan Stratton (among others) were in residence, and the acting company included Diana Belshaw, Doris Chilcott, and Fran Gebhard, who Sharon trained to take over from her in 1979. Her 1978 summer at Banff was a special case because she was also playwright-in-residence and she did some crucial work on "My Name Is Lisbeth." There were nine other writers in the colony that summer, among them Sherman Snukal and a very young Brad Fraser, who wrote Sharon later to thank her for her mentoring and support. The 1979 rostrum included Christian Bruyère, Gaëtan Charlebois, and Margaret Hollingsworth amongst its ten playwrights.

Many years later in *Journeyman* Timothy Findley looked back on the seventies and summed up what they meant for everyone making theatre in Canada and, as if in response to Sharon's 1976 greeting—"hello out there"—he wrote:

> It was in our time that Canadian theatre came of age. It was in our time—and of our crop—that a generation of actors, directors and playwrights stood up, hand in hand, and without apology said: WE ARE HERE. (265)

Certainly Sharon was *here*. She had arrived on the scene with many lessons, learned the hard way, behind her. By the end of the seventies, she had witnessed first hand how some of the large regional theatres operated and she had had her first Stratford fling. She had grasped the politics of theatre in Canada, where Canadian plays and playwrights were rarely acknowledged let alone produced, and she had begun to grapple with the challenges of poor contracts, lack of play publishing, and minimal copyright protection or commission fees. She was writing successfully for the stage, radio, and television, but she was especially keen to direct because, as she explained in a 1979 letter to the ATP Board (54:1.8), "increasing [her] directorial skills and knowledge" would better enable her to assist other playwrights, "enhance and hone [her] own skills in the art and craft of playwriting," and, most importantly, help her "communicate to an audience not only the specific artistic perception of a play, but ... the particular way in which the theatre [provides] insight into human experience and awareness of the human condition."

If this view of directing, playwriting, and theatre work sounds idealistic and wildly optimistic, then so be it. These sentiments, expressed unequivocally in 1977, were genuine, and Sharon has never abandoned them. Her keeping of the faith is all the more remarkable when one goes behind the scenes to understand the vicissitudes of making theatre anywhere, at any time, not just in Canada over the past forty years: casting is always an issue, especially when considerations of race or ethnicity must be addressed; rehearsal time is short, too short for ambitious new plays; workshop opportunities are limited and can be used as a way of avoiding full professional productions; with rare exceptions (as when a playwright has his or her own company or, like Caryl Churchill, is virtually adopted by one), once a play is in rehearsal, the writer is seen as a pariah to be kept as far away as possible. Sharon had quickly acquired vigilance with regard to promotion of her work, house programs, and an appreciation of the need for a voice on national organizations headquartered in Toronto or Ottawa.

But the lessons were not all negative or the tales all cautionary. She had also learned to value and to understand the importance of collaboration amongst all the artists who make theatre, the need for flexibility with a script in rehearsal, and the absolute necessity of responding to an actor's professional demands. On this last matter, living and working with Michael, as well as acting herself, were teaching her how to write lines that an actor could deliver while moving from upstage left to downstage right without running out of space or text. Sitting in the audience it is easy to ignore such minutiae of craft—either a play works, the pace is spot on, or it sags and we feel bored—but these details are fundamental and have everything to do with the way the physical space of a stage is exploited to serve the larger purposes of a play. For Sharon, the complex synergies between physical space, staging, and dramatic structure, or "theatrical envelope," had taken on paramount importance, and finding the appropriate form for the story she wanted to tell remained her chief artistic challenge. By the time she had written and tested *Walsh*, *The Komagata Maru Incident*, and *One Tiger to a Hill*, she had discovered and refined both the framing strategies and the narrator-character figure that she developed through the eighties and nineties. The use of theatrical frames facilitated her exploration of time as non-linear and overlapping, and of memory as private and public interconnection, while her narrator-characters took shape as important vehicles for her theatrical embodiment of perception and understanding: a Pollock play on stage was becoming a theatrical world of memory, imagination, and self-reflexive awareness channelled, for the audience, through the mind of its central character. Moreover, she was coming to see her ideal audience as a participating observer, there to be engaged, to be moved to a greater understanding of their own existence, not to be amused for a couple of hours and sent home in a mood of jocular forgetfulness. On this she was, and remains, uncompromising.

Insofar as Canada's only true national theatre of the day was radio (and to a lesser degree early CBC television), Sharon had acquired a taste for what I call soundscapes. Sound *effects* are not the right term to describe the way she was incorporating the technological possibilities of radio and stage production into the core presentation and meaning of her plays because, like the music, they were not there just for effect. The temporal and spatial fluidity of radio, and the medium's aural capacity to create an inner world of consciousness from the many voices heard intimately in one's head, inspired her to reach for comparable non-naturalistic realities on stage. As we shall see later, the voices that create *Doc* on stage have a lot in common with the voices that *are* the radio play "Constance Kent." But at this point, Sharon is *here*, part of Findley's generation, standing up without apology to announce her arrival. As she reminded the ATP Board in 1977, she had earned her place. By the end of the seventies she was indisputably here, and the Angel in the house was not. The decade ahead would bring major public triumphs and some of her most powerful writing. It would also bring private grief, losses of people important to her, and several new battles.

CHAPTER 6

Murder She Said: Creating *Blood Relations*

I certainly don't understand how a woman with any sense of justice can not be a feminist, but I object to those people who think that 'feminist playwright' means that there is a hidden ideology by which aesthetic choices are being governed. I don't see it as a limiting term at all.

—SHARON POLLOCK, INTERVIEW, RUDAKOFF & RUCH, *Fair Play*, 215

Prior to working in the theatre I was married for some years to a violent man. I spent a great deal of time devising, quite literally, murderous schemes to rid me of him.... I would have killed to maintain my sense of self.... And so it is with Lizzie.

—SHARON POLLOCK, "AFTERWORD," *Blood Relations*, METHUEN, 123–24

I: From "Lisbeth" to *Blood Relations*

In 1983, John Hofsess took Sharon to task for her success. The occasion was the New York premiere of *Blood Relations*, but his chief complaint was that in writing a play that New York audiences *liked*—"a one-sided and bitter" play about middle-class domestic violence—she had sold out to bourgeois tastes. Hofsess was annoyed because she no longer seemed to want to write great-souled plays of conscience about human rights, like *Walsh*, "her best play," and her other plays from the seventies. In an attempt to account for this shift from big, moral plays to bitter family ones, he turned to *the life*. "In happier times," he says, she wrote plays with fine and important parts for male actors and there was always a major role for Michael Ball, but that was the seventies, when she and Ball were poor, surrounded by kids, and supposedly "happy." *Blood Relations*, he argues, signifies an unfortunate change: "By 1980 ... all but one of the children have left home, Ball has departed for an actor half his age, and Pollock's income has become virtually the highest of any playwright in Canada" (3). He insists that *Blood Relations* is an autobiographical play in which the playwright is "revenging her mother's death and ... exposing the patriarchal world that makes such a desperate choice—murder or suicide—the *only* one for some women" (4). Hofsess's linking of Sharon's childhood family situation and her later family/professional life with Michael leads him to the speculation, or that "prurient wish fulfilment" of which biographers are accused, that her personal unhappiness with men triggered her turn to domestic plays.

"Such an embittered view of sexual politics," he announces, "would not likely have come from Pollock in happier times" (3).

On some of these points Hofsess was certainly right: we know about Eloise, about Everett Chalmers, about Sharon's early years in Fredericton. It is true that by 1980 only Bear was still at home and that Sharon and Michael were no longer together by the end of the year. I would even agree that *Blood Relations* has connections with her feelings and thoughts about her childhood and her marriage to Ross Pollock. But autobiography in any work of art, and most definitely in a Pollock play, is not so easily dissected; the autobiographical roots go deeper and are far more complex than a marriage or a relationship gone bad or a family past that was, in Sharon's words, "a ghost story." In fact, as future plays demonstrate, *Blood Relations* was an artistic breakthrough *because* it merged personal experience with political and historical interests to produce a drama that was more, not less, "passionately humanitarian" than her seventies plays.

The woman Hofsess was thinking about and other people remember from the last few years of the seventies and the early eighties was striking. She was wearing her hair cut short, but it was thick, dark brown, and framed her face simply but smartly (except for one brief period during a summer at Banff when she had it tightly curled). Her large brown eyes engaged anyone she addressed with intensity, and she did not yet need the glasses she is now famous for peering over. Her mouth was serious and determined, but her smile, when it came, was wide and generous. Sharon Pollock in her mid- to late-forties was a good-looking woman with style and sex appeal. Diane Bessai vividly recalls meeting her in a Vancouver bar, where she arrived carrying a rose that "some guy on Hastings Street" had given her, but that she seemed, if not unaware of her beauty, indifferent to it and unwilling to trade on it. However, I am not sure how secure she felt as a woman, despite her physical attributes, and I suspect that she did not trust such surfaces because she had seen how little Eloise's beauty had helped her and because, in our culture and especially in the theatre, the ephemeral glamour and attractions of youth are readily available and exploitable commodities. Intelligence, talent, energy, and determination are more reliable coin, and she had all these in spades. But she was not simply the "tough person" she often seemed to be. She was tough, even bloody-minded, but also vulnerable, easily threatened, in some senses even shy, and always reticent about personal troubles.

The private Sharon Pollock was not, I think, at all secure and found it hard to believe that personal happiness could last. She and Michael broke up in 1980 under stressful and wrenching circumstances at almost the same time as her artistic success was assured with *Blood Relations*. The public person who seemed so confident, the writer who was about to have a major new award-winning play to her credit, was also the private human being whose much-loved partner had left her for a younger woman. Sharon felt betrayed and the irony of the situation was bitterly theatrical. In the fall of 1980 she and Michael were both in Winnipeg with the Manitoba Theatre Centre, and it was while she was directing Michael and Leuween Willoughby in MTC's October production of Pinter's *The Betrayal* that the end came. During this quintessential modern treatment of marital betrayal and clandestine love, Michael fell in love with Willoughby while the director looked on. Michael remained in

Winnipeg to perform in the next play of the season, *Macbeth*, and begin his new relationship, but Sharon returned to Calgary. Apparently, her telegram to him on the opening night of *Macbeth* was brief and to the point: she hoped the bard would be with him because she wouldn't. The Ball/Pollock partnership was over. Rick McNair signed over one of his own paycheques to Sharon after Michael withdrew the money in their joint bank account, but Sharon kept the family home in Calgary, which had been purchased in both their names.

In my interview with him, Michael offered two careful reflections on this difficult period: on the one hand, he felt she was extremely suspicious of him and unable to trust in his affection, which led to rows and recriminations; on the other, he did not appreciate the extent of the trauma she had experienced, either in the family home or in an abusive marriage. Because she did not complain about her treatment by Ross or talk about Eloise, he did not realize how scarred and insecure she was. He felt he had to leave to save his own sanity. By 1982 or thereabouts, his new relationship ended, but Michael went on to have a successful career with the Shaw Festival and later married fellow Shaw actor Wendy Thatcher. By the spring of 1982, Sharon had won the first Governor General's Award for Drama, had performed the role of Miss Lizzie in Theatre Calgary's production of *Blood Relations*, and had seen the premieres of a new stage play and a new, award-winning, television play. However, in the years ahead she would never again take a man into her home or heart. If either she or Michael looked back and wondered about what went wrong, they certainly did not do so publicly. After Willoughby left Michael, he and Sharon established a friendship based on their shared interests in the children and the theatre, and within a few years she would again be directing him in her plays. Michael has been a stellar Doc Chalmers and, most recently, he created an oppressively convincing Mr. Borden in the Shaw production of *Blood Relations*. The personal rupture did not become a professional one, which bears testimony to the generosity and capacity for forgiveness of both parties.

Where Hofsess really goes wrong, however, is in his suggestion that *Blood Relations* owes something to the breakup between Sharon and Michael. This play had been in her mind for several years, at least from 1975 when Dorothy Jones commissioned "My Name Is Lisbeth" for Douglas College, and the *conscious* feminist ideas in the play (that "bitter" domestic plot) had been maturing for at least a decade. The artistic roots of the Lizzie Borden play reach back to Sharon's early fascination with murder mysteries and history; she is not joking when she describes her shelves as stacked with books about famous unsolved murders or when she tells stories of searching for such grisly items in the bins of used-bookstores. What's more, murder and violent death (including suicide) are constant subjects in her work—from "Thirty-one for two" and "A Compulsory Option" through *The Komagata Maru Incident*, *Sweet Land of Liberty*, "Portrait of a Pig," and *One Tiger to a Hill* to *Whiskey Six Cadenza*, *Doc*, *Constance*, *Death in the Family*, *Saucy Jack*, *Fair Liberty's Call*, and *End Dream*. Indeed, *Blood Relations* is one part of her unsolved murders trilogy, along with *Constance* and *Saucy Jack*. The real trigger, or smoking gun, for her Lizzie Borden play was the Douglas College commission.

Earlier I described her research for "My Name Is Lisbeth" and one of its rehearsals, but the play itself is worth looking at more closely for what it tells us about the far more subtle and complex play she finally produced. When Dorothy Jones commissioned it, Sharon was not only indulging her "morbid interest" in famous murders, she was also directing, acting, and teaching at Douglas College. 1975 was International Women's Year and Sharon had played the lead in Jones's production of *Lysistrata* and participated in the lively four-woman show "I Am Woman." In the latter, she announced that "it's a man's world all right—and just look what they've done with it," before reading from the work of Isadora Duncan, presumably to provide an antidote to the misogynist platitudes from a long line of male chauvinists in Western history quoted in the show. In other words, she was imagining *her* Lizzie Borden within a very particular, charged context at a time when she was surrounded by women's voices protesting their social inequality. North American feminism was coming into its first bloom under the influence of Simone de Beauvoir (*The Second Sex* appeared in English in 1953), Betty Friedan (*The Feminine Mystique* in 1963), and Adrienne Rich, who captured attention with her provocative book, *Of Woman Born*, in 1976. Well-educated, white, middle-class women were speaking out and laying claim to public lives on their own terms, and "Lisbeth" began as an example of just how far such a woman might go if she is constantly thwarted and infantilized.

At the start, the play was naturalistic, using the kind of structure and style Sharon thought she needed to master—"an exercise to hone my craft"—before she abandoned the form for more expressionist, temporally complex, even allegorical types of play. Her original intention had been to practise using a subject for which she had a secret passion—a murder story— so the play began as an inquiry into why Lizzie did it. But even at its inception, the Lizzie play began to get under her skin. As she confessed in her 1984 Afterword to the Methuen publication of *Blood Relations*, "I am a voracious collector and reader of anthologies entitled *Horrendous Murders through the Ages*. I pore over diagrams of Whitechapel and fuzzy morgue photos. Every cheap and expensive publication detailing contemporary homicides ... finds its way to my bookshelf" (123). And so she came to Lizzie Borden: her secret hobby, her awareness of feminism, and her desire to test her craft on a naturalistic play merged, but that fortuitous coming together was only the beginning of a process that lasted several years. While she was rehearsing her role as Lizzie for Dorothy Jones, she was gaining insight into the larger possibilities of her subject and developing an admiration, even an affinity, for this murderess because Miss Borden was a lady who made decisions, and Sharon likes to make decisions.

By the time Sharon began writing her play, several other major fictional treatments existed, and the recorded facts were familiar. Among the most interesting early recreations of Lizzie are Agnes de Mille's 1948 ballet, *Fall River Legend*, Jack Beeson's 1965 opera *Lizzie Borden*, and the 1975 television movie called *The Legend of Fall River*, starring the beautiful Elizabeth Montgomery. Sharon could not have seen the opera or the ballet (although she could have consulted Agnes de Mille's 1968 book, *Lizzie Borden: A Dance of Death*), but she may have seen the movie dramatization of the trial with its sensational reconstruction of the murders. Montgomery portrayed Lizzie as a fascinating, complex woman who was stubborn and calculating but also pitiable and vulnerable. The movie even hints at an incestuous relationship between Andrew Borden and his younger daughter, and it creates an atmosphere of frustration, confrontation, and claustrophobia in the Borden house at 92 Second Street, Fall River, Massachusetts. Several more factual accounts were available by 1975–76, and by the year 2000, Lizzie Borden had become an industry with new books appearing almost annually—novels, plays, psychiatric/criminology studies, case studies, and even a Lizzie Borden tour guide companion to old Fall River. There is a Lizzie Borden musical, a Lizzie Borden journal called *The Hatchet*, a Lizzie Borden website and, since 1996, a Lizzie Borden Bed and Breakfast in the Second Street house that is decorated in the style of 1892 and can be visited online for a virtual tour of the facilities to the accompaniment of children singing "Lizzie Borden took an axe ...."

The known facts of the case are less entertaining. Lizzie, the thirty-two-year-old unmarried younger daughter of well-to-do Fall River business-man Andrew Jackson Borden, was charged in August of 1892 with the murders of her stepmother and father. Lizzie had an older sister, Emma, and their mother had died two years after Lizzie's birth. Neither daughter was fond of their stepmother, Abby, and both resented their father's transfer of property to this wife. At the time of the murders, Emma was out of town and only Lizzie and the maid, Bridget Sullivan, were in the house when Mrs. Borden and, an hour or so later, Mr. Borden were killed. Lizzie discovered her father's body and called in a neighbour who, together with Bridget, discovered Mrs. Borden's body upstairs. Without any signs of a break-in or any reason to suspect someone outside the family, Lizzie was arrested on circumstantial evidence and tried in June of 1893. During the trial Lizzie fainted when the skulls of the victims were presented as evidence, and the all-male jury, which could not believe that such a frail, well-brought up woman could be guilty of such violent crimes, acquitted her on both charges. Lizzie went back to Fall River a free woman, but a cloud of doubt and suspicion hung over her for the rest of her life. She changed her name legally to Lisbeth Andrew Borden and she bought an elegant house on the hill, which she called Maplecroft. She lived there with Emma until 1905, when something caused such a rift between the sisters that Emma moved out; and for several years Lizzie pursued an intense relationship with the Boston actress Nance O'Neill. At her death, on 1 June 1927, Lisbeth Andrew Borden left her estate to the Animal Rescue League of Fall River; Emma died just nine days later. But perhaps the most astonishing aspect of Lizzie's life, *after* the trial, was her funeral. As Sharon reminded me during a recent conversation, and as she had noted in her "Author's Comments" for the Douglas College production, Lizzie "lived midst rumours, not without foundation, of lesbianism and kleptomania. She died at 64. Those who responded to funeral invitations were confronted with a posthumous statement. She had been buried at midnight the previous evening [with her coffin carried] by six Blacks dressed in black." Sharon also noted that Bridget, who died in her eighties, made "a death-bed confession of withholding information" at Lizzie's trial.

After exhaustive research into these facts and the varying interpretations of Lizzie Borden's story, Sharon's initial decision about the woman was unequivocal: Lizzie did it all right. Moreover, in "My Name Is Lisbeth," Lizzie confesses to Bridget that she has killed her stepmother and we see her kill her father. This double murder is precipitated by the arrival of Mrs. Borden's brother, Uncle Harry (a figure Sharon invented), who persuades

Andrew Borden to change his will so that Lizzie's beloved farm is left to Mrs. Borden while he, Harry, is allowed to occupy it, but many other incidents contribute to Lizzie's mounting despair, anger, and frustration. Her father is pushing her to marry and dismisses her pleas for independence; her stepmother tells her, as she will in *Blood Relations*, that she has no rights; in a fit of rage Mr. Borden slaughters Lizzie's birds; and Emma refuses to support Lizzie concerning their right to inherit the farm. Then, at the beginning of Act Two, Emma leaves for her holiday with friends. Many of the scenes and much of the dialogue in *Blood Relations* are already present in this straightforward, linear, two-act drama of desperation and murder. However, there are some important differences between "My Name Is Lisbeth" and *Blood Relations*, and the crucial one lies in the structure of the play. In "Lisbeth" the entire action takes place over two days in August 1892 in the Borden home. The only hint that Sharon might develop a more complex temporal frame for the play occurs in the opening lines of Act One, when Bridget speaks directly to the audience from an unspecified time *after* the trial to explain where we are: "Where I was at that time, that being 1892, was Fall River." She then proceeds to walk onto the house set to arrange the breakfast table and name the residents of the house. As she works with her back turned to the stairs, Harry sneaks up on her, pinches her bottom, and demands a kiss. From there the play takes off to portray the tension that builds through Act One and spills into Act Two to climax with the murder of Mr. Borden.

Once Lizzie has killed her hated stepmother and confessed to Bridget, the close relationship between the two becomes pivotal. Despite her horror at the deed, Bridget is persuaded to help Lizzie cover up the murder when Lizzie reminds her that she loves her and they can now *both* be free. Lizzie falls on her knees before Bridget and begs:

> I had to kill her, Bridget, to be free. And you can be free too, [if you help me.] Help me and [I'll free you of emptying slop pails,] I'll free you of people like Harry, you can have your own farm. I did it for you too, Bridget—we can both be free if you'll help me. I am on my knees, I am in your power, [I beg you to help me,] this is our chance. If you deny me, then they'll kill me. I ask you for life, Bridget, I beg for both our lives. (54:4.9.2)

The implications here are clear. Lizzie is appealing, across class and economic barriers, to their shared gender position and their need to work together to escape their shackled existence (Lizzie's as a daughter, Bridget's as a maid) and the unwanted attentions of men (marriage for Lizzie and harassment for Bridget). Female solidarity will save them both, or so Lizzie claims. But there is surely something more permeating this intense scene, a something more that remains unstated but that will carry over into the relationship between the Actress and Miss Lizzie in *Blood Relations*. The two women are drawn to each other out of economic and social need, but also out of propinquity and a mutual attraction. So intimately aware of each other are they that Bridget hears the "electronic hum" emanating from Lizzie as she descends the stairs in her blood-stained dress. While there is nothing overt in "My Name Is Lisbeth" to suggest a lesbian liaison, as there is in *Blood Relations*, the possibility of such a relationship hovers over the play and is almost palpable in this scene.

Among other significant differences between "My Name Is Lisbeth" and *Blood Relations*, some warrant attention here because they shed light on what this play became. For example, in the typescript of the 1976 play (54:4.9), the carousel speech, later delivered by Miss Lizzie/Bridget, appears to be missing (at least the one page on which it would occur is missing from the foliation), and the conversation between Miss Lizzie and Bridget that leads into this powerful monologue is shorter and lacks the build-up of frustration that prepares for the speech as we know it now. Consequently, Lizzie's motivation for murder and her reliance on Bridget seem much simpler and more superficial than they are in the later play. The elements of ambiguity, irony, and heightened theatricality that make *Blood Relations* such a complex and devastating portrayal of love, hate, and the will to survive are not yet present, as the abrupt ending and the declarative title confirm. Just as Lizzie and Bridget finalize their alibis in the penultimate moments of "My Name Is Lisbeth," Mr. Borden returns, unexpectedly, to look for his wife, at which point Lizzie has no alternative but to kill him too. He lies down to rest; she forgives him for killing her birds, comments on the fact that he still wears the ring she gave him years ago, and tells him that she "would do anything" rather than have him hate her because she loves him. When he dozes off, she retrieves the axe from upstairs and returns to stand over his sleeping figure. At this point, Sharon calls for the "electronic hum" that accompanied Lizzie while she dispatched Mrs. Borden to be heard again and for a strobe light effect as she hits her father on the head with the axe. When she has finished, she takes off his coat, which she has put on back-to-front to protect her clean dress from the splattering blood, places it behind his head, and calls to Bridget that "Someone's come in and killed papa." Then the stage instructions call for a "BLACKOUT." So much for the "did she, didn't she" question. But even the difference in the titles is revealing. "My Name Is Lisbeth" reminds us that, in Sharon Pollock's view, Lizzie Borden, with Bridget's connivance, got away with murder. As a title, *Blood Relations* is much less literal, much further from the historical record, and many times more evocative and unsettling because, if for no other reason, one cannot change, or escape, one's blood relations as easily as one can a name. "My Name *Is* Lisbeth" exists very much in the present, whereas "blood relations" persist over time and can erupt at any moment to shatter the calm surfaces of life.

"My Name Is Lisbeth" opened at the Surrey Centennial Arts Centre on 31 March 1976. Reviewing it for *The Province*, Bob Allen praised Dorothy Jones and Douglas College for producing such a strong, new play, and he liked Sharon's portrayal of Lizzie, although he found the ending unresolved and Lizzie's motivation simplistic. He was right about the motivation, and Sharon was already beginning to reimagine her play, but she needed time to be able to see just where changes should be made. Above all, she still needed to discover the form that would enable her to explore the subject of a daughter's and a woman's decision to survive at any price. As early as the summer of 1976, not long after "Lisbeth" closed, she told Margo Dunn that this play was her most personal play to date and the only one written from a woman's point of view. For a woman, she explained, writing such a play provides "insight into very clouded things of your own, emotions you feel but can't handle ... insight because someone else has gone the whole way" (Dunn, 4). As the undated typescript of "Lisbeth" with the Pollock papers shows, she began by rethinking the ending and then by modifying the time scheme. This typescript carries many cancellations and changes in Sharon's hand, but the most interesting ones occur for the closing scene and final tableau. She put a large question mark in the left margin beside the stage instructions for Mr. Borden's murder and heavily crossed out the stage instructions where Lizzie stands over the sleeping man and kills him. She only retains these instructions up to the point when Lizzie reappears on the stairs, surrounded by the "electronic hum" and she pencils in—"her hands are behind her. She looks down at her father and starts down the stairs. Blackout." Handled this way, we do not see her kill him and elements of suspense, doubt, and dread—of ambiguity and complexity—enter the play.

But there is another indication of the direction in which Sharon was going, possibly as early as the summer of 1976, and certainly by the time she workshopped the play at Banff in 1978. There is an undated, unaddressed cover note for another copy that indicates where she wanted to take her play. It reads as follows:

> Here's a copy of the Lizzie Borden script I mentioned. I am writing another scene/act which takes place after the trial (in which Lizzie was acquitted but afterwards totally ostracized). The play will be two acts, with I think the second act having two scenes, the first being the present Act II. I have to beef up considerably the characters of Emma, Mrs. Borden, and Harry I think. Ignore stage instructions if you can: some are from the production that Douglas College gave it, and some are rewritten.
>
> Strobe light and actual murder on stage of Mr. Borden is under consideration—I like the strobe, it takes us back to the carousel. (54.4.9–11)

Here is the first unequivocal evidence I have found that the temporal structure was evolving into a framed flashback or play-within-a-play, that Sharon was reconsidering the murder scene, *and* that Lizzie's carousel monologue was linked in her mind, through the strobe light, with the father's murder.

When Sharon took the script to Banff, she had already spent time there in 1976 as a participating playwright, and she had followed Tom Hendry as Head of the Playwrights' Colony, a position she held until Fran Gebhard took over in 1980. Her years as Head coincided with her stint as playwright-in-residence, so these summers were busy. What's more, her rapidly emerging profile and success meant that she was called on to serve on various committees such as the Alberta branch of the National Theatre School's Advisory Committee and the Canada Council Advisory Arts Panel (1978–80), which she chaired in her third year. However, a permanent home base was assured by December of 1978 when she and Michael were able to buy the house on Manora Drive. Despite the breakup with Michael and her extensive travel over the coming years, Calgary was now unequivocally home and Sharon Pollock was an Alberta playwright. Living in Calgary certainly made the logistics of spending six weeks of the summer at Banff, about a ninety-minute drive away, much easier. When she took over from Hendry, she moved quickly to democratize the system so that the acting company, the writers, and the administrators could mix on an equal footing. She invited writers with scripts in varying degrees of development, and she tried to bring the

Colony closer to the professional theatre community. One of the plays that did make the transition from a Colony workshop to full professional production was, in fact, Sharon's Lizzie Borden play, now called *Blood Relations*, and there is no doubt that the experience she gained by serving as a dramaturge for other playwrights and by having the fine acting company at Banff work on her play, helped her to see where and how to transform an intense but straightforward story about murder into a multi-layered psychological drama.

It is probably impossible now to say exactly how the structure of *Blood Relations* emerged from these weeks in the summer of 1978. Guy Bannerman clearly remembers Sharon walking into a workshop rehearsal one day to announce that she had solved the problem with her play by creating the role of an Actress who would interpret Lizzie's 1892 past by *performing* the role of Lizzie while Miss Lizzie watched. However, Diane Bessai believes that Janet Daverne, who was a member of the Banff acting company that summer and played Miss Lizzie opposite Judith Mabey's Actress in the premiere, influenced this shift to some degree. Today it scarcely matters. What does matter is that Keith Digby, the artistic director of Edmonton's Theatre 3, liked this new play immensely and snapped it up for an Edmonton premiere, which meant that it did not go to Malcolm Black, who preferred the linear "My Name Is Lisbeth" and wanted to produce it at Theatre New Brunswick in January 1980. Like Black, Digby had read the "Lisbeth" script, but unlike Black he saw the theatrical power of the revised version and believed he had discovered a challenging and very important new play.

When *Blood Relations* opened at Theatre 3 on 12 March 1980, it was basically the play we have today. There were a number of changes and additions in subsequent productions, but *Blood Relations* as the Actress's re-enactment of what might have happened in 1892 was in place. Fortunately, the Theatre 3 script was published by *CTR* in 1981, so it is possible to see what Digby was working with for the premiere. In this version, the opening instructions indicate that the play begins in 1902, but that *"the year of the 'dream thesis,' if one might call it that, is 1892"* (*Blood Relations*, *CTR*, 48). When the lights come up, it is 4:00 in the morning, the Actress has just arrived from Boston, and she and Lizzie are having a drink. Miss Lizzie breaks the silence by querying her companion about her late arrival; the two women touch each other (Lizzie removing a pin that holds up her friend's long hair, the Actress touching Lizzie's hand); the Actress puts a record on the gramophone, and the women dance *"quite formally some distance from each other"* (*CTR* 50) as they talk. The Actress tells Lizzie about the children outside the theatre in Boston who chant "Lizzie Borden took an axe" and then asks Lizzie to tell her what really happened that August day ten years ago. With mild exasperation at this persistent questioning, Lizzie compares her friend with her sister; Emma, she says, is always asking: "Lizzie ... did you?"

Then, to set the stage for the full-scale re-enactment to follow, Lizzie appears to conjure up Emma so that the two sisters can *show* the Actress how these daily scenes of inquisition unfold. The climax of this mini-performance comes when Lizzie accuses Emma of being her accomplice:

MISS LIZZIE: Did you ever stop and think ... that if I did ... *She whispers* ... then you were
     guilty too?

EMMA: What?

MISS LIZZIE: Well, you brought me up, like a mother to me, almost like a mother. Did you
     ever think that I was like a puppet, your puppet, my head your hand, yes, your hand
     working my mouth, spewing forth all the things you felt like saying, doing all the
     things you felt like doing—as if your boil was lanced but I was covered in the—
     Emma slaps Miss Lizzie's face. Emma walks off. Actress applauds ...
     It's just a theory. (*CTR* 53)

In later versions, Sharon shifted this important exchange to the end of the play, but here it
serves as a way of introducing two crucial elements: that one possible "theory" for what
happened is that Emma was Lizzie's puppet-master and that, through re-enacting the past,
it *might* be possible to gain insight into what happened. But I stress *might* here because the
Actress's "compulsion to know the truth," as she puts it, is fundamentally at odds with
Lizzie's warning that a performance, in fact, *any* performance, is "just a theory." At the
premiere of *Blood Relations*, the suggestion that they play a game to recreate those deadly
days from 1892 in which the Actress will play Lizzie comes from the Actress, whereas in the
play's final version it is Lizzie who seduces the Actress into performing this role. Once the
action shifts back in time and the Actress, gradually warming to the part, becomes immersed
in *her* interpretation of Lizzie's earlier life, events unfold pretty much as they do in the final
version of the play. The Actress/Lizzie argues with her father, flirts with Dr. Patrick, refuses
to contemplate the marriage her father wants, and insults her stepmother (calling her "a fat
cow"). The voice of Lizzie's defence lawyer addressing the jury at her trial is heard, and Miss
Lizzie, playing the part of the maid, Bridget, coaches the Actress in her interpretation of her
Lizzie Borden role and tries to cheer her up. Finally, Miss Lizzie/Bridget delivers the
stunning carousel dream speech, and the first act ends with Mr. Borden slamming the
hatchet into the dining room table in a symbolic slaughter of Lizzie's birds.

Act Two of this version closely resembles the final text until just before the Actress is
about to murder Mr. Borden. At this crucial juncture, Lizzie intervenes to stop the game
before it goes too far. While the Actress goes upstairs to retrieve the hatchet, Miss Lizzie
enters and watches her sleeping father and the stage instructions read:

> *Lizzie [Actress] appears at the top of the stairs, her hands behind her back. She starts down the*
> *stairs. Stops on the stairs, she sees Miss Lizzie/Bridget, a pause, then she looks back to Mr. Borden*
> *and starts down the stairs.*
>
> MISS LIZZIE: No. *Lizzie stops.* No! ... no more ... no more.
>
> ACTRESS: We've moved from the possible to the probable to the necessary, Lizzie.
>
> MISS LIZZIE: It's only a game.
>
> ACTRESS: I never play games.
>
> MISS LIZZIE: No more of this game ... we'll play a new game ... Emma, sister Emma ...

tomorrow while you (*The Actress*) lie in bed ... I'll be there, sitting there, where I've
always sat ... and Emma will say ... (*CTR* 104)

Either Miss Lizzie is alarmed that the Actress has come so close to realizing that she did
do it, or her love for this father trumps her anger and frustration and she cannot make that
final step from what the Actress calls "the probable to the necessary." Either way—and the
ambiguity is inescapable—the "new game" with Emma has little to do with Mr. Borden's
death scene. Instead, it shifts attention to Lizzie's death and her plans for a funeral. This last
bit of game-playing brings us back to 1902, and Emma returns to the action so that Lizzie
can taunt her with the "posthumous statement" she intends to leave behind. She plans to
have the Fall River élite invited to attend her funeral so they can hear Miss Lisbeth Borden's
last words because she knows they will be expecting to hear a confession of guilt. However,
when these "paunches and pursey lips" have gathered, her statement will inform them that
she has already been buried with "six black men" carrying her "coal-black coffin" to its final
resting place. In an addendum she will announce that she has left her estate to the SPCA.
Predictably, Emma is appalled by this "game," but the Actress laughs, and the play ends
with both sister and lover asking Lizzie: "Did you?" while Lizzie sips her drink, smiles, and
"*says nothing*" (107).

Clever as this ending may be—and it does enhance the uncertainty over Lizzie's guilt as
well as the fascination with performance and interpretation—Lizzie's final silence and the
parts played by Emma and the Actress strike me as more contrived than complex, more
superficial and *merely* theatrical than psychologically disturbing and theatrically haunting.
This ending returns us abruptly to the so-called real world of historical fact being
reconstructed on stage and allows the audience to remain uninvolved, to sit back and clap
without feeling co-opted or challenged. This *Blood Relations* comes close to presenting
theatricality for its own sake.

In mounting his production of the 1980 script, Digby was working in an intimate theatre
space with a small thrust stage and minimal sets. Apart from the staircase, which occupied
centre stage and went up but ended nowhere, he relied on scrims and lighting to capture
what he saw as the fundamental "fluidity and nightmare quality" of the play. The carousel
speech was especially important to him because it was "a picture in words" that emphasized
the degree to which Lizzie's nightmare existed inside her head. Sharon joined him and the
cast for the last week of rehearsals, at which point she listened to Daverne's and Mabey's
concerns about their shifting roles and revised the script to address their acting needs. This
willingness to listen to and act upon the practical advice of actors is characteristic of Sharon
and comes from her own acting experience. She also helped Digby to tighten up—"harden
the edges" is how he put it to me—the performances of Mr. and Mrs. Borden, who did not
seem sufficiently cruel and oppressive to please either Digby or Sharon.

Before the premiere closed, Sharon was communicating with Bill Millerd about the
possibility of a *Blood Relations* production at the new Arts Club theatre space on Granville
Island in Vancouver. She sent Millerd some glowing reviews and analysed the production
as she saw it, praising Judith Mabey's performance as the Actress but complaining that the

second act sagged, in part because she felt the supporting roles were not up to Mabey's standard. She offered to send Millerd a new copy of the script to replace the one he had received from Edmonton because she was still modifying here and there. The Arts Club did produce *Blood Relations* but not until 1983, by which time further revisions had strengthened the play. When John Wood directed it for the National Arts Centre in the spring of 1981, he worked closely with Sharon, and the result was a new opening scene and some significant changes to the ending. It was at this point, with Wood's encouragement, that she decided to have the play proper begin as the Actress comes on stage rehearsing Hermione's highly relevant lines from Act 3, scene 2 of *The Winter's Tale*:

> Since what I am about to say must be but that
> Which contradicts my accusation, and
> The testimony on my part no other
> But what comes from myself, it shall scarce boot me
> To say "Not Guilty."

The small changes she made to the last moments of Act Two tipped the play over the edge of clever theatricality into a profound and moving *use of theatre* to explore the process of storytelling and the nature of truth, reality, and responsibility, not only for the things people do but also for their perceptions of themselves, of others, and of the events that connect us. As anyone who has read the play or seen it in a post-National Arts Centre production will know, the Actress's rehearsal of Hermione's speech alerts us—right at the start—to the extended metaphor of performance, of picking up or putting down a dramatic role, that unites structure and action so that the play fully conveys the themes of innocence versus guilt, of giving testimony and bearing witness, and, above all, of seeking truth by telling stories. The revised ending leaves the Actress to carry out her murderous interpretation of Lizzie's story until the raised hatchet is about to descend on the sleeping father, at which point *"there is a blackout"* and the audience hears an increasingly loud and distorted singing of "Lizzie Borden took an axe," followed by *"Silence. Then the sound of slow measured heavy breathing which is growing into a wordless sound of hysteria"* (392). When the lights come up again, we are back in 1902. Mr. Borden is no longer lying on the couch, and the sound is coming from the Actress, not Lizzie, who observes this scenario before taking the hatchet from the Actress's raised hands.

But the play does not stop there. The return to 1902 must include Emma who now comes downstairs to protest the unseemly presence of the Actress and Lizzie's disregard for the fact that she should not give further cause for gossip. Lizzie accepts none of this and proceeds to threaten Emma, accusing her of being the one who was really in control back in 1892 and who was, therefore, every bit as guilty of murder as Lizzie may have been. Now Lizzie's final words—"I didn't. You did."—include Emma, the Actress, and the audience (or reader) who has been present all along, bearing witness to, and participating vicariously in, the testimony of the play. With this ending Sharon created that last touch of aesthetic and thematic consonance that blurs the distinction between outer and inner plays, folds 1892 back into 1902, and returns the entire play to its roots in imaginative performance and interpretation. This ending both concludes the story and leaves its meaning open and troubling. There is no escape for an audience that must face the fact that it has played right along and is now an accomplice after the fact.

II: *Blood Relations* on Stage

The 1980s was the decade of *Blood Relations*. After the premiere, the play was on one or more professional stage across the country almost every year. John Wood gave it a major NAC production in repertory with Ibsen's *Ghosts* in 1981, the same year that Clare Coulter played the Actress in the Tarragon production and Rick McNair directed Sharon as Miss Lizzie for Theatre Calgary (see Illus. 32). In 1982 the play went up at Montreal's Centaur Theatre, on the MTC stage, and at St John's Rising Tide Theatre. In April 1983, Larry Lillo directed it in the Arts Club production that especially pleased Sharon, Keith Digby did it, this time with the Bastion Theatre in Victoria, and it received the New York premiere that Hofsess complained about. By 1985 it was picked up in Australia and England, and in 1986 it received its French-language premiere as "Liens de sang" at the Théâtre de la Commune in Quebec City. The Japanese translation premiered in Tokyo (the first of three strikingly different productions in Japan) in 1987, and Sharon directed the play herself for a Neptune and Theatre New Brunswick co-production in 1988. Then, in January 1989, *Blood Relations* received its definitive Canadian production when Martha Henry directed it at the Grand Theatre in London. Over the years, and up to the present, there have been many amateur productions as well, but the other major professional productions of note took place in Japan in 1994 and 2001 and at the Shaw Festival in 2004. Once this play found its form, the variety of interpretations and designs it has inspired demonstrates just how rich it is. Of all Canada's major professional stages, only Stratford has not yet seen fit to mount *Blood Relations*.

An exhaustive discussion of these productions would become repetitive, but a few do warrant attention, either for what they tell us about the play or because Sharon directed or acted in them. As I have already noted, the premiere at Theatre 3 was well received. Diane Bessai gave it a detailed and expert assessment for the *NeWest Review* (April 1980), stressing the play's "literal exploration (perhaps even parody) of the fundamentals of Brechtian acting technique," and she championed *Blood Relations* at NeWest Press and saw it through the press in its first published book form as *Blood Relations and Other Plays* (1981). Jamie Portman waxed almost ecstatic in his review, calling Sharon's talent "immense" and the play "wonderful"—"a psychological study so subtle and penetrating that it sets off endless re-verberations in performance" (*Edmonton Journal* 1980). Keith Ashwell, in a preview piece (11 March 1980), could not resist comparing Sharon with Lizzie because they are both liberated women and because "while one killed twice, the other has scored twice." He also claimed that with an income now between $30,000 and $40,000 a year, she was earning "good money," for a writer, but in a later review (13 March) he dropped these personal asides and was fulsome in his praise.

32. Sharon performing as Miss Lizzie in
the December 1981 Theatre Calgary
production of *Blood Relations*.
*Photographer unknown. Courtesy of
Theatre Calgary.*

In 1981–82 a good part of Sharon's cachet came from the fact that *Blood Relations* was published and had won the first Governor General's Award offered for drama, and the NAC production, which ran from February through May on the main stage, played to full houses. The *Ottawa Citizen* gave Audrey Ashley's interview a full-page spread, with a colour photograph showing Sharon laughing with the two co-stars (Patricia Collins and Shirley Douglas) opposite a very large and serious photograph of Lizzie Borden. This was prime publicity, of course, but more interesting now are some of the comments Sharon made. Once again she described herself as "a murder freak," but she also explained that she came to Lizzie "in an intimate way" and then added, prophetically as it turned out, that "I could have written about Zelda and Scott Fitzgerald because Zelda had the same kind of internal struggle." However, her Zelda play, *Angel's Trumpet*, would have to wait until she was ready to tackle a subject closer to her own marital experience than anything in the Lizzie Borden story. Perhaps the most interesting aspects of this interview are, first, her insistence that she wants her audience to leave the performance still curious and still looking for more meanings, and, second, her great pride in being Canadian. As she tells Ashley, New York is not the big league it is held up to be, and good professionals there "are no better than good people in Canada." When Ashley reviewed the production, however, her praise was qualified; she called the play-within-the-play a "gimmick," but she liked the somber set, Wood's directing, and Douglas's controlled performance of Miss Lizzie. Judging from the NAC maquette and photographs, Robin Fraser Paye's set design stressed the atmosphere of constraint and repression within the Borden household, but the furnishings were carefully representative of the period and detailed enough to heighten the oppressive middle-class domestic world from which Lizzie longs to escape. Once again, as with the Theatre 3 design, the staircase occupied a dominant centre back position so that the stairs were always visible, and yet, somehow, ominous and sinister long before we realize precisely what they will lead to. The space and design of this production constituted an ideal physical metaphor for the action of the play and the emotional tension of the plot.

The Tarragon production was much less successful, and Sharon was disappointed. She has a habit, as I know from sitting beside her during performances, of groaning quietly and leaning sideways when she dislikes what she is watching, and this was one of those occasions. She found Clare Coulter's Actress loud and one-dimensional and Cecil O'Neal's direction weak, and a hasty retreat to the bar afterwards, where fellow playwright David French refused to speak to her, did not improve her spirits. Predictably, reviews were either lukewarm or damning. Gina Mallet blamed both the playwright and the play, and complained that the play was vague and confusing. I suspect, however, that two other factors contributed to her reaction: the production was weak, and whatever Mallet liked on a stage it was not Sharon's kind of play. Fortunately, on 26 November 1981 *Blood Relations* opened in an excellent production under Rick McNair's direction at Theatre Calgary with Sharon in the role of Miss Lizzie/Bridget on a set designed by Richard Cook. Newspaper interviews with Sharon, and Brian Brennan's review in the *Calgary Herald*, displayed an interest and thoughtfulness that are perhaps more likely when the playwright herself is performing in her own play at the main theatre in her own city. But Brennan was never merely complimentary in his comments on Sharon's work, so I trust him when he describes this production as "establishing a delicious tension ... and maintaining it" and the play as "a new and improved version of the drama" that premiered with Theatre 3. He liked McNair's creation of heightened conflict and violence—without blood—because it threw the dramatic emphasis onto the psychological elements of the plot. About Sharon's acting, however, he had reservations: although she handled the role with "confidence and style," she had difficulties with her voice.

The house program and advertising posters were dramatic, with red splashes across the figure of a woman in black holding a very large axe behind her back, and the program included the main dates and facts of Lizzie Borden's life as well as McNair's statement that the play was "not a documentary" but "an imaginative exploration of the events." It is, in Mc-Nair's words "a second level history play" because on the first level it explored the facts, while on the second it used history "as a starting point" for transcending the facts. I would say that McNair, like Digby, Wood, and later Martha Henry, *got it*; each, in his or her own way, connected with the play and understood where its power lay. In her interview with him before the play opened, Sharon told Louis Hobson how the play had developed and she elaborated on her view that in the staid world of 1892 America an all-male jury simply could not admit that a nice middle-class girl like Lizzie was capable of such rage and violence that she would, or could, commit such crimes. As she told Hobson, she was fascinated by Lizzie's ambiguity and her desire to tease the world with the unanswerable mystery of her life. As a woman who understood the capacity for anger in herself and as an artist who wanted to explore the complexity, fallibility, and manipulation of human perceptions, she found in Lizzie's story the ideal vehicle for examining why we become obsessed by such extreme emotions and the need to understand them. In the last analysis, this need makes us human. And she ended her interview with Hobson by warning him that there was more to come. Although it was only 1981, she was already contemplating her next murder play in the story of Constance Kent.

When *Blood Relations* opened at New York's Hudson Guild Theatre on 2 February 1983, most reviewers seemed stuck on the nationality of the playwright because one after the other felt it necessary to note that Sharon Pollock came from Canada. Some were positive about the play, but Frank Rich panned it in the *New York Times*. "Miss Pollock is a prize-winning playwright in her native Canada," he pontificated, but that "may say more about Canadian theatre than the quality of her work." From there he went on to lay about savagely with his own hatchet, slashing at the play-within-the-play structure, the acting, the directing, and the lesbian subtext. Fortunately, for Americans outside the Big Apple, not everyone agreed with Rich, and *Blood Relations* has often been taught on university courses and produced in the United States. As recently as October 2004, Sharon was invited to Terre Haute, Indiana, by Ann Venable, who directed an amateur community theatre production of the play and organized several meetings for her with students at St. Mary's and Indiana State universities. According to Harriet McNeal, with whom Sharon spent her ten days in Terre Haute, the production had problems, but the play itself and the playwright made a lasting and very positive impression.

A month after the Hudson Guild show, Larry Lillo's production opened at the Arts Club to rave reviews: a "delightful horror story," "remarkable," "top notch," "excellent," "out-standing," "intelligent," "evocative," "first class," and with a "riveting theatrical moment" when the Actress raises the axe over Mr. Borden's head. In an interview for the *Granville Island Times* (*G.I.T.* "Blood Relations"), Lillo described his interest in challenging plays like *Bent*, which he had directed the previous year, and he said that he particularly wanted to direct *Blood Relations*. Because there was both friendship and mutual professional respect between Lillo and Sharon dating back to his work on *The Komagata Maru Incident*, she asked Bill Millerd to have Lillo direct her new play, and Lillo went on to win a Jessie for *Blood Relations*. Up to this point Sharon had been very fortunate to work with some of the country's finest directors, but she felt a personal rapport with Lillo and was convinced of his talent. His death from AIDS in 1993 was a blow, personally for Sharon and certainly for Canadian theatre. This was the first production of *Blood Relations* I saw and I found it truly memorable. Unfortunately, however, I was not in the theatre on closing night, so for the story of what happened I will turn to Suzie Payne who created a complex and interesting Emma. Payne recalls vividly—with a frisson of memory—that on the last night of the show, and *only* that once, Patsy Ludwig, who played Miss Lizzie, delivered her final "You did" and handed

Emma/Payne the axe. Amazed by this sudden, inspired move, she took the axe in a symbolic gesture of reciprocity, complicity, and empowerment. Speaking as the actor who created Emma, Payne told me that by taking the weapon in her hands she actually felt liberated from all the social and familial constraints of a woman's life. In grappling with my reading of this play, I have kept Suzie Payne's Emma before me and found, in this story of one closing night, my own way into the play.

When Sharon directed *Blood Relations* for the Neptune Theatre/Theatre New Brunswick co-production in 1988, she had just completed a stint as associate artistic director at MTC with Rick McNair and taken up her new position as artistic director with TNB. *Blood Relations* was the first play of the season, so the house program served to introduce the new AD as well as the play. And what an introduction! The cover picture shows Sharon perched on her director's chair, cocktail glass in one hand, stiletto heels balanced on the wall, and the ever-present canine pal observing us, and mimicking his mistress, through a pair of glasses. "Welcome to my world!" she says to theatre goers. Others in the TNB company and on the board would end up chafing over her directing (one cast member called her a bully) and sputtering over her bold declaration that this was her world, but what I see in this pose, her right hand extended towards us and glass raised, is a mix of chutzpa, generosity, celebration, and confidence about making theatre and, damn it, about wearing high-heeled shoes. Such heels only emphasize her long, elegant legs, and to this day she can wear them without a hint of backache.

I dearly wish I had seen the production of *Blood Relations* that Martha Henry directed at London's Grand Theatre in January 1989. Henry cast Diana Leblanc as Lizzie Borden opposite Frances Hyland as the Actress, and it is hard to imagine two better actors for these roles. In addition to being superb artists, they made a stunning pair because these two characters are supposed to be so much alike, so intimate, that the one can virtually inhabit the other or, put another way, be convincingly recreated by the other. The Actress and Miss Lizzie need to be *this* close for the drama to unfold at its best and, from all accounts, this production reached that level of synergy. One reviewer stressed the "exceptional rapport" between the two women, and others singled out the uncanny symbiosis achieved by Hyland and Leblanc, who physically resembled each other and played to that mirroring effect. The production received standing ovations after an ending that left audiences in such silence that the entire theatre felt haunted. Robert Reid liked the psychological violence of the play and praised Henry's ability to elicit its multiple layers of irony and ambiguity. Doug Bale put his finger on some of the key design and directorial decisions that gave what was a power-ful play to begin with its "brilliantly expanded" production.

Martha Henry's highly creative interpretation of *Blood Relations* involved reading the script as *theatre of the mind* that inexorably takes over the story until we feel that the play we are watching is the play Miss Lizzie conjures up in her haunted, and possibly demented, imagination. The Actress, once seduced into playing along, becomes taken up, or taken over, by these ghosts from Lizzie's past until she becomes Lizzie's invented self. Performed as a ghost story, the play became a terrifying enactment of something close to possession—a *Turn of the Screw* for the stage. All aspects of the design contributed to and informed this reading of the play. Henry, who reminded me that the Grand Theatre has ghosts (including a live-in female one), wanted to exploit this "conceit" and asked Astrid Janson to design the play to match her (Henry's) vision of Lizzie as slightly mad and living in an abandoned theatre, within which she has created a private space for herself. The result was spectacular.

The entire theatre was used and exposed so the wings, flies, pulleys, and trap door were all visible and the stage levers were operated by Leblanc/Miss Lizzie. The living room furniture was assembled from old Grand sets, which Henry hoped the audience might recognize, and the dominant colour was a rich blood red, carried out in heavy red drapes that were used for a backdrop; the shed was made of plexiglass and as the birds were killed blood could be seen running down its sides. At the start, when the Actress entered the theatre stage in appropriately elaborate Victorian dress, Lizzie was clad only in a white shift-like garment: she could have been dreaming or incarcerated, and she certainly appeared to be ghost-like herself. But as the play progressed and Lizzie conjured up her ghosts, the Actress *became* Lizzie by divesting herself of her elaborate attire until she was in a white shift and Miss Lizzie was the one dressed in the elegant clothes and made up as the Actress. They became mirror images of each other, interchangeable selves, Doppelgänger in an almost Faustian pact. When Henry was describing the production to me, she was enthusiastic about every aspect, but she called Astrid Janson's design work "phenomenal." Janson captured Henry's conception of the play both as existing within the mind of the double self of Miss Lizzie and the Actress and as taking place in a working theatre space. Paradoxically, the bare physical materiality of the stage freed the theatre, the actors, and the audience to see the world through Lizzie's eyes. As the poster for the play suggested (see cover illustration), this was not the most comfortable of positions to occupy. But even before the play began, Grand Theatre audiences were being positioned inside a haunted space and sensibility because they entered the theatre to the sound of a child reciting the "Lizzie Borden took an axe" rhyme. However, the recorded rhyme they listened to was being chanted by the two-and-a-half-year-old daughter of a staff member, and the child would lisp the words, repeat "whack, whack, whack," and then scream with laughter. What was, for such a young child, merely the repetition of a funny sound became, when recorded to repeat over and over, and amplified, a marvellously chilling note on which to start *this* production of this play.

When Jackie Maxwell chose *Blood Relations* for her first season as artistic director of the Shaw Festival, the play had not had a major Canadian production for fourteen years. Maxwell wanted to pay tribute to one of Canada's pre-eminent playwrights, the woman who had encouraged and mentored her twenty years before at the NAC, and to revive a classic Canadian play. The Shaw has a tradition of mounting a British thriller in the Royal George Theatre, but for 2003 Maxwell made the switch to a Canadian thriller (of sorts). She chose Eda Holmes to direct the fine cast drawn from the Shaw acting ensemble, with Laurie Paton as the Actress, Jane Perry as Miss Lizzie, and Michael as Mr. Borden. William Schmuck's set was superb. He created a skeletal, cage-like structure through which the audience could see into the interior of a house, and sitting, in full view, down stage right was an actual bird cage with two live pigeons, a visual reminder of the caged human beings in the play. As the play began, the set opened, its sides swinging back to left and right, as if to provide a temporary release or an invitation to escape for Miss Lizzie and her Actress lover. This doubling of cages intensified the atmosphere of claustrophobia so essential to the play and it also increased the audience's uncomfortable sensation of spying on the creatures inside. The metaphor of watching, and of being watched, enacted as Miss Lizzie/Bridget watches the Actress perform, permeated the production, and the set design pulled the audience into the net of calculated voyeurism and judgement. It was, in fact, a very powerful, *participating* actor in the drama. Emma (a character I always watch carefully) was well done by Sharry Flett as a desperate woman who might easily have aided and abetted Lizzie's murderous acts and who certainly suffered the same sense of entrapment as her sister.

In the final moment of this production, when the Actress takes back the hatchet from Miss Lizzie and says, "Lizzie, you did," Miss Lizzie answered "I didn't. You did," but this time she directed that remark *only* to the Actress. It was, then, the Actress who moved forward and, by looking out directly at the audience, acknowledged our presence, claimed our approval of her performance, and confirmed our bond with her while the final "You did" lingered in our minds. This emphasis may seem slight on the page, but in the Shaw performance it was galvanizing. Simply by looking back *at us* (the audience), returning our gaze, the Actress acknowledged our looking, complicity, and understanding. This emphasis is one that Eda Holmes decided on after discussing the scene with Sharon, who stressed that the play should end by suggesting that, under the same circumstances, anyone *might* be driven to commit murder. For Holmes, who told me that she thoroughly enjoyed directing *Blood Relations* and appreciated what Sharon was saying about the slipperiness of truth, about women's position in society (then and today), and about the power of theatre and performance to capture layers of complexity and ambiguity in perception and experience, this play was not about whether Lizzie did it or whether she was sane or mad, but about our collective—and horrified—realization that there but for the grace of God go I. And that was most definitely what I sensed and then heard around me the night I attended the production. When the Actress looked directly at us, there was an audible gasp from the audience, followed by tense silence, before the applause took over. The chatter and discussion I overheard as the audience walked out confirmed the degree to which individuals felt implicated, caught up, cleverly coerced, and then forced to think about what had just happened *to them* every bit as much as what had happened on stage. This was a Royal George thriller with a bite. Holmes and Maxwell saw *Blood Relations* as a women's play, featuring female artists and women's stories, and at least seventy percent of the audience the night I was there was female. But not all critics welcomed this gender rebalancing of the Shaw. Kate Taylor was particularly *ad feminam* in her critique. She blamed the playwright for the faults she claimed to detect in the production, and she commented on the program notes in which Sharon explained that she had imagined ways of doing in an abusive husband before finally leaving him. For reasons that strike me as irrelevant to the play or a theatre review, Taylor wondered what such a husband would think if he read the program note. Other reviewers, however, stayed on topic and were very positive. Jamie Portman found the play, the acting, the set design—everything—"exemplary": "A stellar performance in a stellar production."

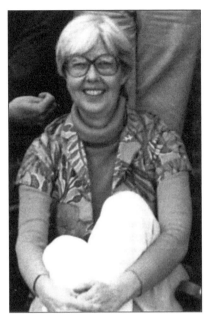

33. Diane Bessai (1982). Bessai is a founder of NeWest Press and the first editor of Sharon's plays. In her introduction to *Blood Relations and Other Plays* (1981), which included *One Tiger to a Hill* and *Generations*, Bessai challenged the perception that Sharon Pollock was a regional writer; "few playwrights," she said, "have her range and technique" (9).
Photograph courtesy of NeWest Press and Diane Bessai.

Sharon has always taken play publication seriously, although not as the most important or urgent requirement for a playwright. She has always recognized that a script is ephemeral, and that if a play is to survive and be produced several times, it needs to exist in concrete form. She is also somewhat unique amongst writers, especially playwrights, in enjoying academic discussions of her work: she often finds such interpretations interesting and she is excellent in conversation with students. In part this tolerance stems from her own intellectual curiosity about ideas, people, and language, and, having watched her interact with academics and graduate students, as well as with theatre colleagues, I believe she genuinely enjoys debates with smart, young people, whether they are acting, writing, or studying. Getting *Blood Relations* published, therefore, was crucial. Without publication the play could not have won the Governor General's Award, and it would not have been studied in universities and generated more than two decades of scholarly interpretation. Moreover, had it not been published in English, it is unlikely that it would have been translated and have travelled abroad.

That said, as Diane Bessai reminded me (with feeling), Sharon took little interest in seeing her play through the press, and Bessai shouldered the brunt of the work (see Illus. 33). NeWest Press was born in 1976 in Bessai's Edmonton home when a group of writers, professors, and theatre people (including Sharon, who was teaching at the university that year, Rudy Wiebe, Doug Barbour, and George Melnick, the founder of the press) gathered to discuss the mandate for such an ambitious venture. Bessai, a theatre specialist, realized that Edmonton theatre at that time was very active and producing quality work, so she wanted to include plays in the publishing portfolio and agreed to become the drama editor for the press. By the time *Blood Relations* premiered at Theatre 3, she already knew Sharon's earlier work through the Citadel's productions of *The Komagata Maru Incident* in 1977 and *One Tiger to a Hill* in 1980, so when she saw *Blood Relations*, she knew immediately that this was an important play. However, getting Sharon to respond promptly to editorial questions was not easy. To this day, it is like pulling teeth to wrench Sharon's attention away from her current writing or directing or theatre work to deal with the fussy, but necessary, details of publication. As she told Suzanne Zwarum in a 1990 interview, "I have what many people consider a flaw in my character. I concentrate on the now, don't worry about tomorrow" (34). To her everlasting credit, Bessai persevered; *Blood Relations and Other Plays* (*One Tiger to a Hill* and *Generations* were the other plays) appeared, won immediate acclaim, made a name and money for NeWest Press, earned Sharon some crucial steady income, and was picked up by Methuen for a 1982 volume of *Plays by Women*. NeWest issued a new edition in 2002, adding *Whiskey Six Cadenza* to the other plays, and a new introduction by Anne Nothof, and the play caps off volume one of the *Collected Works*. Sharon may not have been in the game for the immortality stakes, but she let Diane Bessai play midwife to the future while she concentrated on the now, insisting: "I don't write for posterity."

When she won the Governor General's award, the country paid remarkably little attention. Writing in the *Edmonton Journal*, Dennis Kucherawy seemed more interested in criticizing what he saw as a contradiction in her acceptance of the award. How could she be sincere in her socially and politically provocative work, he muttered, if she accepted the government's $5,000 and a leather-bound copy of *Blood Relations*? Just the asking of the question reminds me of how parsimonious this country is with its praise and of how unwilling so many Canadians are to applaud our own when they succeed. The ceremonies were held in Winnipeg in 1982, so she bought a new outfit and attended, but the location, explained per-haps by the fact that Manitoba's Ed Schreyer was Governor General at the time, meant she was returning to the city still closely associated with personal loss and pain. But she went as a winner, not only for herself but also, as she told Kucherawy, for all Canadian playwrights and for the recognition of Canadian playwriting. This was not her first major award, nor would it be her last, but it signified the arrival of plays on the literary stage in Canada.

The publication of *Blood Relations* meant that a text existed and was easily available for someone who wanted to translate it. When Denise Gagnon, a director with Quebec's Théâtre de la Commune, saw the January 1982 production at the Centaur, she quickly decided to acquire the rights and she asked Francine Pominville to prepare the translation called "Liens de sang." It took Pominville almost two years to complete her work, but the play finally premiered in Quebec City in October 1985 and was remounted in Montreal the next year.[1] Meanwhile, in Vancouver, Toyoshi Yoshihara, a Japanese businessman and theatre *aficionado* who had immigrated to Canada in 1970, saw the 1983 Arts Club production of the play and was completely enthralled. He attended several performances; he persuaded his theatre director friend Takehisa Kaiyama, in Vancouver on a visit, to come with him to the theatre, and together they met with Sharon and Larry Lillo. With Tak Kaiyama's encouragement, Mr. Yoshihara set to work translating Sharon's Lizzie Borden story into Japanese. Through this translation he developed a friendship with Sharon, was able to bring her to Tokyo in 1994 for a festival of Canadian plays, and created the text that led to three successful Japanese productions of the play. He has continued translating Canadian plays, but *Blood Relations*, especially as it was done at its Tokyo premiere by the Bunkaza Theatre, is his favourite. When I asked what the translating process involved and why Japanese audiences might like the play, his answers were direct: Japanese women understood the kind of oppression Lizzie faces because they face it themselves, so the play resonated with their experience. Moreover, from his perspective, it was a pleasure to translate because it is such a well-structured and finely honed play that the language and the scenes are, as he phrased it, tightly knitted together. He made only one change: he shortened the carousel speech because, in rehearsal, the young actor could not carry it through and retain the necessary tension. When Sharon attended the 1994 production with Yoshihara, she noticed that something had happened to that speech, and he then had some explaining to do.

His many reminiscences and production photographs illustrate just how different the three Japanese productions were (see Illus. 34). The 1987 interpretation, directed by Takehisa Kaiyama, was a fairly straightforward period piece with a realistic set design and costuming for an ensemble of young actors who created a family drama about a rebellious daughter and an overbearing father. The Half-Moon theatre production that Sharon saw in 1994 during her visit to Japan, was also directed by Takehisa Kaiyama, but this time he had a cast of experienced, star actors who gave the script a more histrionic treatment. Nevertheless, the play remained, at least to my eyes, a modern Canadian play and certainly not a Japanese drama. The set was more sparse and suggestive than in 1987, the lighting and blocking were more emphatic and intense, and the staircase disappeared into a dark void in a fine symbolic gesture of mystery and fear. Mr. Yoshihara allows that this was a very powerful production. But it is the 2001 Group FOCO production that caught my eye when I examined the photographs, and this is the one I wish I had seen because this *Blood Relations* was not only translated in language but also in sensibility through its extreme simplicity and stylization. There was no attempt at Western periodization in sets or costumes, and the acting itself— postures, gestures, blocking, expression—looks almost classical. But I am reacting to production photographs, whereas Mr. Yoshihara was *there* watching and to his eye the Shake-spearean-trained director, Takayuki Sainoki, reduced the play to a thriller by over-emphasizing the axe, the blood, and the violent murders. It may well be that a *King Lear* aura of father/daughter conflict, greed, and murder seeped into this production of Lizzie's story, and in some ways such a reading of the play is not inappropriate. But whichever production worked best or appealed most to individual audience members, one thing is certain: *Blood Relations* is big enough and flexible enough to meet a directorial challenge, and I believe that Sharon would have enjoyed watching a Goneril-like Lizzie and a Regan-like Actress. The Cordelias and Emmas of this world are not to her taste.

What she most definitely did not approve of was the film version of her play. Late in 1982 Sharon signed a contract with CTV and Robert Barclay of Calgary's CFCN (a CTV affiliate) for a film adaptation of *Blood Relations*, and in December she delivered her screenplay. However, by January 1983 things had gone seriously awry. For reasons that remain vague (Sharon agreed not to discuss the lawsuit that resulted), Barclay said nothing to Sharon but rejected her work and turned to his wife, Jane Barclay, for a new screenplay.[2] In an article about the

34. *Blood Relations* has received three professional productions in Japan using the Japanese translation by Toyoshi Yoshihara:

a) a scene from the 1987 Bunkaza Theatre production in Tokyo;

b) a scene from the 1994 Half-moon Theatre production in Tokyo. Takehisa Kaiyama directed both productions using realistic sets and period dress.

c) By contrast, the 2001 by Tokyo's Group Foco production, directed by Takayuki Sainoki, was highly stylized.

Photographs and descriptions of these productions are courtesy of Toyoshi Yoshihara.

dispute that erupted between the Barclays and Pollock, Marilyn McKinley claimed that CTV/CFCN violated its contract with the author and that the new adaptation distorted and mutilated Sharon's play. And there is no doubt that Sharon was furious for, as she told McKinley, the Barclay screenplay reduced *Blood Relations* to "just another play about Lizzie Borden." Sharon hired a lawyer, Ariel Breitman, and took CTV and the Barclays to court. At the preliminary hearing, Calgary Justice Kenneth Moore granted her a temporary injunction to prevent televising of the play until a decision could be reached on her allegations; however, he also urged both sides to seek mediation and settle out of court. At the centre of this dispute, at least as reported in the newspapers, were Sharon's contract with CTV and Canada's Copyright Act, both of which should have protected her—or so she thought— against the appropriation and misrepresentation of her work. However, apparently Robert Barclay did not like Sharon's screenplay because it was too long, lacked some of the Borden court details he wanted, and was too openly lesbian, so he turned to his wife who wrote a new script without consulting Sharon. This was precisely the kind of situation that Sharon believed her contract protected her against.

When she finally saw the screenplay, she was horrified. After reading the Barclay script both John Murrell and Urjo Kareda agreed to give expert testimony and they submitted affidavits unequivocally supporting Sharon's claim that her play had been bowdlerized. Murrell is quoted as saying that "anyone familiar with Sharon Pollock's work and reputation would indeed be disappointed, disheartened and embarrassed" by the screenplay, and Kareda agreed, saying that it "drastically altered and distorted" both the original play and Sharon's own screenplay (54:1.45). By April 1983 Sharon and her lawyer believed they had reasonable grounds for arguing that her rights had been infringed, her work mutilated, and her reputation potentially damaged. She had received the modest sum of $13,500 for the film and television rights when she signed the contract, but now Breitman was asking for a total of $400,000 in damages. He apparently hoped that a successful 1982 suit brought by Michael Snow against Eaton's for damaging his art by sticking bows and ribbons on it would strengthen the Pollock case. In the end, they settled out of court with Sharon receiving a fraction of what her lawyer had requested, and Canadian copyright law and ACTRA agreements were revealed to be sadly lacking in real protection for the writer. As David Balcon put it in "A Question of Copyright: The Sharon Pollock Case," the lesson for writers is that "there is a confused regime of protection under our existing copyright laws [and] even contracts tend to be an uncertain remedy" (27). For Sharon, who had long mistrusted unions and worried constantly about contractual protection of artists' rights, the entire business proved she had been right all along. Although she gained little from this protracted and stressful business, the temporary injunction and the out-of-court settlement suggest that she had at least won a symbolic victory. The Barclays were required to change the name of their film and to remove all reference to Sharon or to *Blood Relations*.

"Double Play," as the Barclay film was finally dubbed, did have a good director, a fine cast, and it was reasonably well produced. Silvio Narizzano, of *Why Shoot the Teacher?* fame, was hired to direct, and the cast included Maureen Thomas as Nance O'Neill (the Actress is given the real name of Lizzie Borden's friend), Maureen McRae as Lizzie Borden, Suzie

Payne as Emma, Robert Clothier as Mr. Borden, and Lois McLean as Mrs. Borden. Never-theless, the film has never had much of a screen life. Ironically, it had been planned from the start as a way of satisfying CRTC requirements that CTV increase its Canadian content, but the final product ended up looking just like any other sensational portrayal of an old American murder story. Major changes were made to the scenes and structure of the drama, although the shifts between past and present were preserved, large chunks of dialogue were invented, and Mr. Borden's slaughter of the birds was represented in graphic, drawn-out detail, as was Lizzie's murder of Mrs. Borden. The set was obviously false, and the camera's lingering over the axe with hair and blood sticking to it was a perfect example of overkill. "Double Play" may have been a good murder flick, but it was not *Blood Relations*.

III: The Mirror Talk of *Blood Relations*

Over the past twenty-five years, from its publication to the present, there have been many scholarly interpretations of *Blood Relations*. Like the differing productions, these interpreta-tions demonstrate one thing above all others: this play sustains multiple readings and will survive any theoretical approach applied to it. During the 1980s and 1990s more than a dozen major studies appeared in which some scholars argued for contextual, thematic, feminist, Freudian, or Lacanian readings, while others stressed the play's metatheatrical examination of history, truth, and identity, analysed its clever manipulation of narrative, explored its oedipal father/daughter relationship or, in one instance, shifted the oedipal read-ing from the Bordens to the Chalmers to suggest that the playwright was dramatizing her personal struggle with gender and her family's failure to provide positive models for female identity. As different as they are, all these readings make interesting points about the play and help me to better understand why it is so haunting and powerful in performance. Like production styles, critical theories change with the times; what is fashionable in one decade may well be *passé* in another. But if a work of art is good, it will rise above such fashions by saying something important about the human condition and saying it well, regardless of how it is interpreted. *Blood Relations* is such a work.

On certain things, the scholars agree: the play, whether read or watched, is about the nature of truth, reality, personal identity, and memory, and it asks how we can be sure that we know what happened in the past, despite the apparent irrefutability of facts. It is also, unmistakably, about what Rosalind Kerr aptly called "the excluded daughter's revenge" (200). Whatever else it may be, this is Lizzie's story, and in telling it Sharon was constrained by the historical record: that Miss Lisbeth Andrew Borden was a real person who lived in Fall River and had a sister called Emma; that her father and stepmother were hacked to death; and that Lizzie was charged with their murders, but acquitted. What's more, no approach to the play can overlook its intricate structure. Regardless of interpretive emphasis, the doubled role-playing and the time scheme presented through the play-within-the-play, what Sharon calls the "dream thesis," is central to any consideration of the play's meaning. Once Miss Lizzie and the Actress begin their game of role exchange and shift from the present in

1902 into the memories, reconstruction, re-telling and re-enacting of life in that house on Second Street in August 1892, readers or spectators are obliged to ask *how* we can ever know what may or may not have taken place, *why* we are so anxious to know, and *what* such insistent probing of the past can possibly tell us about the present or about who we are as women and as human beings.

As I see it, the Lizzie Borden in *Blood Relations* is Sharon Pollock's creation or, put another way, Sharon has taken upon herself the biographer's task of trying to tell Lizzie's life-story, not the whole story, to be sure, because the daily details are boring, but the life-defining story-within-the-story. As a good biographer she must also be something of an historian, and she had to do her research, but she also had to be attracted to her subject. It may be too much to expect Sharon as biographer to like or identify with Lizzie Borden, but something drew her to this story instead of to a dozen others. In her "Afterword" to the Methuen edition, she suggested that, like Lizzie, she "would have killed to maintain [her] sense of self." Of course, in Lizzie's case the threat to self, as Sharon portrays it, came primarily from the father, aided and abetted by a hated stepmother, whereas in her own case, she felt threatened by her marriage to a violent man and fantasized about "murderous schemes" to free herself of him. However, despite her marital experience, which may go part way towards explaining why she was drawn to Lizzie's story or why she recreates it in the way she does, there are many other subterranean parallels between the Fall River world of the Bordens and the Fredericton world of the Chalmers. While *Blood Relations* is *not* about life in the Grey Street house in Fredericton (that would come in *Doc*), it is informed at deeper emotional and psychological levels by Sharon's understanding of what domestic life in a small conservative town, in a traditional middle-class home, where the mother was absent and the father all powerful could be like for a strong-willed daughter. So my reading of *Blood Relations* is, perhaps inevitably, a biographical one—not in any literal sense, but a biographical one all the same.

I have called this section of the chapter, the "mirror talk of *Blood Relations*": so let me explain what I mean by this phrase. Since the beginning of the seventies, an increasing amount of popular and academic attention has been focused on life-writing or, what I prefer to call, autobiography *and* biography. These genres are extremely popular with readers, and sometimes it seems that every Tom, Dick, and Sally feels compelled to publish his or her memoirs or autobiography. The reasons for this contemporary obsession with the personal story are many and can be traced back to a growing democratization of biography, which is no longer the exclusive preserve of so-called great men in public life, to a comparatively easy access to the media, and to a more diffuse but nonetheless actual anxiety about personal, or even national, identity in an increasingly depersonalized and globalized world. Moreover, the complex dimensions of trauma and of the processes of remembering associated with traumatic experiences have received considerable scrutiny in the aftermath of WWII, the Holocaust, the Vietnam War, and the continuing violence and genocide of the twentieth and early twenty-first centuries. Observing these trends, scholars in Europe and North America, have developed a significant body of theory and secondary analysis of the phenomenon of life-writing and of the roles that memory and trauma play in it, and I have found a few of these concepts helpful in my effort to understand *why* autobiography and biography are so popular, *how* they work as constructions of identity, and *what* they can tell me about Sharon's plays.

In formulating my responses to these issues, I have turned to the theoretical work on autobiography and to some of the current work on memory and trauma. Paul John Eakin's *How Our Lives Become Stories: Making Selves* and Susanna Egan's *Mirror Talk: Genres of Crisis in Contemporary Autobiography* have been especially helpful, but the discussions of trauma by Cathy Caruth and, more particularly, Laurence Kirmayer are also illuminating, especially when they are combined with autobiography theory. I have borrowed the term "mirror talk" from Susanna Egan, and I give prominence to this term here because it embraces theatre and performance. The core of Egan's concept is elegantly simple. Like Eakin, she maintains that storytelling is central to the shaping and communicating of identity, and she goes on to say that it must be intersubjective if it is to work. In other words, a story *must* be heard and acknowledged, as well as told, if it is to give meaning to human experience. Therefore, it takes at least two for a story to exist and this pair must enjoy a high degree of mutual recognition of their similarities and differences if their communication is to be effective. Inevitably, then, such a relationship will be grounded in a dialogue that might start something like this:

> Lizzie? Lizzie.
> What?
> ... Did you?
> Did I what?
> You never tell me anything.
> I tell you everything.
> No you don't!
> Oh yes, I tell you the most personal things about myself, my thoughts, my dreams, my—
> But never that one thing ... (*BR*, *CW*, I, 345)

However, Egan's mirror talk is more than dialogue. Her mirror metaphor reminds us that such talking exists within a context of looking, which immediately evokes, for me, a stage on which characters speak, interact, and watch each other, and where we, the audience, are also engaged in looking. Sometimes, as a spectator, I can be jolted out of my safe, separate, anonymous looking because an actor suddenly looks back at me, acknowledges my presence and makes me realize that I too am seen and that I am both like and different from her. When that connection happens, the mirror has swung (alarmingly in *Blood Relations*) out to include me and my fellow audience members so that we are all addressed and asked to acknowledge our relation to each other and to the storyteller and the tale. In effect, we become active participants in the dialogue, so that our own identities are, to one degree or another, influenced by the story, and the play has entered our "most personal" lives, possibly even our "thoughts" and "dreams." When the story unfolding on stage is obviously, and self-consciously, auto/biographical, as it is in *Blood Relations* and in many other of Sharon's plays, then this mutual recognition occurs *within* the play between the characters who perform their roles of biographer, biographee and autobiographer. Susanna Egan clearly identifies this aspect of mirroring within the story when she tells us that "mirror talk begins as the encounter of two lives in which the biographer is also an auto-biographer" (7).

To the best of my knowledge, Sharon has never described herself as a biographer narrating the life-story of Lizzie Borden, but I believe that when she decided to transform the linear "My Name Is Lisbeth" into a play-within-a-play "dream thesis," she was, in fact, working from the autobiographical premise signalled by the original title—my name is—that in order to tell Lizzie's story, she would also have to tell other peoples' stories. From there it became clear that to tell this story as she saw it, she needed to position a creator of the story—the Actress-biographer—inside the play. The logical consequences of these decisions led her to explore how a life becomes a story through a shared, collaborative telling, a listening and a watching that exposes the autobiographical within the biographical. After all, it is the Actress, at first prompted and then closely watched by Miss Lizzie, who tells us what *she* would do, who enacts her own story, and who apparently murders Mr. and Mrs. Borden. Autobiography overtakes biography. But what of trauma and the memory of trauma, and where, in this complex mirror talk, is Sharon Pollock? On the surface, the actual Lizzie Borden case involved significant trauma; a child does not murder her parents without experiencing a range of extreme emotions, and if she is then charged with the murders, the shock and stress are multiplied. However, by choosing not to worry about what really took place in the Borden house in 1892 and focusing instead on what could provoke or motivate such violent acts, Sharon was pushing beneath the surface trauma to ask questions about a much deeper wound. Such wounds, of course, are the stuff of drama: where would Hamlet be without his psychic wound, or what would Parsifal have to do if Amfortas had no symbolic wound? More to the point, why else would Shakespeare or Wagner have bothered with these rather self-indulgent chaps? But wounds are also the stuff of life and of life-stories, and to heal such trauma one must first remember it, or, as Kirmayer explains about Holocaust and incest survivors, one must find or create a *narrative* "landscape of memory" so that one's memories can be recognized by others because this recognition makes the story believable and meaningful. But if that story is so violent, so traumatic that it resists memory and defies credibility, then telling it becomes almost impossible and a way must be found to allow the telling, the mirror talking, to begin.

When the Actress in *Blood Relations* pesters Lizzie to *tell* or, at the least, "to paint the background," she thinks she is inviting her friend to take up the autobiographer's burden and confess the truth. What the Actress has not yet realized is that autobiography is a slippery genre, that autobiographers can manipulate and deceive, and that it is unwise to trust an autobiographer's professed intentions and truth claims. "And so it is with [Sharon's] Lizzie." When Lizzie tells her lover that she reminds her of sister Emma, the Actress is taken aback but quickly turns to performing a brief imitation of "poor Emma," who also pesters Lizzie with the "did you?" question. But in this exchange, the Actress is about to be out-manoeuvred. Her playing at being Emma gets nowhere, and she is stuck with her "compulsion to know the truth." With this fateful admission, the dialogic ball is back in Miss Lizzie's rhetorical court, and the relationship tightens almost imperceptibly as Lizzie carefully replies—"Sometimes I think you look like me … or how I think I look … sometimes you think like me … do you feel that?" At which point I am tempted to leap up from my seat to warn the Actress: Don't answer that or she'll have you! But, of course, the Actress does answer; she agrees with Lizzie that sometimes they are very much alike. Whereupon, Miss Lizzie pounces:

> MISS LIZZIE: (*triumphant*) You shouldn't have to ask then. You should know.
>   "Did I, didn't I?" You tell me. (347)

But the Actress has not yet fallen fully into Lizzie's biographical trap: "Come on, paint the background," she wheedles; "Perhaps you'll give something away" (347). And then Lizzie makes her move by proposing that they play a game, "And you'll play me." Dismayed, puzzled, the Actress hesitates, but Lizzie knows her partner well and appeals to her professional pride: "It's your stock in trade, my love." In this careful, cat and mouse exchange, Lizzie has got the Actress to agree to the game, to the role that she can play because, while she is different from Lizzie, she is also (as she has agreed) somewhat like her.

Miss Lizzie also needs a role to play as *Blood Relations* seamlessly shifts from 1902 into 1892. She decides to play Bridget, the maid, who "was a great one for stories," and who withheld information at Lizzie's trial, and it is as Bridget that Miss Lizzie begins the play-within-the-play by conjuring up the crude, greedy Uncle Harry and then coaching the Actress, who has been watching this scene closely and waiting for her cue, to become Lizzie. Several stage instructions make it clear that Miss Lizzie/Bridget will provide gestures or words of encouragement to "*guide*" the Actress/Lizzie "*into her role* by '*painting the background*'" (351). As the Actress/Lizzie becomes immersed in Lizzie's story and identity, she needs fewer prompts from Miss Lizzie/Bridget. Then the other family members are conjured up—so realistically does Miss Lizzie/Bridget paint the picture and so convincingly does the Actress/Lizzie play her role—until we have Emma, Mrs. Borden, and finally the *pater familias* himself on stage, each of whom interacts with the Actress *as* Lizzie and treats Miss Lizzie *as* Bridget. There are a few brief moments when this role-playing reverts just long enough to allow the actual Miss Lizzie to speak as herself to the Actress, who remains in her role as Lizzie, and these moments are crucial to the mirror talk between the two women and to our understanding of what lies buried within Lizzie Borden, and possibly within other women. One of these moments occurs when Miss Lizzie muses about the time in her childhood when she no longer had scabs on her knees, which she interpreted as a sign that she was finally becoming "the nice little girl Emma" wanted her to be. But then she turns to the Actress/Lizzie to admit that she was only growing up, falling down less often, and not, in fact, becoming "nice," and she asks her other self a key question: "Do you suppose there's a formula, a magic formula for being 'a woman'? Do you suppose every girl baby receives it at birth [when] the magic formula is stamped indelibly on the brain […] and through some terrible oversight … perhaps the death of my mother […] I was born defective" (362–63)? In response to this appeal, the Actress/Lizzie will quickly say "No," meaning not defective, and then "Just ... born."

However, we and the Actress have been given some important autobiographical information for understanding the rest of Lizzie's story. This daughter lost her mother at or near birth (Sharon places the mother's death at the daughter's birth, whereas Lizzie's real mother died two years after her birth), and from that moment she has seen herself as the abandoned child, possibly blamed for her mother's death, raised by surrogate (Emma) and step (Abby) mothers, and lacking the loving formula, or positive model, she needed to become a happy woman. If there is an original trauma in Lizzie's story (as Sharon imagines it), this is it. This daughter lost the good mother, and she blames herself and the way things are—as she will suggest to her father—for driving this mother away. To make matters worse, this primal loss has left Lizzie vulnerable in many ways; although she rejects the submissive lot in life inculcated by Emma and forced on her by her stepmother, the social order of the day allows her no alternative, no job, no independence, and thus no agency or freedom or secure sense of self. She must marry the man her father has chosen; she must mother his children; she must not presume to question a father's authority, or have a mind of her own; she must submit and obey. Or else. Or else, what? As Sharon Pollock surveyed the historical record, it seemed obvious to her that Lizzie Borden killed the bad mother and the oppressive patriarch, but she also knew that, much closer to home, other far less liberating choices had been made. Eloise, her own mother, largely abandoned her daughter when she descended into the hell of alcoholism because all her outlets for maintaining self-esteem and independence were blocked, before finally killing herself. And Sharon, in her own attempt to conform, to do what was expected of her by society, by Daddy, by the Angel in the house, or by an internalized image of how the nice, dutiful daughter should behave, married very young and lived to rue her decision. The options for Lizzie (or for Eloise or Sharon) seemed severely limited: either you conform and kill yourself (in one suicidal act or slowly, bit by bit), or you kill the parent or husband, or you make a run for it, after which you may succeed in creating a new life, but the gamble is huge because the social restrictions and patriarchal authorities are all still in place.

But let's return to *Blood Relations*. In the speech immediately following Lizzie's memories of her lost mother and fears for herself, the collaborative remembering of the past jumps forward to Lizzie's trial, where her defence lawyer challenges the jury to "look at" Miss Borden and try to imagine such a gracious, well brought up "loving daughter" delivering thirty-two hatchet blows to Mrs. Borden's head followed by "thirteen blows to the head of her father." And he warns the jurors that if they can imagine a gentlewoman like Lizzie committing such violent crimes, then they had better "look to [their own] daughters" (363). Ironically, the formula for being a good girl and a nice woman that Lizzie knows she has not and cannot accept, is so believed in by fathers and husbands that they cannot see Miss Lizzie and cannot imagine her having any other story but one of innocence. What everyone, except the Actress (and we), sees is the mask of submissive, self-less, femininity that threatens to erase the person of Lizzie Borden. And in a crucial scene from Act One, Sharon gets to the core of this dilemma. This scene centres on the carousel speech, which has been a part of this play from its earliest drafts, when Sharon saw it as linked, through strobe lighting, to Mr. Borden's murder.

Surprisingly, most critics say little about this speech and scene, but I believe they lie at the heart, indeed the most private autobiographical heart, of the play. In his article, "Daddy's Girls: Father-Daughter Incest and Canadian Plays by Women," Jerry Wasserman discusses plays by Joanna Glass, Betty Lambert, Sharon Pollock, Judith Thompson, and others, in the light of research on sexual abuse and incest, and he argues that, when the subject is treated in theatrical form, the abused daughter is portrayed as a split-self character (or characters) in what is often a memory play where the daughter blames her mother for betraying or deserting her or even for being complicit in the abuse. At best, Wasserman says, the mother is "simply powerless, an absent presence," whereas the abusive father is "the object of extreme ambivalence" because he is both loved and feared (27). Wasserman understands father/daughter relationships in *Blood Relations*, *Whiskey Six Cadenza*, and *Doc* as explorations of incest that portray different responses from the daughter: in *Blood Relations*, she kills him; in *Whiskey Six Cadenza*, she asks him to kill her; and in *Doc* she forgives him so she can forgive herself. In the case of *Blood Relations*, Sharon knew there were rumours about an incestuous affection (if not incest) between Andrew Borden and his younger daughter, just as there were rumours that Lizzie was a kleptomaniac and a lesbian, so it is conceivable that she drew on those hints to enrich her characters' lives. However, that is not exactly what Wasserman is saying. He sees Mr. Borden's brutal slaying of his daughter's birds as both a prefiguration of her murder of him and as a symbolic representation of his "phallic violation" of Lizzie. Central to his reading of this father/daughter relationship as incest is the carousel speech. Within the logic of his interpretation, the rhythms of the speech, the description of the rigid horse, and the splitting of self into masked rider and anguished observer, all confirm his view that the wound at the core of *Blood Relations* is incest, and although he stops short of speculation, the inference is clear: that Sharon Chalmers knows first hand what such abuse is and that she draws on that knowledge to create this speech and the powerful and disturbing subtexts in three of her major plays.

While I do not agree that the speech is about Lizzie's memory of incest, and I have no reason to believe that Sharon suffered such abuse, there is no doubt that the speech is terrifying and that the nightmare experience described through the metaphors of carousel, horse, and mask is about futile repetition, powerlessness, and the complete erasure of self. Even the possibility of self-recognition from "your birds," which "can see into your heart" and "love you," is unable to replace the horror of the carousel ride. In any case, this speech is delivered by Miss Lizzie/Bridget, the woman split between 1902 and 1982 who knows what happened/is just about to happen to those birds. But before delving further into the meaning of the speech I need to consider what prepares us for it.

Lizzie (the Actress) and Mr. Borden have just had a terrible row, and in a rage he has slapped her and then pushed her to the floor. He wants her to allow the widower, Mr. MacLeod, to court her, but Lizzie is adamantly opposed. She pleads with her father, telling him she does not want to marry or be a mother, that she would prefer to work, that she hates the confining house and wants out. He is deaf to her pleas; he literally refuses to hear her.

So she grows desperate and cries out: "I'm supposed to be a mirror. I'm supposed to reflect what you want to see, but everyone wants something different. If no one looks in the mirror, I'm not even there, I don't exist" (366). Mrs. Borden puts the finishing touch to Lizzie's despair by telling her that she has no rights and must do what her father wants—that is, end up just like this "fat cow" of a hated stepmother, married and raising the man's children. If we are looking for abuse, we need not look much further. This violent confrontation between daughter and father, with the threat of an imposed marriage as the only escape from the father's house, is a classic example of physical, emotional, and psychological terrorism. When the Actress/Lizzie and Miss Lizzie/Bridget are left alone after this terrible scene, Bridget tries to comfort Lizzie by telling her stories about a cook who worked in a fine house on the hill but got around her arrogant employers by smiling sweetly while adulterating the food. As she talks, she clears up the dishes that Lizzie smashed in her fight with her father. Thus, while a petulant Lizzie nurses her grievances, she watches the maid clean up the mess she made and rejects Bridget's realistic advice that she smile, get around the Bordens, and stop dreaming about enjoying life on her own terms.

Just in case we forget who is saying what, it is essential to remember that the Actress is Lizzie—that is, she is playing her version of Lizzie—and that Bridget is being played by Miss Lizzie.

BRIDGET: You dream, Lizzie ... you dream dreams.... Work. Be sensible. What could you do?
LIZZIE: I could
MISS LIZZIE/BRIDGET: No.
LIZZIE: I could
MISS LIZZIE/BRIDGET: No.
LIZZIE: I could
MISS LIZZIE/BRIDGET: No.
LIZZIE: I ... dream.
MISS LIZZIE/BRIDGET: You dream ... of a carousel ... you see a carousel ... you see lights that go on and go off ... you see yourself on a carousel horse, a red-painted horse with its head in the air, and green staring eyes, and a white flowing mane, it looks wild! ... It goes up and comes down, and the carousel whirls round with the music and the lights, on and off ... and you watch ... watch yourself on the horse. You're wearing a mask, a white mask like the mane of the horse, it looks like your face except that it's rigid and white ... and it changes! With each flick of the lights, the expression, it changes, but always so rigid and hard, like the flesh of the horse that is red that you ride. You ride with no hands! No hands on this petrified horse, its head flung in the air, its wide staring eyes like those of a doe run down by the dogs! ... And each time you go 'round, your hands rise a fraction nearer the mask ... and the music and the carousel and the horse ... they all three slow down, and they stop.... You can reach out and touch ... you ... you on the horse ... with your hands so at the eyes.... You look into the eyes! (*A sound is heard from LIZZIE, she is horrified and frightened. She covers her eyes.*) There are none! None! Just black holes in a white mask.... (*pause*) The eyes of your birds ... are round ...

and bright ... a light that shines from inside ... they ... can see into your heart ... they're
pretty ... they love you. (370)

There are several details to keep in mind when trying to understand what is happening
here. First, the exchange leading into the speech is important because in it the
Actress/Lizzie, speaking as the voice of Lizzie's more rebellious and hopeful self, is abruptly,
emphatically denied three times by Miss Lizzie/Bridget, who speaks as the harsh, internalized voice of social and patriarchal authority to insist that Lizzie has no choices and, what is
worse, no "I" with agency. When the outwardly thwarted woman turns inward to dreams,
Miss Lizzie/Bridget will not allow even this avenue of escape from the painful reality of her
life (and here the *her* is both the Actress's imagined Lizzie and Miss Lizzie). She interrupts
again, this time to relate the story of a dream. The emphatic repetition of the pronoun you—
"you dream," "you see," "you watch," "you ride," "you touch," "you look"—anchors the
speech rhythmically at the same time as it splits the self into observer and object observed
and insists on the dream being shared with the Actress/Lizzie. This is Miss Lizzie/Bridget
speaking, and she is once more guiding her partner into the darkest recesses of Miss Lizzie's
life. The Actress/Lizzie begins by watching intently as Miss Lizzie/Bridget delivers this
speech, but she quickly becomes caught up in the story and reacts with terror (as the stage
instruction indicates) at the climactic moment. By the time the story reaches the description
of the mask's eyes, both women are participating fully, each one is "you," and the monologue
has become intersubjective, almost, in fact, a dialogue. This sharing of identity signals that
the mirror talk has worked: unlike the others who only expect Lizzie to reflect them back to
themselves, the Actress mirrors and returns to Miss Lizzie an acknowledgement of her
terror and anguish. Here, more than at any other point in the play, the two women merge,
and the split identity played out thus far is healed because the Actress/Lizzie feels the same
horror as Miss Lizzie. Finally, she understands what it is like to be a woman like (Sharon
Pollock's) Lizzie Borden. Together the women have created a landscape of memory for their
shared trauma. Here, in this mirrored nightmare, is where I locate the core of the "dream
thesis."

But if this is the dream, what precisely is the trauma and what is it that the Actress
understands when she covers her eyes, *"horrified and frightened"*? What is the "thesis"? Every
time I watch or read this scene, I am struck by the speed with which the images and narrative
slide from what should be an innocent, happy child's ride on a colourful carousel into a
story about death, emptiness, and absence. I am also struck by the quality of enforced silence
implied by the description, as if there should be a piercing, shattering scream of self-assertion (instead of the wordless "sound" coming from the Actress/Lizzie). I want to hear an "I."
But that surely is the message: in this dream, there is no "I," no self, because the dreamer
has been reduced to nothing more than a part of the "petrified horse" with a mask that
"looks like" the dreamer's face. The dreamer is one with this "red-painted horse," an
imitation, inanimate, carousel horse, and the eyes of both resemble "those of a doe run
down by the dogs." When this movement stops, the dreamer tries to assert her presence by
taking off the mask, but at this point the full horror of the dream becomes clear. Dreamer,

horse, and mask are all equally petrified, and where the eyes that represent presence, mutual recognition, inner life, and love should be, "there are none! None! Just black holes in a white mask." This dreamer, "you," Miss Lizzie and, now, the Actress have been erased. For Miss Lizzie, this is the deepest wound; as a person, she does not exist because her sense of self is not acknowledged by anyone else, not by Emma, her father, or Dr. Patrick, and certainly not by her stepmother. The thesis of this appalling dream is that to be invisible and unheard is to be nothing. Only by forcing her lover to enter the dream can she be seen, heard, and acknowledged as a precious self. Moreover, only after this crisis of seeing and hearing will the Actress/Lizzie be able to see Miss Lizzie clearly enough to finish performing her life-story.

In this powerful scene of mutual recognition, Miss Lizzie, the autobiographer, gives the Actress, her biographer, the crucial story-within-the-story that she needs to complete her narrative. It is also in this scene, especially in the carousel speech, that Sharon works as an autobiographer within her biography of Lizzie Borden because this is the kind of trauma she experienced. "I would have killed," she has told us, "to maintain my sense of self," and she did. She did not actually kill a husband or a father or a mother, but she did kill Virginia Woolf's Angel who tried to coerce her into selfless submission, into a passive, masked conformity. Like the Lizzie Borden she imagined, she murdered those forces that threatened to erase her identity, and she asserted herself, demanding that she be seen—on stage as an actor—and heard as a playwright. Where the historical Lizzie Borden paid for her self-assertion by spending the rest of her life under a cloud of suspicion, Sharon has paid by needing to create new lives for all her ghosts and by struggling to understand and forgive them. But then Lizzie Borden was not an artist. So, while I do not see the trauma underlying *Blood Relations* specifically as incest, I do see an equally devastating violation of the individual person that strips him or her of self and identity. If those around you refuse to see and hear you, then you do not exist; as Lizzie says, she is reduced to being a mirror in which others choose to see only themselves and, when no one "looks in the mirror, I'm not even there." Sharon's Lizzie suspects that her birth mother may have realized this and chosen to die, just as Sharon was coming to see that Eloise had faced the same erasure and made the same fatal choice.

Once the Actress/Lizzie has shared this dream and Lizzie's birds, who saw into her heart and loved her, have been slaughtered by Papa, she can move, with less coaching into the second act. Act One ends with the slaughter and a blackout; there is no intermission. The lights come up in Act Two on the two women sitting very still. The Actress/Lizzie breaks the silence by asking Miss Lizzie/Bridget to talk to her, but Miss Lizzie/Bridget is still lost in her memories. Speaking in the first person, as Lizzie, she recalls for the Actress how any creature on the family farm that was "different" was rejected by its own kind and killed. When the Actress/Lizzie asks, "Am I different?" Lizzie/Bridget's only answer is: "You kill them" (374). And with that we return to the game of role-playing that has become deadly serious. In Act Two Emma becomes more of a presence to be reckoned with not only because she argues at length with Lizzie and then abandons her, as Lizzie sees it, but also because she is so dramatically included in the final moments of the play.

Now things move quickly. Lizzie begs Emma not to leave her, but Emma stubbornly refuses to listen. Then Lizzie begs Emma to talk to their father, to "make him understand that we're people. *Individual people*" (377), but Emma refuses because she believes that they "can't change a thing." Emma leaves the house as Lizzie screams "Go away! ... I don't like you," and then a calmer Lizzie articulates her most important realization: "I want to die ... I want to die, but something inside won't let me ... inside something says no. (*She shuts her eyes.*) I can do anything" (378). It seems that the Actress/Lizzie, empowered by the insights of the carousel dream, is able to recognize herself and reject the choices made by her dead mother and Emma. Then there is a brief interruption by the voice of the defence lawyer, followed by the breakfast routine in the Borden house on the morning of the murders. Lizzie and Mr. Borden talk and she asks him who she resembles, suggesting that she is "strong-willed" like him. When he tells her she looks like her mother, she immediately asks about her mother's death. Dissatisfied by his vague reply—"it was just something that happened"— she imagines explanations that help her to make sense of this death: her mother was tired, or she wanted to fly away, or she "was caught in a horrible snare," and she bravely took the only way out by *choosing* to die (382). Lizzie, of course, is feeling suffocated and trapped too, but she knows she will not choose her mother's way out. Dr. Patrick enters, thinking he can flirt with Lizzie, but she is in no mood for games. Instead, she confronts him with a life and death question: If he, as a doctor, could only save one of two people, how would he choose? Predictably, he vacillates and obfuscates. She, by contrast, is certain and accuses him of cowardice and hypocrisy because he will not make a decision. Lizzie has reached hers. She will live and someone else will die.

When her father has left the house and Bridget is outside cleaning windows, Lizzie conceals a hatchet under the laundry she carries and follows Mrs. Borden upstairs. When she comes back down moments later and Bridget finds her seated in Mrs. Borden's chair, Bridget (remember this is Miss Lizzie playing the role of the maid) *knows* something serious has occurred, but she is persuaded by Lizzie's begging to go along with Lizzie's plan. When Mr. Borden returns unexpectedly, Lizzie must change her plan, so she persuades Bridget to go upstairs and lie down, and then she concentrates on her father. She convinces him to stretch out on the couch and rest, and a subdued, almost tender scene between the father and daughter ensues. She remarks that he still wears the ring she gave him some years ago, and she forgives him for killing her birds. She undoes his shoes, tells him she loves him, hears him say he loves her, and receives his kiss on her forehead. As he shuts his eyes and drifts off to sleep, she hums a lullaby, moves quietly to the pile of laundry concealing the hatchet, removes it, and returns to stand over his sleeping figure. She raises the hatchet and is just about to bring it down when the lights go to blackout and children's voices are heard singing:

> "Lizzie Borden took an axe,
> Gave her mother forty whacks,
> When the job was nicely done,
> She gave her father forty-one!

Forty-one!
Forty-one!" (392)

When the lights come back up, the play-within-the-play is over. Miss Lizzie, no longer playing Bridget, stands on the stairs watching the Actress who is standing exactly as she was before the blackout with the hatchet in her raised hand. However, the couch is empty; we are back in 1902, and Miss Lizzie takes the hatchet away from the Actress.

This galvanizing scene is performed in silence until Emma is heard calling Lizzie from upstairs. But what we have seen, and heard, is the Actress/Lizzie playing out what she believes to be Lizzie Borden's true story. If we believe that the Actress has understood the truth through her intense mirror talk—her intersubjective connection—with Lizzie, then we will not only conclude that Lizzie did do it but we will also see why and realize that Lizzie did what others could have, would have, done in her place because this mutually remembered and re-enacted story of trauma, rebellion, and murder that is Lizzie's life makes sense. It has been situated within a shared landscape of memory that includes Lizzie, the Actress and us, and is about to include Emma. Our return to 1902 is completed when Emma comes downstairs to confront her sister over the presence of the Actress in their home. On the face of it, Emma forbids Lizzie to have such a person in the house because the people of Fall River are gossiping about their relationship, and Emma wants Lizzie to avoid provoking more gossip. But I suggest that there is a deeper reason for Emma's dislike of the Actress: Emma suspects the two women of being so close, so mutually responsive and understanding, that the Actress has *heard* Lizzie's story and *seen* Lizzie's truth. In the final lines of the play, Lizzie reminds Emma of her role in what has happened, that it was Emma who brought Lizzie up, "like a mother," and that therefore she—Emma—must accept her share of responsibility. Lizzie did, for herself and Emma, what Emma wanted but was too weak to do. Emma, then, is the third party to the murders, the third character alive in the present of 1902 and, as Lizzie's puppet master, *she* and she alone represents the one person who has really been in control of the story throughout—the playwright. Or perhaps I should say that outside the play all three characters are aspects of Sharon Pollock. The Actress is Sharon the actor who interprets the story; Lizzie is Sharon the director who knows the story and works with the actor to reveal it; and Emma is, well, the mother of the plot, the stand-in for the dead mother, who through the semblance of resignation and acquiescent submission to the patriarchal plot inspires the abandoned and betrayed daughter's revenge.

In my reading of *Blood Relations*, the dream *thesis* of the play is that we know ourselves by imagining and telling stories about who we are, what we have experienced, and, there-fore, what we do. However, for the autobiographical story to produce meaning or be effective, the autobiographer *must* have a sympathetic, participating listener, another person who, as a mirror self, collaborates in the story-telling; this listener validates what is being told by giving him- or herself to the storyteller and sharing in, re-telling, or re-performing the narrative, by, in effect, playing biographer to the autobiographer. If one partner to this mirror talk paints the background, the other creates the figures in that ground, and the figure/ground relationship is intimate, mutually supportive, indivisible. The more traumatic the memories in the autobiographical story, the greater the need for a shared landscape of memory through which the narrative can find its legitimizing context and make sense. So, for example, when Lizzie's father tells her to talk sensibly ("Lizzie, you talk foolish!" 366), he is denying her story; he cannot hear her or recognize any narrative landscape for what she is struggling to say. By contrast, the Actress can hear the story and can see the psychological sense of Lizzie's life. To capture this complex understanding of identity, or what Eakin calls "making selves," Sharon employs a memory-mirror (a play-within-a-memory-play) form with a subtle yet strong through-line of visual imagery that braids metaphors of mirrors with images of masks and eyes.

This imagery is most concentrated in the carousel speech, which marks the mid-point and fulcrum of the play and provides the most intense moment of mirror talk. It is here that we are able to see the horror of a petrified existence, where an individual's sense of self is denied and thus destroyed, because for the dreamer trapped in that nightmare, there is no one to acknowledge "you." By telling the Actress/Lizzie this dream story, Miss Lizzie/Bridget gives expression to the pain of that self-less condition and by being seen and heard, and, through the Actress's own horror, acknowledged, Miss Lizzie releases herself from its obliterating void. She *gives* the horror and the release to the Actress, who can act upon what she has seen and heard when she goes on to play out her story of Lizzie Borden in 1892. However, mirror talk within the memory play is only on one side of the mirror. On the other side, in 1902, Miss Lizzie and the Actress are still partners, secret sharers; they are still collaborating in the auto/biography, with a further significant addition: Emma. The 1902 mirror is a three-way glass, one of those mirrors with a central panel and two side panels that includes Emma, the third, living player in the 1902 frame narrative. Just as the Actress resembles Lizzie *and*, as Lizzie says, sister Emma, so Lizzie takes after Emma, who stands in for the lost and the murdered mothers. Emma cannot be ignored because she has been there all along in Lizzie's life, watching, encouraging, questioning, and provoking, in fact, *raising* Lizzie. Instead of being displaced by the Actress in her sister's affection and the mirror story, Emma has been forced to look into the mirror and recognize her role in the narrative landscape. When *Blood Relations* ends, these three interrelated women are all on stage, all connected by the story, all mirroring each other, but the relations do not stop there. With the final words, gestures, and looking from the stage, the audience is seen and forced to see itself; we too are figures in this landscape.

If this play tells us something about Sharon Pollock's life, and I think it does, then we must find that *something* reflected in the roles of these three women and possibly also in the lost mother, and in the murdered stepmother and father. In crucial ways, Sharon's Lizzie suffers childhood trauma and adult frustration and fear that parallel her own experiences. Sharon also lacked a fully present and nurturing mother, and she was taught to behave as a dutiful daughter and wife by denying herself, while seeing, in Eloise, the self-destructive result of such denial. However, the Actress character in the play is given a life and rooms and a profession of her own; she has a distinct, acknowledged identity, the kind of empowering identity Sharon Pollock finally created for herself. But constantly present, in the wings, on the stairs, at the dining room table is Emma, the Angel in the house, abject, yet angry and resentful, advising passive acquiescence while longing for active assertion. Emma is what Sharon might have been, unless she had chosen the mothers' way out. As for the parents, they have to be dispatched because they refuse to see or hear Lizzie and who she wants to be. By murdering them, reducing them to ghosts haunting the 1902 story and called out to play by Miss Lizzie's will, Sharon effectively shatters what they represent as nonreflecting mirrors. She is the one who tells their story in her own performative multi-faceted way. Whether Truth can be found in the telling I cannot say, but power certainly resides there, and it is the power of making theatre.

On several occasions, Sharon has described *Getting It Straight* as her most auto-biographical play, and she should know. But she takes some very important steps towards that play in this one by assuming the role of Lizzie Borden's biographer and only allowing her autobiography to appear indirectly. In the carousel speech and in the fascinating memory-mirror complexities of *Blood Relations*, I hear the voice of Eme and see the terrifying possibility of a life without mirror talk in which one can only speak in tongues or riddles with no one and nothing to address but the void.

CHAPTER 7

Family Trappings

It is a mistake to think that writers create anything from other than the raw material they have to work with, and the raw material they have to work with is their own life.

—SHARON POLLOCK, INTERVIEW WITH KATHLEEN FLAHERTY, APPENDIX 3, 396

May women storm the bastions of men's realm of the theatre establishment? Despite the inhospitable environment, there is dire need of their talent and insight, for the female artistic director is one with the true nature of theatre. —SHARON POLLOCK "REFLECTIONS OF A FEMALE ARTISTIC DIRECTOR," 113

I: Family Trappings—*Generations* and *Whiskey Six Cadenza*

In many ways the 1980s were the most productive, challenging, rewarding, and yet troubled in Sharon's adult life. She saw five major stage plays produced, won two Governor General's Awards, and received her first Honorary Degree—from the University of New Brunswick. And there were other awards and other plays, for radio, television, and children's theatre, as well as opportunities to act and direct. But the decade was certainly not one of unqualified happiness and success. Both personally and professionally, she had to deal with serious challenges beginning with the separation from Michael Ball but going on to include other departures, a serious illness, a sudden death, and a range of acrimonious confrontations with theatre boards, directors, unions, and filmmakers. This is the decade of *Doc*, the play that many consider her finest, but it is also the decade during which her attempts at being an artistic director ended in resignations and when one after another, the children married or left, not just the family home but Calgary. All but one of them eventually returned to take up new roles in her life, but the story of happy, if hectic, family life that John Hofsess presented in his 1980 feature article, "Sticking Together," was over. Sharon was no longer surrounded at home by the smiling daughters in the photograph that Hofsess used for his article. This turbulent decade ended with *Getting It Straight*, which is perhaps fitting. Of all her plays, it was the most difficult to write; it caused the most grief for the playwright and for the artistic directors who commissioned it in its earlier incarnations as "Egg" or "God's not finished with us yet," and it is, finally, her most personal, tormented, and symbolically complex work. The title she chose for this apparently mad monologue belies the play itself, even as it signals her need to understand the pain, losses, and lessons of the preceding years.

But if Sharon's playwriting was drawing increasing power from the "raw material" of her "own life," as she told Kathleen Flaherty, she remained sharply aware of the social, political, and cultural events of the times, many of which had indirect effects on her life and on the kind of theatre she was dedicated to building. Pierre Elliott Trudeau returned as prime minister in March of 1980, but the excitement and optimism that had surrounded his 1971 marriage to Margaret Sinclair were long past; by 1984 he was out of office for good, and their troubled marriage was over. Civil divorce seemed imminent for the country as well, until René Levesque and the Parti Québecois lost their first referendum on separation in May 1980. By September that year, Terry Fox was forced to end his Marathon of Hope in Thunder Bay, and in less than a year he was dead. With hindsight it seems that the private Ball/Pollock breakup was mirrored by these events on the public stage. But there was also a brighter side. In 1981 Canada held its first annual Fringe Theatre Festival in Edmonton, where it continues to flourish, and Louis Appelbaum and Jacques Hébert were appointed to head up a new Federal Cultural Policy Review Committee. Between 1982 and 1983, there were several other signs that the cultural life of the country was in good health: in Toronto, Tomson Highway founded Native Earth Performing ARTS Theatre, One Yellow Rabbit formed in Calgary, the first Chalmer's Children's Play Award competition was announced, and in 1983 the first Jessie Awards were handed out, with Larry Lillo's production of *Blood Relations* winning three. Between 1984 and 1985, three major collections of Canadian plays were published, which meant that Canadian drama had won a secure place on university courses. Finally, Canadian theatre was recognized as a force to be reckoned with and Canadian plays and playwrights were here to stay. In 1985 an all-Canadian *Cats* opened at a refurbished Elgin Theatre in Toronto, R. Murray Schafer's extravagant spectacle *Ra* was revived for an international debut, the XXIst World Congress of Theatre was held in Montreal, and both Theatre Calgary and Alberta Theatre Projects moved into elegant new spaces in Calgary's state-of-the-art Centre for the Performing Arts.

However, this surface energy masked a number of disturbing undercurrents and warning signals that news junkies like Sharon could not ignore. Trudeau was no supporter of the Canadian arts: the so-called Appelbert Report (the *Report of the Federal Cultural Policy Review Committee*) submitted in 1982 had little practical impact, and Rina Fraticelli's important 1982 study, *The Invisibility Factor: Status of Women in Canadian Theatre* was largely ignored. Indeed, efforts in 2006 to reassess the status of women in our professional theatre sector suggest that female theatre administrators and practitioners are only marginally more visible today than they were in the 1980s. While many Canadians applauded their new Constitution, with its Charter of Rights and Freedoms (1982), an improved Canada Health Act (1984), a new Indian Act (1986), the Multiculturalism Act (1988), and the Free Trade Agreement (1988)—a very mixed blessing that would lead to NAFTA in 1994 and do nothing at all to support Canadian culture and the arts—grim revelations were surfacing in the newspapers during 1984 about past practices in the Allan Memorial Institute in Montreal, where psychiatric patients under Dr. Donald Ewen Cameron's care had been subjected to appalling brainwashing *treatments* funded by the CIA during the late forties and the fifties.

In Calgary, Sharon was watching these reports and keeping a clipping file, in part because such an example of the abuse of rights and freedoms by those with medical power pricked her social conscience and aroused her moral indignation and in part because of her more private, personal fears. I have not been able to allay or confirm her fears because only immediate family members can consult medical records, but she is still troubled by the possibility that Eloise suffered at the hands of Cameron in the Allan.[1] I believe that the revelations of what had happened behind the closed doors of the Institute provided the impetus she needed to wrest *Getting It Straight* from the sprawling manuscript of "Egg." What Sharon could not have known about were the crises of political and personal violence that would bring the decade to a close: on 14 June 1989, hundreds, perhaps thousands, of protesters were massacred by the state in Tiananmen Square, Beijing, and on 6 December 1989, at the École Polytechnique of the Université de Montréal, Marc Lepine murdered fourteen female Engineering students, none of whom he knew personally, simply because they were women, what he called "feminists," pursuing their legitimate dreams. It is true, of course, that 1989 also saw the fall of the Berlin Wall, but in Canada and abroad, the decade ended under a dark cloud of repression, violence, and death in what might well be described as very bloody relations.

How eerily peaceful it seems now to return to the other play Sharon premiered at the beginning of the eighties: *Generations*. Six months after the first version of *Blood Relations* opened at Edmonton's Theatre 3, *Generations* received its first production with ATP on 28 October 1980 at the Canmore Opera House under the direction of Mark Schoenberg. It began life as a radio play in 1978 and Douglas Riske commissioned the full stage version. Within the context of Sharon's oeuvre, however, this play remains something of an anomaly. For starters, nothing violent happens (except an offstage fire): no one is murdered or goes mad or commits suicide, and no one is an alcoholic. *Generations* is a relatively gentle, comparatively realistic play set on an Alberta farmstead that tells the story of three genera-tions of the Nurlin family. The grandfather, Old Eddy Nurlin, built the farm and survived the deaths of his wife and infant son, as well as the drought of the dirty thirties. His remaining son, Alfred, returned from WWII traumatized but was content to join his father, run the farm, and marry Margaret, a farmer's daughter. The chief conflict in the play arises in the third generation. The elder of Alfred's and Margaret's two sons, Young Eddy, has left the farm to become a lawyer in Calgary; his brother David, however, has chosen to stay on the farm and fight for a way of life that is increasingly under threat. As the play opens, we learn that the Indians on a nearby reservation have dammed the river that provides irrigation for the surrounding farms to force the government to pay more for their water. Government officials have arrived to hold a meeting, but they are doing nothing concrete to resolve the face-off. When Young Eddy comes home to ask his father for money to establish his own law firm in Calgary, arguments erupt within the family.

Furious with his brother for making such a request—one that can only be met by selling a section of the farm—David lashes out:

What's fair about Eddy and the whole fuckin' city sittin' drinkin' scotch and feedin' their faces
while we bust our ass to put food on their tables! Two-thirds of the goddam world dies of starvation and the farmer's the low man on the totem pole! (*G, CW* I, 320)

And he has a point. In fact, he will drive his point home before the day is over by setting fire
to the back section of the farm (presumably the section Eddy had hoped to sell). But the
generational conflict does not stop with Young Eddy and David. David's fiancé, Bonnie, is
growing dubious about confining herself to the life of a farm wife like her own mother and
Margaret Nurlin. Bonnie is a teacher, and she wants more from life than servitude, as she
sees it, to a man who serves the land. In a telling scene between the two women, Bonnie
marvels at Margaret's ability to agree constantly with the men and submerge her identity in
the farming life. Bonnie sees that this way of life is dying out, and she is unwilling to lose
herself in a struggle to save the farm in a marriage with a stubborn, demanding man like
David. Although Margaret protests, eloquently, that being part of something bigger than an
individual identity is more worthwhile than being self-sufficient, the conversation between
the two generations of women highlights the personal stakes involved and ends in an
impasse. The final confrontation between David and Bonnie also ends without a clear
resolution. He orders her to shut up while he tells her why he chooses to stay on the land
and then warns her—"You can't hack it, you get the hell out." So Bonnie leaves, possibly for
good, and the play ends with Old Eddy reminiscing about the past with an even older Charlie
Running Dog, his sometime friend and neighbour from the reservation. In the closing scene
a timely thunderstorm has stopped the fire in the back section, a new day is dawning, the
two old-timers are standing in front of the Nurlins' *old* cabin (not the new house in which
the family now lives), and the play ends with Old Eddy saying, "We're still here, Charlie.
Hell, we'll always be here." But these words, uttered in this context, offer neither reassurance
about the survival of the farm nor much hope for future generations.

In her description of the characters and setting for the play, Sharon insisted that the land
should be seen as a character and that its "omniscient presence and mythic" power should
be represented through the lighting, which symbolizes the diurnal rhythms of the earth.
Certainly, the mythic qualities of timelessness and cyclic rhythm can be captured on stage,
as they were in the 2004 Theatre North West production that I saw.[2] Sharon was drawing
on personal experience as well as observation to create this play, and she knew full well that
the choices made by Margaret and David would never be made by Young Eddy and Bonnie.
The Nurlins were inspired by the family into which her eldest daughter, Jennifer, married,
and her future son-in-law had left the family farm to become a successful Calgary lawyer.
Moreover, Bonnie speaks for Sharon both in the scene with Margaret, when she protests
that she does not want to lose her identity, and then later when she tells Alfred that "I think
I was born in the wrong place." In a private joke, Sharon has Bonnie tell Alfred that she
should have been born in New Brunswick because it is "domesticated there" (*G*, 329). Of
course, being born in the right or wrong place, and belonging to something larger than the
individual self or safeguarding your independent identity, were not joking matters for Sharon
Pollock in 1980. She had already come through both sets of challenges, learned to appreciate

and adjust to the Prairie surrounding her Calgary home and established a strong independent presence in both her personal life and her career.

Although *Generations* explores perennial questions about life, identity, relationships, and basic values lightly in comparison with her other major Alberta plays like *Walsh* and *Whiskey Six Cadenza*, and while it requires a more realistic set than any of her other stage plays, it is still representative of her kind of theatre. Family members are at odds; the patriarchs expect wives to shut up and behave, to have, in short, no minds or voices of their own; and nothing is resolved or concluded by the end. The upheavals of fire and argument solve nothing because life is too complex and, as always, Sharon can clearly see the grass on both sides of the social/moral fence. In this ambiguity, *Generations* is a subtler and more satisfying portrayal of human relations, individual rights, and married life, than Anne Chislett's *The Tomorrow Box*. Chislett's play is a sharp, even comic, treatment of a bullying man who sells the family farm without consulting his wife because he has the power to do so. However, to his surprise, his elderly, doormat wife, with some legal help, refuses to follow him to Florida, gets a job, pursues her own interests, and manages very well until he returns to insinuate himself back into the family. Chislett ends her play with this manipulative man apparently back in control of his wife, his son, his farm, and their lives. The *happy* ending, with husband and wife reunited, is at best an illusion and at worst a sinister betrayal of the feminist issues raised by the play. In *Generations* Sharon refuses to reach for such answers and conclusions. As the sun rises on her two old men, all we can see is that, like the Prairie, they are still "here," and all we can be sure of is that the conflict between generations in a family, between life on the farm and life in the city, between men and women, between freedom and entrapment, and between races and philosophies will continue. In her next stage play she returned to these conflicts, but with a much darker vision.

Whiskey Six Cadenza, which premiered on 10 February 1983 at Theatre Calgary with the title "Whiskey Six," is the most neglected of Sharon's plays, and yet it is one of her personal favourites. Although it received a CBC-FM radio broadcast on 22 October that year, to my knowledge it has not received another professional stage production since its premiere. This neglect is partially explained by the sheer size and scope of the play: with a cast of thirteen, a symbolically complex set, and the need for music, dancing, and a variety of sound-effects, it is an epic play that is costly to produce. But part of the difficulty also lies in its subject matter and certain aspects of its plot. To a degree *Whiskey Six Cadenza* is about events and figures from Alberta history, and while Sharon takes many liberties with historical fact, the basic story remains rooted in post-WWI, small-town Alberta and cannot be easily transplanted to Toronto, say, or Vancouver. But more importantly, this play tries to do too much, and the various plot lines do not come together in an entirely satisfying manner. Ten years later Sharon again created another epic play, but in *Fair Liberty's Call* she solved the dramatic and structural problems by simplifying and focusing the central dilemma. Like *Fair Liberty's Call*, *Whiskey Six Cadenza* draws on historical events and characters while developing a fictional story of troubled family relations. Indeed, both plays, unlike *Walsh*, *One Tiger to a Hill*, and *The Komagata Maru Incident*, are more about conflicts within families and the moral dilemmas they raise, than about history.

In its earliest incarnation, however, *Whiskey Six Cadenza* was a dramatization of an actual story that ended with murder and hanging in 1920s Alberta, and the scenario Sharon was working on in 1979 stayed close to the known facts. In 1923 Florence Lassandro, an Italian immigrant, whose maiden name was Filumena Costanzo, and Emilio Picariello, a business-man and bootlegger from Blairmore in the Crow's Nest Pass, were convicted of killing Constable Stephen Oldacres Lawson, a WWI veteran and British-born Alberta Provincial Police officer. The two were hanged on 2 May 1923, making Florence Lassandro, aged twenty-two, the only woman ever hanged for murder in Alberta and one of the few women executed in Canada. Florence, who had been married off at fourteen, lived with her husband in the Blairmore Hotel, which was owned by Picariello. Alberta had introduced Prohibition in 1915, but Emperor Pic, as he was called, saw an opportunity to make money and operated a boot-legging business out of his hotel. A large, charming, genial man with four sons, Mr. Pic owned a McLaughlin Six Special, the car known as a Whiskey Six because it was fast and popular with bootleggers. Florence's husband was employed by Mr. Pic to run booze from wet British Columbia into dry Alberta and east as far as Regina. Apparently Florence, together with one of Mr. Pic's sons, would accompany the bootleggers to act as decoys, the idea being that the police would not view a young couple with suspicion. However, and perhaps inevitably, given the sexism of the day and the hostility to immigrants, rumours spread that Florence was having an affair with Mr. Pic or with his son. Neither rumour was ever proven, and Florence's precise role in the shooting was also unclear, but the fact remained that a policeman, whose job it was to stamp out the bootlegging, had been killed by immigrants. A price had to be paid.

Sharon's plans for this story are interesting and shed light on what the play later became. In 1979 she accepted a commission from CBC to create a radio play about the case, which was to be called "Whiskey Six Cadenza: a bittersweet musical," with music by Calgary composer Allan Rae. The "musical" had six main characters—Mr. George (known as Mr. Big), Mama George (his wife), Leah, Johnny McGuire, William Windsor (the police officer known as Bill the Brit), and Gompers, all of whom are involved in the bootlegging story—plus a chorus that would function, "where required," as townspeople, members of the police force, and the McGuire family (54: 12.3–4). The musical was supposed to climax with a fight between the bootleggers and the police in which Leah shoots Bill the Brit to stop him from savagely beating Mr. Big. Interestingly, this early musical was intended to close, as it had opened, with an elderly Johnny sitting on the porch of the abandoned Alberta Hotel in Blairmore telling us how he had waited outside the jail on the morning Leah and Mr. Big were hanged. The entire performance has been his creation, and the characters have been invoked from the past, "57 years ago," brought to life and song by his storytelling imagina-tion. At this point Sharon was not thinking of the Blairmore mines and mining disasters, and the exact nature of the relationship between Leah and Mr. Big remained unclear. What was clear from the start is that Sharon saw her Mr. Big as a charismatic, larger-than-life man who loves Leah, his chosen or adopted daughter, and Johnny, and is loved by them and by his loyal wife Mama George. When CBC funding failed to materialize, Sharon put the script aside. By 1980–81 she was preoccupied with other matters: the production of *Blood Relations*, the separation from Michael, and the less demanding commission from ATP for *Generations*. The history of Prohibition and an Alberta rum-runner and the tragedy of a young woman caught up in these events would have to wait. As it waited, it grew in her imagination until it included aspects of the harsh coal-mining history of the Blairmore area, a second family story, and another set of characters.

By the time Rick McNair, the artistic director of Theatre Calgary and a trusted friend, commissioned her to write a new stage play, she was ready to develop the original radio script in new and larger ways. This time she dropped her plan to write a musical, although music continues to have a more important role in this play than in any other of her works. When the premiere opened in February 1983, the play was simply called "Whiskey Six," and the only actual music was a marching band and a few songs. However, this play remained musical in less obvious structural ways, and a good production should foreground this structure through staging, choreography, and lighting. To understand why the word cadenza is integral to the title and was restored when the play was published, it is necessary to return to the plot. In rewriting it for McNair, Sharon decided to build up a second plot line, *not* a sub-plot, that would develop in tandem with the one about Mr. Big, come into conflict with the first plot at key points, and eventually precipitate the conclusion by bringing the action to its fall (the literal meaning of cadence) or point of rest. This new plot tells the story of the Farley family, the Temperance Movement, and the coal mines, and it centres on Mrs. Farley and her youngest son Johnny. The story proper begins with Johnny's return to Blairmore in 1919 after a futile attempt to find work in Toronto. With the job market flooded by returned soldiers, he is obliged to return home and join his father and surviving brother in the coal mines. His mother is appalled because she has already lost one son to a mine disaster (a second son, Will, dies in the mine during the course of the play) and her husband is clearly dying of lung disease. However, mining is not Mrs. Farley's only obsession. Since the arrival of Prohibition, she has become a Temperance advocate, for which it is scarcely hard to blame her, considering how her husband drinks. When she learns that Johnny's alternative to working in the mines is to take a job with Mr. Big, she decides to co-operate with Bill the Brit in his effort to put a stop to Mr. Big's illegal activities.

Mrs. Farley is anything but a sympathetic figure. When she realizes that her Johnny not only works for Mr. Big but has fallen in love with his adopted daughter Leah, her intolerant and manipulative nature prompts her to accuse Leah of being Mr. Big's whore. The result-ing confrontation between mother and son brings Act One to a painful and dramatic close, but the scene also functions as a pivotal conjunction of the two plots. In musical terms, the Farley plot provides the tonic chord (or feminine chord) and the Mr. Big plot provides the dominant (or masculine) chord for the whole cadence that concludes the play. Given the highly ornate framing of the play in memory, voiceovers, and Johnny's invocation of ghosts, the cadenza itself could be seen as Johnny's solo performance of the remembered story. Other explanations for the cadenza are possible—for example, it could be argued that Mr. Big's long, hyperbolic speeches are cadenza-like—but my point is simply that the concept of cadenza resolved by an authentic cadence is fundamental to the structure of the play. One story is not the sub-plot for the other because they work together, in contrast and yet inseparably, to produce the dying fall and point of rest in the tonic key, which is determined *in relation to* the dominant, the key that calls the shots. Throughout the play it is possible to locate the shared root notes of both chords which, in dramatic and verbal terms, are notes of individual choice and social constraint, of illusion and reality (lies and truths), of male and female, of pride and prejudice, of a life confined to the mines and of a life of freedom on the roads. The problem with such a structure is that while it is clearly visible in musical notation and audible in a concert, it is not so easily seen in the written text of a play (Sharon's "blueprint for performance") or in a live production. Instead, the sheer amount of activity on stage, together with the number of characters, may create confusion. The spectacle is there, but the underlying purpose, and hence the meaning, may be obscured. At no point is this risk of confusion more evident than in the play's penultimate scene when we have shifted from the Farley home to the Alberta Hotel and from a mother/son confrontation to a father/daughter one.

As the play draws to its violent end, Bill the Brit is closing in on Mr. Big's illegal business and Johnny is pressing Mr. Big to tell him the truth about Leah. Although Johnny never asks directly—his interrogation is forestalled by Mr. Big and then interrupted by an armed police blockade—Mr. Big and Leah understand what he wants to know: Have you had and are you still having sexual relations with this young woman who you took into your home when she was eleven and now call your daughter? Yet Mr. Big does answer this question indirectly when he puts the rumour about his relations with Leah into words: his "fantastical comprehension of a cosmic design" is not the result of "revelation or wisdom" but a big lie "to legitimize an on-going affair ... with a child" (*WSC, CW* II, 120). He goes on to insist that Leah "is without flaw or injury" and then, when Johnny has rushed out to break through the blockade in the Whiskey Six, he turns to Leah and tells her to "pretend" he has never touched her. When she refuses to go on living this lie, something has to give way, and the dramatic solution was discovered collaboratively, with Sharon, McNair, and the actors, in rehearsal. The gun that first appeared from behind the bar in Act One is now in full view on the counter. Leah hands the gun to Mr. Big and tells him to "make it right" as she begins to run towards the door and Johnny. Then the stage instructions indicate that "*Mr. Big fires at Leah hitting her in the back. She collapses knocking over a chair*" (*WSC*, 123). Although *Whiskey Six Cadenza* ends not with that shot but with the voiceovers, music, and dancing with which the play opened and gives the final words to a much older Johnny, emotionally and dramatically the structural cadence reaches its dying fall and point of rest with Mr. Big's murder of Leah.

The trouble with this ending is its mixed message, its complexity, and its shift outside the past story into Johnny's present dreamlike memoryscape when he tells us, in the final words of the play, that "It may all have been lies, but that still doesn't mean it weren't true." Unlike the reviewers, audiences at the premiere were genuinely shocked by the murder of Leah, and it still bothers some critics because it *feels* gratuitous, resolves nothing, and leaves the moral emphasis of the narrative squarely on the admission of sexual transgression—the sexual abuse of a female child by a much older man in a position of authority or, indeed, the incest of a father with a daughter.[3] In a scene from Act Two that precedes Johnny's questioning of

Mr. Big, Mama George tells her husband what he has refused to see: that "his great and glorious construction a the universe [is] based on nothin' more than the frail embrace of a child" (114) and that a child grows up, just as Leah has, to love a young man her own age. Mr. Big resists his wife's version of the truth, blaming her for tarnishing his love for Leah out of jealousy. Nevertheless, her charges and her clear-sighted description ring true. She has known about the incest all along because Leah confided in her. Moreover, she understands that as a child Leah was unable to refuse Mr. Big's advances; she admits that she kept silent about this "despicable thing" happening in her family out of love for Mr. Big, and she accepts the reality of Leah's love for Johnny. But Mr. Big cannot accept these truths because his entire identity is built on lies and self-aggrandizement, from his illicit sexual liaison with a child to his bootlegging. If it is possible to argue that Prohibition was nothing more than the arbitrary restriction of individual choice by the state, can it also be argued that no one, least of all the state, should prohibit sexual exploitation or incest? I think not. To equate the two moral questions is to confuse the issues, but the play dangles on the horns of this dilemma at the end. Perhaps Leah or Johnny or Mama George should have killed Mr. Big, or perhaps Bill the Brit should have succeeded in stopping his illegal operation. But the murder of Leah seems only to confirm her existence as a thing shaped by Mr. Big, with no separate value or identity, and as a dependant who is at the mercy of his power. That she hands him the gun and tells him to make things right appears to confirm her insufficiency: the Angel in Mr. Big's house has reappeared to exact her ultimate price. The possibility that Johnny and Leah could live together with the truth is not even glanced at, while the idea that Leah could forget the past and "start fresh" is dismissed out of hand by Dolly who, in an earlier scene, warns Leah that no one can "leave everything behind [and] pretend things never happened" (107).

In *Whiskey Six Cadenza* Sharon seems to be saying that we are trapped by our past, that trying to start over is futile, and that the only way out is to die. But why does she come to such a bleak conclusion? Why is this portrait of women—Leah, Mama George, Mrs. Farley, and Dolly—so utterly hopeless? Why is death the only answer to an ugly childhood? Sharon has said that in the early years of her career she could not imagine women as active agents and that female characters seemed to her to have only two options in life's narrative: to die (be killed or commit suicide) or to kill, to be murderee or murderess, both of which were reactive, not active, roles, or to go mad. She did not see women as able to take charge of their lives and make fresh starts, even though she had done both. So, again, why did she choose to expand and develop the earlier, more historical play that ends with a double hanging, into this complex, ambiguous portrayal of illicit desire and self-destruction? One set of possible answers comes from the play; the other, from the life. Sharon has told me that Leah is not a victim and that shooting her is the only truthful end to the play because it is true to the characters and their situation. By telling Mr. Big to kill her, she destroys his sense of a self-sufficient world in which he is immune from external laws or values or judgements. To the degree that I can see this outcome in the play, then I can imagine Leah as the moral winner who dies true to her values and in dying smashes his illusions. By forcing him to shoot her, she has forced him to accept responsibility for violating her in the first place. By dying, she has rejected him for all time. Just as Leah gets the final word over Mr. Big, so Mrs.

Farley saves her son from the mines *and* the bootlegging. Moreover, Mama George's advice to Mr. Big is proved right, and Dolly is correct when she said that the past can never be left behind. This reading leaves Mr. Big as nothing more than a charming, abusive fraud and Johnny as nothing more than a catalyst and a helpless witness to the unfolding tragedy. He lives to tell us the tale but has no active part in it. But is it possible to show these complexities in a live performance and even if it is, does this reading save the play from seeming to endorse the idea that a woman lacks separate identity from a man and has no agency except in choosing death?

When I turn to Sharon's life, another, rather apposite, set of possibilities arises. On the one hand, the first years of the 1980s were marked by significant highs—the success of *Blood Relations*, the Governor General's award, and productions of *One Tiger to a Hill* and *Generations*. And there were other awards: a Nellie in 1980 for *Sweet Land of Liberty* and a Golden Sheaf in 1981 for her television script, "The Persons Case," a play about Emily Murphy, one of the five Alberta women who led the fight to have Canadian women declared legal persons in 1929.[4] She was appointed artist-in-residence at the National Arts Centre; she was acting, notably as Miss Lizzie; directing at the Manitoba Theatre Centre; and in 1982 she attended the Harbourfront International Festival of Authors in Toronto. The playwright from the West had not only arrived in the East, she had taken her first steps onto the international stage. How she managed to handle personal matters in the midst of such activity—travel, production deadlines, professional obligations—is hard to imagine, especially because to match the highs of these years there were the lows. The separation from Michael represented not only private pain and a severe blow to her pride, but also the challenge of shouldering complete responsibility for the younger children, the awareness that Bear would now be without a father, just as the other five had been, and her personal loneliness that increased as each adult child left home. What is more, she seems to have confided her feelings to no one: with rare exceptions, children and friends alike say that she never complained and seldom spoke about her private life. As she had done with the pain caused by Eloise's absence and alcoholism, she held her emotions in check and kept them hidden. Unless, that is, her writing provided the necessary, even therapeutic release.

It is said that troubles come in threes, and Michael's departure was only the first. In 1981, at the age of seventeen, Michele moved out to live with a boyfriend in Edmonton because she felt she needed to distance herself from her mother whose devotion seemed reserved for her only son and for the favourite youngest child, Bear. In hindsight, the irony of this strained mother/daughter relationship is painfully obvious: Michele was experiencing some of the same sense of grievance and wish to revolt that Sharon had when she was young, but this time the revolt ended in near fatal disaster. In June 1982, Michele collapsed and was rushed to emergency at Edmonton's General Hospital. Her complaints of severe headaches and problems with her vision had been misdiagnosed and doctors discovered that she had a life-threatening infection with six abscesses on the brain. The boyfriend called Sharon, who dropped everything to get to Edmonton, where doctors spelt out the risks of the surgery required: this eighteen-year-old daughter could die on the operating table or survive with brain damage or, God willing, make a full recovery. Might the ethical dilemma of euthanasia for a brain-dead patient that Sharon examined in her radio play "Intensive Care" (broadcast by CBC in June 1983) have begun to trouble her at this time? However, Michele did recover but not without a further period of anxiety. She spent many weeks in intensive care in a coma that was only brought to an end when she was taken off the drugs. Sharon was at the bedside, holding Michele's hand, when one of the drugs was stopped and the nurses had warned her to watch closely for signs of a tremor that would indicate seizures. Hearing Sharon tell the story of this situation was fascinating. With Michele listening, her mother described for me these moments of waiting either for signs of seizures or for awakening from the coma with a matter-of-fact horror. But Michele woke up. With her head shaved, her vision gone, and so weak she had to learn how to walk again, she might not have been described as sleeping beauty, but she did wake up. This Persephone was returned to her Demeter, but like Persephone her return was partial. Michele ultimately moved to Toronto, built a successful life there, married, had her own children, and sees her mother or siblings infrequently. However, on one truly important occasion, when she did come back to Calgary, the circumstances were reversed. This time, in May 2001, Sharon was awaiting quintuple bypass heart surgery and, prior to the operation, realizing how much could go wrong, she said what this daughter still needed to hear: I love you.

The other shock did not have a happy outcome and provided no opportunity for leave-taking or gestures of help or affection. On her trips to Toronto, of which there were several at this time, Sharon sometimes stayed with a young friend, cat lover, and theatre colleague, Catherine Adams. Adams had been at the National Arts Centre but had moved to Toronto to work with Theatre Direct, and she frequently called Sharon to talk. In May 1982, as she prepared for one of her Toronto visits, Sharon called ahead to ask about staying with Adams but she received no answer. Only after arriving in Toronto did she learn that Catherine Adams, who was in her late twenties, had just committed suicide by throwing herself in front of a subway train. Years later this death still troubled Sharon, who vividly recalls the painful memorial service she attended at the Bathurst Street United Church (today the Bathurst Street Theatre) and the fact that Adams had planned a trip with her mother but had left precise instructions with the tickets in her apartment about how to cancel everything. Sharon, however, was left to speculate about what might have driven this young woman to take her own life. Possibly Adams was unable to face a difficult meeting with the board of Theatre Direct, which was scheduled for the day she took her life, or possibly Adams had more private fears about measuring up to others' expectations. Either way, suicide was a response to despair that Sharon understood, and she had not been able to help. Here was another example of a woman who opted for death in the face of the demons that plagued her or the challenges she felt unable to overcome. Catherine Adams was not Sharon's daughter, but she was young enough to have been, and Sharon's sense of loss and regret were keen and lasting.

But what, if anything, do these personal trials say about *Whiskey Six Cadenza*? Can they, in fact, shed any light on that very different world of artistic creation? I believe they do, but the influences are not literal and the light is filtered. In its final form, *Whiskey Six Cadenza* moved a very long way from being a play about Florence Lassandro, Emilio Picariello, Alberta

Prohibition, and the execution of two Italian immigrants in 1923. This play is not as faithful to historical events as John Murrell's and John Estacio's opera *Filumena* or Gisele Amantea's photography and comic-book installation piece called *The King vs. Picariello and Lassandro*. Murrell and Estacio recreate their Filumena (for a lyric soprano) as a beautiful, young, tragic heroine who dreams of a better life. She dies at the end (most opera heroines do), but with something of the pathos of a Manon Lescaut or the nobility of a Marguerite. By contrast, Amantea refuses to romanticize Florence Lassandro or her story. Instead, she uses photographs, many from her own family history, and "imagetexts" to retell the history of Italian immigration, of coal mining in Alberta, of ethnic segregation, and of racist stereotyping. Contemplating *Whiskey Six Cadenza* side-by-side with these two recreations, the differences appear more striking than the similarities. And they are not merely the result of medium. By developing two family stories in which the younger generation is trapped by the obsessions and egomania of the older one, Sharon delves into truths and experiences that she knows intimately. Leah is, in many ways, a girl without a mother to protect her but with a strong, charismatic, loud, popular, and very dominant father, a father who is both loved and resisted when he insists that she be his creation and have a role only in his story. Sharon was not ready to create a fictional daughter who could make an equal but separate life in which she understood, forgave, and loved such a father, so when resistance proved impossible or at least an insufficient basis upon which to escape into a new life, this daughter had to die. Lizzie, of course, chose another avenue of escape and killed both parents. Mrs. Farley represents a mother desperate to save a favourite son at almost any cost, but in trying to save him, she alienates and damages him; the father in this family is present but completely ineffectual.

I hear echoes here of Sharon's private concerns for Kirk and her sympathy for others' sons, such as her brother, Peter, or a half-brother, Bryant, or a young actor friend in Calgary, Graham McPherson (Hopkinson in the teleplay of *The Komagata Maru Incident*), whose family conflicts may have contributed to his early death and possible suicide. Experience showed her how sons might suffer. But at least as important to the underpinnings of this play are her views on family and marriage, especially as these institutions affect daughters and wives, and it is no exaggeration to describe the Farleys and the Georges as dysfunctional families ruled by tyrants. The adults in each case are scarcely happily married: there is neither love nor respect between the Farley parents, and Mama George is both childless and living inside her husband's lie. In each family a parent demands conformity and unquestioning obedience from a child; Mr. Big may appear to be charming and generous where Mrs. Farley is whining and mean-spirited, but of the two his is the greater transgression and betrayal. Leah and Johnny are trapped by their parents' expectations. The Farleys and the Georges are *not* the Chalmers or Pollocks, any more than any couple in the play is the Ball/Pollock duo, but Sharon Pollock knew much of what it was like to live in these homes and families and relationships, and she knew what it took to escape. *Whiskey Six Cadenza* looks back to *Blood Relations* and forward to *Doc*, but in *Doc* she put history aside and reached inside her own family story to examine the politics of being human and of being a wife/mother, a husband/father, and, above all, a daughter.

II: More Family Trappings—*Doc*

For many years I thoroughly disliked *Doc*. My response to the play was visceral, whether I was watching a production or reading and teaching the text, I wanted to strangle Ev, rescue Bob, shake Katie, and argue with Catherine. I could not understand why Sharon had written this devastating portrayal of a marriage and a family. More recently, through my biographical search for Sharon, I have changed my mind. While *Doc* may not be my favourite Pollock play, it is, I believe, her most powerful and courageous one. Reading early drafts of the script, talking with Sharon and others, and weighing the comments she has made in print about the play and its relationship to her family, have all helped me, if not quite to come to terms with *Doc* then at least to make peace with it and to appreciate its beauty. For it is a terrifyingly beautiful work of art, as fine, in my view, as Williams's *The Glass Menagerie* or O'Neill's *Long Day's Journey into Night*, and a more profound play than Miller's *After the Fall* or Pinter's *The Homecoming*. As others have noted, and I agree, *Doc* is Sharon Pollock's *Ghosts*.

But literary comparisons are beside the point, at least in a biography, and none of these plays is a direct influence on *Doc* except insofar as some of them may have inspired her to tackle an autobiographical play about dysfunctional relationships. Moreover, as I noted in "Sharon Pollock's *Doc* and the Biographer's Dilemma," there are risks in a too literal biographical reading of this play, and Sharon's comments in her "Playwright's Notes" for the Theatre Calgary premiere must be kept in mind. "*Doc* is very close to me," she said, but—

> It is not "my" story or the story of my family. There is a lot of my father in Ev, my mother in Bob, and me in Catherine, but Ev is not my father, Bob my mother, nor Catherine me. They are extensions of real people and through telling their story, my personal journey of discovery is hopefully made large enough to communicate itself to you.

Caveat lector. Of course these characters are not Sharon, Eloise, or Everett Chalmers; of course they are extensions, or fictionalizations, of "real people." And there can be little doubt that the play communicates through and beyond the personal. But in what sense can she say that the story of *Doc* is not her story or the story of her family? Surely it is. What's more, I do not believe that anyone but Sharon Pollock could have told the stories in *Doc*.

The challenge with this play, like the biographical trap, lies in that word "story." If, as Sharon has said, the story of a play is the story of "life without the boring bits," then *Doc* is not Sharon's life-story. The dialogue is certainly not a verbatim transcript of Chalmers family conversations, let alone of Ev's and Oscar's arguments, and many details in the play, from the firing of seven or more maids to the specifics of grandmother Chalmers' death and the young brother's name (Robbie), are not factually correct, and Catherine (single and childless, albeit a writer) is not Sharon. But many more details are drawn directly from the facts of family life in the Chalmers house. More important, the truth of *Doc* is not a question of quantifiable facts but of qualitative creation achieved through personal experience, effective dramatic structure, three-dimensional human characters, and poetry. By the time *Doc* premiered at Theatre Calgary in April 1984, it had undergone many permutations and, like all her plays, it changed in and through production as she saw what worked or did not work on stage for the actors who would bring her characters to life. Between 1984 and 1990, *Doc* received several major productions, including one at Theatre New Brunswick, where Sharon directed it, with Dr. Chalmers, his second wife Pegi, and many Fredericton friends, neighbours, and former patients in the audience. On that memorable occasion and only then, the play was renamed "Family Trappings," and in many ways, the story of *Doc* is about such trappings, both in the sense of paraphernalia and the memorabilia of family life and in the sense of entrapment. When the daughter, a woman in her mid-thirties, returns to her home town after a long absence to visit her elderly, ailing father, the two quickly find themselves caught up in a shared recollection of their painful family past. The moment Catherine enters the house she hears voices from that past and remembers herself as a youngster growing up there. She discovers her father sitting alone by an open trunk that contains many of the objects that represent the family past, the trappings, of memory. In his hand he holds an old, still unopened letter, sent to him by his mother shortly before she died on the railway bridge that spans the St. John River. This letter haunts the play and reappears in the final scene when father and daughter agree to burn it without reading it because, by the time the play ends, the ordeal of remembering they have come through has rendered the letter superfluous.

Doc is a memory play with a difference. Instead of one central remembering consciousness, there are two rememberers—father and daughter—and what they remember coincides at times but diverges at others. Each has his or her own version of and perspective on the family's past, and their conversations in the present often escalate into arguments. But the memory structure of the play is still more complex because Ev's and Catherine's memories conjure up ghosts from the past who give voice to their memories and stories and interpretations of events. In effect, *Doc* is a double memory play. It contains and frames another composite memory play in which the ghosts re-enact their stories by interacting with each other and with the present Catherine and Ev in what amounts to a dialogue with the dead. Indeed, the terrible journey that Catherine and Ev take into their past is like a Dantesque harrowing of hell in which the dead come to life to fight, argue, plead with and accuse the living. So palpable, so present are these long dead souls that they take over the stage until they make us listen to their tales of suffering, betrayal, rage, and despair. These souls are Catherine's childhood self, Katie, Ev's younger selves (student, young husband, workaholic doctor, father), Bob, Ev's wife and Catherine's mother, who has killed herself by the end of the inner memory play, and Oscar, Ev's long-time friend, devoted companion to Bob and Katie, who drowned in the Miramichi River some years before Catherine's return. Just as Ev's younger selves still inhabit him and Katie still lives within the adult Catherine, so Bob, and to a lesser degree Oscar, inhabit this house and exist in the minds, hearts, imaginations, and consciences of the surviving father and daughter.

Bob is a particularly potent force in this play, so much so that she almost takes over the story. Despite its title, *Doc* is very much Bob's play because the tragedy of her alcoholism and suicide lies at the root of the questions Sharon is asking about her own life and about the nature of contemporary, patriarchal marriage and the nuclear family. Questions such as: What responsibility for his wife's despair and death lies with Ev whose obsession with his medical practice meant that he refused to spend time with her even though he knew she was seriously depressed? What responsibility for her decline lies with Bob herself for being unable to hold her life together or break away? What responsibility for the early failure of their marriage and the subsequent disasters in their lives can be laid at the doorstep of a conservative, small-town 1940s society in which wives were expected to relinquish any claim to a separate identity and, in the middle-class sphere of a professional man's world, be content with the roles of mother and decorative hostess? When Bob wants to return to nursing after Katie's birth, Ev flatly refuses to allow it, and it is this refusal, more than any other single factor, that destroys her desire to live. But the questions posed by this play extend beyond these three because the casualties of the unfolding tragedy include the previous generation in the person of Ev's mother, who never appears on stage but is present in her unopened letter and in Bob's insistence that she killed herself because of her son's neglect, and in the next generation, which is traumatized by the disintegration of their mother, the absence of their father, and the pretence of their lives. Running like a scarlet thread through the entire play and pulling together the many layers of time and remembrance, is this problem of pretence because, as Catherine and Katie know, the entire fabric of their lives is one of lies. Instead of admitting that Bob is an alcoholic, they must all say she is unwell; instead of being herself, the successful professional, Bob must play at liking bridge and teas and parties and being the doctor's wife; instead of getting better after her various treatments, she only gets worse; instead of confirming or refuting, once and for all, how Gramma died, no one will say; instead of accepting his role in his family's life, Ev pretends Oscar can fill in and that others need him more than his wife and children do. In fact, his is the biggest lie in the play because he will not face the fact that to be successful he has chosen to be ruthless, not simply because he has important work to do or must earn a living but because his own ego demands constant external validation regardless of the cost to those who love him.

Doc is an attempt to ask and answer, or at least to shed light on and open up for scrutiny, some of the most complex questions of human existence. It returns us to Lizzie Borden's question to Dr. Patrick: faced with a choice, which life would you save, which life is more precious? It returns us to the options raised by Bonnie and Margaret in *Generations*: should one lose one's self in something larger or nurture one's individual identity. And it looks unflinchingly at Bonnie's assertion that there are worse things in life than being alone. Both Ev and Catherine are now alone, but what torments them is guilt, regret, the need for love, and the spectre of a woman who was denied the right to be herself. In *Doc* Sharon asks how we can forgive ourselves for hurting and failing others and forgive others for hurting and failing us because, otherwise, we are trapped in the past and unable to make a better future. We may end up like Beckett's Krapp, not only alone but also stuck with a futile replay of pain and loss. However, before asking these questions of us, Sharon asked them of herself, and it is in this honesty that I find the autobiographical heart of the play.

There are three typescript drafts of *Doc* with Sharon's papers, and the first tells us a great deal about where she began in her writing of this play and how far she travelled before it was staged. In this undated typescript (54.6.4–5), the woman who returns to visit her father is called "Sharon" and her younger self, aged fifteen, whose first name is "Mary," is called "Sharnee," Sharon's nickname as a child. The younger brother, who does not appear in this early version or in any later one, is called "Peter," but the other names remain the same: Doc is Ev, Bob is Eloise, and the family friend and fellow doctor is Oscar. The double memory play structure is there from the start, but the role of the adult "Sharon" is much less well developed than Catherine's role becomes, and the play takes place in a "large" house with "gables, bay windows, oddly-shaped rooms," and an "exterior made of clapboard," a house that closely resembles the Chalmers house. "Sharon" enters the house to find her father sitting in the "maid's room ... at the rear of the kitchen," a "forgotten room" used to store things that "belonged to one person" who "has been dead for a number of years." At this stage the play, which was already called *Doc*, is a comparatively literal treatment of Sharon's life and her memories of her mother. After Eloise's death and Everett's remarriage, many of Eloise's belongings remained in the house, so it was in a sense still *her* domain, and her presence lingered long after her death. The letter device is already in place as are many other details: Sharnee hates her mother, knocks her to the floor, and finds and confiscates her liquor bottles; a picture of Bob is produced in which she is feeding a piglet from a bottle— the real photograph still exists (Illus. 9, 51)—and Bob takes her own life; and Oscar is a doctor and a close family friend who supports Bob and Katie. What Sharon does not tell us about Oscar, here or at any later stage, is that the actual man on whom the character was based, Dr. Oscar Morehouse from Keswick, New Brunswick (*not* Keswick, Ontario) was gay and so no threat to the Chalmers' marriage.

The differences between this draft and the play we know as *Doc* are important. For example, the memory play structure was simpler and more linear; it centred on Ev and "Sharnee," much more than on "Sharon," who enters late in the first act, not at the beginning, and never achieves a bond with either her younger self or her mother. The story in this early version is more black and white than it becomes, with the result that there is much less sense of understanding, tenderness, and forgiveness reached by the women, and the mother is viewed more harshly through her daughter's bitter anger. Moreover, there is a less developed sense of sharing and forgiveness between father and adult daughter and Doc, although still a powerful figure, seems less threatening and, therefore, less responsible for the death of his wife or mother. By living with and reworking the play, Sharon found ways to develop her "Sharon" character and to create more space for the stories of Bob, Ev, and Oscar. In the process, she distanced herself from "Sharnee's" anger and hate and created in Katie a more complex portrayal of a child's sense of abandonment and rejection by an alcoholic mother and absent father. Because the structure of the early version was simpler, the nature of time and the role of memory were less apparent and less functional. By the time *Doc* reached its final form, time and memory were so integral to the structure that they had become subjects in the play: *Doc* is, among other things, *about* temporal processes as such and about how time impinges on and shapes individual and family life; it is also *about* memory—why we remember, who we are because we remember, and what remembering does to our understanding of the past, the present, and even the future. In the final *Doc*, the very fabric of time, processed by memory, is a Proustian remembering, reconstructing, and recuperation (however partial and always changing) that must remain fluid, captured in fragments of shifting patterns of sound and light, and carefully evoked by a set design that is not static or literal and by the smoothly interacting movement and blocking of the actors. The greatest risk in staging *Doc* is that it may end up appearing frozen physically and visually, fixed in time and space through separate tableaus of present and past. If this happens, then the flow of memory is stopped and the meaning of the play is reduced to argument, failure, and loss with diminished significance for and impact on the present. The process of learning from the past through memory is reified. But *Doc* is, above all, a play about reparation, and uninterrupted movement is crucial to that reparation.

But while there are significant differences between the early and later versions of *Doc*, and the final play exists at a greater distance from Sharon's stories, there are many points at which biography feeds the play directly and indirectly. The most obvious parallels are in the names, professions, and social context of Ev and Eloise and in the sad failure of their relationship. Everett Chalmers was known during his lifetime as "Doc," and the DECH (the Doctor Everett Chalmers Hospital) sits on a hill overlooking Fredericton. Sharon did not return home for the 1977 dedication ceremony, and her father did have a heart condition. The actual father and daughter were never as estranged as Ev and Catherine, but they did not see each other frequently or correspond regularly after 1966, and their love for each other was not demonstrative. Friends and colleagues who observed the adult Sharon with her father describe her as solicitous of him and as seeking his approbation, but not as arguing with him the way Catherine argues with Ev. Eloise did not return to nursing after Sharon and Peter were born because her husband, the social norms of the day, and her economic status all condemned the idea. Everett, who once told Sharon that if he had collapsed, Eloise would have taken over with expertise, competence, and sober authority, did come to understand how she suffered from the reduction of her identity to decorous helpmate. He knew she was highly intelligent but he accepted the logical conclusion of that fact too late: she would have flourished in her own career. It is also true that Eloise was institutionalized on several occasions, just as Bob is, and that she tried more than once to take her own life. In the play, when she finds the condom in his pocket and accuses him of sleeping with Valma, his office nurse, he cruelly snaps back that if the condom was unused she had nothing to worry about. But in real life, Everett Chalmers was having affairs, or an affair; Eloise's suspicions were well-founded, and once Sharon experienced this kind of betrayal she was better able to understand her mother's anger and grief, if not her withdrawal into alcohol.

As for the other characters in the play, or those family members alluded to but not seen, they too have roots in the Chalmers and Roberts biographies. Sharon's brother was called Peter, not Robbie, but Peter Dann Chalmers was the name he and his mother chose for him in 1947, not the name he was registered with at birth (John Everett Bryan Chalmers), and Dann (the name ridiculed by Ev in *Doc*) was Peter's maternal grandmother's maiden name. So, although the details of his name are not factual, the far more significant business of name changing and parental disagreement corresponds closely with the family story. By bringing such seemingly minor details into the memorywork of the play, Sharon is signalling the deeply divided loyalties within the family that would contribute to her feeling, as Catherine does, that she is like her father and the Chalmers side of the family, while Peter, like Robbie, resembles his mother and the Roberts. One of Eloise's brothers, Edward Clare Roberts, did inherit the Roberts farm, a place Sharon disliked because it smelled strongly of disinfectants, and her father did help his brother-in-law financially. Many small Chalmers background touches also feed the play to the extent that they provide depth and complexity to the character of Ev and contribute to the credibility of the developing tensions between Ev and Bob. Mary Chalmers did fall or jump from the railway bridge in what many believe was suicide, and her husband, George Chalmers, Sharon's paternal grandfather, withdrew and drank heavily in later life. He died in the St. John Provincial Hospital, a psychiatric institution, in 1951, a family detail Sharon drew on for *Getting It Straight*. What's more, Sharon was sent to her Chalmers grandparents at the time of Peter's birth, much as Katie describes things in *Doc*, because something was wrong with "Mummy."

It is unnecessary to trace more of these capillary links between the factual lives of these people and the characters in the play. That they are there is clear, and the purposes they serve are to flesh out the main characters, to establish an intricate context of credibility and motivation for the stories they tell and the decisions they make *as characters*, and to resonate beyond the play and over time—over the playing time of the drama and over time as it is remembered and constructed in the stories—so that we will recognize our common humanity in the acts of storytelling and remembering and in the experiencing of time and space. By the same token, Sharon has left a lot out. Mary Arbeau, Elaine, and Dr. Robert Chalmers, Everett's younger brother do not appear. And nothing is seen of Agnes Roberts; she is only referred to, frequently and with deep regret, by Eloise because she sacrificed so much to give her daughter a good education. It only remains, to linger a bit longer over Catherine and Katie because when a performance or reading of *Doc* is over, it is impossible not to wonder, as Guy Sprung did when he directed the play, just what Sharon Pollock was thinking as she wrote or rehearsed or performed or watched this play.

There are important facts of her own life that Sharon does not draw on to create Catherine. Her character has never been married and separated from a husband, let alone an abusive one, and she has no children. Perhaps the closest Sharon comes to using the external facts of her own adult life are to make Catherine a writer, a point that links her to young Katie who keeps a notebook in which she records what is happening (as Sharon did), to have her sent away from home for her schooling, and to have her current relationship be with an actor. As Ev complains, when he cannot remember the man's name, "this whosits ... an actor, an actor for Christ's sake" (*D, CW* II, 143). When Michael Ball played Ev in the Neptune Theatre and Vancouver Playhouse productions of *Doc*, this was a line he particularly enjoyed. But it is not such autobiographical *facts* that give weight to Catherine's role in the play or to Katie's. What stays with me long after seeing or reading the play is the emotional impact of Catherine's relationships with her father, her mother, and her younger self. Like Catherine, Sharon loved her father and admired his successes in life; she wanted to be like him, to win, but at the same time, she realized that he had not played much of a role in her growing up and had failed her mother. Like Katie, she viewed her mother with anger and contempt and rejected what her mother represented—weakness, self-indulgence, loss of self, and failure. I believe that, like Katie, Sharon feared she was unwanted and unloved by her mother and that her conception may have caused her parents' unhappy marriage. Certainly Bob often refers to the town gossip and her mother-in-law's suspicion that her son would never have married so precipitously if he had not been forced to. When I spoke with long-time residents of Fredericton who had known both Eloise and Everett Chalmers, these tawdry suspicions were still being raised, even though the marriage and birth dates confound such suspicions. As one person said to me, these facts did not mean that Eloise had not *claimed* to be pregnant; small-town, conservative public opinion does not easily give way in the face of facts, and narrow-minded, self-righteous cruelty is all too familiar. Similar gossip later surrounded Sharon's marriage to Ross Pollock and was also repeated to me. But *Doc* puts this gossip in perspective by showing how destructive it can be for a woman who must live in the midst of such chatter. By dramatizing Bob's sharply felt humiliation, Sharon is able to develop Catherine's (and her own) compassion for Bob and for the pain and doubt it causes Katie. The emotional crisis of the play is reached precisely when Katie, who has just screamed that she hates her mother and wishes her dead and then covered her ears to block out Bob's calling of her name, struggles not to cry and turns to her adult self, Catherine, and asks: "Would you want to have me?" To which Catherine replies, "Yes, yes I would" (*D*, 194)

With these simple words of acceptance and affirmation—"Yes, yes I would."—Sharon's Catherine embraces the abandoned child within, acknowledges her mother's pain and her own confused need for Eloise's love, and faces the emotional and psychological trauma of thinking, as a child will, that by wishing for something you can make it happen and are, therefore, responsible when it does. When the scene immediately shifts to the present with Ev and Catherine, Ev's "All over now" is answered by Catherine's "No, Daddy." Sharon's Catherine will not have finished her healing until her father has had to face Oscar's accusations after Bob's death:

> It shouldn't have happened. [...]
> She asked for goddamn little and you couldn't even give her that. [...]
> You got your eye fixed on some goddamn horizon, and while you're striding towards that, you trample on every goddamn thing around you! (*D* 194–95)

Here, in these three statements, Oscar is speaking for Sharon; at least I cannot confirm that someone else actually said these things to Everett Chalmers and that a young Sharnee over-heard them. Sadly, the memorywork of the entire play has shown Oscar to be right. He exits Ev's life for good at this point, refusing to acknowledge, let alone respond to, Ev's rational-ization that his wife's life was not as important as his patients' lives or his own.

In one sense, Sharon takes revenge on this father by exposing his ruthless egoism and by showing him as abandoned by his family and closest friend (something her own father never was), but the play does not end with Oscar's departure or even with Katie's demand that her father send her away "to some school." In what my biographical journey tells me is a wrenching and honest autobiographical moment, Sharon's Catherine describes how Bob destroyed all the family photographs of herself except the one that Oscar kept in which she is feeding a piglet with a baby's bottle:

> Do you remember when she gathered together all the photographs and snapshots, all the pictures of her, and she sat in the living room, and she ripped them all up? So ... after she died, we had no pictures of her.... and Oscar, remember Oscar came over with one ... it was taken at a nightclub somewhere, and she was feeding this little pig—a stupid little pig standing on the table and she—she was feeding it with a little bottle like a baby's bottle [...] Like a baby. She was looking up at the camera. She was smiling a bit. You could see her teeth. She didn't look happy, or unhappy. She looked as if she was waiting. Just waiting. (196)

This photograph, as described in the play, does not coincide precisely with the actual photograph (Illus. 9, 241), but it is close enough. It is not of Bob and Oscar on holiday in the Mediterranean but of Everett and Eloise with family at Au Lutin Qui Bouffe in Montreal. Although this is not the only surviving family photograph, Eloise *did* cut herself out of many such photographs during periods of drinking and depression.

In *Doc*, Sharon reserves this photograph for the closing moments of the play instead of near the beginning where it appears in the early drafts, and Catherine's description of her mother as "Just waiting" leads her father to ask—"For what?" When Catherine answers that she does not know but that "whatever it was [Bob] couldn't grab it," her father tells her that she must "grab" what she wants. Although the rhetoric of grabbing what you want suggests ruthless selfishness, it is important to hear Ev's advice in the larger context of the play and to realize that he is, in effect, telling his daughter not to hesitate as her mother did. Whether his advice is good or bad, he is admitting that *she* who hesitates is lost, and that a woman has a right to her own identity and must not deny her ambitions or lose her sense of self because a father or a husband or society disapproves of her independence. It is too late to say this to Bob, but this Ev has come a long way from the arrogant man who would not countenance his wife's return to her career. Did Dr. Chalmers say this to Sharon Pollock, perhaps in 1964 or 1965, when she returned home an abused wife with five children? Or did Sharon Pollock in her forties still need to imagine patriarchal permission to be the woman she was? Or, is Sharon simply saying that the unconsidered and untold life is an unlived and misunderstood one, that we need to remember who we were and who shaped us in order to see who we are? *Doc* closes with a third gesture of acceptance that completes the reparation (the first and second were Catherine's acceptance of her mother and of her childhood self)—Catherine's acceptance of her father. Just as she has forgiven, by listening to and giving voice to, her mother, so she has listened to the voice of her traumatized childhood self and embraced that child. The final task is to accept her father, with all his successes and failures, and to forgive him, to recognize that in some ways she is her father's daughter, just as she is also her mother's daughter. By forcing him to look at what happened and his role in these events (and by *him* I mean both the character Ev and all those Dr. Chalmers-like men in the audience), she is able to understand herself, understand those who behaved badly (including

Katie/Sharnee), and move on. No, Catherine is not Sharon Pollock, but she is her avatar, her spokeswoman. She says what her creator wants us to understand.

Doc premiered on 6 April 1984. Rick McNair commissioned Sharon to write the play for Theatre Calgary and he chose Guy Sprung to direct and Terry Gunvordahl to design it. McNair is the one we should thank for helping to bring this important play into existence, for believing in it at its early critical stage, and for ensuring that it received the professional production, with talented people, that it deserved. As several reviewers noted, the cast was an off-stage family, which added an extra element of intensity to an ensemble of very fine actors. The naming of Katie fell into place when Kate Trotter was rehearsing the role of Bob which, by all accounts, she performed with devastating emotional strength and honesty. In the house program we are told that the present of the play is 1978 in an "attic room of a house in a small city in the Maritimes [on] the evening prior to the laying of the cornerstone for a hospital named in Ev's honour." In her program "Notes" Sharon explains that she writes "to make sense of the seemingly incoherent and chaotic world we live in, and to discover meaning and purpose in my life," and she adds that until *Doc* she "found [her] personal history too frightening and confusing to confront directly," before presenting disclaimers about the characters not being her parents and herself but "extensions of real people." These comments would be reproduced in the programs for following productions, but they would never entirely convince theatre-goers, reviewers, or scholars.

When I discussed the premiere with Guy Sprung, he vividly recalled his amazement as he watched Sharon at rehearsals observing, with apparent professional objectivity, as *her* father and *her* mother performed on stage. He did not analyse the autobiographical sources with her because doing so would have been too personal, and Sharon is not easy to get that close to, but everyone *knew* those sources were there. Possibly more amazing, when I reflect on it, is that Sharon could also look on while her youngest daughter, just seventeen at the time, played Katie. Bear did not appear in the Toronto or Ottawa productions of *Doc* because she was still in school, but a premiere is special and this was a special role, even for someone "who made her stage debut at the age of two ... in *The Duchess of Malfi*." Bear had acted in several high school plays by 1984, and she seemed poised to follow in her parents' footsteps, a career she did not finally pursue, but this role suggests a mother/daughter bond predicated on considerable intimacy and trust quite beyond inherited acting ability. However, the personal aspects of the play are not what Sprung found most important. It was the structure that impressed him, the subtle time shifts, the balancing and triggering of memories, and the rich layers of characterization, of male and female tensions, of father and mother conflicts, that cannot be reduced to simple good and bad forces. Sprung came to know this play well because he directed it three times in different venues and media and with changes in cast. He is, in fact, the only director to have worked this closely with one Pollock play, and he is the fourth in the set of five excellent directors (Larry Lillo, John Wood, Rick McNair, and Jackie Maxwell) whom Sharon found for her scripts. What is more, he reread the play before our conversation in 2005 and continues to find new insights and new possibilities in it—one of these being the dead grandmother whose haunting presence he now feels should be made stronger and more dramatic in production.

The reviews of *Doc* were mixed, and all stressed the autobiographical subject of the play. While allowing that in this play Sharon was trying to do something "difficult for the stage"— to represent multiple levels of memory through Catherine's perspective—Diane Bessai was unhappy with the constraints on characterization resulting from this point of view and she found the acting disappointing. Mark Czarnecki was more satisfied. He called the acting excellent and Gunvordahl's "stark black and white set a creation of genius." But he concluded his *Maclean's* review by calling the play "a gripping but oppressive exorcism of the demons in Sharon Pollock's past," wondering where she would go next. Writing in the *Globe and Mail*, Ray Conlogue compared *Doc* with *Long Day's Journey into Night* and found Sharon's characters lacking because the memory format restricted their development and left Catherine "nothing more than a passive victim." *Doc*, he felt, was too personal. I find these comments odd because the memory-play structure of *Doc* makes it, finally, a very different play from O'Neill's family saga; the plays are both autobiographical, but in different ways. The most positive and thoughtfully detailed review came from Brian Brennan, who called *Doc* Sharon's "best work yet," a "Chekhovian" exploration of domestic issues that "deals convincingly and compellingly with a story that has echoes for us all" and in which the playwright has made "a strong personal statement with universal implications." Brennan did not get hung up on autobiography (he calls the play "semi-autobiographical") and focused instead on the production. He described the acting as "uniformly superb," the staging "cinematic" and "striking," and the directing as clear and appropriate. Most important, he saw the broader human relevance of the story.

When *Doc* opened at Toronto Free Theatre in October that year, Sprung had to recast Catherine, Katie, and Oscar. As other actors would discover (including Sharon herself) Catherine's role is a difficult one because she can easily become a passive observer of the tragedy rather than an active remembering-participant, but Clare Coulter brought a tough energy to the part. Sharon had thoroughly disliked Coulter's "killer dyke" portrayal of the Actress/Lizzie in the 1981 Tarragon *Blood Relations*, so she must have been dubious about this casting decision, but Sprung was pleased. He liked Coulter's Catherine and sees Sharon and Clare as very similar women. The reviewers, however, showed little interest in any of the characters except Ev and Bob, although Henrietta Ivanans's Katie won praise. According to reviewers, Kate Trotter stole the show with a magnificent performance of Bob, while Michael Hogan's Ev was consistently viewed as a ruthless, compulsive man who by turns neglects and uses his family. Amanda Hale described Ev as "an egomaniac who feeds voraciously on the power of his doctor image." Sprung also had Gunvordahl's stark, ghostly set to work with at Toronto Free and reviewers generally liked it, but Sprung felt the theatre was too small to do justice to the design. In general, however, Toronto seems to have liked *Doc* and while the autobiographical or personal aspects were noted, reviewers zeroed in on the larger message of the play. Stephen Godfrey called it a "superb family drama"; Hale saw the play in feminist terms and the female characters as courageous and triumphant; and Judith Finlayson warned anyone who wanted to return to traditional family values and gender roles to see *Doc*. In November, the Toronto Free Theatre production moved to the National Arts Centre for a two-week run in the Studio Theatre. This was the last time Guy Sprung's interpretation of the play was staged, but he returned to it for the 1991 radio production, with Sharon in the role of Catherine.

Between 1984 and 1991, Sharon directed *Doc* three times, each time learning more about how the play worked. In certain ways the most daring staging was the Theatre New Brunswick production in March of 1986 because Sharon, along with Janet Amos, the company's artistic director, were holding up the proverbial stage mirror to show Fredericton society and one of its leading citizens some rather unflattering reflections of themselves. After discussing the play's title with Amos, Sharon agreed to change it to "Family Trappings" so audiences would not expect a celebratory documentary about a local hero. But apparently neither of them needed to worry about Everett Chalmers's reactions. He had already seen the play at the National Arts Centre, and when Amos called him to discuss her wish to include the play in her 1985–86 season, he was supportive. In fact, he asked to be allowed to contribute a brief statement to the house program and took advantage of the opportunity to comment upon his work with addiction. "I was pleased," he wrote, "to see one of my daughter's plays scheduled for production":

> FAMILY TRAPPINGS is a work dealing with alcoholism and a family in crisis; it is more a manifestation of family love and co-operation than many people realize. This is achieved by exposing some of our frailties to the public.

Of course, *Doc* is no more or less a work "dealing with alcoholism" than is Lowry's *Under the Volcano*. To describe the play in these terms is to duck the most important parts of the issue—the destruction of a talented woman, the repercussions for her daughter, and a husband's/father's role in the tragedy—and to ignore the complex theatrical structure through which his daughter's childhood pain is revealed. Dr. Chalmers was a medical man, not an artist, but his summary of the play makes me wonder what he saw as he watched it in performance or, indeed, what anyone sees. If he saw himself accused and chastised, he did not let on. Instead, he went on to describe his practical work with the disease:

> I have had a great deal of experience with alcoholism, both in family life, and in my practice as a physician. As a result, I developed an obsession with the disease, and hoped someday I would be in a position to do something about it. My appointment as Chairman of the Alcoholism and Drug Dependency Commission of New Brunswick has provided me with a vehicle through which to attack the disease of alcoholism. It is often a family disease and families should be encouraged to discuss it as openly as they would discuss any physical problem.

Audiences, however, reacted emotionally, not clinically, to *Doc*. Some who attended the Fredericton performances were shocked, even horrified, at this portrayal of a local hero and his family, and Amos has described local audiences as "wildly negative." Others, however, were reduced to tears. Peter Chalmers told me emphatically that he saw the play as deeply moving "fact," a depiction of things exactly as they were in that family and that house. He also saw the play as his sister's way of coming to terms with the past, and he admired her ability to do so. His recollection of his father's reaction differs sharply from the sense Janet Amos got of his support. Father, Peter told me, was furious. But because he felt responsible for Eloise's death, he did not blame Sharon for writing the play. Reviews, both in Fredericton and around the province as the played toured, were glowing, even ecstatic: Helmer Bierman called it "emotional dynamite"; Jo-Anne Claus ranked it the "best production" from Theatre New Brunswick in some time; Don Hoyt described it as a "masterful work of theatre"; Lori Redding called it a "powerful" representation of real people but with themes that are relevant to all; and some were at pains to emphasize that this portrayal of "Pollock's father, Dr. Everett Chalmers, [who] is among the most respected and beloved of the province's doctors" (Boisseau) was only partially biographical.

Sharon had a stellar cast for her "Family Trappings." She chose Maritime-born Richard Donat to create a handsome Ev, who was not only credible (for those who knew the real Ev), but also dynamic and even tender; clearly Donat's Ev was more sympathetic than Hogan's had been. Lynn Woodman created what Jo-Anne Claus called such a "heartbreaking" Bob that audience members "wanted to reach out in sympathy to the woman the child Katie is rejecting so furiously," and Cheryl Swarts was rated outstanding as Katie. Sharon brought in Graham McPherson from Calgary to play Oscar, which he did exceedingly well; however, this was his last role in one of her plays. McPherson, who suffered from his own demons, including addiction, was dead within a few years. And that leaves Catherine. Terry Tweed played this role, which is demanding under any circumstances, but she found it especially difficult working with Sharon on the part and, according to Amos, felt "beaten up" by the experience. Lynn Woodman's response to Sharon was very different from Tweed's: "I was excited about working with her," Woodman told Peter Boisseau, because she "struck a fantastic balance. I was very grateful to have her there. She was never an annoyance; she had such insight." Woodman was cautious about stressing the biographical and autobiographical elements in the play, and yet she interpreted Bob by finding out as much as she could about alcoholism and about Eloise—a woman with "enormous energy, vitality and talent," who could not find a fulfilling focus for her life. As Woodman put it, Eloise was treated for her physical and mental condition, but "her soul ... her very being was never attended to." Terry Bennett's set enhanced the universal and spiritual aspects of the story by creating an abstract, non-representational house of stairs and pillars angled to suggest a mirroring and merging of past and present suitable for Greek tragedy: at Theatre New Brunswick, the house of Chalmers recalled the house of Atreus. Writing for Fredericton's *Daily Gleaner*, Redding saw "'Family Trappings' as the creation of a courageous and sensitive playwright who by communicating a part of her own 'journey of discovery' provides the opportunity for those who are willing to discover something about themselves." For Redding, the central "truth" of the play, at least for Catherine and Ev, was that "being reconciled is more important than being alone."

When *Doc* opened at the Neptune Theatre, Halifax, in February 1987, the reviews could not have been more different. Richard Ouzounian, the artistic director and a long-time friend of Sharon's told me that *Doc* caused more protest and uproar than any other play, including *Who's Afraid of Virginia Woolf*, he scheduled during his three years with the Neptune. Theatre patrons wrote angry letters damning the play and expressing their resentment that anyone, let alone a native Maritimer, would portray a prominent Maritime doctor and his family in such a negative light. For this production, Sharon directed Michael in the role of Ev, and Michael knew, and had his own opinions about, Sharon's father, so it is possible that the old synergy between these former partners, coupled with his sense of the real man and his delight in the rich roles Sharon created for male actors, produced a harsher, less sympathetic Ev than Richard Donat's. Although Michael smiled when he told me his story of delivering Ev's caustic line about "whosits" the actor, he may well have enjoyed skewering God-the-doctor on stage. Certainly, when I saw Michael as Ev in the Playhouse production I found the character truly frightening in his ruthless self-centredness. Once again Sharon tried to deflect the prurient autobiographical interest of reviewers by insisting that *Doc* explored larger social and family issues and that she took dramatic licence with the facts. But one reviewer, Dawn Rae Downton, could not restrain her venom and gave the play and Sharon personally one of the most poisonous reviews she has ever received. Downton described the play as "nothing more than the stuff of *Anne of Green Gables* with an unhappy ending," full of "stereotypes" and "shallow insights." She dismissed Goldie Semple's Bob as "competently desperate," Catherine as a "bitchily feminist shrew" that Mary-Colin Chisholm could not rescue, and the whole play as "a mess."

Other productions of *Doc* went well. It was done at the Manitoba Theatre Centre in 1987, directed by Jackie Maxwell, and again in 1987, when Sharon directed it for the Magnus Theatre in Thunder Bay. In February of 1988 Denise Gagnon directed Francine Pominville's French translation for Quebec City's Théâtre de la Commune, and in March 1990 it opened at the Vancouver Playhouse with Michael as Ev and Janet Wright as Catherine. In recalling this production, director John Cooper expressed mixed feelings about his decision to stage the play in an attic with a separation between Catherine and Katie. 1990 was early in his directing career and Larry Lillo, then the artistic director of the Playhouse, warned him to listen to Janet Wright and follow her lead with blocking and staging. His feeling that he failed to heed this advice and that Wright felt immobilized on Pearl Bellesen's static set and unable to fully register the impact of Katie's anguish and Bob's suffering or to *interact* with her young self and her mother, account for the regret he now feels. If he were to direct *Doc* again, he told me, he would do it differently on a simpler, raked set and allow the space-time fluidity of memory its full rein. However, sitting in the audience for performances of the play, I sensed none of the tension or struggle that Cooper remembers. Instead, I was impressed by the superb performances of Michael (see Illus. 35) and Janet Wright (and of Janne Mortil as Katie, Brian Torpe as Oscar, and above all of Donna White as Bob). The physical separation between Catherine and Katie and Bob looked and *felt* right because it captured the emotional and temporal gulf that does separate these people, and it suggested to me the enormous leap of faith and love required to reach across that space. And that gulf is unbridgeable: Bob is long dead by the time Catherine returns home, so for Sharon the recovery of her lost mother can only be symbolic. Katie is a wound that can be healed but that nevertheless leaves an ineradicable scar.

35. Michael Ball as Ev in the 1990 Vancouver
Playhouse production of *Doc*.
*Photograph by David Cooper, courtesy of
Vancouver Playhouse.*

The *Vancouver Sun* reviewer, Elizabeth Aird, also found the set an apt metaphor for the play: the "stage [looked] like bits and pieces of a house, with a jagged-edged wooden floor that could be a bridge over an abyss." The first thing we saw on stage was an elderly man under a bare light bulb surrounded by darkness and a babble of voices, and whether Cooper intended it or not, this production on this set with Michael as Ev, reminded me of *Krapp's Last Tape*. But with a crucial difference: Sharon Pollock is not Samuel Beckett and, dark as this play may be, in her vision of life there is always hope, forgiveness, and a measure of redress for those things in life that are worse than being lonely and alone. In her comments for the house program, Sharon repeated the familiar caveats about a too literal reading of the play as autobiography, and she emphasized that her play was always the result of a process of others' creative interaction and interpretation, a "journey of discovery" that is repeated but never duplicated. What interested her, she explained, was the dramatic articulation of big questions about "those things we live and die by." She also insisted, for the first time in print, that the parents and child in the play "struggle to love one another when things, not necessarily of their own choosing, conspire against it." In the end, she says, "Love triumphs."

My consideration of this play would not be complete, however, without touching on the CBC radio Arts National broadcast on 18 March 1991. I have listened to it several times and its power does not fade. If love triumphs in *Doc* (and I think it does), then it does so after a terrible effort and then only provisionally. The medium of radio emphasizes the long-term, haunting aspects of the play that are more easily ignored during a stage production as we watch the actors. Guy Sprung returned to direct it and, when Sharon wanted to play Catherine, he agreed. She also rewrote parts of the play to introduce a narrator, played by Sharon *as* Catherine, who could move the listening audience from one point of time in the story to others. In her opening remarks, Sharon calls the play we are about to hear the "story of a journey ... home"; she also calls it a "soap-opera" because it is a sadly familiar tale made to seem fresh by its temporal structure and the way it shows "how memories affect our lives." Although Sharon has told me that she was not entirely happy with her Catherine because she seemed to lack an active voice (other actors had struggled with precisely this challenge), I find her voice, doubled as character/narrator, intensely confessional and intimate. In the radio drama, the echoing, overlapping voices from the past, heard through snatches of song, other music, and sound effects, create a shared inner soundscape of memory for Catherine and the listener that is impossible to achieve on stage. For the two hours of playing time, a listener is trapped inside this woman's mind, which is not a comfortable place to be.

Almost at the end of the broadcast, after Katie sings loudly to drown out Bob's calling of her name, after Catherine tells her inner child that she would want her, and when Ev claims that it is all over, we know, even before Catherine speaks, that it is not over, that it can never be "over." What we can distance ourselves from visually, we cannot tune out aurally, and the disembodied voices of the radio play linger, whisper, and echo in a listener's memory. It was not "over" for Sharon either because she would be compelled to return to her story in *Getting It Straight* and to aspects of her parents' story in *Angel's Trumpet*. What she uncovered in *Doc* was a profound truth discovered in all life-writing: identity is always multiple and relational; you are who you are in relation to those around you, and you cannot tell your story without telling theirs or theirs without telling your own. Moreover, she discovered that the way to understand life is reached through telling stories and by juxtaposing different stories about common experiences. *Doc* is precisely this kind of multiple, relational storying; it is Catherine's and Katie's and Oscar's story within Daddy's and Mummy's story, especially Mummy's. By creating such a powerful mother figure, Sharon allowed Eloise a voice and a place in her heart. She did more than forgive this mother, she honoured her, and this is where the necessary *reparation*, as Melanie Klein calls it, lies. Catherine, and through her Sharon, allows herself to love and forgive Katie so that she may ask forgiveness of her rejected mother. The healing and understanding were not over, but they had begun to allow Eloise into her daughter's life in new and productive ways. What's more, this play allows Sharon to say without fear that she *is* like Gramma and Mummy, that, as Margaret Atwood tells us in "Five Poems for Grandmothers," "one woman leads to another" (16).

But perhaps I should give Sharon the last word here because she has said that love triumphs in *Doc*. When challenged by Brian Brennan at the premiere about putting her family's private stories on public view, she replied that she always felt close to her father and believed that neither he nor her brother would be bothered by the play (see Brennan, "Pollock play confirms art follows life"):

I guess I have to hope they would look at the play and see that I've used them to tell a story that's larger than our personal story, a story that other people can relate to. I have to trust that the love and affection with which I've used very personal material is apparent in the play, even though some of the things might not be pleasant for them to recall.

III: Storming the Bastions

During the 1980s, Sharon took on the position of artistic director at two of the country's leading regional theatres. Neither term lasted very long and neither was completely successful. My question has always been *why*: Why would someone like Sharon, who is first and foremost a playwright and an artist, want to take on the administrative tasks demanded of artistic directors in Canadian theatres. An artistic director, as Bill Millerd has assured me (and he wins the prize for AD-longevity in this country), has little to do with being artistic and does not leave much time to direct, but it does require inter-personal tact, diplomacy with boards of directors, a lot of patience, and a capacity to compromise. Now Sharon Pollock has many excellent qualities, but these four are not among them. She is blunt, at times painfully so, opinionated with the sort of folks who often sit on boards and know less about theatre than she does, always in a hurry to get things done, and constitutionally incapable of compromising her artistic principles. All this should have been clear to those who hired her, but as Nancy Coy told me (and she has worked with eight or nine ADs, including Sharon), boards do perverse things and they often fail to choose an AD who compromises cheerfully and has endless and inexhaustible patience. Sharon's first AD-ship was with Theatre Calgary in 1984; she resigned after approximately three months. Then in 1988 she was appointed as the AD of Theatre New Brunswick, a position she resigned from a year later. Both theatres should have known what they were getting into because she had been Associate AD under Rick McNair at Theatre Calgary, and Calgary audiences knew the kind of play she wrote and believed in. Ditto for Theatre New Brunswick. After all, the board members, staff, and fellow Frederictonians had seen *Doc* in May of 1986. What kind of person did they think could write such a difficult, daring, and powerful play?

Why did she take on these two positions, why was she asked to, and why did both attempts end so precipitously and, at least with Theatre New Brunswick, so noisily? I think the roots of the problem lie in the mismatch of personality and job description, in the rigid, hierarchical structure of theatre administration in Canada, in the philosophy and financial control of boards of directors, and finally in gender. This last factor is hard to weigh, but so many individuals have included it in their public and private assessments of Canadian theatre that I must consider it.

When Sharon became artistic director of Theatre Calgary in the summer of 1984, just a few months after McNair resigned, few women had held this position in large Canadian theatres. Joy Coghill had done so with the Vancouver Playhouse for a short period (1967–69) and women had headed up some small companies or children's theatre groups across the country, but the main regional theatres, not to mention Stratford, the Shaw, and the National Arts Centre, had no experience with women in positions of such authority. To be fair, the pool of expert female professionals was comparatively small in the early 1980s. Nevertheless, the barriers for women who wanted to write for the theatre, direct, or become artistic directors were systemic, and the federal government commissioned Rina Fraticelli, then artistic director of Playwrights Workshop in Montreal, to study and report on the situation. Fraticelli released her report, *The Invisibility Factor: Status of Women in Canadian Theatre*, in 1982 with statistics that revealed the paucity of women in key aspects of professional theatre life. Although women comprised 51 percent of the population and 60 percent of theatre audiences, 77 percent of the plays they were watching were written by men, 83 percent were directed by men, and 81 percent of the artistic directors were men. Collectives accounted for 13, 4, and 8 percent in these categories. Women were mostly confined to small, non-profit or children's theatres, and their overall average in Fraticelli's three categories was 10, 13, and 11 percent respectively. Something was wrong. The challenges were to understand how this imbalance occurred and then how to address the problem, but, as Kate Lushington noted in a 1985 article, the Fraticelli "report was devastating in its findings and inspirational in its recommendations. [But] the silence which greeted the release of the report was (and has remained) deafening" (9). Lushington quotes Fraticelli as saying that she had no sense of the impact her report might have on the theatre community because "they in no way supported it, responded to it or even acknowledged its existence" (9). *The Invisibility Factor* remained, by and large, invisible.

Fraticelli studied the period from 1972 to 1980–81 by gathering statistics, conducting interviews, and reviewing the mandates and eligibility criteria and success rates of support institutions such as the Canada Council and university training programs. She also compared her findings with available studies in the United States and Great Britain. Reading the report today, I am impressed by two things—its comprehensiveness and its striking statistics. No matter what sector of professional theatre life and training Fraticelli examined, the conclusion was always the same: "Women form a distinct minority among those employed in the capacities of playwright, director and artistic director in the Canadian theatre community" (114). Despite their numbers in training programs, women ended up in sub-servient positions or simply marginalized at each critical juncture in the wider system—a demographic and employment reality that was true across the board in the professions (the academy, law, and medicine had equally dismal statistics). Compared to men, few women applied for Canada Council grants because they were usually ineligible: an applicant had to have the equivalent of two years experience with a professional company and a playwright had to have "at least one play published or produced professionally on stage" (114). The Catch-22 was that women could rarely satisfy these criteria because the men in positions of authority usually chose other men to work with or plays by men to direct or produce. Consequently, when Fraticelli looked at the jobs done by women, she found that they did the joe-jobs, the support jobs, the low profile, service jobs, and they worked for male bosses. To her surprise, Fraticelli also discovered that a significant number of women were being trained and educated for careers in theatre but that they were not getting these positions in anything like proportional numbers. When she turned her attention directly to Canadian universities, Fraticelli saw that the professoriate was male, the plays taught or chosen for directing were mostly by men and, therefore, that the role models for women were simply absent.

At the root of this systemic problem, however, were the traditions and working conditions of the theatre. All theatre work is collaborative. You can write a play, but if no artistic director selects it, you will never get a professional production (or, very likely, a publication). You can be trained to direct, but if no artistic director asks you to direct a play, you will not gain the experience required to build a career. Moreover, making theatre is risky and expensive; when an artistic director chooses a season of plays, he—or she—must consider the bottom line. What will audiences pay to see? A play by an established male playwright or a play by an obscure female playwright who, it is too often assumed, only knows how to write about women's issues instead of the really significant *universal* ones? And then there are the physical demands of space, of light and of sound technology, of set design, and so forth. If those hired for these tasks are men, they may not want to work for a female director or artistic director. Fraticelli found that professional women working in Canadian theatre between 1972 and 1981 were employed as actresses (if they were not support staff), or else they continued to work in small companies. She concluded that male ADs usually chose men to direct plays by men (a practice Bill Millerd acknowledged), that "without the consent and co-operation of the theatre industry as a whole, no amount of interest, training, and ability on the part of individual women" (115) would enable them to "qualify" for Canada Council support, and that, most important, the gender bias was systemic. "It is no single door," Fraticelli wrote, "but a series of diverse and deeply systemic obstructions which define the exclusion of women from the Canadian theatre" (119). The situation was no better in England or the United States.

These were the challenges Sharon Pollock faced in 1984 when she accepted the job of Theatre Calgary's artistic director. By 1988, when she took on the position at Theatre New Brunswick, things were not greatly different, although she was following Janet Amos in the role. In 2003, when a new generation of female theatre professionals decided to take a second look at the status of women in Canadian theatre, many of the familiar obstacles were still in place. Hope McIntyre, Kelly Thornton, Kate Weiss and their colleagues with the Women's Caucus of the Playwrights Guild of Canada, had difficulty securing funding for a new equity study, but they began gathering data, holding panels, and organizing fora to re-open the debate on the Fraticelli report. Their initial findings, reported by Rebecca Burton in May 2006, supported the view that women had made progress but were still a minority in all the areas Fraticelli considered. Both the Shaw Festival and the National Arts Centre had women at the helm (Stratford remained the hold-out), and some of the major regional theatres, like Vancouver's Playhouse, had women artistic directors, but the larger, more prestigious companies (with sizeable operating budgets and government grants) were at least twice as likely to be run by men, and the "invisibility factor" was still alive and well. Between 1972 and today, a number of major women playwrights have emerged but few of them have enjoyed regular company support (Judith Thompson's relationship with Tarragon is an exception). Vocal feminist playwrights like Margaret Hollingsworth and scholars like Diane Bessai were quick to identify the scope of the problem and to argue, in the context of feminist theory, that there is a distinctly female play structure. During the nineties, scholars like Rita Much, Rosalind Kerr, Judith Rudakoff, and Cynthia Zimmerman focused critical attention on the achievements of women playwrights, and chief among the writers they discussed or interviewed was Sharon Pollock. However, in 1984 Sharon was *understandably* uncomfortable with the label feminist and uneasy about any attempt to classify her or her work by gender, and she remains cautious about any label that might limit her work. I stress *understandably* here because women of Sharon's generation did not grow up with the idea that a woman could achieve things of importance or could assert herself as an individual; Woolf's Angel had a thriving presence in post-WWII Canada. To make matters worse, Sharon did not have positive female role models during her early life. What surprises me is that she emerged when and as she did, not that she shunned overt feminist views or did not create *active* women characters or explore women-centred issues in her plays until, that is, she wrote *Blood Relations*.

Theatre Calgary began in 1968, and from its inception Sharon had an active role in its life. She occasionally performed in their productions, she directed for the theatre, she served as dramaturge and as associate AD, and three of her major plays were commissioned and premiered by this company. During its first twenty years, Theatre Calgary mounted very interesting and often challenging seasons, commissioned several new works, and actively supported Canadian playwrights, actors, and directors. In its mission statement, the theatre emphasized its commitment to Canadian work and to the Calgary artistic community. When the history of Theatre Calgary is written, 1985 may well stand out as a turning point for the company because that was the year it moved to the 750-seat Max Bell Theatre in Calgary's Centre for the Performing Arts, and by the late 1980s it was in serious financial trouble. Theatre Calgary rallied during the nineties, but at the same time its programs became less challenging and more geared to popular fare. To the best of my knowledge, with just one exception, it has hired male artistic directors, beginning with Christopher Newton, who was followed by Harold Baldridge, Rick McNair, Martin Kinch, Brian Rintoul, and Ian Prinsloo, each of whom held the position for several years. The exception to this male succession was Sharon, but hers was not the shortest-lived tenure; Clarke Rogers filled in for one season between Newton and Baldridge. However, Sharon's appointment was not *pro tem*, and her resignation was publicly attributed to a disagreement with the board of directors over the artistic control of productions.

However, her artistic directorship started on an exceptionally high, if somewhat discordant note. In his review of the April 1984 production of *Doc* and her "elevation to the top post" at Theatre Calgary, Alan Hustak stated that her resounding success with *Doc* was "not her biggest recent achievement." He reserved that pinnacle for the position of artistic director, which indicates just how sadly skewed our priorities are if we value administrative prestige over creative work of the highest calibre. In an August interview about her appointment, Gwen Dambrofsky made much of the fact that Sharon was the first female AD at Theatre Calgary—Hustak extended this priority to all of Western Canada, forgetting Joy

Coghill, and asked Sharon what she thought about the fact that two women were running Theatre Calgary: Sharon as AD and Marcia Lane as general manager. Fully aware of trouble behind the scenes, Sharon replied tangentially by explaining her views on feminism—"I don't feel comfortable with that"—but going on to say that "as a woman," she was "more open [than some men] to acknowledging that quality work might be done by a woman." The 1985–86 season had already been established by McNair, with input from Sharon, so it would be some time before she could put her stamp on productions. In the meantime, Theatre Calgary's move into its new quarters was imminent and would keep her busy. Nevertheless, she managed to outline her vision and priorities in this short interview with Dambrofsky: she wanted to produce plays that entertained, but she also expected them to be "meaningful and important" and to address the real concerns of the community, rather than merely providing a form of escape. For anyone who was paying attention, the writing was on the wall. By September it was all over except for the recriminations and the blame. In an article called "A very dramatic exit," Hustak quoted Sharon as faulting the "double-headed" management structure at Theatre Calgary, which gave the general manager equal authority with the artistic director as well as the fiduciary responsibilities for fund-raising and marketing: in short, the general manager controlled the purse strings. Marcia Lane was quoted as saying that she was "devastated" by Sharon's sudden departure, but the chairman of the board, Neil Jennings, was more forthcoming. He criticized Sharon for abandoning the ship while a review was underway and said she should have been well acquainted with Lane and with the basic administrative structure, including its division of labour, and therefore should not have been surprised by the theatre's *modus operandi*. Certainly the impression Hustak gave was that Sharon Pollock was difficult, litigious, and controversial. He stressed the shock and anger felt by many, the problems left in her wake (for example, Richard Ouzounian, who had agreed to guest direct as a "personal favour" for a colleague he respected, withdrew when she resigned), and alluded to the conflicts and personal disagreements between Sharon and Marcia Lane. But as one former artistic director told me, Theatre Calgary was "a court theatre for the oil industry," by which he meant that anyone who was not prepared to acquiesce to the board would be in trouble.

Correspondence between Sharon and the board during July and August of 1984 sheds considerable light on the structural problems and the increasingly strained relations within the company (54:3.36). In a July letter to Bill Patterson, Sharon outlined her concerns about the operation of the theatre, especially with regard to her job description and her frustration with the lack of information she received on vital matters of planning, budgeting, accounting, and so on; she told him that she had to invite herself to meetings where decisions were made or else be left out of the loop. She identified the split between artistic and financial objectives as the root problem and the Achilles heel for the future growth of the company. She also made her own priorities, indeed her *definition* of a quality theatre company, absolutely clear. "As the primary focus of the theatre is an artistic one," she told Patterson, so "it would seem apparent that the artistic programming is the starting point from which all other policy components and practices, as well as resource allocations and decisions are rationalized and related." She concluded this letter by offering to write a new job description for the position of artistic director, an offer that was integral to the review that was under-way of the overall management structure. Patterson replied briefly but warmly, asking her to submit this new job description.

On 2 August she submitted information regarding it and other related concerns to Neil Jennings, but what she wrote amounted to an intelligent and insightful analysis of the evolution of management structures in Canadian theatres. Her comments revealed just how astutely she understood the current dilemma at Theatre Calgary, why she faced the difficulties she did, and what had to change if the company was to be successful in its new facilities and with a new phase in its growth.

Approximately fifteen to seventeen years ago, theatrical companies sprang into professional being across Canada. A great number were founded as a result of Gérard Pelletier's "democra-tization of the arts" policy, and were funded originally through O.F.Y. and L.I.P. grants. Others were the natural off-spring of amateur groups, and such was Theatre Calgary. Those that continued as viable organizations did so as a result of the communal efforts of two or three committed individuals who assumed responsibility to assure accountability to government granting bodies. Sometimes they mortgaged their houses and often their souls. I think it is fair to say that virtually all were individuals who, as a duo or trio, had close and on-going professional relationships with each other prior to their founding of what have now become our "establish-ment" theatres. The duo or trio generally distributed responsibility into Artistic Director, Administrator/General Manager, and Public Relations. At Manitoba Theatre Centre John Hirsch assumed most of the artistic decision-making while playwright Tom Hendry assumed most of the administrative duties. Similarly Ken and Sue Kramer "ran" the Globe Theatre in Regina, Douglas Riske and Lucille Wagner "ran" Alberta Theatre Projects, George Luscombe and June Faulkner Toronto Workshop Productions, Ann Green and Mark Schoenberg Theatre 3. Christo-pher Newton, Pat Armstrong, and Dick Dennison managed Theatre Calgary. What all such duos and trios had in common was virtually a symbiotic relationship with each other, with such cross-overs and mutual decision-making as best fit the occasion, the talents, interests, and aspirations of the individuals, and the mandate of the company as discerned by its founders. Today theatre boards too often find themselves struggling with a structure which was predicated on the existence of a special and unique relationship between its Artistic Director and General Manager. The separation of artistic and administrative management, responsibility, and ac-countability has become fragmenting and divisive, as well as helping to create a false picture of the artist as financially illiterate and administratively suspect. The relationship upon which the dual structure was predicated no longer exists, and the fact that theatre companies, despite unique operational characteristics, can work within a framework of accepted principles of sound management, and that the artist manager, executive producer, call him/her what you will, is the appropriate individual to assume such responsibility and accountability, is obscured by the con-tinuing existence of that obsolete structure of duality. (54.3.37)

Sharon then went on to list the duties of the AD, as she saw them. The bicameral structure she was saddled with needed to be swept away so that a general manager would report to the artistic director who was, above all, responsible for "artistic programming at a quality standard, and within the Board-approved budget." In a follow-up letter of 6 August, she asked for the authority to strike a new budget, to freeze hiring until a new structure was in place, and to set up a series of meetings to organize the pending move. She ended with an apology for seeming to push, but she explained that she was "very nervous" about the urgency of these issues.

Whatever precipitated the final crisis and her resignation, the result was a rift between Sharon and Theatre Calgary that never really healed. She supported the appointment of Martin Kinch as her successor and she spoke out for it during its financial crisis but with the exception of the 1988 *Walsh*, she did not work for the theatre again. Among those with whom I have spoken, not one blames Sharon for the breakdown. Her unhappy experience with Theatre Calgary was by no means unique; McNair was almost certainly fired and Kinch, although he lasted for several years, found the administrative structure difficult and the Calgary scene conservative. Larry Lillo, who was interviewed for the position was disgusted by the narrow-minded atmosphere of mid-1980s Calgary in general and of the Theatre Calgary board in particular. Needless to say, he was not offered the position and probably would not have accepted if he had been. Whether or not gender conflict contributed to Sharon's abrupt departure, the optics were certainly bad. For the first and only time in its history, Theatre Calgary was being run by two women but they were like oil and water. Sharon wanted complete control over the artistic process; she wanted a serious season of plays, the ability to cast the best actors, and the right to hire the best directors whose abilities she knew and trusted. The board and Lane must have had different views. So why did she take on the position? For several reasons: it was a new challenge, something she had not yet tried, and it provided a regular salary with a minimum of travel; it also promised (or seemed to) an opportunity to make a difference in and for theatre. For someone as passionately committed to the art of drama and to its role in society, the position of artistic director, if properly defined, provided the power and authority needed to connect the world of the stage with the community in which it was, or should be, rooted. It sounds overly idealistic, but Sharon hoped to make theatre matter, not just as frivolous entertainment but as an integral part of life. The structural and attitudinal obstacles she faced when she tried a second time with Theatre New Brunswick were similar, and the common denominator was a pervasive smug puritanism accompanied by an anti-artistic mindset that was, and in many ways still is, deeply engrained in Canada's utilitarian soul: theatre as feel-good, decorous entertainment that made money was acceptable; anything more serious or more challenging or more risky was not. To have a strong, knowledgeable, opinionated, vocal woman storming the bastion of such complacent middle-class prudery only added insult to injury. Between the old, immovable object of the Canadian establishment and the irresistible force of Sharon's energy, something indeed had to give.

Act Two in this comedy of manners was just a few years ahead in Fredericton, and it only had two acts because when she set out to run a theatre for a third time, with the Garry, she played by her own rules. The announcement that Sharon Pollock was returning to her home town as the artistic director of Theatre New Brunswick was made with considerable fanfare, especially in New Brunswick, but the *Calgary Herald* also took note of the appointment. In February 1988, some months before Sharon left, Kate Zimmerman described Theatre New Brunswick as the only English-language theatre in Canada to tour all its main stage productions provincewide; she interviewed Sharon about her plans, and quoted Mardi Cockburn, chairman of the TNB board, as saying that everyone was "extremely pleased to have as our new artistic director a person with such a rich background in theatre." Sharon was set to begin in July of 1988, and Zimmerman commented, rather coolly, that "Calgary's theatre community will likely be sorry" to see her go. In the New Brunswick papers, the enthusiasm was unqualified. Again Cockburn was quoted as being full of confidence in this new appointment, and Dr. Chalmers was asked for his opinion: "maybe now I'll be able to get her on the phone," he quipped. In a more detailed piece for *Performing Arts* in July, sub-titled "Sharon Pollock Takes New Brunswick by Storm," Anne Ingram queried her reasons for taking on the position, and some of Sharon's answers are revealing. The fact that she was a woman in a man's profession inevitably came up, and this time, instead of sidestepping the issue, she explained that women are reluctant to admit that they have experienced discrimination but that "it has happened to me and I guess it has made me stronger," although she allowed that "anyone who can't compromise in this business has a big problem" (12). She also confessed that she was "interested in administration ... the nuts and bolts of it all," and she admitted that she had "shot [her] mouth off" about the failings of the contemporary Canadian theatre scene so often "that it was time to either put up or shut up" (13). Clearly, she was under no illusions about the challenges she faced; she knew how conservative the province was, and she knew the company had to tour its productions to nine centres, but her optimism was high: "I want to find a way that this company can respond to the hopes, dreams and fears of the entire province."

The 1988–89 season was partly in place by the time Sharon took over from Janet Amos, and it was a strong one that she made even stronger. Sharon directed *Blood Relations* in September in the co-production with Neptune Theatre, and she performed the role of Eme in *Getting It Straight* on 11 November. When a scheduled play could not be done at the last minute, she put on John Pielmeir's excoriating *Agnes of God* in its place. Other productions included Athol Fugard's *The Road to Mecca*, W.O. Mitchell's *The Kite*, and Brian Friel's *The Faith Healer*. The 1989–90 season offered Beth Henley's *Crimes of the Heart*, David French's *Salt-Water Moon* (a good play that surely pleased Maritimers), O'Neill's *A Moon for the Misbegotten*, Joe Orton's *Loot*, and Wendy Lill's *Memories of You*. Sharon was on record as not wanting too much Neil Simon whipped cream and she did not provide any. Previous seasons, while less serious than these two, were hardly Neil Simon-ish either: Chislett's *The Tomorrow Box* went up alongside "Family Trappings," while David French's *Jitters* and Lillian Hellman's *The Little Foxes* filled out the 1986–87 and 1987–88 seasons along with *Educating Rita* and *Guys and Dolls*. Moreover, Sharon did a lot to improve other aspects of TNB's mandate as she struggled to reverse declining ticket sales and, as Ed Mulally has put it, to "overcome the momentum of audience hostility which had carried over from the last years of her predecessor" (21). She established a playwright-in-residence program, inviting fellow Calgarian and friend, Gordon Pengilly, to spend time in Fredericton working with local authors, and she started a "Brave New Words" program for the reading and workshopping of new scripts, something Ilkay Silk has called Sharon's best "legacy" for TNB. She kept the bilingual school program alive, began a program at Dorchester Penitentiary for would-be playwrights, worked with native groups, gave interviews, and even served pancakes at charity breakfasts (Mulally 21). And, as Nancy Coy has told me, she started TNB's weekly "TGIFs"— Thank God It's Friday gatherings for all the staff—at which colleagues gathered informally over beer to chat and relax.

Despite these efforts, other steps she took and decisions she made did not sit well with many in Fredericton, including members of the board. Productions went over budget, and subscriptions continued to decline. She made a number of changes to the staff, and in at least one case the choice was poor. She brought Lea Learning from Calgary to take the position of public affairs officer, but she was unable to meet deadlines and when Sharon confronted her, she threatened the theatre with a lawsuit. According to Mardi Cockburn, who had been so positive about Sharon's appointment, Sharon's chief shortcomings were her unwillingness to consult, her impatience with fund-raising, and her choice of dark plays that were not suitable for touring and not fun to watch on an evening out. Cockburn was by no means alone in these criticisms. In our conversation in 2004, she still vividly recalled her embarrassment when Sharon, in her view, snubbed Lady Aitken, who had arrived from England to oversee the Beaverbrook trusts (a key source of TNB's funding at about $200,000) and meet people. She had invited Lady Aitken to meet the new artistic director in the theatre lobby so Sharon could take them on a tour backstage, but when they arrived, Sharon was not there, and a message was sent asking them to come to her office, something Mrs. Cockburn refused to do. Whether this was a snub or not, it clearly disappointed the chairman of the board who led the tour herself. Nevertheless, by April 1989, the honeymoon was not entirely over because Fredericton's *Daily Gleaner* ran a two-and-a-half page feature story in their magazine section on "Today's Woman" called "The Many Faces of TNB's Sharon Pollock." The article included five pictures, one of which showed the AD happily climbing on the backstage pulleys. Sharon told Ingram that when a person gave their life to the theatre they were "making a political or social statement" because theatre was "important in peoples' lives." Ingram noted that some people viewed Sharon's passionate commitment and demanding standards as proof that she was "dogmatic and [would] ride roughshod over any opposition" (2), but Sharon countered by explaining why the theatre mattered to her and why it should matter to others. Theatre, she said, is "my home" and she liked that home to be a not-for-profit, non-commercial "environment in which artists can create" and where audiences would be "touched, moved or engaged" and "stimulated into thought." "Theatre will die," she told Ingram, "if all it becomes is live performances of situation comedies. I don't want to see that happen and that's why I'm an artistic director and that's why I'm here" (3).

But opposition was mounting rapidly so, as she told Stephen Godfrey in October 1989, "the board and I began to part company." The deficit had risen from $80,000 to $120,000, and Mardi Cockburn told Godfrey she was not surprised by Sharon's decision to leave because "she's left before" (referring to Theatre Calgary), and Cockburn implied that the board might not want to renew her contract when the season was over. Cockburn went on to complain that plays like *Road to Mecca* and *Agnes of God* were too heavy and that Sharon "was very strong in the feminism line," when all audiences really wanted was "to be entertained. They already get a lot of misery on the TV news." And there is no doubt that the local news was grim during the last months of 1989 with serial killer Allan Legere on the loose. What ultimately caused "outrage" in Fredericton, and has left bad feelings to this day, were Sharon's claim that the board was "insensitive" and the aspersions she cast on her native province. Moreover, Sharon's views appeared (for the whole country to see) in that smug centrist organ, the *Globe and Mail*. She was happy to be leaving early, she told Godfrey, because the things she had disliked and left behind in the fifties and again in the mid-sixties were still there: "the authoritarian, paternalistic attitude toward the disenfranchised, the family compact network, the complacency ... conservatism ... and caution." What Fredericton did not know was that Sharon was already writing the play that would expose these failings—*Fair Liberty's Call*. When Godfrey published this article on 18 October 1989, the jig was up. Sharon's plan had been to leave at the end of her second year, that is, in the summer of 1990; however, by December 1989, she was on her way. She packed her belongings, the cats, dogs, and two rats into a truck and made the 4,000-plus kilometre trek back to Calgary in four days. As a former colleague from Calgary put it, Sharon burned her bridges "with gasoline."

And yet, and yet ... she never burned *all* the bridges. Indeed, she built many that enabled others to cross over into the world of the theatre to make careers there. She had done this for Fran Gebhard and Brad Fraser at Banff, for Jackie Maxwell at the National Arts Centre, for John Murrell, Margaret Bard, Jimmy Leyden, Gordon Pengilly, Barbara Campbell-Brown, and Graham McPherson, to name a few Calgary actors and writers, and she did this for others during her tenure with Theatre New Brunswick. Those who knew her best during her eighteen months in Fredericton were those who lived with her or spent time with her on weekends and in the evenings. When Sharon arrived to take up her new position, she moved into a large, formerly gracious but now rundown, old house in Fredericton that was close to the theatre and where Janet Amos had also lived. Sharon shared it with her daughter Lisa, who spent a year studying at the University of New Brunswick, and then with Clarice McCord, who joined them in January 1989. Sharon had met McCord years earlier at Banff and had encouraged her acting and theatre administration work, so when she asked McCord to join her as the manager at Theatre New Brunswick, McCord did not hesitate. The house was sparsely furnished with K-mart tables and chairs, but they had a television and the evening news was *de rigeur*. Household tasks were shared: Sharon cooked and Clarice cleaned because keeping a house tidy did not interest Sharon who had always been able to function surrounded by the clutter of bills, tax forms, pets, laundry, and dishes. However, the daily routine was orderly. Sharon was up before anyone else, often by 5:00 A.M., would walk the dogs, maybe have a hurried breakfast (prepared by Lisa), and the two women would set off in Sharon's jalopy for the theatre. Sharon always wore fine, tailored clothes (in silk or other natural fabrics) to work, with bright scarves, and she would emerge from the bathroom, looking elegant. If breakfast had been missed, she and McCord would stop at a Tim Horton's for coffee, and Sharon would often arrive with a coffee spill down her front. As

Clarice McCord told me, Sharon was "the best dressed *stained* woman in town." Sharon also brought in Barbara Campbell-Brown, a friend and an actor from Calgary, to play Louise in Wendy Lill's *Memories of You*, and although Campbell-Brown stayed at a separate pension, she and Sharon often cycled around the city and countryside on Sunday mornings. Both the Lill play and the production of *Agnes of God*, in which McCord played Agnes, were judged excellent by those involved, even though some members of the audience found them dark and too feminist. Working as an actor with Sharon was very demanding because she wanted excellence, but as long as you did not put on airs or whine, she was there to help and support you.

In the fall of 1989 Kathleen Flaherty, now a Vancouver producer with CBC, who was working on Prince Edward Island, had applied for the position of associate director at TNB and when she arrived, she was picked up at the train station by a woman driving a boat of a car who was half-in and half-out of a sweatshirt. The woman was Sharon and Flaherty got the job. She moved into the house with Sharon and McCord, but what Flaherty recalls most vividly was arriving home one evening during the rehearsals for *Crimes of the Heart* to find the place in more than the usual uproar and Sharon preparing to depart. Sharon had decided to leave immediately because the board would not release the budget or approve the kind of season she wanted, and both McCord and Flaherty believed she was making the right decision under the circumstances. All the same, they were upset and felt abandoned. They stood together in a dark kitchen, with Sharon leaning against the fridge, and they listened as she told them, simply, to carry on because they could. They did.

Looking back over those busy, even tumultuous months with TNB now, when so many years have passed, my conclusion about Sharon's second AD-ship is that it was a success by her theatre standards. She mounted serious, challenging, even tough plays, thereby offering New Brunswickers some excellent drama; she started several new initiatives, some of which lasted; she brought in a number of talented people to work with her and for Theatre New Brunswick. She worked very hard. She also alienated some board members and offended others who did not share her views about the nature of theatre. Quite possibly her administrative problems were exacerbated by the fact that in Fredericton (as in Calgary), she was sharing key aspects of administrative power with women who were more accustomed to taking orders from men and getting what they wanted *through* men. For such women, having to deal with as strong and professionally oriented a woman as Sharon Pollock, who was not about to become your chum, could be threatening. To some she appeared rigid and uncompromising, but in our conversation Barbara Campbell-Brown stressed her opinion that Sharon was (and is) "the most ethical person I know" and that she never complained or held a grudge. Most of the theatre people who worked with her still describe her as warm, generous, enthusiastic, supportive of others, and always able to make things happen. Some of those who got to see her up close recognized her shyness and vulnerability as well as the long shadow that her early years still cast over her life. To Clarice McCord, Sharon Pollock was a mentor and "the ultimate survivor." If this summary makes Sharon sound too serious or driven, I should quickly push her sense of fun, her quality of innocence, her fascination with those hooded rats because of their intelligence and her insecurity back onto the stage of her life. Being in Fredericton again could not have been easy. From all the stories I have listened to, three aspects of those months stand out for me: the rampage of serial killer Allan Legere; the choice of *Agnes of God* as a last-minute replacement, and the dark, partially finished basement, reached by a steep staircase, where the furnace squatted in the old Fredericton house Sharon shared with Lisa, Clarice McCord, and Kathleen Flaherty.

The basement is the most puzzling because Sharon, who is not easily intimidated by most things and is perfectly capable of long, difficult drives or visits to dangerous parts of the world, was terrified of this basement. If the furnace needed tending, Clarice McCord or Lisa would have to see to it, and Sharon would not explain her refusal to go down the stairs. By contrast, visible and present horrors intrigued her. *Agnes of God* was a play Sharon knew well and had called a "really shitty, yet powerful play" (Dufort). In a 1985 Calgary production, she had played the psychiatrist, Dr. Martha Livingstone, opposite McCord's Agnes, the young nun who has killed her illegitimate baby but whose response to this trauma has led to her loss of memory and sanity. As the doctor struggles to uncover the truth from a protective Mother Superior and to make Agnes remember, she begins to recall tragic events in her own life, her terrible fights with her mother, and her own deep anger. By the end of this wrenching, ugly story, Dr. Livingstone has probed a number of destructive female relationships and decided that Agnes is a hysteric because she had an alcoholic mother and was molested as a child. Dr. Livingstone is a survivor, wounded but functioning and helping others; Agnes is the perfect victim. I can well understand why Theatre New Brunswick audiences might have flinched, but Sharon was not done with it and mounted it a third time at the Garry Theatre. While these grisly tragedies were unfolding on stage, Allan Legere, "the Monster of the Miramichi," was terrorizing the communities of Bathurst and Chatham, not far from Fredericton. Legere was the worst serial killer in Canadian history up to that time. Convicted and jailed for a brutal murder, he escaped from jail on 3 May 1989, and for the next seven months he was on the loose. He raped, tortured, and murdered three women and killed a priest before he was caught on 24 November 1989. So full of fear were New Brunswickers that Hallowe'en was cancelled that year. As fate would have it, Theatre New Brunswick was touring the Miramichi while Legere was on his run from police, and the cast and crew had a narrow escape when he broke into the place where they were staying and stole their equipment before going on a shooting spree. For months the provincial and national newspapers were obsessed with the manhunt and for Sharon this was high drama. Privately, she was processing all these things—the ominous basement, the murderous nun, the serial killer—and eventually they would surface, greatly transformed, in *Constance, Saucy Jack, Death in the Family*, and even in *End Dream*.

Sharon's final word on her two administrative experiences with large regional theatres is preserved in her essay, "Reflections of a Female Artistic Director." She had already commented publicly in a 1990 lecture at Stratford on the difficulties facing women who write plays or want to direct in Canada, and in this lecture she criticized the media who focused on a director's gender, when a woman directed a play, and yet said nothing when plays by men were directed by men and comprised an entire theatre season. In her essay she analysed the gender biases within the profession in more detail and articulated what she saw as fundamental differences between the male and female approach to theatre, from the writing of plays to directing and to the running of theatres. Western theatre, she reminded readers, had traditionally been an exclusively male domain. In our day, when women work on stage and backstage, they are usually confined to administrative support roles in which their talent and vision "is so circumscribed, diminished, and diluted by the male's primary position as artistic director in the realm of mainstream theatre as to render their contribution essentially insignificant" (109). As Fraticelli had shown, women directors usually worked in small, alternate theatres and ended up channelling their energies "into the becoming of others rather than the becoming of themselves" (110). From these observations, and her own experience, she went on to describe female theatre practitioners as holding an "integrated view of theatre" as part of the larger world and being connected with and committed to artistic, political, and social phenomena, whereas "the male-dominated theatre establishment" was obsessed with "theatre as commodity" (110). She even claimed to find a gendered difference in "what constitutes compromise and ... capitulation in the making and sharing of theatre." For Sharon, the kinds of compromises made easily by men would amount to "betrayal and denial of self" for women. In such a system, where theatre is a commodity and where large theatres win big grants to please big audiences and gain status, a female playwright, director, or artistic director has to deny her identity *as a woman* in order "to act like a man" (111).

I think this essay is important because it marks Sharon's coming-to-terms with certain aspects of the making of theatre. Although it was published in 1992, before the Garry experiment, it is the result of twenty-five years of theatre experience at every level. It is also Sharon's statement about the theatre as a *vocation*, rather than an occupation or profession, and her frank avowal of discrimination, as well as her attempt to describe what it is to be a woman first and then a woman artist in the theatre. She takes the opportunity to explore the positive contributions women can make, if they get a chance, to the future of a vital theatre, and she spells out exactly what a woman's vision brings to the kind of theatre that exists within, and is responsive to, its social and political context.

> A woman's life teaches her many things: to trust less the exterior and seek the interior; not to fear multiplicity, having multiple selves within herself; to be suspicious of certainty; and to entertain ideas of contradiction, and diversity, along with unity and singularity. This makes her a positive enabling force. And it requires first an acknowledgement that onc is not complete to begin with, and that totality may not be knowable. Receptive thinking and collaborative actions in the theatre do not represent failures of the imagination, energy or intellect. I see the compelling need to believe that all is contained within, and that, in essence, one generates alone, as male motivating forces in the creation of work, and in the administration of companies. (112)

Sharon does not delve further into feminist or philosophical debates about identity formation or the nature versus nurture controversy, and she does not ask why women, who constitute a significant majority of theatre-goers, might prefer not to see plays like *Agnes of God* or choose not to renew a subscription to a serious season (like hers at TNB) with a number of plays by women. Her focus is on what makes good theatre. She does, however, place the weight of her thought and experience more on the identity-as-socially-constructed side of the argument than on the essentialist, biology-as-destiny side. Women's lives, she says, have depended on their ability to see beyond surfaces to the underlying power structures of social organization to what she calls "substance," and on their capacity to find ways of accessing and trusting impulse and intuition so they can create themselves and their work from those sources. She had taken those steps herself.

By the late 1980s, she understood and could articulate her philosophy; she knew how she had arrived where she was as a woman, an artist, a mother, wife, lover, friend, and a politically aware human being. She was poised to start a new theatre-making venture that would test her principles and her vision. Possibly the most courageous step she took towards that future lay not in leaving a husband or walking away from a position as artistic director, but in the completion and performance of a play that had bedevilled her for years. With this play, she not only confronted her own life and demons but she also *let go* of intellect, rules, and reason, trusting in impulse and intuition and in her ability to reach the *substance* lying "under" and "beneath" the surface displays of masculine power and control. She produced her vision of this substance in the form that meant the most to her and was, therefore, the ultimate forum for personal and professional risk—in the dramatic monologue finally called *Getting It Straight*.

IV: Getting Things Straight

Sharon has said that *Getting It Straight* is her most autobiographical play. Although I am prepared to take her at her word, this claim raises a number of questions. Because *Doc* is about her parents' lives and her childhood, the biographical parallels are recognizable. None of this, however, adds up to an autobiographical portrait of the adult daughter—call her Catherine or Sharon—who we only see from the outside in *Doc*, as an observer of her parents' story because in their biography her autobiography is secondary. But where is Sharon Pollock and what do we see of her in *Getting It Straight*? Is she Eme (M-E), or is Eme her ventriloquist's dummy, the persona or *self* she assumes in order to tell us an inner life-story about memories, fears, motivations, and emotions rather than an external one about actions, events, rational decisions, and the orderly surfaces of life? The answer is complex, and *Getting It Straight* is a challenge *because* it is so intense, so private, so personal, so demanding. I have had to sneak up on it, to eavesdrop on it, and even then to let go of my intellectual tools of facts, analysis, and logical interpretation to hear the play. At a 2004 Workshop at the University of British Columbia called "Putting a Life on Stage," when Sharon reflected on the biographical and autobiographical elements in her work, she said quite frankly that this play was "far more autobiographical than *Doc*. Eme is me and I think I knew it as I was writing it" ("Playwright: Parasite or Symbiont," 300). If she knew it was autobiographical when she wrote it, then I need to listen very closely to Eme because in her many voices and seemingly chaotic words, I may be able to hear Sharon speaking about what matters most to her and about who she believed she was in the eighties (and still is?). I may even be able to understand why this play, of all her plays, proved so difficult to write.

Sharon insists that this play is not linear, that it is actually anti-linear, but I will describe it first as if it were a story with a strong through-line. *Getting It Straight* is a one-act monologue in which Eme (for Emily), a middle-aged woman incarcerated in a psychiatric institution, has slipped away from her fellow patients and their caretakers while on an outing to some form of fair like the Calgary Stampede. On the pretext of going to the washroom, she has taken refuge in a storage area under the grandstand where she sits surrounded by garbage. She knows people are looking for her, but she feels safe enough to deliver her story to us, and it is part confession, part autobiography, part warning, and part exhortation. Eme may be mad—paranoia and schizophrenia are the layperson's terms that crop up in her monologue—and she has almost certainly been subjected to electric shock therapy and drugs and interrogated by doctors, but she is more, or other, than simply deranged. It is clear that she has followed the news on television and in newspapers for many years, so she is well informed about and obsessed with twentieth-century wars and the atrocities committed in the name of war. She is acutely aware of the world as a deadly, dangerous place in which all women and children are at risk because of male power and violence. As a mother and wife who feels threatened and oppressed by her husband, Eme is consumed with the need to warn other women about the dangers facing them, their children, and the world before it is too late. She is also, or has been, violent herself, and it seems likely that she has attacked and perhaps killed her husband. Not only is she convinced that she did kill him, instead of merely imagining or dreaming his murder, but she also insists that to have done so is a lesser crime than to have seen how dangerous he was and done nothing to stop him: "I hope I have killed him, to have known and done nothing? That is the crime that I am not guilty not guilty of that" (*GIS*, *CW* II, 262).

Eme invokes several female heroes and avatars in her monologue, and each speaks through Eme to inform and warn her listeners but also to remind us of the long line of far-sighted, gifted, and intelligent women who have been destroyed, punished, or ignored by the men who hold power, write the histories, and assert patriarchal authority and control over the world. While Lysistrata may be, at some level, an inspiration for Eme, she does not mention her by name. The women she does name are Cassandra, Cassiopeia, and Hypatia, and I will consider the relevance of each later, but at this point it is enough to note that this woman called Eme has several voices and a full range of experience and that she is educated and aware of contemporary history. If she is mad, then there is reason in her madness, and both the monologue form, in its direct address to us, and the impassioned, poetic, allusive rhetoric she uses command our attention. I think of Eme as a bit like Conrad's Marlowe or possibly Lowry's Consul, who was also tormented by war atrocities and by the imminent destruction of the world, with this exception: Eme is speaking especially, if not exclusively, to women. If *Getting It Straight* is Sharon's most privately autobiographical play, it is also her most women-centred play and her clearest feminist statement about life and about women's rights and responsibilities.

Sharon's ideas about individual identity, responsibility, and social protest, not to mention her antiwar sentiments, are as strong today as at any earlier period in her life, but she started to articulate them for the theatre in the mid-1970s. It was then that she began consciously to link her political views with her experiences as a woman, and she first worked with this conjunction of politics and gender in the comic satire she wrote for Christopher Newton, "And Out Goes You?" As I suggested earlier, the character of Goose, that feisty old woman who survived the 1935 Regina Riot, was her first attempt to create a female protester/spokeswoman for the rights of all those who are marginalized, exploited, and even destroyed by the authoritarian, patriarchal state institutions that control our lives. By 1976, Sharon had met Dorothy Jones and starred in Jones's production of *Lysistrata*, and this experience sharpened her understanding of women's narrowly prescribed role and fate within the male-dominated world. By 1979, when she premiered "Mail vs. Female," a simplified, clearer portrayal of the Goose figure and her story of social protest, she understood more about the significance of this Regina Riot survivor who had been silenced by a police bullet and about the potential for exploring the values and priorities of men and women. Both are trapped by the dehumanizing systems of the state, but they respond differently, and, if anything, women are more limited in their options for response than men. However, it was not until *Blood Relations* that she began to see beyond her own view of women as passive victims without agency to the possibility that women could be actively interesting characters in a play, and Goose is the prototype and precursor for the strong, ethically and politically engaged, older women she would ultimately create.

When Michael Dobbin first offered her a commission to write a new play for Alberta Theatre Projects in 1984, he wanted a boardroom comedy that satirized the world of corporate affairs in Calgary. Sharon accepted, hoping she could revisit aspects of "And Out Goes You?" in a new play that she would call "God's not finished with us yet" and then "Egg." As it turned out, she was unable to deliver anything to Dobbin, neither a scenario nor a draft, and he recalls the entire episode with annoyance and disappointment. He also found her uncommunicative and unwilling to sign a contract; her quarrel was with the standard Playwrights Union of Canada contract clause regarding "participation rights," which granted theatre companies (including not-for-profit) a percentage of monies earned on subsequent productions of plays they had premiered. As she saw it, this clause was unfair to playwrights like her self who marketed their own plays.[5] Other reasons for the delays with this commission and her lack of communication must have been that she was busy with *Doc* and embroiled in the conflicts surrounding her tenure as artistic director at Theatre Calgary. However, what Dobbin did not know, and what Sharon did not talk about, was her problem with the play itself: she could not find her way with the material or function with a deadline. Although she had been given an advance for this boardroom satire, she was stuck. Dobbin gave up in frustration, but Sharon was not about to let this play defeat her.

The following year, when Walter Learning, at the time the artistic director of the Vancouver Playhouse, asked her to write a *Lysistrata*-type play for Expo '86, Vancouver's centenary, she accepted and once again began to struggle with this play. For a while it looked as if she would succeed in producing a script, which was now going to focus on war and women's issues, but it was also going to be epic in scope *and* a musical. Learning hired Vancouver-based composer Bruce Ruddell to write the music and, for a short time, Ruddell and Sharon made good progress, even workshopping one act in the Playhouse rehearsal hall while he played a piano reduction of his full score. Ruddell remembers this as a very exciting time and the themes of the play as interesting and timely. He found Sharon intimidating but wonderful to work with; she was fascinated by the composition process and by the evolving non-linear form of the piece. In an important 1986 interview with Lynn Dufort, Sharon provided the most detailed description I have seen of her play as it existed then, and there was no hint that anything was wrong. She told Dufort that Walter Learning had prompted her to call the play "God isn't finished with you yet," but that while she worked on it with the composer the word "EGG" popped up on the computer and she wanted that as her title because "EGG ... actually has something to do with the show" (3). She talked about her delight in being able to work with Ruddell and stressed how important it was for her to do something new, challenging, and different with the form by fully incorporating music. "It was important to me that it wasn't a drama I was doing, but a musical" she explained, before elaborating further: "Everything is underscored by music and sound. It's an opera with no spoken words in it ... a Philip Glass kind of thing" (4).

It seemed as if she was finding or discovering a new form, something that would be "wonderful and different—or a disaster" and that without the right form the meaning of the play could not be conveyed to an audience. But it was not only the form that was evolving. She was also rethinking her subject. "The more I worked on it," she said, "the more I concluded that I couldn't use the model of *Lysistrata* at all" because all those Greek women really wanted was for their husbands to stay home from wars and sleep with them. In the twentieth-century context of war and nuclear threat, such a view was at best "frivolous." And she went on to describe how she was reconsidering issues of war, women, social pressures to conform and acquiesce, and the responsibility to act. Then, in an intriguing aside, she mentioned that she was beginning to imagine a woman who is driven "nuts" by the world we live in and was imagining women with children who go crazy, are locked up, and then medicated "so they function." Here, in these few seemingly casual remarks is the *donné*, or clue, that her moral perspective was taking a radical turn; Eloise's ghost was speaking again, and Sharon was listening. As Sharon continues to summarize her plot, the plurality of women becomes one woman who, Sharon told Dufort, "lives in a constant nightmare, in the constant fear of what is going to happen" (3). The woman, who has been "diagnosed as paranoid schizophrenic," locked up and medicated, believes that she is "living inside an egg," and she hears "the voice of the egg" telling her that the world, not *she*, is crazy and that she must "do something about it." Acting on the egg's orders, she breaks out of the institution and takes over the media so she can persuade the women of the world to unite by "booking off" whatever they are doing. I cannot tell from the interview what Dufort thought about all this or even if she was following Sharon's plot summary, but Sharon was clear about her character: this woman "is in a way a Christ-like figure" who listens to the egg of the entire cosmos rather than to some Jehovah-like father-God. However, as Sharon quickly adds, the story will not end happily. The woman will be recognized, arrested, and pronounced mad. Even at this stage, Sharon seemed stuck with the fate of Goose, who woke up from her coma, in both "And Out Goes You?" and "Mail vs. Female," only to be shot again and relapse into silence and passivity.

Unfortunately, Sharon's enthusiasm for "Egg" did not mean that her fundamental problems with the script had changed. Ruddell recalls that after a period of intense work on the project, when he would arrive at her west end Vancouver apartment to discuss and compose over her favourite brand of beer, she just disappeared. Either she had returned to Calgary, had gone to Regina, where she held a writer-in-residence position with the Regina Library, or she had flown to Fredericton to rehearse "Family Trappings" for its May opening. No one recalls the exact timing of events, and no one told Ruddell what was happening. Walter Learning does remember seeing "dribs and drabs" of script, but Sharon kept missing deadlines and could not be reached by phone. As the weeks ticked by towards the September premiere he had announced internationally, Learning became desperate. He flew to Calgary, went to Sharon's house, and demanded the full script. But Sharon did not have it. God was indeed not finished with this recalcitrant work-in-progress; neither was the playwright. Finally, Learning was left with no alternative but to abandon the play and write-off the money invested in it. He turned to George Ryga's new play, *Paracelsus*, as a last-minute replacement, and like Michael Dobbin he remained angry with Sharon and embarrassed by the situation. Both men understood that a writer cannot always produce to a deadline, but Sharon's inability to grapple with this play was becoming truly awkward for everyone involved.

She was not, however, ready to give up on "Egg." In 1987, Martin Kinch, who had replaced her as the artistic director at Theatre Calgary and was keen to involve her once more in the work of the company, offered her a commission for a new play: she suggested "Egg." This premiere, her first at Theatre Calgary since *Doc*, was to be a central event in Calgary's 1988 Winter Olympics Arts Festival. Billed as a "festival highlight," the news that "one of the country's leading playwrights" was creating a new play for the Olympics made headlines. Liz Nicholls described it as Sharon's "nuclear anxiety satire" about "an escapee from the nut hatch who promotes peace in an insanely bellicose world," and Nicholls noted that as a "musical entitled 'God's not finished with us yet'," it had been withdrawn from Expo '86. Brennan was a bit more thorough in his article, "Pollock play makes debut on TC stage in '88 season." He quoted Kinch who said how important it was to have Pollock back at Theatre Calgary, reminded readers that "Egg" had not been ready for Vancouver, and announced that her new play would open in January 1988. Between April 1987, when Brennan announced the "Egg" premiere, and the late fall of that year, Kinch saw only one act of the script, and he realized from conversations with Sharon that the play was not coming together. He had to make a quick decision on a replacement and he opted for *Walsh*, a play that made a lot of sense as a showcase event for an Olympics being held in Calgary in 1988. Here again, and for the third time, this play had refused to be born, and most writers would have tossed it aside as a lost cause. Not Sharon. She later told Brennan she believed that Theatre Calgary and Martin Kinch understood that a play could not be pushed into production prematurely and that she was expecting them to set a new deadline. Somewhere along the way, the schism deepened between Sharon and the theatre, with Sharon calling them incompetent (over *Walsh*) and the theatre administration responding that in that case "Egg" must be put on a more or less permanent hold. Brennan quoted this exchange in the newspaper and noted Sharon's concern that "Egg" was becoming the festival play that never gets produced. To make matters worse, Sharon elaborated on her criticisms of Theatre Calgary by saying that the most interesting new theatre being done in the city was at alternate theatres like One Yellow Rabbit. Whether this was true or not, it was scarcely calculated to impress anyone at Theatre Calgary. Finally, she told Brennan that she was "working on a new one-woman show, derived from 'Egg'," in which she would perform later that summer. She had arrived at *Getting It Straight*.

In her 1982 conversation with Cynthia Zimmerman, Sharon indicated that she was now ready to write more about women: "I know there's a play that follows *Blood Relations* about what happens to a woman who is unable to kill either her father or her mother or, indeed, even herself. Obviously it is about women and madness." She also felt that Catherine's story had not been told in *Doc*. Running in tandem, then, with all the false starts and attempts to find the right form and the real subject of "Egg," were the many plays she was finishing. During the mid-eighties she was also encountering other playwrights who shared her interest in madness, violence, family secrets, and death; she directed Sam Shepard's *Buried Child* in 1985 for LATA (Calgary's Live Arts Theatre Company) and acted in *Agnes of God* that same year. Other, more personal, matters were also pressing in. In addition to the 1982 scare of Michele's illness, Kirk was facing a major crisis. He had married in the mid-eighties and his daughter, Darryl, was born with a heart defect in 1988. Sharon accompanied Kirk in the medical helicopter that rushed the newborn to Edmonton for surgery. The baby survived, but the marriage did not. Back in Fredericton, quite apart from the professional entanglements of Theatre New Brunswick, it was more and more obvious that Doc Chalmers would not live forever; he was beginning to suffer the heart attacks that reminded everyone in the family about his health and a condition they may have inherited. Sometimes Sharon could get there to see him, but sometimes she could not.

A way through these problems and worries presented itself when the International Women's Festival was announced for Winnipeg in the summer of 1988. Rick McNair had gone to the Manitoba Theatre Centre as its artistic director in 1986, and he was eager to work with Sharon on *Getting It Straight*. Not only did he direct her in her premiere performance of Eme, he also advised her on the shaping of the play, on the cuts needed, and on the set design (see Illus. 36). Sharon trusted McNair more than almost anyone else she had worked with over the years; she respected his theatrical ability and vision absolutely, and he was a dear friend. He had stood by her through the break-up with Michael, he knew her children, her father and stepmother (who, he told me, talked exactly like the Bordens in *Blood Relations*), and he had enjoyed social gatherings in her home. What's more, they shared memories of many things, but in particular of animal adventures—animals rescued in the snow, animals taken in off the streets, the wounded seagull that kept the cats at bay, Ratty (the original Winnipeg Ratty, I believe) who Sharon carried through an airport in her blouse only to have him poke his head out right in an airport security man's face. And there was the frozen puppy, a story McNair delighted in telling. When the little creature died in the

36. Sharon and Rick McNair posing for the camera on the set of *Getting It Straight*, 1988.
Photograph by Bruce Hanks.

winter, Sharon refused to toss it into the garbage, so she froze it until it could be properly buried come spring. But then she forgot until months later. When it surfaced in the freezer, Sharon stuck a note to her coat to remind herself—"take puppy from freezer"—and went out to the local Safeway store, where she noticed people giving her the most puzzled and alarmed stares. Only after arriving home did she realize what was stuck to her coat. Rick McNair knew Sharon happy and joking, outrageous and drunk, surrounded by family and pets, alone and in tears. He also knew her as an actor whom he had directed, as the author of plays in which he had acted, as a playwright whose work he had directed and commissioned, and as his assistant AD at Theatre Calgary. He had been there for her professionally in the past, and he would support her enthusiastically with the Garry. If anyone could help her get this play straight, it was McNair.

For the Winnipeg premiere, produced by Women in the Arts at Prairie Theatre Exchange, McNair added rodeo voiceovers at the beginning and end, not only to provide both frame and context for Eme's monologue but also to create a dramatic contrast between the loud, male public world of physical action and the quieter, female private world of Eme's reflection. The design, created by Linda Leon, served to heighten the idea that out there the world was mad, and that Eme's temporary sanctuary was a pocket of sanity. Instead of using props, McNair wanted his Eme surrounded with real detritus, what he described as "a messy

37. Sharon as Eme in the premiere of *Getting It Straight*, directed by Rick McNair, for the 1988 International Women's Festival held in Winnipeg, Manitoba.   *Photograph by Bruce Hanks.*

conglomeration" of stuff, so that when Eme touched or picked up something it was actually a piece of waste, a fragment tossed away by the loud world, rather like Eme herself (see Illus. 37). McNair remembered *Getting It Straight* as "a wonderful show," and he was proud that she consulted him and followed his advice again when she performed the piece at Theatre New Brunswick that fall. When Anne Ingram interviewed her in early July 1988, Sharon spoke at some length about *Getting It Straight* and her work for the premiere just a few weeks away, and she described the character she would play as "the psychic barometer of her time in her capacity to experience the suffering of women and children ... and in her desire to convince others to help her rid the world of its ugliness" ("Right Theatre at the Right Time," 13). Of course, she told Ingram, this woman may be mad, delusional, paranoid, or what have you, but she may also be "completely rational."

When Rita Much interviewed Sharon in 1990 for the collection *Fair Play: 12 Women Speak*, the play was soon to open in a new production directed by Jackie Maxwell with Susan Wright as Eme. This time, and after doing Eme twice herself, Sharon described *Getting It Straight* in a rather different way. Up to this point, she had stressed the link between women and madness, but now she saw the play and its message for a self-destructive world in more feminist terms:

It's about a woman in an asylum who tries to reconstruct how she thinks she got there. In a sense the play suggests that the ways of knowing—logical, rational, sequential—don't seem to have worked and that perhaps there are other ways of knowing, that women are particularly open to because they give birth and raise children, that are more valid and which should be listened to however they come to people. (Rudakoff and Much, 220)

Jackie Maxwell began rehearsals with Susan Wright in December 1989 for the 10 January 1990 opening at Toronto's Factory Theatre Studio Café. Maxwell was not drinking because she was pregnant, but Wright liked to drink, and this play needed more than a few drinks to see one through. Maxwell summed up the entire process for me with one word: "agonizing." Wright found her role both challenging and "very depressing"; she told Maxwell it felt like a Beckett play. For an actor like Wright, who was most at ease working with a group, a one-hander was always difficult, but this piece was completely draining. For her part, Maxwell knew Sharon well enough to realize that the play was deeply personal; she described it to me as "more naked," "more emotionally bare" than *Doc* and as much closer to the "essence of Sharon." This was a play, or so Maxwell believed, that Sharon had conceived of with herself playing Eme. As a consequence, both she and Wright were extremely anxious about Sharon's reactions to their interpretation of, not just her *play*, but her *self*. When Sharon arrived to watch the dress run, Maxwell and Wright were tense. After it was over, these three amazons of the Canadian theatre retired to the bar to debrief. Maxwell sat quietly with a cup of tea, but Sharon and Susan faced off over much stronger stuff. And they talked, discussed, drank, and disagreed in a lengthy exchange that Maxwell remembers as very intense but always respectful. Sharon was not happy with the set with its recognizable props that left little room for the imagination, and she disagreed with aspects of Wright's interpretation, but she was "generous" all the same. Oh to have been there in that bar, a silent observer and listener (with a camera or a tape recorder) because on that January evening in 1990, Canadian theatre history was playing live with three of the most talented people in the country coming together to make theatre. It was an event, a *tour de force*, a happening that could never be repeated.

The reviews were few and dismal, or very brief. Although some reviewers understood that the play was feminist, non-linear, and yet made a clear statement about our need to accept responsibility for the state of the world and for our lives, Ray Conlogue, writing in the *Globe and Mail* damned the play. In his review, called "Chaotic play offers no answers," he claimed that Susan Wright's "formidable talents" were lost in "80 minutes of unorganized free association," and he accused Sharon Pollock of using Eme "to give vent to her own despair." Conlogue made it clear that he did not approve of professional writers parading their dark moments of the soul in public, especially when the writer was female and was blaming men for the mess things were in. He did catch references to Hiroshima and Nagasaki and to Cassiopeia scattered through Eme's "aimless ... undramatic ... tedious mental wanderings," but he complained that "it never becomes apparent why we are listening to this woman [who] has no point to make, apart from a generalized wish for a millennium of peace." He bristled over the "schizoid rituals" performed while Eme "babbles," reduced the question of madness to an R.D. Laing side effect, and sighed that "the show may strike more of a chord with women than men." Ah Fraticelli, ah humanity! I do not know what Sharon thought of Conlogue's review, if she bothered to read it, but Jackie Maxwell was angry. Basically, he dismissed the play as a trifle, when she was absolutely certain (as was McNair, as am I) that here was "a major writer doing something really different and risky" in a play performed by a brilliant actor in an ideal, intimate venue.

It is no accident that Sharon's own performances of this play were first at a women's festival (July 1988) and then on 11 November 1988, Remembrance Day, for Theatre New Brunswick. As I see it, *Getting It Straight* is Sharon Pollock's personal testament of faith and call to action, addressed by a woman and mother to other women, to save our world from war, especially from nuclear war, which would result in global annihilation. This is Sharon's feminist, antiwar play, and the horror of war motivates Eme to do what she has done and to make her plea to us. Paradoxically, Sharon had returned to the original source for her play, *Lysistrata*, for inspiration, but the play she finally produced is a *cri de coeur* from a twentieth-century woman artist, and it has little in common with its Greek antecedent. Instead, Cassandra and Cassiopeia who, along with the fairy tale heroine, Rapunzel, and, most important, the historical woman Hypatia, are Sharon's touchstones for, and examples of, what men do to women who dare to challenge their authority.

This is her most "naked," autobiographical, play in several senses. As a confessional monologue, it is shot through with allusions, fragmentary and fleeting, to crucial moments in her past life-story and to her ongoing awareness of violence in the present; as an impassioned exhortation, it represents Sharon's willingness to expose the depth of her feelings—of rage, despair, and love—and such a display of passion is always deemed improper or downright dangerous. Sweet Canadians (as Margaret Atwood has called us), living in our self-styled peaceable kingdom, do not behave this way; it is just not done. So when a woman speaks as Eme does, she is seen as an embarrassment, at best, and, at worst, as mad. To speak of madness, however, is to name the risk that Sharon has taken here and the extreme example she is prepared to make of herself in order to make us see things as she does before it is too late. Finally, *Getting It Straight* is an autobiographical play because it functions in terms of memory, a human capacity that has always intrigued Sharon and about which she has always written. Memory, however, is more than a theme here and this play is not, in the usual sense of the term, a memory play. Memory *is* this play—its rhetoric, its structure, its rhythms, its texture of allusions, its message, and its visceral, bodily delivery. In *Getting It Straight*, Sharon has attempted to remember with her body, a body born by a woman, that had born six children, a body that acts, feels, thinks, speaks, and dares us to risk as much, to do the same thing. This play may remind us of Beckett's *Happy Days* or *Mouth*, but it is more like *All That Fall* or *Waiting for Godot* because of its explicit embodiment.

Despite the apparent free association and disjunction of the monologue, with its emphatically non-linear, non-rational (*not* irrational) form, the play is exquisitely structured through repetition, metaphor, internal rhyme, and semiotic rhythms that work to propel the monologue, not forward, but outward through the breath required to express speech in an address. Take almost any set of a dozen or so lines and you will see and hear the poetics of the remembering, breathing body at work:

> all the parts are missing I see the disappeared I
> hear the dispossessed I know we can read a
> magazine you know the one with all the pictures
> of the women
> who have made it
> to the top it's all the rage turn the page
> glossy photos of their children
> very clean
> and smartly dressed smiling
> spouses country
> houses and a long shot
> of some art I lived in a house in the country I lived in
> a house in the country [...] (*GIS*, 240)

You must say these lines out loud to understand them, expend your own breath to feel their significance, to get it straight. Like Eme, Sharon Chalmers had also lived in the country with her family in their cottage on the Miramichi and as Sharon Pollock with her own children when she and Ross bought the house in Keswick on Lake Simcoe. Eme's belief, perhaps only a fantasy, that she has murdered her husband because she believes he is complicit with the militaristic, right-wing forces of patriarchal power that threaten women and children and world peace is rooted in Sharon's desire to kill one of those "smiling spouses [in] country houses," who are dangerous and violent.

Woven into Eme's speech are innumerable references to Sharon's past and present life, to her own plays, and to others' plays (like Alfred Jarry's violent, political allegory *Ubu roi*).[6] Thus, the white rodeo horse with a bulging eye evokes Lizzie's carousel nightmare in *Blood Relations*, and the children's chants or skipping songs that Eme sings recall Katie's songs from *Doc* (see *GIS*, 230 and 241). Eme tells us that she was always close to her "daddy," that her grandfather worked for the railway, but ended up in an institution, where she visited him with her father (236–37)—all aspects of Sharon's life and family story. She riffs on the initials "R.D." (233), which are not Sharon's father's initials but are those of Ross Douglas Pollock, as well as the initials of the popular psychologist R.D. Laing, and she is haunted by people who die of kidney failure (250), as Eloise did.

But one of the earliest childhood memories to surface in Eme's speech predates Eloise's death and possibly even the visits (Sharon's as well as Eme's?) to grandfather Chalmers in the psychiatric hospital in St John. This memory is peculiarly troubling and seems to connect the past of early childhood with contemporary events and with the media images of war that torment Eme. Eme tell us that she sees—

38. The cenotaph at the corner of Queen and Church Streets in Fredericton, with the spire of Christ Church Cathedral in the background. In *Getting It Straight*, Eme remembers visiting the cenotaph as a little girl with her mother. *Photograph by J. Grace, 2006.*

one of those towns on a river
a small little town on a river small little town train
running through and one of those squares in the middle a bite
in the air we walk
to the square my mother my brother and me
it is large and I look up I am small and looking up
old
men marching mothers' tears I am little looking up
wear a poppy hide the grief watch a general lay the
wreath place my hand against the stone
granite grey
mitten sticks
trace the letters carved in stone
here's to those
who lost their lives (257)

The little town could be any number of Canadian towns, but such a town by a river with a train running through it and a town square with a cenotaph that bears the names of its soldier sons killed in the Great War is very likely to be Fredericton (see Illus. 38). The mother with two children who walks to the square wearing a poppy on Remembrance Day is surely

Eloise with Sharon and Peter. When we remember that Eloise's father fought in World War I and died in 1919, quite possibly as a result of his service, and that Sharon's memory of this particular November 11th would be from early in World War II, in which two of her uncles served, then the commemoration acquires a personal, as well as general, significance that magnifies the loss of children in war and mothers' tears into a timeless, universal image of violent death and female suffering. This memory resonates with all the vivid images of contemporary war that Eme, like Sharon, has watched on the television news (notably from Vietnam) and the constant threat of mass annihilation, begun with the American bombing of Hiroshima and Nagasaki and intensified by the threat of all-out nuclear war during the Suez Crisis of 1956, through the Cold War and the escalating arms race, the Cuban Missile Crisis, the threats to Nicaragua, Lebanon, and now Iraq. Eme is obsessed with the news and haunted by the spectres of dying children, weeping women, and those "hungry / silos / [that] seed the skies with death" that are sanctioned by the "state," "the fatherland motherland homeland" (253). The incessant chant she hears and repeats drums the terrors of World War II and of mass destruction into our ears: "cry spare us fat man cry little boy little boy cry / little boy cry little boy littleboyenolagayfatman!" (256). Not until Marie Clements wrote *Burning Vision* (2003) would another Canadian playwright give us such a harrowing image of Little Boy and Fat Man, the nuclear bombs dropped on Japan.

To stop this escalating horror, Eme turns for guidance to female, explicitly maternal, symbols and to myths and stories about women. The symbols she holds out to us are "the ladies" (those rooms where only women can go) and the "oval of blue" that is the egg in which she lives, the egg of the cosmos inside which we *all* live. Within these sacred spaces she listens to the stories of mythical and real women. Cassandra was the daughter who accurately prophesied doom and destruction, but because the god of manly beauty was angered by her warnings, he placed a curse upon her speech and no one believed what she said. That god was Apollo, whose name was given to the first manned American spacecraft program in the 1960s race to explore (meaning to militarize) space. Eme thinks of Cassandra "turned inside out," her prophecies of doom now visible in "cat scans" and "satellite photographs" (231). She places greater faith, perhaps, in Cassiopeia, the Queen of Ethiopia and mother of Andromeda, who, in Greek mythology was punished for being proud of her own and her daughter's beauty. However, this mother outmanoeuvred her first punishment—to appease Poseidon's wrath by having Andromeda sacrificed by her father, the King—but she could not evade male wrath forever. According to the myth, Poseidon placed her in the heavens seated in a chair that revolves around the Pole Star thereby forcing her to spend half her time in an undignified, upside down position. The stories of Cassandra and Cassiopeia, of daughters and mothers, are embedded in larger stories of war and male violence, but Eme looks to them and "to the past for guidance" (256), hope, and inspiration because the stars at the outer edge of the constellation called Cassiopeia's Chair suggest a safety net spun by "women's hands and rapunzel's hair" and the word they spell is "love" (258).

But the story of female wisdom and courage with which Eme identifies most intensely—and the one that terrifies her the most—is not the story of Cassandra, Cassiopeia, or Rapunzel but of an actual fourth-century woman. Hypatia (ca 370–415 AD) was a famous

Egyptian philosopher, astronomer, mathematician, and teacher, who was also reputed to be beautiful and a virgin. She taught at the famous academy in Alexandria at a time of political turmoil between the Christian church, led by the Patriarch Cyril, and the non-Christian, or pagan, state. Because she supported the state and was critical of religious fanaticism, Cyril plotted her murder. Versions of how she was captured and killed vary, but she was seized by Cyril's hit men (dragged from her classroom or carriage), stripped naked, flayed alive, and her body burned. All her scholarly works were destroyed; the church declared her a witch, and Cyril was canonized. We can guess that Eme is seeking empowerment and revenge when she tells us that, as she lies beside her husband, she feels herself "slipping into Hypatia's flayed and discarded skin" (244). The wisdom and almost totemic or magical power that comes from such an investiture enables Eme to look into her husband's brief-case, discover his evil secrets, and ultimately imagine—or carry out—his murder.

I find Sharon's choice of Hypatia interesting. The section of *Getting It Straight* devoted to describing Hypatia's death is disturbing and graphic, and it is juxtaposed with Eme's memories of herself and her husband. Thus, by the logic of this play's woven, non-linear form, the juxtaposition implies their connection. But the story of Hypatia is not well known, so Sharon has made a deliberate choice here. In the 1980s Hypatia gained some attention, however, because a scholarly journal was founded with her name in 1986 and in 1980 Carl Sagan published *Cosmos: A Personal Voyage*, which provided the basis for his immensely popular thirteen-part PBS television series with the same title. One of these episodes dealt with Hypatia, a figure Sagan expressed great sympathy for, so Eme (I mean Sharon) must have discovered Hypatia through the television program, if not the book. Moreover, Sagan was vigorously opposed to the madness of nuclear war with its threat of destruction on a cosmic scale. Hypatia, her wisdom, courage, and violent death at the hands of men, becomes a crucial figure of feminine resistance and of another way, a non-masculine way, of being that can inspire Eme. Her name and fate pull together the threads of the play, but they do so indirectly, covertly, through images and associations, rather than bold statement or argument, because this woman, dimly remembered and called Hypatia, only remains a victim until another woman is brave enough to put on her skin and embody her wisdom. One quotation attributed to Hypatia and preserved in a letter is this: "Reserve your right to think, for even to think wrongly is better than not to think at all." And this is precisely what Eme invites us to do when she slips into the flayed skin of her monologue, and I find it hard to imagine a more apt Sharon Pollock dictum than "Reserve your right to think," unless it were reserve your right to raise your voice and say what you think out loud.

Jackie Maxwell's comment that she and Susan Wright found their work on *Getting It Straight* "agonizing" makes complete sense. Reading and listening to this play is hard, but performing it must be something else. To do this, the actor, a woman, must be prepared to put on the flayed skin of Sharon's language, with its raw shreds and torn fragments and sinews of meaning, and then to think from deep inside her body. When Eme tells us at the end "to go to the ladies / go beneath / go under" (262), she means that to get it at all, to begin to grasp the enormity of the world's crisis and our responsibility, we must relinquish the language of reason with its masculine rhetoric of logic and aggression; we must let go and allow the language of desire to speak.[7] Paradoxically, fittingly perhaps, this very process of going beneath is in itself violent, but like birth it is also creative, liberating, and shared. This process, employing an impassioned, agonistic language, helps to weave the "gossamer net" that holds all of us together in a world of love.

PART III

CHAPTER 8

The Garry Years

Theatre as an art form, which was founded in spirituality, and began as a place to celebrate, question and challenge the gods, is in danger of losing its soul.... [L]et us not expend our energies in maintaining ... theatre as a 'cultural industry.... Let us move on to the rediscovery and examination of our need for theatre—our need as a society, an audience, an artist, a community.

—SHARON POLLOCK, "DEAD OR ALIVE?" 1991, 13

I am attracted to those lives that resonate, sometimes in unlikely or surprising ways, with mine. I sense in certain aspects of their lives and times a lens through which to see more clearly significant issues of my life and times. Focusing that lens involves creation, imagination, and invention.

—SHARON POLLOCK, "PLAYWRIGHT: PARASITE OR SYMBIONT." 2006, 298

I: Life Without the Boring Bits

With the eighties behind her, Sharon turned her attention outwards. She *needed* to do *Getting It Straight*, and when she had completed and performed it, it marked a turning point in her life and work. It is almost as if, once communicated, put down on paper and then published, she could push some of her deepest fears and acutely painful memories aside. She was not necessarily finished with them, or they with her, but after *Getting It Straight* she could move on. For a person so little given to revealing anxiety and so determined to be in control of her life, this play was an astonishing confession of emotional, spiritual, and mental extremity. In one essential way, she had not thrown self-control, inhibition, or privacy to the winds at all because the text of the play had to be winnowed from the uncontrolled mass of the "Egg" manuscript, and the process required precise control. Or to switch metaphors, I am reminded of a comment about her father: he was so skilled and quick as a surgeon that he could operate with a minimum of trauma to the patient. And Sharon had to operate in the same way as she deftly removed her play from its unwieldy source. Performing Eme also took the utmost control and professional skill. Nevertheless, her success with *Getting It Straight* taught her to trust her intuition and creative instincts more than she had before and to rely less exclusively on intellect, and this new balance is apparent in the plays of the nineties: *Fair Liberty's Call, Saucy Jack, Constance,* and *Moving Pictures.*

The eighties had taught her a number of other, less intimate, lessons. She had got her professional life straight in 1982 by abandoning all attempts to work through a literary agency, and after struggling to effect change, she finally resigned from the Playwrights Union of Canada in 1987. By 1987 she had written what may be her last children's play, *Prairie Dragons*, and she had begun her most important play of the nineties, *Fair Liberty's Call*. Major national and international honours (as well as more local prizes) continued to come her way, including the 1986 Governor General's Award for *Doc*, her first honorary degree, awarded by the University of New Brunswick in 1986, and the Canada/Australia Literary Award, which she won in 1987. Her academic recognition by UNB especially pleased her father, perhaps because it came from his hometown university but also because he could understand its importance more clearly than the theatre awards. Her second honorary degree was awarded by Queen's in 1989. By the end of the eighties she had not only learned how frustrating the position of artistic director could be, but she had also gained considerable institutional theatre experience through her adjudication and committee work for the Canada Council and Alberta arts organizations and through her associate artistic director activities with Theatre Calgary and the Manitoba Theatre Centre. Some of these administrative lessons were hard, but others, like her 1986 stint as writer-in-residence at the Regina Public Library were more personally rewarding and more fun because she could spend time helping younger playwrights with their work, a task she has never treated lightly and to which she continues to devote considerable time. Along the way, she was acting and directing, so the cumulative experience of the eighties would result in her renewed dedication in the nineties to the making of theatre in all its forms and in the manner she believed was best. Margaret Bard, an actress in Calgary at this time, describes Sharon as a mentor and an inspiration for her, but she also corroborates what others have stressed—that Sharon Pollock burns her bridges. However, as Bard quickly added: "she rises from the ashes like a phoenix."

It is clear from letters written in 1982 and 1983 that Sharon withdrew from her association with the Toronto-based literary agency Creative Trust so she could take charge of her literary and production affairs herself. Despite the bookkeeping and correspondence entailed, she has never again hired an agent. On the positive side, the decision has meant that 100 percent of royalties are paid directly to her, instead of 90 percent. The first indication of her dissatisfaction with agents I have found comes in an 8 December 1982 letter she wrote to Bill Millerd concerning the Arts Club production of *Blood Relations*: "Bill Boyle, Creative Trust, is no longer empowered to act as my agent," she informed Millerd, and she asked him either to send her the full royalty owed, from which she would send Boyle his 10 percent, or to deduct the agent's fee at source and send her the 90 percent she was owed. Sharon has never seen why a third party should be remunerated for doing relatively little to advance a writer's career, but I wonder why she chose to spend her time doing this kind of clerical work. Over the following years, she had to deal with requests from professional theatres as well as from universities wanting to mount student productions or from publishers wanting to publish or reprint a play or from her translators. Her replies were often tardy because she had been directing, or acting, or out of town. After she got an answering machine callers got the recorded message—in her inimitable, hesitating voice—

saying "uh ... I've been away but now I'm back so ... uh, leave a message. Thanks." At other times, she didn't know what to charge (and sometimes charged nothing at all), or she would lose or mislay a contract. A classic example of the mislaid contract led her to write her 15 May 1983 letter to Jack Lewis of NeWest Press. Micheline Wandor, in England, wanted to include *Blood Relations* in the third volume of *Methuen's Plays by Women*, which was scheduled to go to press by the end of June that year, and, as Sharon told Wandor, she felt "excited and privileged at joining the illustrious company" in the Methuen collection. However, she could not recall the details of her contract and believed she needed clearance from NeWest to be able to proceed. In haste, she told Lewis: "I have lost my copy of our contract (could you send me a copy please?) but believe this [Methuen] publication with non-exclusive rights does not interfere with your rights," and she went on to ask him for a "release" to allow the Methuen reprint or, if that were unnecessary, "a note to that effect." But she was correct in her understanding of non-exclusive rights.

In the midst of all this mundane work, she was tackling CFCN and Robert Barlow over the television adaptation of *Blood Relations* and assuming the responsibilities of artistic director with Theatre Calgary. But as Malcolm Lowry liked to say (paraphrasing Dr. Johnson) "cheerfulness keeps breaking through," and she exercised her particular sense of humour by writing letters to editors and composing play reviews. She sent one especially delicious example of the latter to Brian Brennan at the *Calgary Herald* on 23 January 1986. She had not liked the Theatre Calgary production of *Uncle Vanya*, and she invited Brennan's reaction to her diatribe and asked to see his professional review. She told Brennan that her review was not for publication, which is just as well because she had nothing positive to say; her quip that "even the real dog in Act I looks stuffed" sums up the tenor of her remarks. But it is what she says in the cover letter to Brennan that I find interesting. Having penned her poisonous description of the production, she expressed her satisfaction—"Now I feel much better."— and warned Brennan, or anyone else who might be curious about her reviewing proclivities (like biographers?) that she was going to make a collection of her reviews, most presumably unpublished like this one, to deposit with her papers (recently purchased by the University of Calgary) because "I get some perverse pleasure from the thought."[1] In other words, the private joke between herself and Brennan, who replied that he thought her review was "a gem," always held the potential of becoming circuitously public: for the time being she reserved the right, and the power, to withhold or reveal her views. I have respected this decision by providing only the merest glimpse into what she called her "rabid reaction to *Uncle Vanya*" because she may include it in her archives and because I find it more interesting to contemplate the camaraderie of these two—playwright and theatre critic— that could transcend his criticism of her plays.

There is one more, far more serious, decision that Sharon made in the eighties, the consequences of which would follow her into the nineties and plague her Garry experiment: resignation from the Playwrights Union of Canada. In September of 1987 she sent a seven-page letter to all her fellow playwrights in the Union, outlining the shortcomings, as she saw them, in the Union's proposal for contracts (see 264). She urged them to call for a renegotiation of the proposed contract at the upcoming Annual General Meeting so that it recognized and protected the moral and financial rights of the writer. She ended by stressing the fact that she had personally negotiated many contracts because she did not work with an agent, and she obviously believed she could better protect her rights if she were not constrained by official contracts designed to serve the non-profit Professional Association of Canadian Theatres (PACT) and the Union. She was convinced that the consequences of imposing such minimum standard contracts would be worse for emerging playwrights than for established ones like herself. The result of her letter and subsequent resignation, however, was that she was perceived as having placed herself outside the professional theatre structure in Canada or, worse still, together with her two resignations as artistic director, that she was marginalized not just as a Western or Alberta playwright but as someone altogether beyond the pale. In effect, she had burned another bridge and would have to find a new environment in which to make the kind of theatre she believed in and to write the type of play she valued.

But before I turn to *Fair Liberty's Call*, the play in which I see Sharon reflecting upon and reacting to the artistic constraints, hierarchical pressures, and social expectations of conformity and compromise that she had fought against throughout the eighties, I want to consider a minor play, *Prairie Dragons*. It premiered at Calgary's Quest Theatre in October 1987 and was first published two years later in an edition of children's plays, *Playhouse: Six Fantasy Plays for Children*, edited by Joyce Doolittle. In her introduction to the *Playhouse* volume, Doolittle notes that while the play combines stylized elements from the Asian theatre tradition with modern Western documentary techniques, the play "is written with a completely contemporary sensibility," and she describes it as based on "an audacious premise: that ancient dragons have accompanied Chinese immigrants [to Canada] and dug into the prairie soil to make old paths in a new world" (vi). Equally audacious, if not downright confrontational and personally principled, aspects of this play are Sharon's treatment of women's rights and her portrayal of Chinese immigrants as deeply rooted in the soil of Canadian myth. Indeed, this play for young people is a serious treatment of feminism and of race relations set on the Prairies against the backdrop of World War I. The two teenaged heroines, Sarah Witherspoon and Lily Kwong, are in rebellion against the sexist assumptions of their society, their fathers, and the patriarchal powers-that-be. The fact that the story of the play is told by the colourful, androgynous dragon, who speaks in several voices and represents the actors and the stage manager, in no way disguises the important messages of the play. Quite the opposite. The use of life-sized, cutout figures, which are visibly moved around by the stage manager, and the appearance, or disappearance, of the four actors playing Sarah, Lily, Lily's father, and the greedy banker, Mr. Lowe beneath the undulating shape of the red and orange dragon only serves to highlight the challenge of the story. The innovative form, staging techniques, and the poetic language of the dragon, provide an appropriate vehicle for what Sharon wants to say.

Sixteen-year-old Sarah's story is a sad one. Her mother died when she was only four, leaving her alone on the family farm with her father and an older brother. The year is 1916 and her brother is away fighting. On the day the story begins, Sarah's father is thrown from his horse and killed. In shock and grief, Sarah visits her mother's grave to seek her support and advice; she wants to run the farm herself until her brother returns from the war, and her communion with her dead mother gives her courage. However, the conniving banker, Mr. Lowe, covets the farm and insists that a mere girl can never manage it because he has "never heard of no female farmer" (*PD, CW* II, 216) and because for a woman to farm "goes against nature" (212). He threatens Sarah and attributes the general drought and other problems on the farm to her unnatural self-assertion. Lily's problems are similar. Her father owns the laundry in town and is saving his money to give his son a good education. When twelve-year-old Lily wants to enter a spelling competition to win the $25 prize, both her father and brother tell her she must relinquish all claims to independence or success and drop her education because she is only a girl whose job is to help in the laundry, marry, have children, and obey her father, brother, and husband.

Undaunted by these oppressive men, the two girls team up to defy male authority figures by calling on the forces of nature, in the shape of the dragon and the dead mother, to help them. Lily persuades her father that if Chinese-Canadians can live on the prairie then so can Chinese dragons, and when Mr. Kwong accepts this possibility, all the problems the girls face are resolved: rain comes to relieve the drought, Sarah keeps her farm, and Mr. Kwong accepts his daughter's right to a full life because the Chinese dragon can work its magic—or exact its revenge when displeased—from within its new home. But the play does not end before the Prairie Dragon reminds Sarah to "speak to your Mama" and acknowledge her help. As long as Sarah places her "faith and hope" in her and her pearl necklace (as well, of course, as in the dragon), she will be just fine. Lily's power comes from being *here*, that is from asserting her *Canadian identity* as well as her Chinese traditions. By welcoming the dragon, Lily has freed herself. Underlying the strong feminist message about individual identity is this less overt one about ethnic and national identity. Together these messages make for a positive, empowering female play that I do not think Sharon would have attempted before the eighties, before *Blood Relations, Doc,* and *Getting It Straight.* If I can describe Sharon as throwing down the gauntlet in the shape of a children's play, then that is precisely what she has done in *Prairie Dragons.*

Sharon has told me more than once that the best plays must present "life without the boring bits." However, a biography cannot dismiss these bits in such a summary fashion. Sharon has always managed a great deal of humdrum daily life—housekeeping, cooking, laundry, babies, kids' homework, and frequent moves. In the letters to her father from the late fifties and the early sixties, her fatigue and boredom with domestic routines are palpable. If they were less bothersome through the next two decades, it was not because they vanished but because of her personal happiness with Michael and the challenge of building her career. Managing the business side of her life after 1982, while exasperating at times and certainly time-consuming, was easy by comparison with past domestic chores or with the enormous practical effort she would invest in the Garry. By the end of the eighties, she had gained a new hold on her life as centrally hers and on her time as more exclusively her own. She was living alone, mistress of her daily routine, and the bridges she had burned with the theatre establishment freed her, in a way, from many external expectations and obligations. At fifty-four, Sharon Pollock was still rising early, still exploring her artistic vision, and still keenly interested in world affairs. One personal worry, however, continued to preoccupy her. Although she remained interested and involved in the lives of all her children, she watched Kirk with special concern. Not only had he grown up without his father, but he was dealing with the illness of his daughter and the end of his marriage. On the brighter side, he had begun to write plays and his interest in the theatre looked as if it might develop into a career. For all these reasons—his need for support, his writing ability, his interest in theatre, his isolation in a family of strong, talented women—and for others that are more difficult to explain, the bond between Sharon and her only son was (and continues to be) deep and complex. This relationship was central to her personal life during the 1990s and overshadowed three significant deaths that occurred in 1993: on the political front, the 13 March torture and murder of the Somalia teenager, Shidane Arone, by two soldiers of the Canadian Airborne Regiment with the United Nations humanitarian effort called Operation Deliverance; in the theatre, the death from AIDS of Larry Lillo on 2 June; and, most important for her personal story, the sudden death of her father on 26 April. It is safe to say that by 1990 the boring bits of her life do fall into the background of my story, and that 1993 would explode with a range of emotional challenges, creative work, and new ventures that rival the events of those other, earlier watershed years in her life: 1954, 1966, 1973, and 1981.

The chief theatre achievement of 1993 was her return to Stratford with *Fair Liberty's Call*, but prior to this she had written a new radio play, commissioned by the CBC, and in 1991 she and Kirk had co-founded a small community theatre group in Calgary called the Performance Kitchen, which led directly to the formation of the Garry. The radio play, *The Making of Warriors*, dealt with the story of Canadian Mi'kmaq activist Anna Mae Pictou Aquash and was aired on the 20 May 1991 *Morningside* show in conjunction with the second International Women Playwrights Conference hosted by Glendon College, York University, in Toronto. Sharon's interests in historical events, feminist issues, and native rights, came together for the first time with this play, and while its stage debut belongs to the turn of the century, its roots in her thinking and imagination reach back to the beginning of the nineties. Although she has always been uncomfortable with labels and reluctant to be called a feminist, it is important to remember that she was writing plays like *Getting It Straight*, *Prairie Dragons*, and *The Making of Warriors* between 1987 and 1991—plays different in formal terms but alike in their treatment of women's issues. Moreover, she was prepared to co-chair the international conference for and about women playwrights. It is hard to conceive of a more forthright, public commitment to the creative work and lives of women in the theatre than this role, especially considering the degree of rancour unleashed during the event and Sharon's intervention to halt an altercation that erupted in which white, middle-class playwrights were accused of ignoring other women's problems and of displaying homophobic and racist attitudes. People attending this conference, like Anne Chislett, Cynthia Zimmerman, and Ann Wilson, who described it as a "cautionary tale," remember the scene as ugly and tense, but Sharon (white, middle-class, and senior) remained comparatively unruffled and, temporarily at least, helped return the debate to a civil level. As she told Zimmerman in an interview, "I think it's important that the white woman of privilege's perception of what is the appropriate emotional tone and tenor for dialogue not be allowed to prevail" ("Towards a Better, Fairer world," 1991, 35).

Maybe she felt she had also poured oil on the troubled waters of her own life by writing plays like *Doc* and *Fair Liberty's Call* because when Everett Chalmers died, aged eighty-eight, she did not return to Fredericton. Although he had suffered several heart attacks, in April 1993, he entered hospital for an operation on his knee, and it was his decision to go ahead with the surgery. He knew the risk to his heart, of course, and the instruction on his hospital chart was unequivocal: "Do not resuscitate." Thus far, Sharon has not written about her father's death or what it meant to her, but she had lived with the reality of his heart condition for many years, visited his bedside on other occasions, and would soon face her own cardiac crises. She has, however, described his death and posthumous presence to me with her typical sense of ironic humour and an unmistakable note of satisfaction. As he was dying, Doc Chalmers apparently had enough energy to rebuke the nurse who tried to save him by protesting, "Jesus Christ woman, can't you read!" Possibly this is hearsay, or maybe it is Sharon speaking for her father, but quite possibly these were his exact words—this sounds like the man she captured in *Doc*. When she did go back to New Brunswick a few years later, it was to see Pegi Chalmers. Pegi, who had replaced Eloise in the Chalmers home but had also helped Sharon escape her marriage to Ross Pollock and tried to assist with Sharon's youngest children (despite her own health problems), had been moved to a care facility near Moncton, where she ended her days in a small room with a large painting of Everett staring down at her from the wall facing her bed. Sharon was both amused and appalled by this scene, amused because it captured her father's quintessential presence and appalled on behalf of the woman (and women) he dominated.

II: *Fair Liberty's Call*

When Sharon was invited to give a lecture on *Fair Liberty's Call* for Stratford's Celebrated Writers Series on 11 July 1993, she began by saying that she felt awkward talking about the play because she felt so close to it. Then, in one of her most revealing descriptions of her work, she related the play to her personal experience of leaving the place of her birth to make a new life and a new home in a new place. How long does it take, she wondered aloud, to transplant yourself and to feel you *belong*? From there, she moved into a wider reflection on what forces she believed had shaped Canada, on what values have defined us as individuals and as a nation, and on how her play, in its structural contours and its characters, reflected both her personal journey and the evolution of the country. The personal journey across Canada that she shared with her audience that day included her flight to Calgary at the beginning of 1966 and a number of later trips by car when she could appreciate the topographical variations as she drove from the Maritimes, through Quebec and Ontario, to the Prairies. At first, she regretted the lack of trees and found the mountains ominous; the Prairies felt empty by comparison with the settled, civilized, domesticated East, because she could see little more than absence in the landscape. At the same time, she found the experience of driving West "mystical" because, when you "come out [of] northern Ontario at the Manitoba border [the] landscape opens up and you see great blue sky and horizon." Gradually, this experience of moving westward came to hold for her "a glimpse of infinity full of significance beyond the individual." It was this experience—mystical and humbling—of opening up, of changing, of having to see oneself and the world differently, that lies behind and informs the drama of *Fair Liberty's Call*.

Indeed, the movement and structure of the play do capture this quality of expanding horizons, which in turn symbolize hope, opportunity, and freedom. Towards the end, when John Anderson disappears into the rising sun after choosing forgiveness over retribution, when Joan Roberts accepts her new place by helping him leave and by tasting the earth of her new home, and when Eddie and Wullie decide to stay in New Brunswick to build the future, the play itself seems to open out to embrace a vision of what life in general, and life in Canada, might be. One of the characters in *Fair Liberty's Call*, Eddie, embodies this vision and *performs* it through the course of the play until she/he can be seen (in Sharon's words to her Stratford audience) as a "national metaphor" for a new world. By describing her play and her hopes for it in this way, Sharon once more tried to shift our attention away from such narrow labels as history play and documentary to make us see the symbolic, political, and philosophical dimensions of the work and to focus on its relevance to contemporary affairs. Like Miller's *The Crucible* (the comparison is Sharon's), *Fair Liberty's Call* is "about *now*."

Sharon began writing the play in the mid-1980s, and it has always been called *Fair Liberty's Call*. At the time, she was following the news coverage of revolutionary events in Central America, and she was struck by the hypocrisy of the American response. Despite its own revolutionary history, the United States' reaction to left-wing movements in the area was one of intolerance and interference. In 1989, after years of propping up Panama's right-wing drug-lord, General Manuel Noriega, who worked for the CIA from the fifties to the mid-eighties but had become unco-operative, the United States under President George H. W. Bush invaded the country and captured him. Its activities in El Salvador and Nicaragua during Ronald Reagan's presidency were similarly violent and politically interventionist. Throughout the twelve-year civil war in El Salvador (1980–92), the United States supported extreme right-wing elements, and in Nicaragua they supported, financially and militarily, the violent right-wing forces known as the Contras in their efforts between 1984 and 1990 to defeat the leftist Sandinista government. But perhaps what resonated most powerfully for Sharon was the rhetoric produced by American government interests and reproduced by the media reporting on events both in the United States and in Canada. Labels like the National Army of Liberation, for an extremist group opposed to the Sandinistas, or like the United Nicaraguan Opposition and the Nicaraguan Resistance, for various right-wing political organizations, provided an aura of legitimacy, unity, freedom, and righteousness for these groups and their activities while masking the complex agendas and vested interests at work behind the scenes.

For Sharon, it was a short step from these observations to her critical reflection upon Canada and Canadian history. Never one to throw stones at others when she too lived in a glass house, she focused her attention on New Brunswick and on the intolerance, bigotry, and privilege that had shaped provincial life from its beginnings. As in *Walsh* and *The Ko-magata Maru Incident*, and later with *End Dream* and *Kabloona Talk*, she wanted to expose the darker, untold aspects of Canadian history because they contributed so decisively to what the country was becoming—and might still become as it faced such constitutional crises as the failures of the Meech Lake Accord in 1990 and the Charolottetown Accord in 1992 or the eruption of racism and armed conflict at Oka during 1990. But *Fair Liberty's Call* is neither a history play nor a documentary, if by those terms one simply expects an unexamined dramatization of past events or a faithful reproduction of so-called facts. I see the play as an allegory of Canada and as a treatment of contemporary issues and timeless, if not universal, ideas about liberty, human rights, war and injustice, and many kinds of violence, including the abuse of language to manipulate the facts. Moreover, it has always been this type of play, even in its earliest drafts.

When Sharon was writer-in-residence at the Regina Public Library in 1986, Janet Amos, artistic director of Theatre New Brunswick, wanted a new play and Sharon sent her a draft of *Fair Liberty's Call*. Amos liked the idea enough to commission the next draft, but she also sent Sharon a number of comments and questions. During a Banff workshop in the summer of 1987, Sharon continued to work on the play, but she grew increasingly uneasy about the changes Amos wanted. Her recollection is that Amos had failed to appreciate the scope of the play and the crucial importance of the "gender transcending" significance of Eddie/Emily; for Sharon, Eddie was key to the meaning of the play. For her part, Janet Amos recalls thinking that the draft she saw was neither "new" nor a "deep enough" treatment of history and that the script lacked "a clear through line." The two simply could not agree on what the play should be, and Sharon withdrew it. The script, dated December 1986 and called the "first draft," is in the Banff Archives. Although it has much in common with the 1993 play, and is recognizably an exploration of New Brunswick's United Empire Loyalist past, there are very important differences between it and the final play. This early version is a simpler, more linear and declarative, and more active play. Ironically, given Janet Amos's reservations, *Fair Liberty's Call* began as a comparatively unambiguous history play with a predictable through line. The play opens in the Roberts home near the settlement of St. Anne's on 24 October 1786 as the women of the family prepare a "memorial dinner" to commemorate the Loyalist defeat at Yorktown, Virginia, in 1781. The Roberts family consists of the father George, the mother Joan, an older son Richard, who fought for the Rebels and is now dead, an older sister Annie, the central character of this script, and the younger twins, Edward and Emily. Emily has died of smallpox and Edward, who fought for the British forces, has joined the family exodus to New Brunswick. It would almost seem that the Eddie/Emily character did not yet exist if it were not for some oblique comments made by Joan and Edward towards the end, when Joan remembers her younger son coming home because he could no longer endure the fighting. Then Joan suddenly accuses "Emmie" of killing Edward (while looking at "Edward"), to which "Edward" replies: "He killed himself, mama. (pause) Why do you hate me?" (ts 101). Joan will not answer this question immediately, but when she speaks again she calls "Edward" a liar: "Wearin' his clothes and lookin' like him but not him. No. Liar." (103). And the script ends on this negative note of the mother grieving for her dead sons and resenting the living daughter, Emily, who, it now appears, has assumed her brother's identity, fought for the Loyalist cause, and survived.

At this early stage, the script was nowhere near as psychologically rich and politically complex, let alone as symbolically resonant, as it would become. Major John Anderson, the Patriot, exists, as do Edward's black comrade Wullie, Major Abijah Williams and Corporal Daniel Wilson, who both fought with Tarleton's Legion. Anderson demands revenge but is persuaded by Annie to forgive and leave. However, without a strong Eddie/Emily character and a mother who appreciates her daughters and her new home, the point of the play remains unclear, and the story stops abruptly with Joan lost in the past. It would almost seem as if Sharon was still unable to free herself from her negative image of a mother who is emotionally disturbed, trapped in a lost past, and resentful of her daughter. By calling this mother Joan *Roberts*, a familiar UEL name and Eloise's maiden name, she deliberately connects this mother and family with her own roots. And when one remembers the significance of the name Emily/Emmie/Eme for Sharon herself, it is hard not to see, in the daughter's question, "Why do you hate me?" the shadow of lingering pain and loss in Sharon's life. No wonder she bridled at Janet Amos's apparent dismissal of the Edward character (who is Emily), and no wonder it was this character she developed, empowered, and refined as she reworked her play. This character speaks for Sharon because she is the daughter who could succeed, survive, and be able to imagine a future of fair liberty in Canada just as well as any son could do.

During the 1990 season, Sharon held the position of associate director with the Stratford Festival and she met artistic director David William at this time. 1990 was also the year that John Wood directed his striking production of *One Tiger to a Hill*, so it is no surprise that Sharon and her work caught William's attention. He was a supporter of Canadian plays and considered Sharon one of the most serious and important playwrights in the country; so she was dismayed when he asked her to write a play for Stratford but suggested she adapt a Robertson Davies novel. On reflection, this was an odd idea given the profound differences between the two writers. In any case, Sharon refused and sent William a copy of *Whiskey Six Cadenza* instead. When he did not choose this play, she sent along a draft (probably a second draft at this point) of *Fair Liberty's Call*, and the rest, as they say, is history. Sharon wanted Guy Sprung as her director, and he agreed. Not long after accepting the play, Stratford held a two-day reading of it with Kate Reid as Joan, but with the exception of Reid, who died of cancer on 27 March 1993 and who Sharon recalls as "wonderful," she benefited little from this workshop because the other actors did not focus on the task. Sharon has always been dubious about this kind of workshopped reading, but I have watched her work well with actors she respects on such occasions. This time, however, with this play, she found the process of revision much more satisfying when she was able to work closely with Sprung and with the cast during October 1992 in the preparation for rehearsals. Also attentive and helpful was Stratford dramaturge Elliott Hayes, who wrote to Sharon (in an undated letter probably from October 1992) suggesting some further cuts to historical information and correcting her spelling of Yorktown and the date of its surrender. *Fair Liberty's Call* was announced for the 1993 summer season at the Tom Patterson Theatre in the Stratford

Festival *Friends* newsletter that fall, which contained three pages of detailed, explanatory notes on the American Revolution and the United Empire Loyalists. Clearly, Stratford assumed that the historical elements of the play required explanation, and these aspects continued to dominate many reviews and reactions to the production, and, I think, contributed to the future neglect of this powerful piece of contemporary theatre.[2]

Sharon left the rehearsals in Sprung's hands, not only because she trusted him but also because she was rehearsing her role as Renee Havard in another new play, *Death in the Family*, for its June premiere in Calgary at the Garry Theatre, but she did make it back to Stratford for the final tech rehearsals of *Fair Liberty's Call* and for her July lecture. This time the festival organizers arranged for her to stay at an elegant red-brick Bed and Breakfast at 240 Birmingham Street in southwest Stratford—accommodation that was several cuts above the Church street digs she shared with Michael in 1974 but also several blocks further away from the theatre. Sprung recalls Sharon as being very much on edge at the time because a world premiere at Stratford is a big event for a playwright. He also recalls Janet Wright, who was "tremendous" in the role of Joan, as more than usually tense because of the recent tragic deaths of her sister, Susan, and her parents in a Stratford house fire. There were many technical issues as well, such as candles catching fire and blood grapes disappearing, but the most bizarre glitch involved a large block of ice used on stage as a symbol or literalized metaphor of the story. This block of ice had a perfectly natural tendency to melt during performances, which meant that it had to be regularly replaced. The wagon the men pull on at the beginning to set up their ceremony had to stay on stage in full view, so that every prop essential to the play had to be in the wagon from the start. In short, the stark, symbolic design Sharon called for meant that the behind-the-scene preparations were complex. Despite a nervous playwright, a grieving actor, melting ice, and property challenges, Sprung remembers being told that *Fair Liberty's Call* was "the best thing" of the season, but if it was, that quality did not translate into box office quantity. Of the five plays done at the Patterson that summer (*King John*, *The Bacchae*, *Fair Liberty's Call*, *The Illusion*, and *The Wingfield Trilogy*), it received the fewest performances (sixteen compared with eighteen for *Wingfield* and forty-two for *King John*) and the lowest gross revenue (just under $155,000). However, these statistics say much about Stratford audiences and little about the play.

What was it about this play and its premiere that attracted praise but could not bring full houses? How was it staged, performed, and received? As with all of Sharon's plays, the design was extremely important. She needs to know the space in which a new play will be produced and to see how a designer can work with it in order to imagine the physical reality of her script and to adjust her technical requirements. The careful stage instructions that appear with the published text developed out of production, and in the case of this play correspond closely with what could be done in a theatre like the Patterson, where it was possible to use a long thrust with the audience positioned on three sides of the stage. At the premiere, this area remained empty, except for a play of light across it, which suggested a landscape, and that large block of ice placed well downstage until the actors enter the space to introduce themselves and begin their stories. The fully packed wagon, an echo of Brecht's *Mother Courage*, was then pulled downstage only to be circled back, well upstage again, so that it settled into the background of the action and did not interfere with sight lines. All the props to be introduced into this empty playing area were brought there and finally removed by the cast. The result was a design that fully supported the non-naturalistic atmosphere and symbolism of the play and left almost everything to the mind's eye of each character telling his or her story and to the imagination of the audience.

In the original published stage instructions, Sharon stressed that the stage should be bare at the start, except for a *"swirl of colour"* on the floor to represent *"'virgin' land [that] appears empty and uncorrupted."*[3] As Joan, Annie, and finally, Eddie speaks, *"the swirl of dark colours"* should be *"supplanted by dappled light evoking"* a stand of hardwood trees with *"sunlight filtering through the leaves"* (*FLC, CW* II, 365). At the end of the play, after all the paraphernalia of war and remembrance has been removed, this empty, symbolic space, filled with light and promise for the future, returns. Such a setting and such an imagined place resist historical specificity; the physical space of the play is timeless. The use of music at the premiere was very effective, although Sharon does not call for it in her published stage instructions. Just as the performance was to begin, "Oh Canada" was played, causing audience members to scramble to their feet only to find themselves standing at attention as the violent sounds of battle, followed by "Yankee Doodle Dandy," drowned out the national anthem. Once again Sprung and his designers were trying to wrench the play out of historical amber and locate it in the present. But if Sharon did not include this fine touch in her stage instructions, she was clear about sound effects: *"all sound is impressionistic, even surrealistic, rather than realistic"* (*FLC*, 364), and when the three women deliver the opening incantation—"You want to know where / to put your eye / so you can hear the / heart / beat / of a country / comin' into bein'" (365–6)—they should be speaking *"over a taped montage of their own voices repeating the words"* so that the kind of eerie reverberation, reminiscent of the acoustics exploited in some of her radio plays, would fill up the aural space of the theatre.

In addition to the other songs called for by the script, martial music was played between the two acts, and it seemed to me that the characters were choreographed (rather than blocked) throughout, almost as if they were dancers instead of actors. They began by taking up positions of striking visual isolation from one another, scattered about the long, exposed expanse of the stage; then they were herded together by Anderson, who separates the five men downstage from Annie and Joan, who he keeps close to him upstage. This concentration of characters into two groups is emphasized through lighting when an increasing darkness falls between them. In this way, the staging drew attention to the gendered allegory of the play and complemented the movement of the story from a narrowing into destructive dichotomies (life/death, female/male, hope/despair, future/past) to a celebratory opening out into hope, freedom, forgiveness, acceptance, inclusivity, and the possibility of a new future in the closing scene, where the black man and the man/woman can cross that dark gulf to join forces with the mother and daughter and upstage the quarrelling men. As Sharon told her lecture audience, *Fair Liberty's Call* was written to embody and enact just such an opening out into peace and possibility after the threat of regression and violence because she drew on her own experience of emigrating (after a fashion) from the claustrophobic world of New Brunswick to the comparatively open, liberating world of the West, for the shaping of her play. It is this contracting-in-order-to-expand structure and movement that must be captured on stage, as it was at Stratford, for the meaning of the play to be dramatized as theatre. This symbolic movement, more than plot development or overt conflict, *is* the action of the play. The dramatic tension so necessary in theatre must be built, and relaxed, through lighting, choreography, sound, and speech. Perhaps it was also suggested through that block of ice melting away silently downstage. Sharon did not call for it in her published play, but she told her lecture audience that the director and designer chose this literal metaphor and that she liked it. When she was asked what she thought it meant, she replied that for her it stood for Canada and the North. It might also have suggested the process of acceptance that Joan goes through or of forgiveness that Anderson experiences or the gradually loosening grip of the past on a man like George Roberts. However, if *Fair Liberty's Call* gets a new production in this century of global warming, such a prop would ironically undercut the positive message of the play.

Reviews of the premiere fell into sharply opposed camps with the majority being positive. I cannot think of another Pollock play, with the possible exception of *The Komagata Maru Incident*, that has elicited such opposed reactions. On the negative side, Mira Friedlander called Act One "an expository nightmare," and David Greenberg dismissed the entire play as full of "overdrawn clichéd characters [who] yap left-wing political speeches." Robert Reid went further, calling the play a "feminist attack on the Loyalist experience through the be-smirched spectacles of Political Correctness." On the positive side are reviews that range from ecstatic encomium to thoughtful, judicious praise. Writing in the *Buffalo News*, Terry Doran was positive but thought there was more in the play for Canadians than for "others," but does not say what or why. Other reviewers called it a "formidable challenge," "master-fully written," "excellent," "timeless," and "superb." Clifford Brown gave the production a score of 4.5 out of 5 and predicted that "*Fair Liberty's Call* is destined to become a classic of Canadian theatre"—a prediction I support but am still waiting to see fulfilled. John Coul-bourn described the play as "a refreshing dose of self-honesty, unlaced with hypocrisies," and Bob Verdun proclaimed that "attending this play should be compulsory for all Canadian politicians" because the play was a "brilliant piece of writing" that was "particularly relevant to our nation." In Stratford's *Beacon Herald*, Larke Turnbull praised the production and reminded readers that "despite its historical setting, the play examines issues that are timeless." Indeed, most reviewers, including the few who were negative, got this point: in the guise of a history play, Sharon Pollock was telling us about who we are now and what we might (or might fail to) stand for in today's world. Stewart Brown noted that *Fair Liberty's Call* reminded him of Timberlake Wertenbaker's *Our Country's Good*, which is an interesting parallel, and he concluded that it was "not necessary" to know American history to admire and enjoy the play.

The three reviews I find the most interesting were those by H.J. Kirchoff, Martin Morrow, and Jamie Portman. Kirchoff described the play as a "dramatic gem" that "should be seen by every Canadian, especially United Empire Loyalist descendents with romantic delusions about their forebears." He too stressed the relevance of the subject as well as its universal-ity, and he likened the opening incantatory lines to the "antiphonal poetry of bp Nichol and

Wilfred Watson"—high literary praise indeed! Portman began by calling this play Sharon's "provocative best" and said the play rose "far above the level of polemic" to explore how individuals suffer, cope with guilt and dishonesty, and survive war, betrayal, and terrible loss. Sharon Pollock, he concluded, "is one of the most interesting voices on the Canadian theatre scene." But if Clifford Brown optimistically called the play "a classic of Canadian theatre," Martin Morrow was a bit more skeptical about the impact of such claims. In "Will Audiences Hear Fair Liberty's Call?" Morrow summarized the praise heaped on the play but cited chilling statistics: the houses were only 35 to 50 percent full; money was being lost; David William was leaving the Festival and taking his enthusiasm for Canadian plays with him; and vacationing Americans had no idea who Sharon Pollock or Michel Tremblay were and preferred the fun of chestnuts like *Gypsy* or *The Mikado*. Morrow concluded on a very dark note:

> William has told me that Stratford is our country's national theatre and, certainly, he has attempted to justify that in his commissioning and programming of Canadian plays. But with economics, more than ever, dictating the shape of the festival, it's a sad fact that, while Gilbert and Sullivan and old Broadway musicals have a safe haven at Canada's "national theatre," there's no guarantee we'll see another Sharon Pollock premiere there in the near future.

And we have not, even though she has written several major new plays since 1993.

How is it that a play described in such high terms and cited as a must see by more than one reviewer can disappear so completely? Some of the reasons are not difficult to identify. *Fair Liberty's Call*, with eight characters, is expensive to produce; two-handers come cheap by comparison. It demands sophisticated, even inspired, design work and expert direction, and it is not a good candidate for amateur productions. But perhaps most tellingly, it is not fashionable. It is a demanding, politically and ethically serious, piece of theatre, like Brecht's *Mother Courage* or Frayn's *Democracy*. It is epic theatre—big in scope, symbolic in style, philosophical in meaning—the kind of play only a mature artist could write. Nothing about the play is *feel-good*, not even the tentative and hard-won vision at the end. And it is not theatrically postmodern or superficially innovative. Instead, the play requires polished ensemble acting to portray convincing human beings facing real-life dilemmas. The Roberts family represents millions of families split apart by political feuds, decimated by war, traumatized by violence and betrayal, lied to and exploited, and uprooted from their homes. Since the Second World War we need only think of Central America, which Sharon had very much in mind as she was beginning the play, or events in Chile, Argentina, Sri Lanka, Rwanda, Iraq, Afghanistan, and Lebanon for examples. At the same time, this play is profoundly Canadian because of the hard contemporary questions it asks about our past and our present and because of the nature of the promise it holds out to us at the end. Guy Sprung put this very well in his "Director's Introduction" to the first publication of the play:

> Not only is this the rare work of art that tries to understand present-day English-Canada by exploring the past, but Pollock has dared to examine our identity in relation to our powerful

neighbour to the south without resorting to cheap stereotypes. Rather, she is forcing us to come to terms with ourselves [because] we are all responsible for our own choices.

"Choice"—that most English Canadian of words, because Canada, with geographical, linguistic and racial forces threatening our integrity, is the only country in the world that exists solely by virtue of a choice that must be continually renewed by its citizens. What a postmodern idea of a country that is! Sharon Pollock has, with her extraordinary play, forced us to confront our own nationhood. (9)

I see *Fair Liberty's Call* as the culmination and apogee of Sharon's artistic and political vision and as her most significant theatrical articulation of themes and issues that have always been important to her. It is a family play, but one in which a single family represents a community, a nation, and the human condition. It is a political play that probes and tests the conditions that produce greed and injustice and support class-, gender-, and race-based prejudice and that endorse the exploitation of the many for the benefit of the few. It is a history play insofar as it uses a historical war in one country to examine the impact and consequences of war on the future of another country. It is also a play that is very much about the confrontation between the individual and those in authority, whether that authority rests with a family patriarch, a political interest group, a military establishment, or the apparatus of a modern nation state. In such confrontations, the individual must decide— *choose*, as Sprung notes—whether to comply, possibly at the risk of his or her sanity or soul (like Walsh, Hopkinson, or Bob in *Doc*) or to resist, which brings another set of risks. Choice and responsibility, in Sharon's world, always come down to the individual. Finally, as reviewers like Kirchoff and Portman noted, and as Sprung could see, *Fair Liberty's Call* is about language. It is a poetic play that explores, stretches, and kneads words such as liberty, loyalty, fairness, rebellion, betrayal, and home until they give up some of their complex meaning, until we can hear their rich ambiguity and understand their dangerous slipperiness. Thus, the word *freedom* in George Roberts's mouth does not mean the same thing as it does when Annie or Wullie use it. It is Eddie, the lost son/daughter, who exposes her father's hypocrisy when she demands—

> EDDIE: Is any opposition rebellion?
> GEORGE: It's not the time for questionin'! It's a time for restorin' order and rank and
>   stability. It's time to get on with our lives.
> EDDIE: So our promised land, our great new province, this country will become the fiefdom
>   of a few, is that it?
> GEORGE: Our position—
> EDDIE: Former position—
> GEORGE: —gives us rights, can't you see that?
> EDDIE: It's not what I'm lookin' at. (389)

What Eddie is looking at and hearing is the heartbeat of a country coming into being, and she wants that coming into being to begin on a foundation of fair liberty for all. On this business of honesty and clarity in language, Eddie (who after all is Emily) speaks for Sharon.

In many ways, *Fair Liberty's Call* is an anti-war play. It unfolds against a background of war; all the characters suffer the trauma of losses caused by war, and all have been forced into exile and are obliged to begin again. But it is an anti-war play not only because it portrays such trauma, most poignantly expressed through Joan Roberts's pain and disorientation, but also because Sharon clearly critiques the men's staging of a remembrance celebration as retrogressive, self-serving, and hypocritical. With the exception of Eddie/Emily and Wullie, these ex-soldiers and George Roberts, the father of a Loyalist and a Rebel soldier, are trapped by the past; their uniforms, boots, flags, and other war trophies are stained with blood, like their memories. Nothing productive, the play insists, can emerge from their tawdry re-enactment and maudlin or obscene battle yarns. This message is driven home through the enigmatic but powerful figure of Major John Anderson, the Rebel, or rather, the *Patriot* soldier who has come seeking revenge for the atrocity that claimed his fourteen-year-old brother in the massacre at Waxhaws. Anderson, however, represents more than a man seeking revenge. Reflecting back on the play, Guy Sprung said that he saw Anderson as a mysterious figure who, like the grandmother in *Doc*, represents humanity's "collective guilt and memory." This insight is a good one, and it leads me to think of Anderson symbolically as an avenging angel and yet, morally, as the vehicle for revealing truth and enabling for-giveness instead of retribution. The ugly truth he reveals is not who slaughtered his kid brother but that in war atrocities are perpetrated by all sides, even by and on civilians. He arrives in New Brunswick with an Old Testament desire to take an eye for an eye, but when he leaves he has agreed to help break the vicious circle of retaliation that fuels war. Psycho-logically, he embodies the Freudian return of the repressed; he is more solidly flesh and blood than Banquo's ghost or Hamlet's father, but he serves some of the same functions.

It is no accident that those who sense his importance well before he reveals his identity are the women, and if one is careful about applying the term, then *Fair Liberty's Call* can be called a feminist play. Joan, whose mind is disturbed, imagines she sees in Anderson something of her lost Rebel son Richard, and she is right to do so. Anderson is not her son, but he could have been and he is some mother's son. Annie suspects he is other than he at first appears to be, and he will remind her of and then bring her to recount her story of John Andre, the soldier/spy she liked and yet betrayed, as well as the story of her sexual abuse by Loyalist soldiers holding her brother prisoner. By eliciting these memories, associations, and stories from Joan and Annie, Anderson illuminates the common humanity of shared suffering and love that connects individuals—mother and son, woman and man, sister and brother—despite the violence of war or the prejudices evoked by race, class, and gender. Insofar as this validation of relational identities and interconnectedness can be called feminist, it contrasts sharply with the spectacle of futile dissent and discrimination that the men display as they huddle downstage attempting to rationalize who amongst them is of least value and can thus be sacrificed to Anderson's revenge. Predictably, Major Williams chooses Wullie, the racial other, as his preferred scapegoat. The play's emphatic separation of the men and women in Act Two would imply that the playwright sees life in these simple terms until we remember that Anderson stands with and listens to the women and that Eddie, who stands with the men, is Emily.

Sharon has said that, for her, Eddie is the key to the play. As a woman, this character is able to see through and beyond the prejudices of her father and men like Major Williams, and yet as a man she has experienced firsthand the violence and horror of active combat, something few women do, even today. As a man and an ex-soldier, she claims the status, authority, and agency denied to women, while as a woman she cannot ignore the reality of relationships, and she values the liberty Wullie seeks in racial terms because she knows the gendered limits to freedom with which a woman lives. At least, something like this is what I think Sharon wishes to convey through the androgynous figure of Eddie/Emily. What bothers me about this character, especially when I try to place her as the key to a feminist interpretation of the play, is that Emily's female identity has been submerged in the identity of a man, and a soldier no less. It is almost as if Sharon still needs to clothe a strong woman with the wisdom to imagine an ethical future and the credibility to act on that vision in the shape of a man, and nothing in the play suggests that Emily will re-emerge from her identity as Eddie. But the ending of the play, like a feminist interpretation, does not rest entirely with Eddie/Emily. It is Annie who tells Anderson that neither he nor she can bring back their dead brothers by seeking revenge. She tells Anderson that they "oughta be lookin' to a better world for our children," and she *tells* him to "Go." (414). And it is the mother who releases him: "You can go now," Joan says, and she holds out her hands for his pistol. It is not Eddie/Emily who acts decisively at this critical point. It is Annie who holds the men at bay with Anderson's rifle and gives the orders: "Take all the guns, Mama. Take them down to the water. Throw them in where it's deep and scatter the horses" (414). In the penultimate moments of the play, when the stage has been cleared of the war trophies and remembrance totems, Joan will ask for her lost daughter Emily, and Eddie will reassure her mother that Emily is "still here" but "changed" (417). And it is at this moment that the real feminist heart of the play beats. In the 1986 draft of *Fair Liberty's Call*, Sharon ended the play with the mother's rejection of the daughter and all she stood for. In the final version, Joan comes up close to Eddie/Emily, touches her child's face, and accepts her daughter, her daughter's change, and the "new world" in which she now lives.

That new world is, of course, Canada. But if Sharon has always been reluctant to be labelled a feminist, she has been equally uneasy with the label of nationalist. Yet almost every reviewer of the Stratford premiere saw this play as a meditation on the Canadian nation and on the history and values that define Canada. Indeed, *Fair Liberty's Call* is her exploration and affirmation of her country and its national identity. By setting the play in 1785 New Brunswick, she chose a strategic moment when one part of the emerging Canadian nation was being created, and she deliberately focused on a United Empire Loyalist family fleeing to the safety and promise of New Brunswick to remind contemporary Canadians that, with the exception of the First Nations, all Canadians originally came here from somewhere else and many arrived with the hope of making, or finding, a better, fairer world. Of course, not all non-aboriginal settlers were thinking in these terms because there have always been the speculators in furs, land, timber (as New Brunswickers know), and other sources of wealth, who came to advance their own interests and to seize control and power at the cost of every-one else. As usual, Sharon did her homework on the subject, and New Brunswick really did begin with a struggle between a select group of Loyalist families who wanted patronage and preferment and the less privileged families. Moreover, the treatment of African-Canadian Loyalists, like Wullie, was racist, and many of these men and women accepted Britain's offer of transport to Sierra Leone, an offer Wullie rejects. Just as Sharon exposed originary events on the Prairies with *Walsh* and in British Columbia with *The Komagata Maru Incident*, so she dug deeply into the soil of her own origins in *Fair Liberty's Call* to tell us more about how Canada came to be, to show us how much blood (spilled elsewhere, as well as here) has contributed to building the country, and to warn us about contemporary abuses of power in the name of liberty, patriotism, and democracy.

Although the plight of First Nations or the relations between Indians and white settlers do not receive close attention in this play, as they do in *Walsh* and *The Making of Warriors*, she has not ignored this dimension of Canada's history. Joan Roberts senses the presence all around her of these other inhabitants—the red woman with her baby, the burial sites, the bones—but she cannot appreciate these signs or see in them the chance for a new under-standing of who she might be and where she is until the end of the play. To reach this deeper, racial connection, she must first look "up close" at Eddie/Emily; to see who was always here before her, she must first touch her daughter's face and accept *her* as *him*. In other words, Sharon makes the feminist message inseparable from the national one: accepting Eddie leads her to forgive her husband and acknowledge his love, which enables her to "feel [her] feet pressin' flat 'gainst the surface of the soil now," to hear "the words spoke by the man with the missin' jaw bone," and to see that, when she kneels, her "knees make a small indentation in the dirt" (418). To stay in Canada, to *belong* here, means realizing that there were others here before you and that this new country must be inclusive and above all shared. Instead of a remembrance ceremony that celebrates war and looks to the past or an oath of citizen-ship that legitimizes privilege and merely bestows a legal status recognized by the authorities (and perhaps not always or equally by them), Sharon's mother figure enacts a very different ritual.

> JOAN: I see the red woman with the babe on her back step out from under the glade of trees. She holds out a bowl. She offers a bowl full of dirt. Eat, she says. Swallow. And I do.
> (418)

In the original publication of *Fair Liberty's Call*, as in its premiere, the play ended with Joan's words of commitment—"And I do."—after which she raised her hands, fingers spread, in front of her face. When it came time to reprint the play in *Collected Works*, Sharon adjusted this ending, not by cutting or adding lines, but by re-ordering them; she also modified her stage instructions just enough to give her feminist/nationalist message a small, but significantly different inflection. In the modified version the final words are dialogue shared between Eddie and Wullie who collectively choose to "stay right here" and make their place. The future of New Brunswick, of Canada, will belong to the mothers and children, to the son/daughter whose symbolic transgendering includes the wisdom of both sexes in one identity, and to the ex-slave who will be free because together they decide to stay and make a better place. As the stage is returned to its uncluttered state, free of imported values and an imposed past, Eddie *"begins slowly lowering the English flag as lights go to blackout"* (418). This ending is less woman-centred and less ambiguous than in the first published text, but the symbolism is just as powerful: the British flag, like American revolutionary rhetoric, is foreign. To build this country, to see or hear it coming into being, we must work together from the ground up; we must *choose* to stay here not simply by rejecting elsewhere but by relinquishing the grip of *there* on our lives *here*. And to preserve what we have got today, we must know our own past and listen to fair liberty's call. Which brings me back to Martin Morrow's question: "Will Audiences Hear Fair Liberty's Call?" The answer is no, they will not, if the play is not produced. Perhaps Sharon's vision is too idealistic, maybe even too romantic, to be taken seriously now. Perhaps we have gone too far down other roads of privilege, patronage, political appeasement, cultural globalization, a so-called war on terror, and *Free* Trade. When I asked Guy Sprung why he thought this play had not received another major production or why Sharon had to do it herself as the final show at the Garry, he replied with anger: "Woe to the country that doesn't have room for Sharon Pollock. Anywhere else in the world and they'd be on their knees asking how they could help her, but in Canada, she's been ostracized."

III: Making Theatre at the Garry

I first met Sharon Pollock at a small greasy spoon café on a run down street in east end Calgary in the summer of 1995. I had taken a taxi to this spot at her request, but I did not know the city and had no idea where it was, relative to the rest of the town, or what the playwright was doing there. The neighbourhood was Inglewood. Sharon was taking a lunch break to meet with me; two or three doors away was the Garry Theatre. Although I already sensed that this meeting was going to lead to others, I had no clear idea of what lay ahead and so, unfortunately, I paid little attention to the Garry, did not ask to see inside it, or quiz her on why she chose this theatre space on this street at this time in her life. Two years later the Garry Theatre had closed. It was a small venture that only lasted for five years and received little attention during its life, but I believe that it marked an inevitable and significant development in Sharon's life and work and has a lot to tell us about theatre in Canada. In fact, it has a lot to tell us about the other arts in this country, especially the visual arts, because the Garry was created by artists for artists and for the immediate community that gave it a home, and in all these ways it resembled the small, independent art galleries that spring up in our cities in sleazy, low-rent parts of town, to exhibit new works, which are often cutting edge, by the best local artists. These little galleries have nothing in common with the swish, private, commercial galleries on our upscale streets, and their connection with the public, museum galleries—those counterparts to the major regional theatres—is always through the back door. If the right artistic director or curator sees and likes your show, you may be on your way instead of downing your tools to wait on tables or drive a taxi. But the price paid by the dedicated people who run such establishments is exceedingly high. They cannot make a living, not even the minimum wage, and it is fair to say that the Garry Theatre proved all-consuming for Kirk and exhausting for others, and that it nearly killed Sharon Pollock.

Before the Garry opened its doors in September 1992, Sharon had taken the first steps towards creating her kind of artist-run, community theatre with a tiny storefront operation called the Performance Kitchen and with a rousing call-to-arms. This training-centre-cum-theatre that she set up with Kirk—or K.C. Campbell as he called himself—and Barbara Campbell-Brown only lasted for a year, but it whetted her appetite for a form of volunteer, art-centred work that she saw as the heart and soul of genuine theatre. The call-to-arms appeared in the form of an important article, really more of a theatre manifesto, first called "Something in the Wind," which she published in the Alberta Playwrights' Network news-letter *Rave Review* in 1990 and reprinted a year later in *Theatrum* with the title "Dead or Alive? Feeling the Pulse of Canadian Theatre." This little-known essay has a close relation-ship with the Performance Kitchen and Garry experiments because in it she sets forth her reasons for dissatisfaction with the past twenty-five years of theatre development in Canada and identifies the principles upon which a lively, honest theatre must be based. All the main-stream theatres, she insists, have become safe, homogenized, market-driven culture palaces, where the élite go to experience "a diversion from life." Many of the ostensibly non-profit theatres "have abdicated their responsibilities, obligations [and] *raison d'être*" to "cuddle ever closer to corporations and multinationals for financial support and operational models" (42). Ironically, in light of some of her own best work, she chastises her fellow playwrights for becoming incestuous and self-centred because they are churning out "plays about making plays, neurotic dramas about neurotic families, and biographical reconstructions" to the exclusion of "the new, the expansive, and the other-worldly" type of play and those that reflect the multiracial reality of the country (42). Quite simply, in Sharon's view (and many would have agreed with her), theatre in Canada was "in danger of losing its soul." The pact being made by the profession was Faustian; theatre was degenerating into a flashy commodity, "a rose on society's lapel" (43).

To save its soul, the theatre had to return to its roots in community and spirituality, she said, and if such a claim sounded messianic, it was. For Sharon, theatre was more than a way of life; it was akin to a religion, something you were (almost) ready to die for. She concluded her remarks, sent out to her fellow playwrights through the APN newsletter, by urging them to wake up and rededicate themselves to the highest goals of their art, to make theatre that was as important to life as health and education and to write plays that offered "an immer-sion in life" instead of mindless entertainment by responding to the needs of society and community "in this time and place." With such a rededication, "a truly living theatre" would survive; "otherwise," she said, "I'm not so sure" (43).

Even more to the point, she was poised to put not just her own money but also her time and energy where her mouth was. The kind of theatre she envisaged would not rely on

Canada Council grants, Alberta government subsidies, or corporate sponsorships, which was just as well because the 1990s was not a good time for arts funding. The Canada Council experienced budget freezes followed by cuts in the early nineties; the Alberta government was making huge cuts to the Performing Arts Centre and other large arts organizations around the province; and established companies like Theatre Calgary were running large deficits. By 1996, Alberta arts funding was in crisis, and the Herald Arts Alliance (headed by the *Calgary Herald* with Theatre Calgary, Lunchbox Theatre, Alberta Ballet, Alberta Theatre Projects, the Calgary Opera, the Philharmonic Orchestra, and the Banff Centre) formed as a consortium of sorts in an emergency measure to market and assist the Calgary arts community. Looked at from a different perspective and with hindsight, however, the crisis was at the top of the arts chain, where productions and overheads were costly. For its size, Calgary actually had a lively and varied theatre scene by the mid-nineties. In addition to Theatre Calgary and Alberta Theatre Projects, there were smaller theatres like Lunchbox, Loose Moose, LATA (Live Arts Theatre of Alberta), One Yellow Rabbit, Theatre Junction, and the Garry.

ATP did mount some important contemporary plays such as David Henry Hwang's *M Butterfly* in 1993 and Alan Ayckbourn's *Man of the Moment* in 1995, and Alberta's *wunderkind*, Brad Fraser, was making waves at home and abroad with *Unidentified Human Remains and the True Nature of Love* and *Poor Super Man*. Theatre Calgary had by no means sold out to musicals and comedies; they were still prepared to risk *Waiting for Godot* in 1995, a great classic, but hardly a saccharine crowd pleaser. None of this was enough to satisfy Sharon, however, even if she did find some satisfaction in the fact that Fraser (whom she had mentored years earlier at Banff) was having success. In an early newspaper piece about the Garry, she complained to Brian Hutchinson that "an accomplished playwright like Wendy Lill" should not have had to premiere her new play, *All Fall Down*, in ATP's annual PlayRites Festival. Sharon knew Lill's work, had directed *Memories of You* for Theatre New Brunswick, and strongly believed that this new play about allegations of child sexual abuse belonged on a main stage during a regular season instead of receiving what she called "the affirmative-action treatment." The real sticking point for Sharon, and part of the reasoning behind her appeal for a theatre with its finger on the pulse of its own community, was that Canadian theatres were not supporting new or proven Canadian plays and playwrights, especially when they addressed tough subjects of serious concern to contemporary Canadian society. As she told Rena Cohen, "the more contact I have with people from across the world, the less I [feel] that we [have] our own theatres [because] our theatres are isolated from the pulse of the community [and are] just elitist theatre," which should never be our only kind of theatre. "We're in the process of becoming," she continued with reference to the Garry, of finding "another way of making theatre, or another kind of place that theatre can be made" ("The Garry Theatre," 35).

Enter the Performance Kitchen. Enter the Garry. No matter who you were or whether or not you could pay for your ticket, you were welcome. The Performance Kitchen opened in 1991 in what had been a Chinese corner store in the Ramsay area of Calgary. The front section, where the "theatre" was installed, held a tiny black box affair with room for no more than fifty people; the tech facility was set up in a telephone booth, where Kirk would stand with the dimmer board and a six-pack. He lived behind the theatre in two small rooms with a sink and a minimal kitchen, which gave the space its name. The creative team (they did not assume administrative titles) were Sharon, Kirk, and Barbara Campbell-Brown, with help from professional actors such as Grant Linneburg and Jimmy Leyden. They began their clean-up of this space and their first plays with about $4,000, $2,000 of which they raised by staging a forty-eight-hour, non-stop reading fund-raiser. Props and other furnishings were scrounged from the garbage or donated. Call it bare bones theatre or non-profit or shoestring—all the work was volunteer and no one made a penny. At fifty-five, a two-time winner of the Governor General's Award for drama, recipient of honorary degrees and many prizes, Sharon Pollock described herself as "head cook" in this democratic, walk-in, work-shop kitchen, where theatre people could learn to write, act, direct, and just take part. Before it closed in the summer of 1992 in time for the "team" to transfer its operations and philosophy to the Garry, it had staged, among many readings and works-in-progress, at least one masterpiece: *Krapp's Last Tape*, directed by Sharon with Jimmy Leyden as Krapp.

Anyone familiar with Sharon's career knows the privileged position Beckett holds in her universe, so I will venture the speculation that her decision to do this play was carefully weighed. The space was ideal—small, cramped, dark, and unadorned—but choosing this tough classic also meant returning to her theatrical roots and earliest inspiration as a play-wright. Krapp, isolated with his tape-recorder, memories, light bulb, and bananas represents twentieth-century man, and people like Krapp could be found living just next door to the the-atre and a few blocks away in Inglewood. Krapp represented the community, and his story was an immersion in life. There is little written record of the Performance Kitchen, and few memorabilia have survived, but one night of the Beckett run stood out in the memories of those I talked with. Sharon, Kirk, and Jimmy Leyden vividly recall the night when only one person turned up. Shortly before 8:00 P.M., Kirk explained that they would have to cancel that night's performance and they invited the man to return, but he was catching a plane to Vancouver later in the evening and he begged them to go ahead with the performance. He loved Beckett and, as Leyden told me, "Beckett was smiling on us that night." So the show went on, and Leyden performed for his grateful and delighted audience of one.

Inglewood is one of Calgary's oldest neighbourhoods with a lively community spirit; it is bounded by the Bow River to the south, the railway tracks to the north, a freeway to the east and the Elbow River on the west between Inglewood and downtown. It is only about a twenty-minute walk from the Garry Theatre to the Performing Arts Centre. During the Garry years, the area and the street were decidedly seedy and run down, but when Sharon and Kirk attended a "visioning" session and talked with John and Oreal Kerr, who owned property in the area, they were won over by the optimistic plans for making Inglewood safe and liveable. In the early nineties, the community had begun a process of urban renewal. Merchants and landlords, anxious to improve their streets, had invested over half a million dollars on improved street lighting and other amenities, and they were working with police to clear the area of prostitutes and drug-related activities. The building that would become the Garry Theatre had begun life in 1936 as a smart cinema, with a sophisticated sound system, where customers could enjoy the latest Hollywood flicks. By the fifties, however, Inglewood had a bad reputation and the cinema had deteriorated into the Hyland International porn movie house. By 1992, when the Kerrs bought it and Sharon and Kirk took it over, the place was a mess: the stucco walls were covered with painted sheet metal; the washroom was indescribably filthy; the basement was piled high with discarded film cases, reels, and X-rated movies. Kerr charged the mother and son team a low rent on the understanding that they would transform this space into a venue for respectable live theatre. Looking back on this beginning, Sharon can laugh about the washroom, the porn films, and the general mess, but at the time she "swung between despair and euphoria." As she told Rena Cohen, she "realized that it would be a huge undertaking," but she was attracted to the Garry because it could be "a storefront operation that connects with the real world [to make] theatre a part of life as opposed to a space that you go to escape from life" (33).

Earlier in this story I described Sharon as having done every possible theatre job, but the kind of work she put into the Garry stretches the meaning of the term "theatre job." This time even her housekeeping skills came in handy because that bathroom had to be scoured before the theatre could open and then maintained once it was in use. GGs and LLDs notwithstanding, she worked not only as artistic director (without claiming that title), director, and renovator, but also as the charwoman. And she had essential help from Kirk, from dedicated volunteers, and from the landlord. They did most of the renovations themselves. They installed a new ceiling, sanded the floor, expanded the stage, and refurbished the tiny lobby—with no public funding. In short, Sharon was putting into practice the principles she had espoused in her APN *Rave* article. She gathered around her "my own damn theatre group" of local people who wanted to make theatre, including talented young Calgary actors, who could showcase their work in plays they might not otherwise get a chance to do, and playwrights with new scripts who would benefit more from a professional production than from a workshop reading or the festival treatment Wendy Lill's *All Fall Down* had received. Above all, she was running a theatre that was physically and artistically integral to its community. Anyone could attend the shows, and when someone asked about the dress code, Sharon would assure them that they were welcome as long as they wore clothes. If a person could not pay the ten or twelve dollars for a ticket, they could help out with chores or pay up next time. The "Garry team" kept the theatre afloat for five exhilarating years, from 1992 to 1997, because the rent was low, the labour was largely voluntary, and they combined a regular season of six plays with a rental system for visiting arts groups, fashion shows, lectures, and regular Sunday meetings of the Rocky Mountain Bible Church. Kirk handled the rental bookings, managed the actors' fees and contracts, built sets, ran most of the productions, and kept the building open on Sundays; his *quid pro quo* for all this work was to have rent-free living space above the theatre. In time, he and Sharon established a small office up there. The other members of the core team were Tim Culbert, who had met Sharon and Kirk at the Performance Kitchen, Craig Hansen, and Mark Dawson. The set designer, often credited in house programs as "E.E. Roberts," was in fact a Pollock family in-joke: most of the sets were designed by Kirk with the help of the team or volunteers because every-

39. The home of the Garry Theatre in Ingelwood, Calgary, as it appeared before renovation. The venue was a movie house, as the advertisement for *Rose-Marie* indicates.

Photograph courtesy of K.C. Campbell.

one at the Garry had to be able to *multi-task*. "We like to think of ourselves as theatre workers who do various jobs," Sharon told Rita Much.

After renovations, the theatre had an attractive street entrance, a 236-seat auditorium, and a small, shallow stage (see Illus. 39, 40, 41). There were no wings or proper dressing rooms and the storage room, dubbed "the fire hazard room," was crammed with paints, chemicals, and junk. The lighting system, such as it was, was improvised, and in the last two years the roof began to leak; despite the team's best repair efforts, it was not advisable to sit in rows M, N, O, or P. However, audience members could get up in mid-performance to go to the washroom without attracting stares or complaints. On the night that the local biker gang decided to attend, things were a bit less relaxed. The play was Albee's *Zoo Story*, and Rocky, the gang leader, made it very clear that he expected to be entertained—or else! He parked his Harley-Davidson in the lobby and then occupied the front row with his burly friends. Through the performance the gang laughed loudly, sang, and chatted with the actors, but when the play ended, the Garry team and the rest of the audience held their collective breath. There was a delay with the house lights, a long pause, and silence. Then the lights came up and Rocky shouted "Fuckin' eh—CLAP!" and started to clap. Everyone else quickly followed suit. But a leaking roof and a biker gang were not the only challenges at the Garry. During the premiere of *Saucy Jack* in October 1994, the theatre almost blew up. It was a Saturday night and the audience had just taken their seats when a substantial explosion shook the place, sent window glass flying into the street, and brought dust and debris down

40. The Garry Theatre, ca July 1995, with its signature false front and name. Playbills and house programs often reproduced this design. A Garry summer live theatre show is advertised instead of an old-time movie. *Photograph by Tammy Roberts. Courtesy of K.C. Campbell.*

41. K.C. Campbell, General Manager, with Sharon Pollock, Artistic Director (more commonly known as members of the Garry team) in the tiny lobby of the Garry Theatre, ca 1995. *Courtesy of K.C. Campbell.*

onto the stage. Kirk and some others grabbed fire extinguishers and rushed out to discover the adjacent slum apartment building engulfed in smoke. When Kirk rushed in, he found that an elderly tenant had tried to commit suicide by disconnecting a gas line, but while he stumbled around in the dark, smoke, and fumes, back in the theatre the show went on as usual until the firemen showed up and evacuated the place.

On the evening that I met with Sharon, Kirk, Tim Culbert and Alyson Pauley Culbert to discuss the Garry and look through Kirk's box of photographs and programs, Tim and Aly called the Garry years the "glory years." But not everyone would agree. Martin Morrow tried to review the productions regularly so there is an objective record of what worked well and what did not, but the quality of the productions was mixed, not surprisingly given the ad hoc circumstances under which the team worked, and by the end of the second season the Garry's finances were in serious trouble. Of the approximately $3,000 they owed in benefit dues to the Canadian Actors' Equity Association, they had been unable to pay the final $800, and the Association served the Garry with a Defaulting Managing Notice for the sum. It fell to Kirk to take care of such business matters, but he had a cash flow problem. The theatre owed roughly $5,000 in salaries to non-equity actors, and he wanted to pay that off before turning his attention to the Association, but the money, already minimal from box office, was just not there. The consequence of the Actors' Equity action, however, was tantamount to blacklisting, and although the dues were eventually paid, the unfortunate episode is among the things remembered when the Garry Theatre is mentioned. Actors sometimes got no pay at all for their work, and contracts for productions were hit and miss. Equity accused Sharon of exploiting non-equity actors, but she responded angrily by pointing out that Equity was inflexible and made life for a small community, or semi-professional, theatre without government subsidies next to impossible. Her point was that many young non-equity actors gained valuable experience at the Garry, which provided them with the hours of professional training they would need should they choose to join Equity. Another battle line was drawn between Sharon and the theatre establishment, but she stood her ground. When actors auditioned, they were told how the Garry operated, and whether Equity liked it or not, as she told Martin Morrow, "We'll keep on doing what it is we do." What they were doing was producing serious plays from Shakespeare to contemporary classics to new work by Sharon and other writers. She had no illusions about the future or about the judgement of her peers: "If we fail to make this work, there is no one to blame but ourselves. If we succeed, we will know that value-driven theatre has a future." When she made this brave pronouncement to Brian Hutchinson at the beginning of 1993 ("Staging a comeback in Inglewood"), he believed that the odds were in her favour, but in the final analysis the play is the thing, and only the seasons would tell the artistic story.

During its five-year life, the Garry Company consisted of K.C. Campbell, Sharon Pollock, Tim Culbert, Jarvis Hall, Mark Dawson, Jeff Jenkins, Craig Hansen, Alyson Pauley, Christopher Youngren, and "E.E. Roberts." Others came and went. Rick McNair came back to Calgary to direct Sharon's *Death in the Family*; Paul Gélineau, currently the artistic director with Keyano Theatre in Fort McMurray but in the nineties working in Edmonton, directed, wrote for the Garry, and designed the logo art work of the Garry façade that was reproduced on its posters and house programs (see Illus. 40); and many actors, some of whom have built successful careers, worked at the Garry. They put on a number of summer shorts—*The Zoo Story* so enjoyed by the biker gang was one of these—Thursday night readings, and children's plays. Their five regular seasons were demanding: six major stage plays each year, often with sizeable casts; most of these were serious dramas, and many were Canadian. They opened in October 1992 with a fine production of *Billy Bishop Goes to War* that Sharon directed. Martin Morrow gave the play and the Garry debut a warm review that firmly placed

Gray's and Petersen's play in the context of Canadian views of war by drawing comparisons with the McKenna brothers' controversial 1993 CBC documentary *The Valour and the Horror*. He praised Brian Brennan's "nimble-fingered, resourceful" work as the Piano Player and concluded that the production made "a strong debut for the new Garry Theatre company." Brennan recalls the whole experience fondly; he had never actually worked with Sharon before and was impressed with her directing, her preparation, and her careful director's notes in which she never told Grant Linneburg (who played Billy) or himself how to act but encouraged them to think through what they were doing.

The other plays in that first season were T*he Other Side of the Pole*, *The Tomorrow Box*, *Macbeth*, *Jack's Daughters*, and *Death in the Family*. In addition to *Billy Bishop*, Sharon directed *The Other Side of the Pole*, *Macbeth*, and *Jack's Daughters*, four very different plays within a nine-month period during which she was travelling back to Stratford to work with Sprung on *Fair Liberty's Call*, coping with the deaths—especially her father's—mentioned earlier, and creating the Garry. I find it hard to comprehend, let alone capture in words, the extent of this workload or to measure the amount of passion, energy, and sheer determination required to get her through these months. And yet there was always the adrenalin rush of getting a play up. Working like this as playwright, director, artistic director, and actor (in *Death in the Family*), with her son at her side, her granddaughter, Darryl, often in the theatre, surrounded by talented, young theatre people, and observing the Inglewood street folk come and go would have come close to Sharon's idea of heaven. She was beholden to no granting body and had no board of directors to please. For the first time in her professional life she could do what she wanted. It seems to me, however, that the taskmaster she answered to was more demanding, less compromising, and decidedly more relentless than any granting body or board could be. Now she had to satisfy herself, the gods of theatre art, and the community she had *chosen* to serve.

The Other Side of the Pole, which opened on 17 December and ran through the Christmas season until 3 January, was a holiday musical imported from Edmonton (something Calgarians were loathe to do because of the famous rivalry between the cities). Written by Stephen Heatley and Marney Heatley, with music by Edward Connell, the piece was a light-hearted play-within-a-play treatment of Christmas inspired by the Dr. Seuss story *How the Grinch Stole Christmas!*. It had a worthy message: first of all, it celebrated Christmas by setting its story in small town Alberta, where Christmas had been banned for its objection-able commercialism, and it emphasized the true spirit of the season. Morrow gave it a good review, focusing on the all-Calgary cast and the degree to which the Garry drew upon and provided work for the Calgary theatre community. But there were problems; cracks had already begun to appear on the management side of things. Stephen Heatley (currently a theatre professor at the University of British Columbia) first met Sharon in the 1970s in Edmonton and then reconnected with her at a 1982 PACT conference in Banff where, as he recalls, he received his "baptism by Sharon." Star-struck by all the theatre luminaries gathered at Banff, thirty-one-year-old Heatley approached Sharon at a reception to tell her how delighted he was to meet her and that he had all her plays on his shelf. Sharon replied brusquely—"Oh, yeah!"—and dumped her glass of red wine down the front of his white shirt (Sharon recalls a white sweater). He was shocked; she was unapologetic. But they did chat about this little scene the next day, when Sharon explained that she had thought he was being facetious ("smart ass" was her term). This time she did apologize and offer to clean the shirt (or sweater), an offer he gracefully declined, saying he would treasure the stained garment. This remark tempted her to baptize him again, but she resisted and they have remained friends. Doing *The Other Side of the Pole* put some strain on this friendship, however, because the writers could not get a contract from the Garry. This may have been the first of such problems but it was by no means the last. Yet in our 2004 conversation, Heatley praised the Garry effort and attributed the company's demise, in large part, to a Canadian failure to value serious theatre, especially when it is homegrown.

The Tomorrow Box, billed as a "light-hearted comedy," opened on 21 January 1993, making the first three shows at the Garry contemporary and Canadian. It had another all-Calgary cast, but Morrow was reserved in his comments. While he liked what he saw as the gentle feminism and universal appeal of Chislett's play, he was dubious about transferring the action to an Alberta setting and he faulted the acting. Nonetheless, the house program for the play is of note because it indicates the Garry's commitment to community: the substantial list of acknowledgements included local actors, the Garry landlords (John and Oreal Kerr), members of Sharon's family, and many people from Inglewood. Notably missing from the credits were corporate sponsors or governments, and the advertisers were Inglewood small businesses and nearby eateries. The program also announced upcoming events such as an evening of theatre and monologue with Woodland Cree from northern Alberta, a series of kid's plays, and the next plays of the season. *Macbeth* was the Garry's first serious gamble or, as Morrow put it in his largely negative review, this play "is a risk for the low-budget, non-subsidized Garry." Wisely, Sharon opted for a bare-bones design, and she helped create a simple but dramatic poster: that life-sized red hand-print on the black ground is hers (see Illus. 42-A). But why choose Shakespeare and why *Macbeth*? Perhaps simply because any Shakespeare play is a draw; perhaps because it was on the high school curriculum and there is no better way to teach a play than to take students to a live production. Perhaps. But after the comparatively light fare of the first part of the season, *Macbeth* allowed Sharon to announce other purposes and predilections with a splash. After all, *Macbeth* is a classic masterpiece, a large, serious drama, that is also about murder and mystery—favourite Sharon topics—that explores marriage, ambition, violence, war, madness, and death. Following seasons would return to these themes.

In her "Director's Notes" for the house program of *Jack's Daughters*, Sharon provided some clues as to why she liked this piece by contemporary Australian playwright Patricia Cornelius:

> It's been said that family life is a battleground, a source of pain and anguish, while, at the same time, it's acknowledged as the source, perhaps the greatest source, of love and sacrifice. I think we all share complex and contradictory feelings as we grow older and critically contemplate our parents and our past. And when our family life falls short in memory and

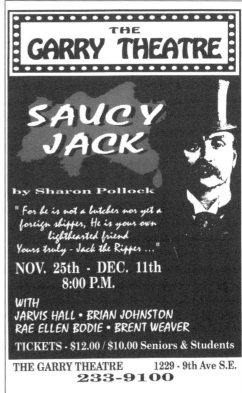

42. Two posters advertising Garry productions:
    a) Sharon directed the March 1993 production of *Macbeth*, and the life-sized imprint of a hand, in red on a black background is Sharon's contribution to the image.
    b) This dramatic poster advertising the premiere of *Saucy Jack* is in red, black, and white.
                                        Both illustrations are courtesy of Tim and Alyson Culbert.

experience, acceptance, compassion, healing and positive movement into a future unrestricted by the past are difficult.

I like "Jack's Daughters" because it deals with three sisters engaged in such a struggle, and I like to think they emerge bloody, but victorious.

Sharon considers *Jack's Daughters* one of the best productions the Garry did. The play reminds me of Beth Henley's *Crimes of the Heart* because it is about three sisters who have been abused by their father, a traumatized hero of the Second World War, and they gather to remember and make sense of their lives after his death. The subject was bound to catch Sharon's attention because of its powerful portrayal of home-front, post-war experience and because it examined this experience in terms of family, notably of father and daughter relationships. The house that this Jack built turns out to be the house in which he has been murdered by one, or all, of his daughters. *Blood Relations, Whiskey Six Cadenza, Doc*, and other plays Sharon was working on, like *Saucy Jack* and *Constance*, or about to produce, like *Death in the Family*, are close affiliates with *Jack's Daughters*, and it was here, with this play, that "E.E. Roberts" made "his" first appearance as a set designer at the Garry. According to the house program, "E.E. Roberts (set designer) is a recent newcomer to Calgary. He's worked with numerous amateur and semi-professional companies in Canadian cities in which he's resided. This is his first venture in Calgary and he's happy to be working with the *Garry Theatre* in Inglewood." Of course, everyone knew that "E.E. Roberts" was a *nom-de-plume* for Kirk. What they did not know was that this name and initials had belonged to Eloise Elizabeth Roberts.

Mr. Roberts also designed the next Garry production—the premiere of Sharon's *Death in the Family*, directed by Rick McNair with Sharon as the central character, an eccentric, alcoholic, middle-aged woman who lives alone on an isolated farm with her retarded brother Gillie. This play, which began as a television script and was finally produced by Nomadic Pictures and shown on BRAVO TV on 4 November 1998, is about the past returning to haunt the present in the shape of a twenty-three-year-old man, who suddenly arrives at the Havard farm to solve the mystery of his birth and to find his real parents.[4] As the story unfolds, we discover that twenty-three years earlier, during World War Two, Renee had an illegitimate son and gave him up for adoption. The child's father, Gino, was an Italian immigrant labourer with whom she fell in love, but when her father caught them together he urged Gillie to beat up the man and drive him away. However, Gillie, who is large, strong, and simple-minded (rather like Lennie in *Of Mice and Men*) kills Gino. When the play opens, Renee herself seems slightly demented after years of grief and loneliness spent tending her demented murderer brother and hiding her personal past. Tragedy seems about to repeat itself on the day that the young son, Warren, shows up and approaches the farm house because Gillie spies him in the driveway and thinks it is Gino come back for Renee—so much does this young man resemble his dark, handsome father. Once again, Gillie attacks the man but this time leaves him lying bloodied in the road while he runs away to hide. When neighbours find the young man they bring him to the farm house, where a host of terrible secrets surface, the key one being that Warren is Renee's son. He, at least, has found what he was looking for—his mother. *Death in the Family* ends with Renee, who has cancer, settling back into what remains of her life and her sad routine of caring for Gillie. The only review I have found is "Lower Depths Unprobed" by Rena Cohen, who says that "Pollock turned in a believable performance as a pathetic, worn alcoholic with a tragic history, and Tim Culbert matched her as the demented, tormented brother," but she found little else of value in the script or the production. The film version, in which Sharon plays Renee opposite Rick McNair as Gillie, was more successful because Sharon and Rick worked well together and because the camera captured the beauty and isolation of the physical landscape that holds this family together.

Death in the Family has not received another staging, but it is included in volume three of *Collected Works*, and it is more than a mere melodrama or a thriller or a lesser version of Shepard's *Buried Child*, which Sharon had directed for LATA in 1985. This play belongs with

Blood Relations, Doc, and *Constance* because of its subject: a family torn apart by their guilty past, a past that returns to exact its price in truth and, possibly, reconciliation. The dramatic conceit of the orphan child grown to adulthood and searching for the truth about his past is as old as theatre, but there are aspects of this script, such as its visceral realism of setting and elemental directness, even simplicity, in character portrayal and language (all clearly present in the film version), that make me think back to Sharon's New Brunswick past, her own mother's story, and the Roberts family. In his final years, Everett Chalmers told Peter that Eloise had had another child, a daughter, born before their marriage, and both Sharon and Peter believed that he had fathered a son, who grew up with many problems, in an extra-marital relationship. Dr. Chalmers' death in April 1993 may have freed Sharon to test her story about illegitimacy, alcoholism, psychological frailty, and tragedy on the stage in the form of this play. At the beginning of this biography I promised not to indulge in those biographer's sins of speculation and prurient wish-fulfilment, so I hesitate to do so now. Nevertheless, the narrative nakedness of this play, its lack of literary polish and artistic trans-formation compared with her best work, suggests to me that Sharon was probing things like sexual guilt, alcoholism, mental illness, and family grief that she still struggled to confront and understand. A psychoanalyst might say—of this play, if not of its author—that the return of the son symbolizes the return of the repressed, except that the same claim might be made about many murder mysteries. Like fairy tales, such stories appeal to our desire for titillation, dark secrets, danger, and excitement, as well as to our need to get things straight.

If the first Garry season closed on a serious and somewhat qualified note, the 1993–94 season opened on an upbeat one with the popular *Come Back to the Five and Dime, Jimmy Dean, Jimmy Dean* by Ed Graczyk. This play about the reunion of a group of Dean fans certainly had its flaws and clichés, but it was also very funny. Christopher Foreman, its director, was working with the Garry for the first time and seems to have enjoyed the experience because it reminded him of community theatre in his hometown of Yellowknife. He was less than amused, however, when Sharon's dog, who had free range of the theatre, pooped on the set on opening night. Foreman also directed *Agnes of God* in January, with Sharon as Dr. Livingstone, but he did not stay with the Garry. As he told Morrow, it gave him "a bit of a turn to come in and see this award-winning Canadian playwright bent over, scrubbing a toilet" ("Five and dime full of problems"). The season continued with *Saucy Jack*, which Sharon directed, *Agnes of God*, Allan Stratton's comedy, *Nurse Jane Goes to Hawaii, Headin' Out*, written and directed by Kirk, with the final play, *Death of a Salesman*, directed by Sharon and designed by "E.E. Roberts," who "after a brief stint in Vancouver looking for work and finding none, returns to the Garry, where audiences may remember his former designs for *Jack's Daughters* and *Death in the Family*" (house program).

The premiere of Sharon's new play, *Saucy Jack*, began on 25 November 1993, and the Garry Theatre was in many ways an ideal venue for it (see Illus. 42-B, 307). In her "Director's Notes," Sharon explained that her approach to the story of Jack the Ripper, while certainly drawing on historical facts, was not to come up with a theory about the murderer's identity. "I'm uncertain," she said, "of what draws me to Jack the Ripper":

> I'm never able to map the process whereby casual interest in an event or individual is transformed into fanatical absorption and ultimately a play. It seems that I do not so much choose the play to be written as it chooses me, and Jack, for whatever reason, has had me by the neck for a number of years. I do know I'm not interested in putting forth a personal theory as to his identity. The play SAUCY JACK is more an extrapolation and variation based on the Ripper theme, and mixing historical characters, probable relationships, possible events, with the magic of theatre to entertain and provoke.

In fact, as she later said in the introduction to the play in *Collected Works*, her Ripper play is more about predation by the upper classes on the lower and by men on women than it is about murder as such, and it returns agency to those lower-class women victimized by the killer.

Sharon was aware of a string of prostitutes slain in Calgary at the time (and of similar serial killings in Edmonton and Vancouver), and she realized that these women remained nameless victims whose fate meant little to mainstream, middle-class Canadian society. Like so many of her plays, this one was not just a thriller or an 1880s documentary-cum-history play; *Saucy Jack* was about Canadian indifference and the murders of vulnerable women in Canada in the 1990s. It is also a strong feminist play. The three male characters, Montague Druitt, James Kenneth Stephen, or Jem, and Prince Albert Victor, or Eddy, are based on actual people, two of whom were suspected of being the killer or of being involved in the Ripper's crimes, but the fourth character is Sharon's fictional creation. She is an actress called Kate, who is hired by Jem to play the parts of some of the murdered women, to enact their stories, name them, and give them voices. Kate is the most interesting character in the play because she develops from a helpless hireling, ordered by the men to perform or remain silent, to the one person who can really see what is going on. As Sharon noted, Kate is "the only vital or potent figure or force in the play"; she has refused to become a victim, and by the end, as the men die or become impotent and insignificant, Kate "lives" (*SJ, CW* II, 312).

Martin Morrow gave the play prominent billing with his preview article, "The Ripper hits Inglewood," and the play was well produced and received. Paul Gélineau, who worked for a time as Sharon's assistant director and as the fight director for *Saucy Jack*, remembers the play as terrific, and judging from the published text I would definitely agree. *Saucy Jack* not only belongs with *Blood Relations* and *Constance* as part of Sharon's famous murders trilogy, but it also conveys a powerful social and feminist statement that harkens back to *Blood Relations* and points forward to *End Dream*. It is a tightly crafted play about memory and truth that explores a woman's, and an artist's, ability to see through the homosocial manipulations and power struggles of men and beyond their delusions to a wiser, fairer, more honest appreciation of what matters most in life.

The next play of the season was the hard-hitting *Agnes of God*, so it was probably wise of Sharon to schedule Stratton's 1980 Harlequin Romance comedy, *Nurse Jane Goes to Hawaii*, as the next item on the Garry season. However, Morrow damned Stratton's play—"that rare thing in Canadian theatre: a crowd-pleasing Canadian comedy"—for "lapsing into sitcom blandness." He also panned *Headin' Out*, written and directed by K.C. Campbell, and advised

Kirk to forget the influence of Pinter and Beckett. The fact that Sharon played the role of Frances, an elderly, deranged, homeless woman who camps in a dump (which may be an underpass, but makes me think of *Getting It Straight*) with a young man, Earl, who has destroyed his life, makes it tempting to imagine some form of existential exploration of mother/son relations in Campbell's play, but I have not seen the script and Morrow's description does not shed much light. Thankfully, the closing play of the season, *Death of a Salesman*, was a welcome sell-out success. Sharon directed it, with some young untried actors in the cast, and the play, despite its sentimentality, presents a disturbing portrait of family disintegration, loyalty, betrayal, and suicide. Morrow called the revival "respectable and often highly effective," and he was heartened by the Garry's (and Sharon's) ability to bring it off. Although the season ended with a solid production of this familiar classic, there was an alarming thread running through the reviews. Over and over again, Morrow noted the hiring of non-equity actors and the low-budget, sometimes amateurish, productions at the Garry. And he had not missed the fact that Sharon was producing her own and her son's plays there. Behind the scenes, problems and financial worries were escalating.

Nevertheless, the Garry's third season opened right on cue in October with Joe Orton's dark comedy *Loot*. Though Sharon directed the play, Morrow was unimpressed. He called the production "static, tedious and as tepid as a neglected cup of tea," and he dismissed the acting of Garry's "informal resident ensemble" as no more than "fair to middling." After *Loot* closed, the record becomes less clear but *The Komagata Maru Incident*, directed by Sharon, was staged that November. In the new year, the season continued without a hitch, and the Garry produced four plays: Dale Wasserman's stage adaptation of *One Flew Over the Cuckoo's Nest*, *The Diary of Anne Frank*, *Saint Joan*, and, finally, a remount of a new play written by Paul Gélineau, Janet Hinton, and Sharon called "Highway #2, the Great Divide" about the rivalry between Edmonton and Calgary.[5] Morrow, who disliked the story of *Cuckoo's Nest*, nevertheless had high praise for the Garry revival, which he described as "one of the best things" the company had done. Stephen Massicotte made his first appearance at the Garry in a bit part, and Sharon, who started out as the director, had to take over the role of the hateful Nurse Ratched when the actor who had been cast for the role could not cope. The show sold out. Morrow gave the next production, *The Diary of Anne Frank*, a mixed review, and he was decidedly admonishing when it came time to review *Saint Joan*. The Garry, he warned, was becoming sloppy (he had already spotted a 1970s school book and a saran-wrapped lettuce in *Anne Frank*), and if it did not pay more attention to production details it would not be taken seriously. What strikes me as a problem is the sheer size of the cast for both *Cuckoo's Nest* and *Saint Joan*. Even if salaries had not been an issue (and they were), the small Garry stage, the need for an experienced stage manager under such circumstances, and the necessity of having expert ensemble acting for these plays must have presented major challenges.

In 1995–96 the Garry opened earlier and the season was divided evenly with three plays before and three after Christmas. Again Sharon included Canadian plays—David French's *Salt-Water Moon* and *Danceland* by Glen Cairns—side-by-side with thrillers and serious imported drama. Patricia Hamilton's *Gaslight*, directed by Sharon, prompted Morrow to make comparisons between the humble Garry and Calgary's Pleiades Mystery Theatre with its superior resources, but he liked the production and praised the design, which had none of the previous year's failings. *Salt-Water Moon* is a fine play and a two-hander (no need for a cast of fifteen), but the Newfoundland accents and understated characters are challenging for inexperienced actors. According to Morrow, however, Jeff Jenkins brought the play off well and preserved its magic. The next show, *Dracula*, drew yawns and groans from Morrow. He complained about the boring plot—it "recalls one of those low-grade monster movies that makes you laugh instead of shudder"—and nearly threw in the towel when the dry-ice fog got out of control. Thankfully, January 1996 started off with an excellent production of *The Killing of Sister George*, and Sharon stole the show in the role of the cigar-smoking, gin-swilling lesbian actress June Buckridge, aka Sister George. Morrow was enthusiastic. He urged people to see the play and praised Sharon for performing the bellicose, yet pathetic, actress, who is being forced out of her job, with "compelling conviction."

With *Danceland*, the Garry took a risk, a calculated one perhaps, given the high praise this play, which is set on the Prairies and was written by a little-known writer, had received in the *Times* after its 1994 London Fringe production, but a risk all the same. Few people had heard of Glen Cairns and his 1990 play had received little attention in Canada. The Garry production was its Western Canada premiere. But this kind of risk with a play, written by a young Canadian using a local setting, was precisely what Sharon had wanted to do at the Garry. The play is set in an historic Saskatchewan dancehall in 1934 after Lily, a local girl and now a nightclub singer, has fled Chicago with her musician husband who has been crippled by a mobster's bullet. From that situation, a raw drama of sex, alcohol, and corruption unfolds in small-town Saskatchewan. The season closed with another dark, sexually charged drama—*Of Mice and Men*—and Morrow called the final play in the Garry's fourth season "accomplished and affecting" with excellent acting. After the successes of *Sister George* and *Danceland*, this was the Garry's third hit in a row and the future looked bright. In her "Director's Notes," Sharon made no reference to the play or the production. Instead she spoke to her audience about the Garry's history and vision. Although "it's been a struggle and many's the time we've teetered on the edge of extinction," she declared that they were forging ahead without grants or subsidies. She thanked everyone, from the Kerrs to the local businesses, the loyal supporters, actors, and volunteers, and she urged her audience members to buy the up-coming fifth season package and to join the "Friends of the Garry." She sounded happy and optimistic, but in the photograph that accompanied this note she looked exhausted.

Ironically, the 1996–97 Garry season would be its last. I say *ironically* because so many things seemed, finally, to have come together: the plays selected were challenging, varied, and, judging from the few reviews I could find, very well done. Moreover, the Garry had finally made good on its debt to Actors' Equity and been removed from the blacklist. The last play of the season was, in fact, an Equity co-production with six of the eight actors being Equity members. Once more they mounted six big plays; starting in September, they again ran three before and three after Christmas, with Sharon directing four and acting in one. They opened with James Goldman's *The Lion in Winter*, a perennial light drama favourite, directed by Sharon who also played Eleanor of Aquitane. But the reviewing of Garry productions appears to have dwindled, or perhaps just been slow to start in 1996 because I can find little newspaper coverage of this production, which also had serious competition from some of Calgary's professional theatres; part one of Tony Kushner's *Angels in America* was on with ATP and One Yellow Rabbit was grabbing attention with Ronnie Burkett's "Tinka's New Dress." The next Garry play, *Equus*, did bring Morrow back to Inglewood, but he was lukewarm about the production, which he described as "intelligent, but not gripping." Although he liked the "stark symbolism" of the design and Darin Gregson's score, he criticized the acting, calling it capable at best and more often than not "amateurish." The *Equus* run ended on 9 November to be followed by the sixties Broadway comedy *Luv*, a silly (albeit popular) piece about failed suicide and hopeless marriage.

The three plays done in 1997 were *Scotland Yard*, *A Moon for the Misbegotten*, and *Fair Liberty's Call*. The first piece continued the Garry tradition of producing mystery plays, and the O'Neill addressed Sharon's interest in troubled family dramas. Sharon had directed *Scotland Yard*, taken a break to let Trevor Rueger direct the O'Neill, and then, for this last play, one of her most important ones, she again took over. This was the Western Canadian premiere for *Fair Liberty's Call*, and it did put the Garry back on the reviewing map. The production was a Shoestring Co-operative one, and Sharon used Equity actors with non-equity actors from the Garry company. As Martin Morrow noted in "Play finally comes to town," this was not only a premiere for Calgary but, in fact, only the second production that the play had ever received. When he asked her about this prodigal daughter treatment by her hometown, she replied: "To be brutally honest," artistic directors tell "me that *Fair Liberty's Call* is an important play, it's great to see you doing this kind of work, but no, I don't think there's room on my stage for it." Then, she quipped, they inquire about more Norm Foster. Of course, not having "room on my stage" had nothing to do with physical dimensions and everything to do with fashion and box office. So, rather like the little red hen, Sharon did it herself. Morrow gave the production a good review, as well as a preview article, and the house program included an excerpt from Guy Sprung's Stratford comments, in which he had stressed the contemporary relevance of the story to Canada, and a list of significant dates. But the program contained not a word from the director/playwright, and no mention was made of summer shorts or the next season. The play opened on 22 April with regular tickets at $12.00 and $10.00 for seniors and students. When it closed on 4 May, the Garry Theatre experiment, at 1229 9th Avenue, S.E., in Inglewood, was over.

I have used the word *over* here, rather than ended or dead or closed or failed because the experiment was complete. The theatre itself did not close for good—Loose Moose took over the space—and it did not come to a dead end, with all that implies, and I do not think it is fair to say that this little community theatre experiment failed. Patently it did not fail, if one's measures for success are some fine productions of serious plays, the training of young actors and designers, and the evidence of local community support. Moreover, the number of Canadian plays produced by the Garry is, in itself, a measure of its success: there were ten out of thirty main season plays. And if I could count and identify all the summer shorts and children's plays and Garry revues, that ratio would be higher. But the problems the Garry faced were many and real. Sharon's insistence on operating without grants and subsidies may have allowed her greater artistic freedom, but it also meant that the company could neither meet its salary costs nor spend enough to polish its productions. And yet, debt and deficit are not strangers at large regional theatres, as everyone in the Canadian theatre world during the nineties knew. Like her big sister, fully professional companies, Sharon's Garry was obliged to offer varied seasons that included a fair number of mystery plays and light comedies, as well as a few familiar chestnuts, in order to put, as the saying goes, bums on seats. Despite those compromises, the money ran out, and so did the patience of local reviewers. At ten and twelve dollars a ticket, the Garry could not turn a profit, not even with *Luv*. Being blacklisted for almost four years did not help; it not only meant that more experienced actors could not work at the Garry but also that no one *should* work there because, according to Actor's Equity, the theatre was exploiting non-equity people. In short, the PR was bad because it was easy to misrepresent, or simply ignore, the objectives of this grassroots, storefront theatre.

I have asked many theatre people what happened at the Garry and why it lasted for just five years, and their responses have differed sharply. Some onlookers described the entire effort as a terrible embarrassment; they were horrified that someone of Sharon's stature would be involved with such a thing. Others felt that her efforts, however noble, were not sufficiently experimental or alternative. Closer to the operation itself, opinions were just as divergent: either the experiment was a disaster or it was the chance of a lifetime; either it was exploitative and personally debilitating or it was exciting and courageous. For example, Tim Culbert and Alyson Pauley, both left Calgary in 1996 and went on to do their own community theatre work in London, Ontario, where they applied the many lessons they had learned from working closely with Sharon. Nevertheless, by the end of *Fair Liberty's Call* in the spring of 1997, everyone actively involved in productions was completely burnt out. The building was in desperate need of renovations, but the Kerrs could not carry out repairs while charging very low rents. The early excitement had worn off; reality had set in, and reality meant an almost derelict building, a chronic shortage of money, exhaustion on everyone's part, new opportunities to study or work that drew members of the team away, and Sharon's personal position. For months, she told me, she had been saying "we can't go on" and "I don't want to go on"; most lunch times she was rushing from the theatre to Jennifer's home to help her grandchildren with lunch; and her health was deteriorating under the stress. Although most people I spoke with were cautious about what they said and did not wish to be quoted, some certainly felt that Kirk had difficulty carrying out the administrative tasks or handling money, although how he juggled all his responsibilities is hard to imagine. He told me himself that he was drinking too much, but like everything about the Garry, drinking must be seen in context. The regular Garry team, the triumvirate of Kirk, Tim Culbert, and Craig Hansen, all liked to drink and all worked hard—no one harder than Kirk. Sharon is categorical about the situation: she could not have replaced Kirk because no one else would have given so much to the Garry. During the five years of its life, the mother and son duo worked together on every theatre job imaginable, including front of house, and on many unimaginable jobs as well. By 1997 "the grand adventure" (as Sharon calls it) was over.

This is Sharon's story, not Kirk's, but the Garry years are inseparable from him and from his role in her life. At times during the running of the Garry, they had colourful rows, but for them this was business as usual and through it all they stuck together—she supportive and loyal; he loyal and *there*. On the evening that Kirk, Sharon, and I gathered at the home of Tim and Aly Culbert to remember the Garry, he was anxious that I treat his mother's story with the utmost respect. I saw between them a camaraderie forged from shared memories and a love of theatre, and when she spotted two copies of a photograph of him amongst his Garry materials, she asked to keep one. In it he is young, happy, and handsome. Later that evening she told me how much Kirk is like his father in appearance, as well as in irritating qualities, and she worried aloud about what Kirk might have missed by not having that father. There are also times, she told me, when Kirk reminds her of *her* father. What she did not speak of was the fact that Kirk was born on May 12th, the day Eloise had died, three years before her grandson's birth. When I asked her for her assessment of the Garry years, Sharon insisted that without Kirk at her side she would not have "embarked on that journey." She told me that he put his own plans on hold to work with her and that the task consumed all his time and energy. While she was comparatively free to come and go, able to travel to Stratford, to give readings, or to work at home on new plays, he was *always there*.

IV: Life after the Garry

When Martin Morrow interviewed Sharon in January 1998, he described her as "feisty again" with the Garry only five months behind her. She reminded him that "in the beginning it was a wonderful way to make theatre," but that by the end "it was sucking everybody dry." "I've never felt that companies should be kept alive past their time," she continued, because "there's nothing wrong with shutting down." She was already deeply engrossed with the script of a new play, *Moving Pictures*, from which she was going to be reading, along with John Murrell, for a fundraiser in aid of the Calgary Women's Emergency Shelter at the end of the month. However, her feistiness and the excitement of a new project were tempered by the fact that before the end of 1997 she had suffered a major heart attack and been told she needed bypass surgery.

Sharon knew that heart problems ran in the family. She must also have known that her life-style was hardly conducive to good health. For many years she had been working non-stop, pushing her considerable energy to the limit, and managing extremely high levels of stress. She drank a fair bit, as so many Canadians did in those years, and paid little attention to how she ate. Public awareness about healthy diets, low in cholesterol, was less common than it is today. By April 1997 she was sixty-one and the preceding seven years had certainly been strenuous. In addition to the Performance Kitchen and the Garry, she had travelled a good deal, not just to Stratford or other places within Canada, but abroad. In 1994 she visited Tokyo to attend a festival of Canadian plays, which included the Half-Moon Theatre production of *Blood Relations*. She took in the other festival productions of Tremblay's

Albertine in Five Times and an avant garde production of Ryga's *The Ecstasy of Rita Joe* that she liked but feared would have caused "poor George to whirl in his grave." She lectured at the Canadian Embassy, where her audience quizzed her about Lizzie's sexual orientation. They wanted to know if Lizzie was gay, and Sharon's answer was frustrating: as the playwright, she told them, she did not care, but as a person she thought that Lizzie was having an affair with the actress and that there was also a sexual attraction between Lizzie and Bridgit. Toyoshi Yoshihara, who was translating this exchange, felt uncomfortable because the audience wanted a clear answer and *his* playwright would not provide one. After the festival, Sharon spent time touring Japan and visiting Kyoto; she had planned carefully for this trip in the hope that she would do things correctly for her gracious host and his wife. And she must have succeeded because *Blood Relations* has been highly appreciated in Japan, and in 1995 she won the Japan Foundation Award for her theatre work. She had not stopped acting, as the Garry record shows, and she was always directing something, not just for the Garry but for other companies too, and in 1992 she directed *Look Back in Anger* for Theatre Calgary. Most important of all, there was never a year when she was not writing, and in addition to *Fair Liberty's Call*, *Death in the Family*, and *Saucy Jack*, she polished off two radio scripts: *Constance* and *The Making of Warriors*. Through it all, as Jimmy Leyden has told me, her home continued to be open to actors and her parties memorable. The pets to be cared for never seemed to be fewer in number or to be low maintenance: Bear's horse did not live in, but the other creatures did; the seagull, the cats, the dogs, and the rats were regular residents, but the pot-bellied pig, which grew too fat to climb the stairs, lived outside with heaters to keep it warm through Calgary winters. This pig created more than one crisis and inspired a Garry children's play called "Fizzy Pop." Leyden remembers Sharon's outrage when he fed it bacon bits: he was turning her pig into a cannibal! And Kathleen Flaherty recalls Sharon coming to Edmonton with the creature in tow and parking it in her apartment. When the pig expired, Sharon was both grieved and incensed because she had to pay to have the carcass removed from her yard.

In the summer of 1997, when she realized something too serious to ignore was happening, she was nevertheless unwilling to *acquiesce*—an important word and an important state of mind for Sharon Pollock in the nineties. She was walking to a drugstore on 12th Avenue near Jennifer's home when she realized she was feeling very ill. But as she told me, the episode was most inconvenient: no one was home at Jennifer's, and it would be difficult to reach the other children in the middle of the working day. She decided to call Melinda and left a message asking to be picked up. Then she told the drugstore clerk to call an ambulance if she fell over while waiting for her daughter to arrive. Melinda arrived, quickly sized up the situation, and drove her mother directly to the hospital. Later, when she wrote to Barbara Campbell-Brown, Sharon transformed this crisis into a comic satire with touches of ironic humour, but there had been nothing funny about the situation. In every play she wrote during the nineties, death was a major character or a theme, and a brush with death was something to make sense of, to use rather than be nervous about. She looked the idea of death in the face with special truculence in *Constance* and with unflinching anger and compassion in *The Making of Warriors*. Moreover, in an important interview with Kathleen Flaherty dating from the mid-nineties (see Appendix 3), she spoke from a perspective of self-assessment and summation that is not in any of her earlier interviews, or, for that matter, in any she has given since that time. While part of her was frantically busy with new projects and with the Garry, it almost seems that another, personally prescient, part of her was beginning to weigh what she had done and what she was going to do with her life. Before I consider the interview, however, let me go back to her radio plays of the nineties: *The Making of Warriors* and *Constance*.

After *The Making of Warriors* received its CBC radio premiere on 20 May 1991, it was rebroadcast twice that fall, on October 20th and 27th. The script was unusual because it involved a collapsing of time and the parallel unfolding of two seemingly separate stories about women "warriors" from the past, and these stories are held together by the voice, mind, and memory of a third woman—a contemporary Canadian who may have witnessed a murder but failed to stop her car to investigate or help. This third woman functions as the active conscience or consciousness that registers events and connects directly with the audience. The two historical stories, separated in time by more than a century, mirror each other thematically insofar as each explores the rights, and thus the responsibilities, of women and the oppression of African and native peoples in North America by whites. Stylistically, the play combined fact and fiction, objective reportage and subjective story-telling, the kind of combination and temporal fluidity that should be easily and effectively accomplished on radio. However, listening to the tape I found the documentary voice too declamatory and the voice of the contemporary woman too didactic. The most moving story is the one about Anna Mae Pictou Aquash (1945–75), the Nova Scotia Mi'kmaq woman who was active in the American Indian Movement (AIM) and at the Wounded Knee standoff between AIM and the FBI in the early seventies. Anna Mae was found murdered, in what looked like an execution-style slaying, by the side of a South Dakota road, and the case has still not been satisfacrorily solved. The parallel story concerns a nineteenth-century American abolitionist and activist for women's rights, Sarah Moore Grimké (1792–1873). Grimké, who was born in South Carolina into a wealthy, slave-owning family, became famous for her refusal to agree with the legal views of the day that American slaves could not, and should not, read or write, and she went on to fight for their rights and for the rights of women during her long life.

The Making of Warriors was inspired by a number of atrocities and political crises of the seventies, such as the assassination of Anna Mae and the brutal murder of Helen Betty Osborne (1952–71), whose white male killers were not charged, let alone tried for their crime, until 1987. Sharon was aware of the sexual violence and racial intolerance around her, but she also believed that white women who had achieved a measure of power, legal status, the franchise, and the right to education had responsibilities. As she had told Cynthia Zimmerman in 1991, through writing *The Making of Warriors*, she wanted "to find a way for women to transcend the injustice without trivializing or diminishing their enormous struggle" (*CTR*, 1991, 38). No longer were women like herself voiceless and powerless; therefore, they could not remain, as the woman observer has been, innocent passersby. This character understands what she saw at the side of the road—the body of Anna Mae—and accepts the challenge to become, like Sarah and Anna Mae, a woman warrior who must try to change the world. When this play was transferred to the stage in 2000, it presented some serious challenges: dramatic point of view, didacticism, and spatial and temporal fluidity all had to be rendered theatrically convincing and visually, rather than aurally, credible. Despite these challenges, the play worked on stage and I examine the productions it has received in the next chapter. In fact, to my eye (and ear), *The Making of Warriors* is *more* powerful as live theatre, not less so, and the issues driving the play and motivating Sharon have, sadly, not disappeared.

Constance was directed and produced by Kathleen Flaherty and aired on CBC's *Arts Tonight* on 15 June 1992 with Sharon in the role of an elderly Constance Kent, or Miss Kaye as the woman calls herself. Sharon knew Flaherty from her time as artistic director at Theatre New Brunswick. By 1992, Flaherty had moved to Edmonton, where she was working as a pro-ducer/director with CBC radio, and when she wanted a good play for her Monday night drama series, she simply picked up the telephone and called Sharon. Flaherty put no limits on what Sharon could do; she was not asking for a murder mystery, just for a good radio script of the sort she knew Sharon could provide. Sharon immediately said yes and soon sent Flaherty a copy of *Constance*, a one-act play about a famous English murderess named Constance Emilie Kent. Constance had been accused of killing her three-year-old half-brother in June of 1860, when she herself was only sixteen. She was acquitted of the crime, but some years later, and under odd circumstances, she confessed to killing the child. Many aspects of this confession were puzzling, contradictory, and never fully investigated, but this time Constance was found guilty and spent twenty years in jail. After her release, she apparently disappeared, but stories and theories abound, and one of these stories is that she moved to Australia, changed her name to Ruth Emilie Kaye, worked as a nurse, founded a nursing home, and lived to be one hundred. True to form, Sharon explored the story of Constance Kent from a fascinating angle because she was not interested in whether or not Constance had murdered her little half-brother. Instead, she wanted to explore the broader context of what might have led a teenager to commit such a crime and to examine the contradictory circumstances surrounding the case. On these issues, Sharon had much to say. As usual, she did the necessary research, but the story she finally created goes far beyond the documented facts. The actual Constance Kent was the second youngest surviving child of Samuel Kent and his first wife, who had borne ten children in fifteen years and become ill and possibly mentally unstable. William, her younger brother, was the last child born to this marriage, and he and Constance became close, especially when their father quickly married the family nursemaid with whom he began a relationship before his wife's death. In her interpretation of these facts, Sharon created a mother/daughter relationship of intense devotion, and a father/daughter relationship of active abuse and dislike.

As the play opens, we hear adults quarrelling violently and two children whispering as Constance tries to calm her frightened brother William. These sounds fade into what we re-alize is a present time, many years later, when an unidentified male voice interrupts the reverie of the hundred-year-old Miss Kaye, who has been hearing these voices of her parents from eighty-four years ago, while in the present she listens to and watches children playing outside her nursing home window. We will never know who this visitor is: Miss Kaye suspects he is Death come to take her at last, but he may simply be a prying writer, looking for a juicy story, or a father confessor, or a lawyer, or even the manifestation of her conscience—a harsh superego figure who embodies the forces of social retribution and condemnation. Whoever he is, he has arrived at her side to accuse her of murdering the child and to wring further confession and repentance from her. Under the pressure of his accusations, Miss Kaye (Constance Kent) tells her tragic story as she knows it and makes her own accusations as the narrative shifts back and forth over time and she relives the events. When the play ends, Miss Kaye stubbornly insists that she has told the truth, as she sees it, that Constance Kent "transcended guilt … not by denying it, but by assuming it" (*C, CW* II, 309), and that she, Constance Kent, has never acquiesced.

On radio, the sound effects of remembered voices, or of voices overheard and overlapping with snatches of children's song, heard now and back then, of shifts in time and place and in dialogue, from Australia in 1944 to England in the 1860s, are dramatically convincing and powerful because they serve to position the listener inside that room with Miss Kaye and her visitor and, more privately still, inside the mind of Constance Kent. Listening to the play, I find it impossible not to be caught up in the haunted memory of this woman, all the more so because Sharon Pollock played Miss Kaye.[6] Flaherty cast Sharon in this role because she needed a strong, older female voice for the central character, and Sharon is formidable as the tough yet tormented Miss Kaye. In fact, Flaherty found directing Sharon unnerving, not because she wanted to control her play or was in any way difficult but because she knew the script so well and brought intense emotion and understanding to the role. The characters Sharon has created for her Constance and Miss Kaye are deeply sympathetic and complex. As a girl, Constance is the abused daughter who has every reason to suspect that her philandering father poisoned his first wife so he could marry the sexually available nurse-maid, who is already pregnant with the child who will be murdered. The scenes in which Miss Kaye remembers Constance visiting her ailing mother's room, and then staying by her bedside as she lies dying, are harrowing. Constance pleads with her beloved mother to stand up to her husband, but Mrs. Kent is too weak in body and mind to do so. Instead, she asks her daughter to save herself and her brother William from the clutches of her violent husband. "The others acquiesce, give in, accept, never question!" she tells Constance. "And I in my isolation and illness can do nothing, nothing. You do not acquiesce, Constance, and I place my faith in you" (*C*, 283). Reluctantly, Constance agrees to her mother's plan to escape with William after she has inherited the money her mother will leave her, but she remains furious with her father and with the intrusive, conniving maid. In her final moments, the mother tries to warn her daughter not to eat the food prepared by the maid and Mr. Kent, but the father orders her out of the room and she is dragged away screaming for her mother. In the present of 1944, as the male visitor repeatedly demands that Miss Kaye confess and repent, the old woman persists in offering her interpretation of what happened: her violent father poisoned her mother and then killed his second wife's child so he could hide his philandering. However, the autocratic male visitor dismisses these theories as lame excuses; he cannot "believe the father capable" of killing his own son, but he has no difficulty believing Constance guilty because she was then and remains "perverse," "deviant," and incapable "of regret, apology or compassion" (302). For him, such intransigence in a woman is more intolerable than the crime of murdering a child.

In *Constance*, Sharon created a companion piece to *Blood Relations*, but she did much more. She pushed behind the documented story, with all its inconsistencies and ambiguities, to establish an intense mother/daughter relationship in which the mother places her faith in her daughter, who then believes she must take some form of revenge on an abusive, adulterous father who has caused her mother's suffering and death. But the form of this revenge may not have been a child's murder. Certainly, in Sharon's hands it becomes an unflinching condemnation of a patriarchal system that uses and discards women and children. The Constance/Miss Kaye that Sharon creates is intelligent and courageous but also loyal and loving. Her tender devotion to her younger brother is unqualified, and she never wavers in her devotion to her mother's memory or in her mistrust and dislike of her father. Because we hear her version of the truth, filtered by her memory, the father is seen as a monster and his wife as his helpless victim. By the end of this story, we have little choice but to believe Constance because she has given us her life-story. The play ends with the old woman telling her male inquisitor to "go to hell," and she interrupts his closing sentence— "I accuse you Constance Kent alias Ruth Emilie Kaye of the murder"—with a final refusal to acquiesce: "(*Her voice strong and clear.*) Not! Guilty!" (309). Constance has had enough punishment for telling the truth as she knows it and for challenging male authority. As children, she and William were often punished by being locked in a dark cellar—the basis for an especially chilling scene in the play—she was robbed of her mother, supplanted in her own home by a hated stepmother and a new family, and then hounded by police and the church into confessing to murder, for which she spent twenty years in jail. Now, after fifty years of an exemplary life, she again faces a male authority figure expecting her to do his bidding. But Sharon's Constance stands her ground, forceful, clear-sighted, and non-acquiescent to the end. This powerful play deserves its place with Sharon's best work, especially beside *Blood Relations*, *Doc*, and *Fair Liberty's Call*, because it so successfully dramatizes the story of an individual woman who refuses to be coerced or destroyed by a corrupt system.

After the successful broadcast of *Constance*, Flaherty asked Sharon to write a new detective series for CBC radio. However, the idea Sharon came up with was not approved by Flaherty's boss, Bill Howell. Sharon's proposal was for a series called "A.J. Jones," and it featured a young, female, would be detective and her talking cat, but when Howell read the pilot script he did not like the idea and did not want this kind of spoofing in a detective story. Sharon stuck to her guns; she wanted the cat. Flaherty could not persuade either her boss or her playwright to change their minds, so "A.J. Jones" was never aired. However, Flaherty worked closely with Sharon once more to create the profile/interview of 1994. Like the detective series, this profile was never broadcast, but it is a remarkable document for many reasons. Kathleen Flaherty conducted the interview portions in Sharon's upstairs office at the Garry Theatre sometime in 1994 after the April production of *Death of a Salesman*. Immediately after Flaherty's introduction to "the Sharon Pollock that I know—an artist of power and substance and a person of passion, generosity and largeness of spirit"—we shift to a series of unidentified women's voices that belong to characters in *Whiskey Six Cadenza* and *Doc*. The most significant lines spoken, at the outset of this dramatic profile are Dolly's from *Whiskey Six Cadenza*—"that's what you wanna do. Leave everything behind, pretend things never happened," which almost seem to be answered by Katie's words from *Doc*: "I used to pray to God but I don't anymore. I write it all down in here." In other words, Flaherty has carefully selected passages from the plays (up to and including *Saucy Jack*) to set up, contextualize, interact with, and respond to Sharon's autobiographical reminiscences. For me, the effect of this innovative structure is twofold. It places Sharon's playwriting at centre stage, defining the woman who is the subject of the program *through* her art and her artistic vision. It also complements the very personal first-person voice of the woman, who tells us about herself in lengthy monologues, first, by providing an objective set of others' voices (the actors interpreting fictional characters) running parallel with the subjective, ruminating voice of the artist and, second, by suggesting that the life itself, like the plays, exists in performance and story. Sharon Pollock is making theatre *and* making up her life by telling stories. There could hardly be a more appropriate way for interviewing this particular playwright.

Although I do not want to review the contents of those monologue sections of the profile, I want to note just how revealing they are; they illustrate Sharon's acute self-awareness, as well as a vulnerability and honesty that typify her. Beginning with her New Brunswick roots and her family, she focuses in on her father and her mother before moving on to her own life and work as if to remind her listeners (Kathleen and us) that *that* is where it all began, *there* and with those people. At the end, she returns to her early childhood, to Eloise, and to her mother's gift of a special pair of "plaid shoelaces" for her saddle shoes, a gift that made her feel self-conscious and embarrassed. As a child, Sharon confesses, she was quiet, introverted, insecure; she felt different (in a negative way) because of what was going on at home, and she was anxious that something like these shoelaces would single her out, mark her as a misfit. Can this be Sharon Pollock? Indeed it can, and is. Inside the confident, seemingly extroverted, successful artist of today, there is still this little girl who is afraid to speak up, afraid to look different, afraid that her home life of pain and confusion will show. Her last monologue ends with this little girl surfacing in the grown woman, albeit surrounded by self-ironic laughter, to tell us that she is "horrified to think what I might be like when I get to be seventy-five but maybe I'll regress. I have a terrible feeling that ... I'll end up looking for plaid shoelaces and feeling outside the game."

Three years later the game was almost up. After Melinda drove Sharon to Calgary's Foothills Provincial Hospital in 1997, she underwent various tests. The family gathered and the news was not good. But she had been lucky. She had survived the attack, and there were medical alternatives that she could consider. Her coronary arteries were blocked and she would eventually require bypass surgery. An interim measure was a procedure called angioplasty, which involves dilating an obstructed artery to relieve a blockage or narrowing of the vessel to facilitate the flow of blood to the heart, and then inserting a stent into the vessel to keep it open. She opted for angioplasty because it would buy her time. On the one hand, she was terrified, as who would not be, at the prospect of quintuple bypass surgery: it might well be successful, but it was also possible that she would die on the operating table or after the surgery. On the other hand, she was impatient with the idea of how much time she would lose over such major surgery when she had so bloody much to do. She did not have time, not in 1997 or in 1998, for major heart surgery and months of convalescence. Fortunately, the angioplasty worked, relieved the strain on her heart, and, with the help of medication, she was off again. In 1998 *Death in the Family* was shown on BRAVO TV and she was elected president of Alberta Playwrights Network, a position she held through 1999, when she became executive director in this organization that she had always supported. As she told Martin Morrow in his January 1998 interview ("TJ to stage new Pollock play"), she was busy writing her new play *Moving Pictures*, which would preview with Mark Lawes's company, Theatre Junction, on 10 March 1999. What she did not tell Morrow was that there were two more new plays waiting in the wings, *End Dream* and *Angel's Trumpet*, and that her 1991 radio play, *The Making of Warriors*, would have its stage premiere, which required some revisions to the script, with Calgary's Crazy Horse Native Theatre in October 2000. And as if all this were not enough, when the chance came to direct Pinter's *Betrayal* for Theatre Junction in 1999, she jumped at it. Pinter, and especially *this* Pinter play, held special significance in her personal life and for her work.

1999 was in many ways a good year. The Theatre Junction premiere of *Moving Pictures* was very successful, and *Betrayal* was well received. Sharon had, in fact, begun a new relationship with a vibrant new company and its young, ambitious artistic director, who recognized the treasure he had in local senior playwrights like Sharon Pollock and John Murrell. Sharon had good reason to be optimistic, and when she won the Henry and Martha Cohen Award for "significant and sustained contribution" to Calgary theatre, her stature at home, in her own city, had finally been recognized. Family life was rich and rewarding as well. Her grandchildren were a constant source of pride and joy. Bear, who had married a few years earlier, had the first of her two boys, little Calem, in 1999, and grandma was prepared to commit some of her time to babysitting. Pre-Christmas parties at Jennifer's home were massive affairs for which the Calgary Pollock women—Sharon, Jennifer, Melinda, Lisa, and Bear—gathered to prepare for hours, each with her allotted tasks. Sharon sliced tomatoes, among other things, and met the guests (often strangers to her) at the front door because the hosts were never quite ready on time. Christmas day had become the time when the extended family gathered, usually at Jennifer's, where food, laughter, constant talk and what would have seemed to outsiders like noise and chaos reigned. On these occasions, Sharon Pollock was just Mum and Grandma, pitching in to work with her family in the kind of happy domestic celebrations that she herself had not experienced as a child. Life was very good, and the future would take care of itself.

CHAPTER 9

Still Making Theatre

Meaning is derived from the act of telling the story. Meaning is not derived from living the story.
—SHARON POLLOCK, INTERVIEW, NOTHOF, 2000, 174

What interests me is the ownership of a life and its transformation into a literary (or dramatic) text. … Perhaps more important for me is the question, where does the truth lie? In the living of our lives, or in the multiple ways and means we have of recording them?"
—SHARON POLLOCK, "PLAYWRIGHT'S NOTES," *Angel's Trumpet*

I: Theatre Junction

1999 marked Sharon's debut with Theatre Junction as a playwright, but she had already directed for the company (*Look Back in Anger* in 1992) and would direct their production of *The Betrayal*. Her friendship with Mark Lawes, its artistic director, went back to 1991, when he returned to Calgary from Toronto with the dream of creating a new theatre company. As its name implies, and as the company explained in its advertising and mission statement, "Theatre Junction aspires to produce theatre of quality, theatre whose lodestone is the text, whose focus is the actor [and] theatre that illuminates humanity to an inquiring and demanding audience." Moreover, the term "Junction" was deliberate because the new company intended "to be a crossroads" for *Calgary* theatre artists, art, and their immediate community. Although they did not limit their choice of play to Canadian works, new and established plays by Canadian playwrights were, and remained, a regular feature of Theatre Junction's programs. Having nationally and internationally recognized playwrights like Sharon Pollock and John Murrell at hand was a gift.

The core group to join Mark Lawes in 1991 included many young actors and directors as well as Calgary veterans like Grant Reddick and Terry Gunvordahl, and during the company's first four years they produced lively repertory seasons, including the first professional production of Judith Thompson's *I Am Yours* and in 1995 her more challenging play *White Biting Dog*. By 1997 the company had grown by 50 percent, had doubled its box office revenue and private donations—a clear sign of community buy-in—and produced the premiere of Murrell's *When They Stop Dancing*. They were mounting their productions in the intimate 200-seat house of the Dr. Betty Mitchell Theatre and beginning to win awards. By the 1999–2000 season, Theatre Junction was a force to be reckoned with, not just in Calgary, but in Alberta and Western Canada. They had created an honorary patrons' council, a community outreach program, and premiered a new Pollock play. By 2000, Mark Lawes had added an office manager to his administrative staff and put together a formal artistic ensemble of actors to present the company's 2000–2001 season. Although Theatre Junction could not be described as Calgary's version of Stephen Joseph's Scarborough community theatre, which has nourished the long career of Alan Ayckbourn, it performed something of this supportive role for Sharon's next major period of writing and production, the four years that saw the workshopping, rehearsing, revising, and the premieres of *Moving Pictures*, *End Dream*, and *Angel's Trumpet*. However, after the 2001 premiere of *Angel's Trumpet*, which suffered from the constraints imposed by the ensemble approach, Sharon distanced herself from Lawes and his company. At the end of 2003, Theatre Junction was evicted from the Betty Mitchell Theatre to make way for renovations to Calgary's Jubilee Auditorium. They had to find a new home, so Lawes raised funds to buy the old Grand Theatre (built in 1912 and the oldest theatre in Western Canada) in downtown Calgary and renovated the building to transform it into a permanent home for his company. Theatre Junction opened its doors at the Grand in January 2006 with a production of Caryl Churchill's *Far Away*.

Even before the end of the Garry Theatre adventure, Sharon had begun working on more than one new script, but when Brian Richmond approached her in 1997 with an idea, she was intrigued. Richmond was fascinated by the life of Canadian-born silent film star and filmmaker Nell Shipman (1892–1970), who became famous for her roles in films with wild animals and was billed as "the girl from God's country." She had tried to become an independent filmmaker at a time when the Hollywood industry was taking control of the business, but like many others she could not make a success of the venture and disappeared from the film scene. Richmond, however, liked her films and had read her autobiography, *The Silent Screen & My Talking Heart*. He wanted to commission a play about Shipman that would have a good role for Lory Wainberg, who was prepared to invest in the play if the right playwright could be found. As far as Richmond was concerned, Sharon was the right play-wright, and when she agreed to take the commission, he and Wainberg flew to Calgary to discuss terms. Soon after, Mark Lawes was brought aboard so that Theatre Junction would premiere the play. Richmond gave Sharon a free hand with the material—no doubt she would not have accepted the commission under any other terms—but, as he told me, what she ultimately wrote was not at all the play he had imagined. Through each of her drafts and a series of consultations, when Sharon, Mark Lawes, and Terry Gunvordahl travelled to Toronto to work with Richmond, Sharon's script evolved into a vehicle for examining a set of issues and questions that interested her but that had relatively little to do with the actual Nell Shipman. True to form, Sharon did extensive research. Like Richmond, she read Shipman's autobiography but, as she told Anne Nothof, she did not find the woman sympathetic or perceptive, and she was not interested in simply retelling Shipman's life-story. But the idea of autobiography and the underlying compulsion to tell one's story resonated, and what captured her imagination was the process by which a person comes to find, or make, meaning in their life by telling stories: "My basic idea was that of an older woman telling her story, at the end of her life saying that it didn't mean anything, and wondering what she lived for" (Nothof, "Interview" 174). Once she had established this premise, Sharon created the three-person character of Nell Shipman with Shipman as an old woman, Nell as her younger filmmaker-self, and Helen as the teenager who dreams of acting in the "flickers." She then placed this multiple character in the context of the silent film era, the emerging Hollywood industry, and the discoveries of Thomas Edison. The play she wrote was *Moving Pictures*, which Richmond sees as Sharon's own life-story, insofar as it portrays an older artist looking back on her life and assessing its meaning while her younger selves press forward to challenge and support the old woman they have, in fact, become.

One of the practical advantages of working with Theatre Junction was its workshop and rehearsal policy for new plays. From the start Lawes tried to allow for longer rehearsals than the usual two- to three-week period common in professional Canadian theatre, and he held a successful workshop on *Moving Pictures* with the cast in December 1998 for a production that opened on 10 March 1999. He also secured a $10,000 Canada Council grant, and tickets sold well throughout the run. To be sure, he had a pretty safe bet on his hands because a new play by Sharon Pollock was an important event. Moreover, *Moving Pictures* was part of an ambitious Theatre Junction season in 1998–99; for the fall, they mounted another Stoppard (*The Real Thing*) followed by Mamet's *The Cryptogram*, with Chekov's *Ivanov* in February, *Moving Pictures* in March, and *The Betrayal* in April-May. As Martin Morrow noted, Theatre Junction was taking on the "big guys." Although neither Sharon nor Richmond was entirely satisfied with the final production—she was not happy with the casting and he found the relationship between the Edison material and Shipman's story less than clear—the play was beautifully produced, well received by reviewers, and it belongs with her finest work, both as a stage play and as a literary text.

Moving Pictures is an autobiographical memory play with a dramatic structure so tightly integrated with the action that the structure is the action. In it Sharon tells the story of an aging artist who is alone, forgotten, and impoverished, and who is prompted to remember and evaluate her life when she receives a letter from her doctor with bad news about her health. This could well have been Sharon's situation in 1997–98 because she had received bad news about her heart, which must have led her to look back and ask herself what she had achieved. But the details that her character in the play remembers and judges belong, by and large, to Nell Shipman not to Sharon Pollock, even though some of the parallels between their lives are striking. Where Sharon veers away from the facts of Shipman's life as recounted in *The Silent Screen & My Talking Heart* is in the context for that life and in the meanings wrung from re-examining it. Nell Shipman's autobiography is notable for its *lack* of critical self-reflection and for its seeming ignorance of the business realities of the film industry. These are the gaps in the book that irked Sharon when she first read it. She felt that Shipman failed to grasp the economic environment of production and distribution monopolies, the star system, and the capitalist investment ideology of the emerging industry because she stubbornly insisted on making films her way and "couldn't understand why it wasn't working" (Nothof, "Interview" 173). Although Nell Shipman became a parka-clad star, famous for her rapport with wild beasts and nature in the Canadian North, her decision to reject the Hollywood system to make wildlife films on her own terms was foolhardy and, finally, a disaster for the animals as well as for herself. Thus, it is not the bare facts of her autobiography but what Sharon does with the story that makes *Moving Pictures* such a fine play. In creating her Shipman, who is a female Krapp, and prodding her to recall her past through the younger figures of her earlier selves (Nell and Helen) Sharon makes Shipman's story come alive in the present. But these younger selves are by no means mere puppets; as soon as they step forward out of the shadows and into the limelight, they assert their own versions of their life and make their own claims about what happened and why. This life-story, like others, is multi-faceted, contradictory, and complex. Its meaning lies in its telling and performance.

The play opens in darkness, then the lights come up to pick out an old woman sitting behind a desk reading a letter. In the shadows behind her are two younger women, and on the periphery two men stand watching. In this dimly lit silence the woman directly behind Shipman leans down to her and whispers: "Play." When Shipman refuses, Nell snaps her fingers, and a silent, black-and-white film (one of Shipman's old movies) flickers across the set while the three women look out together (three-as-one) towards the audience "*as if they are watching a film*" (*MP, CW* III 83). At this point the voice of Thomas Edison breaks the silence "*describing his greatest achievement*": "The Illusion of Continuous Movement through Persistence of Vision" (*MP*, 83). Reminded of her own failure with this new medium by his confident assertion, Shipman insists that "she has nothing to say." She thinks she has come to the end of stories; the doctor's news is bad, she is alone, poor, and finished. But her younger self, Nell, a driving force that still inhabits her memory and imagination, has not given up. Nell is still writing; inside her head she is writing, creating, telling new stories, and she will challenge her aging Shipman-self to rise to the occasion by embracing the ongoing story of her own life. Meanwhile, the youngest woman, Helen Barham (Nell Shipman's original name), is studying a script and paying only intermittent attention to the argument between Nell and Shipman. The mounting tension breaks when Nell loses patience with her cantankerous older self, and her younger self, Helen, steps forward to announce that if Shipman won't play, she and Nell will. And *Moving Pictures* is off and running as the thirteen-year-old Helen begins her first audition in the role of Lady Teazle.

From this point on, Shipman remembers key events in her life-story as it is played out before her by Nell and Helen. She is coaxed into playing along, into singing and dancing with Helen; she finds herself trying to warn Nell about some of her hasty decisions; she suffers with Nell when her mistakes have consequences or when deals fall through. But perhaps most significantly, and certainly most dramatically, she challenges Helen and Nell to face some harsh truths about her (their) life. This excruciating, uncompromising capacity to face up to her failings, while at the same time forgiving herself and moving on lies at the heart of the play. It is what Sharon Pollock could not find in Nell Shipman's autobiography, and it is what produces the meaning in this character's life. Part confession and self-defence, and part fictional recreation, the stories of Shipman's life help her, and us, to understand why she made the choices she made, what price she paid, why she made certain mistakes, what her ambition has cost others, and why she has been driven all her life to be an artist. And Sharon does not pull her punches: her Nell Shipman is ruthless, driven, and ambitious but also honest, courageous, hard-working, and talented. She has neglected her son; abandoned and denied her "Mummy" and "Daddy"; changed husbands when it suited her (Sharon gives her Shipman one husband and one lover, but the actual Shipman had more); burned her bridges with the men who run the movie industry—Ernie Shipman, Sam Goldwyn, and Carl Laemmle; thrown away a lot of her own money on her independent movie-making schemes and on her private animal farm-cum-film set in Idaho (where Shipman built her Lionhead Lodge); and she has worked herself, and those around her, almost to death in her drive to make her own kind of movie her way. Now, with her doctor's letter in hand, she is being called—is calling herself—to account. Where Sharon used a male visitor in *Constance* as the reason for that old woman to recall her past and explain her life, in *Moving Pictures* no such device is required. Shipman is her own accuser, confidante, witness, confessor, and autobiographer.

If all this sounds familiar, it is. The events that Sharon selects for her story of Shipman's life, while they are in or can be inferred from *The Silent Screen & My Talking Heart*, parallel her own life-story and capture many of her personal doubts. She too began as an actress in imported period plays and she also knew something of the touring life; she too took on a husband to escape an uncongenial, dead-end life. When the marriage failed, she left, and when acting in second-rate plays became intolerable, she decided to write her own, better material. Because of her hard work and her drive to succeed she often left her children to fend for themselves, and because of her emotional scars and insecurities she pushed her partner until that relationship came to an end—not violently as happens in *Moving Pictures* when Bert attacks and tries to kill Nell—but painfully, and irrevocably, all the same. Sharon has never run an animal farm, but her home has always been shared with pets, and she sank her own money into the Garry Theatre. Deeply buried within the layers of Sharon's treatment of Shipman's life, lies a complicated relationship with the parents. In her interpretation, Sharon's Nell refuses to visit her elderly father because she is too busy, but, worse still, she has marginalized her mother, the very mother who died so that she could live. This mother, about whom Nell Shipman says very little in her autobiography, becomes a private focus of longing, loss, and guilt in Sharon's play. So powerful is the dead mother, so overwhelming are the emotions associated with her, that the play almost stops when the truth is put into words and Shipman forces Nell, Helen, and herself to listen to the story that only she is prepared to tell—"The real Mummy story" called "How Mummy died for Nell" (102).

To insist that because the story itself is not Sharon's or Eloise's story misses the point and ignores the psychological crisis dramatized by the "Mummy story." Mrs. Barham died so her daughter could live insofar as she caught the flu (in the 1918 epidemic) from nursing her daughter and, superstitiously perhaps, the mother remembered a promise she had made years earlier that she would gladly sacrifice herself if God would spare her new baby. As Sharon's Shipman tells the story, the Mother "went up and lay on her bed ... and in the morning, you woke up. She didn't" (102). So devastating is this revelation, this saying out loud of what has been repressed, that the ebullient Nell is silenced and unable to go on.

Faced with this anguish, Shipman announces—"I win"—although the stage instruction for this statement is "*defeated*," and her assertion is followed by "*silence*" on the part of all three characters. After an electric pause, held just long enough to allow the impact of this moment to register and sink in, the play goes on—as life always does, as Sharon's has, as Shipman's did. Helen helps Nell and Shipman gather their emotional resources (she is the youngest, the least burdened, and the most resilient part of the self), so they can resume their "play," and the story continues to unfold right up to the end, after Bert's attack, after the deaths of the animals and the loss of Lionhead Lodge, and after Nell has escaped into the wintry night to start life all over again. The real Nell Shipman carried on; she published stories and novels; she wrote more screenplays. Most important, she never stopped believing in her chosen art. She never gave up. And this is the note on which Sharon concluded her story about Nell Shipman reliving/telling her life-story: *Never*. In the final moments of the play, all three voices agree that they will never give up or give in, never stop being what they are—an artist—and never acquiesce. Paradoxically, given that the final word is negative, *Moving Pictures* ends in self-knowledge and affirmation. It also ends with its heroine poised to keep right on playing. Before the final blackout, after Shipman's "Never," we once more see the play of black-and-white flicker images and hear the music hall piano playing along as this three-in-one woman begins, once more, to write.

Despite the charisma of Nell and the boisterous optimism of Helen, Shipman is the dramatic lynchpin of this play. It is Shipman's mind and memory that we enter as the lights come up, and it is Shipman's story that constitutes the play. Shipman, in short, is a strong presence; even when she appears to be merely watching her younger selves perform her story, argue with the various men—husband, lover, movie moguls—and re-examine key events in her life, she is never passive. This role is an older actor's dream, one in which she can and must call the shots. When Sharon performed the role of Shipman in the 2004 production, this is precisely how she interpreted the part. Her Shipman was indomitable, acutely aware, and totally engaged at all times. At the premiere of the play, however, the dramatic energy seemed more dispersed or distributed across the three female characters, and Shipman often seemed to be a somewhat milder, faded version of Nell. In large part this presentation of character was the result of casting and directing, and it explains why Sharon was not entirely happy with the production.

Nevertheless, the premiere received praise. Terry Gunvordahl designed a stunning set, which, at Richmond's urging, recreated a film sound stage by using vintage cameras and a black and white colour scheme for costumes and props, and he bathed everything in silvery light to suggest Shipman's remembering of personal and professional history. The visual impact was appropriate and powerful without slipping into nostalgia. Thea Gill was so beautiful and fierce as Nell and Shawna Burnett's Helen was so lively and captivating, that between them, the slim, older Lory Wainberg had little dramatic room to make Shipman's presence felt to the degree that Sharon wanted. Watching the play, I was not troubled by this portrayal of Shipman but Sharon, who was sitting beside me, was unhappy with what *she* observed. It was not until I saw Sharon's Shipman in 2004 that I grasped what she had found lacking and had wanted in the play.

In "Pollock's new play impressive," Martin Morrow described the premiere, and the play itself, as ambitious and powerful. He praised the design, the acting, and the "sophisticated, densely layered" writing. He was quick to point out that the play was not "a flat biography of Shipman" because, in Sharon's hands, the real woman's story became a vehicle for exploring creativity. Sharon's Shipman is, above all, not a victim of the Hollywood system but an artist who stubbornly refuses to compromise and only arrives at a more complete understanding of her mistakes and compulsions by reliving the story. Morrow felt Sharon took her cue for the structure of the play—portraying three stages in the life of one woman—from Michel Tremblay and Edward Albee, and while I see his technical point, *Moving Pictures* is far more celebratory and constructive than either *Albertine* or *Three Tall Women* because Sharon's woman is a highly articulate artist whose insights, hard won and painful, enable her to accept herself and carry on.

When Jan Selman, chair of the Theatre Department at the University of Alberta and a long-time admirer of Sharon's work, decided to remount *Moving Pictures* in the Timms Centre Studio Theatre's 2004–2005 season, she wanted Heather Inglis to direct and they both wanted Sharon to play Shipman. As it turned out, these decisions produced an important event for Edmonton theatre and for Sharon. The production process itself was fascinating; a symposium took place around the production; and Sharon, appearing in a demanding role for the first time after her quintuple bypass surgery, had a first-hand opportunity to test her blueprint for performance. The final product was significantly different from the premiere. This time Shipman was always the controlling, remembering, focusing presence, and it was Shipman who could and would learn from the storytelling. I sat in on rehearsals, listened and watched as Inglis worked with her cast and crew, and then attended three performances. For anyone interested in the making of live theatre, never mind for Sharon Pollock's biographer, this was a rare opportunity (see Illus. 1, 23).

Rehearsals for this 2004 production of *Moving Pictures* began at the end of October with the preview on December 1st and opening night on the 2nd. This gave the director and the student cast and production team from the Theatre Department, a longer than usual rehearsal period, and they needed the time. As the actors told me, it was, at first, intimidating to be working alongside Sharon Pollock—this living icon of Canadian theatre—and they needed time to relax with each other as they explored the complex, demanding script. However, when I entered the rehearsal room for the first time on November 19th, what I saw was three actors—Kelly Spilchak, Candice Woloshyn, and Sharon Pollock—working in front of a large mirror as they practised the song sequence for "Alexander's Ragtime Band." They were struggling to co-ordinate their movements with the song while complementing each other: Helen, young and frisky; Nell, middle-aged but energetic and still flexible; Shipman, old now, ill, stiff and awkward. By this point, which occurs late in the play, Shipman has been persuaded to "plaaay," but the actors knew they still had a lot of work to do. As they worked, what I saw were three people who had established good rapport, who were patient with each other, and who laughed as they tried out this or that posture. Sharon was unpretentious and down to earth, just one of the girls. I could detect no hint that she was pulling rank and no need for her young colleagues to feel intimidated, although as others have told me, Sharon could be, and was, demanding.

When the men joined this rehearsal to work on an early scene between Ernie Shipman and the young Helen Barham, everyone was comfortably off-book, and the sequence went well. Inglis seemed content, but she stopped the actors at the point when the scene shifts to Sam Goldwyn's encounter with Nell. This is one of those crucial transitions that keep this play moving (or kill it if not done just right). There is no scene break and the action must flow seamlessly from Ernie and Helen at one point in time past to Sam and Nell at a later point. This is, after all, a memory play, and Pollock is a master at creating these temporal shifts. Inglis gently reminded them all of this temporal dimension; she suggested some blocking changes to maintain rhythm and pacing, and they tried again ... and again. By the time they called it quits, it seemed to me that this sequence was *there*, secure, in place and working well. During this process, Sharon watched from the side of the room (Shipman does not speak during these exchanges), quietly observing the director at work with her actors. Would Sharon have done this differently, I wondered? Did Inglis feel as if there was an *eminence grise* in the room observing? Each of them seemed to be totally absorbed in the task at hand. At the next break, Sharon mixed easily with the students while they gathered around the director for a few notes. Here was a major, senior artist behaving as part of the team in a rehearsal with students of one of her own finest plays, and what I saw was her desire to work very hard in service of the production. This was Sharon Pollock making theatre.

The next stage in the rehearsal process was to move into the theatre. It was too soon for the tech people to take part, but the set was up with a revolve, a screen, a table and type-writer, a desk and chair, and a gramophone—a period piece with a large cone speaker—and above the revolve there was a much higher platform reached by stairs at both sides of the stage. When work started, Inglis picked up the action from the point when Shipman interrupts her impetuous, younger self, Nell, who has just insulted Sam Goldwyn (110). The scene that follows this sharp exchange is extremely important and Shipman is its driving force. It peaks when Nell and Shipman literally face off over the life-story they are replaying. Nell, some self-doubt seeping in from her older, wiser self, insists: "This is the beginning! ... I am going to make movies that'll make people laugh and cry, and think a little. What the hell is wrong with that story?" But Shipman answers her with just one word, and I watched Sharon deliver it with a devastating mixture of cold calm, finality, and hindsight: "Incomplete." (112). Shipman knows the subtext, both what Nell is repressing from the past and what the future will bring, and the actor playing Shipman must capture all that knowledge in three syllables—*in-com-plete*. At that rehearsal, Sharon paused, looked at Nell, then turned away, and with a necessary stillness that was *not* repose but intense focus and with a lowered voice, said—*incomplete*. The word she had, as the writer, put down on the page had come alive in ominous overtones of threat qualified by undertones of pain.

Everyone seemed satisfied with the result, so the rehearsal moved to a scene where two movie moguls identified only as Man #1 and Man #2, played by Stephen Kent and Mark Jenkins, appeared on the catwalk platform, up stage, centre, and I could see how the distance between levels was going to work to suggest both the masculine backroom control of the movie-making business *and* the movement of Shipman's memory as she recalls that world from which she was excluded. However, there was a problem. Mark, who also plays Ernie, had to get from the platform to downstage centre for a scene with Nell, and he could not cover this distance without rushing. The timing needed work and I was intrigued to see Sharon advise the actor, while Inglis was busy helping Nell and Helen. Although it was impossible to hear exactly what Sharon said, when Mark repeated his scene as Man #2 and shifted into Ernie for his scene with Nell, the timing worked. What had seemed to be dead space between the two men now vibrated with an energy that carried him down the stairs and into his next lines with panache. I already knew that Sharon could write spatially, by which I mean, write for the physical realities of a stage, but at that rehearsal she stepped outside her play and her role to achieve the right, practical solution to a concrete physical problem. By 10:30 P.M., after some final discussion and director's notes, a gruelling day's work was done, and anyone who thinks making theatre is easy is seriously mistaken. On the following morning, Inglis began putting them through their paces, with particular attention to the use of physical space. To a degree this is a matter of blocking, having one actor occupy the right place relative to another. However, Inglis was after something else that could be discovered through space, and when a heightened tension and quality of electric connection flared among the three women, I understood what she wanted. Sharon clearly knew this already for she was listening viscerally, with her entire body, to every word uttered by Nell and Helen (and by herself), and when Inglis got the trio to do this together the drama of confrontation leading to acknowledgement and acceptance (of past grief, losses, mistakes, and joys) that produces the play's cumulative self-awareness became dynamic. When Shipman told Nell that she was "a danger" to herself and others because she believed she could do anything she chose to, all three women registered the significance of the word *danger*.

As an actor, Sharon's voice is strong, her enunciation clear; she listens, engages, and reacts with her entire body, even when her physical movements seem stiff and awkward (as they must be for the elderly Shipman). Watching her rehearse, I saw a carry-over from (and back to) real life because certain facial expressions or mannerisms (like peering intently over the top of her glasses), or certain hand movements, are so basic to the person that they persist on and off stage. But perhaps most surprising was the realization that she could turn on a dime from the actor to the director to the writer, see what was needed, and do it. She has often told me that working on a play frees her to see how and where to improve the script, to make better theatre. A small tweak, a minor cut, some rearranging or redistribution and something almost imperceptible falls into place. In these rehearsals changes were made without histrionics or demands or ego. Which is not to say Sharon was entirely satisfied. The revolve continued to vex her; the screen (behind which the shadow of Nell's son Barry would pass) seemed awkward; the lighting cues wanted more work.

Although the opening night performance took place on 2 December, the gala evening was the 6th, when the performance was followed by a reception with speeches and a Q and A. The 6th was also the first of my three nights in the audience, and I was caught off guard by the final moments of the play. In the original publication, the stage instructions call for

Shipman to look up to the lighting booth and give the order: "Gooo—to black" (133). As the lights start to fade, Nell contradicts her: "Never!" and the lights come back up. Nell and Helen want Shipman to continue playing, to go on living and telling stories (to live by telling stories), but Shipman protests: "Would you give me one moment's peace? I'm an old woman you know. *You're* an old woman!" "Never" is their joint response. And Shipman must agree (after all, they are her): "Alright. You've got me. Never! So—Play!" (133). And the play ends with a minute or so of piano music and the *play* of the flickers over the women, who look out "*as if watching a film*" (133). They are held like that in "*hot pools of light*" before the final blackout. All this closing dialogue and stage business occurs rapidly. However, that night things were suddenly different. Shipman gave no command for the lights to go to black, so the lights did not dim; instead, we moved directly from Nell, Helen, and Shipman agreeing that they will never stop because they "have no choice" but to go on telling stories, to the shared sequence of repeated nevers. Shipman took a notebook from Nell, as Nell and Helen gathered around her, to start writing, telling, scripting a new story, and the play closed with them looking out over the audience while the flickers played across them and, accompanied by the piano music, they prepare to begin again. Only then did the lights fade.

This shift might seem small, but it bothered me, so I asked Sharon if she had cut that "Gooo—to black," and, if so, why? Her reply was swift: yes, she had cut it because it did not work for her as the actor who had to perform the role of Shipman. As Shipman, she found the emotional distance between resignation and renewed hope too great to be made credible in the time available. What the playwright wrote simply did not work for the actor, and the actor won. Also, there was, she felt (as the actor), something slightly "hokey" (her word) about lowering the lights briefly. I was not entirely convinced (so fixed had I become in my sense of the play), but I did not argue. I had been reminded, forcibly, that to make theatre is to make changes, to adapt, to be flexible, and that the play can be well served when the playwright listens to the actor. Over a drink the next night, Sharon insisted that she saw Shipman as a woman who could use even the bad news about her health as the impetus for a story, but she was not certain she could "make that 'read' for the audience in performance." She could, I responded; indeed, she had. This message had been especially clear in the night's performance, which made theatrical reality of the idea that the play we watch is the one this indomitable old woman writes.

Before tackling *Moving Pictures*, Sharon had already begun work on the script that premiered with Theatre Junction in 2000 as *End Dream*, and while she turned her attention to directing this new play, she had yet another project underway, one that had fascinated her for some time: the tragic story of Zelda Fitzgerald. As early as October 1999, she knew that she wanted this play, already called *Angel's Trumpet*, to premiere with Theatre Junction, but *End Dream* was ready first. In its own way, *End Dream* is as powerful a play as *Moving Pictures*, but it is more visual, less reliant on language or dialogue than its predecessor because Sharon allows more of the story to emerge from a wider range of gestures, sound effects, and detailed choreographing of the actors' bodies than she had in any of her earlier plays. This shift in *End Dream* is not new to Sharon's work; it is more a matter of balance, of slightly more emphasis on one set of theatrical strategies instead of another. And in production this stress on the visual was highly effective *for this play*. Indeed, its March production in the Betty Mitchell Theatre was breathtaking, if anything, more impressive *as theatre* than *Moving Pictures*.

End Dream explores the 1924 death of a Scottish nanny whose body was found in the basement of her wealthy white employers' Vancouver home, but whose death was never satisfactorily investigated or explained. Janet Smith was ultimately assumed to have committed suicide, but the circumstances of her death strongly suggested murder, and, in fact, a young Chinese man who worked for the same family was charged with her murder but eventually acquitted. The story of Janet Smith remains a popular chapter in Canada's history of mysterious deaths and unsolved murders, and the subject naturally appealed to Sharon because of its rich possibilities, ambiguities, and social inequities. Both in its historical basis and in her dramatic treatment of the subject, this play belongs with *Blood Relations*, *Saucy Jack*, and *Constance*. By its end we will not know for certain whether Janet killed herself or, if she did not, who murdered her, but Sharon will have complicated the question nicely and raised important moral, social, and psychological questions for good measure. *End Dream*, as its title warns us, is less a history play than a nightmare from which one would like to awake, with or without answers.

One day in 1985 or 1986—or so the story goes—Sharon was browsing in a used bookstore when a bright yellow dust jacket with a deliciously lurid title caught her eye: *Who Killed Janet Smith?* Now Sharon not only adores murder mysteries but must also have something to read with her at all times. She is always on the lookout for likely items. This time, however, she got more than she bargained for. To be sure, the book was marketed as a sensational thriller; the cover showed a pretty young blonde, in profile, with a hand gun, a hypodermic needle, and full cocktail glasses beside her head and behind her face the picture of a handsome young Chinese man, the face of a distinguished judge, and a cluster of smaller male figures wearing hoods that resembled the Klu Klux Klan. Beneath the title, in large black lettering, was a boxed notice that shouted: "THE 1924 VANCOUVER KILLING THAT RE-MAINS CANADA'S MOST INTRIGUING UNSOLVED MURDER." On the back dust jacket there was a black and white photograph of a rather plain young woman, clearly the inspiration for the blonde on the front cover, and several testimonials to the effect that this book is a "true-crime ... thriller," "mysterious," "fascinating," and "sensational." Of course, Sharon bought the book, but as soon as she began to read she realized that she should not have judged this book by its cover. The author of *Who Killed Janet Smith?*, Edward Starkins, had carefully re-searched the death of Janet Smith. He had dug deeply into the background of the Baker fam-ily, who had lived on Osler Street in the wealthy Vancouver neighbourhood of Shaughnessy Heights and had hired the girl and paid her passage from England to British Columbia, and he had investigated the actions and comments of various policemen and studied the sensa-tional newspaper reports. He had uncovered information about Janet Smith's family in Eng-land, explored all possible clues concerning the treatment of the Baker's Chinese houseboy, Wong Foon Sing, and included several fascinating photographs in his book. What Starkins did not do was answer the question posed by his book's title. Instead, at the end of his study, he tantalized the reader with one possible answer after another, offering up for the reader's consideration one *perp* after another, before concluding that "all such theories are speculative and will likely remain so forever" (329).

However, Starkins's book gave Sharon a host of facts about the story of Janet Smith, including revelations that R.P. Baker had been involved in drug smuggling and that high-placed men in provincial and municipal governments were aware of this illicit activity, possibly even implicated, and therefore anxious to protect the Baker family and to hush up gossip and scandal. Starkins also recounted, in detail, the racist attitudes that made it easy for police to throw the blame for the nanny's death on Wong Foon Sing, who was kidnapped by police, brutalized, and slandered before being acquitted of trumped-up charges and secretly shipped back to China. The picture Starkins creates of 1920s Vancouver social life with the heavy drinking and excessive partying of the wealthy set and the rigid class system shot through with ethnic prejudice is compelling and disgusting. Certainly the brave new world of Canada, with its promises of Gold Mountain, equality, and freedom, was a lie. For Sharon, who is always quick to see through the pretensions of those in power and to expose the injustices carried out in the name of law and order, Janet Smith's story was irresistible. As she has explained, *End Dream* is "a story from our past, and the way it relates to today is that those whom we trust, our betters, our politicians, our worthy employers, often betray us" (see Doig, "Digging in the past"). In a sense, she was once more exposing Canadian history, as she had with *Walsh*, *The Komagata Maru Incident*, and *Fair Liberty's Call*, to remind us all about things we might prefer to forget.

Although the play begins at the point just seconds before Janet dies and replays key events leading up to this moment, it is not *about* her murder or even *about* the historical case as such.[1] In *End Dream*, Sharon uses the case to examine the nature of facts or truths and to consider how these are manipulated, not just by those with political, legal, or economic power, but by each of us depending on our personal point of view, our assumptions, and our knowledge. Along the way, this play provides disturbing glimpses into the racist attitudes of white Canadians (and of the working class Brits they employ), and a chilling portrait of family life and marital relations hiding behind the elegant façade of Vancouver's élite. The husband and patriarch, Robert Clarke-Evans is a seductive, but threatening, Bluebeard figure, secretly involved in the drug trade, who dominates everyone around him, including his alcoholic wife, Doris. Janet's arrival in this sinister household is a shock to her because she seems to expect more from Robert than he will give her; Doris immediately suspects her husband of having seduced the young woman, and, to make matters worse, Janet finds she must live side-by-side with a "Chinaman." Her initial racist response to Wong Foon Sing is as virulent as her employers', but by the play's end it is possible that she has come to accept him, to ally herself with him, and possibly to care for him. However, *End Dream* is not a linear, straight-ahead account of events in the Clarke-Evans' home. It is a psychodrama with many expressionistic qualities, presented from Janet Smith's unbalanced perspective in a series of flashbacks just before she dies. Sharon has summarized her play as "a kind of theatrical exploration inside the head" of Janet Smith, who finds herself "in this weird house-hold and who may or may not be having a nervous breakdown" (see Wilton). As she relives, or replays, her story from the day she arrived in this house to the moment when the play begins, what we see is the life of bullying, vague threat, and constant accusation that is tantamount to domestic abuse. Janet is by turns tormented and attacked by the suspicious wife and bullied and exploited by the oily husband, who has so much to hide but to whom she seems sexually attracted. She would like to escape her situation, but she cannot: Robert Clarke-Evans has paid her passage to Canada and she is in his debt. Might this psychological and emotional pressure push Janet to commit suicide? Has the jealous, drunken wife killed the girl? Or has the husband who suspects the nanny has discovered his illicit drug business done her in to shut her up? Or has some drunken party guest—the son of the lieutenant-governor of the province maybe?—tried to rape Janet and killed her in the process? In Sharon's portrayal of the characters, the least likely murder suspect is Wong Foon Sing whose words open and close the play: he tells us he did "*not want this*" (words to be delivered in Cantonese). But the meaning of "this" is left wide open; it could refer to Janet's death, his treatment by his boss, or by the police who mistreat him, or even to his separation from Janet. And yet, in the play's final moments, it seems entirely possible that he has killed her, on Robert Clarke-Evans's orders, or that she has, as Foon Sing will always insist (also on his boss's orders?) killed herself. The play recalls Henry James's masterpiece *The Turn of the Screw* insofar as it establishes a terrifying household and then suggests a number of horrible explanations for what happened but resolves nothing.

Although the dialogue, imagery, and allusions are all powerful, this play is a theatre vehicle that can only come alive in performance, and it carries detailed stage instructions to guide designers. The flashback structure, further complicated by the replaying, with significant differences, of the key scene just prior to Janet's death, reminds me of film, especially Kurosawa's *Roshomon* (1951), with its multiple versions of a murder, or Bergman's *Sarabande* (2003), which is a memory-film that unfolds layers of its story through a series of dance-like exchanges between two people: estranged husband/wife, father/daughter, father/son, and granddaughter/grandfather. *End Dream* is built in a similar way. It too is a memory play that presents what is remembered through a delicately balanced sequence of pairings: Janet/Foon Sing, Janet/Doris, Robert/Doris, Janet/Robert, Robert/Foon Sing, and so on. As audience members (or readers), we must shift our attention constantly from one couple to the next, while noting that someone on the periphery is always watching those who are performing and, sometimes, also, the audience. The sensation of watching and being watched is unsettling and so critical to the play that, however fine its language, it must be *seen* to be understood. While this is true of any play, it is especially so with *End Dream* because the story is about playing with perceptions and interpretations of so-called facts. What's more, Terry Gunvordahl's set and lighting perfectly captured the ominous, nightmare quality of the play's form and subject. Gunvordahl, who has worked with films and had designed other Pollock plays, created a set design for *End Dream* that became a palpable presence, almost another character, and in her published description of the "place" for her play, Sharon retained Gunvordahl's design in virtually every detail.

The set, at once the interior of the Clarke-Evans home and an "infinite space" that leaves room for the imagination, is designed as a series of mirror-effects. The paired dark red, wing-back chairs that occupy centre stage are mirrored in a second, identical set placed upstage; the black and white floor, suggestive of a chess board, is glossy and reflective; the walls, or what serve as walls, are translucent; and around the periphery, defining and pressing in on the central playing area, "are twelve straight-backed chairs ... tightly bound with heavy black cord" and a crate covered in a light-coloured sheet (*ED* 138). The dominant colour, apart from the floor, is red—maroon upholstery and crimson dust covers. At every point in the action someone will be watching and listening to what transpires in the space framed by these trussed chairs. To add to this menacing scene, the sound effects Sharon calls for are explicit throughout as are her requirements for blackouts, spots, and precise gestures and movements by the actors when they are not speaking. With this play, Sharon was working, if not quite with a different palette, then with a new conception of the entire visual dynamics of the play within the particular space of the Betty Mitchell Theatre. Certainly, when I attended performances during the March 2000 run, I was completely absorbed by the total experience—aural, verbal, visual, and spatial—of the production. While the characters are all compelling and I was intrigued by Sharon's use of Cantonese (without translation) for Wong Sien, the interpreter, and at times for Foon Sing, it is the total sensory impact of this play that remains with me. Sharon's directing, her fine cast, and Gunvordahl's inspired vision of the play, made *End Dream* a theatrical *tour de force*.

Reviews of the production were both positive and disappointing. Lisa Wilton was the least qualified in her praise, calling the play "mesmerizing" even though she would have preferred a simpler story; Cybèle Creery, however, was completely put off by the play's ambiguity. Bob Clark described it as "a beautiful piece of writing" and "a rare pleasure" to listen to, but he questioned whether or not *End Dream* was actually good theatre. Although he had picked up on an important allusion in the play (to Hans Christian Andersen's "The Red Shoes"), he concluded that the play was too intellectual. This business of the red shoes, introduced by Doris in the second act as she teases and tempts Janet, is not a minor detail. Andersen's disturbing fairy tale about a young woman who covets a pair of fancy red dancing shoes received a stunning film interpretation in the 1948 British film *The Red Shoes*, starring Moira Shearer as the ballerina who is danced to her death by the supernatural shoes of her art. It is this movie version, with its story about making art within the main film narrative, that should remind audiences about Sharon's all-consuming passion for making theatre, no matter how factual, historical, or political the surface subject may be. Is such an allusion too intellectual? Surely not. Moira Shearer's fate in *The Red Shoes* was a cautionary tale for any little girl of Sharon's generation: if you refuse to be an obedient, subservient wife and insist on being an artist, then you will die. So who, or what, killed Sharon's Janet Smith, or Nettie, or Nursie, as her employers called her? Her own passion killed her; she died because she dared to venture forth, to take risks, to become someone new and different from a working-class girl with a boozy mum. She may not have been an artist, but she wanted more from life than she was offered, and that desire was her undoing. *Angel's Trumpet* would return to this theme of the woman who wants more from life than to play second fiddle to a husband, but in Zelda Fitzgerald Sharon had another artist, as she had in Nell Shipman, and the tragedy she explored in her last play for Theatre Junction was that of a wife who wants to write her own story and a husband who will not allow it.[2]

As Sharon said in her "Playwright's Notes" to the published play, *Angel's Trumpet* is her interpretation of the lives of Scott and Zelda, in which she considers crucial questions about the right of one person to transform another person's life-story into a work of art and the conflicting right of that person to use this story in his or her own "urge for self-expression." As always, she was keenly interested in the problem of truth and where or how it could be found—"in the living of our lives, or in the multiple ways and means we have of recording them?" (*CW* III, 186). Informing these large philosophical issues, however, was a more emotional and human problem because Zelda's story had fascinated Sharon for some time: "in the end the only thing that really interests me," she has said, "is the complex and compelling relationship between two talented and passionate people locked in a struggle born of love, hate and circumstance, and from which it seems neither can emerge victorious" (*AT* 186). In *Angel's Trumpet* Sharon follows the facts about Scott and Zelda, but the play is also a study in how two artists use and destroy each other, in how a husband exploits his power (economic, social, and sexual) to control a wife, and in how the desire for self-expression in one's own voice can, if repressed, appropriated, or denigrated, drive a person mad. In this play, even more than in *Blood Relations*, *Doc*, or *Constance*, Sharon has pared everything down to the barest, most deadly essentials. *Angel's Trumpet* is a dance of death masquerading, at least until its final moments, as a *pas de deux*.

The play has only four characters: Francis Scott Key Fitzgerald, Zelda Sayre Fitzgerald, Dr. Michael Renton, Zelda's psychiatrist, and Miss Laheursa, the stenographer who says only one word—"Zelda"—the word that opens the play, but who is present throughout to record the meeting that comprises the action. As the other characters talk, argue and erupt, she types, and the sound of her work provides, at times, *"an aural counterpoint"* (188) to the dialogue. Although such a role may seem odd in a play, it is an extremely important one because it provides an increasingly unsettling focus for the drama unleashed by the main protagonists. Sooner or later, an audience (or reader) must wonder what will be done with the final report the stenographer is preparing and how such an account could capture what is taking place. I recall someone protesting to me that the role of the stenographer was a waste of a good actor, but I strongly disagree. Miss Laheursa is fundamental to the play; she represents, in a sense, those who witness, who listen, who dare to think it is possible to report truthfully on what happens in life. She might even represent that faculty of the artist that enables him or her to stand apart like God paring his fingernails or, more ominously, like Nathaniel Hawthorne's artist coldly observing the suffering souls of human beings so he can write about them.

The date of the action is 28 May 1933, less than a year after Zelda's release from the Phipps Psychiatric Clinic of Johns Hopkins Medical School in Baltimore, shortly after her novel *Save Me the Waltz* (1932) was published. Nine months later Fitzgerald began serial publication of *Tender Is the Night* in 1934, which coincided with the time Zelda was recommitted to the Phipps. The playing time, approximately seventy-five minutes, equals the time required for the meeting. The setting is the living room of the Fitzgerald home, La Paix, near Towson, Maryland, but the set that Sharon calls for is very simple: two armchairs, one straight-back chair, a small desk with a chair and a machine for recording the meeting, a coffee table, a bar with liquor (*"primarily gin, no mix"*) and glasses, one pouf or small art deco bench, and a sculpture. This sculpture is important, and Sharon is precise about what she wants:

> A minimalist sculpture a portion of which (or the sculpture itself depending on size) lies on the floor as if thrown there. It has a skeletal appearance like a fragment of skull and looks as if it's been exposed to extreme heat. Beneath it is a red slipper. (188)

Zelda will eventually pick up this ominous work of art as well as the red slipper. She will eventually dance wearing the slipper and its mate. That sculpture and those red slippers are potent images of Zelda's life, metaphors of her ambition and indices of her fate. Once again, the warning notes from that cautionary tale about women artists, husbands, red shoes, and death are struck, and it behooves an audience to notice these props.

Sharon's version of Scott and Zelda Fitzgerald's story was inspired by an actual event. On 28 May 1933, Scott Fitzgerald did hold such a meeting and attempted to coerce Zelda's psychiatrist into viewing her case entirely from his perspective. He demanded that he be supported as *the* writer, a genius, and the sole artist who could have complete access to the raw materials of the couple's, and his wife's, life for use in his work. She was to confine herself to the role of wife, mother, and possibly muse, to abandon all attempts at writing and publishing, and to follow every rule governing her activities set forth by Scott and endorsed by the clinic. In short, Fitzgerald demanded absolute control over Zelda, and absolute ownership of her life, actions, and words so that he could mine them as sources for his current novel, *Tender Is the Night*. The biographers Sharon consulted in her research all discuss and quote from the actual transcript of this terrible meeting at La Paix.[3] By selecting this one event for her play, however, Sharon signals her interest, not in the jazz age as such, the novels of Scott or Zelda, or even the full trajectory of the Fitzgeralds' biographies, but in the deadly psychological battle between a controlling husband and a rebellious wife who, beneath all their marital recriminations, are fighting over the ownership of their shared, interconnected life-story. Each is also fighting for survival as an individual and as an artist: Zelda wants to *do something* (as she insists with mounting distress) more than to be a passive, voiceless muse, but Scott jealously guards what he sees as his superior talent, and he (as Sharon depicts him) is unable to accept the possibility that his demands may have caused, or contributed to, her mental collapse. Worse still, as he tells Dr. Renton, Zelda's sanity is a price he is willing to pay, and he expects Renton to agree with him: "Because ... you see, if... if the ultimate price to be paid for my survival, is her sanity ... then that is the price that must be paid" (199).

In the claustrophobic atmosphere of *Angel's Trumpet*, the focus shifts back and forth between Scott and Zelda. They hurl accusations at each other, almost as if they are performing pre-scripted roles. At one point, he seems to have the upper hand, at another she does. Indeed, Sharon's Zelda is not merely a helpless victim, and Scott is more than a ruthless monster; if we are to be moved by her situation, she must be portrayed as a woman with strength, will, and something real to lose, and we must also see that he too has suffered and has much to lose, whether or not we think the actual F. Scott Fitzgerald was an important writer. Renton's role is to witness, comfort where possible, and above all to agree with and endorse Scott's views. From time to time he tries to temper Scott's self-serving interpretation of Zelda's condition and rejects Scott's suspicions that he has assisted Zelda in the writing and publication of *Save Me the Waltz*, both of which Scott had expressly forbidden. But in the final analysis, he becomes complicit in Scott's demand for complete control over Zelda's life. Throughout the play, Scott reminds Renton, in carefully calculated and entirely sober (despite his constant drinking) manoeuvres, that Renton will not receive the promotion he seeks at the clinic if he chooses to side with Zelda. In Sharon's interpretation of this story, the good doctor, a bit like Major James Walsh, capitulates. At the very end of the play, just as the lights go to black, Renton picks up the pen to sign, and thereby legitimize, the transcript of this meeting, which contains Scott's demand: "She will not indulge in artistic endeavors without my express consent" (234).

This ending closes *Angel's Trumpet* on a truly horrifying note because it emphasizes the ability of men, be they artists, husbands, or doctors, to force their will upon others, especially on women whom they see as failing to conform, obey, or do what society expects of them. Of course, we know that the real F. Scott Fitzgerald died of alcoholism and heart failure in Hollywood in 1940, and today few would claim that he was a literary genius. We also know that Zelda was recommitted to the Phipps, that she later recommitted herself to another institution, and that she burned to death in a fire at the Highland Hospital of Nervous Diseases in Asheville, North Carolina, on 11 March 1948. Her charred remains were identified from dental records and from a slipper found under these remains. Sharon does not depict these deaths. She does not need to. Her focus is on the deadly struggle between these two people while they are alive and during the seventy-five minutes running time of the meeting and the play. But while the final gesture shows Renton preparing to sign Scott's document, the closing vision of the play belongs to Zelda, who will see, almost prophesy like Cassandra, the deaths of herself and Scott. In other words, Sharon salvages from the wreckage of Zelda's mind and the destruction of her individuality, a kind of creative power—the power to predict the future and by predicting it to retain some control over their story. Like the ballerina in *The Red Shoes*, she will play out her vision to the end—her own death and her husband's demise—and while it may not qualify as revenge or even as a satisfactory image of female agency, it does underscore Sharon's larger point that a thwarted life will return to haunt and destroy those who thwart it and that a woman must express herself or go mad.

Angel's Trumpet provides Sharon's most chilling exposé of the figure of the artist and of just how far the artist must be prepared to go for his (or her) art. It also explores the terrible cost of creativity and probes, uncompromisingly, the value of art, its utility, its contribution to the world, its ethics, and its *raison d'être*. Sharon does not answer these questions about art and artists, if by answers we expect clear affirmation or condemnation. What she gives us is an experience, a search for answers, a thoughtful consideration, and a double portrait, layered with complexities, of the human need to create. I do think, however, that she comes close to answering the ethical question about who has the right to a life-story when everyone's story is both singular and multiple, when each person's story necessarily includes others' stories. As in *Moving Pictures*, *Saucy Jack*, *Doc*, and *Blood Relations*, in this play she has dramatized her conviction that a life is precious, that we all have the right to a voice of our own, and that by telling stories—creating art—we make meaning. But the terrible question of whether Scott's novel was worth the price of Zelda's sanity haunts this play much as Ev's question in *Doc*—tell me was my utter devotion to my medical practice worth Bob's loneliness and suicide?—lingers in the mind unanswered, unanswerable, long after that play is over. Perhaps the only way to answer such questions is personally, and my answer would be no.

As a portrait of a marriage, *Angel's Trumpet* is excoriating, more distressing even than *Doc*, and at least as shocking as Albee's *Who's Afraid of Virginia Woolf*. It may yet be as close as Sharon will come to recreating her marriage to Ross Pollock or her relationship with Michael Ball, and if it is, the question is: Who in *Angel's Trumpet* plays Sharon? As the female partner she is Zelda, and if she had stayed in her marriage to Pollock, she might well have ended up mad or dead. But as the successful artist who controls the raw materials of life—her own and others' lives—and fashions her stories from these materials ... as *this* artist, she is Scott. She may even, at some level, find herself in the psychiatrist, analyzing and building a career on others' problems, or she may locate herself in that silent stenographer who presumes to capture the action, the story, the meaning of what she observes in a written document. In Martin Morrow's preview/interview article, "Examining the toxic flower," Sharon explained that through *her* characters she was exploring "a crisis of faith" she was experiencing about the value of her own art. Like Scott Fitzgerald, like most artists at some point, she had come to doubt the value of theatre, of art itself. She had already asked this question through Nell Shipman in *Moving Pictures*, but with this play she explored the darkest corners of her own obsession with creativity and self-expression. Whether we begin by stressing the play's focus on two historical people, on the value of an individual life, or the stresses of a marriage, *Angel's Trumpet* always returns us to this fundamental issue of art. The toxic flower that Morrow referred to is called an angel's trumpet, a member of the lily family that Zelda liked to paint. But in Sharon's hands it becomes a metaphor for art—beautiful, self-sufficient, evanescent, seductive, and potentially deadly.

Sharon's interest in Zelda Sayre can be traced back at least to 1981, when she linked Zelda's story to Lizzie Borden's in some comments she made to Audrey Ashley in an *Ottawa Citizen* interview of 23 February. Nancy Milford's 1970 biography *Zelda* was the first book to focus on Zelda's life and work, instead of on F. Scott Fitzgerald's. Sharon knew it and over the years she continued to follow publications about the doomed jazz age couple. As recently as the winter of 2004, when she was performing Shipman in the Edmonton revival of *Moving Pictures*, she could not resist buying another Zelda book. I well remember her enthusiasm as she showed me her latest find—a handsome coffee table book of Zelda's surviving paintings (including images of the poisonous flower). She particularly wanted me to see this book and, I think, agree with her that Zelda had been a talented, if not a great, artist. Leafing through the book together, our conversation turned from Zelda's art to the therapeutic efficacy of painting, and from there to Eloise. Just as Zelda had been encouraged to paint as part of her treatment, so too had Eloise, but this mode of self-expression failed to *save* either woman. In both cases, painting offered too little self-expression too late, and the general problem of how a woman could avoid or surmount the constraints imposed on her life because of gender and social expectations remained unacknowledged and unaddressed. I am sure Sharon saw in Zelda, as she had in Eloise, a fate she had narrowly escaped herself.

By 1999 she was ready to commit herself to finishing this play and eager to premiere it with Theatre Junction. On 14 October 1999, she stated in a letter included with the company's application for a Canada Council grant, that it was her "strong desire" to work on "Angel's Trumpet" with Mark Lawes and his company because she approved of their script creation process; she valued the opportunity to work with the director, actors, and designers well ahead of the eventual production because she believed such a process improved the final play. As it turned out, Theatre Junction received a $12,000 grant from the Council's Canadian Creation Program, with the express purpose of increasing the rehearsal time for *Angel's Trumpet*, and Sharon wanted to direct the premiere herself.

In the weeks leading up to the 28 February to 17 March 2001 run, problems began to surface and tensions increased. Perhaps Sharon was partly responsible for the difficulties with rehearsals, but some of the problems lay with the cast. Mark Lawes had assembled a group of actors who were functioning as an ensemble company for the first time in the 2000–2001 season, which meant that Sharon felt obliged to cast her play from this group. But as the days ticked by, the actor she had chosen for the role of Scott was floundering; he could not memorize his lines and less than two weeks before opening night he was not off book. Sharon was growing increasingly anxious but she was unable to resolve the situation. Other conflicts and complications were brewing behind the scenes; Lawes was out of town, and no one was able to make the necessary, tough decision to fire this actor and find a replacement. Eventually, however, Trevor Leigh was parachuted in to take over the role a week before the play opened. Not surprisingly, the reverberations caused by this late change may have compromised some aspects of the production and the distress the situation caused has stayed in the memories of all involved. Ironically, the very process of development through rehearsal that Sharon wanted, and that Theatre Junction provided, fell short.

Terry Gunvordahl had worked on many of Sharon's plays, but he was unhappy with the result this time; he felt rushed, and the set, featuring a large wall-sized mirror hanging above and tilted out over the playing area, seemed unnecessarily complicated and metaphorically unclear. In retrospect, Lawes attributes some of the problems with the production to the fact that Sharon was directing a premiere of her own new play at a sensitive point in the play's development, but he also told me that the late change in the casting of Scott, painful as it was, made for a better production. Maev Beaty, who reviewers found to be a moving Zelda, was honoured to be chosen by Sharon for this demanding role but felt increasingly intimidated as rehearsals progressed. Working on the play was tough; Sharon seemed uncertain (at least to some of the cast) about what she wanted, and the late casting change meant that Beaty also had to adapt so she could re-establish the essential dynamic with her new stage partner for a relationship that is the dramatic centre of the play. Nevertheless, the show went on. To his credit, Trevor Leigh brought off his Scott and Beaty created a passionate, vulnerable Zelda that earned her a standing ovation on opening night. If she did not win Sharon's praise that night—and she did not—it may have been precisely because her Zelda was too vulnerable, too much the victim which is not Sharon's vision of the character. Indeed, the depiction of a woman—or a man—as a victim has never appealed to her. For someone who has always refused to see herself that way and who has little patience with any trace of self-pity, Beaty's Zelda, however theatrical, may simply have annoyed her. In the green room after the play closed on opening night, a jubilant Beaty faced an angry Pollock who insisted that she toughen up her Zelda, or else.

If *Angel's Trumpet* reveals a great deal about Sharon's investment in being an artist and a woman, and about her trauma as the former wife of a bullying husband or as the watchful, and not always sympathetic, daughter of a mother who was rather like Zelda, it is small wonder that this play, with its professional challenges in casting and design, caused her anxiety, even anger. She had a lot riding on *Angel's Trumpet*. She always strove for the very best in any play she wrote, directed, or acted in; she always sought perfection. But this play, for all she knew, might be her last. Just ahead loomed her heart surgery, and for *Angel's Trumpet* she had dug deeply into the sources of her own life and work. Was she wrong to become angry and demanding? Was she wrong to direct this play herself? To the first question I would reply, no, or at least that it scarcely matters. To the second, the answer is more complex and only a new production of the play under someone else's direction will help to clarify that issue. The questions underlying her interest in the lives of Scott and Zelda Fitzgerald and informing her version of the story troubled this production from the start: Can one artist claim ownership of a life and control its transformation into art? Can one individual's self-expression be justifiably sacrificed to the needs of another? When there are competing claims, whose claim to the story takes precedence? Where can any of us draw the line between control and freedom, silencing and expression, life and art? And when these opposites conflict, can anyone emerge victorious?

II: Being Away and Coming Back

Since *Angel's Trumpet*, Sharon has not worked again with Theatre Junction. But the three plays she premiered with them are major pieces, and despite problems they all got good productions. Critics and other theatre people have often wondered what became of Sharon Pollock after the sensational productions of *Doc* in the 1980s. They have sometimes lamented the years she gave to the Garry and wondered why a two-time winner of the Governor General's Award for Drama who had been produced at Stratford, the National Arts Centre, and in major houses across the country, would end up working with a new, small company like Theatre Junction. The implication of such reflections is either that she has lost her cachet because her kind of play (as if it could be easily categorized) is out of date, or that the world of Canadian theatre has a short memory. The theatre world is indeed fickle; people move on to other places, and artistic directors champion (and receive funding for producing) young writers and new scripts. Nevertheless, I have been surprised by the general unfamiliarity I have encountered with Sharon's work after *Doc*. Working with the Garry and then with Theatre Junction seems to have done little to enhance her reputation. And yet *Moving Pictures, End Dream*, and *Angel's Trumpet* confirm her stature as Canada's leading senior English-language playwright. These plays display an exciting range of characters with splendid, challenging roles for actors; they explore serious, timeless human issues and pose fundamental questions about existence. Moreover, they are beautifully crafted: the prose, dialogue, and dramatic structure of these plays are confident, polished, and rewarding to listen to, watch, read, and perform. When I wrote the introduction to *Sharon Pollock: Three Plays* fresh from seeing their premieres and working closely with the scripts, I described them as evidence that Sharon Pollock belonged with the best contemporary English-language playwrights in the world. Time, distance, and measured reflection have only strengthened my early opinion. But now I see something more in these three plays. As a trilogy, they now strike me as containing a set of final statements about issues that had concerned Sharon all her life; they also fuse aspects of history play, memory play, domestic or family play, political theatre, and personal, autobiographical play; they trust more to showing than to telling, employ a wide range of theatrical styles, and do more with less. In their very economy of form, Sharon has distilled her art, reduced it to its essentials. The challenge she faced with the surgery would be a test of another kind, and if she failed that test, she knew that with these plays she had nailed her colours to the mast where, in due course, we would see them.

But there was more. Indeed, there is always more in any story about Sharon Pollock, and in the year 2000 she had one more play, this one rescued from the archives of the CBC, to see safely on to the stage before her surgery: *The Making of Warriors*. There is nothing especially *auto*biographical about this play, but when I finally saw a production in a tiny hole-in-the-wall space in Edmonton in February 2003, it was the handling of voice, the name of the central witnessing character—now called *Eloise*—and the play's insistence on personal perspective that both fascinated and troubled me. To appreciate this play, as I saw it, I found it necessary to go back twelve years to the radio version the CBC commissioned in 1991 to coincide with the International Women's Playwrights' Festival. For the radio play, which I discussed in the last chapter, it was possible to imagine the stories of Sarah Moore Grimké and Anna Mae Pictou Aquash overlapping and connecting to suggest a commonality of experience over time. However, problems inherent in the structure and subject matter of *The Making of Warriors* were real, and Sharon was aware of them. From the start she was anxious not to appropriate the First Nations voice and she strove to find ways around flattening the real differences between Sarah and Anna Mae. Her primary goals were to remind today's audiences about injustice, about our continuing responsibility to take action against it, and about the stories of two women whose lives she found exemplary. To avoid appropriation in the radio script, most importantly for Anna Mae's story, she had introduced the third, contemporary woman (called simply Woman One), who could witness and comment upon events, and created three distinct modes of narration for her women who, at times, also speak together as a chorus. Woman One, a fifty-four year-old white woman (Sharon's age when writing the play) was the only character to speak directly to us as herself; she was also the person who, unlike a Good Samaritan, drove by the Pine Ridge Reserve in South Dakota one afternoon and did not stop when she saw a group of men at the side of the road gathered around what may have been a body. Woman Two, however, was not Anna Mae. Sharon created an objective, reporter-style role to suggest a neutral telling of Anna Mae's story. Only Woman Three, who had a warmer, more intimate manner and who introduced us to Sarah, actually took charge of the dramatization of what amounted to a story within the story or a play within the play—the story of Sarah Moore Grimké. This inner play had five characters, all identified by name: Sarah, her brother Thomas, her father, the Judge, her younger sister Angelina, and Angelina's husband, Mr. Weld.

As Sharon explained, for the radio script she wanted to "have voices that [were] speaking directly to the listener, some of it seeming like objective news, and some of it seeming like very subjective experience and some of dramatization," and she hoped she "could tell Anna Mae's story without assuming the voice of the other, by making it objective and making evident my white perspective as much as possible" (Jansen, *Airborne* 101). To my ears, however, the radio play was flawed. Sarah Grimké's enacted story came alive but Anna Mae's more urgent tragedy was lost in the objective reporting of her case. Sharon's desire to make us hear and attend to the stories of these three women, to urge us to action, was weakened by her choice of voices and by the inconsistency in perspectives: subjective/objective/dramatized. When the radio play was published by Ann Jansen, Sharon noted that she wanted to expand her script into a two-act play. In the event, she did rewrite it for the stage but not by adding a second act. The changes she made were in one sense more limited but in another more creative, and they transformed the play into a complex and moving blueprint for performance in the live theatre.

When Crazy Horse Theatre in Calgary decided to mount *The Making of Warriors* as a stage play, the script Sharon gave them had no stage instructions. As Michelle Thrush, who played Anna Mae, put it, the actors had to work from the ground up to create everything. The stage instructions that now appear on the script and with the play as published in *Collected Works* evolved out of this October 2000 premiere. First, she gave her contemporary middle-aged white woman who drives by the Pine Ridge murder scene a name: Eloise. Together, Annie (this slight shift in name recalls that Anna Mae once said that Annie was her more personal, intimate name), Sarah, and Eloise orchestrate the opening and closing frame of the play, and in the process they give priority to the story of Anna Mae Pictou Aquash. The three women address the audience directly, urging us to remember lost stories and lost women and, finally, exhorting us to bring meaning and courage to our lives through storytelling. Gone is Sarah Grimké's extended family, now represented as "the Others" who will deliver the lines of a number of different participants in the stories. These Others may be played by two or more actors, by men or women, and they occasionally contribute lines, or fragments of lines, to the choral frame of the play. At one and the same time, Sharon found ways of reducing the enacted power of Sarah's story and of enhancing a more general, symbolic sense of the ghostly voices haunting the stage, our memories and imaginations, and our forgotten or silenced history. The result is a more engaging recreation of memory that puts

Anna Mae's life and death at the centre of the remembering process, and the effect, theatrically, is one of celebration as well as of mourning.

However, one especially difficult issue remained. Although Sharon had abandoned the objective, reporting third-person speaker who told us about Anna Mae in the radio play in favour of a flesh and blood actor who would be called Annie and certainly *represent* Anna Mae, she insisted on having this actor speak about herself in the third person. For Thrush, who had to create the role on stage, this decision caused considerable frustration. Thrush is Cree and, therefore, did not feel she would be appropriating the voice of a woman who had become an iconic First Nations figure in Canada and the United States. She felt ready and able to speak *as* Annie, and she believed her work as an actor would be better if she could do so. When Sharon came to rehearsals, Thrush pressed her about this odd voice, but Sharon would not budge. Her reasons were clear: she, Sharon Pollock, simply could not write the voice of this native woman, and she would not try to speak *for* the First Nations. Thrush had little choice but to accept the playwright's ethical position, and she told me that she finally managed to channel her frustration with the voice into the interpretation of the role until she was able to perform Annie as *if* from the inside.

The Crazy Horse production ran for ten nights, with an all-native cast and a white director (Coral Larson Thew) to largely white, middle-class audiences in Calgary's Pumphouse Theatre. Given the audience demographics, it was perhaps wise to maintain a third-person voice for Anna Mae because her story is both horrifying and deeply moving, and if mishandled could become the vehicle for accusations and race-based antagonism that would turn the play into a tract and obscure Sharon's central point, which is that we must all work together to resist injustice and violence and to stand up for human rights. In its second stage production, directed by Heather Inglis with Edmonton's Absolutely YES Cooperative, many of the challenges faced by Thrush and her colleagues remained, but there was now a design concept to build on, further revisions to the script by Sharon, and a very different venue to play in for a very different audience. In its 2003 Edmonton revival, the space was a narrow, tiny (not just intimate) refitted garage, and on the night I attended at least half the audience was of First Nations or mixed-race background. Of the thirty people there that night, easily two-thirds were women, and many of them already knew Anna Mae's story. For me, this *Making of Warriors* was memorable. The acting was very fine, the direction sensitive and clear, and the design (if somewhat overproduced for the space) effective, but it was, above all, the audience members that lifted the play beyond good theatre into a moving communal experience.

When I asked Heather Inglis why she wanted to do a new stage production of *The Making of Warriors*, a Pollock play that few had ever heard of and a difficult piece to perform as live theatre, she replied by stressing her personal commitment to serious Canadian plays and her desire, as a director, to respond to the political and human crises of our time. She saw *Warriors* as addressing such crises by linking atrocities and injustices that were distant in time and place with the present lives of contemporary Canadians who lead comparatively safe, comfortable lives and pay little attention to these injustices. For Sharon such injustices and atrocities included crimes such as the murder of Helen Betty Osborne, ethnic cleansing in Kosovo, and the torture of Shidane Arone in Somalia; in 2003, for Heather Inglis, the troubling events were the invasion of Iraq, the so-called war on terror, and the aggression perpetrated in the name of democracy. Directing *Warriors* allowed Inglis to test herself on a smaller Pollock play with a strong ethical vision before tackling *Moving Pictures*. Inglis is also an admirer of Sharon's kind of theatre; she is, unlike John Wood, Guy Sprung, or Rick McNair, at the beginning of her career, but like them what she wants to create in the theatre has as much to do with important social issues as with entertainment. That said, *Warriors* was a challenge. Because she found the play to be more narrative than most stage plays, Inglis wanted to *stage* it in an unconventional way, preferably in an unusual space. Her initial concept was to create a gravel playing area that would suggest a road, the road that Eloise had driven along in 1976 when she failed to stop; the characters would meet on it and the audience members would sit separately in chairs placed on the road's metaphorical shoulders. In the end, she could not realize this design, but she devised other ways of high-lighting the central conceit of a road. She also wanted to blur the good/bad distinctions between women and men and to expand the ethnicity of the characters through her casting. In short, she wanted to make her production true to Sharon's script and as inclusive and non-judgmental as possible.

Sharon drove to Edmonton for several hours of rehearsals; she was highly supportive of the actors, who were struggling to find their way, but she also expected carefully thought-through reasons for every decision. Yes, Inglis admitted: working with this icon of Canadian theatre was tough because Sharon knew what she wanted, what would work (and would not), and her approach to the process was analytical and cerebral, whereas Inglis works more intuitively. And yet, Sharon enjoyed the work and saw herself as a collaborator and participant with the director, cast, and crew. Because the script still lacked detailed stage instructions for the actors, the role of Eloise presented the team with many questions, but this role was key to the play and Inglis came to appreciate its importance as the play's chief link to an audience: Eloise must relate and react to—that is, she must register and learn from—both Sarah's and Annie's stories. Indeed, as Sharon explained, Sarah's story helps Eloise under-stand Anna Mae and see that she could have done more than merely pass by. As *The Making of Warriors* developed from radio script to full stage play, the character of Eloise became more integral to the larger purpose of the storytelling—to help us learn and take action.

On the night I attended the play, Alison Wells in the part of Eloise, who describes herself as "nobody in particular [but] maybe you" (*MW*, *CW* III, 233), was excellent. She held my attention throughout, guiding my perspective and reactions while she shifted from being a passive observer, staring at the news on the television, to an engaged person who bears witness to the stories she (and we) hear and is changed by them. Interestingly, the role of Annie, played by Julie Golosky, was not a problem for me because she managed the third person voice Sharon insisted on so well that she almost seemed to be speaking as the ghost of Anna Mae from beyond the grave, and this eerie quality added a disturbing edge to her performance. When the play ended, with Eloise exclaiming that Anna Mae Pictou Aquash "Lives!" followed by the chorus of voices (the Others, Annie, Sarah, and Eloise), who faced each other before turning towards us to urge us to remember, the house (if I can call the garage-space that) sat in silence. Behind me I heard muffled weeping. Finally, a few people began to clap tentatively, and this applause grew warmer as each actor was acknowledged. Nevertheless, the sense that something unusual had transpired lingered. There was a break of several minutes, with no place for cast or audience to disperse to, before anyone was prepared to ask a question. Then I was astonished to hear a self-identified First Nations woman speak about the importance of Anna Mae's story, and then a man, of mixed race, contributed his views about the importance of the play, and so it continued. This was not a conventional Q and A but a testimonial by participants who needed to affirm what they had seen and establish their connection with the play. Unfortunately, Sharon was not present that night because, when I finally gathered myself together to pose a question, I wanted to know what Julie Golosky thought about using the third-person voice for Annie. Her answer was that initially this had been a real challenge but that eventually she had found her way (as had Michelle Thrush) inside the role; she understood why Sharon had made this decision, and then she worked from there. But I think what surprised everyone at the play that night was an interjection from the audience member who had wept: she wanted to thank the white woman who had created this play because too much worry about appropriation could lead to silence and silence would not help anyone. Others in the audience applauded this state-ment.

When all is said and done, making theatre is never a one-shot process. Live theatre is what *lives* and what can bring a constantly changing play to a wide range of audiences. I was not taken with the radio play, and I doubt that *The Making of Warriors* would suit today's Arts Club audiences in Vancouver or Theatre New Brunswick or Neptune audiences because I suspect they would find the play too serious, too didactic, too *in your face*. After all, *The Komagata Maru Incident* has always evoked this kind of criticism. I suspect this would be the reaction, but I may be wrong and, in any case, I am not likely to see another production of this Pollock play. But on a cold February night in 2003, in a converted garage in downtown Edmonton, a small group of people gathered to experience what live theatre can do. The Absolutely YES Cooperative brought Anna Mae Pictou Aquash and Sarah Grimké and this woman called Eloise to life. Further south, in Calgary, the white middle-class playwright was busy getting her injections against malaria, typhoid, and other diseases, in preparation for a new adventure and a totally new challenge. She was about to leave for Sierra Leone to see what making theatre in a third world country might do. Her warriors in Edmonton were almost on their own, *almost* because Sharon was there through her persona, the woman (voice, figure, role, E-me) her alter ego, the mother-figure who does not die or give up or fail, but who speaks out finally as Eloise.

***

Once she had seen the first production of *The Making of Warriors* onto the stage with Crazy Horse Theatre in 2000 and had finished directing *Angel's Trumpet* in 2001, Sharon could no longer ignore her heart. When she visited Vancouver to speak at the Vancouver Institute in March 2000 and to meet with graduate students, she was clearly not well. I met her plane expecting to see her familiar, feisty, energetic figure stride into the arrivals area, but instead she smiled briefly and had to sit down because she felt faint and could not get her breath. I was alarmed but had no clear sense of how serious the situation was or that the medications she had been on since the angioplasty were no longer doing the job. And Sharon was not about to give me chapter and verse. When I think back over her three-day visit that spring, her public and social appearances, and her unfailing generosity with my students, it is a shock to reflect on how differently things might have turned out. She said little, kept going (from 5:30 A.M.), and asked for no special consideration. On the 30th of May, two months after *Angel's Trumpet* closed, she entered Calgary's Foothills hospital again, this time for quintuple bypass surgery. She has refrained from descriptions of how she felt going into surgery, and she has said little about the long process of recuperation, but doctors described the risks and challenges involved, which the family was warned about. Had things gone badly on the operating table or in the recovery room, she had made her wishes clear: like father, like daughter—her instructions were that nothing extraordinary should be done to keep her alive. This was not quite as peremptory as her father's "Do not resuscitate," but the message was much the same. Recovery from such surgery takes many weeks, several return trips to see the doctors, and a carefully calibrated arsenal of drugs. Recovery, with continued good health, also requires certain lifestyle changes in food, alcohol, and stress. For a person like Sharon these changes would present a problem because she thrives, artistically and psychologically, on stress and she finds French fries and beer hard to resist.

After her discharge, she moved in with Jennifer where she could rest and always have a family member at hand. However, on one famous occasion, early in July, everyone was out, and Sharon was resting happily on a sofa. The crisis came when she had to get up from a recumbent position to visit the bathroom; she found that rising from such a position when your breastbone and chest have been stapled closed was no laughing matter. Later, telling me about this, she did laugh because she was rescued by a grandson who arrived home in the nick of time, but for what seemed like an eternity, literary tropes about the shocks that flesh is heir to were cold comfort. By the end of that summer, she returned home to begin picking up the pieces—feeding the cats, walking the dog, and, inevitably, beginning work for at least one new play. A year after the surgery she described her health as excellent: "I'd recommend bypass surgery to the world at large." Her elevated heart beat was under control; her meds were organized; and she was acknowledging the necessity for some serious changes in diet and lifestyle. With these changes and her many pills, she was, as she put it, "good for years." But she knew she had been lucky:

> It turned out that I had a number of 100% blockages, which I thought meant you had a heart attack. Not so. It's the sudden blockage that produces the attack as I understand it. Mine was sort of cumulative and as I kept busy I had built some subsidiary vessels around the blockages which were sustaining me. It did mean the heart itself was not damaged which is why they ended up doing the quintuple—"the full meal deal" as the surgeon put it.[4]

I guess the moral of the story is that her high-stress, high-activity level kept her going, protected her heart, and forced her body to develop "subsidiary vessels." At least, this is one interpretation of the story, when it has a happy ending! But Sharon is a touch superstitious about this happy ending so she keeps a private totem with her. When I visited her in Edmonton during the run of *Moving Pictures*, there was a small, stuffed bear in her otherwise extremely spartan apartment. A small stuffed bear, I asked? She picked it up, hugged it to her chest, and wrapped her arms around the bear and herself. Then she explained: these bears were given to heart patients who participated in drug trials to control arrhythmia, something she had experienced that is common after heart surgery. Patients were also given heart-shaped cushions, but she disposed of hers after one of the cats threw up on it. Now all she has left to placate her troubled heart is this bear, so here he was in Edmonton, clasped to her chest as she chuckled and told me the story. The drug she was administered during the trials was a placebo. The bear, well, he is something else.

By the end of 2002, Sharon had begun to travel again and to give readings and talks. She went to the Maritimes to read from *Getting It Straight*, to California for a production of *Blood Relations*, and to Stratford for the 50th anniversary celebrations of the festival and, in particular, of Canadian plays produced there. With three productions over the years, Sharon is one of the most produced Canadian playwrights at Stratford. There was no sign of any slowing down. She spoke, she argued and contributed to discussions; she read from her work and attended plays, and she enjoyed fries and beer. In Calgary she was also enjoying her youngest grandchild, Bear's second son Spencer, who arrived in 2001. Visits with Spencer had become a regular feature of her life. He called them "*aventures* with grandma"; she delighted in reporting his new words and their shared exploits. During these months she put the final touches on the published texts of *Moving Pictures*, *End Dream*, and *Angel's Trumpet* for their appearance in the 2003 volume *Sharon Pollock: Three Plays*, and she wrote a new Playwright's Note for the Shaw Festival program for *Blood Relations*, which opened in May. Both *Doc* and *Fair Liberty's Call* were coming out in new editions, and this process also required her attention, as did the remount of *The Making of Warriors*. In November she was to receive an honorary degree from the University of Calgary, and while this was her third such honour, she had to give her talk on home ground, with most of her family assembled and for the same convocation at which her eldest daughter received her law degree. It was a very happy occasion followed by a formal photography session and a long family dinner. But stressful as it may have been, it was nothing compared to her trip to Sierra Leone in February with CAUSE Canada.

"People ask me why did I go," Sharon has said. "People ask me what it was like. People ask me what do I think.... What have I made, or will I make, of my experience in Sierra Leone." These are the comments with which she began a speech she gave for CAUSE Canada after she returned, and she has now published it as "A Memoir: Sierra Leone, 2003." As she went on to explain, she knows why she went though she cannot yet find, or organize, the words to make something of her experience, never mind to make theatre from it. She went to Sierra Leone to meet the people who live there, people in so many ways like herself, like us, and she also hoped to see their theatre work and speak with theatre people. I think she also went because she suspected it would be a tough experience and, therefore, one she should not shirk: "The danger in going was to the self, and not to the person," which is "more frightening" because "it's easier to take a bullet to the body than a blow to one's prior conceptions or political or cultural assumptions" ("A Memoir," 18). In this memoir/speech, and in other pieces she has written or delivered about her trip, she has struggled to find meaning in what she saw by relating it to life in Canada, to what is familiar, to her personal sense of family, identity, and work. This is not a matter of comparing lifestyles but of testing the limits of perception and understanding, and ultimately—critically for a writer—of testing language. So, for example, she continues to ask herself if a little boy she saw, who was about four and whose leg had been amputated at the knee, "is my grandson"? She had watched the child hobble around a makeshift soccer field following a string of older boys and men, also amputees, because he loved soccer, like her little grandson, and his desire to join in made sense to her *through* the personal connection with the child back home. At the same time, she confesses that "if in my heart I feel he is [a member of my family], what follows can be so overwhelming that it defies translation into action" (19).

This image of the boy still haunts her. It is one of the first things she described to me after her return to Calgary. This image haunts her along with other staggering observations, many of them critical, about first world aid and white folks helping in places like Sierra Leone, where the needs are so great and long term, and the comparisons so shocking. In the early months of 2003, the wealthy, powerful nations of the world were launching a bloody invasion of Iraq in the name of peace, freedom, democracy, and the war on terror. Although it was almost impossible to get news in Sierra Leone because of power failures, she tried to follow developing events in the Middle East. As a result, the incommensurability of First World actions compared to her Third World surroundings was always on her mind. Being Sharon Pollock, in her CAUSE Canada talks, her "memoirs" about Sierra Leone, her conversations, and, I am certain, in any play she may write out of this experience, she could not help but draw invidious comparisons, name inconsistencies and hypocrisies (the millions of dollars spent on war, the violence, the innocent victims), connect the dots, expose the realities behind the official upbeat stories. As she told her audience for the "Memoir" talk, she could not help but be a "pain in the ass" because she has always seen through the façades and rhetoric that shield the fortunate few from reality.

CAUSE Canada is a Christian NGO based in Canmore, Alberta, with projects in Honduras, Guatemala, Ivory Coast, and Sierra Leone. CAUSE is an acronym for Christian Aid for Under Assisted Societies Everywhere. It was founded in 1984 by Paul Carrick who, with his wife Bev, the executive director and a nurse, lead a small team that supervises the work in these four countries. Their mission is "to alleviate poverty and injustice through long-term partnerships that empower communities to respond to their own needs," and they rely on volunteer help, individual donors, community support, and CIDA (Canadian International Development Agency) grants. When Sharon went to Sierra Leone the organization was focusing their efforts on education and training for women and girls who had survived the torture, rape, and sexual slavery they endured during the country's violent civil war (1992–2002). They were also sponsoring a theatre program to bring performances about important health issues to people living in a country where the basic infrastructure and communications systems were in disarray. Through Carrie MacLeod, CAUSE Canada's Calgary Director of Development Education, a young woman who studies drama, they contacted Sharon to ask of she were interested in making such a trip. Carrick and MacLeod had recently begun to invite donors and others from the local community to join them on selected short-term visits, and they believed that Sharon's profile and stature would help them in their work. Sharon listened to the proposal, read the background materials they provided, and did her own homework on the recent war in Sierra Leone. She had not forgotten the distant link between New Brunswick and this African country or that her character, Black Wullie, in *Fair Liberty's Call* had chosen to stay in the new Canadian province rather than emigrate there. She said yes, she would go.

On 26 February 2003, Sharon, Bev Carrick, and Carrie MacLeod boarded their plane in Calgary for the flight to Heathrow. They spent a day and an evening in London, attended a play, and then caught their next flight from Gatwick to Freetown, the capital of Sierra Leone. In just forty-eight hours, they had gone from a Calgary winter to another world. Sharon was based in Freetown but made trips to smaller cities in the company of MacLeod or with both MacLeod and Carrick and their intrepid driver Bramba. They left Sierra Leone for the long journey home on March 10th, just under two weeks after they had set forth, but a lifetime away in experience. This abrupt telescoping of time and space make such a journey very difficult to register, comprehend, or categorize, and judging from her conversations and written reports, she must have felt a bit like Alice falling down the rabbit hole from this safe world into another reality. She has described feeling ill at ease, privileged, well fed, and therefore guilty, when so many around her had nothing. Visiting a community, where women would greet her singing about how happy they were (as indeed they may have been, relative to their lives during the war), was, to say the least, jarring. Sitting down to a welcoming meal at which only the visiting whites were served food and the leftovers from the visitors' plates were scraped together for their hosts, made swallowing anything an ordeal, even though refusing the food was out of the question. So she worried, constantly. Not about the heat or the water or even the mosquitoes, but about the incongruities, inequalities, inconsistencies, and injustices of our world, which she nonetheless wanted to see as one: "despite our differences in colour and culture, I remembered One World."

Two things enabled her to hold onto this vision of One World: the children and the theatre. From her perspective, the women could only be helped temporarily unless outside aid reached the men, but it was the children who touched her most profoundly and held out a promise for the future. Somehow the mothers, impoverished though they were, sent their youngsters off to school (when school was available) dressed in wonderfully white, meticulously clean, pressed clothes. The streets may have been a shambles, the open sewers filthy, but the children were beautiful (see Illus. 43). And in Freetown's Amputee Refugee Centre, where that small boy hobbled around the soccer field, there was theatre. CAUSE Canada supported the Amputee Theatre Group, which used the universal language of theatre to present plays about trauma and healing or about HIV/AIDS that employed improvisation, dance, song, storytelling, and drumming, all traditional and familiar

43. Sharon in Sierra Leone, 2003. It is the children she saw that Sharon most often remembers from this trip. *Photograph courtesy of Bev Carrick, CAUSE CANADA.*

techniques in Sierra Leone. Education through theatre reminded Sharon of One World too because the developed Western countries—like Canada—have such theatre. Her visit to Freetown's Culture Village, or what remained of it, was less reassuring. The original, pre-war Sierra Leone Dance Troupe had once been world famous for their performances, but by 2003 they were struggling to regroup and retrain in a slum area of the city with mud streets, open sewers, tin huts, and a dilapidated amphitheatre. Sharon met and talked with Sam Sillah, who was working desperately "to keep the dream alive, a dream of foreign tours and recognition at home and abroad for the troupe's celebration of traditional Sierra Leone culture" ("A Memoir: Sierra Leone, 2003," 24). This was a kind of work and a dream she could understand. Much harder to accept was the near impossibility for the serious writer, whether in English or the vernacular Krio, to create a personal, individual, artistic vision or to write politically challenging plays instead of plays that addressed immediate social problems and aimed at educating audiences. But as one playwright asked her, who would produce or perform such work, who would attend or read it, or, for that matter, how would their work get published?

She has said that she is glad she went to Sierra Leone, that her "head is full of strange reactions," that going confirmed her belief that making theatre is common to all people and can unite us, and that she carried this confirmation back home with her as "a gift from the people of Sierra Leone." But she has said much more. At the end of "A Memoir: Sierra Leone, 2003," she describes reviewing the day's activities with Carrie MacLeod one evening, tossing aside the mosquito netting, trying to unwind in their room, where the solitary light bulb blinks on with "a brownish glow for 30 seconds with 2-minute intervals of total darkness," and laughing,

> Till tears come.
> Tears come.
> Tears.
> I think of Samuel Beckett. "We laugh so as not to cry."
> That doesn't always work. (27)

III: Still Making Theatre—2004 to 2007

For the Shaw Festival production of *Blood Relations* in 2003, Sharon agreed to write a short essay about the genesis of her play. Much of it was already familiar: for example, she told her new audiences that she had always been fascinated with famous murder cases, that she preferred non-linear dramatic structures to straightforward ones, and that she always saw a play script (even one like *Blood Relations*, which had been in print and produced for more than twenty years) as a blueprint for performance. But she began this essay with a set of observations that are less familiar. She began by recalling her father and his good advice over the years, much of which she had studiously ignored. "However he did instill in me one thing," she confessed, one she attributed to his "dour Scottish Protestantism": "that doing what you don't like to do is inherently good for you" (Shaw program, 2003). As a child, this meant finishing everything on her plate; as a teenager, it meant rising early, even on weekends; as an adult playwright, it meant forcing herself to write a well-made, realist play because it would be *good for her*. That well-made play was the first version of her Lizzie Borden play, and I would have thought that was enough of doing what she disliked because a dour old Scots voice said it was good for you. But apparently this bit of fatherly advice stuck because in December 2004 I was astonished to learn that she had agreed to be interviewed on the Edmonton radio show "Wild Rose Country." I was astonished because this was one of those call-in shows with hosts who are long-winded and callers who are even worse; often the hapless guest is ignored, trivialized, and *used*. I could not see how it would be good for Sharon by any dour yardstick.

But she had agreed to do this; she even went down to the radio station in person. I sat with Diane Bessai in her Edmonton kitchen and listened for about an hour, and what we heard was neither edifying nor good for Sharon or anyone else. But I did learn several things about *my subject*. Under dismal circumstances and thoughtless provocation, Sharon Pollock could remain patient, tolerant, articulate, and clear-headed. At the time, Canada was in the throes of compiling a list of the ten greatest Canadians, and the host kept prodding his distinguished guest about why no women had made the top ten, why Nell Shipman had been utterly forgotten, and what Sharon *felt* about all this? She tried a brief answer but he kept interrupting. I wished she would strangle him. But I guess she could hear Everett advising her—this is good for you!—so she explained that Shipman had moved to the United States, that much of early film history is unknown, and that telling women's stories is a relatively new phenomenon. Then she pointed out, in a rather mild way, that the media must share the blame for this silence and marginalization because when women are successful and have authority, they are portrayed by the media as "bitchy." She gave her host examples—Charlotte Whitton, Sheila Copps. But the host was not listening; he was interrupting. Sharon Pollock, he exclaimed, is a star! A lengthy groan was audible over the air waves as she reiterated her views about competitions to choose stars: "I am not interested in being a star; stars are a pain in the ass." And she elaborated on the point. Stars are not useful people to work with because they are worried about surfaces and about how others see them, instead of concentrating on the work at hand and having a secure inner sense of who they are. For herself, she was interested in substance, flaws in character, depths, human motivations, and storytelling, and she tried to bring the host's line of questioning to a close by insisting that when she won awards, she thought of them as signs of "our society valuing" not only what she does but also what theatre, as a collaborative art, does.

The host persisted: Who were her role models? Does she feel neglected? How did she become a star, by which he meant, how did she get her start in theatre? Sharon patiently answered: Nancy Drew was her role model (and she was not being merely facetious), although she rejected the very term *role model*; neglect in Canada is cultural not personal and, therefore, the artist (although she did not use this word) must persist (ah, this is where doing what's good for you surfaces). And then she went on to correct his garbled version (yes, he told his version before allowing her to answer his question) of how she got here from there. This story is the one about "Acne, Alberta," the smelly school locker room, the silly Broadway play, the girl who asked for a signature and wanted to know how Miss Pollock "got here," and Sharon's answer: "By bus." Then, her voice firm with sincere conviction, she told anyone who was listening that "plays must have significance for us and for the world." I have heard her say this so often that I wondered if she did not feel like a voice crying in the wilderness, but then, I reminded myself, she *believes* that good theatre is good for us. If I had to select just one key to this woman's life, that would be it: her unshakeable conviction about good theatre. This is why she subjects herself to interviews and talk shows and, more importantly, why she has carried on making theatre.

Between 2004 and the present, Sharon has remained extremely busy. In addition to shows like this one and her performance in *Moving Pictures*, she participated fully in the one-day symposium held in her honour and on her work at the University of Alberta, she gave a keynote lecture and was actively engaged in a Workshop on theatre and autobiography held at the University of British Columbia in the spring of 2004, and she has done further acting (for example, Miss Tracey in Calgary's Vertigo Mystery Theatre, April 2004 production of J.B. Priestley's *Mystery at Greenfingers*). In 2006 she began a term as playwright-in-residence with APN, and she continues to work with them, and with other emerging playwrights, like Kevin Loring, as a dramaturge. She has returned to Banff to assist Mark Lawes on a new project; she has appeared on professional panels (in Edmonton and Toronto), travelled to the United States (Terre Haute, Indiana in 2004) to speak, meet students and attend rehearsals for a semi-professional production of *Blood Relations*, and she flew to Hungary for the 2007 launch of the translation of this play. She has served on juries for Calgary's Random Acts one-act play competition, given university lectures and playwriting workshops in both Calgary and Edmonton, and she continues to win prizes, such as the Gwen Pharis Ringwood Award for Drama in 2006 for volume one of the *Collected Works*, and to be awarded honorary degrees (her fourth was from the University of Alberta in 2005). Much of this work helps to pay the bills and, of all her plays, *Blood Relations* has continued to be the most produced and profitable. But this work will never allow her to retire in style, buy an Audi convertible, or attend soirées in furs—even if she wanted to. What she does want to do (because it is good for her and for us) is make theatre. So she continues to write new plays and to explore new directions in the theatre. She is also quietly experimenting with prose, about which she will say very little. Volume three of *Collected Works*, on which she worked closely with her editor Cynthia Zimmerman, appeared in 2008, and a new play called *Man Out of Joint*, premiered in May 2007 with Calgary's Downstage Performance Society. In April 2007 she turned seventy-one, but she remains formidable, funny, feisty, and full of opinions. She has neither slowed down nor shut up.

When Sharon arrived in Vancouver for the February 2004 Workshop, "Putting a Life On Stage," she seemed in excellent spirits. The event had been planned around a production of Joy Coghill's *Song of This Place*, an autobiographical portrait of Emily Carr. Sharon was to give a keynote lecture on the relationship between theatre and auto/biography at this event, which had brought academics and theatre practitioners together in one space for three days. The atmosphere was charged, even before things began because these two worlds rarely rub shoulders and cannot always speak the same language. Inevitably, sparks flew, tempers flared, voices were raised, debates erupted, and through it all the senior stateswoman (I will not say *star*) of Canadian theatre listened attentively, intervened tactfully to explain one group to the other and smooth ruffled feathers, and offered sharp insights into the questions being discussed. She did all this, moreover, while scarcely able to see. When she arrived in Vancouver all seemed fine; at least, there were no heart problems this time. By the first evening, however, it was clear that all was not well. Sharon Pollock was rapidly losing the sight in her good eye (the other one being weak). After a few phone calls and trips to different hospitals, I finally got her to an eye specialist at the Vancouver General Hospital who came in especially to see her. By midnight, when I returned her to her room at the University of British Columbia's Peter Wall Institute, where all the writers were staying, she only knew that there was too much blood gathered in her eye for a firm diagnosis and that she would have to sleep sitting up and return to the hospital in the morning, when, it was hoped, enough of the blood would have drained away for the doctors to assess the damage, do an ultrasound test, and be certain about what had happened. The following morning, the keynote speaker, without a word of complaint or fuss, was driven back to the doctors. Sharon's only requests had been that Linda Griffiths read from *Moving Pictures*, so her eyes could rest—

she was both grateful for this help and very impressed with Griffiths's Nell Shipman—and that her speech be blown up as large as possible so she could manage to read it the following morning. Which she did, standing close to the window, so her weak, but unaffected eye could decipher the large type. By the third day, Melinda had quietly arrived from Calgary to accompany her mother home, but Sharon protested that the eye was slowly clearing and she was not leaving until after the closing panel (at which her biographer was scheduled to speak) and the closing dinner, at which she enjoyed a long evening over wine with the other participants. By 11:00 that night both the daughter and the biographer were tired and went to bed; Sharon Pollock, I later heard, was still going strong at 2:00 A.M.

She did leave early the next day in the care of Melinda, but no fuss could be made, no discussion of details indulged in, and no public acknowledgement made of this health problem. The show had to go on and it did. A few weeks later, after further medical care in Calgary, she had recovered most of her sight and was driving again, despite grey areas that would obscure her vision when she tried to focus. This sudden crisis, caused by a haemorrhage but, luckily, not a detached retina, subsided into a faint memory. I cannot imagine her ever mentioning it again, but I will never forget her unflappable determination to carry on. If she was terrified, she did not show it. Her reactions were all practical: find a doctor, get a diagnosis, and take it from there. Very sensible. Once back home, she turned her attention to other tasks, to the cats and dogs, to two tiny finches she had been given, to her grandson, to her writing, to revising the autobiography lecture for publication.

The title of Sharon's lecture and published essay is both provocative and puzzling. "Playwright: Parasite or Symbiont" does not end with a question mark, although the rhetorical question conveyed by that "or" colours everything that follows. The essay itself, however, answers this implied question by claiming that this playwright, Sharon Pollock, is both and that all serious art (all art that is good for us) will be both parasitic and symbiotic to some degree. She begins by acknowledging the "multitudinous voices" she always hears in her head, except when she is actually writing, and she describes herself as "legion" because of these conflicting voices. While this state of inner dialogue or debate might sound odd, even alarming, to others, for Sharon the "simultaneous broadcast," as she calls her voices, is useful. Rather like an internal devil's advocate, they force her to question what she means and to wonder if she will believe tomorrow what she believes today. Most important of all, these voices want to know why—why things are as they are in the complex world out there or in the play or essay or lecture she is writing. Listening to inner, debating voices characterizes both the woman and her work, so when confronted with the subject for this essay-lecture she could only proceed by respecting both sides of the debate. On the one hand, there were the voices that considered her a parasite for ransacking the lives of historical figures (all the way from Walsh and Lizzie to Scott and Zelda) and of her family (notably in *Doc*) to use as stories in her plays. On the other, there were the voices that protested this designation, reminding her of her intimate, sympathetic, possibly subconscious desire to create meaning through these stories by establishing symbiotic relationships between herself, as a person and a writer, and the lives of these people, between her life-story and theirs, and then between her play and the larger society in which that play would live.

To clarify this fine, mutually supportive balance between parasitism and symbiosis, she described her understanding of biography and autobiography in the theatre by placing them on a spectrum: the more biography and autobiography emerged, or was used in a play, the more she saw herself as a parasite; the less biography and autobiography was identifiable in the play, the more she felt she had achieved a symbiotic relationship with it and the more that play would live in symbiosis with its audience or reader. And yet, the goal, *her* goal, always, was to create a work of art that would have meaning for others regardless of whose life-story it featured. In her words, a play is

> like a cake made up of eggs, butter, flour, a bit of vanilla. Show me any of these once the cake is baked. You may draw assumptions about the real-life people as easily as you may draw the egg in its shell from out of the cake.
>   *Doc* is baked. (298)

And indeed it is. Baked to such perfection that, as Sharon told us that day, reading beside the window from her magnified text, Everett Chalmers insisted that what happened in *Doc* happened in his life, even when Sharon knew it had not.

However, in compliance with her voices all demanding to be heard, she had no sooner made this statement about *Doc* and, thus, about the power of theatre, then she had to face the "shadow of autobiography" (299) because she had to admit that she did not like to think of bits of her life popping up in her plays. The very idea, in fact, was irksome: "the playwright should have asked me," she protested (299). Which raises another clamouring issue: ethics. In the lecture, she wondered out loud what James Walsh or Janet Smith or Zelda Fitzgerald would say if she bumped into them at one of her plays: "is there an ethical dimension to my cutting and pasting their lives to make a better dramatic point?" (299). The answer was that her "primary ethical obligation (if one can prioritize ethics) is to the integrity of the work" (299). She also wondered out loud (and with refreshing honesty and generosity) about *Getting It Straight* because it is "far more autobiographical than *Doc*," and it reveals, presumably with the playwright's permission, a great deal about Eme, who "is ME when spoken" (300). Can you be parasitic of yourself? Can you be a self-symbiont? These are questions Sharon did not play with directly on this occasion. However, she did say (and write) that "the closer the work comes to me and the more closely it is self-reflective, the more I suspect the worth of doing it" (300). Why? Because the *you* for which the making of good theatre (as in well-baked theatre) must be good is legion; the you must be singular *and* plural, inescapably parasitic but ideally symbiotic.

Sharon continued to wrestle with these questions about life stories and theatre in the interviews and panel discussions held in Edmonton later that year. Indeed, the ability to *wrestle with* multiple perspectives and conflicting views characterizes Sharon. It is an ability that has caused some people to see her as simply argumentative. However, what stands out about these reflections from 2004 in Vancouver and Edmonton is the degree to which she entered into a debate with herself about the nature of creativity and, thus, about the sources of her own work, and that kind of debate is dangerous. At the start of her conversation with

Pat Demers and Jan Selman, she admitted her discomfort with plays (like *Moving Pictures* and *Angel's Trumpet*) that probe and expose why a writer writes and how the writing is done (see "An interview," Demers, 15). Nevertheless, she did create such plays with an honest and uncompromising examination of the creative act and the artist's motivations. For Sharon, the question her Nell Shipman faced is valid: "if you can't make the movie [or the play], or nobody sees it, what are you then?" (Demers, 17). By performing the role of Shipman herself, she took on the extraordinary challenge of working through such a question in public because while deeply personal for her, it is ultimately common to us all, whether or not we have the talent and dedication to be artists. As Sharon sees it, we "experience life when we tell stories about our lives and we find meaning in those experiences through the creation of story; everyone is a storyteller" (Demers, 16). However, not everyone has the courage to make of themselves the vehicle, on a public stage, of such an experience.

There is one more comment in her interview with Demers that jumps out now because I can see that it points towards the new work she was already doing. This work pulled her away from stories about artists and creativity towards stories about injustice, political violence, and the abuses of power. When Demers asked her if she did not think a play like *Walsh* could still be relevant in Canada, or indeed the world, at the end of 2004, she began by laughing. Of course it was relevant; if she wanted to see it produced again, she had to agree that it was. Then, she went on to tell Demers that she had always seen in James Walsh, who is the kind of man who merely follows orders, parallels with Nazi Germany and with the Americans in Iraq (16). Sharon was turning her attention outwards again after a decade of inner reflection, perhaps even of self-doubt about her work. She was assessing major and horrifying world events: Rwanda, Darfur, Canadian peacekeeping disasters, the "9/11" World Trade Centre tragedy, the invasion of Iraq, the war in Afghanistan, the prison in Guantanamo, Maher Arar's torture, conflict in Lebanon and Israel, and racial-profiling in the name of the war on terror. Her time in Sierra Leone had brought her face to face with the real and lasting consequences of ethnic cleansing, war, extreme poverty, social collapse, and unimaginable trauma. Back home, she began talking to refugees from Afghanistan and the Middle East to try to better understand what Muslims in Canada were facing. Now she had to *make something* of these events.

Kabloona Talk and *Man Out of Joint* are the most recent results of her need to *make something* by making theatre. The first of these plays goes back to an episode from early twentieth-century Canadian history; the second focuses on the struggles of a Canadian lawyer who decides to defend alleged terrorists. Both plays explore the injustices of the law and the dilemmas faced by individuals who become caught up in the juggernauts of political and judicial systems and of pervasive social prejudice and paranoia. There are many capillary links between these new plays and *Walsh*, *The Komagata Maru Incident*, and *One Tiger to a Hill*, not the least of which are Sharon's focus on male characters and on dramatic trials. In her seventies she is once more exploring her vision of humanity in crisis and of fair liberty on trial to show us that the greatest shock is not a blow to the body but an assault on our dearly held and unexamined beliefs about what, and who, is right or wrong. This blow shakes the very foundations of the self, but sometimes it needs to be struck.

When Ben Nind, the artistic director of Yellowknife's Stuck in a Snowbank Theatre, approached Sharon about writing a play, he had a famous subject in mind: the 1913 murders of two Roman Catholic priests by two Inuit from the area of Kugluktuk (formerly called Coppermine) in Nunavut. The Inuit were brought to trial in August 1917, first in Edmonton and then in Calgary, and the trial was both sensational and bizarre. The appearance of two *savages* or *cannibals*, as they were called by whites of the period, in a southern, predominantly white city like Edmonton, escalated into an international *cause célèbre* when the first of the Inuit to be tried, Sinnisiak, was acquitted of the charge of murdering Father Rouvière. A new trial was ordered with a change of venue to Calgary and the sequestering of the jury, and this time both Sinnisiak and Uluksuk were found guilty of killing Father Le Roux. They were sentenced to death by hanging, but their sentences were commuted to imprisonment and they finally served two-year terms at the North West Mounted Police detachment at Fort Resolution on Great Slave Lake in the Northwest Territories. However, this bald summary of the basic facts conveys nothing of the complexity of the trial, and it barely hints at why the case of *Rex vs. Sinnisiak and Uluksuk* has become so significant in the annals of Canadian law, in the history of the Canadian North, and in popular stories of gruesome murders. For Canadians with a taste for such things, there are colourful accounts of these "Eskimos" and the priests they murdered; for scholars and historians, the case is an informative example of a clash between cultures and political interests; for Nind, a theatre man and a northerner, it is one of the many fascinating stories to come out of the North. For Sharon Pollock, the subject appealed on all these grounds and on several others besides. Once she had agreed to write a play, she set to work on her research, reading court records, newspaper coverage, popular and serious treatments of the story, and background information about the geography and history of the Northwest Territories in the early twentieth-century.[5]

The play that resulted is called *Kabloona Talk*, a title that signals Sharon's approach to her subject. The term "Kabluna" or "Kabloona" (*qallunaaq*) means white man and indicates that only white men will speak in her play, although the combination of the Inuit word for whites with "Talk" also suggests the alienation of the Inuit, who were subjected to a barrage of white men talking non-stop in a setting and a language completely foreign to them. In *Kabloona Talk*, Sinnisiak and Uluksuk do not appear; instead, they are talked *about* (argued, even shouted, about) by four white men who have gathered after Sinnisiak's acquittal to review the proceedings and the jury's surprising verdict. While she has stayed close to the facts of the case, right down to details of physical evidence and a debate about the translation of a key phrase, she has invented her four characters and imagined a scene that *might* have occurred because it supplies the dramatic context she needs to explore a host of issues— social, cultural, political, and ethical—that she finds embedded in the larger story of white men pushing ever further into the North to pursue their own goals of exploration, adventure, wealth, and Canadian sovereignty over a vast and remote area of the continent. It is easy to see why an early twentieth-century murder trial appealed to her now because issues of internal colonization, legal jurisdiction, economic control of valuable resources, and of Canadian sovereignty in the Arctic are very familiar today. Moreover, the confrontation of one cultural system with another and the inevitable clash of values, rights, and languages, which lies at the heart of this case, fuels contemporary conflict in Canada and around the world. As one of her characters insists, there are "immigrants, foreigners from a range of countries" living in Canada right now, and regardless of the "laws and customs they once lived under, they must conform to the law of this land, British [today we would say, Canadian] law" (*KT*, *CW* III, 288).

In the early years of the last century, both the Protestant and Roman Catholic churches were sending their clergy into ever more remote corners of the North to convert the heathen "Eskimos." There was, in fact, a competition for souls of the kind Herschel Hardin castigates in his satire of white behaviour in *Esker Mike and His Wife, Agiluk*. Two Belgian Oblate missionaries, Father Jean-Baptiste Rouvière and Father Guillaume Le Roux, were based at the Roman Catholic mission located at Fort Norman, northwest of Yellowknife and Great Slave Lake, on the Mackenzie River. Rouvière had already spent four years with the Dogrib further north and he was reputed to be kindly. Le Roux, however, was younger, highly educated, inexperienced in the North, and irascible. In November 1913, the two priests travelled from Fort Norman northeast to Coronation Gulf to work among the Killiniqmiut. But something went very wrong. The priests failed to return to Fort Norman, and rumours began to circulate that these remote people had been seen wearing cassocks and in possession of other Catholic accoutrements.

The Catholic bishop asked for an investigation, and in June of 1915, Inspector Charles Deering LaNauze of the Royal Northwest Mounted Police, left his base on Great Slave Lake with two constables and an interpreter to travel by canoe and dogsled across more than six hundred miles of arctic tundra to investigate. LaNauze discovered that the priests were dead, apparently murdered, and in May 1916 he found and arrested Sinnisiak and Uluksuk, who admitted to the killings and tried to explain what had happened near Bloody Falls on the Coppermine River in November 1913. According to Sinnisiak, and other Inuit who were questioned, the priests had had a disagreement with the Inuit and decided to return south alone, although they were close to starving and knew little about survival in an Arctic winter. Sinnisiak and Uluksuk followed them and were persuaded (possibly at gunpoint by Le Roux) to pull the priests' sled, but when they reached Bloody Falls, the priests were killed and the Inuit returned north to their people. According to Sinnisiak and Uluksuk, they became frightened by Le Roux, who lost his temper and threatened them with his rifle, and they believed the white men were very dangerous, possibly even deranged. They were hundreds of miles from any white settlement and utterly isolated; therefore, the reasonable thing for the Inuit to do was to kill the priests before Le Roux killed them, an action they would have taken within their own culture when faced with irrational behaviour. Sinnisiak stabbed Le Roux and shot Rouvière in the back as he ran away; Uluksuk stabbed both priests. Once the white men had died, the Inuit opened their abdomens and ate small pieces of each priest's liver in a ritual they believed would protect them from the spirits of the dead men. To white, southern, Christian eyes, of course, this macabre communion was cannibalism.

Three and a half years after the murders, Sinnisiak appeared in a sweltering Edmonton courtroom on trial for the murder of Father Rouvière before Judge Horace Harvey and a jury of six white men. The prosecuting attorney was C.C. McCaul; the lawyer for the defence was James Wallbridge. Sinnisiak was dressed in his traditional skins and provided with a bucket of cold water to cool his feet, while McCaul delivered a lengthy, decidedly racist, opening statement about how these cannibals of the Arctic must be taught to recognize the authority of white law. McCaul was confident of a guilty verdict. When the jury returned with an acquittal, McCaul was outraged. So was Judge Harvey, who had reminded the jury that there was no question but that Father Rouvière had been shot in the back—the accused had admitted it. Nevertheless, the situation was not lost because McCaul had split the charges, so that each Inuk was charged separately for each crime. By a process that is still not entirely clear, McCaul sought and received a change of venue to Calgary with Judge Harvey still presiding, but with a new jury and a new charge: both Sinnisiak and Uluskuk were charged with the murder of Le Roux. This trial was held on 24 August 1917 and both Inuit were found guilty as charged. The penalty was execution, but clemency was recommended and the death sentence was commuted to a prison sentence to be served in the North. The Inuit were released in 1919.

Even during the tumultuous years of the Great War, these trials created a media frenzy. Of course, the United States was not as focused on the war as Canada and Great Britain, but there was clearly much more at stake than the deaths of two priests in the frozen North. In any case, the battle for British law, Canadian sovereignty, and the safety of Christian white men who wanted to develop the North had been won. Or so it seemed. But many questions hovered over the whole affair: Why did the Edmonton jury acquit Sinnisiak? Was public sentiment in favour of these strange Arctic men and, if so, why? Did the all-Protestant jury not care what had happened to two Catholics? Under what backroom pressures was the second trial moved to Calgary? What did it *mean* to try and then convict two Inuit, who had killed to save themselves in accordance with their own customs, in a southern court where they understood neither the language spoken nor the legal system? Was *justice* served at these trials, and how can justice be defined under such circumstances? These are among the questions facing Sharon's four characters in *Kabloona Talk*.

The play opens in a sparsely furnished chamber adjacent to a court room. The set includes plush drapes, a liquor table with glasses, and a somewhat incongruous, bare, utilitarian, wooden table at centre stage. Beside this table sits a stack of five chairs, and the table is raked and lit to draw attention to its surface. When the door opens, an impeccably dressed man enters who, we later discover, is simply called Smith. He carries a rusted Winchester rifle and a box labelled "Rex vs. Sinnisiak." During the few minutes of silence that follow, he arranges objects on the table—a blood-stained cassock, some wrinkled pages from what looks like a diary, and a human lower jawbone. When the Judge (who is not identified by name) enters, he sees the man, appears to know both who he is and why he has come, and then reads an important, official letter given to him by the silent man. Enter the Prosecutor (which is all he will be called) who is furious about the acquittal. He and the Judge commiserate about the preposterous verdict until the Judge reflects that they "have options" (*KT* 262). Through all this, Smith watches the Judge and Prosecutor in silence. Enter the Defence (also not named), who is delighted with his success. Sharon calls for her defence lawyer to be a young man at the beginning of his career who, unlike the prosecuting attorney, did not graduate from prestigious Osgoode Hall, back east. He has joined his colleagues thinking he will celebrate until he spots the stranger. At this point, well into the play and with the four men assembled, Smith introduces himself as "Just Smith" (266). The young lawyer is instantly suspicious as well he might be because during the sixty-odd minutes of the action, Smith will take command of these new, ex-officio deliberations. Smith is a "fixer"; he is there to put things straight. His task, since he did not attend the trial, is to gather as much information as possible and then find a legal way to convict the Inuit.

By the end of the play, Smith has solved the dilemma created by the acquittal by facilitating an arrangement whereby certain affidavits will be sworn suggesting improper influence on the jury, which clears the way for a change of venue to Calgary and a new, sequestered jury. The Prosecutor quickly presents a new charge—*Rex vs. Sinnisiak and Uluksuk*—for the joint murder of Le Roux, and the Defence realizes he has been *used*. As Smith tells him in their final exchange, "without men like you the system would never work" (299). The young lawyer realizes he has been stripped, not only of his arguments but also of his personal dignity and belief in justice. Through the course of the play, as the Prosecution and the Defence reiterate their arguments for the benefit of Smith, we learn more about this bizarre murder case and its underlying issues (as Sharon sees them). Chief among the factors at work, and the real reason for Smith's ominous presence, is the simple necessity for the powers-that-be to establish firm control over the Northwest Territories and everything under the surfaces of its land and water. Ottawa does not want a repeat of what happened in the Yukon during the 1890s Gold Rush, when unruly Americans flooded into the area threatening Canadian sovereignty and control of resources. The Christian Church and the British legal system both serve political interests by establishing authority in such distant places, by staking claim to all aspects of life in the North, and by extending and legitimizing Euro-Canadian, southern control. Fundamentally decent young men like the Defence, who are able to present sincere arguments for cross-cultural miscommunication and to argue for a culturally sensitive sympathy in a way that is convincing, allow the system to appear fair, impartial, and just.

Sharon's choice of a courtroom-like setting and a retrial context provides an appropriate structural conceit for her play because it implicates the audience in the arguments, brings them face to face with the evidence, both the history and the gruesome physical objects displayed on the table, and casts viewers and readers alike as jury members. Implicit throughout are these questions: What would we have decided in August 1917, and what would we do today? To sharpen her inquiry, Sharon has the Defence introduce the seventeenth-century case of William Penn, a Quaker who was arrested and tried for disseminating his religious views, but who was acquitted by the jury despite the judge's instruction to convict. As a result, the men of the Jury were thrown into jail in an effort to force them to reverse their decision, but they refused, and both they and Penn were freed. This case, in effect, established the independence of a jury which should listen to, but is not bound to follow, a judge's instructions. In the eyes of the Defence, a jury had the power and duty to think for itself, and he wanted the Calgary jury to be informed of this right. But this judge dismisses the "little history lesson" as "irrelevant and without merit" (298). Sharon, needless to say, does not agree. In this new play she returns to issues of individual freedom and responsibility that plagued Walsh, Hopkinson, and the Roberts family in *Fair Liberty's Call*, but she has her eyes focused on the present and immediate future, both in Canada and abroad. Her question to us is: When you see an idealistic person being manipulated by a cynical fixer and a ruthless system, where will you stand and what will you do? Will you, like Eloise in *The Making of Warriors*, simply look the other way, or will you, like the lawyer in her next play, take action?

I cannot, of course, answer such large questions, and perhaps answering them is not the point. I can describe the 16 May 2005 Workshop organized by Alberta Playwrights Network as part of their play development program during which Sharon met with four Calgary actors in a small, windowless room in the APN offices to work through her script. Veteran actors were hired to read the script and then discuss it with the playwright. Sharon had arrived well ahead of time with refreshments and by 10:00 A.M. they began. Seated around a bare table with their scripts and nothing else to use but their voices, eye contact, and hand gestures, these actors put *Kabloona Talk* through its paces. Sharon sat silent and completely engrossed, registering every word, every pause. To my eyes and ears, Stephen Hair was stunning as Smith, and the success of the play turns on this key role. We need to fear this man even before he speaks because we sense his power over us. He must be like the mythical basilisk—quiet, calm, assured, irresistible, and inescapable.

After a short break, everyone returned to the room for a general discussion. Each actor identified what he liked, what he felt worked and what did not. They debated several questions: Was there enough contextual information for an audience to follow? Was there too much? Was there enough dramatic action, and where did that action lie? Why was the Defence a young man when the real lawyer, Wallbridge, had not been? Who wrote the letter Smith shows to the judge and what did it say? Should it be a letter or a telegram, given the communications systems of the period? Sharon was anxious to know if the actors had enough back-story to perform and reveal their characters because she saw each man as changing, or even as learning, as the play unfolds, and she most certainly saw them losing or gaining the upper hand in their relationships with each other. For her, that is where the drama lies, in that intense but subtle interaction of the four men. They considered the racist views of the Prosecutor, but Sharon told them that the real McCaul wanted to see changes in the way the law was introduced in the North and that his views were representative of his time and place. All four men wanted to know—*WHO IS SMITH*? A heated discussion followed, with Sharon putting a word in here and there. Then someone asked why Smith was in town anyway and how he got his hands on the evidence (the rifle and other exhibits)? Ah, said Sharon, now there's the real problem, and she carefully reviewed her reasons for creating Smith while the actors interjected with suggestions and more leading questions. She wrestled with what could be changed and how; everything had to be *there*, be clear, *inside* the play. The table was essential to her vision. It represents the North after Smith meticulously lays out the rivers, lakes, and key sites, such as Bloody Falls. On this table, Smith will map the co-ordinates of the crime scene in a part of the country few people have any knowledge of, and by doing so he will reveal his own character. She wants Smith to be human because, she explained, his humanity, fussiness about details, and obvious pride in his work make him more frightening. The Nazis, she reminded us, are more appalling when we see them as normal, with wives, children, and a love of classical music.

After lunch, everyone returned for a page-by-page reading and analysis that did not conclude until 5:30. On the one hand, Sharon wanted feedback on almost every line so she could develop stage instructions that make sense for actors; on the other, she needed to know where an actor might stumble so she could alter a line, add a look or a gesture, or cut a word. After a thorough discussion of Smith's letter, she agreed to rethink this device. Her comments about the table and the North clarified just how vitally important it is for her to *see* the physical space of her play and, in this case, how crucial it is to enable a southern audience to imagine and grasp the vast distances of the Northwest Territories and the realities of life there in the early twentieth-century. Because she is throwing new light on a northern story, the space of that story must be spotlighted—literally, theatrically. Here again, and at an early stage in the process, was Sharon Pollock making theatre, and it was evident that, for her, this was a collaborative process in which she works best with actors she trusts and respects and with theatre people who can engage with her on an equal footing. She takes nothing for granted and is prepared to question, defend, cut, or sharpen everything in the script. No wonder she has always been so dissatisfied with one-shot productions, hurried rehearsals, amateurish readings of scripts, and dramaturgical interference with a playwright's (especially a young, vulnerable playwright's) script. Working, as she just had, with her peers, other seasoned professionals, is the ideal Pollock process for improving a script, which goes on being tested, shaped, and improved with each professional production.

The next time I listened to *Kabloona Talk* was in November when a dramatic reading of the play was the final event in Theatre Alberta's and APN's 2005 PlayWorks Ink conference and workshop. This time the cast was different and the venue, a public auditorium in the Glenbow Museum, seemed to flatten the script, and the absence of the all-important table with its exhibits and mapping (even when only imagined) reduced the impact of the story. Perhaps the larger space, the flat playing area, with the four men standing in a semi-circle, raised an expectation of performance that could not be realized. Nonetheless, there were important lessons here: this play wants an intimate theatre space for its intense interactions to have power, and it needs that raked and spot-lit table on which to lay the grisly exhibits and to map the North. Sharon seemed on edge, preoccupied, and she said little. Maybe she was troubled by the script or the space. Maybe her thoughts were elsewhere because she knew that immediately after the reading we were moving across the street to the Auburn Bar to celebrate the launch of her *Collected Works* by Playwrights Canada Press. Nevertheless, when I asked her to pose for a snapshot with the actors (all long-standing friends) after the reading, she agreed easily and smiled happily (see Illus. 44). In shared moments like these, with other theatre people, Sharon relaxes.

Shortly after we adjourned to the Auburn, Cynthia Zimmerman began the launch with an assessment of the playwright's career and the reasons for preparing this collection at this time. When it came Sharon's turn to speak, she looked desperately uncomfortable. I thought back to that radio call-in show and to her insistence that she did not want to be a star because

44. Sharon with friends—the actors who read *Kabloona Talk* at the Glenbow Museum, 6 November 2005. Left to right: Larry Reese, Joe-Norman Shaw, Sharon, Peter Strand Rumpel, and Grant Reddick. After the reading of the play, people gathered to celebrate the launch of the first volume of Sharon's *Collected Works*.   *Photograph, S. Grace.*

stars were a pain in the ass. Her first words this time were: "I feel like I should be dead." For this woman of such accomplishment, energy, and vision, who is also shy in many ways and insecure in others, this moment was a trial. Of course, she rose to the occasion; the show always goes on. But to be publishing your collected works, with your editor and biographer looking at you, might seem *final*. Except that the editor and the biographer did not see her this way. As it turned out, two more launches lay ahead (for volumes two and three) and there were more plays—*are* more plays—still to come. No end was in sight because, like Shipman, Pollock always says "Never." As her biographer, I have no choice, happily, but to follow suit. And so this is not an ending to the biography, at least not in the sense of closure. The ending is open, her story continues. My story about her just stops, but in stopping I want to look ahead and watch Sharon as she disappears over a new horizon, beckoning and teasing me with hints or clues about where she will go next.

***

Years ago, Marshall McLuhan warned us about our obsession with rearview mirrors. Because we potter along staring insistently in a rearview mirror, we miss what is right in front of us or just ahead down the road. Sharon Pollock has never made this mistake. Down the road ahead of her are new projects and new challenges. In the summer of 2006 she launched volume two of *Collected Works* (this time there were no worries about being alive), and she began to work with the artistic director of the Atlantic Ballet of Canada, Igor Dobrovolskiy. This company, founded by her half-sister, Susan Chalmers-Gauvin is new and innovative. Sharon got her toes wet, as it were, by serving as dramaturge for the company's opening production of their 2006–07 season: the premiere of Dobrovolskiy's *Phantom of the Opera*.[6] There had been talk of this kind of collaboration in the past because Sharon has long been fascinated with the place of music in the theatre and the dramatic links between music, movement, and story. She has toyed with the idea of a musical, or even an opera, at least as far back as the early 1980s with her Lysistrata/Egg manuscript and the musical structure of a play like *Whiskey Six Cadenza* or *Getting It Straight*. Even her use of songs and sound effects in *Blood Relations*, *Doc*, *Fair Liberty's Call*, and *Moving Pictures*—not to mention "T.S.'s" antics in *The Komagata Maru Incident* or Zelda's passionate dance in *Angel's Trumpet*—all stem from Sharon's sensitivity to music and movement and their potential to convey meaning, beyond and apart from dialogue, on stage. Often her plays invite a form of choreography that is more than the usual blocking. I suspect that her early, and continuing, work with radio drama also enhanced her awareness of acoustic power. The results of this new direction in her making of theatre remain to be seen, but I predict that we will see more work combining dance, music, and theatre from her.

Meanwhile, she is busy helping Kevin Loring with his new script, "The Ballad of Floyd," mentoring and assisting another young playwright, as she did years ago with Brad Fraser, and as she has done with so many emerging playwrights over the years. In September 2006 she began reviewing Calgary's theatre scene for CBC radio; you can find her at www.sharonpollock.com/Reviews. And she is writing. In her head (like Nell), she is always writing. Ask her about O.J. Simpson, Jennifer and Melinda suggest. Ask her about Iraq, or Maher Arar, or Rocco Galati. Ask her if she is writing a novel. (Privately, I wonder: if she is writing prose, will she publish it under the pen-name of E.E. Roberts?) Sharon is not telling. What she is saying publicly, apart from her CBC reviews, is contained in speeches. One of these, about Canadian women playwrights (see "Reflections") was delivered at the May 2006 Playwrights' Guild of Canada Conference in Toronto; another, which is unpublished and has no title, was the eulogy she delivered in February 2007 at the Calgary celebration of Rick McNair's life. At the Guild conference, she spoke personally about who she was and why making theatre matters. She reminded her audience that she is an Albertan and a regional playwright insofar as her "region is people." She reflected upon her past plays, on how she finds meaning through telling stories, on why she had to move beyond "judging myself and other women" before she could create principal female characters, and on how uneasy she feels about her work if it is self-reflective. She recalled the good old days of CBC radio drama and some of the people who first encouraged her, and she stressed her love of Pinter, Beckett, and Brecht, whose work, she explained, gave her "permission" to believe that serious theatre had a role to play in the world. And while not mentioning feminism as such, she reiterated what I see as one of her most salient self-defining comments: "I come from a country of mothers, of daughters and grandmothers" (*CW* III, 15).

When Rick McNair died suddenly at sixty-five on 1 February 2007, Sharon was devastated. They had been friends and colleagues for thirty years, and they had shared some of the best and some of the worst of times. Difficult though it was to summarize her memories of him for a speech at the 12 February memorial in Calgary, she was determined to do so and adamant that his life and work should be remembered and attention paid. She began her remarks, characteristically, with a touch of ironic humour: because of her heart problems, she and Rick had assumed that he would be the one saying something about her, and they had laughed about the possibilities. Then she went on, as the genre of such occasions dictates, to review his life, his enormous generosity (in fact, she recounted the occasion when he had signed over his pay cheque to a nearly destitute Sharon), his creativity, his love of books, of conversation, and of family. But it was her closing remarks that stay with me because she ended by describing the movie they made together in 1998—it was the film version of Sharon's play *Death in the Family*—and she evoked an image of Rick as Renee Havard's beloved brother Gillie lying in a field of golden canola with arms outstretched and smiling like a leprechaun. This scene is striking. In the film, with Rick as Gillie opposite Sharon as his older sister Renee, these two friends had enacted an aspect of their real-life friendship. Rick's untimely death, when it came, was like a death in Sharon's family: "I shall miss him terribly," she said.

By the spring she was ready to premiere another new play with a small Calgary company run by Simon Mallett called the Downstage Performance Society. Downstage wants to do plays that most other companies refuse to touch, and in their 2006–07 season they did George F. Walker's *Heaven*, *This is for You, Anna*, created by the Anna Collective of Toronto's Nightwood Theatre, and Sharon Pollock's *Man Out of Joint*. These are not cheery, feel-good plays. *Heaven*, with its exposé of racism and religious extremism, *Anna*, with its feminist focus and non-linear confrontation of domestic abuse and revenge, and *Man Out of Joint*, which explores paranoia in the current context of the war on terror, are all tough plays about urgent social issues. These are plays that expect audiences to think and to leave the theatre debating what Mallett has called "hot-button" topics (see Kubik, 2006).

So it was on 9 May 2007 that I took my seat beside Sharon at the Vertigo Studio Theatre in downtown Calgary for the premiere of this new Pollock play. Although I had read the script, I was not sure what to expect in staging, and I wondered how many shocks it would deliver to my assumptions. And the play did not disappoint. *Man Out of Joint* is hard-hitting theatre about universal issues and perennial Pollock themes. It is the story of an Italian-Canadian lawyer who decides to represent a group of young Muslims accused of terrorist activities. The more deeply he is drawn into the dark world of the war on terror, paranoia, and the abuse of detainees at Guantanamo Bay, the more his private life collapses around him. This man, called Joel Gianelli (loosely based on Toronto lawyer Rocco Galati), is the heart and soul of the play, and watching the premiere I was reminded of earlier Pollock characters of conscience like Walsh, Hopkinson, Doc, and Eddie/Emily. Like these characters,

Gianelli is a good person with a social conscience who struggles to do what he believes is right, and his fate, or moral dilemma, remains as familiar today as it was in Walsh's because humanity, or society, has not changed. We are as easily manipulated by those in power, or as selfishly indifferent to the consequences of our inaction as we have always been. Sharon has said that she did not intend to write a play about "Guantanamo or 9/11 because [she] had no human connection." It was not until the character of the lawyer took shape in her mind that she knew she had found the right story about how politics can infiltrate and destroy an individual's life. For me, one of the most gripping aspects of Gianelli's story is his haunting by the voice of his Italian-Canadian father who was interned by the Canadian government during the Second World War, as were so many groups of suspected enemy sympathizers. This father is one of those insistent Pollock ghosts (like Anderson in *Fair Liberty's Call*, the grandmother in *Doc*, Clarence in *Walsh*, or the dead in *One Tiger to a Hill*, *Whiskey Six Cadenza*, *Saucy Jack*, and *Constance*); he will appear frequently to remind his son about past injustice, and the son will have no choice other than to oppose the racial profiling that is excused as a measure of anti-terrorism in contemporary society. What happened during the war is happening once more, and someone must have the courage to stand up against it, regardless of personal sacrifice.

When the performance ended and the lights came up, there was a tense silence before the audience began to applaud. The actors, as well as many audience members, knew that the playwright was there, but no special notice was taken of her. It was enough to have been present when a major new play by one of the country's pre-eminent artists had come to life. It was satisfying to see that Sharon Pollock was still angry with the way things are, still eager to embrace the region she calls "people," still trying to make the world a better, fairer place for our children, and *still making theatre*.

CHAPTER 10

Taking the Fingerprints of Her Sources

I look back over what I've written and I know it's wrong, not because of what I've set down, but because of what I've omitted. What isn't there has a presence, like the absence of light.

—MARGARET ATWOOD, *The Blind Assassin*, 498

This comment from Atwood's novel is made in the first person by a character called Iris Chase. Iris is concluding a story about her life (autobiography) and about her sister, their parents, her husband, sister-in-law, and the man who, we will finally realize, was her lover and the father of her child (biography). *The Blind Assassin* is an intriguing, complex narrative about biography and autobiography that intentionally and provocatively blurs the lines between truth and falsehood, revelation and subterfuge, reality and imagination, so-called fact and so-called fiction, one kind of storytelling and another (indeed, several others). It is a novel that *closes* on questions unanswered, with lives and stories untold or still to be told. It ends with a lingering afterglow of *to be continued*, and the final words send the reader scrambling back to the beginning for clues, details, the presences of absence, which we must surely have missed as we read. It leaves us hungry, longing to know more, scrutinizing the narrative for silences, gaps in the manuscript, almost suppressed traces, or what Sharon Pollock once described as fingerprints.

Sharon used the phrase "the fingerprints of my sources" when answering a question at the February 2004 workshop on autobiography, biography, and theatre at UBC. As far as I know, she has not (yet) written it down anywhere; to my frustration I can only find this comment in my notes, hastily scribbled down during the event. Did I really hear her say this, or something like this? Or am I wishing she had and attributing to her something she might have said? In the last analysis, I will have to trust my memory and good intentions because I cannot provide a reference. All I can offer is circumstantial evidence: the fingerprints of *my* source. And, of course, at many points in this story of Sharon's life, fingerprints are what I have studied and written about: her fingerprints, my fingerprints, others' fingerprints that are smudged by time, faint traces or presences that point to something else, to what I have knowingly, and unknowingly, omitted.

As I come to the close of my story about her life, I have reached a number of working conclusions, some of which are more definitive than others. I have no doubt now that biography is a demanding and perverse art: demanding because the biographer must tell a good story while observing the duty, ethical and scholarly, to be accurate where accuracy is possible; perverse because the biographer, whether parasite or symbiont, must devote his or her life (or substantial portions of it) to someone else's life. To claim that Sharon Chalmers was born in Winnipeg in 1937, had four children, and spent the last forty years living in Toronto, would be factually wrong. To say she wrote novels, disliked cats and dogs, and poisoned her husband would be worse than getting the facts wrong; it would be gratuitously untrue, possibly libellous. And yet, I have begun to realize just how quickly, almost imperceptibly, a biographer leaves the *terra firma* of verifiable facts and accepted truths for the tempting shallow water of a safe beach and then, by degrees, is seduced into the deeper waters offshore. One begins happily enough, swimming confidently, looking at this delight or that curiosity on the surface when suddenly the water becomes dark and deep; then there is an undertow, a strong current pulling one out further or under. The adventure becomes frightening, even dangerous. So why take the risk? Why attempt to *tell* this story, to *write* a biography, or an autobiography for that matter?

I think biographers take these risks, or at least that I have, for several reasons. As human beings we all have lives and life-stories and we want others to be interested in them. When we protest that we (or you) should "get a life," we really mean we should get a life that is worth telling a story about: stop complaining, stop hiding in your work (hiding from what?); take time, do things, enjoy yourself, then tell me about it. As human beings we need stories, and we are always making up our lives as we go along (as Malcolm Lowry told me years ago, as Scheherazade knew, as Homer knew). Human beings are curious, some much more so than others. We want to know how and why and what. Some of this curiosity may be little more than nosiness about a neighbour's or a friend's life; some of it involves self-reflection; and much of our curiosity concerns the world at large. At its best and most productive, human curiosity becomes creativity, and the results can be splendid medical discoveries, amazing feats of engineering, and superb works of art. However, to live life creatively is as rare as is the ability to transform the life lived into art; therefore, I have come to believe that some lives are more worth the risk of writing about (because more interesting, more illuminating, more representative, more dramatic) than others.

Telling an important, significant life-story should provide insight into much more than one person's daily life. In fact, as Sharon has said when describing a good play, it should be life without the boring bits. A good subject for a biography should satisfy far more than idle, prurient curiosity insofar as the events of that life—its significance—have a wider meaning. The events in the life of a good subject for biography should resonate on several levels of common experience and illuminate both the world in which we live and the strengths and weaknesses of the human spirit. I would go further and say that some biographees are especially illuminating for their time and place, their culture, and perhaps even for a sense of national identity. Biography is one of the ways in which we tell ourselves who we are and what we stand for (even if we fall short of that ideal), and biography has long been used for such national and ideological purposes, hence, the long tradition of saints' *lives* or the secular *lives* of prime ministers, generals, influential scientists, artists, and philosophers. Biography, like autobiography, is a form of history, about a person, a family, a community, a nation, or a civilization, but, like history, it is incomplete. Such stories are, as Shipman tells us in *Moving Pictures*, always incomplete. Until very recently, Western biography and history have been too narrowly focused because both narrative genres have tended to explain us to ourselves in terms of one gender (male) and one class (the ruling class, the élite, with its homogeneous ethnicity). Consequently, the stories told have not accounted sufficiently for the diversity within communities or nations.

Canadian biography has been no different in its limitations than the biographies of any other Western country except, perhaps, in its comparative paucity—which brings me to another of my conclusions, albeit a more tentative one. As a training regime for the writing of Sharon Pollock's biography, I read as much modern biography as possible, not just Canadian, but specifically literary and theatre biography in English. This in itself has been a fascinating journey. Unfortunately, however, my observations suggest that Canada has produced too little biography and too few biographers, especially for artists and theatre practitioners. Thankfully, there are some wonderful exceptions to this low profile of Canadian biography, and some of our artists, including theatre artists, have written interesting autobiographies, but so much remains to be done that I feel reasonably safe claiming (*pace* Iris Chase) that the presence of what has not been written engulfs us in an "absence of light." Moreover, this observation about biography in Canada is corroborated in other areas of cultural endeavour. Take, for example, the Portrait Gallery of Canada. As I write in 2007, few Canadians will have heard of such an institution, and among those who care about the arts, few will be aware that Canadians have a national collection of over 20,000 portraits and self-portraits, plus over four million photographs and related pieces. But we do. So why do we still not have a portrait gallery, which is surely one of the more benign, overt, and public expressions of individual and national biography?

When it comes to the visual arts, I suspect that one answer to this question lies in our national obsession with land, landscape art, and the physical spaces of geographical regions, but as I suggested at the beginning of *this* biography, Canadians are also reticent about themselves; they harbour deep-seated reservations about the self and about displaying images of the self. In this respect, Sharon Pollock is quintessentially Canadian. We (for I really should say we) are reluctant, even skeptical about celebrating ourselves, telling our own stories, or giving artistic expression to individual and national identity. As Sharon has said on many occasions (most recently in "Reflections"), she is uncomfortable with autobiography because "the closer the work comes to [her] ... the more [she] suspects the worth of doing it" (17). We are more comfortable agreeing with Pierre Berton, who believed that we found ourselves as Canadians, en masse and almost anonymously, at Vimy Ridge, where we fought not for Canada *per se* but for the mother countries of England and France.

Despite our rather thin crop of biographies and autobiographies, and our lack of awareness about Canadian portraiture, and regardless of the reasons I have set forth to explain these absent presences, I am optimistic about the future. I am optimistic because, like the portrait paintings, there are actually more concrete examples of our life-stories out there than we currently realize, and I am optimistic because over the past twenty-five years we have written an increasing number of biographies and produced a few stellar biographers. When I am tempted to become discouraged by absences, I remind myself of Rosemary Sullivan, John English, François Ricard, Claude Bissell, Sandra Djwa, Paul Wyczynski, or of Ira Nadel, Kevin Bazzana, and Paula Sperdakos. We are developing a significant body of biographical evidence, which includes a few of our artists. We are also beginning to pay attention to Canadian women artists of distinction such as Atwood, Carr, Johnson, Laurence, MacEwen, and Watson. What's more, our best biographers have placed their subjects' lives in a rich narrative context of time and place; they have told a larger, collective, national story by telling us about Gwendolyn MacEwen, Gabrielle Roy, Harold Innis, Pierre Elliott Trudeau, Leonard Cohen, and Glenn Gould. And we have produced some innovative forms of biography in plays like R.H. Thomson's *The Lost Boys*, comic-strips like Chester Brown's *Louis Riel*, memoirs and autobiographies like Margaret Atwood's *Moral Disorder*, Charles Comfort's *Artist At War*, Mary Pratt's *A Personal Calligraphy*, or Mavor Moore's *Reinventing Myself*, and in what I call composite biography. My favourite example of this form is Sandra Gwyn's superb *Tapestry of War* in which she speaks in her own voice to tell us the stories of a few famous and not so famous Canadians who lived through, or died in, the Great War. The wider landscape of Gwyn's composite (auto)biography is a multi-faceted portrait of Canada with a complex, moving story about the nation at a critical period in its history, about what it meant to be Canadian at that time, and how that period from the past continues to affect our national story.

The field in which we are most grievously lacking biography is theatre, and through the writing of Sharon Pollock's biography I have found myself wrestling with two questions. What, if anything, is distinct about the craft of biography for a playwright (or a major director or artistic director like Christopher Newton) that is not relevant to the life-story of a politician, scientist, military man, or poet? What, that is specific to the theatre and to theatre history, does a playwright's biography have to tell us about our time and place, about culture in Canada, and about being Canadian? My answers to the first question are still cautious and tentative, but my answer to the second question is simple and unequivocal: a lot. As I hope this biography demonstrates, a major playwright's life holds a mirror up to geography and history, first and foremost because it is a life lived publicly—the playwright will not exist professionally unless other theatre professionals (and amateurs) produce her or his plays, and a play will not be produced unless the public comes to see it. Theatre is a communal art form, brought to life by a team and shared in performance with a live audience; thus, what is selected for a theatre season, as well as its success with audiences and reviewers, says much about current social attitudes and personal tastes. A playwright's biography also con-tributes to the understanding of a larger communal, national, and human story in especially incisive ways when the playwright reflects upon and dramatizes significant events from a personal or public history. I am not thinking narrowly of history plays but of those great plays that take important private or public human stories and transform them into mean-ingful art—Shakespeare's *King Lear*, Goethe's *Faust*, Ibsen's *Ghosts*, Chekov's *The Cherry Orchard*, Shaw's *Major Barbara*, O'Neill's *Long Day's Journey into Night*, Beckett's *Waiting for Godot* (which showed my generation so much about our lives), Brecht's *Mother Courage*,

Pinter's *The Homecoming*, Tremblay's *Les Belles Soeurs* (which spoke to women of my generation in Canada as few other plays would do), Highway's *The Rez Sisters*, Pollock's *Doc* and *Fair Liberty's Call*, Churchill's *Cloud 9*, and Frayn's *Democracy*.

Trying to discover and then capture in my narrative exactly what might be distinct or special about the biography of a playwright has been more difficult. I am intuitively aware that there are real differences between, say, writing Pollock's biography and writing Atwood's or Trudeau's or even Gould's, and this difference does not depend on whether the biographee is alive or dead. Gender matters greatly here, but so do the artefact and the archive, and something about the art of theatre and playwriting sends up warning signals to a biographer who seeks to confirm facts and reach beyond illusion to something we call *reality*. Let me put gender aside for the moment to consider artefact and archive because the profession of playwright does not produce reliable or definitive artefacts, and a playwright's archive, while invaluable, is partial and misleading in important ways. If a biographer begins from the premise that the biographee must have a life worth writing about and, when the biographee is an artist, there must be a significant oeuvre that makes the artist important, then the artefacts of a playwright's life—the plays—are extremely slippery and evanescent. If you miss the premiere of a play, you miss it, period. The moment or hours can never be recaptured or repeated; each performance night will be different in subtle ways, and each new production will be different in obvious, even strategic, ways. Unlike a painting, a novel, or a poem, a play escapes a biographer's grasp. We can, of course, discuss the published text, which I have done, but such a discussion is limited by the fact that no play exists on the page the way other literary genres do. We can also consult reviews or watch videos of performances or study production photographs, but each of these ways of approaching live theatre only reminds us about how much we are missing. The problem faced by a playwright's biographer quickly resolves itself into an impossible task of recreating and discussing a vanished artefact by locating its traces, fingerprints, and absences.

But what about the playwright? Where in this realm of performance and illusion is she? And does the fact that a playwright has also been a director of and an actor in her own plays further complicate the question? If the artist is still alive and is co-operative, a biographer will shift into interview mode, or will ensconce herself in the archive, assuming the subject has organized his or her papers and sold them to a library. However, all archives have innumerable limitations, gaps, and unacknowledged (but very deliberate) structures, and in this sense the archive is no different for a politician, playwright, or poet. Sometimes archival materials are restricted and the owner of the archives will have decided what to include and what to withhold—this letter will be included, but not that one; this draft can be seen, but not that one. What is different for a playwright is the status of the creative works contained in the archive. Drafts of a play tell us much but never the whole story because a play will be changed in minor or even major ways by the director, actors, and designers who mount it and by the logistics of the physical space and resources available for performance. Even the most controlling of playwrights—Beckett or O'Neill—are overruled, after their deaths, by the exigencies and realities of theatre production. And that is exactly as it should be with theatre.

There is another aspect to this quixotic endeavour called biography that worries me. While it may be true that all human beings are, to varying degrees, self-conscious performers—Trudeau with his rose sliding down banisters or giving the Canadian public the finger certainly was—playwrights are often skilled, professional performers. A playwright, I suspect, knows more about creatively pushing the "theatrical envelope" (as Sharon would call it) and manipulating story, back-story, character, and visual and aural effects, than most of us, including consummate, canny escape artists like Atwood or the best actors. It is not just that the playwright/actor/director plays roles (we all do that some of the time) but also that he or she *creates* roles through convincing, fictional characters who must be embodied, live, on stage. The better the professional playwright, the more powerful, numerous, and *authentic* the roles. I do not know, or have not yet discovered, how or where to draw the line between what Virginia Woolf described as the "six or seven selves" that comprise a "complete" biography, the "thousand" selves that a biographee may have, and those many other performed selves that are and *are not* the playwright, but are most certainly the playwright's stock-in-trade.

In the case of Sharon Pollock, three performance moments stand out vividly for me, but they are not scenes from her plays. The first of these moments occurred in April 2000. We were having breakfast together when I told her I wanted to write her biography. She immediately responded that such a thing should be done, but then she paused before adding that, in her case, the story should also be the story of Canadian theatre and of her life as part of that larger story. She did not laugh at me, and she most certainly did not refuse to allow me to carry on with my chosen task. Instead, she peered at me over her glasses for several seconds, half-sighed, half-groaned (a uniquely Sharon sound that I have often heard since and have come to realize translates—depending on the inflexion of the groan—roughly as: aahhh, that's an idea to ponder, or good Lord what next?) and changed the subject. She is never at ease talking about herself. The second moment took me by surprise. Towards the end of that February 2004 theatre and auto/biography workshop, after I had spoken about writing her biography while she sat in the audience listening, she rose to her feet and declared, quite cheerfully, that I would never know her, that even her children did not know her. She put this in kindly terms ("I love Sherrill but ... "), and one of her children, Melinda, was also in the room listening to her mother's comments. Of course, Sharon had simply spoken the truth: one person can never *know* another; indeed, we can never fully know ourselves. But Sharon's declaration reminded me, not only of Virginia Woolf's observation, but also of the profession of my subject, who was also an actor and a director. I came away from that scene wondering if I was becoming nothing more than a Pirandellian figment of my own imagination, or, more unsettling still, a character in Sharon's carefully crafted and directed script. Perhaps I had been cast as the Actress opposite Sharon's Lizzie Borden, which is not a reassuring thought!

However, moments one and two were intriguing, even enjoyable, compared with moment three, which remains disconcerting. During her Edmonton radio interview in December 2004—the one where the garrulous talk-show host kept pestering her about gender—Sharon pronounced that a book about a woman written by a man carried more authority than a book about a woman written by a woman. If that is true, then where does that leave Sharon's biographer and what, more importantly, does that mean for *this* biography? Was she saying that I was wasting my time because nothing I said about her would carry much weight? Or was she actually talking about something else altogether, such as the sexist biases of our culture (notably, in light of this radio-show occasion, our media), about some of her own plays which explore the life-stories of strong women, or about what she sees as the unnecessarily deep divides between men and women. I have continued to reflect on this comment by reminding myself that I am a woman writing about a woman. Moreover, I am writing about a very strong woman who has succeeded in a heavily male-dominated profession that Virginia Woolf saw as the one most closed to women.

Sharon has always been cautious about making categorical feminist statements, and she has also been very clear regarding her personal ambivalence about being a woman or creating female characters in her plays. Nevertheless, she recognizes that all aspects of professional theatre are dominated by men and that the canon of major playwrights is almost exclusively male. I believe that Sharon's reluctance to adopt, or certainly her qualified identification with, twentieth-century feminisms (for there are many), stems from two realistic considerations. Being Sharon Pollock, she is aware of the many sides to any position or argument as well as the complex nature of human experience, and being an artist, she refuses to have her work limited by a label or slotted into one category or another. She also knows and has always accepted the fact that to succeed in the theatre a playwright *must* rely on and work with others and that the great majority of those others will be men, many of whom are very talented. At the beginning of Sharon's career, men in positions of influence recognized and encouraged her talent, and her early professional mentors were men. As the decades passed, she made her own attempts at climbing the theatre ladder, which places the artistic director at the top, and she was, for her time, one of the few women in Canada to succeed in the assault on this bastion of male power. Ironically, when she was forced out of these positions other women played the key offensive roles. As the decades passed, Sharon never forgot who had helped and mentored her, and she has never stopped admiring and praising the many talents of these men, but as her own opportunities to mentor others multiplied she often chose to encourage younger women, while also watching for creative ability in men.

In the public sphere, the status of women in Canadian theatre remains low. When Rina Fraticelli submitted her report in 1982, she described the general lack of female directors, artistic directors (notably in the large, professional Canadian theatres), and produced playwrights as "the invisibility factor," and she published hard statistics to support her claim that women were discriminated against by the Canadian theatre establishment and by the wider system of arts funding and cultural priorities. With the cards stacked against her, Sharon had to establish her career during precisely those years, between 1967 and 1981, which were characterized by a gendered invisibility factor. In the quarter century that has passed since Fraticelli's report, precisely the period during which Sharon would achieve some of her greatest successes, the scenography of Canadian theatre has changed for the better. According to the follow-up study jointly undertaken by Nightwood Theatre, the

Playwrights' Guild of Canada, and PACT, in 2006, 28 percent of produced playwrights were women (compared with 10 percent in the Fraticelli Report), 34 percent of directors were women (compared with the earlier 13 percent), and 33 percent of Canada's artistic directors were women, some of them at the helms of our best-funded, largest, and most prestigious national and regional theatres (as compared with a mere 11 percent in 1981, when most female ADs ran small local companies or children's theatres).[1] When I look at Sharon's career through the optic of gender against the 1981 and 2006 reports for the years 1967 to 2006, I am both cheered and dismayed. On the one hand, she has indisputably reached the top as a playwright with an impressive oeuvre, which continues to be performed at home and abroad, has been translated, is published, and is studied in universities. On the other hand, however, at the peak of her career, she had to run her own small theatre, the Garry, only one of her new plays from the nineties has thus far received a production at a major Canadian theatre—*Fair Liberty's Call*—and only two of her plays from this richly creative period in her life—*Moving Pictures* and *The Making of Warriors*—have received professional premieres plus remounts. Few Canadians outside Calgary, even among those who are active in the theatre, know that she was writing through the nineties and is still writing. They associate her with *Walsh, Blood Relations,* and *Doc.*

No doubt there are other factors at work here besides gender. In Canada, the theatre world is regional, and in general, as I have noted, the theatre world is fickle and audiences are easily seduced by what looks new. Canadian granting councils (as well as other economic and administrative structures) favour the new play and the emerging playwright over the established writer or a new production of a play from the Canadian canon. But issues relating to gender cannot simply be dismissed. Perhaps, with hindsight, it will be possible to measure the ways in which Sharon's career has cleared the way for the next generation of women playwrights in Canada. In any case, I believe that her personal discomfort with labels and gendered explanations for the status quo and her ambivalence about writing roles for women characters, have contributed as much to the gender dynamics in her work and career as any external, systemic pressures. When asked why she did not create leading roles for women in her early plays, she always provides two answers: that the kind of play she wants to write requires action and that, in her early years, she found it difficult to imagine women as dramatically active or interesting characters. Moreover, she could not create women characters until she had come to terms with herself, learned to like herself, and to know herself better. Only then could she channel her creative energies into a Lizzie or a Bob, an Eme or an Eddie, a Shipman or a Zelda.

Although she has not, to my knowledge, ever put the matter quite this way, I believe she had to come to terms with Eloise and with what her mother meant to her before she could begin to respect or trust herself. She had to *forgive* her mother for, in a real sense, abandoning her, and forgive herself for rejecting and disliking this mother. She had to manage her own guilt, and this process took a long time—decades in fact. By growing up, escaping a bad marriage, forging an independent career, then experiencing a mutually loving relationship with a man she respected, and by having five strong, successful, capable daughters, she could plumb the depths of Eloise's nightmare from a position of relative safety, resist any

temptation to follow in her mother's fatal footsteps, and surface with the insight and compassion that helped her to write *Blood Relations, Doc*, and *Getting It Straight*. These plays, in
turn, made it possible for her to imagine the women in *Fair Liberty's Call, Moving Pictures,
The Making of Warriors, Saucy Jack*, and *Angel's Trumpet*. In short, the steps that took her
from facing the pain of loss, rejection, and guilt, which she identified with her mother, to
an essential reparation with that mother achieved in *Doc* and *Getting It Straight* freed her (insofar as one is ever free of the past) to write all the plays that followed, most of which have
superb roles for women as well as men. *Doc* also allowed her to look carefully at a much
loved and admired father, to forgive him his role in Eloise's tragedy, and to understand and
accept the fact that she is very much like him. In her best-selling 1976 book *Of Woman Born*,
Adrienne Rich wrote that "the cathexis between mother and daughter—essential, distorted,
misused—is the great unwritten story" (225). When I asked Sharon if she had read the book,
she said no. At first I suspected that she might have rejected a book with such a title, but now
I think that she did not need to read it because she was preparing herself to write that story
in *Doc*, which means I too have had to grant this play an important, even decisive, place in
my version of her life.

If Eloise E. Chalmers (née Roberts) is the woman behind the woman Sharon Pollock
would become, the absent presence who would haunt her, and the mother who would leave
her fingerprints on her daughter's life, she is definitely not the only such presence, and she
is in no way among the professional *dramatis personae* of her daughter's life-story. The
fingerprints of Eloise's influence lie elsewhere, in Sharon's emotional and psychological
script where I can never fully *know* them. By withdrawing from her daughter and then finally
from life itself into alcohol and suicide, Eloise showed Sharon what *not* to be: a self-
destructive victim. I have often wondered what role, if any, other women of her generation
might have played in prompting, challenging, or supporting her in her determination to
live and succeed. Were the suicides of Sylvia Plath and Gwendolyn MacEwen warnings? Did
she follow the Vancouver newspapers in September 1975 as the details of Pat Lowther's
murder came to light? And if she did, for she was living in the same city at the time, was
keenly interested in the news, and was part of the artistic scene (although poets and
playwrights seldom crossed paths), did she think about this murdered woman writer and
reflect: there but for the grace of God go I? They were of an age (Lowther was born in 1935);
they were just beginning their artistic careers in the early seventies, and they each had several
children to tend while trying to write. More to the point, Sharon well knew what it was like
to live with an abusive husband who seemed to want to kill her. The stark difference between
the two women was that Sharon escaped. Christine Wisenthal does not mention Sharon
Pollock in her 2005 biography, *The Half-Lives of Pat Lowther*, but I find the parallels—except
that crucial one—between their lives remarkable, and what this comparison suggests to me
is that Sharon's defiant response to Eloise's tragedy strengthened her to the point that she
could escape to reinvent herself where many other talented women of her generation could
not.[2]

On the list of professional *dramatis personae* in her story, however, there are very few
women, and among the playwrights there are none. Sharon's primary influences are men,

and her significant, positive, and formative influences are Beckett and Pinter. Beckett's plays reached her in the mid-sixties when she was just starting out and was very receptive, and from Beckett she learned what serious drama could be and how powerfully non-realistic dramatic structures could convey the most common, poignant, and timeless of human dilemmas—loneliness, failure, futility, despair—as well as the cruel and comic twists of fate. Pinter taught her lessons in staging these dilemmas through the manipulation of temporal sequences and through dialogue that suggests unspoken (and unspeakable) truths and ambiguities without naming them. Like Beckett, he too showed her how to work with nuanced words and effective pauses and gestures to achieve her ends. Indeed, when it comes to this business of creating contemporary dramatic language that frequently rises to the level of poetry, Sharon, at her best, is as good as these writers. Both Pinter and Ibsen, and to a lesser degree Brecht and Miller, confirmed for her the vital importance of writing political plays, by which I mean plays that explore the politics of our lives and of human history, a range of social issues of immediate and perennial importance, and the inextricable ties that connect an individual with his or her general context, the private with the public sphere, and the family with the nation. However, in my search for her sources, I can only find faint traces of their fingerprints on her work because, like all the best artists, she has made them her own by transforming their influences or lessons into her individual vision. I could, as a few reviewers and scholars have, compare a Pollock play with a play by a contemporary woman playwright such as Caryl Churchill, Timberlake Wertenbaker, Beth Henley, or Anne Chislett, but these are not the playwrights who have influenced her craft, and if there are women playwrights who I could cast in this role they would be those whose work—like Jean Kerr's *Mary, Mary*—she reacted against. The smudge of fingerprints on Sharon's plays reveals relatively few major playwrights, but I have found ample evidence of a host of other sources, from her work in radio drama, and her keen interest in history, politics, and world events, to her fascination with popular films, television programs, and books about Canadian history, Vietnam, Wounded Knee, human aggression, the prison system, and tales of unsolved murders and infamous murderers. It must also be said that a few women, albeit not playwrights, have played crucial supporting roles in her story: Joyce Doolittle, whose encouragement and skill provided early training and inspiration; Dorothy Jones, who believed in Sharon and her work during the early seventies in Vancouver; Diane Bessai, who midwifed *Blood Relations* into print, thereby securing its place in the canon; Kathleen Flaherty, who put her own considerable talents as director/producer and interviewer at Sharon's service in the nineties; and Cynthia Zimmerman, scholar and editor of the *Collected Works*.

***

As I look back over what I have written and reflect on what I have omitted, I see a few details in my portrait of Sharon Pollock that need further work or at least some minor touching up. This is by no means a matter of airbrushing or overpainting. I have no desire to make her seem better or nicer or less complex and driven than she is or to willfully suppress the facts, although I have chosen to remain silent on some matters. In her essay, "Playwright: Parasite or Symbiont," Sharon addressed the question of ethics in autobiography and biography, as well as in her own auto/biographical plays, and she concluded that for her, as a playwright, "acknowledging ... my theft and manipulation of their lives meets my ethical obligation to them [because] my primary ethical obligation is to the integrity of the work" (299). And so it is for me. Although I have tried, scrupulously, to acknowledge my sources, right down to my own and Sharon's fingerprints, I too have an ethical obligation to the "integrity of the work." This obligation tells me that I cannot end my story without some further observations about Sharon's contributions to our theatre and her position on the rostrum of national and international English-language playwrights.

It is no exaggeration to say that through the seventies and eighties, Sharon Pollock broke new ground and led the way to new pinnacles of achievement for Canadian theatre. She was the first, not just the first woman, to win a Governor General's Award for Drama, and she remains one of the few Canadian playwrights to have three plays produced at Stratford (one of them a world premiere). But productions, prizes, and honorary degrees are only a few of the more visible signs of success. Where her contribution to the theatre is most impressive and lasting is in her plays, in their range of styles and subjects, in their uncompromising, often courageous, exploration of extremely sensitive historical and personal issues, and in what I can only call her vision. Despite the challenges and disappointments in her early private life and her acute awareness of the inequities and injustices of our world, Sharon is an optimist. She is an optimist in that each of her plays gives us something worthwhile to think about, challenges our smug complacencies, informs us about things we should know but might prefer to ignore, and inspires our faith in the moral and creative potential of being human. While some of her characters make bad decisions or selfish choices, none of them is merely evil, and most of them struggle with the responsibility of their own individuality. Unlike Beckett, who I believe is her primary and constant dramatic influence, the playwright to whom she herself grants artistic pride of place, Sharon never depicts the human lot in tones of pessimistic despair or as an utterly bleak affair of life reduced to silence.[3] Her plays are full of vitality, noise, voices (even in a monologue like *Getting It Straight*), argument, and a range of conflicting perspectives, questions, and laughter. She never lets us off the hook; watching, or even just reading, a Pollock play makes us more alive.

As I travelled the country interviewing theatre people, I always asked how they would situate Sharon's work within the Canadian or international English-language canon. In asking such a question I was not anticipating categorical answers—a ranked list of names— as much as insight into what theatre professionals value in a play and a playwright. Those, like myself, who placed her among the very best in Canada, wanted serious, political, epic theatre that jolts us into a heightened awareness of ourselves and our society; they were bored or disgusted with our current surfeit of entertainment and spectacle masquerading as theatre. Those who hesitated, or qualified their praise, described her plays as too overtly political, even preachy, or too conventional; they preferred more cutting-edge, ironic, and innovative kinds of plays. Seeing her work within an international context is more difficult, but again those interviewees who were willing to run with the question mentioned a small number of living playwrights—Pinter, Churchill, Frayn, Shepard, Wertenbaker, Albee, and Nowra—as her peers. The common denominators here are fairly obvious: a willingness to confront important moral and socio-political issues (by which I do not mean agitprop politics and propaganda); a sympathetic yet critical exposure of human strengths and weaknesses; and creativity—the gift of language, the understanding of gesture, the heart and wisdom to imagine convincing characters, and an ability to exploit the medium of live theatre to its fullest, not for the sake of innovation but for the sake of meaningful theatre.

To see Sharon in the round, however, is to look beyond the playwright to the actor, director, artistic director, mentor and friend to many. It is also necessary to see her outside the theatre, as a daughter, wife, and lover, and as a sister, mother, and grandmother. Whichever of these selves she inhabits at a given moment, she is, above all, fully engaged with life, whether she is having an adventure with her youngest grandson, delivering a speech as one of our senior artists, or receiving another honorary degree. She does her grocery shopping, walks her dogs, and reads the daily paper, just like the rest of us. She agonizes over world affairs, the state of contemporary theatre, or the progress she is making with a new script. She drinks too much coffee. She gets too busy, or too preoccupied, to answer her mail and phone messages. She drives, well, absent-mindedly, gesticulating, talking, and on occasions I recall vividly, detailing the horrors of driving with one or another of her daughters who will speed along, chatting on a cell phone, balancing coffee, answering the children, and chastising the dogs. Like mother, like daughter. In her seventies she is a woman full of energy, surrounded by love, which she happily returns, and yet she is still angry, still driven to speak out and to create, still determined to make a difference in the world through art. The anger, which has its roots in that gracious house on Grey Street in Fredericton, has been both a curse and a blessing because it inspires and focuses her attention. She can be almost shockingly direct and frank, and she can be overbearing and intimidating, but she can also be painfully shy and insecure. She is one of the most opinionated and formidably intelligent people I know, but she is also at times awkward, anxious, and vulnerable. She can be abrupt, abrasive, and argumentative, but she is also generous, thoughtful, and extremely loyal. She is funny. Yes, indeed, she is funny in the sense that she is quick to see the ridiculous side to life, including her own, and her laughter, which is hearty, is seldom directed at others. Her funniest stories are the ones she tells on herself.

It is impossible, of course, to capture such a person in a biography. But then biography, as Elinor Langer reminds me, "is not taxonomy with the specimen to be reclassified according to the latest findings—it is the story of one life as seen by another, with both always growing and changing" (13). If I have succeeded in presenting those six or seven selves that Virginia Woolf saw as comprising most biographies, then I will rest my case. The real Sharon Pollock has many more selves than I will never know. The *real* Sharon Pollock is alive and well and living in Calgary, where she is still making theatre, and in my life I look forward to sitting beside her once more as someone tells us to turn off our cell phones and pagers, the house lights go down, the audience falls quiet, and the stage lights come up on another Pollock play.

Two early stories by Sharon Pollock: "Things I Like To Do" (1954) and "How Things Are" (1973)

The first of these two stories appeared in *Per Annos* (1954), the school magazine of King's Hall, in Compton, Quebec, the private girls' school that Sharon attended from 1952 to 1954. Sharon wrote both poetry and prose during her school years in Fredericton and Compton, but short essays or essay-like stories, such as "Things I Like To Do," are among her earliest published pieces. This story is not remarkable, but it captures aspects of her personality and style that would characterize the adult, such as her love of cars and of walking and her persistent way of bringing opposites together to develop an idea.

Things I Like To Do

All of us have our "likes" and "dislikes." As long as our "dislikes" never outnumber our "likes" the result is pleasant. If our attitude were the same towards all activities, think how dull life would be! It would be like trying to eat luke-warm soup—not hot enough to give any real enjoyment, not cold enough to be thrown away.

One of my "bowls of hot soup" is walking in the rain at night. As darkness falls and it begins to rain I pull on my raincoat and boots and step outside into another world. A moist breeze greets me and the branches of near-by trees bend and bow to show me their leaves— shiny, wet and sparkling with minute drops of rain. The street, black and glistening, holds small puddles which, instead of carefully avoiding, I slosh through taking secret delight if some of the water enters my boots, for everyone knows that no sound compares with that of sopping shoes in warm rain. I stop and test a shoe by placing my heel on the sidewalk and slowly bringing my toe down. A gentle, soft squi-i-i-sh is heard and with a smile on my face I continue. I am not afraid of the night as I usually am, for to-night it is not dark and mysterious but warm, wet and sparkling. Each tiny droplet of rain catches the lights from the streets and homes as it falls and mirrors happiness and contentment. A car slowly passes me and as it disappears down the street, two red eyes from its back bumper wink coyly at me and are reflected in the glistening road. A cat sitting on the curb gravely contemplates the small leaves and sticks carried by in eddies of water. On catching sight of me she shakes her head and with a complacent air licks one paw. Looking up again to find me still standing there she gives me a curt nod of dismissal and I turn towards home and bed.

Another of my "likes" is entirely different. It requires four friends, one convertible, and a hot, dry day. I put on my bathing suit and hop as quickly as possible over the hot pavement and into the car. Four short stops to pick up passengers, and we're off! The destination is unknown, but the difference between six miles and sixty seems small when you have a day ahead of you to go where you please. Our red, sticky faces are cooled by the brisk breeze blowing into the car, and the radio blares in our ears. Although we have to shriek to be heard above it, no one would dream of turning it down for the same reason that none of us wear kerchiefs on our heads. Our wind-blown hair is snarled and knotted and to-night we will wonder why we did not wear that kerchief, but somehow it would spoil the day. Songs are sung, each person singing a slightly different tune with slightly different words. Each tries to outdo the radio, but doesn't quite succeed, although a wonderful discord is produced.

Suddenly someone sees a sign "Lake George—five miles!" We turn off the pavement and slowly make our way down a dirt road to find a small lake at the end of it. There's a sudden rush from the car to the water, and after an exhausting swim we collapse on the beach. No noise disturbs the silence except the occasional call of a bird from the nearby woods. Each of us lies there, thinking our own thoughts, some wondering at the beauty of the spot we've found, others thinking of what they'll wear to-morrow at the dance. The sun beats down on us; we turn a delicate shade of lobster-red; but what does it really matter?

A scream shatters the silence, a whoop answers it, and the mad rush is repeated, only this time from the beach to the car. The radio blares forth its nasal tones again, the songs begin even more heartily. It takes only a fraction of the time to return, for now we know where we're going. Half the thrill of going away for the day is turning towards home when the day is over. We're home! Four short stops to let off my passengers and then I drive into my own driveway. My mother gasps at my beet-red face and tangled hair.

"Did you have a good time, dear?"

"Uh-uh."

"Where did you go?"

"O-o-o-o-oh, I don't know—some lake or other, I guess."

I dash upstairs and Mother thinks it has been just another day. I know differently. If it weren't for days like this, what would be the adventure in being young? Indeed, if it weren't for likes and dislikes what would be the adventure in living?

SHARON CHALMERS, MATRIC

© SHARON POLLOCK

"How Things Are," written in the late sixties or early seventies, was published in 1973 by *The Fiddlehead*, a literary magazine begun in 1945 with editors from the University of New Brunswick and St Thomas University. The magazine continues to publish poetry, fiction, original drawings, and reviews, and in the winter 1973 issue there were poems by writers who have since become major figures on the Canadian literary scene—Robert Kroetsch, Anne Marriott, Susan Musgrave, and Alden Nowlan. "How Things Are" is distinguished by its economy, complex, understated emotion, and its disturbing glimpse into a child's world and the past.

How Things Are

Have you ever noticed how we prefer children resembling the young of household pets? Cuddly and cute. Pert, you might call them, with wide, expressive eyes, small noses, and winning ways. I suppose that's why infants in furry coats are so appealing.... The child I met last summer was not like that. Had I been in Ireland and approached by such a creature, I would immediately have categorized her as one of the "little people" and put out a bowl of milk. A characteristic of children of the poor is the look of the leprechaun with iron-poor blood. That she had. The prematurely old face belying an immature form. Sharp nose. Pinched mouth. Eyes leaden and dull I thought, until I caught the cautious look she cast about, and then, as she met my glance, I saw that acuity dart away and hide beneath passive pupils.

I had stopped early that day. You had to, to be sure of a camp-site for the night. The sun was high and hot. I sat on a stump and stared at the leaves dappled dark green and lime, the redwood table bright with shellac, the chalky pebbles outlining my temporary home, and the everpresent galvanized garbage can. I was deep in what my mother would term "a brown study."

The loud hum of wasps exploring the garbage can in a desultory fashion formed the only sound. By focusing carefully, I could see into the bordering undergrowth. With my magic microscope eyes in my brown study, I viewed tiny black beetles with crunchy backs depositing opalescent eggs in the dark earth, and large ants carrying larger burdens of dear departeds. I sniffed the fenny smell hovering on the very edge of the grey-white gravel.

I didn't hear her approach. She seemed to spring out of the no where into here, and I was first aware of her when she spoke, breaking my self induced stupor.

"What're you starin' at?"

The voice was flat, expressionless, and harsh, hardly a welcome intrusion.

"Eh?" I turned, at first saw nothing, and then distinguished, standing in the shadows outside the whitish margin, a small slight figure.

"You're starin' at somethin'."

A statement of fact. Whoever spoke seemed little interested in whether I replied or not, which I did, with a rather uncommunicative, "Oh."

"I been watchin' ... I seen you."

"Oh. Well. I wasn't really ... I was.... " I tried shading my eyes hoping for a better look at my interrogator, but it did no good.

Then she stepped onto the gravel and into the sun, squinting and screwing up her face. "You was awful quiet. I seen you sittin' here, starin' and being so quiet. So I came over."

Poor thing, so pale and drawn, as if she, like my beetles and ants, spent too much time hidden from the sun, and preoccupied with an oppressive reality.

A-ha, thought I, pity is a poor foundation upon which to build a friendship; it's doubtful if it serves any better as causation for conversation. (I am prone to such ornate musings.)

The gnome-child drew nearer to me. She began, "Are you ... " hesitated, then plunged onward, "are you feelin' sad? Cause I can go, if you feel sad ... if you want me to."

I studied her, then it struck me. There's "a wrinkle in time." She's fallen out of Dickens' England.

At first glance you might assume that her skin's greyish cast would disappear with a good scrub. Closer scrutiny indicated the need for something more than soap and water to dispel the pallor. Her hair was clean and combed, but exceedingly thin and baby-fine. The hem of her dress just cleared the knees, which, because of their protrusion, gave the general appearance of grapefruit supported on popsicle sticks. And whoever heard of hollow cheeks on a child of six?

"Are you?"

"Am I what?"

"Are you sad?"

"No, I'm not sad," said I, filling with an immense sadness.

What the hell. Frank Lloyd Wright made a name for himself building a hotel on sinking sand. What could be worse foundation than that?

I smiled at her, and she smiled back; both efforts were rather second-class surface smiles, but you have to start somewhere.

"What's your name?"

"Phyllis. Do you know what?" Her voice gained a little animation.

"What?"

"We was shopping just now. And on the way back we saw an accident. Did you know that? A motorcycle went round a corner and hit this here car."

"That's too bad."

"Yeah. There was a lot of blood."

"I bet."

She remained standing very close to me and staring into my eyes. Silence fell for a few seconds while I gazed into her enigmatic pupils. Did she find my gloss, shadow, and mascara as inscrutable as I found her shuttered eyes? The idea made me faintly uncomfortable, and I broke the sonorous hush.

"People should be more careful."

"It was his head ... and one of his legs was funny. What was you starin' at when I came over?"

I had to laugh at her persistence.

"Bugs, I guess. I was thinking."

"What were you thinkin'?"

"I don't know. Where do you come from, Phyllis?"

"We been campin', oh, for a long time now. We're movin', and when Pops finds work, well, that's where we're gonna come from."

"Are you tired of camping?"

"My mum is…. Last place we come from was Minto. That's far away."

My heart gave an extra pit-a-pat, and my stomach, a slight churn. I had passed the old Rambler with the New Brunswick plates on the way into the campsite. It's strange how one always picks out plates from home. I can spot them a hundred yards away. I risk life and limb, plus two demerits for tail-gating to confirm my suspicions. Occasionally I'm disappointed when it turns out to be Saskatchewan or Florida, but as a rule, I'm dead on. New Brunswick plates have emanations for me.

I had passed that old Rambler, noted it loaded to the gunwales; I had followed it far too closely attempting to read the name and location of the garage at which it had been purchased, and I had scanned the elderly man driving on the off-chance he might be familiar. All to no avail. (It has never been to any avail; however, I keep on.)

I smiled, a first-class smile this time, and felt a great warm wash of Maritime kinship sweep over me and roll like an Atlantic breaker towards my scrawny little confrere.

"I know Minto," I said, with far more emotion than the situation called for.

She continued to stare solemnly into my face. I caught a flicker of something—she was probably wondering how anyone who knew Minto could wax enthusiastic about it. I tried to explain.

"You see, I come from New Brunswick too. I haven't been home for years and years … and when I meet anyone from there … "

She gave all her attention to scratching a mosquito bite at the top of her arm as if my display of sentimentality was a lapse she'd prefer not to witness—or perhaps she simply found it uninteresting; I couldn't tell.

I finished with a feeble, "Well … I … like to talk to them."

She glanced up at me, then quickly turned away. In that fraction of a second, our eyes met. It was as though someone had dealt me a crushing blow to the chest.

Can you imagine the sensation experienced when, after lying in bed convincing yourself it's the wind and that same old squeak in the hall, a shadow falls on your bedroom door?

Or conceive that moment when, after countless nightmares of falling elevators, you actually step into one, watch the door slide shut, and feel the cable slip?

I shut my eyes.

I don't believe in souls. How can I say I saw her soul?

I felt … her mute anguish at how things are, and a sick yearning for how they ought to be.

I saw a little wild thing, not like my fluffy kitten prancing serenely under the most belligerent dog's nose, but more like the timid field mouse for whom the beating of the owl's wings is never far off.

When I opened my eyes, she stood in the shadows on the road, her hand in the hand of a man stooped and grey. She didn't speak, but raised her arm and gave a small wiggle to the fingers.

The man inclined his head. She may have smiled.

They turned slowly and walked away. I could barely make them out, and in a few steps they had disappeared completely.

Perhaps they've never been, I thought.

I wish I could believe that.

© SHARON POLLOCK

The Garry Theatre, 1992–1997

The Garry Theatre, at 1229 9th Avenue S.E. (known as Atlantic Street), in the Inglewood area of Calgary, was a 250-seat theatre located in the building of a former neighbourhood cinema. Its box office telephone number was: 233-9100, and ticket prices ranged from ten to twelve dollars during main seasons. The original cinema opened in 1936, but by the 1950s it had deteriorated into a porno-movie house under names like the Rialto or Hyland International. Pollock took it over in 1992 when John and Oreal Kerr bought the property so it could be renovated into a live theatre. It opened its first season in October 1992 and closed in May 1997. After the Garry Theatre Company closed, Loose Moose occupied the space. By 2004 the building was slated for demolition, but it has survived into 2007 as a design space.

During its five years of life, the Garry Theatre offered five main seasons with six plays per season. They also offered seasons of summer shorts, children's plays, and revues. When the company was not using the theatre, they rented the space to a wide range of community and cultural events, from bible meetings to concerts. The Garry Theatre Company employed many non-equity actors, some amateurs, and some university theatre students, as well as some Actors' Equity members. All information provided below has been drawn from house programs, posters, and photographs in the files held by K.C. Campbell or from reviews of shows in the *Calgary Herald*. It is a pleasure to thank K.C. Campbell (Kirk) for sharing his files with me, Sharon, Tim Culbert, and Alyson Pauley Culbert for their memories of the Garry years, and Sharon and Kirk for reading this summary of the Garry years and making additions and corrections to the record.

ARTISTIC DIRECTOR: Sharon Pollock

PRODUCTION AND GENERAL MANAGER: K.C. Campbell (Kirk Pollock)

MEMBERS OF THE COMPANY

(*not all members stayed for the full five years and other directors and actors occasionally worked for the theatre*): K.C. Campbell, Tim Culbert, Mark Dawson, Jarvis Hall, Craig Hansen, Jeff Jenkins, Robert Kirik, Kristian MacInnes, Alyson Pauley, Bill Preston, Sharon Pollock, Trevor Rueger, and Christopher Youngren.

Main productions by season:

1992–1993

Billy Bishop Goes to War by John Gray and Eric Peterson
DIRECTOR: Sharon Pollock
OPENING: 22 October 1992
CAST: Brian Brennan (at piano) with Grant Linneburg (Billy)
SET AND LIGHTS: Terry Gunvordahl

The Other Side of the Pole by Stephen Heatley, Marney Heatley, and Edward Connell
DIRECTOR: Sharon Pollock
PREMIERE: 17 December 1992
CAST: Paul Cowling, Katharine Venour, Duval Lang, Jane Husak, Yvonne Friedrich, and Lyle St. Godard
SET: Jarvis Hall; Music: Valerie Pearson

The Tomorrow Box by Anne Chislett
DIRECTOR: Chris Youngren
OPENING: 21 January 1993
CAST: Judith Betzler, James Charal, Jim Cox, Val Planche, and Alison Whitely
SET: Brad Leavitt; Lights: Craig Hansen

Macbeth by William Shakespeare
DIRECTOR: Sharon Pollock
OPENING: 18 March 1993
CAST: Paul Cowling, Brenda Finley, Jim Leyden, Dean Dobirstein, Lyle St. Goddard, Gail Whitehead, Estelle Dickinson, Carol Douglas, Esther Purvis-Smith, Darcy Johnstone, Alan Van Sprang, Stephen Spender, Richard Cox, Michael Hentges, Teresa Cook, and Joel McNichol
SET AND LIGHTS: Craig Hansen; Music: Doug Berquist
COSTUMES: Helena Armstrong

Jack's Daughters by Patricia Cornelius
DIRECTOR: Sharon Pollock
OPENING: 22 April 1993
CAST: Jane Husak, Katharine Venour, and Catherine Myles
SET: E.E. Roberts*; LIGHTS: Craig Hansen

---

* E.E. Roberts was the maiden name and initials of Eloise Elizabeth Chalmers (Sharon Pollock's mother) who died in 1954. When this name is given for a Garry set design, it actually refers to design work done by the Garry design team, which included K.C. Campbell, Sharon Pollock, Tim Culbert, and Craig Hansen. The house program identified Roberts as follows: "E. E. Roberts is a recent newcomer to Calgary. He's worked with numerous amateur and semi-professional theatre companies in Canadian cities in which he's resided. This is his first venture in Calgary and he's happy to be working with the Garry Theatre in Inglewood."

Death in the Family by Sharon Pollock
DIRECTOR: Rick McNair
PREMIERE: 3 June 1993
CAST: Sharon Pollock, Tim Culbert, Alyson Pauley, Peter Strand Rumple, and
    Fred Kakish
SET: E.E. Roberts; LIGHTS: Craig Hansen

1993–1994

Come Back to the Five and Dime, Jimmy Dean, Jimmy Dean by Ed Graczyk
DIRECTOR: Christopher Foreman
OPENING: 8 October 1993
CAST: Katrin Bowen, Mary Hennigan, Katrina Perry, Ann Ray Poulsen, Allison Smith,
    Andrea Gooding, Diane White, and Cheryl Gooding
SET: Jarvis Hall; Lights: K.C. Campbell

Saucy Jack by Sharon Pollock
DIRECTOR: Sharon Pollock
PREMIERE: 25 November 1993
CAST: Jarvis Hall, Rae Ellen Bodie, Brian Johnston, and Brent Weaver
SET: K.C. Campbell; Lights: Craig Hansen
COSTUMES: Christopher Foreman

Agnes of God by John Pielmeier
DIRECTOR: Christopher Foreman
OPENING: 5 January 1994
CAST: Rae Ellen Bodie, Katrina Perry, and Sharon Pollock as Dr. Livingston, the
    psychiatrist
SET: K. C. Campbell; LIGHTS: Craig Hansen

Nurse Jane Goes to Hawaii by Allan Stratton
DIRECTOR: Paul Gélineau
OPENING: 10 February 1994
CAST: Carol Douglas, Jim Dobbin, Ania Danylo, Tim Culbert, and
    Trevor Rueger
SET: Jarvis Hall; Lights: Jeff Collins

Headin' Out by K.C. Campbell
DIRECTOR: K.C. Campbell
PREMIERE: 16 March 1994
CAST: Sharon Pollock as Frances, Tim Culbert, and Darrin Myers
SET: Darrin Myers and Leah Van Loon; LIGHTS: Craig Hansen

Death of a Salesman by Arthur Miller
DIRECTOR: Sharon Pollock
OPENING: 21 April 1994
CAST: Douglas MacLeod, Mary Hennigan, Trevor Rueger, David Chapman, Robert Kirik, Teresa Cook, Stephen Eric McIntyre, Bob Armstrong, Darrin Joncas, Nicole Libin, Lesia T. Bear, and Chris Kelly
SET: E.E. Roberts—"After a brief stint in Vancouver looking for work and finding none, E.E. returns to The Garry where audiences may remember his former designs for *Jack's Daughters* and *Death in the Family*."
LIGHTS: Tim Culbert

1994–1995

Loot by Joe Orton
DIRECTOR: Sharon Pollock
OPENING: 11 October 1994
CAST: Tim Culbert, Trevor Rueger, Robert Kirik, Shari Wattling, and Mark Dawson
SET: K. C. Campbell; LIGHTS: Craig Hansen

The Komagata Maru Incident by Sharon Pollock
DIRECTOR: Sharon Pollock
OPENING: November 1994
CAST: David Chapman, Jarvis Hall, Nicole Kelly, Viktoria Koganova, Tim Culbert, and Alyson Pauley
SET: K.C. Campbell; LIGHTS: Craig Hansen

One Flew Over the Cuckoo's Nest adapted by Dale Wasserman (1963)
DIRECTOR: Sharon Pollock (assistant director, Alyson Pauley, took over)
OPENING: 12 January 1995
CAST: Sharon Pollock as Nurse Ratched, Tim Culbert, Robert Kirik, Mark Dawson, Alyson Pauley, Jon Raitt, Cindy O'Neill, Joseph Tulley Kerr, Jennifer Peterson, David Chapman, Dan Jones, Rick Brien, Michael Cornish, Greg Schneider, Stephen Massicotte, Big Bear Keewatincappos, Nicole Kelly, and Diane White
SET: K.C. Campbell; LIGHTS: Craig Hansen

The Diary of Anne Frank by Frances Goodrich and Albert Hackett
DIRECTOR: Ania Danylo
OPENING: 23 February 1995
CAST: Mauri Bell, Eric Moseley, Stanley Argue-Simes, Jennifer Holder, Lorette Clow, Stan A. Simes, Sandra Seltsam, Cara Mullen, Jon Raitt, Kevin Chinook, Ryan Belshaw, and "30" (the cat)
SET: K.C. Campbell; LIGHTS: Craig Hansen

Saint Joan by G.B. Shaw
DIRECTOR: Sharon Pollock
OPENING: 4 May 1995
CAST: Mark Dawson, Robert Kirik, Ravonna Dow, Trevor Rueger, Bob Armstrong, Michael Cornish, Brent Weaver, Stephen Massicotte, David Chapman, Chris Kelly, Rick Brien, David Laplante, Tim Culbert, and Darryl Leigh Pollock
SET: Jarvis Hall; LIGHTS: Mark Hansen

Highway #2, the Great Divide by Paul Gélineau, Janet Hinton, and Sharon Pollock
DIRECTOR: Sharon Pollock
PREMIERE: 15 June 1995
CAST: Mark Dawson, Robert Kirik, Alyson Pauley, Trevor Rueger, and Shari Wattling
SET: E.E. Roberts; LIGHTS: K.C. Campbell

1995–1996

Gaslight by Patrick Hamilton
DIRECTOR: Sharon Pollock
OPENING: 7 September 1995
CAST: David Chapman, Alyson Pauley, Kathleen Roach, Jane Husak, Jon Raitt, and Mark Patton
SET: E.E. Roberts; LIGHTS: Craig Hansen

Salt-Water Moon by David French
DIRECTOR: Jeff Jenkins
OPENING: 12 October 1995
CAST: Rowan Fisher and C. Adam Leigh
SET: K.C. Campbell; LIGHTS: Craig Hansen

Dracula by Patrick Deane and John L. Balderston
DIRECTOR: Sharon Pollock
OPENING: 16 November 1995
CAST: Michael Cornish, Julie Hamilton, Mark Paton, Michael Shepherd, Jane Husak,
    Andrea Gooding, Robert Heimbecker, and Tim Culbert
SET: K.C. Campbell; LIGHTS: Craig Hansen
MUSIC: Darin Gregson; VOCALS: Julie Duerichen

The Killing of Sister George by Frank Marcus
DIRECTOR: Christopher Youngren
OPENING: 11 January 1996
CAST: Sharon Pollock as June Buckridge/Sister George, Jane Husak, Lorette Clow, and
    Ania Danylo
SET: K.C. Campbell; LIGHTS: Craig Hansen

Danceland by Glen Cairns
DIRECTOR: Jarvis Hall
OPENING: 22 February 1996
CAST: Jennifer Webber, Douglas MacLeod, Michelle Morros, and John Stewart
SET: Mark Dawson; LIGHTS: Brian MacNeil

Of Mice and Men by John Steinbeck and George Kaufman
DIRECTOR: Sharon Pollock
OPENING: 18 April 1996
CAST: Jarvis Hall, Tim Culbert, Rob Kirik, Michael Cornish, "Woozle" (the dog), Trevor
    Rueger, Ravonna Dow, Mark Dawson, Randy Lawrence, John Stewart, and Alfred
    Connolly
SET: Garry Design Team; LIGHTS: Brian MacNeil

1996–1997

Lion in Winter by James Goldman
DIRECTOR: Sharon Pollock
OPENING: 12 September 1996
CAST: Tim Culbert, Melanie Windle, Rob Kirik, Matt MacDonald, Kevin Chinook, Trevor
    Rueger, and Sharon Pollock as Eleanor of Aquitane
SET: Garry Design Team; LIGHTS: Brian MacNeil

Equus by Peter Schaffer
DIRECTOR: Sharon Pollock
OPENING: 17 October 1996
CAST: Christopher Youngren, Trevor Rueger, Kimberley Faires, Mary Hennigan,
    Leonard Stanga, Diane White, Rob Kirik, Melanie Windle, Aiden Flynn, Rick Biren,
    and Tammy Roberts
SET: K.C. Campbell and the Garry Design Team; horse masks by Dean Bareham of the
    Green Fools Mask Troupe

Luv by Murray Schisgal
DIRECTOR: K.C. Campbell
OPENING: 21 November 1996
CAST: Tammy Roberts, Adam Leigh, and Aiden Flynn
SET: Garry Design Team; LIGHTS: Craig Hansen

Scotland Road by Jeffrey Hatcher
DIRECTOR: Sharon Pollock
OPENING: 9 January 1997
CAST: Robert Kirik, Yvonne Friedrich, Melanie Windle, and Sandra O'Neill Brown
SET: K.C. Campbell; LIGHTS: Craig Hansen

A Moon for the Misbegotten by Eugene O'Neill
DIRECTOR: Trevor Rueger
OPENING: 20 February 1997
CAST: Robert Kirik, Leanne Padmos, and Terry Lawrence
SET: K. C. Campbell; LIGHTS: Craig Hansen

Fair Liberty's Call by Sharon Pollock
DIRECTOR: Sharon Pollock
CO-PRODUCED with Shoestring Co-operative
OPENING: 22 April 1997
CAST: Barbara Campbell-Brown, Catherine Myles, Carmen Distefano, Paul Cowling,
    Christopher Youngren, William Melathopolous, Brad Loucks, and Dave Anderson
    Richards
SET: K.C. Campbell; LIGHTS: Brian MacNeil; MUSIC: Darrin Gregson

The Garry Theatre also ran Summer Shorts and Late Night productions and rented their
space. I have not compiled a list of these shows or rentals but some examples of the Summer
Shorts are: *Lone Star* and *Laundry & Bourbon* by James McClure; *The Zoo Story* by Edward
Albee; *Audience of Animals* by Tim Culbert; *Aquadude* by Mark Dawson; *The Star-Spangled
Girl* by Jarvis Hall; and the *Garry's Own Goon Show*.

Kathleen Flaherty, currently a director/producer with CBC in Vancouver, had worked with Sharon at Theatre New Brunswick in the late 1980s and had produced *Constance* for CBC radio in 1992. She conducted the following interview in Sharon's office at the Garry Theatre in 1994. This interview is unusual because Flaherty is an almost invisible, or inaudible, presence throughout and because she has chosen to juxtapose Sharon's stories about her life with passages from the plays. On the disk, a copy of which Flaherty prepared for me, these passages are not identified, which contributes to their aural quality of existing as voices within Sharon's imagination and memory. Sharon has frequently described her art as deriving from a host of voices inside her head clamouring for embodiment in a play, and this interview, when listened to, captures that artistic origin and motivation quite beautifully. Regrettably, this fascinating portrait of an artist was never aired, and I am grateful to Kathleen Flaherty for sharing it with me and to both Kathleen and Sharon for their permission to print a transcription of it here. The tape was initially transcribed by Michelle La Flamme; my thanks to Michelle for undertaking this task. I have edited the transcription and supplied sources for the quotations from Sharon's plays; these appear in square brackets and refer to *Collected Works*. The title is mine, but it has been approved by its authors.

The Many Voices of Sharon Pollock
—*As interviewed by Kathleen Flaherty*

KATHLEEN FLAHERTY: Many people are familiar with the name Sharon Pollock. More people are familiar with her plays *Walsh*, *The Komagatu Maru Incident*, *Blood Relations*, *Generations*, *Doc*, *Whiskey Six Cadenza*, *One Tiger to a Hill*, and *Fair Liberty's Call*, just to name a few. Big plays with big ideas and strong emotions. Plays about people caught in the defining moments of life—the moments that test them. But Sharon Pollock is not only an award-winning, internationally acclaimed playwright. She's an actor and director. She's an often-quoted commentator on, well, every subject you can imagine. She's a mother, a rescuer of animals, a catalyst. She is visible on our cultural horizon. And she's been controversial for most of the nearly thirty years we have been paying attention because she's articulate, outspoken, and compelling. When I finally met Sharon Pollock in 1988, she was interviewing me for a job at Theatre New Brunswick. I was expecting her to be a bit larger than life—and I guess she is. Meeting Sharon is starting a conversation that has no boundaries of time or subject. In a single sitting you can touch on the Young Offender's Act, interpretations of *Death of a Salesman*, bad television, and fashions in naming children. Some of my favourite evenings in Fredericton—yes, I got the job—were spent with Sharon surrounded by her dozen cats and a couple of the dogs watching video detective thrillers. Sharon naturally could out-predict me on the plot twists ten-to-one. When she left TNB in the middle of winter driving a twenty-foot U-Haul headed for Calgary, her instructions were simple: keep the community outreach programs going, get the school tour out, make the visiting artists feel welcomed and supported, and feed the stray cat that's hanging around the theatre. What you are about to hear [read] are some of Sharon Pollock's words. Most are from a recent interview in her second-floor office at the Garry Theatre in Calgary, the rest are from her plays. They are intended to introduce you to the Sharon Pollock I know—an artist of power and substance and a person of passion, generosity and largeness of spirit.

> (*SFX: Voices montage*)
>
> [*Whiskey Six Cadenza, CW* II, 106–7]

DOLLY: But you're who you are and who you were and who you met and what you did and ...

LEAH: Will ... is ... dead.

DOLLY: He's alive right inside a me, and caught in this picture is a little bit a him, and he's sittin' right over there where we used to sit, and in the mine where he used to work, and if you listen real close, which I know we can't but if we could, you could hear him, things he used to say and would make everyone laugh and you could hear us laughin' too.

LEAH: Why can't you just leave him?

DOLLY: That's what you wanta do, leave everything behind, pretend things never happened. But I don't want to do that and you can't do it either!

> [*Doc, CW* II, 174]

KATIE: I used to pray to God, but I don't anymore. I write it all down in here.

> (*SFX: Drum sound*)

SHARON POLLOCK: I think that every time we recall something even that happened yesterday we are not so much re-creating as creating what that past was. If you have children you know ... you know that. We sit around a table at Christmas or Thanksgiving and talk about something that happened in the past, and everyone around the table has a different version of what it is that occurred. And ... when you write, whether it's your own past or something you've drawn from ... whether history has been the catalyst for it or something you read in the paper ... I don't see any real difference. I only see perhaps an ordering—you know—the choices that you make which are not always rational when you create a work and may be intuitive, but it is in a search for meaning. It's in a search to find significance in something that confused you at the time you experienced it, whether you experienced it through reading, or whether it was something you saw on the street, or whether it was something you lived in your own life; you're looking for a way to encapsulate it and make it significant so it isn't lost, so that you come away from it richer than when you actually just lived it. I think it is a mistake to think that writers create anything from other than the raw material they have to work with, and the raw material they have to work with is their own life.

(*SFX: Voices*)

[*The Making of Warriors*, RADIO SCRIPT, *Airborne*, 105]

Collage: The making of Warriors. The making of Warriors. The making of Warriors. An exploration of—a story about—a personal reminiscence.

WOMAN 1: Come on.

WOMAN 2: Now. Now.

(*SFX: Car driving away. Voices.*)

WOMAN 1: Now listen. I ... I am a white woman. Age? Age 54 ... a little overweight. I don't mind saying that. Well I do but I am so ...

SHARON POLLOCK: Well I did little things in high-school and things like that. And then when I was married I belonged to a community theatre. Ah ... there was a theatre beginning down in New Brunswick, the Beaverbrook auditorium had been built there and there was a small company. A guy by the name of Alex Grey and a woman by the name of Elizabeth Orion, who interestingly enough now heads the Graduate Program at Carnegie Melon. Anyway, she and Alex worked with Joan Littlewood's theatre in England and they opened up a whole idea, you know, of theatre that I had, that was news to me. And then because I had come from a kind of a political background in terms of my father, politics always played a large role in our house and because I then was sort of a single mom and really poor and (*laughter*) ... all of a sudden a whole different *version* of the world started to open up to me. Ahhh, not that I hadn't ... sort of been a good Marxist (*laughter*) from the time I suppose I was about fourteen, but from a theoretical point of view, right? (*laughter*) It was always very important for me to explain to my father why, when the revolution came, how he understood and accepted that if he were shot up against a wall that this was the right thing to do. But then, when I was sort of on my own, all of a sudden, to live, to be desperately poor and living in a house that in the winter time, here in Calgary, the living room literally got ice on the inside of it, it probably had more ice than the ice box had or the fridge had, and then when the Chinook came in your walls would defrost, right? (*laughter*) Ahh and I just, I mean I gradually began more and more to see theatre as a vehicle, I would have said at that time, *for change*. That you would change the world, and that partly explained my starting to write—in a way I started to believe.... Gee, I guess I could change the world doing *Mary, Mary*, but it's going to take a *very* long time. And I started to see the absurdness in a way I used to feel about doing *Mary, Mary* in a one grain elevator town. And I thought oh this is such a powerful experience and ... and why are we desecrating it with *(laughter)* ... when every time I speak on the stage I can't use my own voice. I speak in that kind of mid-Atlantic accent that denoted an actor at that time or a CBC announcer. And I began to form some opinions about what that did to us *(laughter)*: you know? And also because of, I suppose, my personal situation at the time, I wrote because I wanted to understand the world around me. I wanted ... I couldn't understand, I still don't understand, you know, why good people do bad things. We all aspire to be noble and we choose different means. We want the best and yet terrible, terrible things happen in the world, and ... inside myself the conflicting emotions or actions that I might undertake that don't really reveal what it is I desire or even what I want to do.

(*SFX: Children singing*)

[Doc, *CW* II, 189; 172–73; 189]

BOB: The more you do of certain things, the less it seems you do. You fill your time up, my time's filled up. I sit at these tea luncheons, s'always ... sherry. I hate sherry. I never have any sherry. I know what they think, but that's not the reason. I just don't like sherry. No. No sherry. (*beat*) Children are important.

EV: I cared about those little kids! I looked into their faces, and I saw my own face when I was a kid ... was I wrong to do that? So goddamn much misery—should I have tended my own little plot when I looked around and there was so damned much to do—so much I could do—I did do! Goddamn it, I did it! You tell me, was I wrong to do that!

BOB: —everything's working for them and everything can work for me too. I can be them. It isn't hard, I can do it. I can. If I ... if I want to.

SHARON POLLOCK: Growing up in a small town, in a poor province, in a very conservative province, where it seemed to me image was everything, surface counted for a lot and substance not so much ... how you presented yourself to your neighbors who knew everything about you or else they thought they did. And if your own inner life—whether it was inside you or inside the living room or, you know, the closed doors and windows of the house that you lived in—if that didn't conform to what it ... to the image that was presented outside in public ... if the private and the public did not equate.... In my own case, with my father being in that time and place an important man, a doctor who was a priest and a banker and a psychiatrist and a medical savior, who people thought highly of and who I worshipped, I would say, myself.... And yet he was someone whose father had worked for the railroad, who put himself through McGill by playing semi-pro hockey for part of the year, who had first got himself a pair of boots and then hauled himself up by his own boot straps *(laughter)*! You know? Who I sensed never really felt at ease in this circle—the social circle that he moved in, in that town. And my mother who came from a large family in a very small village where all of the resources really went towards her making something of herself as the youngest and the smartest, and she became a nurse, and married a doctor, and made a success of her life. You know: win the golf championship, play wonderful bridge, be President of the IODE, and an alcoholic, who eventually killed herself. And to know what the kind of *truth* was behind all of this and yet see how the outer world viewed, for example, my family. At that time, of course, I probably thought my family was unique, that [with] all the other families on the street their interior matched their exterior. It was only as I grew older that I started to realize that there was probably as much discrepancy there as there was in my family, or some discrepancy at any rate. And to see what I thought ah ... my father was very active politically ... to be aware of how elections were run in that province in the forties and fifties, where you could buy a vote for a pint of rum, where ballot boxes were stuffed, where the day after the election patronage was so pervasive that even people who worked on the road crews didn't bother reporting to work if the other party went in. Anyway, I think that that is what ... that is what informs a lot of my work. And then I do believe that coming to the West, where there is a scope and scale to the environment around you, where the frontier mentality, particularly in the mid-sixties when I first came West, was prevalent, where who you were in terms of your family didn't matter. It was what *you* did that counted. Ah ... nobody knew (*laughter*), in fact, the past of a lot of people; they'd come here from away and, therefore, you created your own. And that really appealed to me. Where it seemed to me there was less discrepancy between what people really thought and what they said. It ended up that some people were labeled red-necks, but it was easier to address someone making a red-neck statement than someone who in fact denies that they feel that way and yet every action they take reveals that, in fact, that is their true philosophy. So there was less façade, I felt. And also the environment itself, that huge sky, the mountains, and the Prairies are a constant reminder of where you stand in the greater scheme of things. Humans are very teeny. Your car can stall on the wrong road at the wrong time of year and you can freeze to death, and if the snow comes you might not be found for a while. And so you're constantly reminded of this force (*laughter*) that is larger than you are, and you're only a bit player with a lot of other bit players.

(*SFX: quiet voices talking*)

[*Whiskey Six Cadenza*, CW, II, 120]

MR. BIG: ... if all mankind could read the skies as I can, do you know what they'd do? They'd never lift their eyes from off the path in front of them! They fear dimension. They live in cracks between the baseboard and the wall in one corner of a mansion whose beauty and proportion is as boundless as the heavenly firmament!

(*SFX: voices gradually getting louder*)

[*Blood Relations*, *CW* I, 393]

EMMA: ... ought not or ought not do.

MISS LIZZIE: Common sense is repugnant to me. I prefer uncommon sense.

EMMA: I forbid her in this ...

[*Constance*, *CW* II, 284]

MALE: ... behaviour and yet reports an obstinacy and passion.

MISS KAYE: Oh yes. Contradiction.

MALE: Where does the truth lie?

MISS KAYE: Truth lie? Oh yes.

[*Blood Relations*, *CW* I, 393]

MISS LIZZIE: You could always leave.

EMMA: If I only—

MISS LIZZIE: Knew.

MISS LIZZIE: ... Emma, do you intend asking me that question from now till death us
do part?

EMMA: It's just—

MISS LIZZIE: For if you do, I may well take something sharp to you.

EMMA: Why do you joke like that!

SHARON POLLOCK: I was drawn to write about not expedient questions but ethical questions. That that constant reminder, because of the natural environment, of something
considerably larger than yourself that made me concentrate on ... on not *how* you do
something but why you do it and then how the how you do it affects the why you do it.
You are not the centre. There *is* something a whole bunch bigger than you are—I
suppose it's a spiritual thing really (*laughter*). I don't know, I just kind of [get a] feeling
that people do strive to be noble. People do strive to achieve ideals. That lives are based
on principles and maybe if you're in downtown Toronto surrounded by manmade
structures, where the natural world, except for the lake, is sort of almost obscured, you
can begin to believe that corporate agendas and money markets and political decision-
making are all based on a kind of pragmatic way to get things done. As soon as you step
outside of that environment and you're in a natural environment that is not man-made,
you start to understand that those are shoddy reasons for doing things. That the end you
choose and the reason why you choose that as a desirable end is horrendously
important. And pragmatism ... oh this sounds really corny—like you can't build a better
world, I don't think, (*laughter*) around ... around pragmatism.

(*SFX: rattle*)

[*Fair Liberty's Call*, *CW* II, 390–91]

GEORGE: That sense of justice and fair play, that's a good thing, but it's got to be tempered with a sense of reality, Eddie. You'll learn.

EDDIE: You don't know who I am or what I think.

GEORGE: 'Course I do.

EDDIE: You think you do but you don't.

GEORGE: What kind of crazy talk is that?

EDDIE: Let's talk about smashin' a man's skull with the butt of my gun, and wipin' his brains off of my sleeve. Or leanin' down from my horse and slicin' a man who's run out of powder, knowin' to stay my arm can mean my own death or the death of my friends. Let's talk about sightin' down the barrel of my gun and seein' the face of a neighbour knowin' I might see the face of my brother sightin' down the barrel of his gun at me! And for what? That's what's crazy!

GEORGE: No more, no more!

MAJOR: There's some things have to be done and we had to do them.

EDDIE: To stop and think then was to die, but now? Now I ask, what did we do it for?

MAJOR: Loyalty to our country, trust in Parliament and the King.

EDDIE: Are they to be trusted?

GEORGE: Eddie—

EDDIE: *You know* nothin' about it and you know nothin' 'bout me.

GEORGE: I'm your father, I know you better than anyone! You sit down, sit down! The rum's gone to your head.

(*SFX: Music fading*)

SHARON POLLOCK: I think that I ... well, this probably sounds really pretentious but I think that one of the terrible traps—and I would say of our time, although God knows it may have been the trap of every time for all I know—is that in recognizing conflicting realities and conflicting truths we have stepped back from the individual responsibility of saying which one we believe in. And so, I feel that there is a difference between recognizing the sincerity with which different people hold conflicting views of the universe and reality and the necessity to believe that yours is the one *true* one.

(*SFX: soundscape with tambourine, drum and emerging collage of voices*)

[*Whiskey Six Cadenza, CW* II, 89; *Constance, CW* II, 276]

MR. BIG: I've mastered the art a seein' the multiple realities a the universe, and more than that. I have embraced them, though they be almost always conflicting but equally true ...

MALE: Do you remember Constance Kent, Miss Kaye?

MR. BIG: —how far is it? Fifteen feet, [...]

MISS KAYE: What?

MALE: I was asking [...]

MISS KAYE: Yes! ... yes yes yes. Yes. I remember. How could I forget? They said ... they
said she ... was a strong and obstinate character, and ... even as child, her ...
nature was ... irritable and—and impassioned.

(*SFX: music*)

SHARON POLLOCK: I'm a believer in that ... kind of ... I don't know, silly little theory perhaps ... that really what I am is ... I have found a way to structure and funnel my madness that allows me to function. Some people who find the world too painful rearrange
it in ways that end up with them being diagnosed and locked up or medicated or ... you
know? And through some quirk of nature, I managed to find a way that, when I look at
the pain and the anguish in the world, I take it in and try to manage it or control it or
transform it, and so I ... I write plays.

(*SFX: Rattle and drum*)

[*Getting It Straight*, CW II, 230–31]

EME: [...] I think
of ubu roi of the nightmares of the blind of the nutcracker suite turned sour I think
of a very large collection of string puppets
hung
in a very small
room
backstage I think
of mime
and
panto-mime
and of
mirrors and of
wings
I think of the layman's guide to Schizophrenia and of
ubu roi
again but I remember camus! I think
of
brown skin and tubercular chests and smallpox
blankets bought from the bay I say
how did you get here?
I think of giants and
of animals that speak and of people who remain
silent I think of cassandra turned inside out I think
of cat scans of the brain of satellite photographs of

the earth I think!
of real
and
unreal
shuffled
like a deck of cards play the hand I say!

SHARON POLLOCK: I think of writing as a political act. I mean if I didn't write I would have to do something else that was more overtly political, like plant bombs or do things that were seen as much more anti-social. And my great good luck was that I was born into a family that ... you know and I went to school, and I was given certain tools. And so it wasn't necessary or, for some reason, I chose not to stick needles in my arm, to shoplift or do any number of other things that would constitute a kind of a destructive act. Because I think of writing as first of all a destructive act, saying this world isn't good enough. Who created this mess? God? Well, I could make a better world that would have much more sense to it than this, and now I am going to sit down and put page one and here's my world I am creating that makes more sense than your world. (*laughter*) You know? So there is an incredible act of ego I think in anyone who [says] there isn't another play in the world that, in fact, has actually said this: although, of course, you don't think like that.

[*Constance, CW* II, 281; *Saucy Jack, CW* II, 323]
MOTHER: (*singing*) "Hi said the little leather-winged bat. I'll tell you ... "
JEM: Knowledge is a terrible thing. It calls for action. And one must act. Or not act and live with that.

[*The Making of Warriors*, RADIO SCRIPT, *Airborne*, 119]
WOMAN 1: To speak in public I—
WOMAN 2: Take courage Sarah.
WOMAN 1: I—
    (*SFX: breathing and singing*)
WOMAN 1: I will speak.

SHARON POLLOCK: I love the inside of theatres, too. And I think there's a reason why Pinter and Mamet and Brecht ... we could go through a lot of people who write for the theatre and have been theatre workers in other areas. And that's the kind of theatre person I think of myself as. I don't want to send the play in and then come in if somebody decides to do it, and then ... and then go away. I want to be ... I want to be there for all of it. (*laughter*).

(*SFX: music rattle and flute*)

[*Getting It Straight*, CW II, 262]

EME: This is the egg talkin' to all members a the female
Sex whether you be operatin' in a corporate world
surrounded by the pressures of the 8 to 4 the 9 to
5 swing shift night shift day shift not forgettin'
those with ambition and drive who aspire to
executive positions slave to the 13 and one half
hour day I'm talkin' to you!
I'm includin' in this call for action all women who toil
in the home the field the factory on and offa the
street in and outa the jungle every race colour
and creed first second and third world, under or
over on top or on bottom the egg is talkin' it's
talkin' to you!
What are you gonna do?
(*beat*)

I say
go to the ladies
go beneath
go under
you'll find others there
I do have this stain on my skirt
but myrna will answer twice on the bus while
you
and I
spin a gossamer net of women's hands and rapunzel's
hair and that net will encircle the globe and if a
person stood on the far left star of the utmost
edge of cassiopia's chair that net would twinkle
in the inky cosmos like fairy lights on a Christmas
tree—and what would it spell?
(*beat*)
what would it spell?
(*beat*)
what would it spell?

SHARON POLLOCK: I never think of my playwriting as serving my acting or my directing, but
I always think of acting and directing as serving playwriting. I think that it's so easy for
playwrights to forget that someone has to live the role you've written. Ah ... and that
you can dismiss really bona fide questions (*laughter*) as a playwright. Or be irritated by

what you think are dumb comments, etcetera. Or you forget that you leave the show, in some respects, after opening night and the actor continues on in that show. And the same thing is true of directing. I mean, I think that I am a better playwright because I direct, and I'm constantly reminded that it's so easy to get word-oriented when you write plays. And actually I think that words—even though I think I write, I can write pretty powerful words, I think—but nevertheless I think that words have lost a lot of their power because they've become the coinage of duplicity and hypocrisy in our world through the world of advertising or ahh ... "collateral damage" for dead civilians. You know, all of those euphemisms that have been created by various corporate or military or, you know, or medical arenas, and so no longer do words have the same power that they used to have. I always think of a word like fluff, for which I used to have an image in my mind of a dandelion when dandelions go from seed and you blow that fluff away. And now the word fluff, in my mind, quite often ... what comes into my mind are sanitary napkins because of advertising ... right? *(laughter)* And the image somehow has been corrupted. The word has been corrupted and now it doesn't have the same meaning to me as it once had. And I have to always remember that the most powerful things on the stage are often things that are not said, but things that are revealed, just as in life you can say anything you like but action *reveals* character. So directing always reminds me of that, always keeps reminding me of all of the wonderful things that you can do on a stage that illuminate or counterpoint text, as we think of it, and that enlarge the meaning of the text. You know, I also like to act because what the actor brings to it ... I think it keeps me open, as a playwright and as a director, to the incredible things that actors can come up with ... and that, and the need to give them *room* to do that. I don't think there's anything more exciting. And usually that excitement, for me, comes sometimes more as a director because you're sort of on your feet, right? But I can't think of anything as exciting as being in a rehearsal and having a major door open in terms of the discovery of something around what it is you're doing, whether it's an actor breakthrough or a moment where somebody just does something and it rings so true. And how energizing that is when you're working on material. And you just come away really invigorated and vitalized by that wonderful discovery. I always think of, you know, and it's been said before, creation is not a destination: it's a journey and there are many ways of taking the trip. And the least interesting way is to get on the Trans-Canada highway. But it isn't too good to sort of go from Calgary to Ottawa via Tiajuana either. You know? *(laughter)* So it's trying ... it's sort of finding all those byways that somehow you're covering the ... you know, you're taking the trip. In fact, I use that in rehearsal hall a lot: "Getting on the train" I call it. And you sometimes get on the train, and you gotta ride the train; you can't get off. I saw you get off at a station 'cuz you were afraid to go on to the next piece of track. But the train will take you there if you'll just get on it and go.

(SFX: *woman singing a lullaby*)
[*The Making of Warriors*, RADIO SCRIPT, Airborne, 125]

MAN: I tell you when Angelina first introduced us, I thought what manner of woman—if women it b—is this?

[*Walsh, CW* I, 81]

WALSH: I've always thought of myself as a man of principle ... Honour, truth the lot ... They're just words, Harry.

SHARON POLLOCK: When I began writing I used to ... I tried to analyse, I suppose in some way, how it is I write, partly because you can get paid for doing workshops and sharing that sort of useless information. So I would look at what it was I did and then kind of try and put that into some kind of form that I could share with other people. At the same time, I always said, you know, that everybody has their own method, so go with your own method. And now, as I get older, I rely much more on the intuitive part of me. I'm only interested in analyzing and being objective after that intuitive self has done whatever it is that it does. (*laughter*) Ahhh ... something is going around that is a question: "How come?" and that is where the intuitive bit comes in. At one time, I might have tried to understand what that question was before I started to accumulate stuff from which a play might grow. Now, I don't bother with trying to figure out what the question is. I just start accumulating stuff, reading whatever I'm moved to read, seeing what my eye catches on the street, recognizing when my mind drifts where it is it drifts to, what kind of people I start to notice, what kind of pictures I start to look at, what kind of things strike me when I sit in a room with a lot of other people, what it is I hear and is important to me, and what it is I'm not interested in, in what people are saying, who it is I notice in the room with me; I just sort of start to track all that stuff and eventually a story will start to grow. It may come out of a character, or a conglomerate usually of something. Or little bits and pieces begin to fill in this sort of puzzle, and at some point I have enough pictures in the puzzle to start to ... I don't know, put them in the box. And then to start to recognize that a lot of blue means it belongs in the box, but a lot of black means it doesn't belong in the box. And I just still don't know what the real picture is; I'm just sort of saying—Oh, some part of me has criteria for this and I know, it knows, what belongs and doesn't belong. And so I keep piling this stuff in the box. And eventually, when I have enough things in the box, I say now I have enough to make a picture, so I start to put the pieces together. Now, before I can start to put the pieces together, like I always say writing the dialogue is the simplest thing. That's the last thing I do. Putting the pieces together means sometimes my having to start to put down on a piece of paper who it is that I think is in the play, and what it is that happens in the play, and at that point I still don't know what the question is that's moving me. And the more I try to *phrase* the question, the more I restrict the possibilities of the question, so I don't want to phrase the question (*laughter*), you know? Because then I've closed off the possible implications, or meanings, or depth of the question, by trying to define it. Then I have to think: I call it "The Gimmick." What's the gimmick? And what ... and then sometimes at universities I say: what's the theatrical envelope, and (*laughter*) what

I'm really talking about is how I tell the story, the structure of the story. Because the story might be three feet long, but I may only be going to tell two inches of it, right? But I need the whole story in order to do the two inches. And how am I going to? ... The order in which I am going to tell, you know, the parts of the story—how I string them on the line, has meaning in itself. So until I come up with the way, the structure, the theatrical envelope, how I'm going to tell the story, I can't write anything. And that's the most difficult part. And sometimes I think it will never happen; it won't come to me. (*laughter*) And almost always it comes to me as a gift ... right? (*laughter*) I'm ... I don't know, cleaning the kitty litter and I have a brilliant piece of insight that's says: Oh my God, this is what happens! The circus sideshow in *Komagatu Maru* ... a kind of the inside out of the rodeo in *Getting It Straight*, and then the kind of the freefall through that. With *Blood Relations*, the exchange of roles by the actress and Miss Lizzie, and the bookending.... So they aren't great profound insights; it's just something, a little hook, that I start to say, Oh. And then, with *Blood Relations*, it's the observer and the observed, and the audience member and the performer, and there's the ramifications of that; so at the same time the play unfolds in *Blood Relations*, you also have the multiple levels of playing with theatre *itself*, and points of view *itself*. And then once I have that, well then, I can write sort of a scenario and a French scene unfolding, and then I just sit down and start to type, right? At that point, then, I can look back and start to say I have ten pages now, okay: Editorial self look at this etc, etc. I imagine by the time I get really old I'll probably think that I'm ... ah, I don't know, an oracle (*laughter*). In other words, everything will be coming to me, you know, through a special rock that I have in the garden.

(*SFX: voices and rattle*)

[*Saucy Jack, CW* II, 322]

JEM: Would an unimpaired intellect recognize it's impairment? Might, perhaps, the failure to recognize be the most compelling symptom of its impairment, everything starts in the home! On the other hand the unimpaired intellect can state with certainty "the intellect is unimpaired." In either case the intellect's assessment is "the intellect is unimpaired" so one can tell nothing from that. It seems the only proof of the soundness of one's intellect would be the firmly held belief that one's intellect is impaired!

SHARON POLLOCK: If your own view of the world is never played back to you, do you exist? Are you *real* in this world? It seems to me, as somebody who lives here, in Calgary, Alberta, and has lived for periods of time, I think, in every province except the North West Territories and, you know, the Yukon and Newfoundland, I feel as if there is a big void in the sense of who we are. That somehow people have been silenced in terms of celebrating and throwing up in the air all of our stories and experience and what significance they have when they're codified (*laughter*), you know? Say, in my own field in the making of plays or performance art. And that until we're able to play back to ourselves who we are in the same way that I write, in terms of trying to find out where I am really and who I am really, that as a, I hate to use the word *nation*, but as a people, that, that's something that's been missing in our lives. That in a way we're barren. And so I see a lot to do in that area. Not because I exactly want to do it. (*laughter*) You know what I mean? More as if I'm, once again I am sort of reluctant to speak those words, but it's almost as if I'm *called* to do it. I can't imagine doing anything else. I look at people on the street, or I read the paper, or I read about our past, or about our present, or I think about people's lives or people call me on the phone trying to sell frozen meat for a freezer, and then they ask me: "Are you Sharon Pollock the person who writes?" and I say, "Yes" and then they say: "I lost my job" and they want to tell me about their life and say: "You should write a play about that because this is what happened to me." And everybody has that story, and often nowadays the stories have to do with what's happening in this country. The kind of commodification of everything. Even people being replaceable parts or, or parts we don't need any more and now they're just chucked out, and I think there is ... this great need for that sense of social cohesion and community, which is in fact one of the greatest feelings you can have—to be part of something larger than yourself, I think. Whether it happens at the Flames game (*laughter*), you know? Or when somebody wins the Stanley Cup. And I feel as if that is missing in my life in terms of a community sense that isn't around sports or organized religion, but just in terms of being who I am here sharing this place with a lot of other people. And so I see a lot to do in trying to find the role that theatre plays in that nurturing of community.

(SFX: *flute and drum*)

SHARON POLLOCK: I think the other thing we have done, of course, is marketed theatre as an escape, right? We celebrate work that disturbs in other countries and we damn it in our own. If not damn it we just make sure it's produced in an inappropriately small hall that would not lead to a major riot, you know? (*laughter*) But that's the other thing that the big halls do, they in fact render impotent disturbing work that happens in them. In the environment of our great culture palaces, the medium is the message and the medium is not just what happens on the stage; it's, you know, the medium happens as soon as you buy the ticket and walk into the lobby. And if you go to see *Mother Courage* or *The Rez Sisters* in the major house in one of our major regional theatres, that environment shapes the experience. It makes it palatable and non-threatening and we can discuss the costumes, you know, and the performances, but the content is safely removed from us. I think the other thing, too, is that people often go to the major houses to have their view of life and times validated—not to have it challenged. And then, when they go to an alternate space, quite often they're open, more open to just the very fact that it isn't their idea of a theatre. (*laughter*). They've already opened a tiny door. Therefore, what can happen in it does not have to conform so rigidly to a preconceived idea of what should occur in that kind of a setting. I think the lack of human scale in major houses is a major problem in terms of an audience, or for people who may be thinking of going to the theatre, but are not regular theatre goers, or have never been to the theatre, you know? That it diminishes you, where in a way, the theatre is saying "Hey every little sparrow that falls" you know ... (*laughter*) means something. Your life is significant. And yet, you go to a place in which the size of everything says you're insignificant. We've had people come in here [the Garry Theatre] who will talk about why they might not go down to the Centre and I find, quite often, their reasons are always interesting. Sometimes they're for reasons that I would not think of like ... one being how hard it is to read the ticket. And then other people will talk sometimes about the difficulty of trying to get into the place. They're always like rabbit warrens, those places. Like if we were rats and it was an experiment in a maze we'd all of us be flunking. I've always sort of thought that they were meant for, you know, as kind of pseudo-shelters of some sort, should the revolution come, that the city council would retreat to over at the Centre for Performing Arts, which has a kind of mediaeval fortressy feel to it; it seems to me. Keys get so important. I went in once to the Centre and they gave me one of those little name tags, you know? I was going for some sort of a meeting, so they ascertained that I had a right to be there and then they gave me one of these little badges you wear. And some place between the time I got there and the time I left I'd lost the badge. And when I came down to leave they said, "Where is your little clip-on badge?" and I said, "Oh dear I've ... I've lost it" and they said to me "You can't leave until you find it" and I said "Good, send out for pizza. Where will I sleep? I am not going to go up and look for that stupid badge for one minute! And I guess I'll just have to live here then," you know? (*laughter*)

[*The Komagata Maru Incident*, CW I, 119]

T.S.: Ladies and gentlemen! It walks! It talks! It reproduces! It provides cheap labour for your factories, and a market for your goods! All this, plus a handy scapegoat! Who's responsible for unemployment? The coloured immigrant!

[*SFX: xylophone*]

[*The Making of Warriors*, RADIO SCRIPT, *Airborne*, 110]

SARAH: I'm so aggravated Thomas because slaves can so read.

THOMAS: No they can't.

SARAH: Well I taught Kitty to read just as you and my brother taught me.

THOMAS: It's against the law to teach readin' and writin' to slaves, Sarah.

[*The Komagata Maru Incident*, CW I, 119]

T.S.: Can we afford to be without it? I say "No!" It makes good sense to keep a few around—when the dogs begin to bay, throw them a colored immigrant! It may sound simple, but it works. Remember though—the operative word's "a few."—For reference, see the Red, the White, the Blue and Green paper on Immigration, whatever year you fancy!

SHARON POLLOCK: I believe there is a place for what I think of as righteous anger. That as a society we've lost the capacity for righteous anger. And I think that anger fuels a lot of work, not just my own. It's anger about how things are and the sense you have of how they ought to be. And if you don't feel anger at that ... I think anger often leads to action, you know? (*laughter*) And if you don't feel anger ... I mean might you feel, I don't know, what might you feel? Sorrow? I don't think of the ... as sorrow perhaps as the ... I think that what we are attracted by is a passionate voice. Maybe not anger but passion. You know, I feel passionate about lots of things and I would feel much more comfortable with that word, in fact, than ... than anger. And sometimes I wonder if anger isn't a Canadian anglophone word to say what Quebecois people express as passion ... (*laughter*) you know? And ... and it comes from caring ... caring tremendously about what happens, and at the same time feeling as if there's not much you can do about what happens.

[*Generations*, CW I, 319–20]

DAVID: I dunno. I feel we oughta be doin' better—why aren't we?

ALFRED: We do alright.

DAVID: We just get by every year. Some years are better, some years are worse, but it's always something. How can you spend your whole life like that, and then say that we do alright?

ALFRED: I got two fine boys and we've never gone hungry.

DAVID: That's not what I'm talkin' about—two fine boys never gone hungry—what's that got to do with the price of farm machinery or crop insurance?

ALFRED: What are you sayin'? Are you sayin' you think we should quit?

DAVID: No!

ALFRED: Then, what're you sayin'?

DAVID: I don't know what I'm sayin'! I'm sayin' ... we gotta remember one thing ... my grampa came over in the hold of a ship in 1908 ... and he worked his butt off from the time he was seven ... and we got something worthwhile here.

ALFRED: But—if, someday you weren't to keep on, there'd be no reason to keep it together.

DAVID: Now what're you sayin'?

ALFRED: ... It hardly seems fair to Eddie if—

DAVID: Fair? You wanna talk fair! What's fair about Eddie and the whole fuckin' city sittin' drinkin' scotch and feedin' their faces while we bust our ass to put food on their tables! Two-thirds of the goddamn world dies of starvation and the farmer's low man on the totem pole! You wanna talk fair?

ALFRED: That's not the way things are!

DAVID: I don't like it!

ALFRED: You can't change it!

DAVID: Who says I can't change it!

SHARON POLLOCK: I don't know whether it's my greatest … it probably is my greatest flaw and a kind of strength: that it's been more important for me to try and be as honest as I can. And it's always been a journey of discovery for me, too. I mean I discover what it is … what my answer is, as I'm trying to construct my answer as truthfully as I can at that particular moment. And I've never really been very good at … like accumulating anything or thinking of anything other really than today. And so I've never really thought of the repercussions of just saying what it is I actually think or feel. So I don't, I suppose, guard my tongue or frame my thoughts by thinking well, if I say this, then that might happen. (*laughter*) Right? And this would not be good if you wanted that job tomorrow. I've never been concerned with that sort of thing. And I always think: oh well, I guess I will write 'til I die in order to pay my mortgage. I would rather not be doing something if I don't believe in it, and even though it might make good financial sense, or it might even make career sense not to say—well this isn't what it is I thought it was and so I don't know if I want to waste my time and energy in order to keep up appearances and then move on so many years from now. I've always said, oh time is too precious, your energy is too precious. What's to be done is too large so why, why waste time, if the light dawns and if you've thought about it for a bit. Then move on or speak out. I've never been afraid of saying I'm wrong, either. Maybe sometimes I've been wrong and I haven't realized it. But discovering that you're wrong, I always think of as a great leap forward. I've always said I've never learned anything from anything I've done well.

> (*SFX: music*)
>
> [*Fair Liberty's Call*, CW II, 389]
>
> EDDIE: I speak of the betrayin' of what we was promised and you call me a Rebel? Me who's killed Rebels from Waxhaws to Camden, King's Mountain to Yorkton?
>
> MAJOR: What you speak of is sedition and treason and best forgot by all of us here.
>
> EDDIE: Is any opposition rebellion?
>
> GEORGE: It's not the time for questionin'! It's time for restorin' order and rank and stability. It's a time to get on with our lives.
>
> EDDIE: So our promised land, our great new province, this country will become the fiefdom of the few, is that it?
>
> (*SFX: discordant music*)

SHARON POLLOCK: When I think of when I was little or, or in high school, I remember myself as being very reticent, very quiet. I can remember hating to stand up in school because my face always turned bright red and I never wanted to stand up and say anything because I turned beat red and felt silly and stupid. And my big fear was always that somehow I would be dressed imperfectly or wrongly, you know, like I would be wearing the blue sweater with the black, plaid, pleated skirt, but it was the wrong colour of blue. Or my mother had brought me plaid shoelaces in New York when she was there, and I had put them into my saddle shoes but no one in the rest of the school was wearing plaid shoelaces. And that didn't mean that I thought I was ahead of the game; I thought that I was terribly outside the game. I feel as if I was introverted, is what I would feel. And I think that what turned me around, what changed for me in some respects was ahh ... marriage, right? And my absolute inability to be what it was that I was supposed to be in that marriage. And so part of that meant that I turned more and more inward until I had an epiphany washing dishes one day and suddenly thought: no, I am a person who is as valid as he is. Why is it me who has to turn myself into somebody that I'm not? And perhaps it was my absolute inability to do *that* that also led to that [epiphany]. And I suppose from that came a feeling that I would not ever present myself as anybody but who I actually was, and, if that didn't fit well, then better that we got that out of the way right away and not have to deal with it later. People still have a great desire sometimes to think that I am other than I am, for whatever reason. They might express surprise at something, and I always think ... but why would you be surprised that I would say or do that. That is exactly what I said I would do and now I'm doing it. (*laughter*) You know? But I, but for me, you know it came at a moment at which I felt I either was going to kill myself, if not literally then metaphorically, or else I was going to allow myself to be born and live, even though I suppose I was twenty-six or twenty-seven at the time. And I had a choice and it seemed to be a very clear choice—die or live. And if you live then don't ever pretend anything other than what it is you actually feel and think, and maybe you'll be wrong. You know often you are wrong and you say things that are stupid and afterwards ... ah the only thing I always say is I reserve the right to say I was wrong. Sometimes I ... and probably my children more so might be quite horrified to think what I might be like when I get to be seventy-five ... but maybe I'll regress. I have a terrible feeling that I might go full circle (*laughter*). I'll end up looking for plaid shoelaces and feeling outside the game.

(*SFX: woman singing quietly*)

[*Doc, CW* II, 191]

BOB: Listen Katie. I want ... I want to tell you—when—when I was little, do you know, do you know I would sit on our front porch, and I would look up, look up at the sky, and the sky, the sky went on forever.

[*The Making of Warriors*, RADIO SCRIPT, *Airborne*, 132]

VOICES: We won't forget. The struggle. Remember. Remember.

BOB: That was me, Katie. That was me.

Sharon Pollock Chronology

1936 — born Mary Sharon Chalmers,19 April 1936, Fredericton, New Brunswick; has one
   brother, Peter Chalmers (1938–); father: Dr. George Everett Chalmers, OC (1905–1992),
   physician, Tory MLA from 1956 to 1972; mother: Eloise Elizabeth Roberts (1913–1954)

1939–40 — family moves to Grey St. home in Fredericton

1940 — 5 August, Mary Branch Chalmers dies: "accidental drowning" in Saint John River

1942–50 — attends Charlotte St. Public School, Fredericton

1950–52 — attends Fredericton High School, grades 9 and 10

1952–54 — attends King's College School (called Compton) for Girls in Compton, Eastern
   Townships, Quebec, grades 11 and 12

1954 — 12 May: Eloise Chalmers dies; September, enters the University of New Brunswick
   in Arts and completes one year, taking History, Philosophy, and Classics

1955 — marries Ross D. Pollock and enrolls as a "special student" at UNB

1956 — daughter, Jennifer, born and couple moves to Toronto

1957 — son, Kirk, born on 12 May (anniversary of Eloise's death)

1958 — family moves from Toronto to Keswick, Ontario

1959 — Melinda born

1961 — Lisa born; SP joins local amateur theatre in Keswick

1963 — Michele born; SP directing for amateur theatre in Keswick

1964 — June, leaves Ross Pollock and returns to Fredericton with her children

1964–65 — begins working and acting, with Company of Ten, at the Playhouse Theatre in
   Fredericton; meets Michael Ball

1966 — January, joins Ball in Calgary; begins touring with Victor Mitchell's Prairie Players;
   wins Dominion Drama Festival Award for Best Actress in Ann Jellico's *The Knack*;
   summer tours with MAC 14 Touring Company

1967 — performs in Beckett plays at University of Calgary; Amanda born

1967–71 — living in Calgary with Ball and children; continues acting, and begins writing
   radio scripts and first play: "A Compulsory Option"

1971 — wins Alberta Department of Culture Playwriting competition for "A Compulsory
   Option"; moves to British Columbia with Ball and children

1972 — August, premiere of "A Compulsory Option"; does research for *Walsh*

1973 — *Walsh* premiere at Theatre Calgary, 7 November; writing children's plays; moves to 116 Granville, New Westminster, B.C. (across from former penitentiary, begins work on *One Tiger to a Hill*); teaches playwriting at Douglas College

1975 — 24 March premier of "And Out Goes You?" at Vancouver Playhouse (main stage), directed by Christopher Newton; is acting at Douglas College

1976 — premiere of *The Komagata Maru Incident* for the Vancouver Playhouse (at the VECC stage), directed by Larry Lillo; plays Lizzie in "My Name is Lisbeth" at Douglas College; moves to Sherwood Park, Edmonton; holds position of instructor in Theatre Department, University of Alberta for 1976–77 academic year

1977 — returns to Calgary; Dr. Everett Chalmers Hospital has official opening in Fredericton; named playwright-in-residence at Banff Centre Playwrights' Colony

1977–79 — playwright-in-residence, Alberta Theatre Projects, Calgary

1978 — purchase of the Manora Drive house in Calgary

1977–80 — Head of Playwrights Colony, and playwright-in-residence, at Banff Centre School of Fine Arts

1980 — premiere of *One Tiger to a Hill* at Citadel Theatre, Edmonton, directed by Richard Ouzounian; premiere of *Generations* at Alberta Theatre Projects, Calgary, in Canmore Opera House; premiere of *Blood Relations* at Edmonton's Theatre 3, directed by Keith Digby; wins Association of Canadian Television and Radio Artists (ACTRA) award for *Sweet Land of Liberty*

1981 — separation from Michael Ball; wins first Governor General's Award for Drama for *Blood Relations*; wins Golden Sheaf Award for television script, "The Persons Case"

1981–83 — artist-in-residence, National Arts Centre of Canada

1983 — premiere, *Whiskey Six Cadenza* at Theatre Calgary, directed by Rick McNair; wins injunction against CFCN and Robert Barlow for adaptation of *Blood Relations*; wins Alberta Achievement Award in "Excellence Award" category

1984 — premiere of *Doc* at Theatre Calgary; wins Chalmers Canadian Play award for *Doc*; wins Alberta Writers' Guild Award for *Doc*; wins 1984 Governor General's Award for Drama for *Doc*

1986 — writer-in-residence at the Regina Public Library; begins working on drafts of *Fair Liberty's Call*; LLD, University of New Brunswick

1987 — wins Canada/Australia Literary Award; resigns from the Playwrights Union of Canada; "Egg" commissioned by Martin Kinch for Theatre Calgary's 1988–89 season

1988 — Associate Artistic Director at the Manitoba Theatre Centre; appointed Artistic Director at Theatre New Brunswick; July 1988 performs Eme in premiere of *Getting It Straight*, directed by Rick McNair, for International Women's Festival in Winnipeg

1988–89 — Artistic Director at Theatre New Brunswick, Fredericton

1989 — LLD, Queen's University

1990 — Associate Director, Stratford Festival; Stratford production of *One Tiger to a Hill*, directed by John Wood

1991 — attends second International Women Playwrights Conference, in Toronto at Glendon College, as co-Chair; founds Performance Kitchen in Calgary

1992 — opens the Garry Theatre, at 1229 – 9th Ave, S.E., in Inglewood district of Calgary, with son Kirk Campbell

1993 — 26 April, Everett Chalmers dies; premiere of *Fair Liberty's Call* at Stratford, directed by Guy Sprung

1994 — *Blood Relations* performed in Tokyo (Half-Moon Theatre); SP lectures on "Contemporary Canadian Theatre" at Canadian Embassy in Japan

1995 — wins Japan Foundation Award

1996 — continues as Artistic Director, Garry Theatre, directing and acting

1997 — the Garry Theatre closes on 22 April 1997; SP has angioplasty for heart condition; begins writing *Moving Pictures*

1998 — elected President of the Alberta Playwrights Network; 4 November 1998, *Death in the Family* on BRAVO TV, with SP as Renee Havard and Rick McNair as Gillie

1999 — premiere of *Moving Pictures* at Theatre Junction, Calgary; wins Harry and Martha Cohen Award (for significant and sustained contribution to Calgary theatre)

2000 — premiere of *End Dream*, directed by SP, at Theatre Junction; premiere of *The Making of Warriors* for Crazy Horse Native Theatre in Calgary

2001 — premiere of *Angel's Trumpet* at Theatre Junction; 30 May 2001: has quintuple bypass heart surgery

2003 — 26 February to 10 March, travels to Sierra Leone with CAUSE Canada; LLD, University of Calgary

2004 — February, gives keynote lecture at UBC "Putting a Life on Stage" workshop; December, performs role of Shipman in *Moving Pictures* at Studio Theatre, University of Alberta; completes draft of *Kabloona Talk*

2005 — LLD, University of Alberta; 6 November, launch of volume 1 of *Sharon Pollock: Collected Works* in Calgary

2006 — appointed playwright-in-residence with Alberta Playwrights Network; wins Gwen Pharis Ringwood Award for Drama for *Collected Works*, volume I; volume 2 of *Collected Works* published; speaks at theatre panel at CanStage (Toronto); gives address at Playwrights Guild of Canada conference (Toronto); works as dramaturge with Atlantic Ballet of Canada; September, begins reviewing plays for CBC radio in Calgary

2007 — premiere of *Man Out of Joint* by Downstage Theatre Company at Vertigo Studio Theatre, Calgary; death of Rick McNair; continues work with Atlantic Ballet of Canada; elected, Fellow of the Royal Society of Canada

2008 — publication of volume 3 of *Collected Works*; continues writing, acting, speaking engagements, CBC reviewing.

Notes

Chapter 2

1. William Maxwell Aitken, first Baron Beaverbrook (1879–1964), was the son of a Presbyterian minister who moved his family to New Brunswick in 1880. Max grew up in Newcastle and began legal training in Chatham, where he made connections with two other New Brunswick men who would become powerful and influential friends—R.B. Bennett, a future Canadian Prime Minister, and James Dunn, a wealthy New Brunswick businessman.

2. I am grateful for the assistance of Don Dixon for these details. Professor Paul Delaney from the University of Moncton has confirmed that the French Robert(s) were not Acadian and that the official records have lacunae and inconsistencies. When Eloise's parents, John Roberts and Agnes Dann, married in 1903, John gave *his* father's name as John Roberts; therefore, it is possible that Elizabeth Roberts was married to a John Roberts, thus doubling the Roberts name, but it is also possible that two different Roberts families existed in the same area. Unfortunately, family documents are scarce and memories spotty; neither Sharon nor her mother knew grandfather Roberts, and Sharon was not close to this side of the family; Peter Chalmers, who was devoted to grandmother Roberts, cannot recall hearing details about genealogy or a French connection. Grandmother Roberts, who both Sharon and Peter knew, was Church of England and her home was filled with royal memorabilia.

3. By 1980, federal politics, including the Conservative party, had some high-profile female members such as Flora MacDonald and Ellen Fairclough, who Diefenbaker named as a cabinet minister in 1957. Alberta's Emily Murphy led the battle for suffrage and female "person" status as early as the 1920s—a victory Sharon would explore in a television play—and Jeanne Sauvé, first elected as a Liberal MP for Montreal in 1972, was appointed Canada's first woman Speaker in the House of Commons on 14 April 1980 and in 1984 she became our first woman Governor General.

4. Peter Chalmers is certain that Elaine was Eloise's much-loved daughter and that the circumstances surrounding her birth lay behind his mother's unhappiness. He bases this conclusion on the fact that the two women looked so much alike (see Illus. 8), that Eloise was very fond of Elaine, and that, in old age, Everett told Peter that Eloise had this daughter before their marriage. Sharon recalls Elaine's time with her family and has discussed this possibility with Peter, but she is not convinced.

5. The school was modeled on British schools for girls and developed during an era when education for women began to be important. The philosophy of the school was always pro-British, Anglican, and royalist. The name was changed from Compton Ladies College to King's Hall in 1902 to mark the coronation of Edward VII and the school motto became "Pactum Serva" (Keep Troth). From 1939 onwards the permanent teachers and the Lady Principal were chosen from a Canadian pool of applicants. By Sharon's day, the school uniform was a navy tunic, white blouse, black stockings and shoes, with the school's crest on the tunic and a light blue sash tied at the waist. The girls, mostly from wealthy English-speaking, Montreal families, all wore the school tie with blue and gold stripes. The name of the yearbook *Per Annos* was chosen in 1951 and is Latin for a popular song of the day, "Through the Years." King's Hall closed its doors in 1972.

6. Medical specialists assure me that the kinds of silver polish used today are not fatally toxic and I have not been able to confirm what it was that Eloise consumed. Sharon believes her mother swallowed something containing mercury; however, I wonder if arsenic may not have been the substance because

it was available in various kinds of pest control powders, including weed killer, because Eloise was a gardener (as well as a nurse) and would have known what substances were on hand, because the descriptions I have been given of her dying (acute pain, extreme dehydration, length of time) resemble arsenic poisoning and, finally, because she read widely and may have known Flaubert's *Madame Bovary* and seen in that story of an unhappy wife married to a doctor, a mirror of her own existence.

Chapter 3

1.   Peter is now retired and living in Fredericton, where he is active in volunteer and church activities. He and Sharon share a strong family resemblance in looks and manner, and his pride in her achievements is clear. Peter is convinced that the son born in 1950 and brought to his father's marriage with Pegi, which took place on 14 February 1956, was Everett's. Because of his devotion to his dead mother and his grief—still keen today—at her loss, his time at home after this marriage was not happy, but he told me that Everett Chalmers tried to spend more time with his second family and in his Will left everything to Pegi and his children with her.

2.   I made numerous efforts to locate Ross Pollock until a member of his family asked me not to persist. I have respected that request, but I cannot explain why it was made.

3.   Bob Haley, an actor and friend of Sharon's from Calgary days, and himself the adult child of alcoholic parents, drew my attention to the American organization known as ACOA (Adult Children of Alcoholics) and to the possibility that Sharon had suffered serious trauma as a result of her childhood experiences with alcoholism. I have found the studies by Cermak, Ackerman, and Velleman and Orford useful, but care is needed in applying any of the findings of these authors because the characteristics they isolate as typical of the children of alcoholics are found in the so-called normal population. When assessing the relevance of such studies, it is important to remember that the children of alcoholics are resilient and more often than not go on to lead successful, happy lives.

4.   Sharon is vague about whether or not she was finally divorced from Ross Pollock. She has told me that a lawyer contacted her regarding a divorce when she was living in Calgary, by which time the grounds of adultery were clear, but that she refused to agree to adultery unless Ross agreed to provide some support for his children. When she heard nothing further, she assumed that there was no divorce. However, she also believes that Ross remarried and began a second family, and she recalls that in about 1972, when Kirk was visiting in Toronto, he tried to see his father, who turned him away at the door.

Chapter 4

1.   The actors in "Thirty-one for Two" were Jack Goth as Peter, Pat Reid as Liz, his wife, Donald Truss, as Don and Kay Grieve as Betty, Don's wife; Stephen Cook played the son, Alan, who is killed by the Organization, and Andrew Allan was marvellous as the "the Geezer's Voice"; the goons were played by Clint Jarboe and Bill Speerston. Several of these actors were frequently cast in the Calgary radio dramas of the time, and some of them performed in others of Sharon's early radio plays.

2.   Dave Barrett became leader of the provincial New Democratic Party in 1970 and premier of British Columbia in 1972. He was defeated by Bill Bennett and the Social Credit Party in the 1975 election after imposing back-to-work legislation to end labour strife. Bennett, the son of former premier W.A.C. Bennett, became leader of the Socreds, a right-wing, business-oriented party in 1973, and after the 1975 election he stayed in power until 1986. He privatized a number of public assets, imposed wage restraints, cut budgets, and launched a number of megaprojects. Philip Gagliardi, an evangelist preacher, who served in the Socred government as minister of public works and minister of highways,

became known as "flyin' Phil" because of his use of government planes and his many speeding tickets.

3.   In April 1935 residents of federal relief camps in British Columbia went on strike in a protest over their conditions and treatment. When this strike got no results, they began a journey to Ottawa to present their case to the federal government in what would be know as the "On to Ottawa Trek," led by Arthur Evans from the Workers' Unity League (WUL). When they reached Regina, the demonstrators, now two thousand in number, waited for word from Ottawa, but when talks broke down, the Prime Minister, R.B. Bennett, decided to send in the RCMP to arrest the leaders, and the rally called by the WUL for 1 July 1935 in Regina turned into the Regina Riot when trekkers assaulted police and police fired back. The Trek was finally repressed and a majority of trekkers returned to Vancouver without any change in their situation. To this day, the trek and riot are significant reminders of state repression in Canada.

4.   I am grateful to Dorothy Jones for sending me a copy of this rough working script, as well as several photographs and other materials about Sharon's time at the College. Her clear memories of those years and her generous assistance with details have helped to flesh out a little known period in Sharon's life and in the greater Vancouver's theatre scene.

5.   The story of Holiday Theatre and its demise needs to be told and the resources for such a story are in the City of Vancouver Archives, Holiday Theatre/Playhouse Holiday Fonds, where, among other documents there are records and a newsletter history of the theatre by Margaret Rushton. The merger of the smaller company with the Playhouse was only one factor in its demise; their building was sold, funding was tight, Playhouse priorities shifted with each new artistic director and with changes in the administration of the theatre. Moreover, the wider theatre scene in Vancouver had changed considerably since the early fifties, and there was arguably less of a role for a children's theatre wing of Playhouse operations once Green Thumb Theatre for Young People had opened in 1975. Few of Sharon's children's scripts appear to have survived but I was able to obtain a complete one, with music, of "The Great Drag Race, Smoked, Choked and Croaked," from the B.C. Lung Association.

6.   The full name of the play is "A Great Noise, A Great Light," and the production took place in the summer of 1976 for ATP at Calgary's Canmore Opera House. Murrell also recalls that occasion and the way he felt when Sharon supported him: he told me "it was what I needed to hear to be able to go on."

Chapter 5

1.   Baldridge did not receive a Canada Council grant for the play but the Alberta RCMP Century Celebrations Committee provided some funding support. Sharon was anxious to see Métis and/or First Nations actors cast for the roles of the Sioux, so she and Baldridge were both pleased to secure Schellenberg, Denis LaCroix, and Frank Turningrobe for this production. Casting would prove problematic in later productions, especially in the 1988 Theatre Calgary revival.

2.   The script for this production shows that these characters were used near the beginning to sketch the historical background of the play. Presented as dialogue, the facts nevertheless remain flat information and these exchanges do nothing to forward the plot or create dramatic interest. The stage business—a making of camp beds—is lame. When the play was published in a third printing and slightly revised edition in 1976 it followed the structure of the Stratford production: the Prologue was in tact and there was no four-character recitation of history; the ending is the one retained through to the 1998 reprint; and the scenes with Mary Walsh and Pretty Plume that were there in the Stratford production are retained. Further changes appear in the 1998 reprint, which should really be called a new edition, and the most significant of these is the addition of a lengthy scene with Colonel Terry and Pretty Plume, who speaks for her people; see the 1998 edition of the play, pages 67–72.

3. As if the various problems that beset this production were not enough, on one evening a First Nations member of the cast was arrested by the Calgary police, allegedly for drinking, and when Martin Kinch went to the police station to secure his release, he was lectured by the police on keeping the city clean of Indians for the duration of the Olympics.

4. Very early Sharon understood the importance of publishing and she resented the fact that after its successful premiere no one would publish *The Komagata Maru Incident*. She told Margo Dunn that Talonbooks rejected it because of its length, and she goes on to challenge this response by noting that *Krapp's Last Tape* is even shorter and that length is irrelevant: "Someone in this country should be publishing every play that has had a professional production," she insisted (Dunn, 6). The play was first published as a script in 1978 by Playwrights Co-op; it appeared in book form in 1992, when Tony Hamill included it in *Six Canadian Plays* and is now in volume one of *Collected Works*.

5. No one was charged with Mary Steinhauser's murder because the guns used by the tactical squad were shuffled and could not be identified with the guards who had used them. The most important interview Sharon has given concerning this play is her 1990 one with Pat Quigley.

6. Her original working title for the play was "Deposition," but she was persuaded to find a more interesting title and came up with "One Tiger to a Hill." She had been reading Lorenz and Ardrey, both of whom describe human beings as inherently violent, so the phrase just "sprang to mind." It is, however, an ancient and familiar Chinese saying, and it was also the title for a September 1962 episode in the popular American television series *Route 66*, which Sharon may have seen.

Chapter 6

1. This translation and production marked a rare event in Quebec theatre because it is not often that Francophone theatres and audiences show much interest in anglophone work. But Gagnon, who knew the Lizzie Borden story, was fascinated by the play and found her work on it profoundly engaging. The cast was Denise Verville (Miss Lizzie), Micheline Bernard (Actress), Janine Angers (Mrs. Borden), Louis Fortin (Mr. Borden), Claude Binet (Uncle Harry), Johanne Bolduc (Emma), and Jacques Lessard (Dr. Patrick and the Defence) with scenography by Carole Paré. The translation (a copy can be read at the National Theatre School in Montreal) is fairly literal with a few exceptions; one of the most interesting of these is the swearing which is considerably more pungent in French. Ray Conlogue, who reviewed the production for the *Globe and Mail*, noted the rarity of Quebec interest in English-Canadian plays but went on to call *Blood Relations* old-fashioned by Quebec standards.

2. In the following discussion I have relied on information that has appeared in print (see Balcon, Hayes, McKinley, and Solomon), and Balcon's piece is the most informative. As he notes, no one wants to talk about what was happening behind the scenes, and neither party was allowed to disclose details of the out-of-court settlement. Archival materials are restricted, but on 23 May 1983 the Guild of Canadian Playwrighting issued a news release on the subject. They announced that, together with Playwrights Canada, they had established a legal fund to support Sharon, and they noted that this case would be the first time in Canadian legal history that a playwright had invoked Section 12-7 of the Copyright Act, which "allows an author to restrain from broadcasting" a work that is deemed to have mutilated their original or that would harm the author's reputation. I have seen a print of the film "Double Play" and in my view it is a travesty of Sharon's play, but it is hard to imagine how a good film could be made of this play because it is not a filmic text; its power resides in its language, in the theatricality of performance and in physical, live enactment.

Chapter 7

1.   From 1977, when the truth of what had happened in the Allan began to leak out, until as recently as 2004, allegations and reports have surfaced about the number and identity of victims who were subjected to damaging electric-shock treatments, placed in insulin-induced comas, and held in what were known as "sleep rooms" for weeks on end. It appears that the CIA was funding mind control experiments that could not legally be conducted on American soil. Compensation has been paid to families by the CIA and by the Canadian government, but both bodies deny any direct responsibility for the fate of patients. Cameron (1901–67) left the Allan quietly under a cloud of suspicion in 1964, and no document has been found, to date, that links him directly with the CIA; many documents are still classified and others are suspected of being lost or mislaid. The Allan still exists and today it houses the Psychiatry Department of McGill University's Royal Victoria Hospital. It is a large mansion, built by wealthy Montreal businessman Sir Hugh Allan and given to the hospital in 1940.

2.   Theatre North West, in Prince George, B.C., produced the play in October 2004 under the direction of Ted Price. It was a nicely nuanced and well acted production, and through seeing it and discussing it with Price and the actors, I gained a new respect for the play. Clearly, the subject had not dated and the characters appealed to local audiences because there was a lot of fellow feeling for the farmers' dilemma in Prince George, which is not far from Dawson Creek, where Nick Parsons lived. Parsons, a local farmer, had recently driven his tractor to Ottawa to put up a sign saying: "If you don't support agriculture—stop eating." Price posted photographs of Parsons and newspaper articles about his protest in the lobby to underscore the play's topicality; audience response on the evening I attended was very warm, and the reviews were glowing. In this production, the role of Bonnie was critical because she became the focal point for the conflict between generations, between men and women, and between two incompatible ways of life.

3.   Theatre scholars have had different responses: in "Sharon Pollock's Women," Diane Bessai sees Leah and the other women as defined by men and the personal relationships in the play as "sadly destructive"; in "Postcolonial Tragedy in the Crowsnest Pass," Anne Nothof argues that Leah makes her own choices (for Johnny and then for death), thereby subverting the historical victimization of Florence Lassandro and killing Mr. Big's dreams. However, in "Daddy's Girls: Father-Daughter Incest in Canadian Plays by Women," Jerry Wasserman makes a strong case for seeing Leah as trapped within Mr. Big's story and as lacking the power to create her own; in *Blood Relations*, the daughter kills the abusive father, whereas in *Whiskey Six Cadenza* she is killed by him. Not until *Doc*, says Wasserman, was Sharon able to imagine another way: "To save their own lives, Sharon Pollock's daughters must either kill the abusive father or forgive him" (33).

4.   Emily Murphy (1868–1933), together with Henrietta Muir Edwards, Nellie McClung, Louise McKinney, and Irene Parlby, challenged the exclusion of women as "persons" under the BNA Act. She first took the case to the Supreme Court of Canada, which ruled that women were not persons and therefore could not hold public office and were denied many other rights and privileges enjoyed by men. Undaunted, the five women turned to the Privy Council in England, which ruled in their favour on 18 October 1929. Sharon received a $4,500 commission fee to write "The Persons Case" for Alberta ACCESS television, which showed the sixty-minute teleplay starring Frances Hyland in October 1981. Her original title had been "Free our sisters, free ourselves," but the final title better captures the nature of the story and its symbolic significance. Sharon told Robert Sibley that her Emily is a leader who is very human but who nevertheless fights for what she believes in. Sharon's Emily was "strained through [her] subjective interpretations" of the facts (Sibley, 5).

5.   On 6 September 1987, Sharon wrote a detailed seven-page letter to her fellow member-playwrights in the Union, outlining her many concerns with the "standard minimum contracts for commissioned work, for premiere productions, and for subsequent productions." She pointed out that as an established playwright who did not work with an agent (she had terminated such relationships by 1982), she

was less vulnerable than emerging playwrights, but she believed in her responsibility to remind her colleagues that "as playwrights and artists" they held the moral and economic rights to their own work, and she quoted the provisions of Bill C-60 with its amendments to the Canadian Copyright Act. One particular worry for Sharon was the standard contract provision on "participation rights" that gave an originating company, including not-for-profit companies, a percentage of all world stage royalties earned by the playwright. (In current Playwrights Guild and PACT standard premiere contracts, "participation rights" are optional and negotiable.) Sharon's letter is a fascinating and thoughtful document, and I am grateful to Jim DeFelice for sharing his copy with me because, as he says in his cover note, her letter "contains a lot of her philosophy." This letter is now with the Pollock papers.

6. There are several literary echoes and allusions in the play and it would require a literary exegesis to trace and explain all of them. Jarry's 1896 play, however, is particularly noteworthy: the play is a violent, grotesque satire on men's greed, thirst for power, and warlike nature; the players are meant to be puppets or life-size marionettes. When W.B. Yeats saw the play, he worried that nothing more was left to art but a regression to the Savage God and, in theatre history, this play is seen as a forerunner of later forms of subversive art. Eme's (Sharon's) naming of Ubu, however, plus her memories of "string puppets / hung / in a very small room / backstage" (230), suggests that this play represents the wrong kind of subversion because of its masculinist, military agenda. *Ubu roi* is part of the nightmare of history from which Eme is struggling to awake. There are references to children making paper cranes that evoke Colin Thomas's popular children's play *One Thousand Cranes* (1983) and the legend of Sadako and the cranes of world peace, to the fairy tale of Rapunzel, and to the *Nutcracker Suite*, all works of art for children. Eme also names Camus and, possibly, R.D. Laing, whose popular study of schizophrenia, *The Divided Self* (1960), Sharon knew. Carl Sagan's work, book and television series, serve as a type of underground sprinkler system nourishing many of the concerns and images that surface in Eme's monologue.

7. I doubt that Sharon has drawn on the work of Romanian-French linguist and theorist, Julia Kristeva, but Kristeva's concepts in *Desire in Language*, and the distinctions she makes between the paternal mode of symbolic language and the maternal mode of semiotic language, help me understand how this play functions and how a female, bodily language may communicate wisdom and experience. Social communication requires both the symbolic and semiotic sign systems to work in a given sentence, speech, or text; however, Kristeva argues that the symbolic function represses instinct and the identification of the individual with the mother, whereas the semiotic function releases the instinctual and maternal elements, especially in what Kristeva calls poetic language, by disrupting the paternal, syntactic, thetic function of language. See *Desire in Language*, chapter 5, 133–36.

Chapter 8

1. My thanks to Brian Brennan for sharing this letter and its enclosure with me.

2. The illustrations and information in the house program defined *Fair Liberty's Call* as a history play. The cover carried the image of a sword and feather crossed with a blurred period map of North America behind this image. The production photographs showed the eight-member cast in period dress and the program included a map showing the battles mentioned in the play, described each of them in annotations, illustrated the map with period pictures of the officers mentioned in the play and of King George III, and printed Sharon's own summary of the historical setting for the action of the play. Only Guy Sprung, in his short essay "Choice and Responsibility, eh?", alerted the audience to the contemporary parameters of the play they were about to see.

3. These instructions appeared in the first publication of the play (19), but she dropped the reference to "virgin land" when she revised it for volume 2 of the *Collected Works*. She made other interesting

changes as well, such as inserting the instruction that "God Save the King" be played as the play begins and that this should be followed by terrifying sounds of battle.

4. *Death in the Family* began as a film script called "This Is Now" (54: 10–18). It was produced by Nomadic Pictures and directed by Douglas Berquist with Sharon as Renee Havard, Rick McNair as Gillie, and Frank Kakish as the son, Warren, who has been given up for adoption and has come to find the truth about his past. Amanda Pollock played the young Renee Havard who has the love affair with Gino, and Paul McNair—Rick McNair's son—played the young Gillie. The film version has some good points— sound effects and merging of past with present are striking in the film—but the narrative is unresolved and Sharon's acting is too much on one level of intensity. McNair gives a moving portrayal of the disturbed Gillie. The reasons for the attack on the Italian Gino are more complex than his affair with Renee; the Havard brother, Gerald, has died in the war and the Havard men are angry about his death.

5. As Albertans know, this highway runs between Edmonton and Calgary, and the play grew out of interviews held with a range of people in both cities. It combines monologues, songs, and sketches in a form reminiscent of *The Farm Show* or *Paper Wheat*, and it attempts to create a community or communal form of theatre about a local subject of interest.

6. The play, originally called "Constance Kent," was aired on 15 June 1992 with Sharon as Miss Kaye, Kate Ryan as young Constance, Blair Haynes as the male visitor, Lindsey Schneider as William, Anne McGrath as Mrs. Kent, and Wendell Smith as Mr. Kent; original music was written and performed by Doug Blackley. There are a number of small differences between the radio script and the published text; for example, in the broadcast Miss Kaye does not tell her male visitor to "go to hell," and in the published text the final stage instruction suggests a stronger, more decisive old woman than the Miss Kaye of the radio version. The case of Constance Kent is known as the Road Hill Murder; many books have been written about it, and the British film, *Constance Kent*, was released in 1981. To my knowledge it has never been proven that Constance Kent became Ruth Emilie Kaye, but that is one of several explanations about her life after her release from prison in 1885. Other theories identify her as the real Jack (or Jill) the Ripper because she hated women, or have her moving to the United States and marrying. Sharon had to pick and choose what to use in her play, but she kept to the facts on several points. The first Mrs. Kent was subjected to yearly pregnancies and became unwell; she was incarcerated in her own home and died of a bowel obstruction in 1853. Her husband quickly married the nursemaid and began a second family. The real Constance did run away from home dressed as a boy, did resent her stepmother, and her father did send her to a convent school in France. After her return to England, she made a public confession of her guilt in killing her half-brother, but this confession was made under pressure and was riddled with inconsistencies. A woman called Ruth Emilie Kaye immigrated to New South Wales, Australia, where she worked as a nurse and founded the nursing home in which she died at one hundred on 10 April 1944.

Chapter 9

1. Another play about Janet Smith, called "Disposing of the Dead," written by Katherine Schlemmer, with Sandhano Schultze and Wayne Specht, was produced by Vancouver's Axis Theatre Company and Pink Ink at the Waterfront Theatre in November 1996, with sets by Robert Gardiner. Although this play was striking, it did not move beyond the thriller genre. *End Dream* is very different. Sharon's aim is not to say who did it but to explore how it could have happened and why it was never thoroughly investigated; she focuses on the social context and on the frightening male authority figure of the employer whose home becomes a trap for both the houseboy and the nanny.

2. In the program notes for *Angel's Trumpet*, Sharon is described as currently writing an adaptation of Ibsen's *Enemy of the People* (a work that has not yet seen production), as doing research for a series of plays to celebrate Alberta's centennial in 2005, and as "tentatively dipping her toe into prose fiction

which she finds a bit scary." Sharon has not been willing to divulge the nature of this prose fiction, which is still underway.

3. In her fictional recreation of what happened that afternoon at La Paix, Sharon made changes to the historical record. For example, Zelda's psychiatrist from the Phipps was Dr. Thomas Rennie, and it was Rennie, not Scott, who arranged the La Paix session. Another Phipps doctor, Dr. Mildred Squires, had encouraged Zelda to write *Save Me the Waltz* because she believed that writing would help Zelda; Zelda dedicated her novel to Squires. Fitzgerald was indeed furious about this book and he saw to it that Dr. Squires was removed from Zelda's case. The stenographer at La Paix was Isabel Owens, an associate of Fitzgerald's, and she used a dictaphone from which she later prepared the 114-page transcript.

4. To my knowledge Sharon has said nothing publicly about this period in her life. These comments are quoted from an email she sent me on 14 June 2002 in reply to my inquiry about her health. I am thankful for her willingness to discuss the surgery at all; other details I have recounted here come from conversations with her over the telephone or in person. I am also grateful to my brother-in-law, Dr. Archie Grace, for his help in understanding the procedures and risks of angioplasty and bypass surgery.

5. Nunavut became a separate Canadian territory in 1999 when the former Northwest Territories was divided and a new boundary drawn; the area around the former Coppermine is now located in Nunavut. This change, and the return to Inuit place names, are recent developments, as is the current usage of Inuit, instead of Eskimo, but in the early twentieth century the entire geographical area of this story was part of the NWT. Thus, in the play, which is set in Edmonton in August 1917, Sharon uses the terminology of the period.

6. This original ballet, conceived and choreographed by Dobrovolskiy, is based on Gaston Leroux's 1910 novel, with music by Francis Poulenc. It opened in October and went on tour across Canada. In the summer of 2007, Sharon returned to Moncton to work with the company again.

Chapter 10

1. In her Executive Summary of *Adding it Up: The Status of Women in Canadian Theatre*, Kate Weiss notes that despite improvements between 1981 and 2006, women are far from achieving equity with their male colleagues in any part of Canadian theatre. Although women comprise almost 60 percent of Canadian theatre audiences, professional productions of plays by women, especially Canadian plays by women, are still relatively rare and women are still concentrated in the support roles of assistant directors, stage managers, and administrative staff, where they earn less money than men. Research for this report was done by Rebecca Burton under a national advisory committee headed by Hope McIntyre and Kelly Thornton for Equity in Canadian Theatre: The Women's Initiative, which began in 2004 and also examines the under-representation of people-of-colour in all aspects of our theatre.

2. Both Sharon and Pat Lowther lacked a post-secondary education and married young; these marriages failed. Both established new relationships—Lowther married her second husband Roy Lowther—both had several children, and both developed careers as writers while juggling family, poverty and the need to hold jobs. Both were keenly interested in politics and world affairs, although Lowther's views were farther to the left than Sharon's, and both women refused to cast themselves as victims. But the most striking parallel is their husbands. Sharon fled her marriage because she feared for her life, as well as for her basic identity or self; Lowther stayed in the hope she could establish herself economically and provide a home for her children after she left Roy. However, he murdered her before she could reach economic independence. Perhaps Sharon had a stronger sense of self-preservation, instilled by her mother's example, and she certainly had a protective father to come home to, but Lowther's story is close enough to Sharon's to remind us of the pressures and real threats that women of Sharon's generation often faced if they wished to be anything more than passive helpmates.

3. I realize that Beckett scholars may not share my opinion of Beckett's vision as pessimistic, and I know that there are moments of humour in some of his plays. Nevertheless, I see a fundamental difference between his work and Sharon's that I discuss in "Shipman's Last Take: or Why Sharon Pollock is Not Samuel Beckett": Where he leaves us hanging over an abyss of nothingness and silence, especially in plays like *End Game*, *Happy Days*, and *Not I*, she fills up the world of her plays with life, affirmation, hope, and noise. This is not to say that she is happier than he was about the cruelty and violence in this world, but that she insists on countering this awareness of emptiness and possible annihilation with a vision of hope and abundance.

Sources

In addition to the archives acknowledged in my Preface, I have consulted information from the following organizations: the B.C. Lung Association; Bishops College School; Cause Canada; the City of Vancouver Archives (Holiday Playhouse, New Play Centre, and Playhouse Theatre *fonds*); the Department of Drama, University of Calgary; Fredericton High School Library; the Georgina County Public Libraries (Keswick, Ontario); the National Archives of Canada; the University of Guelph Library (Canadian Stage, Toronto Free Theatre, and Centre Stage *fonds*); the University of New Brunswick Archives, Harriet Irving Library; the National Theatre School Library; and theatres across the country, including the Arts Club Theatre (Vancouver), the Bastion Theatre (Victoria), the Centaur Theatre (Montreal), the Citadel Theatre (Edmonton), the Grand Theatre (London), the Manitoba Theatre Centre (Winnipeg), Tarragon Theatre (Toronto), Theatre Junction and Theatre Calgary (both in Calgary), and Theatre New Brunswick.

Individuals across the country, and abroad, generously gave me their time and assistance with archival records or in interviews, in person or by telephone, email, and letter. I owe much of my understanding of Sharon Pollock's life and work and the Canadian theatre history of which she has been such an important part to: Hrant Alianak, Murph Allen, Carol Ames, Janet Amos, Mary Arbeau Adams, Sheila Atkinson, Shauna Baird, Harold Baldridge, Michael Ball, Guy Bannerman, Margaret Bard, Maev Beaty, Diane Bessai, Allan Boss, Jim Bowman, Brian Brennan, Barbara Campbell Brown, Norman Browning, R.D. Burgess, Paddy Campbell, Bev Carrick, Ellen Charendoff, Marlys Chevrefils, Donna Coates, Mardi Cockburn, Joy Coghill, John Cooper, Nancy Coy, David Craig, Tim Culbert and Alison Pauley Culbert, Jan Dales, Violet Dales, Jim DeFelice, Paul Delaney, Patricia Demers, Keith Digby, Don Dixon, Michael Dobbin, J. Douglas Dodd, Joyce Doolittle, Jim Dugan, Bob Eberle, Jaimie Eberle, Jane Edmonds, Ed Ellis, Glen Erikson, Howard Fink, Kathleen Flaherty, Christopher Foreman, Robert Fothergill, Fran Gebhard, Paul Gélineau, Mallory Gilbert, Jerry Grace, Bill Gray, Jane (Hickman) Green, Doreen Grinstead, Terry Gunvordahl, Bob Haley, Mary Hall, Bruce Hanks, Pamela Hawthorne, Peter Hay, Stephen Heatley, Tom Hendry, Martha Henry, Jane Heyman, Eda Holmes, Heather Inglis, Mark Jenkins, Dorothy Jones, Donna Juliani, Stephen Kent, Martin Kinch, Teresa Kind, Katalin Kürtösi, Mark Lawes, Walter Learning, Jim Leyden, Christopher Loach, Kevin Loring, Clarice McCord, Scott McKowen, John McLean, Rick McNair, Harriet McNeal, Jackie Maxwell, Bill Millerd, Victor Mitchell, Mavor Moore, Martin Morrow, Ed Mulally, John Murrell, Christopher Newton, Glen Nichols, Anne Nothof, Richard Ouzounian, Peter Pacey, Malcolm Page, Jane Parkinson, Suzie Payne, Gordon Pengilly, Veda Peters, Damiano Pietropaolo, John Pflance, Mary Pratt, Ted Price, Ken Puley, Pat Quigley, Angela Rebeiro, Brian Richmond, Douglas Riske, Bruce Ruddell, Mark Schoenberg, Janet Sellery, Jan Selman, Shirley Sibalis, Charlie Siegel, Ilkay Silk, Merrylou Smith, Kelly Spilchak, Guy Sprung, Apollonia Steele, Dor-Lu Stephens, Michelle Thrush, Jennifer Prosser Wade, Candice Woloshyn, Reuben Ware, David Watmough, Jackie Webster, Pat Webster, Rob Wellan, Meaghan Whitney, Don Williams, John Wood, John Wright, Odette Yazback, Toyoshi Yoshihara, and Cynthia Zimmerman.

For complete information on reviews and secondary works referred to in the chapters, endnotes, and sources, see the Bibliography.

Chapter 1:

My understanding of biography and autobiography has developed over many years and for the discussion of both I have drawn upon the work of many biographers, autobiographers, and theorists. These sources are listed in the Bibliography, but of particular importance are the theoretical discussions by Sara Alpern, Helen Buss, Paul John Eakin, Susanna Egan, William Epstein, Leigh Gilmore, Laurence Kirmayer, Philippe Lejeune, Sharon O'Brien, Thomas Postlewait, Mary Rhiel and David Suchoff, and Linda Wagner-Martin. The contributors to *Theatre & AutoBiography*, edited by Grace and Wasserman, and those authors named in this chapter and in chapter 10 have provided me with insights and inspiration.

Chapter 2:

For my discussion of New Brunswick history, politics, and culture, I have drawn upon several studies, memoirs, and interviews. The most useful published works for my purposes are by Dalton Camp, Steven Frick and Elizabeth Shilts, Tim Frink, Christopher Moore, Mary Pratt, Dan Soupcoup, W. Austin Squires, David Taylor and Glenn Rodger, James Walter, Esther Clark Wright, and Graeme Wynn. I also found Peter Howard's biography of Beaverbrook and Beaverbrook's memoir helpful. Elizabeth Milner's history of King's Hall School is an invaluable resource, as are the school's yearbooks and other archival materials.

Chapter 3:

For background and context on the Red Barn Theatre, the Beaverbrook Playhouse, and Theatre New Brunswick, Vernon Chapman's memoir *Who's in the Goose Tonight?* was helpful, and I also consulted a 1964 essay by Gray, old programs and clippings from the Theatre New Brunswick *fonds* in the New Brunswick Provincial Archives and benefited from interviews with Mardi Cockburn and Doreen Grinstead, who also lent me materials from their private collections, and with Walter Learning and others in Fredericton. The literature on alcoholism and on the adult children of alcoholics is extensive, but I have listed a few that I found useful in my endnotes.

Chapter 4:

Excellent studies of Canadian culture and theatre history, as well as memoirs, autobiographies and biographies, have appeared in recent years and many of these works are fundamental to my understanding of our cultural history. See studies in the Bibliography by Pierre Berton, Diane Bessai, Susan Crean, Joyce Doolittle, Ken Dyba, Karen Finlay, Daniel Francis, James Hoffmann, Denis Johnston, Vincent Massey, Mavor Moore, Malcom Page, Ginny Ratsoy, Don Rubin, Ross Stuart, Maria Tippett, Renate Usmiani, Anton Wagner, and George Woodcock. Between 1966 and 1970, the Drama Department at the University of Calgary published a magazine called *Drama at Calgary*, and this publication provided important background on productions Sharon was part of and her early exposure to Beckett. Studies of radio are comparatively rare but I have benefited from the work of Howard Fink, Alice Frick, Frances Gray, Jill Tomasson Goodwin, Gerry Gross, Peter Lewis, Mary Jane Miller, Anne Nothof, and Damiano Pietropaolo. Andrew Allan's autobiography is essential reading, and I greatly appreciated my conversations with former CBC directors Kathleen Flaherty and Bill Gray. The Centre for Broadcast Studies at Concordia University is an invaluable resource for the study of radio in Canada. For reviews of "A Compulsory Option," see Ashwell, Chatelin, Dafoe, Erdelyi, Fraser, Galloway, Mallet, Maskoulis, and Sherman.

Chapter 5:

For information on Major James Walsh and Sitting Bull, I consulted studies by Ian Anderson, Dee Brown, Vine Deloria, Black Elk, and Grant MacEwen. The Fort Walsh National Historical website has useful photographs and information: http://www.rcmpmuseum.com. For my discussion of *Walsh* and its main productions, I have benefited from my conversations with Harold Baldridge and John Wood and from reviews in the archives of Theatre Calgary, the National Arts Centre, and the Stratford Festival Archives. Detailed discussions of images of Mounties and Indians in popular culture can be found in Berton's *Hollywood's Canada*, Daniel Francis's *The Imaginary Indian*, and my book *Canada and the Idea of North*. For background on the historical context and treatment of the *Komagata Maru*, see the article by Grace and Helms, the book-length study by Hugh Johnston, and the *Encyclopedia of British Columbia* edited by Daniel Francis. Ali Kazimi released his documentary film *Continuous Journey: The Story of the Komagata Maru* in 2005. Sharon has drawn upon religious texts by Sikh prophets for Hopkinson's final speech, and she kept a clipping file for her research on the incident and on racist events in 1970s Vancouver (54:7–12). For reviews of productions of *The Komagata Maru Incident*, see Ashwell, Gillese, and Hopkins. Information about the hostage-taking used by Sharon for *One Tiger to a Hill* can be found in the Murphys' *Sentences and Paroles*.

Chapter 6:

The literature about Lizzie Borden is voluminous, but I relied on works by Arnold Brown, Angela Carter, Robert Flynn, Ann Jones, David Kent, William Masterton, Leonard Rebello, Frank Spiering, and Douglas and Olshaker's forensic psychiatric study. My discussion of "My Name Is Lisbeth" is based on the typescript with the Pollock papers (54:4.9). For New York reviews of *Blood Relations*, see Barnes, Burgi, Leahey, Massa, Rich, and Thrall, and for the interview with director David Heefer, see McBryde. Among the most interesting studies of biography and autobiography are works by Leigh Gilmore, Philip Lejeune, and Helen Buss, and I have drawn directly on the theories of Susanna Egan and Paul John Eakin; see also essays by Sherrill Grace, Ira Nadel, Sharon O'Brien, Mary Rhiel, and W.B. Worthen. *Blood Relations* has received close critical study by theatre specialists; see, in particular, articles by Diane Bessai, Susan Clement and Esther Beth Sullivan, Rosalind Kerr, André Loiselle, Madone Miner, Susan Stratton, Erin Striff, Jerry Wasserman, and Herb Wyile.

Chapter 7:

The most useful sources for productions of *Generations* are reviews by Dolphin, Mallet, and Milliken, and Geeta Budhiraja provides a useful account of the 1994 production directed by Robert Fothergill at M.S. University Baroda in India. The 1983 premiere of *Whiskey Six Cadenza* was reviewed by Brennan, Conlogue, and Hobson, but to date the play has not received much critical study. For background information and production history I considered the John Murrell and John Estacio opera *Filumena*, which premiered with the Calgary Opera in February 2003, scholarly articles by Peter Oliva and Anne Nothof, a new essay by Mark Diotte, and Nancy Tousley's review of Amantea's installation piece, *The King vs. Picariello and Lassandro*.

   For an understanding of the history of women in Canadian theatre, I found the Fraticelli report and several discussions of and responses to it indispensable; see the special issue of *CTR* 43 (1985) devoted to the report, with articles by Diane Bessai, Lynne Ferney, Mira Friedlander, Margaret Hollingsworth, Kate Lushington, and Eleanor Wachtel. I also consulted several important studies of women and theatre by feminist scholars; see books and articles by Diane Bessai, Hélène Cixous, Jill Dolan, Josette Féral, Maggie Gale, Lucie Joubert, Rosalind Kerr, Rita Much, Judith Rudakoff, Ann Saddlemyer, Paula Sperdakos, Heidi Stephenson and Natasha Langridge, Susan Stratton, and Cynthia Zimmerman. Recent work by Hope McIntyre, Kelly Thornton, Kate Weiss, and Rebecca Burton has helped me appreciate the challenges still faced by women in Canadian theatres. *Getting It Straight* has not received the critical attention it deserves, but for Sharon's comments on the play, see interviews with Ingram and in Wallace and Zimmerman and in Rudakoff and Much. The best article on the play to date is by Craig Stewart Walker.

Chapter 8:

For information on the genesis of *Fair Liberty's Call*, I consulted the early draft of the play in the Banff archives and interviewed several people who saw the Stratford production as well as director, Guy Sprung. An audio tape of Sharon's lecture, a video of the premiere, and many other production documents are held in the Stratford archives. Other helpful sources are articles by Cathy Chung, and Sherrill Grace ("Imagining Canada"). My information about the Garry Theatre has been gleaned from interviews, production reviews by Martin Morrow and Brian Hutchinson, articles by Rena Cohen and Rita Much, Morrow's article, "Garry Theatre runs afoul of Equity rules," and the files kept by Kirk Pollock and the Culberts. For a checklist of Garry productions, see Appendix 2.

Chapter 9:

The essential sources for background on Nell Shipman and *Moving Pictures* are Shipman's autobiography and Kay Armatage's biography of Shipman. I discussed the play in detail in three articles published in 2001, 2002, and 2005, and Anne Nothof's articles from 2001 and 2005 are especially helpful for production history. Shipman's most famous film is *Back to God's Country* (1919). For my understanding of the 2004 production I found interviews with Heather Inglis, Jan Selman, and members of the cast invaluable, and the proceedings of the symposium organized by Patricia Demers provide important context and analysis; they appear in the on-line journal *wwr: Women Writing and Reading* (Summer 2005). I also consulted reviews of the premiere and of the Edmonton production; see Evans, Finstad, Matwychuk, Morrow, and Nicholls.

   The case of Janet Smith is mentioned in many general histories of British Columbia, but the most important sources are Edward Starkins's book and the unpublished play script, "Disposing of the Dead," by Kate Schlemmer, which was produced at Vancouver's Waterfront Theatre in November 1996. To date *End Dream* has not received much scholarly analysis, but I found reviews of the premier useful (see Clark, Creery, and Wilton) and Anne Nothof's 2001 article helpful. The most useful sources for *Angel's Trumpet* are the biographies by James Mellow, Nancy Milford, and Kendall Taylor, but I relied on reviews of the premiere by Clark, Goffin, Mandel, Morrow, and Wilton for further understanding of reactions to the production. Anne Nothof's 2004 article is the only scholarly study to date. I found my interviews with Sharon, Mark Lawes, and cast members very helpful. I list other sources, including Tennessee Williams's play about the Fitzgeralds, in my article, "The Art of Sharon Pollock."

   For historical and biographical information on Anna Mae Pictou Aquash, my main sources are the NFB documentary *The Spirit of Anna Mae*, Yvette Nolan's play *Annie Mae's Movement*, and Michelle La Flamme's "Indigenous Women Beyond the Grave," but I have also followed media coverage of the story and found "Word Warriors" by Gloria Anzaldua and Cherrie Moraga helpful. Ann Jansen's essay on the radio version of Sharon's play provided useful production history, and for information on the stage play productions I relied on interviews with cast members and directors and on reviews by Matwychuk, Nicholls, and Sassano. The chief source for historical background on the murders of Father Rouviére and Le Roux is R.G. Moyles's *British Law and Arctic Men*, and I discuss this and other treatments of the case in my 2007 article "White Men Talking." Sharon's comments on *Man Out of Joint* are from her interview with Stephen Hunt in "Playwright heads downstage."

Chapter 10:

Works that I have drawn on for my conclusions and summary in this chapter are all identified in the text or endnotes. However, I must emphasize how valuable I found the discussion and presentations at the 2004 Workshop "Putting a Life on Stage," which led to the book *Theatre & AutoBiography*, edited by Grace and Wasserman. All the main speakers are included in the book, but the book cannot capture three days of lively debate or the impact of those days on my appreciation of theatre.

Sharon Pollock:
A Comprehensive Bibliography

The following bibliography of primary work by Pollock and of reviews of her productions has been checked many times against available records. Unfortunately, some details could not be confirmed and review clippings often lack identification of sources, but I have retained entries for all items I have seen in archives so that future scholars might add or correct as necessary. The bibliography is separated into the following categories: Primary Sources, with A: interviews; B: works by Sharon Pollock; and Secondary Sources, with A: production reviews, book reviews, and newspaper commentaries; and B: all other works consulted such as books, chapters, critical articles on Sharon Pollock, on Canadian theatre and cultural history, and on biography, autobiography, and theory.

Primary Sources

A: Interviews

Anon. "A Conversation with Sharon Pollock." *Canadian Literature: A Guide.* Calgary Access Network (CMEC 1986): 139–43.

Anon. "Spicing up 'bland pap' of Canadian history." *The Beacon Herald* 19 July 1974. 3.

Ashley, Audrey M. "Sharon Pollock ... from the inside." *Ottawa Citizen* 16 Nov. 1984. D12.

Bale, Doug. "Walsh playwright swears she has written her last three-act play." *London Free Press* July 1974.

Brennan, Brian. "Pollock play confirms art follows life." *Calgary Herald* 1 April 1984. F10.

Clark, Bob. "Playwright Likes 'Simple Stories'." *Calgary Herald* 10 March 2000. C9.

———. "Beautiful Damned: New play explores the ill-fated marriage of Scott & Zelda Fitzgerald." *Calgary Herald* 3 March 2001. ES.6.

Dambrosfsky, Gwen. "Artistic director uneasy about feminist 'equation'." *Globe and Mail* 22 August 1984. M7.

Demers, Patricia. "An interview with Sharon Pollock and Jan Selman." *wwrMagazine* 2.1 (Summer 2005): 15–19.

———. "An interview with Sharon Pollock, Kelly Spilchak & Candace Woloshyn." *wwrMagazine* 2.1 (Summer 2005): 20–25.

Doig, Ian. "Digging in the Past." *Avenue* March 2000. 13.

Dudley, Wendy. "Pollock joins Lubicon protest." *Calgary Herald* 13 January 1988. F2.

Dufort, Lynn. "Sharon Pollock Talks About Her New Work." *Foothills* 2.2 (1986): 3–5.

Dunn, Margo. "Sharon Pollock: In the Centre Ring." *Makara* 1.5 (August/September 1976): 2–6.

Flaherty, Kathleen. "Profile of Sharon Pollock." Taped interview with play excerpts, made at The Garry Theatre, ca 1994. Published as "Sharon Pollock on Sharon Pollock: As Interviewed by Kathleen Flaherty" in *Making Theatre: A Life of Sharon Pollock*, Appendix 3. 394–411.

G.I.T. "Blood Relations." *Granville Island Times* 4.4 (Spring 1983). 1–2.

Goffin, Jeff. "F. Scott and Zelda Fitzgerald exposed." *Fast Forward* (Calgary) 1–7 March 2001. 24.

Grace, Sherrill. "How Passionate Are You? An Interview with Sharon Pollock." *CTR* 114 (Spring 2003): 26–32.

Hobson, Louis. "Lizzie Borden took an axe ... " *Calgary Sunday* Sun 6 December 1981. S15.

Hofsess, John. "Playwright Sharon Pollock: mother, lover, artist." *Calgary Albertan* [Magazine] 9 March 1980: 10–12.

———. "Families." *Homemaker's Magazine* 15 (March 1980): 41–60.

———. "Sharon Pollock: writing for the illegitimate theatre." *Other Stages* 5.11 (February 1983): 3.

Hohtanz, Marie. "Passionate playwright." *Calgary Herald* 29 November 1987. 6–10.

Hunt, Stephen. "Keeping her edge." *Calgary Herald* 18 June 2006. C 1–2.

———. "Pollock heads downstage." *Calgary Herald* 9 May 2007. C 1–2.

Lewis, Nicholas. Dir. "From Script to Stage: The Diary of 'My Name Is Lisbeth'." Douglas College: Video, 1977.

MacMillan, Shannon. "Sharon Pollock." *Where* (Calgary) 18.10 (March 1999): 78.

Metcalfe, Robin. "Interview with Sharon Pollock." *Books in Canada* 16.2 (March 1987): 39–40.

Mitton, Roger. "Interview with Sharon Pollock." *The West Ender* (Vancouver) 21 April 1983. 26.

Montgomery, Lori. "So far from her beginnings." *Fast Forward* (Calgary) 9 March 2000. 9.

———. "End Dream." *Fast Forward* (Calgary) 16 March 2000. 8.

Morrow, Martin. "TJ to stage new Pollock play." *Calgary Herald* 13 May 1998. F2.

———. "Pollock examines life of forgotten star." *Calgary Herald* 11 March 1999. F6.

———. "Examining the Toxic Flower." *Globe and Mail* 2 March 2001. R7.

———. "Jazz Age Tragedy of Scott & Zelda." *Calgary Straight* 1–7 March 2001. 7.

Nothof, Anne. "Interview with Sharon Pollock." Nothof, ed. 2000: 167–79.

Quigley, Pat. "Musings of a Political Playwright: A Conversation with Sharon Pollock." *Stratford for Students.* Fall 1990. [n.p.] Rpt. *Sharon Pollock: Critical Perspectives on Canadian Theatre in English.* Ed. Sherrill Grace and Michelle La Flamme. 33–40.

———. [abbreviated version of "A Conversation with Sharon Pollock"] *Stratford Fanfares Bulletin* 24.3 (1990).

Read, Nicholas. "A murky kind of inspiration." *Vancouver Sun* 13 April 1983. E1.

Rempel, Byron. "Not a diplomat, Pollock returns, dismayed at Canadian theatre." *Alberta Report* 6 November 1989. 56–57.

Rudakoff, Judith, and Rita Much, eds. "Interview with Sharon Pollock." *Fair Play: 12 Women Speak: Conversations with Canadian Women Playwrights.* Toronto: Simon and Pierre, 1990. 208–20.

"Sharon Pollock." Richmond, B.C.: ACCESS Television, 1984.

Sheppy, Nikki. "Playwright's life a symphonic score." *Fast Forward* (Calgary) March 1999. 23.

Solomon, Howard. "Theatre figures back Pollock injunction." *Calgary Herald* 29 April 1983. E1.

———. "Pollock suit is settled." *Calgary Herald* 3 June 1983. F11.

Taylor, Kate. "Firebrand playwright still sizzles." *Globe and Mail* 9 March 2000. R1, 5.

Telenko, Sherri. "Why is Sharon Pollock so dissatisfied with the state of Canadian theatre?" *Performing Arts in Canada* 30.4 (Spring 1997): 14–15.

Wallace, Robert. "Sharon Pollock." In Robert Wallace and Cynthia Zimmerman. *The Work: Conversations with English-Canadian Playwrights*. Toronto: Coach House Press, 1982. 115–26.

Wasserman. Jerry. Telephone interview. September 1993. Ts. 20 pages.

Wilton, Lisa. "Real Canadian Mystery. Strange case inspires TJ's latest play." *Calgary Sun* 9 March 2000. 51.

———. "Trumpet hails turbulent love affair." *Calgary Sun* 27 February 2001. 41.

Women Writing and Reading/wwrMagazine 1.2 (Summer 2005). Special issue on Sharon Pollock. www.womenwritingreading.org

Zimmerman, Cynthia. "Towards a Better, Fairer World: An Interview with Sharon Pollock." *CTR* 69 (Winter 1991): 34–38.

Zwarum, Suzanne. "The Cats Came Back." *Western Living* (Vancouver) 20.9 (September 1990): 40–41.

CBC Radio Interviews:

"Morningside." Peter Gzowski. 6 April 1984.

"Variety Tonight." Vicky Gaboreau. 18 October 1984.

"Morningside." Peter Gzowski. Panel with Sharon Pollock, Urjo Kareda, and Patrick O'Flaherty. 13 September 1985.

"Morningside." Peter Gzowski. Panel with Sharon Pollock, Robert Enright, and David Barnett. 24 January 1986.

"Morningside." Peter Gzowski. Panel with Sharon Pollock, Janet Amos, and Daphne Goldrick. 19 September 1986.

"Morningside." Peter Gzowski. Panel with Sharon Pollock and 2 actors. 16 February 1989.

"Morningside." Peter Gzowski. Sharon Pollock about the Garry Theatre. 3 December 1993.

"The Arts Tonight." Sheila Rogers. Sharon Pollock about *Saucy Jack*. 6 December 1993.

"This Morning." Sheila Rogers. Sharon Pollock about *Angel's Trumpet*. 15 March 2001.

B: Works by Sharon Pollock

Essays, Speeches, Short Stories (published and unpublished):

Chalmers, Sharon. "Shaking Hands." *Fredericton High School Yearbook*. 1951. 71.

Pollock, Sharon. "If at first." Ts. story ca 1970–71. Sharon Pollock Archives.

———. "How Things Are." [short story] *The Fiddlehead* 96 (Winter 1973): 81–84.

———. "A Note from the Playwright." In "Study Kit for the Playhouse Production of 'The Komagata Maru Incident'." Compiled by Camilla Ross, Margaret Whitford, and Lendre Rodgers. January 1976. 3.

———. "The Komagata Maru Incident." Program note, Citadel Playbill. 21 March–2 April 1977. 3.

———. "The Canadian Playwright Today." 1981. Speech given at the meeting of Canadian English-language International Theatre Institute Centre conference, Montreal. Audio tape. Sharon Pollock Archives.

———. "Canada's Playwrights: Finding Their Place." *CTR* 32 (1982): 34–38. Rpt. in Rubin, ed. 389–93.

———. "Afterword." *Plays by Women: Volume Three*. Ed. Michelene Wandor. London: Methuen, 1984. 123–24.

———. "Theatre critic must call production as he sees it." *Calgary Herald* January 1988.

———. "Something in the Wind: Burning Desire? Or the Smouldering Remains of Once-Vital Canadian Theatre?" *Rave Review: Albert Playwrights' Network Newsletter* 2.5 (1990): 2–3.

———. "Dead or Alive? Feeling the Pulse of Canadian Theatre." *Theatrum* 23 (April/May 1991): 12–13. Reprinted in S. Grace and M. La Flamme, eds. 41–43.

———. "Reflections of a Female Artistic Director." *Women on the Canadian Stage: The Legacy of Hrotsvit*. Ed. Rita Much. Winnipeg: Blizzard, 1992. 109–14.

———. Untitled Lecture [Celebrated Writers Series, Stratford] Stratford Archives Cassette. 11 July 1993.

———. "Many Brave Spirits." *Theatre Memoirs: on the occasion of the Canadian Theatre Conference*. May 21–23. Toronto: Playwrights Union of Canada, 1998. 13–17.

———. "The Evolution of an Authentic Voice in Canadian Theatre." *Canadian Culture and Literature: A Taiwan Perspective*. Eds. Steven Tötösy de Zepetnek and Leung Yiu-nam. Edmonton: Research Institute for Comparative Literature, University of Alberta, 1998. 114–24.

———. "Genesis of *Blood Relations*." "*Blood Relations*. Shaw Festival Program." 2003. n.p.

———. "Trip to Sierra Leone." Public lecture, 1 May 2003, Calgary, for CAUSE Canada.

———. "The Universal Language of Theatre." *CAUSE Canada in Sierra Leone*. Newsletter, 2003. n.p.

———. "One World, One Theatre." *APN Bulletin* June 2004: 1–4.

———. "A Memoir" [originally "Many Brave Spirits"]. In *Collected Works*. Vol I. 2005. 17–21.

———. "Playwright: Parasite or Symbiont." In *Theatre and AutoBiography: Writing and Performing Lives in Theory and Practice*. Eds. Sherrill Grace and Jerry Wasserman. Vancouver: Talonbooks, 2006. 295–300.

———. "A Memoir: Sierra Leone, 2003." *Collected Works*. Vol. II. 2006. 17–27.

———. "Reflections." [originally "Canadian Women Playmakers: Tributes and Tribulations," speech delivered to 4th Annual Playwrights Guild of Canada Conference, May 2006]. *Collected Works*. Vol. III 2006. 15–24.

Published Plays:

———. *Angel's Trumpet*. In *Sharon Pollock: Three Plays*. 165–224. *Collected Works*. Vol. III. 185–225.

———. *Blood Relations*. [1980 script] CTR 29 (Winter 1981): 46–107.

———. *Blood Relations and Other Plays*. [*Generations, One Tiger to a Hill*]. 1981. Edmonton: NeWest Press, 2002.

———. *Blood Relations*. In *Plays by Women*. Vol. 3. Ed. Michelene Wandor. London: Methuen, 1984. 91–122.

———. *Vérkötelékek*, with Foreword and 18 January 1982 letter by Sharon Pollock. Trans. by Katalin Kürtösi. Budapest: Napkút Kiadó, 2007.

———. *Blood Relations*. *Collected Works*. Vol. I. 337–94.

———. *Collected Works*. See *Sharon Pollock: Collected Works*.

———. *Death in the Family*. *Collected Works*. Vol. III. 33–78.

———. *Doc*. Toronto: Playwrights Canada Press, 1984. *Collected Works*. Vol. II. 125–97.

———. *Doc*. *Modern Canadian Plays*. Ed. Jerry Wasserman. Vancouver: Talonbooks, 1994. 129–67.

———. *End Dream*. In *Sharon Pollock: Three Plays*. 97–163. *Collected Works*. Vol. III. 135–84.

———. *Fair Liberty's Call*. Toronto: Coach House Press, 1995. *Collected Works*. Vol. II. 359–418.

———. *Generations*. In *Blood Relations and Other Plays*. 138–98. *Collected Works*. Vol. I. 277–335.

———. *Getting It Straight*. In *Heroines: Three Plays*. John Murrell, Sharon Pollock, Michel Tremblay. Ed. Joyce Doolittle. Red Deer, Alberta: Red Deer College Press, 1992. 85–126. *Collected Works*. Vol. II. 227–62.

———. "'It's all make believe, isn't it?'—Marilyn Monroe." *Instant Applause: 26 Very Short Complete Plays*. Winnipeg: Blizzard, 1994. 91–95. *Collected Works*. Vol. II. 263–69.

———. *Kabloona Talk*. *Collected Works*. Vol. III. 255–99.

———. *Komagata Maru Incident, The*. Script. Toronto: Playwrights Co-op, 1978. In *Six Canadian Plays*. Ed. Tony Hamill. Toronto: Playwrights Canada Press, 1992. 223–86. Reprinted in *Playing the Pacific Province: An Anthology of British Columbia Plays, 1967–2000*. Ed. James Hoffmann and Ginny Ratsoy.

Toronto: Playwrights Canada Press, 2002. 107–37. Excerpted for *The Literary Half-Yearly: A Journal Devoted to Comparative Literature* xxiv. 2 (July 1983): 164–77. *Collected Works*. Vol. I. 97–137.

———. "Making of Warriors, The." *Airborne: Radio Plays by Women*. Ed. Ann Jansen. Winnipeg: Blizzard, 1991. 99–132. *Collected Works*. Vol. III. 227–54.

———. *Man Out of Joint*. *Collected Works*. Vol. III. 301–65.

———. *Moving Pictures*. In *Sharon Pollock: Three Plays*. 13–96. *Collected Works*. Vol. III. 79–183.

———. *Prairie Dragons*. In *Playhouse: Six Fantasy Plays for Children*. Ed. Joyce Doolittle. Red Deer, Alberta: Red Deer College Press, 1989. 100–124. *Collected Works*. Vol. II. 199–226.

———. *Saucy Jack*. Winnipeg: Blizzard, 1994. *Collected Works*. Vol. II. 311–58.

———. *Sharon Pollock: Three Plays* [*Moving Pictures, End Dream, Angel's Trumpet*]. Toronto: Playwrights Canada Press, 2003.

———. *Sharon Pollock: Collected Works*, 3 vols. Ed. Cynthia Zimmerman. Toronto: Playwrights Canada Press, 2005, 2006, 2008.

———. *Sweet Land of Liberty*. *Collected Works*. Vol. I. 177–212.

———. *Walsh*. Vancouver: Talonbooks, 1973.

———. *Walsh*. 3rd printing with revisions. Vancouver: Talonbooks, 1976.

———. *Walsh*. In *Modern Canadian Plays*. Ed. Jerry Wasserman. Vancouver: Talonbooks, 1993. 237–71.

———. *Walsh*. 9th printing, revised. Vancouver: Talonbooks, 1998. *Collected Works*. Vol. I. 30–95.

———. *Whiskey Six Cadenza*. In *NeWest Plays by Women*. Ed. Diane Bessai and Don Kerr. Edmonton: NeWest Press, 1987. 137–247. Reprinted in *Blood Relations and Other Plays*. Edmonton: NeWest Press, 2002. 225–330. *Collected Works*. Vol. I. 35–124.

———. "Wreck of the National Line Car." Play script. Toronto: Playwrights Union of Canada, 1977. *Collected Works*. Vol I. 139–75.

Unpublished scripts for stage, film, and radio:
(for scripts held in the Sharon Pollock *fonds*, see *The Sharon Pollock Papers First Accession*)

Stage:

———. "A Compulsory Option." [1971]; premiere at New Play Centre, Vancouver. 1972; Dir. Pamela Hawthorne; production in 1975, Citadel Theatre, Edmonton, Dir. Keith Digby; production at Festival Lennoxville, 1977, Dir. Bill Davis; production as "No! No! No!" at Theatre Passe Muraille, 1977, Dir. Hrant Alianak.

———. "A Lesson in Swizzelry." Dir. Sharon Pollock for OFY-funded caravan troupe, touring parks in summers of 1974 and 1975. Dir. Dorothy Jones, Douglas College, April 1975.

———. "And Out Goes You?" Vancouver Playhouse. Dir. Chris Newton. Premiere: 24 March 1975.

———. "Chautauqua Spelt E-N-E-R-G-Y." Children's play, 1979. Premiered by Alberta Theatre Projects, 1979; Dir. Douglas Riske.

———. "Doc." Trans. Francine Pominville. Ts. National Theatre School of Canada. 1988.

———. "Egg." Typescript. University of Guelph Archives. n.d.

———. "Highway #2: The Great Divide." By Sharon Pollock, Paul Gélineau, and Janet Hinton-Mann. Premiere: 1994, Phoenix Theatre, Edmonton. Dir. Paul Gélineau.

———. "Liens de Sang." [*Blood Relations*] Trans. Francine Pominville. Ts. National Theatre School of Canada. 1985.

———. "Mail versus Female" March 1979; premiere at Lunchbox Theatre, Calgary. Dir. Bartley Bard.

———. "New Canadians." Premiered at Playhouse Holiday, 1973. Dir. Don Shipley.

———. "Star-child." (adaptation of Oscar Wilde) 1974. Children's play. Premiered at Playhouse Theatre School, 1974. Dir Don Shipley.

———. "Superstition Thru' the Ages." 1973. Children's play, premiered at Playhouse Holiday, 1973. Dir. David Barnett.

———. "The Great Drag Race, or Smoked, Choked and Croaked." 1973. Lyrics and music by Marjorie Morris. Play commissioned by the B.C. Lung Association [formerly British Columbia Christmas Seal Society] for B.C. schools.

———. "The Happy Prince." (adaptation of Oscar Wilde). 1974. Children's play. Premiered at Playhouse Theatre School, 1974. Dir. Don Shipley.

———. "The Rose and the Nightingale." (adaptation of Oscar Wilde). 1974. Children's play. Premiered at the Playhouse Theatre School, 1974. Dir. Don Shipley.

———. "Tracings: The Simon Fraser Story." Written by Sharon Pollock, dramaturge for SFU students. Adapted for Television by Theatre Network. ITV Productions. 1978.

———. "Wudjesay?" 1974. Children's play. Premiered at Playhouse Holiday, 1974. Dir. Don Shipley. Toured lower mainland B.C. schools with theatre-in-education program, January to March 1974.

Radio:

"31 for 2." CBC AM: broadcast, 7 February 1971. Producer/director Fred Diehl.

"A.J. Jones." CBC AM: radio series pilot episode. Prod/Director Kathleen Flaherty. c1992. Not broadcast.

"Constance Kent." CBC FM Arts National: broadcast 15 June 1992. Producer/dir, Kathleen Flaherty.

"Doc." CBC FM: broadcast 16 March 1991. Dir. Guy Sprung; Producer, Heather Brown. Re-broadcast, CBC AM: 12 June 1992.

"Generations." CBC AM: broadcast, 10 December 1978. Producer/director, Bill Gray.

"In Memory Of." CBC AM: 1975. Broadcast date unconfirmed.

"Intensive Care." CBC AM: broadcast, 5 June 1983. Producer/director, Bill Gray.

"In the Beginning Was." CBC AM "Soundstage" 1980. Broadcast date unconfirmed. Producer/director Bill Gray.

"Mary Beth Goes to Calgary." CBC AM:1980. Broadcast date unconfirmed. Prod/Dir Bill Gray.

"Mrs Yale and Jennifer." Commissioned script 1980. Seven episodes. CBC. Broadcast date unconfirmed. Calgary. Prod/Dir: Bill Gray.

"One Tiger to a Hill." CBC AM: broadcast, 12 August 1985. Producer, Greg Rogers.

"Split Seconds in the Death Of" CBC AM Radio: broadcast, 22 November 1970. Producer/director Fred Diehl.

"Sweet Land of Liberty." CBC AM: broadcast, 2 December 1979. Producer/director Bill Gray. Re-broadcast for CBC FM 22 April 1990.

"The B Triple P Plan." CBC AM: broadcast, 21 September 1974. Producer/director Irene Prothroe. [also "The Larsens" TV play.]

"The Making of Warriors." CBC AM: broadcast 20 May 1991. Producer, James Roy. Re-broadcasts: CBC FM 20 October 1991; CBC AM 27 October 1991.

"The Story of the Komagata Maru." CBC AM: Western Profiles series, broadcast 31 January 1978. Adapted from stage play ca 1976–77.

"Waiting." CBC (Vancouver) Anthology. July 1973. Dir. Don Mowatt.

"Walsh." CBC AM Radio: broadcast 23 March 1974. Producer/director Claudia Gibson.

"We to the Gods." CBC AM Radio: broadcast, 5 September 1971. Producer/director Fred Diehl.

"Whiskey Six." CBC FM: broadcast 22 October 1983. Producer Greg Rogers.

Television:

"Country Joy." Episodes by Sharon Pollock and others. CBC TV. 19 November 1979 to 4 January 1980.

"Death in the Family." Dir. Douglas Berquist. Nomadic Pictures Productions. Bravo TV. 4 November 1998.

"Death in the Family." Dir. Douglas Berquist. Nomadic Pictures, Calgary 1998.

"Double Play." Telefilm loosely based on *Blood Relations.* Dir. Silvio Narrizano. Producer Robert Barclay. CFCW, 1983. Script adaptation by Jane Barclay.

"Portrait of a Pig." [Sharon Ball]. CBC TV (Winnipeg). Broadcast date unconfirmed. 1974. Producer/director, Don S. Williams.

"Ransom." For *The Magic Lie.* Adapted for TV by Sharon Pollock from story by Lois Duncan. CBC (Edmonton), 22 March 1978.

The Komagata Maru Incident. ACCESS Alberta. September 1984.

"The Larsens." CBC TV (Winnipeg). 27 November 1976. Dir. Donald S. Williams.

"The Persons Case." ACCESS Alberta. October, 1981. Dir. John Wright.

"Walsh". Producer/director, Gene Packwood. Access Alberta. 1986.

Secondary Sources

A: WEB sites; Collections; Production Reviews; Book Reviews; Newspaper Commentaries.

"Sharon Pollock." *The Literary Enclyclopedia and Literary Dictionary.* http://www.LitEncyc.com

"Sharon Pollock." Alberta Playwrights. http://www.Albertaplaywrights.com

"Sharon Pollock." Encyclopedia of Canadian Theatre. http://www.CanadianTheatre.com

Sharon Pollock Papers, The, First Accession. Ed. Apollonia Steele and Jean F. Tener. Calgary: University of Calgary Press, 1989.

***

Abdalla, Laila. "Saucy Jack." *Canadian Book Review.* Toronto: P. Martin, 1994: 231–34.

Ackerman, Marianne. "Quinzaine leaps culture, language barriers." *Montreal Gazette* 31 May 1986: C5.

Aird, Elizabeth. "*Doc* sits us head down in mud." *Vancouver Sun* 24 March 1990. D7.

Albers, Sandra. "*Komagata* must be seen." *Kamloops Daily News* 4 February 1977. 4A.

Allen, Bob. "*Walsh* passable, by College standards." *Vancouver Sun* 14 November 1974. 31.

———. "Stratford Discovers the West." *Vancouver Province* 5 April 1974. 3, 18.

———. "Laughs aimed at politicians in a new play." *Vancouver Province* 21 March. 1975. 35.

———. "'Out' has purpose and wit but precious little slashing." *Vancouver Province* 25 March 1975. 25.

———. "Play reveals shame of *Komagata Maru.*" *Vancouver Province* 16 January 1976. 31.

———. "Douglas College Theatre turns Lizzie loose." *Vancouver Province* 1 April 1976. 29.

———. "*The Komagata Maru Incident*: 60 years hasn't changed much." *Vancouver Province* 21 January 1976. 8–9.

———. "SFU's Tracings has potential." *Vancouver Province* 20 June 1977. 21.

———. "Playwright treated poorly: Pollock." *Vancouver Province* 13 April 1983. A9.

———. "Arts Club takes theatre awards." *Vancouver Province* 13 June 1983. B6.

———. "*Blood Relations* strong, evocative." *Vancouver Province* 15 April 1983. B5.

Anon. "Pantomime Starts This Week." *Fredericton Daily Gleaner* 21 December 1964. n.p.

Anon. "Shiretown Audience Praises 'Mary, Mary'." *The Bugle* May 1965. 12.

Anon. "'Provok'd Wife' Solid Success; On Again Tonight." *Fredericton Daily Gleaner* 27 February 1965. 1, 2.

Anon. " 'Provok'd Wife' Ends Three-Night Run." *Fredericton Daily Gleaner* 2 March 1965. 16.

Anon. "Calgary play wins DDF." *The Albertan* 24 May 1966. 2, 9.

Anon. "Asian Role Examined." *Vancouver Province* 21 January 1976. 24.

Anon. "*The Komagata Maru Incident*: You can look for a message made palatable." *Vancouver Sun* 16 January 1976. 31.

Anon. "Three boring non-people in flimsy excuse for a play." *Ottawa Citizen* 2 August 1977. 33.

Anon. "Compulsory Option, demanding on the funny bone." *Ottawa Journal* 14 July 1977. 38.

Anon. "ATP Theatre-in-Education run starts Feb. 13." *The Albertan* 9 February 1978. 22.

Anon. "Playwright Pollock's a hit in San Diego." *Alberta Report* 23 November 1979. 46.

Anon. "Sharon Pollock's *Blood Relations*." *New York Magazine* 2 February 1983. n.p.

Anon. "TNB Play Opens March 1." *Fredericton Daily Gleaner* 21 February 1986. 9.

Anon. "Pollock honoured." *Calgary Herald* 30 January 1986. D4.

Anon. "Guild honours Pollock, Van Herk." *Globe and Mail* 13 May 1987. C5.

Anon. "Writer explores mother's suicide." *Winnipeg Free Press* 4 February 1987. 35.

Anon. "Dramatic Feuding: Theatre Calgary's *Walsh* garners controversy." *Alberta Report* 15 February 1988. 41.

Anon. "Home-town gal stages own play." *Toronto Star* 14 April 1988. B4.

Anon. "Did you do it, Lizzie Borden?" *The Exeter Times Advocate* 11 January 1989. 7.

Appelbe, Alison. "Reality finally comes to Canadian plays." *Vancouver Sun* 14 August 1972. 27.

Ashley, Audrey M. "Stratford Director, Cast and Playwright's Delight." *Ottawa Citizen* 25 July 1974. 50.

———. "A Hostage-taking drama gets lost in welter of words." *Ottawa Citizen* 7 July 1980. 42.

———. "Ambiguous murder drama expertly staged." *Ottawa Citizen* 24 February 1981. 54.

———. "Axe-slaying case turned into play by 'murder freak'." *Ottawa Citizen* 23 February 1981. 30–31.

———. "Revised version of *Walsh* lacks impact." *Ottawa Citizen* 11 May 1983. 78.

Ashwell, Keith. "Establishment play funny but not absurd." *Edmonton Journal* 21 October 1975. 37.

———. "Shame helps play shine in ingenuity." *Edmonton Journal* 24 March 1977. 63.

———. "Playwright Pollock set to score with *Blood Relations*." *Edmonton Journal* 11 March 1980. D2.

———. "Borden's Notoriety is Pollock's Notability." *Edmonton Journal* 13 March 1980. C9.

Astington, John. "Drama" *University of Toronto Quarterly* 51.4 (1982): 374–84.

Atkey, Mel. "Blood Relations." *Georgia Straight* 22–29 April 1983. 16.

"Author plans play." *Winnipeg Free Press* 18 December 1987. 38.

"Awards." *Quill & Quire* 54.3 (March 1988): 69.

Balcon, D. "Question of copyright: the Sharon Pollock case." *Cinema Canada* 102 (1983): 26.

Baldridge, Harold. "Calgary" [review of *Walsh* premiere, 1973]. *CTR* 2 (Spring 1974): 118–20.

Baldwin, Carol. "Stratford play really does have it all." *The Post* (Burlington, ON) 28 July 1993. B7.

Bale, Doug. "Longshot Steals Show at Stratford Festival." *London Free Press* 25 July 1974. D2.

———. "Theatrical metaphor brilliantly expanded." *London Free Press* 7 January 1988. D2.

Bannon, Anthony. "'Walsh' is American Indian Drama, Totem Ritual Confession of Sham." *Buffalo Evening News* 25 July 1974. n.p.

Barnes, Clive. "Lizzy Borden Does It Again." *New York Post* 15 February 1983. 33.

Baron, Clifford. "*Fair Liberty's Call*: excellent ensemble piece." *Our Community Press* (Stratford) 21 July 1993. 8.

Berting, Nerine. "Sharon Pollock stars in saucy production." *The Pinion* (Douglas College) 3 April 1975. 5.

Bertoia, Susan. "Lizzie! Lizzie! Lizzie!" *The Ubyssey* 26 September 1986. 6.

Bessai, Diane. "Theatre Provocateur." *NeWest Review* (April 1980): 6, 10.

———. "A playwright comes into her own." *NeWest Review* (June 1981): 9–10.

———. "A Family Affair." *NeWest Review* (June 1984): 16.

Bierman, Helmer. "'Family Trappings' is emotional dynamite." *The Evening Times Globe* 21 March 1986. 29.

Billington, Dave. "Canadian playwright's *Walsh* revives history of the west." *Windsor Star* 26 July 1974. 16.

Blakey, Bob. "Sitting Bull's stay in the West comes to life." *Calgary Herald* 25 February 1986. D1.

———. "Pollock's Egg won't be done in time for festival." *Calgary Herald* 23 April 1987. D1.

[*Blood Relations*]. Selections from newspaper and periodical reviews and articles. *Canadian Drama* 11.1 (1985): 188–95.

Boisseau, Peter R. "Pollock's play strikes close to home." *Times-Transcript* 8 March 1986. 10.

Bradbury, Joy. "Guilty—or is she?" *Vancouver Courier* 20 April 1983. 20.

Brady, Owen E. "*Fair Liberty's Call*." *Theatre Journal* 46 (May 1994): 272–74.

Brenna, Dwayne. "Playing for Time." *NeWest Review* 13.10 (Summer 1988): 17.

Brennan, Brian. "*Komagata Maru Incident* heavily laced with propaganda." *Calgary Herald* 13 January 1979. A8.

———. "Playwright's account of Lizzie Borden effective drama." *Calgary Herald* 1 November 1980. C9.

———. "Playwright stars in her own play." *Calgary Herald* 19 November 1981. D14.

———. "Tension energizes *Blood Relations*." *Calgary Herald* 27 November 1981. C1.

———. "Tourist pamphlet inspired new Pollock play." *Calgary Herald* 5 February 1983. H1.

———. "Whiskey Six is Pollock's best play yet." *Calgary Herald* 11 February 1983. F1.

———. "Pollock play getting warm N.Y. response." *Calgary Herald* 15 February 1983. D1.

———. "Pollock offers best work yet." *Calgary Herald* 8 April 1984. F2.

———. "Playwright's father gives *Doc* the nod." *Calgary Herald* 29 November 1984. D1.

———. "Calgarians make mark in British theatre." *Calgary Herald* 7 May 1985. D1.

———. "Busy playwright always ready for new challenge." *Calgary Herald* 6 September 1985. F1.

———. "Pollock is tops again." *Calgary Herald* 27 May 1987. A1.

———. "City thespian lands role in *HMS Pinafore*." *Calgary Herald* 22 September 1987. C9.

———. "Pollock play makes debut on TC stage in '88 season." *Calgary Herald* 23 April 1987. D1.

———. "Award winning playwright still feels uneasy about arts award." *Performing Arts in Canada* 24.4 (1988): 24.

———. "Playwright quits the scene of her greatest triumphs." *Calgary Herald* 19 March 1988. F1.

———. "Play bogs down in enigmatic, historical difficulties." *Calgary Herald* 17 January 1988. E2.

———. "Historic award winner revived." *Calgary Herald* 23 January 1988. 14.

———. "ATP in lead on road to the Games." *Calgary Herald* 6 January 1988. B8.

———. "Pollock came from birthplace to home: Award-winning playwright says there's no place she'd rather live." *Calgary Herald* 6 April 1998. 4.

Brousseau, Jean-Paul. "Drame de la famille et dramaturgie." *La Presse* 19 Janvier 1982. n.p.

Brown, Stewart. "Staging sets eerie mood at Grand." *Hamilton Spectator* 10 January 1989. F5.

———. "Excellent cast a boost for *Fair Liberty's Call*." *Hamilton Spectator* 16 July 1993. C6.

Browning, Fred. "Grand Theatre." *Courier Press* (Wallaceburg) 8 January 1989. 20.

Brunner, Astrid. "Getting it Straight." *Arts Atlantic* 9 (Spring-Summer 1989): 59.

Burgi, Adrienne. "When she saw what she had done she gave her mother forty-one." *Barnard Bulletin* 9 February 1983: 4.

Chapman, Geoff. "Fair Liberty's brave call." *Toronto Star* 16 July 1993. C10.

Chatelin, Ray. "Experiment in theatre succeeds with new play." *Vancouver Province* 15 August 1972. 17.

Clark, Bob. "Pollock turns Nanny's Death into mesmerizing drama." *Calgary Herald* 12 March, 2000. B17.

———. "Mystery returns playwright to stage." *Calgary Herald* 1 April 2004. E3.

———. "Cast's stylish stagecraft keeps comedy buoyant." *Calgary Herald* 3 April 2004. E3.

———. "Pollock finds power in joint." *Calgary Herald* 12 May 2007. C 8.

Claus, Jo Anne. "Theatre N.B.'s 'Family Trappings' Strongest Production in Some Time." *Telegraph-Journal* 3 March 1986. 6.

Clements, Jim. "Western history comes alive." *Hamilton Spectator* 25 July 1974. 28.

Cohen, Joy-Ann. "Tearing Adanac apart seemed more fun." *Calgary Herald* 15 February 1978. C9.

Cohen, Rena. "Jack the Knife." *NeWest Review* (April–May 1984): 35.

———. "The Garry Theatre: playwright Sharon Pollock takes on new challenges as a director of a troubled theatre in Calgary." *NeWest Review* 19.2 (December–January 1993–1994): 33–35.

———. "Lower Depths Unprobed." *NeWest Review* (December–January 1993–1994): 35.

———. "Sharon Pollock's political satire could be an annual event." *NeWest Review* (December-January 1995–1996): 30.

Cohen, Ron. "Blood Relations." *Women's Wear Daily*. 19 February 1983. 19.

Conlogue, Ray. "How Western audiences are won." *Globe and Mail* 1 November, 1980. 16.

———. "Victorian production bustles into confusion." *Globe and Mail* 2 October. 1981. 22.

———. "Theatrical Gem Reflects the Last, Best West." *Globe and Mail* 7 March. 1983. 15.

———. "A highly personal drama." *Globe and Mail* 10 April 1984. M7.

———. "Lizzie Borden comes to Quebec." *Globe and Mail* 11 June 1986. D5.

———. "Chaotic play offers no answers." *Globe and Mail* 12 January 1990. C7.

———. "Tiger's impressive when it roars." *Globe and Mail* 31 August 1990. D6.

Corbeil, Carole. "Some truth among clichés." *Globe and Mail* 3 April 1981. 19.

Corrivault, Corinne. "L'étrange histoire de Lizzy Borden telle que racontée par Sharon Pollock." *Le Soleil* 28 September 1985. C3.

Côté, Marc. "Remembrances of Things Past." *Books in Canada* 16.2 (March 1987): 17–18.

Coulbourn, John. "Loyalist Legacy." *Toronto Sun* 16 July 1993. 53.

Coveney, Michael. "Blood Relations." *Financial Times* 13 May 1985. In *London Theatre Record* 5.10. 8–21 May 1985. 484–85.

Cowan, Cindy. "*Doc*." *CTR* 52 (Fall 1987): 95–96.

Creery, Cybèle. "Where Dreams End and Begin." *Calgary Straight* 16–23 March 2000. 8.

Crew, Robert. "*Doc* examines a shattered family." *Toronto Star* 4 October 1984: F2.

Czarnecki, Mark. "Ghosts in a family attic." *Maclean's* 97 (23 April 1984): 52.

Dafoe, Christopher. "First production almost a play." *Vancouver Sun* 15 August 1972. 27.

———. "Political comedy too true to be good." *Vancouver Sun* 25 March 1975. 37.

Davis, Robert. "*Blood Relations* script at fault." *Toronto Star* 7 April 1987. 16.

Deakin, Basil. "TAG's *Walsh*: Should be Stuff of Good Theatre." *Halifax Chronicle-Herald* 14 June 1984. 42.

———. "*Doc* changed treatment with author Pollock." *Halifax Chronicle-Herald* 5 February 1987. 29.

De Bono, Norman. "Pollock: Festival could become national theatre." *The Beacon Herald* 1990. 34–35.

Demers, Edgard. "'Walsh' manque trop souvent la cible." *Le Droit* (Ottawa) 17 May 1983. 40.

Dibbelt, Dan. "*Walsh*." *Windspeaker* 5 (29 January 1988): 14.

"*Doc*." *Arts Atlantic* 7.4 (1987): 64.

Dohy, Leanne. "Graduates urged to get involved early." *Calgary Herald* 9 November 2003. D4.

Dolphin, Ric. "Windy Clichés." *Alberta Report* 14 November 1980. 52.

Doolittle, Joyce. "*Walsh*." *NeWest Review* 13 (April 1988): 13.

Doran, Terry. "Hard issues in 'Liberty's Call,' but you've heard them before." *Buffalo News* 21 July 1993. B6.

Downton, Dawn Rae. "*Doc*." *Arts Atlantic* 7.4 (1987): 64.

———. "*Blood Relations*." *Arts Atlantic* 33 (Winter 1989): 62–63.

"Dramatic Feuding: Theatre Calgary's *Walsh* garners controversy." *Alberta Report* 15.9 (15 February 1988): 41.

Dudley, Wendy. "Supporters and detractors hope that TC will survive." *Calgary Herald* 24 August 1988. C9.

Dykk, Lloyd. "Drama with the feminine touch." *Vancouver Sun* 25 January 1984. D1.

Elliott-Dyke, Nancy. "Moving Performance of 'Doc' Opens." *The Telegraph-Journal*. 10 February 1987. 12.

Erdelyi, Joseph. "Comedy, atmosphere, tension? No! No! No!" *Ottawa Citizen* 15 February 1977. 60.

Evans, Michael. "Sharon Pollock: theatre icon stars in her own *Moving Pictures*." *See Magazine* (Edmonton) 2–8 December 2004. Cover, 10.

Faulder, Liane. "Strands of stories stitched together." *Edmonton Journal* 17 August 2003. B3.

Feldberg, Robert. "An engrossing look at Lizzy Borden." *The Record* 15 February 1983. B9.

Filewod, Alan. "Saucy Jack." *CTR* 86 (Spring 1996): 60–61.

Finlayson, Judith. "*Doc* explores social ailment." *Globe and Mail* 26 October 1984. D11.

Finstad, Kristine. "Moving Pictures." *Calgary Straight* 18–25 March 1999. n.p.

"For the Record." *Calgary Herald* 14 February 1988: D5.

Frank, Rich. "Theatre: 'Tiger to a Hill': Canadian Prison Drama." *New York Times* 14 November 1980. C3, 5.

Fraser, John. "Bad traps and hard knocks for 2 actors on the theatrical ladder." *Globe and Mail* 12 February 1977. 37.

———. "Shaggy dog comedy fetchingly manic." *Globe and Mail* 14 February 1977. 17.

Fraser, Matthew. "Theatre breaks new ground." *Globe and Mail* 15 February 1986. D9.

———. "*Doc* may be a tough pill for New Brunswick." *Globe and Mail* 7 March 1986. A12.

Freedman, Adele. "NAC brings little to wild west yarn." *Globe and Mail* 12 May 1983. 25.

Freeman, Brian. "In Review: *The Komagata Maru Incident*." *Scene Changes* V.9 (December 1977): 20.

Frey, Cecelia. "Power play: Sharon Pollock plays to win." *Calgary Herald* 10.5 (January 1988). 17–18.

Friedlander, Mira. "Stratford cast turns 'fair' script into worthy performance." *Today's Senior* September 1993. T.

Fuller, Patty. "The Problem of Sharon Pollock: Calgary's free-market playwright faces a union blacklist." *Alberta Report* 6 September 1993: 24.

Galloway, Myron. "Pollock play a riotous fantasy." *Montreal Star* 13 July 1977. C-11.

———. "A big improvement, but early-day lustre's gone." *Sunday Express* 12 July 1980. 32, 36.

Garebian, Keith. "Festival Lennoxville: *One Tiger to a Hill*." *Scene Changes* 6 (September/October 1980): 37–39.

[*Generations*] Selections from newspaper and periodical reviews and articles. *Canadian Drama* 11.1 (1985): 197–202.

Giles, Valerie. "Conflict fuels *Generations*." *The Prince George Citizen* 4 October 2004. 13.

Gillese, Kevin. "Incident closer than admitted." *The Gateway* (University of Alberta) 24 March 1977. 11.

Gluck, Victor. "Blood Relations." *Back Stage* (New York) 6 March 1983. 58.

Godfrey, Stephen. "*Doc* a superb family drama." *Globe and Mail* 4 October 1984. E5.

———. "Debate soars above earthbound historical drama." *Globe and Mail* 29 January 1988. A18.

———. "Pollock set to call the shots." *Globe and Mail* 25 February 1988. D13.

———. "Pollock pulling up stakes at Theatre New Brunswick." *Globe and Mail* 18 October 1989. C11.

———. "Sharon Pollock packs her bags and leaves TNB early." *Globe and Mail* 13 December 1989. C9.

Goffin, Jeff. "Once Were Warriors." *Fast Forward* (Calgary) 5–11 October 2000. 32.

———. "F. Scott and Zelda Fitzgerald exposed." *Fast Forward* (Calgary) 1–7 March 2001. 24.

Gold, William. "Canada poised to fight culture war." *Calgary Herald* 20 July 1993. A5.

Goodwin, Jill Tomasson. "Dramatic Memory." *Canadian Literature* 116 (Spring 1988): 157–59.

Goodwin, Lee. "Childsplay: *The Wreck of the National Line Car*." *The Albertan* 17 February 1978: 6.

"Governor General's award winner." *Quill & Quire* 53.7 (1987): 54.

Graham, Gord. "*Blood Relations* plays with nagging question." *Now Magazine* (Toronto) 8–14 October 1981. 11.

Green, Richard. "*Komagata Maru Incident*: An Irreconcilable Mix of Styles." *Georgia Straight* 29 January–5 February 1976. 20.

Greenberg, David. "*Fair Liberty's Call* not a good example of Pollock's best work." *The Goderich Signal Star* 4 August 1993. 8.

Greenwood, Robert. "You don't have to be young to like kids' plays." *The Albertan* 29 May 1978: 22.

Griffiths, Trevor R. *Bloomsbury Theatre Guide*. London: Bloomsbury, 1988. 243.

"Guild honours Pollock, van Herk." *Globe and Mail* 13 May 1987. C5.

Hale, Amanda. "Family Flashback." *Broadside* 6 (November 1984): 11.

Hammerstedt, Josh. "Theatre North West presents a play for every generation." *PG this Week* 10 October 2004. 13.

Hanni, K. "Grand Presents Psychological Portrait." *SOGS [UWO Society of Graduate Students] Advocate* 12.1 (February 1989): 10.

Hayes, Christopher. "Miss Pollock gives CFCN 40 whacks: the court freezes the TV adaptation of her Lizzie Borden play." *Alberta Report* 16 May 1983: 38.

———. "Miss Pollock downs her axe: she settles out of court: the Borden film goes on." *Alberta Report* 20 June 1983: 45.

Hobson, Louis B. "Slick prairie soap: good clean fun." *Calgary Sunday Sun* 31 October 1980. 39.

———. "Prairie stage is set for new play." *Calgary Sunday Sun* 26 October 1980. S9.

———. "Soap with a hope." *Calgary Sunday Sun* 2 November 1980. 51.

———. "Whiskey Six trifle boring." *Calgary Sunday Sun* 13 February 1983. 42.

———. "Pollock production finally set free." *Calgary Sun* 4 May 2007. 7.

Hoffman, Peggy. "Centaur takes the edge on great theatre for '82." *The Suburban* 13 January 1982. A22.

Hofsess, John. "Seduced not raped." *The Albertan* 14 January 1979. 8.

———. "Families." *Homemaker's Magazine* 15.2 (March 1980): 41–44, 48, 49–50, 52, 54, 58, 60.

———. "Sharon Pollock Off-Broadway: Success as a Subtle Form of Failure." *Books in Canada* 12 (April 1983): 3–4.

Hogg, Carol. "Canadian historical play strives for non-textbook realism, drama." *Calgary Herald* 3 November 1973. 43.

"Home-town gal stages her own play." *Toronto Star* 14 April 1988. B4.

Hopkins, Mark. "Well played, Sharon Pollock." *Swerve: Calgary Inside and Out* 4 May 2007. 10.

Hopkins, Stephen. "The Ugly Canadian—It's tough making a play 'with a message.'" *Saint John's Edmonton Report* 21 March 1977. 40–41.

Hoyt, Don. "Family Trappings: A Masterful Work of Theatre." *Telegraph-Journal* 6 March 1986. 4.

Hunt, Stephen. "Pollock heads downstage." *Calgary Herald* 9 May 2007. 7, 1–2.

Hustak, Alan. "Lizzie Borden with a pen … " *Edmonton Sun* 1980.

———. "Sharon Pollock's triumph: A hit for Theatre Calgary's new boss." *Alberta Report* 30 April 1984: 54–55.

———. "A very dramatic exit: Playwright Pollock quits Theatre Calgary." *Alberta Report* 10 September 1984: 40–41.

———. "The first time." *Alberta Motorist* September/October 1984: 8.

Hutchinson, Brian. "'Somewhat democratic' theatre: playwright Sharon Pollock launches her own theatre company." *Alberta Report* 30 September 1991: 50–51.

———. "Restored 'theatre of risks': maverick director Sharon Pollock gives Garry Theatre new lease on life." *Financial Post* 87:12 (20 March 1993). S5.

———. "Staging a comeback in Inglewood." *Western Report* 7.51 (1993). 42–43.

Ingram, Anne. "Pollock Named TNB's New Artistic Director." *The Daily Gleaner* 11 February 1988. 19.

———. "Right theatre at the right time: Sharon Pollock takes New Brunswick by storm." *Performing Arts in Canada* 24.4 (July 1988): 12–13.

———. "The Many Faces of TNB's Sharon Pollock." *The Daily Gleaner* 22 April 1989. 2, 3.

Irish, Paul. "Lizzie Borden staged in Pickering." *Toronto Star* 24 March (1987). 14.

Jansen, Ann. "Change the Story: Narrative Strategies in Two Radio Plays." *Contemporary Issues in Canadian Drama.* Ed. Per Brask. Winnipeg: Blizzard, 1995. 86–102.

Johnson, Audrey. "Critic's Choice." *Victoria Times Colonist* 10 November 1983. D3.

Johnson, Bryan. "Sikh's play, Komagata Maru, bitter and austere, but true." *Globe and Mail* 24 October 1977.15.

J. W. S. "Centaur Theatre starts its new season with a bang." *Westmount Examiner* 21 January 1982. n.p.

Kaplan, Jon. "Pollock's emotional Tiger bites close to the bone." *Now Magazine* (Toronto) 16–22 August 1990. 43.

———. "*Blood Relations* retells Borden tale." *Now Magazine* (Toronto) 1 October 1981. 9.

Kareda, Urjo. "Canadian history drama thick with atmosphere." *Toronto Star* 25 July 1974. E10.

Karp, Zen. "Play explores Canada's Loyalist heritage." *The Beacon Herald* 12 July 1993. 3.

Kirchoff, H.J. "Canadian History Dull? Not on the stage at Stratford." *Globe and Mail* 17 July 1993. C6.

Knelman, Martin. "Daddy Dearest: Sharon Pollock's *Doc*." *Saturday Night* 99 (October 1984): 73–74.

Knowles, Richard Paul. "Sharon Pollock: Personal Frictions." *Atlantic Provinces Book Review* 14 (February–March 1987): 19.

Kubik, Jeff. "Plays the other companies won't run." *Fast Forward* (Calgary) 13–19 July 2006. 54.

———. "Confronting injustice through story." *Fast Forward* (Calgary) 3–9 May 2007. 39.

———. "Fury or whimper?" *Fast Forward* (Calgary) 17–23 May 2007. 56.

Kucherawy, Dennis. "Pollock faces a contradiction in taking GG award." *Edmonton Journal* 31 May 1982. B6.

Kudera, Wendy. "The enigma of Lizzy Borden." *The Tillsonberg News.* 9 January 1989. 3.

Lacey, Liam. "Looking back at a tragedy." *Globe and Mail* 2 April 1987. C5.

Lakevold, Dale. "*Saucy Jack*." *Prairie Fire* 17.1 (Spring 1996): 118–19.

Land, Mary. "Axe-murder drama a macabre success." *The Newspaper* (Toronto) 14 October 1981. nd.

Law, Alex. "Production of *Blood Relations* offers electric performances." *Toronto Star* 7 April 1987. E12.

———. "Memory, reconciliation subjects of play." *Toronto Star* 1 March 1988. E12.

Leahey, Mimi. "Did you, Lizzy, Did You? *Other Stages* (New York) 24 February 1983. 7, 77.

Lefebvre, Kenneth P. "Play about Lizzy Borden examines the logic of murder." *The Expositor* 14 January 1989. 7–8.

Lévesque, Robert. "Théâtre." *Le Devoir* 2 February 1988. 9.

Loiselle, Andre. "Paradigms of 1980's Québécois and Canadian Drama: Normand Chaurettes's *Province-town Playhouse, julliet 1919, j'avais 19 ans* and Sharon Pollock's *Blood Relations*." *Québec Studies* 14 (Spring-Summer 1992): 93–104.

London Theatre Record. "Blood Relations." [Production Reviews] 6–19 November 1985. 1124–25.

Loucks, Randee E. "Whiskey Six: Observations of a First Performance." *ACTH Newsletter* 7 (Fall 1983): 17–18.

———. [Untitled] Review of *Doc. Dandelion* 14.2 (1987): 147–50.

MacBryde, Phyllis. "Hudson's Guild Heefner Produces Quality and Quantity." *Manhattan Plaza News* February 1983. 8.

MacLean, Colin. "Stark Backdrop highlights Warriors." *Edmonton Sun* 13 February 2003. 50.

Macpherson, Margaret. "Family's dark secrets on stage." *SEE Magazine* (Edmonton) 11–17 November 1999. 27.

Macrae, Scott. "Goosing it into shape." *Vancouver Sun* 21 March 1975. A8–9.

McCoy, Philip. "Arts West and Arts National." CBC radio review of *Generations*, 31 October 1980.

McKinley, M. "Sharon Pollock's bloody relations: a TV adaptation of her hit play enrages the Calgary writer." *Alberta Report* 28 February 1983: 36.

Mallet, Gina. "No! No! No! a thousand times No!" *Toronto Star* 16 February 1977. F1.

———. "*Generation*'s muddled writer needs advice." *Toronto Star* April 3 1981. C3.

———. "Vague play trips up actors." *Toronto Star* 2 October 1981. D1.

———. "Critic axes Lizzie Borden." *Toronto Star* 3 October 1981. D1.

Mandel, Charles. "*Angel's Trumpet* a bit out of tune." *Calgary Herald* 9 March 2001. C3.

Marson, Claire. "Borden Murder case opened at Centaur." *The Link* 12 January 1982. 9.

Maskoulis, Julia. "'Compulsory Option' is just kid stuff—but fun." *Montreal Gazette* 13 July 1977. 31.

Massa, Robert. "Did She or Didn't She?" *Village Voice* 1 March 1983. 84, 86.

Matwychuk, Paul. "The making of *The Making of Warriors*." *Vue Weekly* 6 February 2003. 49.

———. "The Shipman News." *Vue Weekly* 5 December 2004. 56.

Messenger, Ann P. "More Utile than Dulce." *Canadian Literature* 65 (1975): 90–95.

Milliken, Paul. "In Review: *Generations*." *Scene Changes: The Theatre Magazine* IX 4 (June 1981): 39–40.

Mitten, Roger. "Go see it." *The West Ender* 5 May 1983. 26.

Montgomery, Lori. "On Stage." *Fast Forward* (Calgary) 16–22 March 2000. 22.

Morrow, Martin. "Playwright pulls name from show." *Calgary Herald* 7 January 1988. F4.

———. "Pollock winner skilfully revived." *Calgary Herald* 19 March 1988. F6.

———. "Her Way." *Calgary Herald* 8 June 1993. D6.

———. "Pollock play better suited to big screen." *Calgary Herald* 11 June 1993. C9.

———. "Will audiences hear Fair Liberty's Call?" *Calgary Herald* 28 July 1993. E8.

———. "Play finally comes to town." *Calgary Herald* 23 April 1997. C8.

———. "Pollock's dark drama raises audience: *Fair Liberty's Call* pits families against families caught in the bloody fissure of our history." *Calgary Herald* 27 April 1997. C4.

———. "Pollock feeling feisty again." *Calgary Herald* 28 January 1998. F1.

———. "TJ to stage new Pollock play." *Calgary Herald* 13 May 1998. F2.

———. "Pollock examines life of forgotten star: Play looks at Canadian-born figure in early film history." *Calgary Herald* 11 March 1999. F6.

———. "Pollock's new play impresses." *Calgary Herald* 14 March 1999. C5.

———. "Who's Afraid of Zelda Fitzgerald?" *Globe and Mail* 9 March 2001. R6.

"Mrs. G.E. Chalmers Dies in Hospital; Funeral Friday." [Obit.] *Fredericton Daily Gleaner* 13 May 1954. 3.

Musselwhite, Bill. "Radio and Television." *Calgary Herald* 17 November 1979. C7.

Nelson, James. "High drama highlights *Walsh*." *The Beacon Herald* 25 July 1974. 1.

———. "Critics have kind words for Canadian play *Walsh*." *London Free Press* 25 July 1974. 40.

———. "*Blood Relations*, high melodrama." *Montreal Gazette* 6 March 1981. 22.

Nicholls, Liz. "Doc's the only character who really comes across." *Edmonton Journal* 15 March 1985. 44.

———. "Theatre schedule announced for Olympic Arts Festival." *Edmonton Journal* 1 May 1987. D2.

———. "Smart direction, great acting in *Doc*." *Edmonton Journal* 6 November 1999. C5.

———. "Awakening the Warrior within." *Edmonton Journal* 12 February 2003. C2.

———. "Balance of virtues and flaws fascinates playwright Pollock." *Edmonton Journal* 2 December 2004. C2.

———. "*Moving Pictures* gives many voices to silent star." *Edmonton Journal* 2 December 2004. C2.

———. "Sharon Pollock's *Moving Pictures* practically stands still." *Edmonton Journal* 4 December 2004. E5.

Nothof, Anne. "Lizzy Borden's Trial By Theatre." "*Blood Relations*" in Shaw Festival Program. 2003. n.p.

Nunn, Robert C. "Sharon Pollock's Plays: A Review Article." *Theatre History in Canada* 5 (Spring 1984): 72–83. Nothof, ed. 2000: 26–43.

Oliva, Peter. "How Do You Grow an Opera?" *Alberta Views* (March/April 2002): 38–42.

Page, Malcolm. "He Never Lost a Man." *Toronto Theatre Review* October 1977: 15.

Parker, John F. "*Walsh*." *B.C. Library Quarterly* 37.3 (1973): 29–30.

Pawagi, Manjusha. "A haunting look at Lizzy's legend." *Montreal Gazette* 10 January 1989. 11.

Pennington, Bob. "40 Whacks for obscure Relations." *Toronto Sun* 6 October 1981. 52.

———. "A dream role for veteran McNamara." *Toronto Sun* 6 April 1981. 44

Peterson, Maureen. "Actress Terry Tweed can, and does." *Montreal Gazette* 16 January 1982. n.p.

———. "Centaur's *Blood Relations* everything a play should be." *Montreal Gazette* 9 January 1982. 34.

Plant, Richard. "Precious Blood." *Books in Canada* 11 (April 1982). 8–12.

"Pollock honoured." *Winnipeg Free Press* 6 September 1986. 27.

"Pollock at odds with TC." *Globe and Mail* 25 January 1988. C7.

"Pollock wins Australia prize." *Toronto Star* 28 January 1988. B4.

"Pollock wins literary award." *Globe and Mail* 29 January 1988. D6.

"Pollock honoured." *Calgary Herald* 30 January 1988. D4.

"Pollock named to direct TNB." *Globe and Mail* 11 February 1988. D1.

Porter, MacKenzie. "Adults Beware." *Toronto Sun* 26 July 1974. 24.

Portman, Jamie. "*Walsh* signals red-letter event for TC." *Calgary Herald* 8 November 1973. 76.

———. "Calgary I" *CTR* 1 (Winter 1974): 118–20.

———. "Calgary II." [review of 1973 premiere of *Walsh*] *CTR* 2 (Spring 1974): 121–23.

———. "Sharon Pollock demonstrates immense gifts with latest play." *Calgary Herald* 20 March 1980. C9.

———. "Pollock's immense talent shines in *Blood Relations*." *Edmonton Journal* 22 March 1980. L2.

———. "Pollock's play three times unlucky." *Vancouver Sun* 28 August 1990. C6.

———. "Stratford revival can't save Pollock's Citadel bust." *Edmonton Journal* 31 August 1990. C9.

———. "Pollock at her provocative best." *The Windsor Star* 17 July 1993. F4.

———. "Pollock's Lizzie Borden thriller, *Blood Relations*, gets the blue-ribbon treatment at the Shaw Festival." *CanWest News* 22 May 2005.

Prosser, David. "*Saucy Jack*." *Quill & Quire* November 1994. Q8.

Rae, Lisbie. "Review of Anthologies." *Canadian Drama* 13.2 (1987): 229–31.

Randy, William. "Skillful 'Blood Relation' cast gives sharp edge to Lizzie Borden legend." *Newark Star Ledger* 13 February 1983. 48.

Rankin, Lee. "Play Hits Racism." *The Peak* 5 February 1976. 13.

———. "*Tracings* prove Simon Fraser not a shmuck." *The Peak* 15 June 1977. 7.

———. "*Tracings* show curious picture of enigma." *The Peak* 22 June 1977. 6.

Read, Nicholas. "A delightful horror story." *Vancouver Sun* 15 April 1983. E6.

Redding, Lori. "Family Trappings Debuts: TNB New Play Powerful." *The Daily Gleaner* 3 March 1986. 16.

Reid, Robert. "Intrigue of psychological violence permeates tale of Lizzie Borden." *Kitchener Waterloo Record* 7 January 1989. D2.

———. "Serpentine tale, convoluted plot, feminist bias undermine story of Loyalist clan." *Kitchener-Waterloo Record* 16 July 1993. E1, 9.

Rich, Frank. "Theatre: *One Tiger to a Hill* Canadian Prison Drama." *New York Times* 14 November 1980. C3.

———. "Stage: 'Blood Relations,' The Lizzie Borden Case." *New York Times* 16 February 1983. C24.

Richer, Shawna. "It's too little, too late for *Fair Liberty's Call*." *London Free Press* 17 July 1993. C 6.

Robinson, J. Rebecca. "Give 'em one for me Lizzie." *Ottawa Revue* 5–11 March 1981. n.p.

Rowan, D.F. "*Separate Tables*, Stimulating Performance." *Fredericton Daily Gleaner* 8 April 1965. 24.

Rubin, Don, and Alison Cranmer-Byng, eds. *Canada's Playwrights: A Bibliographical Guide*. Toronto: Canadian Theatre Review Publications, 1980. 134–37.

Rubin, Don. "Portrait." *CTR* 32 (1981). 8.

Saddlemyer, Ann. "Sharon Pollock: National Arts Centre." *Globe and Mail* 12 May 1983. 25.

Sasauo, Mari. "On Stage: *The Making of Warriors*." *See* (Edmonton) 6 February 2003. 32.

Schaefer, Keith. "*Blood Relations* has strong performances but lacks excitement." *The Beacon Herald* 10 January 1989. 3, 6.

Schelstraete, Nancy. "Convicts & convictions." *NeWest Review* (April 1980): 7, 10.

Schmaltz, Ken. "Where The Play Is, Again, The Thing." *Western Living* (November 1994): 26–28.

Schoenberg, Mark. "Theatre Stages: One Tiger Dissected." *Interface* (Edmonton) April 1980. 17.

Schwann, Shirley. "Lizzie Borden Hacks Her Way to Success." *Brooklyn College Kingsman* 18 February 1983. 25.

"Script Writing Continues As Opening Night Looms." *Simon Fraser News* 9 June 1977. n.p.

Shaw, Phil. "GCTC's *Komagata Maru Incident*." *Ottawa Review* 19–25 July 1979. 154.

Sherman, David. "A Compulsory Option: objectionable." *Sherbrooke Record* 13 July 1977. 3.

Sheppard, Allan. "One Rose Among the Thorns." *Interface*. October 1980. C26.

Shorter, Eric. "Blood Relations." *Daily Telegraph* 14 May 1988. In *London Theatre Record* 5.11. (22 May-4 June 1985). 533.

Sibley, Robert. "ACCESS produces 'The Persons Case'." *ACCESS Magazine* January 1981: 1–5.

Sidnell, Michael J. "Designers' Texts and Other Plays: The Stratford Festival 1990 [*One Tiger to a Hill*]." *Journal of Canadian Studies* 25 (Winter 1990/91): 136.

Siskind, Jacob. "Hostage Play Fascinates." *Ottawa Citizen* 23 March 1981. 59.

Skene, Reg. "MTC shows ability with *Doc* production." *Winnipeg Free Press* 6 February 1987. 29.

Smith, Patricia Keeney. "Looking Back." *Canadian Forum* 64 (January 1984): 39–40.

Spiegel, Clive. "*Blood Relations*: a Brainteaser." *The Paper* 19 January 1982. 6.

Sprung, Guy. "Director's Introduction." *Fair Liberty's Call*. Toronto: Coach House Press, 1995. 7–9.

Stanton, Victor. "Stratford Third Stage production of Canadian play strong, artistic." *Kitchener-Waterloo Record* 26 July 1974. n.p.

Stone, Martin. "Farming, a way of life." *Canadian Tribune* 13 April 1981. 10.

Strong, Greg. "Sinking Maru Play." *The Ubyssey* 23 January 1976. 5.

Sweet, Louise. "Playwright's life provided the tools of her trade." *Toronto Star* 3 March 1984. D1.

———. "Writer explores mother's suicide." *Winnipeg Free Press* 4 February 1987. 35.

Swimmings, Betty. "Play about Canadian cruelty recalls plight of 'boat people'." *The Ottawa Citizen* 12 July 1979. 62.

Syna, Sy. "Lizzy Borden play bloodless." *The News World* (New York) 17 February 1983.

Tatham, Ruth. "'Fair Liberty's Call' explores early history." *The Listowel Banner* 28 July 1993. 9–10.

Taylor, Kate. "Firebrand playwright still sizzles." *Globe and Mail* 9 March. 2000. R1–5.

———. "Lizzy Borden, how could you?" *Globe and Mail* 23 May 2003. R4.

"The Ugly Canadian. It's tough making a play 'with a message' more than a sermon." *Saint John's Edmonton Report* 21 March 1977. n.p.

Thornber, Robin. [Review: *Blood Relations*]. *Guardian* 3 May 1988. *London Theatre Record* 5.11. 22 May–4 June 1985. 534.

Thorne, Bernhard. "An 'acceptable' Canadian play." *The Beacon Herald* 25 July 1974. 1.

Thrall, Judy. "Fine Performances in 'Blood Relations'." *Washington Market Review* 16 March 1983.

Tivy, Patrick. "Backstage wizardry makes Theatre Calgary's show." *Calgary Herald* 11 February 1983. F 10.

Trick, Bernice. "Theatre North West opens season with family drama." *Prince George Citizen* 29 September 2004. 13.

Turnbull, Larke. "Pollock's Latest Play." *The Beacon Herald* 16 July 1993. 1, 5.

———. "Pollock play paints tough picture of life in prison." *The Beacon Herald* 25 August 1990. 1, 13.

Turney, Carolyn. "Celebrated Playwright Returns to City." *The Daily Gleaner* 21 February 1986. 17.

———. "City Woman's Play to Open in New York." *The Daily Gleaner* 26 September 1980. 10.

van Luven, Marlene A.D. Lynne. "Paved with good intentions." *NeWest Review* 11.4 (1986): 19.

Verdun, Bob. "The roots of Canadian conservatism." *The Independent National Edition* (Elmira, ON) July 1993. 8.

[*Walsh*]. Selections from newspaper and periodical reviews and articles. *Canadian Drama* 11.1 (1985): 94–101.

Wagner, Kit. "Shocking Tiger growls but lacks teeth to bite." *Toronto Star* 26 August 1990. C4.

Wasserman, Jerry. "Drama." *University of Toronto Quarterly* 57.1 (Fall 1987): 67–69.

———. "Heel Thyself: Sharon Pollock's Doc left his compassion in the waiting room." *Pulse* (Vancouver) 6–19 April 1990. 22.

Webster, Jackie. "Another Stage Triumph for Sharon." *Atlantic Advocate* 64 (August 1974): 50.

Weir, Ian. "The director's vicious circle. It's not that easy being a young director." *Kamloops Daily Sentinel* 28 January 1977. 6A.

———. "*Komagata Maru Incident* very Brechtian." *Kamloops Daily Sentinel* 1 February 1977. 9.

Wellan, Rob. "So You Want to be a Playwright … " *Stage: National Arts Centre* 8.3 (1982). 8–9.

Whittaker, Herbert. "*Walsh* Beautiful, Tedious Too." *Globe and Mail* 13 November 1973. 16.

———. "Canadian West at Stratford." *Globe and Mail* 22 July 1974. 14.

———. "*Walsh* Serves Up Sad History Straight." *Globe and Mail* 25 July 1974: 13.

Wilton, Lisa. "Mesmerizing Dream." *Calgary Sun* 10 March 2000. 43.

———. "Real Canadian Mystery. Strange Case inspires TJ's latest play." *Calgary Sun* 9 March 2000. 51.

———. "Tragic inspiration." *Calgary Sun* 9 March 2001. 6.

Winston, Iris. "Theatre Review: *Blood Relations* forces audience into Lizzie Borden's shoes." *Ottawa Citizen* 4 March 1994. E6.

Wintle, Adrian. "Who gave the Bordens the chop?" *The Australian* 15 March 1985. 10.

Woloshen, Richard. "Dramatic feuding: Theatre Calgary's *Walsh* garners controversy." *Alberta Report* 3.4 (15 February 1988): 40.

"Writers Guild of Alberta awards." *Quill & Quire* 53.7 (1987): 53.

Wyman, Max. "Something to hold in our minds as Habitat hits us." *Vancouver Sun* 18 May 1976. 37.

———. "*The Komagata Maru Incident*: You can look for a message made palatable." *Vancouver Sun* 16 January 1976. 31.

———. "*Komagata Maru*: the clash of symbols." *Vancouver Sun* 21 January 1976. 43.

Yungblut, Andrea. "Festival plans three more Canadian plays for 1992." *The Beacon Herald* 26 June 1990. 2, 9.

———. "Pollock: Theatre has lost community roots." *The Beacon Herald* 11 September 1990. 17.

Zimmerman, Kate. "Pollock lands job back 'home.'" *Calgary Herald* 11 February 1988. D2.

B: Other Works

Abbott, H. Porter. *Beckett Writing Beckett: The Author in the Autograph*. Ithaca & London: Cornell University Press, 1996.

Ackerman, Robert J. *Perfect Daughters: Adult Daughters of Alcoholics*. 1989. Revised ed. Deerfield Beach, Florida: Health Communications Inc., 2002.

Agnew, Eleanor and Sharon Robideaux. *My Mama's Waltz: A Book for Daughters of Alcoholic Mothers*. New York: Pocket Books, 1998.

Agnew, Theresa. *Let Her But Breathe: Changing Representations of Women in Plays by Prairie Women Playwrights*. MA Thesis. Edmonton: University of Alberta, 1994.

Albee, Edward. *Three Tall Women*. New York: Dutton, 1994.

Albers, Sandra. "Sharon Pollock heads Playwrights' colony." *The Kamloops News* 28 February 1977. 20.

Alien Thunder. Film. Dir. Claude Fornier. Onyx Films, 1974.

Allan, Andrew. *A Self-Portrait*. Toronto: Macmillan, 1974.

Allen, Paul. *Alan Ayckbourn: Grinning at the Edge, A Biography*. London: Methuen, 2001.

Alpern, Sara, Joyce Antler, Elizabeth Israels Perry, and Ingrid Winther Scobie, eds. *The Challenge of Feminist Biography: Writing the Lives of Modern American Women*. Urbana and Chicago: University of Illinois Press, 1992.

Amantea, Gisele. *Reading History Backwards (The King vs. Picariello and Lassandro)*. Installation comic art. Walter Phillips Gallery, Banff Centre, 2003.

Andersen, Hans Christian. *The Red Shoes*. London: Neugebauer, 1983.

Anderson, Benedict. "Introduction to Part Two: Staging Antimodernism in the Age of High Capitalist Nationalism." In *Antimodernism and the Artistic Experience: Policing the Boundaries of Modernity*. Ed. Lynda Jessup. Toronto: University of Toronto Press, 2001. 97–103.

Anderson, Ian. *Sitting Bull's Boss: Above the Medicine Line with James Morrow Walsh*. Markham, ON: Fitzhenry & Whiteside, 2000.

Anzaldua, Gloria and Cherrie Moraga. "Word Warriors." *The Sacred Hoop: Recovering the Feminine in American Indian Tradition*. Ed. Paula Gunn Allen. Boston: Beacon, 1986. 51–83.

A Question of Guilt: Constance Kent. Film. Dir. Paul Annett. BBC TV, 1981.

Ardrey, Robert. *African Genesis*. New York: Dell Publishing, 1961.

Armatage, Kay. *The Girl from God's Country: Nell Shipman and the Silent Screen*. Toronto: University of Toronto Press, 2003.

Armstrong, Pat, ed. "The Newsheet of the Playhouse Theatre Centre of B.C." 2.1 (October 1974): 1–4; 2.2 (February 1975): 1–4.

Arnott, Brian. "Performing Arts Buildings in Canada." Wagner, ed. 82–94.

Artfacts/Artifaits. Toronto: Ontario Arts Council/Conseil des arts de l'Ontario. 31 October. 7.2 (2003): [4 pages].

Ashley, Audrey and Boyd Neil. "Ontario." Wagner, ed. 137–47.

Aston, Elaine. *Caryl Churchill*. Plymouth: Northcote House, 1997.

Atwood, Margaret. "Five Poems for Grandmothers." *Margaret Atwood: Selected Poems II. Poems Selected & New, 1976–1986*. Toronto: Oxford University Press, 1986. 16.

———. *Cat's Eye*. Toronto: McClelland & Stewart, 1988.

———. *The Blind Assassin*. Toronto: Random House, 2000.

———. *Moving Targets: Writing with Intent, 1982–2004*. Toronto: Anansi, 2004.

———. *Moral Disorder*. London: Bloomsbury, 2006.

Ayckbourn, Alan. *Woman in Mind. December Bee*. London: Faber & Faber, 1986.

Back to God's Country. Film. 1919. Restored print. Idaho Film Collection, Hemingway Western Studies Center, Boise State University, 1996.

Bair, Deirdre. *Simone de Beauvoir: A Biography*. New York: Summit Books, 1990

Baldridge, Mary Humphrey. "Lunchbox Theatre Calgary." *CTR* 13 (Winter 1977): 121–23.

Baldridge, Harold. "Calgary." *CTR* 2 (Spring 1974): 118–20.

Bannerman, Guy. "Indirections: Evolution, Not Revolution, at the Shaw Festival." *CTR* 121 (Winter 2005): 82–85.

Baxter, Arthur Beverly. "The Birth of the National Theatre." 1916. Rubin, ed. 38–43.

Bayefsky, Aba and Humphrey N. Milnes. "Fields of Force in Canadian Art, 1930 to 1980." Keith and Shek, eds. 135–45.

Bazzana, Kevin. *Wondrous Strange: The Life and Art of Glenn Gould*. Toronto: McClelland & Stewart, 2003.

Beaverbrook, Lord (Max Aitken). *My Early Life*. Fredericton: Brunswick Press, 1965.

Beckett, Samuel. *Collected Shorter Plays*. New York: Grove Press, 1984.

Belliveau, George. "Daddy on Trial: Sharon Pollock's New Brunswick Plays." *Theatre Research in Canada* 22.2 (2001): 161–72.

———. "Investigating British Columbia's Past: *The Komagata Maru Incident* and *The Hope Slide* as Historiographic Metadrama." *BC Studies* 137 (Spring 2003): 93–106.

Berger Thomas. *Little Big Man*. New York: Fawcett Crest Books, 1964.

Berton, Pierre. *Marching As to War: Canada's Turbulent Years, 1899–1953.* [2001] Toronto: Anchor Canada, 2002.

———. *Hollywood's Canada: The Americanization of Our National Image.* Toronto: McClelland & Stewart, 1975.

Bessai, Diane. "Introduction." *Blood Relations and Other Plays.* Edmonton: NeWest Press, 1981. 7–9.

———. "Women, Feminism and Prairie Theatre." *CTR* 43 (1985): 28–43.

———. "Sharon Pollock's Women: A study in dramatic process." *A Mazing Space: Writing Canadian Women Writing.* Ed. Shirley Neuman and Smaro Kamboureli. Edmonton: Longspoon/NeWest Press, 1986. 126–36. Nothof, ed. 2000: 44–67.

———. "Introduction." *NeWest Plays by Women.* Ed. Diane Bessai and Don Kerr. Edmonton: NeWest Press, 1987. vii-xvii.

———. "Sharon Pollock." *The Oxford Companion to Canadian Theatre.* Ed. Eugene Benson and L.W. Conolly. Toronto: Oxford University Press, 1989. 424–26.

———. "Women Dramatists: Sharon Pollock and Judy Thompson." *Post-Colonial English Drama: Common-wealth Drama Since 1960.* Ed. Bruce King. New York: Macmillan, 1992. 97–117.

———. *Playwrights of Collective Creation.* Toronto: Simon and Pierre, 1992.

Billington, Michael. *The Life and Work of Harold Pinter.* London: Faber and Faber, 1996.

Bird, Kym. *Redressing the Past: The Politics of Early English-Canadian Women's Drama, 1880–1920.* Montreal: McGill-Queen's University Press, 2004.

Bissell, Claude. *The Young Vincent Massey.* Toronto: University of Toronto Press, 1981.

———. *The Imperial Canadian: Vincent Massey in Office.* Toronto: University of Toronto Press, 1986.

Black Elk. *Black Elk Speaks: Being the Life Story of a Holy Man of the Oglala Sioux, as told through John G. Neihardt.* Illus. by Standing Man. Lincoln: University of Nebraska Press, 1961.

Bolt, Carol. "The Zimmerman Report: Canadian Women in the Theatre." *CanPlay* (July-August): 6–7.

———. *Cyclone Jack.* Toronto: Playwrights Canada Press, 1972.

Boyden, Joseph. *Three Day Road.* Toronto: Penguin Canada, 2005.

Bradley, Pat. "The Status of Women in Theatre—The Ontario Experience." *Art Facts/Artifaits* 8.1 (January 2004): 1–4.

Brennan, Brian. "Sharon Pollock: One play slated for Calgary while another opens off Broadway." *Calgary Herald* 25 October 1980. B9.

———. "Sharon Pollock delighted; David Cassidy plays West." *Calgary Herald* 18 May 1982. A15.

———. "Finishing school: the Banff playwrights' colony." *CTR* 49 (1986): 30–35.

———. "The Prairie Provinces." Wagner, ed. 159–66.

———. "Art travelled province with projector." *Calgary Herald* 6 July 1994. B2.

———. *Boondoggles, Bonanzas, and Other Alberta Stories.* Calgary: Fifth House, 2003.

Broadfoot, Barry. *Ten Lost Years, 1929–1939: Memories of Canadians who Survived the Depression.* Don Mills, ON: Paper Jacks, 1973.

Brodersen, George. "Towards a Canadian Theatre." Rubin, ed. 147–52.

Brown, Arnold. *Lizzie Borden: The Legend, the Truth, and the Final Chapter.* Nashville, TN: Rutledge Hill Press, 1991.

Brown, Chester. *Louis Riel: A Comic-Strip Biography.* Montreal: Drawn and Quartered Publications, 2003.

Brown, Dee. *Bury My Heart at Wounded Knee.* New York: Henry Holt, 1970.

Brown, Randy. "The Porchlight." CBC AM Radio, "Nightfall" series: broadcast, 26 February 1982. Producer/director Bill Gray.

Brownstein, Marilyn L. "Catastrophic Encounters: Postmodern Biography as Witness to History." Rhiel and Suchoff, eds. 185–99.

Bruyère, Christian. *Walls.* Vancouver: Talonbooks, 1978.

Budhiraja, Geeta. "Glimpses of Canada in India: Sharon Pollock's *Generations* and George F. Walker's *Love and Anger.*" *CTR* 105 (Winter 2000–01): 24–26.

Buss, Helen. *Repossessing the World: Reading Memoirs by Contemporary Canadian Women.* Waterloo: Wilfrid Laurier University Press, 2002.

Butler, Judith. "Performative Acts and Gender Constitution: An Essay in Phenomenology and Feminist Theory." *Performing Feminisms: Feminist Critical Theory and Theatre.* Ed. Sue-Ellen Case. Baltimore: Johns Hopkins University Press, 1990. 270–82.

Byatt, A.S. *The Biographer's Tale.* London: Vintage, 2000.

Bye, Bye Blues. Film. Dir. and producer. Anne Wheeler. Alberta Motion Pictures Development Corp., 1989.

Cairns, Glen. *Danceland.* Toronto: Playwrights Canada Press, 2002.

Camp, Dalton. *Gentlemen, players, and politicians.* Toronto: McClelland & Stewart, 1970.

Canadian Arts Consumer Profile, 1990–1991. Findings. Decima Research and Les Consultants Culture Inc. May 1992.

Carlson, Marvin. *Places of Performance: The Semiotics of Theatre Architecture.* Ithaca: Cornell University Press, 1989.

———. *Theatre Semiotics: Signs of Life.* Bloomington & Indianapolis: Indiana University Press, 1990.

Carroll, Francis M. "Drawing the Line." *The Beaver* 83.4 (August/September 2003): 19–25.

Carter, Angela. "The Fall River Axe Murders." *Black Venus.* London: Picador, 1985. 103–21.

Caruth, Cathy. *Unclaimed Experience: Trauma, Narrative, and History.* Baltimore: Johns Hopkins University Press, 1996.

Case, Sue Ellen. "From Split Subject to Split Britches." *Feminine Focus: The New Women Playwrights.* Ed. Enoch Brater. New York: Oxford University Press, 1989. 126–46.

CAUSE Canada. *Celebrating 20 Years of Challenging Global Poverty.* Annual General Report 2003–2004.

Cermak, Timmen L. *A Time to Heal: The Road to Recovery for Adult Children of Alcoholics.* New York: Avon Books, 1988.

Chapman, Vernon. *"Whose in the Goose Tonight?" An Anecdotal History of Canadian Theatre.* Toronto: ECW Press, 2001.

Chislett, Anne. *The Tomorrow Box.* Toronto: Playwrights Canada Press, 1980.

Chodorow, Nancy. *The Reproduction of Mothering: Psychoanalysis and the Sociology of Gender.* Berkeley: University of California Press, 1978.

Chung, Kathy K.Y. "'A Different Kind of the Same Thing': Narrative, Experiential Knowledge, and Subjectivity in Susan Gaspell's *Trifles* and Sharon Pollock's *Blood Relations.*" *Theatre Research in Canada* 20.2 (Fall 1999): 159–80.

———. "'Lookin' to a better world for our children': The Concept of Inheritance in Pollock's *Fair Liberty's Call.*" Nothof, ed. 2000: 151–66.

Churchill, Caryl. *Cloud 9.* New York: Routledge, 2000.

Cixous, Hélène. "Aller á la mer." Trans. Barbara Kerslake. *Modern Drama* XXVII 4 (December 1984): 546–48.

Clark, Sally. *Saint Frances of Hollywood.* Vancouver: Talonbooks, 1996.

Claycomb, Ryan. "Playing at Lives: Biography and Contemporary Feminist Drama." *Modern Drama* 47.3 (Fall 2004): 525–45.

Clement, Susan, and Esther Beth Sullivan. "The Split Subject of *Blood Relations.*" *Upstaging Big Daddy: Directing Theatre as if Gender and Race Matter.* Ed. Ellen Donkin and Susan Clement. Ann Arbor: University Michigan Press, 1993. 259–76.

Clements, Marie. *The Unnatural and Accidental Women.* Vancouver: Talonbooks, 2005.

———. *Burning Vision.* Vancouver: Talonbooks, 2003.

Cohen, Nathan. "Stratford After Fifteen Years." 1968. Rubin, ed. 259–77.

———. "Theatre Today: English Canada." 1959. Rubin, ed. 228–50.

Comfort, Charles. *Artist at War.* Pender Island, B.C.: Remembrance Books, 1995.

Conlogue, Ray. "Michael Ball shuns 'bland young man' tag." *Globe and Mail* 28 November 1981. 23.

Conolly, L.M., ed. *Canadian Drama and the Critics.* Vancouver: Talonbooks: 1987. 135–44, 259–76.

Conolly, L.M, and D.A. Hadfield, eds. *Canadian Drama and the Critics.* 2nd Ed. Rev. Vancouver: Talonbooks: 1995. 135–44, 259–76.

Continuous Journey: The Story of the Komagata Maru. Dir. Ali Kazimi. 2001.

Cook, Michael. "Ignored Again." Rubin, ed. 362–74.

———. "The Painful Struggle for the Creation of a Canadian Repertory." Rubin, ed. 367–74.

Cornelius, Patricia. "Jack's Daughters." Unplublished script. nd.

Coulter, John. "The Canadian Theatre and the Irish Exemplar." Rubin, ed. 121–26.

———. "Toward a Canadian Theatre." 1945. Rubin, ed. 132–34.

———. "Theatre Needs More than a Pat on the Head." Rubin, ed. 184–87.

Crean, Susan. "The Invisible Country." Rubin, ed. 332–40.

———. *Who's afraid of Canadian Culture?* Don Mills, ON: General Publishing, 1976.

CTR: Canadian Theatre Review 124 (Fall 2005). Special issue. "Calgary's High Performance Rodeo: 20 Years of New Performance." Eds. Susan Bennett and Penny Farfan.

Cushman, Robert. *Fifty Seasons at Stratford.* Toronto: McClelland & Stewart, 2002.

Czarnecki, Mark. "The Regional Theatre System." Rubin, ed. 278–92.

Darlow, Michael. *Terence Rattigan: The Man and his Work.* London: Quartet Books, 2000.

"David French." Wallace and Zimmerman, *The Work.* 305–16.

Davies, Robertson. "Fifty Years of Theatre in Canada." Keith and Shek, eds. 69–80.

Day, Douglas. *Malcolm Lowry: A Biography.* New York: Oxford University Press, 1973.

DeFelice, Jim. "Remembrance of Things Past: Time, Space and Character in Sharon Pollock's *The Komagata Maru Incident, Blood Relations,* and *Doc.*" *wwrMagazine* 2.1 (Summer 2005): 8–9.

Deloria, Vine, Jr. *Custer Died for Your Sins: An Indian Manifesto.* New York: Macmillan, 1969.

De Mille, Agnes. *Lizzie Borden: A Dance of Death.* New York: Atlantic Monthly Press, 1968.

Deringer, Ludwig. "Kulturelle Identität im zeitgeossischen anglokanadischen Drama." *Wozu Wissenschaft heute? Ringvorlesung zu Ehren von Roland Hagenbuchle.* Tubingen, Germany: Narr, 1997. 39–53.

Diotte, Mark. "Constructions of Masculinity in Sharon Pollock's *Whiskey Six Cadenza.*" *Theatre in Alberta.* Ed. Anne Nothof. Toronto: Playwrights Canada Press, 2008. 129–43.

Dolan, Jill. *Presence and Desire: Essays on Gender, Sexuality, Performance.* Ann Arbor: University of Michigan Press, 1993.

———. "Geographies of Learning: Theatre Studies, Performance, and the 'Performative'." *Theatre Journal* 45.4 (1993): 417–41.

Doolittle, Joyce. "Theatre for the Young: A Canadian Perspective." *CTR* 10 (Spring 1976): 6–21.

———. "Calgary: Cowboys, Culture and an Edifice Complex." *CTR* 42 (1985): 7–16.

————. "Counterparts: An Introduction." *Heroines: Three Plays*. Ed. Joyce Doolittle. Red Deer: Red Deer College Press, 1992. 7–10.

————. and Zina Barnieh. *A Mirror of Our Dreams: Children and the Theatre in Canada*, with a chapter on Quebec by Hélène Beauchamp. Vancouver: Talonbooks, 1979.

Douglas, John and Mark Olshaker. *The Cases That Haunt Us*. New York: Scribner, 2000.

Drainie, Bronwyn. *Living the Part: John Drainie and the Dilemma of Canadian Stardom*. Toronto: Macmillan, 1988.

Drama at Calgary. A Quarterly Journal. 1966–1970. University of Calgary, Calgary, Alberta.

Dyba, Kenneth. "The MAC 14 Story." In *MAC 14 Theatre, 1967–68 Season*. A souvenir program. Calgary: Rothmans, 1967. No pag.

Eakin, Paul John. *How our Lives Become Stories: Making Selves*. Ithaca: Cornell University Press, 1999.

Edel, Leon. *Henry James, A Life*. New York: Harper & Row, 1985.

Edmonstone, Wayne E. *Nathan Cohen: The Making of a Critic*. Toronto: Lester & Orpen, 1977.

Edwards, Murray. D. *A Stage in our Past: English-Language Theatre in Eastern Canada from the 1790s to 1914*. Toronto: University of Toronto Press. 1968.

Edwards, Peter. *One Dead Indian: The Premier, the Police, and the Ipperwash Crisis*. 2001. Toronto: McClelland & Stewart, 2003.

Egan, Susanna. *Mirror Talk: Genres of Crisis in Contemporary Autobiography*. Chapel Hill: University of North Carolina Press, 1999.

————. "The Company She Keeps: Demidenko and the Problems of Imposture in Autobiography." *Who's Who? Hoaxes, Imposture and Identity Crises in Australian Literature*. Ed. Maggie Nolan and Carrie Dawson. *Australian Literary Studies* 21.4 (2004): 14–27.

Eight Men Speak and Other Plays from the Canadian Workers' Theatre. Richard Wright, ed. Toronto: New Hogtown Press, 1980.

Elk, Black. *Black Elk Speaks*. 1932. Lincoln, Nebraska: University of Nebraska Press, 1961.

Epstein, William, ed. *Contesting the Subject: Essays in the Postmodern Theory and Practice of Biography and Biographical Criticism*. West Lafayette, Indiana: Indiana University Press, 1991.

Euringer, Fred. *A Fly on the Curtain*. Toronto: Oberon, 2000.

Evans, Gary. *In the National Interest: A Chronicle of the National Film Board from 1949 to 1989*. Toronto: University of Toronto Press, 1991.

Fenwick, Ian. "Touchstone: The Way It Was, 1975–80." *CTR* 39 (Spring 1984): 31–43.

Féral, Josette. "Writing and Displacement: Women in Theatre." Trans. Barbara Kerslake. *Modern Drama* XXVII. 4 (December 1984): 549–63.

Ferguson, Ted. *A White Man's Country: An Experience in Canadian Prejudice*. Toronto: Doubleday, 1975.

Fick, Steven and Elizabeth Shilts. "Return of the Dispossessed." *Canadian Geographic* (March/April 2004): 30–36.

Filewod, Alan. "National Theatre, National Obsession." Rubin, ed. 424–31.

————. "Simulations of Nationhood; Spectacles of Postcoloniality: The Show Boat Controversy as Imperial Pageant." *The Performance Text*. Pietropaolo, Domenico, ed. 41–56.

————. *Performing Canada: The Nation Enacted in the Imagined Theatre*. Kamloops, B.C.: Textual Studies in Canada, 2002.

————. "The Face of Re-enactment." *CTR* 121 (Winter 2005): 9–16.

Findley, Timothy. *The Wars*. Toronto: Clarke Irwin, 1977.

————. *Journeyman: Travels of a Writer*. Ed. William Whitehead. Toronto: HarperFlamingo Canada, 2003.

Fink, Howard. "The sponsor's vs. the nation's choice: North American radio drama." Lewis, ed. 185–243.

———. "A National Radio Drama in English." Wagner, ed. 176–85.

———. "Canadian Radio Drama and the Radio Drama Project." *CTR* 36 (Fall 1982): 12–22.

Finlay, Karen. *A Force of Culture: Vincent Massey and Canadian Sovereignty.* Toronto: University of Toronto Press, 2004.

Fitzgerald, Zelda. *Save Me the Waltz.* 1932. Carbondale: Southern Illinois University Press, 1967.

Flahiff, F.T. *Always someone to kill the doves: A Life of Sheila Watson.* Edmonton: NeWest Press, 2005.

Flynn, Robert. *The Borden Murders: An Annotated Bibliography.* Portland, ME: King Philip Publications, 1992.

Foucault, Michel. *Discipline and Punish: The Birth of the Prison.* Trans. Alan Sheridan. London: Allan Lane, 1977.

Francis, Daniel. *The Imaginary Indian: The Image of the Indian in Canadian Culture.* Vancouver: Arsenal Pulp Press, 1992.

———. *National Dreams: Myth, Memory, and Canadian History.* Vancouver: Arsenal Pulp Press, 1997.

———. ed. *Encyclopedia of British Columbia.* Madeira Park, BC: Harbour Publishing, 2000. 389.

Fraticelli, Rina. "The Invisibility Factor: Status of Women in Canadian Theatre." *Fuse* (September 1982): 112–24.

French, David. *Soldier's Heart.* Vancouver: Talonbooks, 2002.

Freud, Sigmund. "Mourning and Melancholia." *The Standard Edition of the Complete Psychological Works of Sigmund Freud.* Vol. xiv. Trans. James Strachey, Anna Freud, Alix Strachey, and Alan Tyson. London and Toronto: Hogarth Press and Clarke, Irwin, 1957. 238–58.

Frink, Tim. *New Brunswick: A Short History.* Saint John, N.B.: Stonington Books, 1997.

Frye, Northrop. "Across the River and Out of the Trees." Keith and Shek, eds. 1–14.

Fulford, Robert. "Beautiful Dreamers: Canadian cultural icons figure in an increasing number of biographies." *Maclean's* 6 October 1997: 73–75

Gale, Maggie B. "Autobiography, Gender, and Theatre Histories: Spectrums of Reading British Actresses' Autobiographies from the 1920s and 1930s." Grace and Wasserman, eds. 185–201.

Garber, Marjorie. "Bisexuality and Celebrity." Rhiel and Suchoff, eds. 13–30.

Garebian, Keith. *William Hutt: A Theatre Portrait.* Oakville, ON: Mosaic, 1988.

Garrison, Dee. "Two Roads Taken: Writing the Biography of Mary Heaton Vorse." Alpern, et al., eds. 65–78.

"Gaspé Manifesto, The. A Strange Enterprise: The Dilemma of the Playwright in Canada." 1971. Rubin, ed. 302–6.

Gass, Ken. "What is a Canadian Play?" 1974. Rubin, ed. 404–10.

Gelinas, Gratien. "Le Crédo professionel d'un homme de théâtre." Keith and Shek, eds. 81–89.

Gems, Pam. *Three Plays: Piaf, Camille, Loving Women.* London: Penguin, 1985.

Gilbert, Helen and Joanne Tompkins. *Post-Colonial Drama: Theory, Practice, Politics.* London: Routledge, 1996.

Gilbert, Reid. "Sharon Pollock." *Profiles in Canadian Literature,* 6. Ed. Jeffrey Heath. Toronto: Dundurn, 1986. 113–20.

———. "Sharon Pollock." *Contemporary Dramatists.* 4th Ed. Rev. Ed. D.L. Kirkpatrick. London: St. James Press, 1988. 434–36.

———. "Sharon Pollock." *Contemporary Dramatists.* 5th Ed. Rev. Ed. K.A. Berney. London: St. James Press, 1993. 538–40.

———. "'My Mother Wants Me To Play Romeo Before It's Too Late': Framing Gender On Stage." *Theatre Research in Canada* 14.2 (1993): 123–43.

Gilbert, Sky. "Canadian Actors' Equity: Recognize What Is 'Canadian' about Theatre practice in this Country." *CTR* (Summer 2005): 15–18.

Gilmore, Leigh. *Autobiographics: A Feminist Theory of Women's Self-Representation*. Ithaca: Cornell University Press, 1994.

———. *The Limits of Autobiography: Trauma and Testimony*. Ithaca: Cornell University Press, 2001.

Glover, Guy. "Film." Ross, Malcolm, ed. *The Arts in Canada*. 104–13.

Godard, Barbara. "Between Performative and Performance: Translation and Theatre in the Canadian/Quebec Context." *Modern Drama* XLIII. 3 (2000): 327–58.

Goodwin, Jill Tomasson. "Andrew Allan and the Stage series." *Canadian Drama* 15.1 (1989): 1–24.

Gottried, Martin. *Arthur Miller: His Life and Work*. Cambridge, Mass.: Da Capo, 2003.

———. *Balancing Act: The Authorized Biography of Angela Lansbury*. Boston: Little, Brown, 1999.

Gould, Warwick and Thomas E. Staley, eds. *Writing the Lives of Writers*. New York: St. Martin's Press, 1998.

Grace, Sherrill. "Constructing Canada: An Introduction." *Painting the Maple: Essays on Race, Gender, and the Construction of Canada*. V. Strong-Boag et al., eds. Vancouver: UBC Press, 1998. 3–15.

———. "Sharon Pollock's Portraits of the Artist." *Theatre Research in Canada* 22.2 (2001): 124–38.

———. "Creating the Girl from God's Country: Sharon Pollock's Nell Shipman." *Canadian Literature* 172.33 (2002): 98–117.

———. "Imagining Canada: Sharon Pollock's *Walsh* and *Fair Liberty's Call*." *Performing National Identities: International Perspectives on Contemporary Canadian Theatre*. Ed. S. Grace and A. R. Glaap. Vancouver: Talonbooks, 2003. 51–69. Reprinted in *Sharon Pollock: Critical Perspectives on Canadian Theatre in English*. Ed. Sherrill Grace and Michelle La Flamme. 133–50.

———. "The Art of Sharon Pollock." *Sharon Pollock: Three Plays*. Toronto: Playwrights Canada Press, 2003. 1–11.

———. "Staging Lives: Sharon Pollock's Theatre and the Autobiographical Impulse." *Canadian, Literary, and Didactic Mosaic*. Ed. Michael Heinze and Elke Müller-Schneck. Trier: WVT, 2004. 35–45.

———. "Shipman's Last Take: Or Why Sharon Pollock is Not Samuel Beckett." *wwrMagazine* 2.1 (Summer 2005): 10–14.

———. "Performing the Auto/biographical Pact: Towards a Theory of Identity in Performance." *Tracing the Autobiographical*. Ed. Marlene Kadar et al. Waterloo: Wilfrid Laurier University Press, 2005. 65–79.

———. "Sharon Pollock's *Doc* and the Biographer's Dilemma." *Theatre and AutoBiography*. Ed. Sherrill Grace and Jerry Wasserman. 2006. 275–88.

———. *Canada and the Idea of North*. 2001. Montreal: McGill-Queen's University Press, 2007.

———. "White Men Talking." *Journal of Northern Studies* 1–2 (2007): 9–26.

Grace, Sherrill, and Gabriele Helms. "Documenting Racism: Sharon Pollock's *The Komagata Maru Incident*." V. Strong-Boag, et al., eds. 85–99.

Grace, Sherrill, and Albert-Reiner Glaap, eds. *Performing National Identities: International Perspectives on Contemporary Canadian Theatre*. Vancouver: Talonbooks, 2003.

Grace, Sherrill, and Jerry Wasserman, eds. *Theatre and AutoBiography: Writing and Performing Lives*. Vancouver: Talonbooks, 2006.

Grace, Sherrill, and Michelle La Flamme, eds. *Sharon Pollock: Critical Perspectives on Canadian Theatre in English*. Toronto: Playwrights Canada Press, 2008.

Grant, George. *Lament for a Nation*. 1965. Montreal: McGill-Queen's University Press, 2005.

Gray, Alexander. "The Playhouse." *The Atlantic Advocate* (September 1964): 65–69.

Gray, Bill. Producer/director. "Gerald." CBC AM Radio, "Nightfall series." 1982.

Gray, Frances. "The Nature of Radio Drama." Lewis, ed. 48–77.

Gray, Jack. "The Performing Arts and Government Policy." Wagner, ed. 24–34.

Gray, John and Eric Peterson. *Billy Bishop Goes to War*. Vancouver: Talonbooks, 1981.

Grey, Charlotte. *Flint & Feather: The Life and Times of E. Pauline Johnson*. Toronto: Harper, 2002.

Griffiths, Trevor R. and Carole Woddies. "Sharon Pollock." *Bloomsbury Theatre Guide*. London: Bloomsbury Publishing, 1988.

Gross, Gerry. "Matters of Conscience: The Radio Dramas of Reuben Ship." *Canadian Drama* 15.1 (1989): 25–39.

Gussow, Mel. *Edward Albee: A Singular Journey*. New York: Applause Theatre Books, 2001.

Guthrie, Tyrone. "A Long View of the Stratford Festival." Rubin, ed. 204–15.

Gwyn, Sandra. *Tapestry of War: A Private View of Canadians in the Great War*. Toronto: HarperCollins, 1992.

Hamill, Tony, ed. *Six Canadian Plays*. Toronto: Playwrights Canada Press, 1992.

Hampton, C.C. "Staging All That Fall." *Drama at Calgary* 2.1 (November 1967): 48–52.

———. "All That Fall: Productions II and III, Final Report." *Drama at Calgary* 2.4 (May 1968): 37–41.

Hardin, Herschel. *Esker Mike and His Wife, Agiluk*. Vancouver: Talonbooks, 1973.

Harron, Martha. *Don Harron: A Parent Contradiction*. Toronto: Collins, 1988.

Hay, Peter. "Cultural Politics." Rubin, ed. 309–17.

———. "Vancouver." *CTR* 1 (Winter 1974): 113–15.

Hendry, Tom. "The Masseys and the Masses." Rubin, ed. 188–92.

———. "Trends in Canadian Theatre." Rubin, ed. 251–58.

———. *Fifteen Miles of Broken Glass*. Vancouver: Talonbooks, 1975.

Henighan, Tom. *The Presumption of Culture: Structure, Strategy, and Survival in the Canadian Cultural Landscape*. Vancouver: Raincoast Books, 1996.

Henley, Beth. *Crimes of the Heart*. New York: Viking Penguin, 1981.

Herbert, John. *Fortune and Men's Eyes*. New York: Grove Press, 1967.

Herr, Michael. *Dispatches*. 1968. New York: Vintage, 1991.

Hirsch, John. "Directing in Canada." *CTR* 1 (Winter 1974): 49–55.

Hirsch, Marianne. *Family Frames: Photography, narrative, and postmemory*. Cambridge, Mass.: Harvard University Press, 1997.

Hodgins, Jack. *Broken Ground*. Toronto: McClelland & Stewart, 1998.

Hoffman, James. *The Ecstasy of Resistance: A Biography of George Ryga*. Toronto: ECW Press, 1995.

Hoffman, James and Ginny Ratsoy, eds. *Playing the Pacific Province*. Toronto: Playwrights Canada Press, 2003.

Hofsess, John. "The primary playwrights' class." *Sunday TAB* 10 December 1979. T 07.

Holder, Heidi J. "Broken Toys: The Destruction of the National Hero in the Early Plays of Sharon Pollock." *Essays in Theatre/ Etudes Theatrales* 14.2 (May 1996):131–45. Nothof, ed. 2000: 100–127.

Hollingsworth, Margaret. "Why We Don't Write." *CTR* 43 (Summer 1985): 21–27.

Howard, Peter. *Beaverbrook: A Study of Max the Unknown*. London: Hutchinson, 1964.

Hutchinson, Ann M. "*Doc*." *Canadian Woman Studies* 8.3 (1987): 96–98.

Innes, Christopher. "In the beginning was the Word: Text versus Performance." *The Performance Text*. Pietropaolo, Domenico, ed. 9–19.

Jackson, B.W. "The Avon and Third Stage." *Journal of Canadian Studies* XI (1975): 57–62.

Jameson, Sheilagh. *Chautauqua in Canada*. Calgary: Glenbow-Alberta Institute, 1979.

Jansen, Ann. "Introduction." *Airborne: Radio Plays by Women*. Winnipeg: Blizzard, 1991. vii–xix.

Jarry, Alfred. *Ubu roi. Tout Ubu*. Ed. Maurice Saillet. Paris: Livre de poche, 1963.

Jellicoe, Ann. *The Knack*. 1962. London: Faber and Faber. 1968.

Jessup, Lynda, ed. *Antimodernism and Artistic Experience: Policing the Boundaries of Modernity*. Toronto: University of Toronto Press, 2001.

Jenkins, McKay. *Bloody Falls of the Coppermine: Madness, Murder, and the Collision of Cultures*. Toronto: Random House, 2004.

"John Palmer." In Wallace and Zimmerman, *The Work*. 329–41.

Johnson, Barbara. "Introduction" to "Whose Life Is It, Anyway." Rhiel and Suchoff, eds. 119–21.

Johnston, Denis W. *Up the Mainstream: The Rise of Toronto's Alternative Theatres*. Toronto: University of Toronto Press, 1991.

———. "Totem Theatre: AutoBiography of a Company." Grace andWasserman, eds. 225–48.

Johnston, Hugh. *The Voyage of the Komagata Maru: The Sikh Challenge to Canada's Colour Bar*. Vancouver: UBC Press, 1989.

Jones, Ann. *Women Who Kill*. New York: Holt, Rinehart & Winston, 1980.

Joubert, Lucie, ed. *Trajectoires au Féminin dans la Littérature Québécoise, 1960–1990*. Montréal: Éditions Nota Bene, 2000.

Keaney, Patricia. "Living with Risk: Toronto's New Alternate Theatre." Rubin, ed. 411–19.

Keith, W. J. and B.-Z. Shek, eds. *The Arts in Canada: The Last Fifty Years*. Toronto: University of Toronto Press, 1980.

Kennedy, Adrienne. *People Who Led to My Plays*. New York: Alfred A. Knopf, 1987.

———. *The Adrienne Kennedy Reader*. Minneapolis: University of Minneapolis Press, 2001.

Kennedy, Brian. *The Baron Bold and the Beauteous Maid: A Compact History of Canadian Theatre*. Toronto: Playwrights Canada Press, 2004.

Kent, David. *The Lizzie Borden Source Book*. Boston: Branden Publishing Co., 1992.

Kerr, Jean. *Mary, Mary and Other Plays*. New York: Doubleday, 1963.

Kerr, Rosalind. "Borderline Crossings in Sharon Pollock's Out-law Genres: *Blood Relations* and *Doc*." *Theatre Research in Canada* 17.2 (Fall 1996): 200–215.

Kilbourne, William, Jean Roberts, David Gardner, David Peacock, Claude des Landes, and Walter Learning. "The Canada Council and the Theatre: The past 25 years and Tomorrow." *Theatre History in Canada* 3.2 (1962): 165–92.

Kilgour, David, ed. *A Strange Elation: Hart House, the First Eighty Years*. Toronto: Hart House, 1999.

King's Hall. Booklet compiled by the King's Hall Memorial Committee. 1972.

Kirmayer, Laurence J. "Landscapes of memory: trauma, narrative, and dissociation." *Tense Past: Cultural Essays in Trauma and Memory*. Ed. Paul Antze and Michael Lambek. London & New York: Routledge, 1996. 173–98.

Klein, Melanie and Joan Riviere. *Love, Hate and Reparation*. 1936. New York: W.W. Norton, 1964.

Knowles, Richard Paul. "Replaying History: Canadian Historiographic Metadrama." *Dalhousie Review* 67 (1987): 228–43.

———. "Towards a Materialist Performance Analysis: The Case of Tarragon Theatre." Pietropaolo, Domenico, ed. 205–26.

———. "Celebrating Canadian Plays and Playwrights." *CTR* 114 (Spring 2003): 3–5.

Knowlson, James. *Damned to Fame: The Life of Samuel Beckett*. London: Bloomsbury, 1996.

Kogawa, Joy. *Obasan*. Toronto: Lester & Orpen Dennys, 1981.

Kristeva, Julia. *Desire in Language: A Semiotic Approach to Literature and Art*. Ed. Leon S. Roudiez. Trans. Thomas Gora, Alice Jardine, and Leon S. Roudiez. New York: Columbia University Press, 1980.

Kritzer, Amelia Howe. *The Plays of Caryl Churchill: Theatre of Empowerment*. New York: St Martin's Press, 1991.

Kroetsch, Robert. "A Conversation with Margaret Laurence." *Creation*. ed. Robert Kroetsch. Toronto: New Press, 1970. 53–63.

La Flamme, Michelle. "Indigenous Women Living Beyond the Grave: From Pollock to Pechawis." Grace and La Flamme, eds. 160–75.

Lahr, John. *Prick Up Your Ears: The Biography of Joe Orton*. London: Penguin/Allen Lane, 1978.

Laing, R. D. *The Divided Self*. 1960. London: Penguin, 1963.

Langer, Elinor. *Josephine Herbst: The Story She Could Never Tell*. Boston: Little Brown, 1983.

Leavitt, Robert. *Maliseet & Micmac First Nations of the Maritimes*. Fredericton, N.B.: New Ireland Press, 1996.

Lee, Betty. *Love and Whisky: The Story of the Dominion Drama Festival and the Early Years of Theatre in Canada, 1606–1972*. 1973. Toronto: Simon & Pierre, 1982.

Lee, Hermione. *Virginia Woolf*. London: Chatto & Windus, 1996.

Lefebvre, Paul. "Playwrighting in Quebec." Trans. Barbara Kerslake. Wagner, ed. 60–68.

Legend of Lizzie Borden, The. Film. Dir. Paul Wendkos. George LeMair Productions. Paramount, 1975.

Leighton, David and Betty Leighton. *Artists, Builders, and Dreamers: 50 Years at the Banff School*. Toronto: McClelland & Stewart, 1982.

Lejeune, Philippe. "The Autobiographical Pact (bis)." *On Autobiography*. Ed. Paul John Eakin. Trans. Katherine Leary. Minneapolis: University of Minnesota Press, 1989. 119–37.

Le Vay, John. *Margaret Anglin: A Stage Life*. Toronto: Simon & Pierre, 1989.

Lewis, Peter, ed. *Radio Drama*. London and New York: Longman, 1981.

Lill, Wendy. *Memories of You*. Toronto: Summerhill Press, 1989.

Lillo, Larry. "From the director." In "Study Kit for the Playhouse Production of 'The Komagata Maru Incident'." Compiled by Camillia Ross, Margaret Whitford, and Lendre Rodgers. January 1976. 4–5.

Lincoln, Victoria. *A Private Disgrace: Lizzie Borden By Daylight*. New York: G.P. Putnam's Sons, 1967.

Lind, Jane. *Joyce Wieland: Artist on Fire*. Toronto: James Lorimer, 2001.

Lister, Rota. An interview with Joyce Doolittle about Sharon Pollock. Unpublished ts., 22 June 1988.

Litt, Paul. *The Muses, the Masses, and the Massey Commission*. Toronto: University of Toronto Press, 1992.

Littler, William. "Developing Opera as a Musical Theatre." Wagner, ed. 274–82.

Little Big Man. Film. Dir. Arthur Penn. 1970.

Littlewood, Joan, and Theatre Workshop, Charles Chilton, and the members of the original cast. *Oh What a Lovely War!* London: Methuen, 1965.

Loiselle, André. "Paradigms of 1980s Québécois and Canadian Drama: Normand Chaurette's *Provincetown, Juillet 1919, J'avais 19 ans* and Sharon Pollock's *Blood Relations*." *Québec Studies* 14 (1992): 93–104.

Lorenz, Konrad. *On Aggression*. Trans. Marjorie Latzke. London: Methuen, 1966.

Loucks, Randee E. "Sharon Pollock 1973–1985, Playwright of Conscience and Consequence." M.A. Thesis. University of Calgary, 1985.

Lower, Arthur R.M. *Colony to Nation: A History of Canada*. Toronto: McClelland & Stewart, 1977.

Lowry, Malcolm. *Under the Volcano*. London: Jonathan Cape, 1947.

———. *Sursum Corda! The Collected Letters of Malcolm Lowry*, 2 vols. Ed. Sherrill Grace. London and Toronto: Jonathan Cape and University of Toronto Press, 1995, 1996.

Lushington, Kate. "Fear of Feminism." *CTR* 43 (Summer 1985): 5–11.

MacEwan, Grant. *Sitting Bull: The Years in Canada*. Edmonton: Hurtig, 1973.

MacLeod, Joan. *The Shape of a Girl / Jewel*. Vancouver: Talonbooks, 2002.

McInerney, Vincent. *Writing for radio*. Manchester: Manchester University Press, 2001.

McIntosh, R. Dale, B.A. Hanley, P. Verriour, and G.H. Van Gyn. *Arts Literacy in Canada: A report prepared for the Canada Council and the Social Sciences and Humanities Research Council.* Victoria, B.C.: Beach Holme, 1993.

McIntyre, Hope. "Women Playwrights Speak." *CanPlay* 20.4 (2003): 8–12.

MacLennan, Hugh. *The Watch That Ends the Night.* New York: Scribner's, 1959.

———. "Fiction in Canada-1930 to 1980." Keith and Shek, eds. 29–42.

Malpede, Karen. "Theatre at 2000: A Witness Project." *The Year 2000: Essays on the End.* Ed. Charles B. Strozier and Michael Flynn. New York: New York University Press, 1997. 299–308.

"Martin Kinch." In Wallace and Zimmerman, *The Work.* 343–59.

Massey Commission Report. See Report: Royal Commission.

Massey Report [excerpts]. Rubin, ed. 176–83.

Massey, Vincent. "The Prospects of a Canadian Drama." Rubin, ed. 50–63.

———. "Canadian Plays from Hart House Theatre." Rubin, ed. 70–71.

———. "Art and Nationality in Canada." *Transactions of the Royal Society of Canada.* Third Series vol. xxiv. Ottawa: Royal Society of Canada, 1930. 59–72.

———. *On Being Canadian.* London and Toronto: J. M. Dent, 1948.

Masterton, William L. *Lizzie Didn't Do It!.* Boston: Branden Publishing Co., 2000.

Meisel, John and J. Van Loon. "Cultivating the Bush Garden: Cultural Policy in Canada." *The Patron States: Government and the Arts in Europe, North America and Japan.* Ed. M.C. Cummings and R.S. Katz. New York: Oxford University Press, 1986. 276–310.

Mellow, James. *Invented Lives: F. Scott and Zelda Fitzgerald.* Boston: Houghton Mifflin, 1984.

Milford, Nancy. *Zelda: A Biography.* New York: Harper & Row, 1970.

Miller, Arthur. *After the Fall.* New York: Viking, 1964.

Miller, Mary Jane. *Turn Up the Contrast: CBC Television Drama Since 1952.* Vancouver: UBC Press, 1987.

———. "Television Drama in English Canada." Wagner, ed. 186–96.

———. "Radio's Children." *CTR* 36 (Fall 1982): 30–39.

Miller, Nancy K. *But Enough About Me: Why Do We Read Other Peoples' Lives.* New York: Columbia University Press, 2002.

Milner, Elizabeth Hearn. *The History of King's Hall, Compton, 1874–1972.* Lennoxville, Quebec: Bishop's College Schools Association, 1979.

Minami, Yoshinari. "Canadian Plays on the Japanese Stage." Grace and Glaap, eds. 181–97.

Miner, Madonne. "'Lizzie Borden took an Ax': Enacting *Blood Relations*." *Literature in Performance* 6 (April 1986): 10–21.

Montgomery, Lori. "By the light of the misbegotten moon." *Fast Forward* (Calgary) 20–27 February 1997. 22.

Moore, Christopher. *The Loyalists: Revolution, Exile, Settlement.* Toronto: McClelland & Stewart, 1984.

Moore, Mavor. *Reinventing Myself: Memoirs.* Toronto: Stoddart, 1994.

———. "An Approach to Our Beginnings: Trans Plant, Native Plant, or Mutation?" Rubin, ed. 139–46.

———. "Theatre in English-Speaking Canada." Ross, ed. 68–76.

———. "Radio and Television." Ross, ed. 116–24.

———. "A Theatre for Canada." Rubin, ed. 238–50.

———. "Dora Mavor Moore and the New Play Society (c. 1946)." Rubin, ed. 155–64.

Morrow, Martin. "Canada's Billy Bishop still flying high." *Calgary Herald* 24 October 1992. D1.

———. "Violence links two plays at Garry Theatre." *Calgary Herald* 15 November 1992. C2.

———. "Edmonton export." *Calgary Herald* 17 December 1992. C1.

——. "It's *Agnes of God* at the Garry Theatre." *Calgary Herald* 5 January 1993. B5.

——. "The Worm Turns." *Calgary Herald* 23 January 1993. F21.

——. "Headin' Out should head back." *Calgary Herald* 20 March 1993. C3.

——. "City's newest theatre defies curse." *Calgary Herald* 21 March 1993. C3.

——. "Alberta playwright gets rave reviews." *Calgary Herald* 21 April 1993. D14.

——. "Her Way." *Calgary Herald* 8 June 1993. D6.

——. "Garry Theatre runs afoul of Equity rules." *Calgary Herald* 18 August 1993. A16.

——. "Five and Dime full of problems for director." *Calgary Herald* 8 October 1993. D11.

——. "The Ripper hits Inglewood." *Calgary Herald* 25 November 1993. C11.

——. "Ripper a chiller under Pollock's Hand." *Calgary Herald* 29 November 1993. C5.

——. "Nurse Jane's a single joke." *Calgary Herald* 12 February 1994. F5.

——. "Garry's *Death of a Salesman* grips." *Calgary Herald* 23 April 1994. E9.

——. "*Loot* proves tepid farce." *Calgary Herald* 9 October 1994. C3

——. "Calgary Baffles Britain." *Calgary Herald* 9 November 1994. C7.

——. "'Cuckoo' takes over Garry nest as best effort yet." *Calgary Herald* 20 January 1995. C4.

——. "Young actress explores terror." *Calgary Herald* 23 February 1995. C11.

——. "Small flaws tarnish effective Holocaust drama." *Calgary Herald* 25 February 1995. A15.

——. "Gaslight's old, but it still works." *Calgary Herald* 10 September 1995. D8.

——. "*Salt-Water Moon* shines like a gem." *Calgary Herald* 14 October 1995. E12.

——. "*Dracula* needs a shot of juice." *Calgary Herald* 20 November 1995. B1.

——. "*Saint Joan* rises again." *Calgary Herald* 4 May 1995. D1.

——. "Trial scene true strength of play." *Calgary Herald* 8 May 1995. B15.

——. "Enjoy a brisk ride down Highway #2." *Calgary Herald* 24 June 1995. B9.

——. "Sister George a rich, juicy delight." *Calgary Herald* 15 January 1996. B5.

——. "Garry mounts bold new play." *Calgary Herald* 22 February 1996. D16.

——. "Play finds home on the Prairies." *Calgary Herald* 22 February 1996. D16.

——. "Acting is excellent in Garry's *Of Mice and Men*." *Calgary Herald* 20 April 1996. F8.

——. "Dark probe into the psyche intelligent but not gripping." *Calgary Herald* 18 October 1996. B6.

——. "TJ takes on big guys." *Calgary Herald* 7 September 1998. C9.

——. "Pollock wins Cohen Award." *Calgary Herald* 31 January 1999. C3.

——. "Theatre Junction season marks the millennium." *Calgary Herald* 24 April 1999. J7.

——. *Wild Theatre: The History of One Yellow Rabbit*. Banff: Banff Centre Press, 2003.

——. "Calgary's Wild Ride: How the High Performance Rodeo Inspired and Transformed a Theatre Community." *CTR* 124 (Fall 2005): 35–38.

Morton, Desmond. *Fight or Pay: Soldiers' Families in the Great War*. Vancouver: UBC Press, 2004.

Moyles, R.G. *British Law and Arctic Men: The Celebrated 1917 Murder Trials of Sinnisiak and Uluksuk, First Inuit Tried Under White Man's Law*. Saskatoon, Sask: Western Producer Books, 1979.

Much, Rita. "Theatre by Default: Sharon Pollock's Garry Theatre." *CTR* 82 (Spring 1995): 19–22.

Mullaly, Edward. "Sharon Pollock at Theatre New Brunswick: The Return of the Native." *CTR* 63 (Summer 1990): 20–24.

Murphy, P.J. and Jennifer Murphy, eds. *Sentences and Paroles: A Prison Reader*. Vancouver: New Star Books, 1999.

Murrell, John. *Waiting for the Parade*. Vancouver: Talonbooks, 1980.

————. *Memoir. Heroines: Three Plays.* Ed. Joyce Doolittle. Red Deer, Alberta: Red Deer College Press, 1992. 13–84.

Murrell, John, and John Estacio. Opera. "Filumena." 2003.

Nadel, Ira. *Tom Stoppard: A Life.* New York: Palgrave Macmillan, 2002.

————. *Various Positions: A Life of Leonard Cohen.* Toronto: Random House, 1996.

————. "Biography and Theory, or Beckett in the Bath." Noonan, ed. 9–17.

Nagel, Thomas. *Concealment and Exposure, and Other Essays.* Oxford: Oxford University Press, 2002.

Nolan, Yvette. *Annie Mae's Movement.* Toronto: Playwrights Canada Press, 1999.

Noonan, James, ed. *Biography and Autobiography: Essays on Irish and Canadian History and Literature.* Ottawa: Carleton University Press, 1993.

Nothof, Anne. "Canadian Radio Drama: Prick Up Your Ears." *Theatre History in Canada* 11.1 (Spring 1990): 59–70.

————. "Crossing Borders: Sharon Pollock's Revisitation of Canadian Frontiers." *Modern Drama* 38.4 (Winter 1995): 475–87. Nothof, ed. 2000: 81–99.

————. "Gendered Landscapes: Synergism of Place and Person in Canadian Prairie Drama." *Great Plains Quarterly* 18.2 (Spring 1998): 127–38.

————. ed. *Sharon Pollock. Essays on Her Works.* Toronto: Guernica, 2000.

————. "Introduction: Illuminating the Facets." Nothof, ed. 2000. 7–11.

————. "Staging the Intersections of Time in Sharon Pollock's *Doc, Moving Pictures,* and *End Dream.*" *Theatre Research in Canada* 22.2 (2001): 139–50.

————. "Ironic Images: Sharon Pollock's Stratford Productions." *CTR* 114 (2003): 21–25.

————. "Appropriated Voice in Sharon Pollock's *Angel's Trumpet.*" *Theatre Research in Canada* 25. 1–2 (2004): 136–47.

————. "The Artist as Moving Target in Sharon Pollock's *Moving Pictures.*" *wwrMagazine* 2.1 (Summer 2005): 4–7.

————. "Postcolonial Tragedy in the Crowsnest Pass: Two Rearview Reflections by Sharon Pollock and John Murrell." *Great Plains Quarterly* 26.4 (2006): 235–44.

Nowell, Iris. *Joyce Wieland: A Life in Art.* Toronto: ECW Press, 2001.

Nunn, Robert C. "Performing Fact: Canadian Documentary Theatre." *Canadian Literature* 103 (1986): 51–62.

O'Brien, Sharon. "Feminist Theory and Literary Biography." *In Contesting the Subject.* Ed. William Epstein. 123–33.

Oglov, Linda. "John Wood." *National Arts Centre: Stage* 8.1 (1981): 4–5.

O'Grady, (Nothof), Anne. "Sharon Pollock: Theatre Relationships." *The Athabasca University Magazine* 8.3 (Winter 1983/84): 21–23.

Ondaatje, Michael. *The English Patient.* Toronto: McClelland & Stewart, 1992.

Orton, Joe. *Loot.* London: Methuen, 1967.

————. *What the Butler Saw.* London: Methuen, 1969.

Osborne, John. *A Better Class of Person: An Autobiography, 1929–1956.* London: Faber & Faber, 1989.

————. *Almost a Gentleman: An Autobiography, 1955–1966.* London: Faber & Faber, 1991.

Ouzounian, Richard. *Stratford Gold: 50 years, 50 Stars, 50 Conversations.* Toronto: McArthur & Co., 2003.

Pachter, Marc, ed. *Telling Lives: The Biographer's Art.* Philadelphia: University of Pennsylvania Press, 1985.

Page, Malcolm. "British Columbia." Wagner, ed. 167–74.

————. "Sharon Pollock: Committed Playwright." *Canadian Drama/ L'Art Dramatique Canadien* 5.2 (Fall 1979): 104–12. Nothof, ed. 2000: 12–25.

———. "Vancouver in 1983: Summer Success and Winter Worries." *CTR* 39 (Spring 1984): 15–22.

Pavis, Patrice. "Théâtre autobiographique." Dictionnaire du Théâtre. Paris: Dunod. 361–62.

Per Annos: King's Hall, 1953. School Magazine & Directory.

Per Annos: King's Hall, 1954. School Magazine & Directory.

Perkyns, Richard. "*Generations*: An Introduction." *Major Plays of the Canadian Theatre, 1934–1984*. Ed. Richard Perkyns. Toronto: Irwin, 1984. 605–8.

———. "Nova Scotia." Wagner, ed. 106–11.

Peterson, Leslie. "Our Forgotten Shame." Review of Ted Ferguson's *A White Man's Country*. *Vancouver Sun* 12 December 1975. 32A.

Pielmeier, John. *Agnes of God*. New York: Plume, 1985.

Pietropaolo, Damiano. "Narrative and Performance in Radio Drama." Pietropaolo, Domenico, ed. 70–77.

Pietropaolo, Domenico, ed. *The Performance Text*. New York, Ottawa, Toronto: LEGAS, 1999.

Pinsent, Gordon. *By the Way*. Toronto: Stoddart, 1992.

Pinter, Harold. *The Homecoming*. New York: Grove Press, 1965.

———. *The Betrayal*. London: Methuen, 1978.

Plant, Richard, ed. *The Penguin Book of Modern Canadian Drama*. Markham, ON: Penguin, 1984.

Podbrey, Maurice, as related to R. Bruce Henry. *Half Man, Half Beast: Making a Life in Canadian Theatre*. Montreal: Vehicule Press, 1997.

"Pollock, Sharon." *Contemporary Canadian Authors*. Vol I. Ed. Robert Lang, Pamela Willwerth Aue, and David M. Galens. Toronto: Gale Canada, 1996. 373–75.

Portman, Jamie. "Theatres lack new directors." *Edmonton Journal* 22 March 1977. 63.

Posner, Michael. *The Last Honest Man, Mordecai Richler: An Oral Biography*. Toronto: McClelland & Stewart, 2004.

Postlewait, Thomas. "Autobiography and Theatre History." *Interpreting the Theatrical Past: Essays in the Historiography of Performance*. Ed. Thomas Postelwait and Bruce A. McConachie. Iowa City: University of Iowa Press, 1989. 248–72.

Pratt, Mary. "Another time, another place, another me." *Globe and Mail* 19 August 1998. C 12–13.

Pratt, Mary. *A Personal Calligraphy*. Fredericton: Goose Lane Editions, 2000.

Pumpkin Eater, The. Film. Dir. Jack Clayton. 1964. Produced by James Woolf.

Raban, Jonathan. "Icon or symbol: the writer and the 'medium'." Lewis, ed. 78–90.

Rabillard, Sheila, ed. *Essays on Caryl Churchill: Contemporary Representations*. Winnipeg: Blizzard, 1998.

Radin, E. D. *Lizzie Borden: The Untold Story*. New York: Simon and Schuster, 1961.

Rashomon. Film. Dir. Akira Kurosawa. 1950. Daiei Japan.

Rattigan, Terence. *Separate Tables*. *The Collected Plays of Terence Rattigan*, 3 vols. Vol 3. London: Hamish Hamilton, 1964. 95–195.

Raymond, Rev. William O. *The River St. John: Its Physical Features, Legends, and History from 1604 to 1784*. St John, N.B.: Strathmore Press, 1910.

Rebello, Leonard. *Lizzie Borden: Past and Present*. Al-Zack Press: Fall River Press, 1999.

Red Shoes, The. Film. Dir. Michael Powell and Emeric Pressburger. Archers Production, 1948.

Redfern, Jon. "The Case for Children's Scripts." *CTR* 10 (Spring 1976): 36–39.

Report of the Federal Cultural Policy Review Committee. [Appelbaum-Hébert] 1982.

Report: Royal Commission on National Development in the Arts, Letters and Sciences, 1949–1951. [Massey-Levesque Commission] Edmond Cloutier, 1951.

Rewa, Natalie. "Running Time: Scenography and Temporality in Performance." *The Performance Text.* Pietropaolo, Domenico, ed. 178–204.

Rhiel, Mary and David Suchoff, eds. *The Seductions of Biography.* New York and London: Routledge, 1996.

———. "Introduction: The Seductions of Biography." *The Seductions of Biography.* 1–11.

Rhodes, Richard. "On Calgary Time." *Canadian Art* 22.4 (2003): 36–39.

Rich, Adrienne. *Of Woman Born: Motherhood as Experience and Institution.* New York: W.W. Norton, 1976.

Ricou, Lawrence. *Vertical Man, Horizontal World.* Vancouver: UBC Press, 1973.

Ridout, Godfrey. "Fifty Years of Music in Canada? Good Lord, I Was There for All of Them!" Keith and Shek, eds. 116–34.

Riviere, Joan. "Hate, Greed and Aggression." *Love, Hate and Reparation.* Klein and Riviere. 4–41.

Roberts, Sir Charles G.D. "Tantramar Revisited." *The New Oxford Book of Canada Verse in English.* Ed. Margaret Atwood. Toronto: Oxford University Press, 1982. 27–29.

Robinson, Guy. "A Study of the New Play Centre and Playwright John Lazarus." Honours Graduating Essay, SFU, April 1982.

Robson, Frederic. "The Drama in Canada." 1908. Rubin, ed.11.

Rose, Phyllis. "Confessions of a Burned-Out Biographer." Rhiel and Suchoff, eds. 131–35.

Ross, Malcolm, ed. *The Arts in Canada.* Toronto: Macmillan, 1958.

Ruban, Douglas H. *Treating Adult Children of Alcholics: A Behavioural Approach.* San Diego: Academic Press, 2001.

Rubin, Don. "Creeping Toward a Culture: The Theatre in English Canada Since 1945." Rubin, ed. 318–31.

———. "The Toronto Movement." Rubin, ed. 394–403.

———. "Training the Theatre Professional." Wagner, ed. 284–92.

———. ed. *Canadian Theatre History: Selected Readings.* Toronto: Copp Clark, 1996.

Rudnick, Lois. "The Male-Identified Woman and Other Anxieties: The Life of Mabel Dodge Luhan." Alpern et al, eds. 116–38.

Russell, David. "The Direction of Whiskey Six." MFA Thesis. Edmonton: University of Alberta, 1987.

Rushton, Margaret. "Holiday's Twenty-one magical Years, 1953–1974." Newsheet of the Playhouse Theatre Centre of B.C. 2.2 (February 1975): 3.

Rutherford, Paul. *The Making of Canadian Culture.* Toronto: McGraw-Hill Ryerson, 1978.

Ryan, Toby. *Stage Left: Canadian Theatre in the Thirties.* Toronto: CTR Publishers, 1981.

Ryga, George. *The Ecstasy of Rita Joe.* Vancouver: Talonbooks, 1970.

———. "Theatre in Canada: Three Statements." Rubin, ed. 348–61.

Saddlemyer, Ann. "Circus Feminus: 100 Plays by English-Canadian Women." *Room of One's Own* 8.2 (1983): 79–91.

———. "Two Canadian Women Playwrights." *Cross-Cultural Studies: American, Canadian and European Literatures: 1945–1985.* Ed. Mirko Jurak. Ljubljana: English Department, Filozofska Fakulteta, 1988. 251–56.

———. "Crime in Literature: Canadian Drama." *Rough Justice: Essays on Crime in Literature.* Ed. M. L. Friedland. Toronto: University Toronto Press, 1991. 214–30.

———. "Sharon Pollock, *Blood Relations*: Schuld und persönliche Verantwortung." *Das moderne english-kanadische Drama.* Ed. Albert-Reiner Glaap. Düsseldorf: Schwann Verlag, 1992. 219–28.

———. *Becoming George: The Life of Mrs W.B. Yeats.* Oxford: Oxford University Press, 2002.

St. Pierre, Paul Matthew. "Sharon Pollock." *Canadian Writers Since 1960.* Ed. W.H. New. 2nd ser. DLB 60. Detroit: Gale Research, 1987. 300–306.

Sagan, Carl. *Cosmos: A Personal Journey*. New York: Random House, 1980.

Salter, Denis. "(Im)possible Worlds: The Plays of Sharon Pollock." *The Sharon Pollock Papers, First Accession: An Inventory of the University of Calgary Libraries*. Ed. Apollonia Steele and Jean F. Tener. Calgary: University of Calgary Press, 1989. xi-xxxv. Rpt. in Grace and La Flamme, eds. 13–32.

Salutin, Rick. "The Meaning of it All." Rubin, ed. 381–88.

———. *1837: The Farmers' Revolt*. Toronto: James Lorimer & Co., 1976.

Sandwell, B. K. "The Annexation of our Stage." Rubin, ed. 16–20.

Sarabande. Film. Dir. Ingmar Bergman. 2003.

Schoenberg, Mark. "Edmonton." *CTR* 1 (Winter 1974): 121–23.

Senda, Akihiko. "Tokyo Festival of Canadian Drama." Trans. Cody Poulton. *CTR* 83 (Summer 1995): 69–71.

Shadbolt, Doris. *The Art of Emily Carr*. Toronto and Vancouver: Clarke Irwin and Douglas & McIntyre, 1978.

Shanks, Connie. "Dr Chalmers: Medical Pioneer, Tireless Campaigner." *Fredericton Daily Gleaner* 27 April 1993. 19–20.

Sharon Pollock. Special issue of *wwrMagazine* 2.1 (Summer 2005). www.womenwritingreading.org

"Sharon Pollock: *Doc*." *Contemporary Literary Criticism: Yearbook 1987*. Vol. 50. Ed. Sharon K. Hall. Detroit: Gale Research, 1988. 222–27.

Shaw, Marion. "Invisible Presences: Life-Writing and Vera Brittain's Testament of Friendship." *Women's Lives/Women's Times: New Essays on Auto/Biography*. Ed. Trev Lynn Broughton and Linda Anderson. Albany, N.K.: State University of New York Press, 1997. 244–57.

Shepard, Sam. *Buried Child*. *Sam Shepard: Seven Plays*. New York: Bantam, 1981. 62–132.

Sherriff, R.C. *Journey's End*. 1929. London: Penguin, 1983.

Shewey, Don. *Sam Shepard*. Updated edition. New York: Da Capo Press, 1997.

Ship, Reuben. *The Investigator: A Political Satire in Documentary Form*. New York: Broadside, 1954.

Shipman, Nell. *The Silent Screen & My Talking Heart*. Boise, Idaho: Boise State University Press, 1987.

Sidnell, Michael. "Authorizations of the Performative: whose Performances of What, and for Whom?" *The Performance Text*. Pietropaolo, Domenico, ed. 97–112.

Siggins, Maggie. *Riel: A Life of Revolution*. Toronto: HarperCollins, 1994.

Smith, Mary Elizabeth. "New Brunswick." Wagner, ed. 112–17.

Soucoup, Dan. *Historic New Brunswick*. Lawrencetown Beech, NB: Potterfield Press, 1997.

Soule, Donald. "Vancouver II." *CTR* 1 (Winter 1974): 115–17.

Speaking of our Culture: Discussion Guide [Applebaum/Hebert Report guide]. Ottawa: Federal Cultural Policy Review Committee, 1980.

Sperdakos, Paula. *Dora Mavor Moore: Pioneer of the Canadian Theatre*. Toronto: ECW Press, 1995.

Sperdakos, Paula. "Untold Stories: [Re]Searching for Canadian Actresses' Lives." Grace and Wasserman, eds. 202–24.

Spiering, Frank. *Lizzie*. New York: Random House, 1984.

Spirit of Annie Mae. Film. Dir. Catherine Anne Martin. NFB, 2002.

Squires, W. Austin. *History of Fredericton: The Last 200 Years*. Ed. J.K. Chapman. Fredericton, N.B.: City of Fredericton, 1980.

Starkins, Edward. *Who Killed Janet Smith?* Toronto: Macmillan, 1984.

"Status of the Artist Act." 1992. Bill C 33. http://laws.justice.gc.ca/en/S-19.6

Steele, Apollonia, and Jean Tener, eds. *The Sharon Pollock Papers: First Accession. An Inventory of the Archives at the University of Calgary Libraries*. Calgary: University of Calgary Press, 1989.

Stephenson, Heidi and Natasha Langridge. *Rage and Reason: Women Playwrights on Playwriting*. London: Methuen, 1997.

Stevenson, Anne. *Bitter Fame: A Life of Sylvia Plath*. 1989. London: Penguin, 1998.

Stewart, Alan. "A look at family affairs." *Globe and Mail* 26 October 1984. 11.

Stone-Blackburn, Susan. "Character in Context." *Canadian Literature* 96 (Spring 1983): 130–32.

———. "Feminism and Metadrama: Role Playing in *Blood Relations*." *Canadian Drama* 15 (1989): 169–78.

Stoppard, Tom. *Arcadia*. London: Faber and Faber, 1993.

Stouck, David. *Ethel Wilson: A Biography*. Toronto: University of Toronto Press, 2003.

Stratton, Susan. "Feminism and Metadrama: Role Playing in *Blood Relations*." Nothof, ed. 2000. 68–80.

Striff, Erin. "Lady Killers: Feminism and Murder in Sharon Pollock's *Blood Relations* and Wendy Kesselman's *My Sister in This House*." *New England Theatre Journal* 8 (1997): 95–109.

Strong-Boag, V., S. Grace, A. Eisenberg and J. Anderson, eds. *Painting the Maple: Essays on Race, Gender, and the Construction of Canada*. Vancouver: UBC Press, 1998.

Stuart, E. Ross. *The History of Prairie Theatre: The Development of Theatre in Alberta, Manitoba, and Saskatchewan, 1833–1982*. Toronto: Simon & Pierre, 1983.

Sturken, Marita. "Personal Stories and National Meanings: Memory, Reenactment, and the Image." Rhiel and Suchoff, eds. 31–41.

Sullivan, R. *Goodbye Lizzie Borden*. Brattleboro, VT: Stephen Green Press, 1974.

Sullivan, Rosemary. *The Red Shoes: Margaret Atwood Starting Out*. Toronto: HarperFlamingo, 1998.

———. *Shadow Maker: The Life of Gwendolyn MacEwen*. Toronto: HarperCollins, 1995.

Sunter, Robert. "Starvation of the Arts, B.C. Style." *Vancouver Sun* 3 December 1966. 6.

Taylor, David and Glenn Rodger. *Fredericton: A Postcard Trip to the Past*. Fredericton: Atlantex Publications, 1995.

Taylor, Kate. "A Canadian stamp on the Shaw playbill." *Globe and Mail* 17 May 2003. R11.

———. "Nancy Drew: Feminist or daddy's girl?" *Globe and Mail* 16 June 2007. R5.

Taylor, Kendall. *Sometimes Madness Is Wisdom: Zelda and Scott Fitzgerald, A Marriage*. New York: Ballantyne, 2001.

Thacker, Robert. "Erasing the forty-ninth parallel: nationalism, prairie criticism and the case of Wallace Stegner." *Essays on Canadian Writing* 61 (Spring 1997): 179–202.

Theatre for Young Audiences. Special issue, ed. Joyce Doolittle. *CTR* 10 (Spring 1976).

Theatre Research in Canada. 22.2 (2001). Special issue on Sharon Pollock. Guest Ed. Anne Nothof.

Thomson, Colin. *One Thousand Cranes*. Toronto: Simon & Pierre, 1989.

Thomson, R.H. "Standing in the Slipstream: Acting in English Canada." Wagner, ed. 293–99.

———. *The Lost Boys*. Toronto: Playwrights Canada Press, 2001.

———. "Never Not Narrative." Grace and Wasserman, eds. 324–28.

Tippett, Maria. *Making Culture: English-Canadian Institutions and the Arts before the Massey Commission*. Toronto: University of Toronto Press, 1990.

"Tom Hendry." In Wallace and Zimmerman. *The Work*. 172–83.

Tousley, Nancy. "Gisele Amantea: Tracing a History." *Canadian Art* 20.1 (Spring 2003): 62–65.

Tremblay, Michel. *Forever Yours, Marie-Lou*. Trans. John Van Burek and Bill Glassco. Vancouver: Talonbooks, 1975.

———. *Albertine in Five Times*. Trans. John Van Burek and Bill Glassco. Vancouver: Talonbooks, 1986.

———. *The Real World?* Trans. John Van Burek and Bill Glassco. Vancouver: Talonbooks 1988.

Turner, Victor. *Dramas, Fields, and Metaphors: Symbolic Action in Human Society*. Ithaca: Cornell University Press, 1974.

———. *From Ritual to Theatre: The Human Seriousness of Play*. New York: Performing Arts Journal Publications, 1982.

Urquhart, Jane. *The Stone Carvers*. Toronto: McClelland & Stewart, 2001.

Usmiani, Renate. "The Alternate Theatre Movement." Wagner, ed. 49–59.

———. *Second Stage: The Alternative Theatre Movement in Canada*. Vancouver: UBC Press, 1983.

Vanbrugh, Sir John. *Four Comedies [The Provoked Wife]*. London: Penguin, 1989.

Vanderhaeghe, Guy. *The Last Crossing*. Toronto: McClelland & Stewart, 2002.

———. *Dancock's Dance*. Winnipeg: Blizzard, 1996.

van Luven, Marlene A.D. Lynne. "Charting the Territory: A Study of Feminism in English-Canada Drama from 1967–1991." Ph.D. thesis. University of Alberta, 1991.

Velleman, Richard and Jim Orford. *Risk and Resilience: Adults Who Were the Children of Problem Drinkers*. Amsterdam: Harwood Academic, 1999.

Voaden, Herman. "A National Drama League." Rubin, ed. 76–78.

———, ed. *Six Canadian Plays*. Toronto: Copp Clark, 1930.

———. "The Theatre in Canada: A National Theatre?" Rubin, ed. 135–38.

Wachtel, Eleanor. "Two Steps Backward from One Step Forward." *CTR* 43 (Summer 1985): 12–20.

Wagner, Anton, ed. *Contemporary Canadian Theatre: New World Visions*. Toronto: Simon & Pierre, 1985.

Wagner-Martin, Linda. *Telling Women's Lives: The New Biography*. New Brunswick, N.J.: Rutgers University Press, 1994.

Walker, Craig Stewart. "Women and Madness: Sharon Pollock's Plays of the Early 1990s." Nothof, ed. 2000: 127–50.

Wallace, Robert. "Writing the Land Alive: The Playwrights' Vision in English Canada." Wagner, ed. 69–81.

Wallace, Robert and Cynthia Zimmerman. *The Work: Conversations with English-Canadian Playwrights*. Toronto: Coach House Press, 1982.

Walter, James W. St. G. *The Black Loyalists*. Halifax: Dalhousie University Press, 1976.

Wandor, Michelene, ed. "Introduction." *Plays by Women: Volume Three*. London: Methuen, 1984. vii-x.

Wang, I Chun. "Historiography of War and Suffering in Pollock's *Walsh*." *Canadian Culture and Literature: A Taiwan Perspective*. Ed. Steven Tötösy de Zepetnek and Leung Yiu-nam. Edmonton: Research Institute for Comparative Literature, University of Alberta, 1998. 145–54.

Wasserman, Jerry. "Daddy's Girls: Father-Daughter Incest and Canadian Plays by Women." *Essays in Theatre* 14.1 (November 1995): 25–36.

———. ed. *Modern Canadian Plays*. 2 vols. Vancouver: Talonbooks, 2000, 2001.

———. "Where Is Here Now? Living the Border in the New Canadian Theatre." *Crucibles of Culture*. Ed. Marc Maufort and Franca Bellarsi. Brussels: Peter Lang, 2003. 163–73.

Webster, Jackie. *The Coleman Frog: A Tribute*. Fredericton: Otnabog Editions, 2003.

Wegscheider, Sharon. *Another Chance: Hope & Health for the Alcoholic Family*. Paolo Alto, California: Science and Behaviour Books, 1981.

Weiss, Kate. "Adding it up: The Status of Women in Canadian Theatre. Executive Summary." 2006. www.playwrightsguild.ca/pgc/c_pgc.asp

Wertenbaker, Timberlake. *Our country's good*. London: Methuen, 1995.

Whittaker, Herbert. "The Theatre." Rubin, ed. 216–27.

Wicker, Tom. *A Time to Die: The Attica Prison Revolt*. 1975. Lincoln, Nebraska: University of Nebraska Press, 1994.

Williams, Joyce, Eric Smithburn, and Jean Peterson, eds. *Lizzie Borden: A Casebook of Family and Crime in the 1890s*. Bloomington, Indiana: T.I.S. Publications, 1980.

Williams, Sherley Anne. "Telling the Teller: Memoir and Story." Rhiel and Suchoff, eds. 179–84.

Williams, Tennessee. *The Glass Menagerie*. 1945. New York: New Directions, 1970.

Wilson, Ann. "The Politics of the Script." *CTR* 43 (Summer 1985): 174–79.

Wilson, Ann. "Canadian Women Playwrights: (Inter)national Contexts." *CTR* 69 (Winter 1991): 3–4.

———. "Boards of Directors: Who's in Charge?" *CTR* 123 (Summer 2005): 19–24.

Wisenthal, Christine. *The Half-Lives of Pat Lowther*. Toronto: University of Toronto Press, 2005.

Woititz, Janet Geringer. *Adult Children of Alcoholics*. Pompano Beach, Florida: Health Communications, Inc., 1983.

Wood, Barbara L. *Children of Alcoholism: The Struggle for Self and Intimacy in Adult Life*. New York and London: New York University Press, 1987.

Wood, John. "Canadian Sensibilities." *Stratford Fanfares Bulletin* 24.2 (1990): 2.

Woodcock, George. "When the Past Becomes History: The Half-Century in Non-Fiction Prose." Keith and Shek, eds. 90–101.

———. *Strange Bedfellows: The State and the Arts in Canada*. Vancouver: Douglas & McIntyre, 1985.

Woolf, Virginia. *A Room of One's Own*. 1928. Harmondsworth: Penguin, 1945.

———. *Orlando: A Biography*. Harmondsworth: Penguin, 1942.

———. "Professions for Women." *The Death of the Moth and Other Essays*. 1931. London: Hogarth Press, 1942. 149–54.

———. "The Art of Biography." *The Death of the Moth*. 119–26.

Worthen, W.B. "Drama, Performativity, and Performance." *PMLA* 113.5 (1998): 1093–1107.

Wright, Esther Clark. *The Loyalists of New Brunswick*. [privately printed] Fredericton, N.B., 1955.

Wyile, Herb. "'Painting the Background': Metadrama and the Fabric of History in Sharon Pollock's *Blood Relations*." *Essays in Theatre/ Etudes Theatrales* 15.2 (May 1997): 191–205. Rpt. in Grace and La Flamme, eds. 81–97.

Wynn, Graeme. *Timber Colony: A Historical Geography of Early 19th Century New Brunswick*. Toronto: University of Toronto Press, 1981.

Yeo, Leslie. *A Thousand and One First Nights*. Oakville, ON: Mosaic Press, 1998.

Yoshihara, Toyoshi. "A Personal Attempt to Introduce Canadian Theatre to Japan." *CTR* 85 (Winter 1995): 19–21.

Zemans, Joyce. "Establishing the Canon: Nationhood, Identity, and the National Gallery's First Reproduction Program of Canadian Art." *The Journal of Canadian Art History* XVI. 2 (1995): 6–35.

———. "Envisioning Nation: Nationhood, Identity—The Wartime Prints." *Journal of Canadian Art History* 19.1 (1998): 6–47.

Zichy, Francis. "Justifying the Ways of Lizzie Borden to Men: The Play Within the Play in *Blood Relations*." *Theatre Annual* 42 (1987): 61–81.

Zimmerman, Cynthia. "Tom Hendry." *The Work*. Robert Wallace and Cynthia Zimmerman. 173–83.

———. "Sharon Pollock: The Making of Warriors." *Playwrighting Women: Female Voices in English Canada*. The Canadian Dramatist. Vol. III. Ser. Ed. Christopher Innes. Toronto: Simon and Pierre, 1994. 60–98.

———. "Sharon Pollock: Transfiguring the Maternal." *Theatre Research in Canada* 22.2 (2001): 151–60.

Ziraldo, Christina. "Replaying History: A Study of Sharon Pollock's *Walsh*, *The Komagata Maru Incident*, and *Blood Relations*." M.A. Thesis. Guelph: University of Guelph, 1996. Rpt. in Grace and La Flamme, eds. 114–22.

Index